THE BUILDINGS OF ENGLAND

FOUNDING EDITOR: NIKOLAUS PEVSNER

# NOTTINGHAMSHIRE

NIKOLAUS PEVSNER

REVISED BY ELIZABETH WILLIAMSON

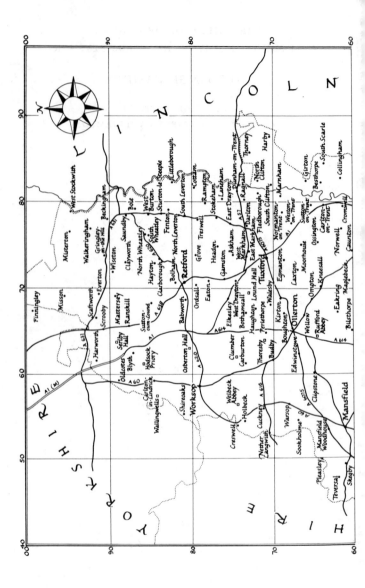

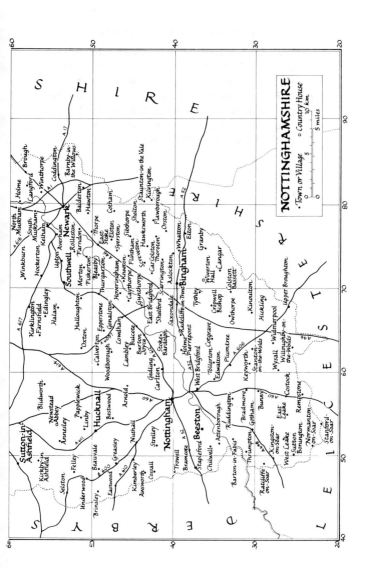

NOTTINGHAMSHIRE

• Town or Village    □ Country House

0    5 miles
0    5 km.

THE BUILDINGS OF ENGLAND

# Nottinghamshire

BY

NIKOLAUS PEVSNER

★

REVISED BY ELIZABETH WILLIAMSON

YALE UNIVERSITY PRESS
NEW HAVEN AND LONDON

YALE UNIVERSITY PRESS
NEW HAVEN AND LONDON
302 Temple Street, New Haven CT 06511
47 Bedford Square, London WC1B 3DP
www.yale.edu/yup
www.yaleup.co.uk
www.pevsner.co.uk

—

Published by Penguin Books 1951
Second edition 1979
Reprinted with corrections 1997
First published by Yale University Press 2003
2 4 6 8 10 9 7 5 3 1

—

ISBN 0 300 09636 4

—

—

Printed in China
through World Print
Set in Monotype Plantin

—

TO THE DRIVER WHO GAVE SATISFACTION

# CONTENTS

## Map References

*

The numbers printed in italic type in the margin
against the place names in the gazetteer of the book
indicate the position of the place in question on the
index map (pages 2–3), which is divided into sections
by the 10-kilometre reference lines of the National
Grid. The reference given here omits the two initial
letters (formerly numbers) which in a full grid
reference refer to the 100-kilometre squares into
which the country is divided. The first two numbers
indicate the *western* boundary, and the last two the
*southern* boundary, of the 10-kilometre square in
which the place in question is situated. For example,
Stapleford (reference 4030) will be found in the 10-
kilometre square bounded by grid lines 40 (on the
*west*) and 50, and 30 (on the *south*) and 40; Blyth
(reference 6080) in the square bounded by grid lines
60 (on the *west*) and 70, and 80 (on the *south*) and 90.

The map contains all those places, whether towns,
villages, or isolated buildings, which are the subject
of separate entries in the text.

# FOREWORD TO THE FIRST EDITION

*First of all I have to thank Dr R. Schapire for the way in which she extracted and compiled most of the facts which will appear in the pages to follow. In addition Mr M. W. Barley has been most helpful in reading my text, correcting mistakes, and adding from his unique knowledge of brickwork and slate gravestones. I feel it to be my duty also to place on record my great gratitude to the Thoroton Society and the libraries of Nottingham, Newark, and Worksop, and especially to Mr Duncan Gray of Nottingham, who put at my disposal his library's exemplary collection of county photographs. The windmills mentioned in my text are based on a list provided by Mr Rex Wailes (who, incidentally, advised me to leave out all derelict windmills gutted inside).\* Church plate in the text is taken from the incomplete manuscript list compiled by Messrs A. Jones and F. Needham, and only plate registered by them is referred to by me.‡ Dovecotes are mostly taken over from J. Whitaker's book of 1917. Moreover, I was helped by the photographic collection of the National Buildings Record,§ by Mr H. S. Goodhart-Rendel's manuscript notes on Victorian churches which he kindly allowed me to use, by Mr T. D. Kendrick's manuscript notes on Victorian glass, which he was good enough to place at my disposal, and by the late Mr Nevil Truman's articles from the* Journal of the British Society of Master Glass-Painters *on 'Ancient Glass in Nottinghamshire,' including proofs of their future instalments. Moreover, by the courtesy of the Ministry of Town and Country Planning,¶ who have a statutory duty to compile lists of buildings of architectural or historic interest, I have had access to unpublished lists and much other information collected by the Chief Investigator of the Ministry and his staff. This was most useful for checking my results and in a few cases for references to buildings not inspected by me. Such references are given in my text in brackets and specially marked* MTCP.¶ *Similarly information coming from Mr*

---

\* Shells of windmills are included in the second edition since remains of any kind are now so rare. There is one working windmill in the county and altogether only thirty in any condition.

‡ Church plate has been deleted from this edition (*see* foreword to the second edition).

§ Now National Monuments Record (NMR).

¶ Now Department of the Environment (DOE).

*Goodhart-Rendel is marked* GR, *and information from Mr Kendrick* TK.

Many rectors and vicars of churches and owners of houses had to be pestered with letters for information on minor points, and most of them have been sympathetic. Some have gone to much trouble in the interests of this book.

# FOREWORD TO THE SECOND EDITION
## (1979)

*The revised edition of Nottinghamshire, like all volumes of The Buildings of England, owes a great debt to local experts who freely give us so much new information. In this instance I have been most fortunate to have been helped by three such experts, Professor Maurice Barley, Dr Norman Summers, and Mr Keith Train, whose combined knowledge of the history of the county and its buildings is formidable.\* I am grateful to them all for their unflagging interest. I must first thank Dr Summers for devoting so much of his time to visiting and revisiting buildings throughout the county in order to correct and amend our descriptions of secular (and particularly vernacular) buildings. His name or initials in the text denote his contributions, but he gave me much other help in improving my text. Professor Barley has made some important contributions to both editions, to this one most notably the descriptions of Holme Pierrepont Hall, of Newark Castle, of the medieval boroughs of Newark and Nottingham, and of the Archbishop's Palace at Southwell. Mr Train supplied me with copious notes and kindly checked numerous historical details. I also owe many thanks to Mr H. V. Radcliffe (Curator, Newark Museum) who spent two days giving me an exhaustive tour of Newark and district and to Mr H. A. Johnson, who drove me round the north of the county and gave me much new information. I would like also to thank Mrs Radcliffe and Mrs Johnson for their generous hospitality. We are very grateful to Mr Alec Clifton-Taylor for, as usual, undertaking to write about Building Materials for us, this time in collaboration with Professor Barley. Mr Malcolm Todd wrote the essay on Early Settlement and the corresponding entries in the gazetteer, Mr Keith Reedman those concerning Industrial Archaeology. Mr J. P. Bartlam provided excellent material from his research about T. C. Hine and Victorian architecture in Nottingham, indicated in the text by his initials. Mr R. Alvey kindly visited parish churches all over the county and recorded many details omitted from the first edition. Mr G. Beaumont of the Nottingham County Council Planning and Transportation Department answered a stream of inquiries.*

\* Their contributions are acknowledged in the text by their initials: MWB, NS, KT.

*I am grateful to Mr H. T. Swain (County Architect) for informa-
tion about the work of his department, and to Mr Brian T. Collins,
Director of Planning and Transportation, Nottinghamshire County
Council, Mr S. P. Byrne, Nottingham City Planning Officer, Mr
F. H. Molyneux, Director of Planning, Ashfield District Council,
Mr G. M. Ball, Director of Development, Bassetlaw District
Council, Mr K. A. Smith, Principal Architect, Broxtowe Borough
Council, Mr J. L. Parry, Chief Planning and Estates Officer, Ged-
ling Borough Council, Mr D. H. Jagger, Director of Technical Ser-
vices, Mansfield District Council, and Mr G. Stobbs, Newark Dis-
trict Council Architect, for answering my extensive queries. I have
also received a great deal of help from local librarians, namely Miss
B. M. Attenborough (Worksop), Mr D. Crute (Mansfield), Mr
E. J. Lingwood (Hucknall), and Mr R. H. Venner (Bingham), and I
must thank especially Mr Michael Brook, Special Collections
Librarian, Nottingham University, Mrs Sheila Cooke, Local
Studies Librarian, Nottinghamshire County Library, and Mr P. R.
Cousins of the County Education Resources Service. I was greatly
helped in my task by all the people in the county who generously con-
tributed information about their own localities or special interests,
in particular Mr G. Beaumont (windmills), Mr W. Clay-Dove (Sut-
ton-in-Ashfield and Teversal), Mr D. Durant (Bleasby), Mr A.
Henstock (Bingham), Mr D. S. Kilner and Mr D. Golberg (Watson
Fothergill), Mr F. W. Patmore (Mansfield and Skegby), Miss
Lorette Russenburger (The Park Estate, Nottingham), and Mr B.
Twelvetrees (Sir Thomas Parkyns). In addition, the officers of the
local societies gave me information on behalf of their members: Mrs
R. Spaul (Caunton Local History Society), Mr A. R. D. Arden
(Clifton History Society), Mrs V. Ayres and Mrs J. Stafford
(Kirkby and District Conservation Society), Mr F. J. Fletcher
(Mansfield Civic Society), Mr B. Wells (Old Mansfield Woodhouse
Society), Mr T. Leafe (Nuthall and District Local History Society),
Mrs A. Richardson and Miss J. V. Stafford (Ruddington and Dis-
trict Local History Society), and Mrs S. A. Mason (Wollaton Vil-
lage Preservation Society). Dr D. G. Williams, Dr B. J. Biggs, and
Messrs B. Hardy, R. Moore, and W. Storrs of Retford and District
Historical Society provided details about their area.*

*I am indebted to all the incumbents, owners of houses, principals
of schools and colleges, directors of business concerns, and hospital
secretaries who have spared some of their valuable time to answer
my questions. Dr R. Coope and Miss P. Wood thoroughly revised
my description of Newstead Abbey, Mr Gervase Jackson-Stops gave
me additional facts about Clumber, and Colonel Matthews kindly*

*entertained me at Welbeck College. Colonel T. Blagg (Brunsell Hall, Car Colston), Mr R. Brackenbury (Holme Pierrepont Hall), Mr L. Godlewski (Shireoaks Hall), Mr M. T. Hildyard (Flintham Hall), Mr P. V. Radford (Langford Hall), and Mr G. F. Seymour (Thrumpton Hall) all gave me detailed information about their homes.*

*As usual, many corrections and additions have been sent to us since the first edition was published. We thank all contributors, especially Mr M. Airs, Mrs R. Aldred, Mr T. Beaumont, Mr L. A. Butler, Mr T. L. Butler, Miss S. Calthrop-Owen, Mr J. W. Chambers, Mr H. M. Colvin, Mr R. Dixon, Mr W. G. Doubleday, Mr P. Howell, Mr R. L. Lewis, Mr N. Llewellyn, Mr S. G. Luff, Mr J. V. Machin, Mr R. Marks, Mr G. McHardy, Mr P. Middleton, Mr Ian Nairn, Mr R. McD. O'Donnell, Mr D. Palliser, Mr Charles Ogden, the late Mr S. Race, Mr S. E. Rigold, Mr M. R. Robbins, Mr J. M. Robinson, Mr E. Saunders, Mr C. W. Sex, Mr F. Smith, the Rev. G. W. Staunton, Mr C. Suffolk, Mr W. G. Syson, Mrs F. M. Wilkins-Jones, and Mr Christopher Wilson. Information about particular architects has been generously provided by Mr Paul Joyce (G. E. Street), Dr P. Leach (James Paine), Mr Hugh Meller (Blore), Mr Mervyn Miller (Parker & Unwin), and Dr R. B. Wragg (Carr of York). Mr C. Stell compiled a list of Nonconformist places of worship and Mr R. Hubbuck notes about Victorian stained glass: their initials in the text denote their contributions. The county map and the plans of Newark, Nottingham, and Southwell were drawn by Mr R. Piggott. Mr John Kilday redrew the plans of Newstead Abbey and of Southwell Minster (with kind permission of Dr Norman Summers). Mrs Mary Gage and Mr Peter Mawson gave me valuable secretarial help.*

*In the following gazetteer, as in all the other volumes, information ought to be as complete as space permits for churches prior to 1830, and for town houses, manor houses, and country houses of more than local interest. Movable furnishings in houses are not described, but church furnishings of before 1830 are, with the exception in most cases of bells, chests, royal arms, hatchments, altar tables, plain fonts and plate.\* Small Anglo-Saxon and Anglo-Danish fragments and coffin lids with foliated crosses are included where they are of special interest, post-Reformation brasses are mentioned only rarely. Village crosses are omitted where only a plain base or stump of shaft survives. As for churches, chapels, and secular buildings erected after 1830, examples of architectural value or significance in the light of architectural history have been selected.*

---

\* Plate has been included in all previous volumes. We have omitted it from this volume because understandably requested to do so by many incumbents.

*A note is necessary on how all the alterations to the first edition have been incorporated. Minor factual corrections or additions have been made without comment. For more extensive changes the source of information has been indicated. Other additions, unless they are in brackets, are the result of my own visits.*

*In this edition is printed for the first time a revised and expanded glossary which will be standard in all subsequent revised editions of The Buildings of England.*

*Finally I thank Mrs Bridget Cherry and Mrs Judy Nairn for their advice and constant encouragement. Once again corrections and additions will be welcome.*

## FOREWORD TO THE 1997 REPRINT

*We have taken the opportunity of this reprint to correct some of the inaccuracies in the 1979 edition. I have especially to thank Mr L. D. Butler and Mr Neville Hoskins for their comments. News from the county is generally good. Since 1979 few buildings of importance have been demolished and many have found new uses (not usually noted here). Several high-quality buildings have been restored, e.g. Serlby Hall by* Simpson & Brown, *1990–5; the White Hart, Newark, by* F. W. B. Charles, *1982; the front portion of Owen Williams's pioneering building for Boots at Beeston, extensively restored to much acclaim for use as labs and offices in 1995 by* Jan Sosna; *and warehouses in Nottingham's Lace Market, which has been revived as a lively urban quarter. Nottingham has also benefited from some exceptional new architecture, notably* Michael Hopkins & Partners' *Inland Revenue HQ, 1992–5,* Renton Howard Wood Levin's *Royal Concert Hall, completed c. 1978; and* Nicholas Grimshaw & Partners' *Castle Park warehouses, mid 1970s. On a more modest scale,* Robert & Brenda Vale's *attractive family house at Southwell was, when completed in 1993, judged the most energy-efficient house in the UK. Important research has been undertaken by Dr Rosalys Coope and Ms Pamela Wood at Newstead Abbey and by the University of Nottingham's tree-ring dating laboratory. Their county survey, begun 1977, has more precisely dated a number of timber-framed houses, including six of the late c13 and c14 (see* Trans. of the Thoroton Society 99, 1995, pp. 45–54).

# INTRODUCTION

NEITHER the architectural nor the picturesque traveller would place Nottinghamshire in his first dozen or so of English counties. It has no ancient cathedral, though the collegiate church of Southwell has been made one, and none of the most spectacular medieval castles or post-medieval country houses. As far as natural attractions go, there is indeed Sherwood Forest, though its existence underlines the county's lack of natural wealth, prior, that is, to the exploitation of coal (and gravel) in modern times.* Sherwood Forest has become a romantic concept since the growth of the legend of Robin Hood in the C18; the truth was far different. The Bunter sandstone soil, dry and sterile, makes up more than a quarter of the county's area, and it was so poor that by 958 it was already 'the wood belonging to the shire', useful only for common and for hunting. Villages were few and small, parishes enormous. The Norman kings made it royal forest, subject to special laws administered by a hierarchy of aristocratic officers which lingered on into the C18. The forest was not naturally dense and the trees (birch and oak) grew to girth rather than height; as the timber was consumed (the best of it for royal and ecclesiastical buildings, the rest for fuel) the glades turned into open heath. For the peasantry, the timber was neither good nor plentiful enough to generate a rich tradition in vernacular building (*see* Building Materials, p. 48). When the monasteries (Rufford, Newstead, Welbeck, Worksop) were dissolved, their sites and lands returned as a matter of course to the aristocracy. In 1769 Sir George Savile of Rufford Abbey told Lord Rockingham that four Dukes, two Lords, and three rabbit warrens took in half the county. The rabbit warrens eventually disappeared under afforestation and agricultural improvements. Now the Dukeries has neither dukes nor lords, and new coal mines and mining villages (Ollerton, Blidworth, etc.) have transformed the forest scene.

Of early architectural remains the tower of Carlton-in-Lindrick 3 is the most important, its details characteristic of the transition from late SAXON to Norman. Foundations of Saxon churches have been excavated at East Bridgford and at Ruddington (St

* For an account of early settlement in the county *see* p. 40.

Peter Flawford). The best example of Saxon decorative sculpture
4 is undoubtedly the Stapleford cross, but fragments survive in
several churches (Bilsthorpe, Carlton-in-Lindrick, East Bridg-
5 ford, Hawksworth, Hickling, Kneesall, Rolleston, Shelford, Shelton). Of NORMAN figure sculpture the most important is the early
historiated capitals at Southwell, comparable with those at Hereford, Westminster Abbey, and Reading. The contemporary tym-
11 pana at Southwell and Hoveringham, probably by the same
workshop, show traces of the 'Urnes' style. Other sculpture of
the early C12 seems in no essential way different (tympanum at
12 Hawksworth, lintel at Kirklington). Of later C12 sculpture the
representations of the occupations of the seasons at Calverton
are of more than local interest. Of Norman fonts there are plenty,
so many that those which are wholly undecorated are not men-
16 tioned in this book. The one at Lenton is among the best and most
interesting in the whole country, that at West Markham belongs
to a well-known type.

To NORMAN ARCHITECTURE Notts contributes more than
6–10 people usually realize. Blyth is a first-rate example of late C11
severity at its grimmest, Southwell nave equally fine of the early
C12, just keeping a nice balance between the bleakness of Blyth
19 and the busy Transitional of late C12 Worksop. In addition Notts
8, 20 has the only two complete surviving Norman two-tower façades
in England: at Southwell and Worksop. Southwell, the best preserved, also has a large tunnel-vaulted two-storeyed Norman N
porch, a very rare thing. Of equal distinction in the field of secular
architecture is what is left of the Bishop of Lincoln's Newark
17 Castle of c. 1133–9, with a gatehouse matched by few. The town
itself has an easily distinguished Norman plan, and under the par-
13 ish church is an early Norman rib-vaulted crypt. Minor Norman
appears in many places. Littleborough and Sookholme should be
specially mentioned, and the arcades of South Collingham and
18 South Scarle. South Leverton has a Norman W tower, rare in
Notts. Of Norman doorways Cox counted over fifty, more or less
complete. The best is at Teversal, and the best porch (forgetting
14, 15 Southwell) at Balderton. Chancel arches (Everton, Halam, South
Wheatley) and tower arches (Mansfield, Plumtree (rebuilt 1906),
Warsop) occur here and there. Specially interesting is the display
which some places make of herringbone masonry, one of the
characteristics of early Norman workmanship. The most conspicuous examples are Averham, East Leake, Farndon, Flintham,
Laneham, Littleborough, and Rolleston.

The C12 was a time of much enthusiasm for the founding of

RELIGIOUS HOUSES in the county. After the Benedictine Blyth of 1088 came Lenton (Cluniac, the richest monastery of Notts, founded by William Peverel in 1102–8), Thurgarton (1119–39, Augustinian), Worksop (c. 1120, Augustinian), Broadholme (1135–54, Premonstratensian canonesses), Wallingwells (c. 1140–4, Benedictine nuns, no remains), Rufford (1146, Cistercian), Felley (1156, Augustinian), Welbeck (1153–4, Premonstratensian), Shelford (c. 1160–80, Augustinian), Newstead (c. 1163–73, Augustinian), and finally Mattersey (c. 1185, Gilbertine). The Knights Hospitaller were established at Ossington before 1154 and at Winkburn before 1199: no remains. There are remains of most of the houses mentioned and some are of interest. The cloister layout at Rufford with a remarkably complete cellarium is very close to that of Fountains Abbey. Beauvale (founded 1343), though not thoroughly excavated, is one of the least encumbered of the English Charterhouses. More complete remains (cloisters, chapter house, etc.) are incorporated in Newstead Abbey. The new orders of the C13, that is the friars, had only three houses, and of these there is nothing left: Nottingham (Franciscan, before 1230, and Carmelite, before 1271) and Newark (Observants 1507, then Austin Friars 1534). There were no major hospitals, and nothing remains of those that there were. At Southwell, the buildings round the minster reflect its important collegiate status.

GOTHIC CHURCHES have no characteristics wholly peculiar to the county. They partake of styles whose centres lie outside Notts, notably in Lincolnshire and south Yorkshire, but also (only locally relevant) in Derbyshire and Leicestershire. The SPIRES of Notts for instance are not as spectacular or frequent as those of Lincolnshire or Northamptonshire, although good examples survive, especially Newark. The chief types are broach-spires (for example Gedling, a preparatory early form at Gotham, and one with minute broach-spires as pinnacles at Ratcliffe-on-Soar) and thinner octagonal spires rising far recessed behind battlements (for example St Peter, Nottingham). Spires may have from one to four (Newark) tiers of openings. Crocketed spires are rare (Balderton, etc.). Crossing towers are equally rare (Clifton, Langar, St Mary Nottingham, and, with spires, Normanton-on-Soar and Whatton). WEST TOWERS on the whole are not high. A few ambitious compositions with large Perp bell-stage windows occur particularly in the E part of the county (Dunham, South Muskham, Rolleston, etc.). Minor specialities are a large group with eight instead of four pinnacles on the battlements (St Mary Nottingham, etc.),

one with nine (Upton), and one with twelve (Sturton-le-Steeple), another group with a panelled and decorated frieze below the
32 battlements (Newark and many others), and yet another with a plain horizontal band connecting the tops of the buttresses below the battlements (Attenborough, Barton-in-Fabis, Bunny, Sutton Bonington).

THE STYLE OF THE C13 has more work of first-rate national
21 significance in Notts than any other: Worksop Lady Chapel (mid
22–5 C13), Southwell E arm of c. 1250–60, Southwell chapter house
27–9 (after 1288) with its unforgettable leaf capitals, the tower of
32 Newark (completed only in the mid C14), and (far too little known) the classically perfect façade of Newstead Abbey. The w portals of Thurgarton Priory of c. 1230 are also in impeccable E.E. taste. In smaller churches a surprising variety of pier shapes can be found, well worth recording, in contrast to the so much more marked tendency towards standardization which came with the C14 and C15.

An early example is the use of three types at Cuckney (octagonal, circular, quatrefoil) c. 1200.* A mixture of circular and octagonal piers is quite common in the C13, perhaps reflecting the influence of Worksop (see e.g. Barnby-in-the-Willows, Orston, Sutton Bonington). Other types include quatrefoil, quatrefoil with four detached shafts in the diagonals, square with four attached shafts, or with four shafts and deep hollows between, or with four major and four minor shafts, octagonal with four shafts in the main or the diagonal directions, etc., and most of these shafts either plain or keeled or provided with fillets. The sources are Southwell, Beverley, and Lincoln (especially its parish churches). Good places to look are Laneham, Rolleston, North and South Collingham, South Leverton, and Thurgarton. The font at Lowdham is no doubt also work of the Southwell lodge.
30 The charming figure corbels at Whatton on the other hand seem to derive from the workshop of the Angel Choir at Lincoln. Geometrical tracery becomes specially interesting around 1300, when the perfection of lancets and circles with inscribed trefoils and quatrefoils, etc., is given up in favour of slightly more complicated, more wilful and less balanced forms. Some study of the restless variation of geometrical motifs in the Southwell chapter house, the upper floor of the chapter house corridor, and then at Burton Joyce, Averham, Ratcliffe, Normanton-on-Soar, Stapleford, East Leake, Eakring, etc., can be recommended.

* Earlier still are the unique C12 piers excavated at Lenton Priory (see p. 252 n).

It leads on to the delights of the early C14 in Notts, that is the
DECORATED style. Here also the county is in close relations with
Lincolnshire and south Yorkshire, that is with Lincoln, Beverley,
Selby, and so on. The most excellent monuments are the stone
screen of Southwell, vaulted with rarely found flying ribs, c. 1320– 37, 38
40, and the chancel of Hawton with its ornate Easter Sepulchre 39, 40
dating from soon after 1330. This chancel and those of Sibthorpe,
Car Colston, Woodborough, and Arnold all belong together (cf. 41
also the niche arrangement in the W tower at Thoroton). Easter
Sepulchres are in more or less fragmentary forms at Sibthorpe,
Arnold, and Fledborough. They obviously come from the same
workshops as those of Heckington, Irnham, and Navenby in Lincolnshire. Two relief panels at Mattersey are also by the same 36
masons. Crocketing is everywhere of the most luxuriant, and window tracery often of fantastic, sinuous shapes (Cromwell, Eakring, and East Leake (E windows), North Leverton, South Leverton, and Sutton). The tiny mid-C14 porch attached to the early
C14 Worksop Priory gatehouse is exquisitely complete. Spatially
more interesting than these vagaries of decoration is the growing
tendency towards breadth as against height, characterized impressively by the addition about 1300 or 1310 to the early naves of
Blyth and Newark of aisles as wide as the naves had been. Their
width and their large windows altered the spatial character of the
buildings completely. From the middle of the C14 onwards Notts
liked to emphasize this change of predominant dimension by giving up the pointed heads of windows which had been a matter
of course in Gothic architecture until then and remained so in
other countries and counties. In Notts straight-headed windows
appear as early as c. 1356 (at Strelley). They soon became very
usual though by no means universal. On the largest scale they were
never used, not even in the late C15 and early C16 (Newark and
St Mary Nottingham, W window Southwell). What, however, did
happen in some of these late churches, and which reflects the same
mentality, is that the curves of the sides of a pointed window head
are replaced by straight lines (North Muskham, Colwick (Nottingham), Norwell, Sutton-in-Ashfield, Sutton-on-Trent).

These last remarks have already taken us to the PERPENDICU-
LAR style, and it was then that the Notts parish churches came
into their own. A few points of detail may be mentioned at once
before passing to some more general remarks. Clerestory windows
are occasionally doubled as against number of bays inside (St
Mary Nottingham, Newark, East Markham, Laxton), the same 46, 48,
lively rhythm as is found, for example, at Melton Mowbray close

to the Notts border and in so many of the larger churches of East
Anglia. Pier sections are not on the whole very interesting.
Newark is quite ordinary, St Mary Nottingham and North Musk-
ham are lozenge-shaped, East Markham (and also Clayworth)
have octagons with two reed-like hollows in each of the diagonals.
About a dozen porches exist with stone roofs supported by trans-
verse arches: at Babworth, Bunny, East Bridgford, Hayton,
Linby, North Collingham, Scrooby, Sutton-cum-Lound, Trowell,
West Retford, and (without ribs) at Gedling. They are headed by
47 St Mary Nottingham, early C15.

      St Mary Nottingham and Newark, which took nearly eighty
47–52 years to build, are the paramount examples in Notts of rich town
churches. Newark was in the late Middle Ages as populous and
prosperous as Nottingham. Village churches may not be up to
the standards of, say, the Nene Valley, but some of them are none
the less of a size and finish surprising in what now seem such
remote villages. However, it should not be forgotten that owing
to the wealth accruing to the lords of the manors and the farmers
from sheep farming, villages were quite often bigger than they
are now (this applies specially to the wolds in the s and se; see
the evidence of depopulation in the reduction of sizes of village
churches at Upper Broughton, Colston Bassett, Edingley, Elton,
Granby, Langford, Owthorpe, Sibthorpe, Stanton, Stokeham),*
and that the families of the lords of the manors sometimes
belonged to a class well aware of, and connected with, developments in the rest of England and indeed of Europe. A characteristic case is Laxton, where in the C13 Richard de Lexington had
one son who was Keeper of the Great Seal and went on political
missions to the Emperor Frederick II and the King of France,
one who became Bishop of Lincoln, and another who became
Abbot of Clairvaux, one of the most illustrious monasteries in
Europe. No wonder, then, if occasionally village churches are
far from modest in architecture and decoration. Lambley, built
in the 1460s by Ralph Cromwell, High Treasurer of England, is
a good example of that unusual thing, a completely Perp village
church. In Notts, however, the most perfect example of a village
church essentially the gift of one man is due not to a peer but
to a tradesman, the rich wool merchant John Barton of Newark
53, 54 † 1491, who rebuilt and re-equipped Holme-by-Newark about
the end of the C15. The church is almost complete with its
stained glass, its screens, and its stone monument to the bene-

      * The best deserted medieval village site is at Willoughby-on-the-Wolds
(Thorpe-in-the-Glebe).

factor, and it was, moreover, uncommonly well restored to SPAB principles.

For outstanding CHURCH FURNISHINGS one would hardly go to Notts, although the old doors with their decorative ironwork at Southwell (and in other places: Attenborough, Hickling, Laneham, Teversal, Worksop) deserve more than passing notice. But neither fonts, nor stalls, nor bench ends, nor stained glass are of the first quality. The few things of interest can be enumerated briefly. There are numerous poppyhead bench ends at Balderton; the best misericords at Newark, Southwell, and, from St Mary Nottingham, at St Stephen Sneinton (Nottingham). Of stained glass the most substantial fragments are at Halam (C14), Newark (c. 1300–C15), Southwell (C13–15), East Retford (C14 and C15), and Fledborough (C14). More unusual are the C16 painting of the Dance of Death on the Markham Chantry at Newark, the C15 coat of arms of Christ with a Spitting Jew at Clifton (Nottingham), the fine brass lectern belonging to a series made in East Anglia c. 1500 at Southwell, and the rare shawms or vamping horns at East Leake and South Scarle.

As for MONUMENTS, nothing worth looking at remains earlier than the C14, and then also hardly more than minor objects: a group of monuments to laymen holding their hearts in their hands (Averham, Stanford, West Leake), a group of priests, their busts enclosed in quatrefoils (Tuxford, Gamston; cf. Gedling), and a group of figures in a curious form of recessed relief as if lying in a shallow trough with a broad band across, hiding the middle parts of their bodies (East Markham, North Collingham, Staunton c. 1330). Especially attractive C14 monuments are at Skegby (to a Sherwood Forest official), Laxton (Sir Adam de Everingham † 1341), Gonalston, and Norwell (two ladies wearing wimples 35 c. 1300). At Strelley Sir Sampson de Strelley † c. 1390 provided 43 himself with a lavish tomb in the chancel he rebuilt, but in general later monuments are better. That at Holme to John Barton † 1491 is of good quality, with a corpse on the lower tier and the effigy on the upper, as are also those of about the same date at Wollaton († 1528) and Strelley († 1501). In both Wollaton († 1471) and 56, 57, 59 Strelley († 1487) churches there are also good C15 brasses, but the show-piece amongst brasses in Notts is the uncommonly large plate to Alan Fleming at Newark, which is foreign, probably Flemish, and dates from 1363. Good also are one of 1419 at East Markham and two of 1478 and 1491 at Clifton. The 45 earliest surviving English brass seems to be the remains of one of c. 1360–80 at Bothamsall. As to alabaster sculpture, Notts has twenty effigies of pre-Reformation date, and surprisingly few of those characteristic small panels with such scenes in relief as the Annunciation, Crucifixion, Deposition, Trinity, etc., which were exported from Nottingham right through the late Middle Ages to destinations as distant as Spain, Italy, and Germany. The Nottingham Museum preserves a good number (besides the outstandingly good C14 figures of the Virgin and Saints from Flawford), but it looks oddly as if the industry, which chiefly used the alabaster quarried at Chellaston in Derbyshire (*see* Building Materials, p. 47), worked almost entirely for export.* The early incised alabaster slabs are not usually well-preserved enough to comment on, though the one to a priest of *c.* 1150 at Selston is one of the earliest to have a figure. This changes with the later C15, but the largest collection (eleven slabs *c.* 1490–1524 at Ratcliffe-on-Soar) is in bad condition.

Of church furnishings of the late Middle Ages the SCREENS are the most noteworthy. There are about thirty-five in Notts. Newark's (1508) is the only surviving work of the famous *Thomas Drawswerd* of York, but the earlier screen (*c.* 1400) at Strelley perhaps deserves the palm. West Bridgford is exceptionally early, evidently C14, Laxton remarkably late, dated 1532. The design of the Notts screens is far from standardized. Only occasionally can two or three be recognized as belonging to one and the same type: Blyth and Sutton; Rolleston and Halloughton; Sutton-on-Trent and Laxton; and Ordsall and East Drayton (with lively tracery). Laxton also has a lavish though not particularly high-quality Perp roof. On the whole it is the *ensembles* of churches that impress us more than the individual monument or stained-glass window or screen.

All the MEDIEVAL SECULAR BUILDINGS of any consequence are in ruin. What survives is the C12 to C15 fabric of Newark Castle, slighter remains of 1212–13 and the C14 at Nottingham Castle, the outer walls of the Archbishop of York's Palace (later C14 and 1426–36) at Southwell, and a fragment of a royal hunting lodge in Sherwood Forest, at Clipstone.‡ At Laxton is the largest and best preserved motte-and-bailey castle in the county. At Castle Farm, Greasley, are the remains of the Cantilupes' fortified manor of *c.* 1341. The intact C13 and C14 tower house at Halloughton and the stone hall-house of *c.* 1500 at Bleasby are unusual for

---

* At least some were intended for private houses.

‡ Only earthworks are visible of another hunting lodge, Kingshaugh, Darlton, so very little evidence remains of this building type which was important from the C12 to C16 in a county with so much area covered by royal forest.

the county; the circular C13–14 dovecote at Sibthorpe is unusually 42 large. There are few remains of timber-framed buildings in Notts (*see* Building Materials, p. 48) and none of national importance except the late C15 front range of the White Hart Inn at Newark 55 with its superb purlin roof. The TUDOR period sees the advent of brick in secular building (*see* Building Materials, p. 49), in the only surviving range of the early C16 courtyard house at 58 Holme Pierrepont, at Old Hall Farm Kneesall, *c.* 1522–6, at Hodsock gatehouse, and before 1553 in the demolished 'Red Prebend' at Southwell. Old Hall Farm, probably built as a courtier's hunting lodge, can claim two innovations: the lobby-entrance type of plan* and the structural use of terracotta (which is employed decoratively for tracery in Granby church, in a *tour de force* of decoration on the gateway at Rampton, *c.* 1540, and later (1573) for a finely carved panel at Staunton Hall). At Hodsock *c.* 1525, Renaissance ornament makes an early and isolated appearance in the county. In the plasterwork, *all'antica* motifs are combined with conventional diaper work.

The RENAISSANCE seems to have taken hold in Notts late. Still in the 1530s neither the Laxton screen (1532) nor the Sacheverell tomb of 1539 at Ratcliffe have any Renaissance detail. The Mering Chapel of 1525 at Sutton-on-Trent represents the last stage of the purely Perp style church building, but the gorgeous, if somewhat barbarous, Babington chantry at Kingston-on-Soar of *c.* 1540 betrays familiarity with the new fashion in its ornament. It appears elsewhere also only in odd details such as the angle balusters in the Sacheverell tomb of 1558 at Ratcliffe, and then is straightaway swamped by the craze for Flemish strapwork (Clayworth, 1559). The conduit-head at Newstead (the priory remodelled by Sir John Byron in 1539) has the characteristic combination of late medieval and Renaissance motifs. The pure Renaissance forms of, say, the chancel stalls of King's College Chapel, Cambridge, do not occur at all. The transition from Perpendicular to Elizabethan appears without hiatus.

ELIZABETHAN MONUMENTS, chiefly of alabaster, and those continuing the Elizabethan style into the C17, until the time when the style of Inigo Jones belatedly arrived as a second thrust of Renaissance ideas, are numerous: the other Sacheverell tombs at Ratcliffe and Barton, the Chaworth tombs at Langar, Cliftons at 65, 71 Clifton, Byrons from Colwick (now at Newstead), and others at

* This plan became popular in the later C17 in smaller village houses and can be easily identified by the chimneystack rising from the centre of the roof ridge. The type is most common at Cossall and Thrumpton.

Wysall († 1572, cf. Ratcliffe † 1558), Screveton († 1583), Shelford
66 († 1587; cf. Southwell), Southwell (Archbishop Sandys † 1588),
68 Saundby († 1599), Cotham († 1601, now at Newark), Ossington
(† 1602), Averham († 1607; cf. Newstead † 1604), Tuxford
(† 1625), Selston (late, † 1630), and Stapleford (very late, † 1639).
The two tombs by known designers are not outstanding. They are
by *John Smythson* at Holme Pierrepont (1615), and by *Edward
Marshall* at Walkeringham, which is dated 1659 but is still in the
60 Jacobean tradition. More original and moving is the shrouded
C16 figure at Annesley. The Scroope monument of 1609 at
Langar is as good as any in the country, as good, e.g., as the
Rutland tombs at Bottesford in Leicestershire. In other cases the
decoration is much better than the figure work (for example
67 Sibthorpe, 1590); the bulk is decidedly provincial.

ELIZABETHAN AND JACOBEAN ARCHITECTURE must have
been far more abundant than it is now. Of the Holles's Haughton,
one of the greatest mansions in the country, and of Lord Shrewsbury's Worksop Manor nothing survives. Wollaton Hall (1580–
63, 64 8) is so spectacular that it promises much for the buildings we
can now only study in part or in remaining drawings and engravings. Wollaton is exceptional among Elizabethan houses and
characteristic in more than one way of its designer, the architect-
mason *Robert Smythson*: in its raised central hall, a more deter-
minedly symmetrical feature than was usual before the C17, and
in its Gothic tracery and medievalizing angle *tourelles* (cf. Bolsover
Keep). The origin of the plan is in a French pattern-book, but
otherwise it has plenty of hearty and somewhat coarse strapwork
decoration and windows as large and with as many mullions and
transoms as Hardwick.* Robert Smythson was patronized by
Lord Shrewsbury, his wife Bess of Hardwick, and their own
circles of friends and protégés who dominated this part of the
61 north Midlands. He developed at Worksop Manor (completed
1585–6), and over the Derbyshire border at Barlborough (1585),
Hardwick (1590), and probably at Bolsover (begun 1612), a style
which is regional without being the least provincial in a derogatory
sense. Its distinguishing feature was, as described at Wollaton,
a tall, compact, ingeniously symmetrical plan. This, and most
62 probably Smythson's hand, can be seen at Worksop Manor Lodge
and at Shireoaks Hall, which has a plan akin to that of Bolsover
Keep. What exactly the Shrewsburys did at Rufford is unknown.
Smythson and his son *John* worked for Bess of Hardwick's son,

* Possibly not Smythson's first Midlands house, as was once thought.
Worksop Manor has a claim to precedence.

Sir Charles Cavendish, at Welbeck, where part of Robert's court-yard plan house survives in the C18 structure, and one room and the remodelled riding school (1622) are by *John*. The evidence of John's work elsewhere in Notts is slight. He designed a tomb (*see* p. 147) at Holme Pierrepont, where a fragment of the 1628 hall suggests his hand. At Clifton Hall there is no trace of his 1632 banqueting house and stables, though a chimneypiece may be his. His plans for Haughton (1618) were unexecuted, and there is nothing of his to see in what is left of Wiverton Hall nor was there at Grove Hall after *Carr* set to work in 1762.

Almost nothing is left of INTERIOR DECORATION of the period either. At Wollaton all that survives is the stone screen. At Newstead are three early C16 overmantels (possibly from Colwick) and a plaster ceiling of 1631–3. 70

One of the most important POST-RESTORATION HOUSES, Nottingham Castle, was also erected by a member of the Shrews- 79 bury clan, the Duke of Newcastle, grandson of Bess of Hardwick. This, built in 1674–9, may be far from polished in its architecture, but it has much character and certainly not a provincial one. Its revolutionary Baroque silhouette (cf. the Duke's buildings at Bols-over) and details owe a debt to Italy, and predate Thoresby, which is usually thought to have been the first building of this type in England. Thoresby, built in 1685–7, was burnt down in 1745. Probably designed by Wren's Office of Works, it was of impor-tance in the evolution of the so-called Office of Works style (at Hampton Court, Greenwich, etc.). Its decoration by *Cibber* and *Laguerre* also set a fashion.* The detail at Nottingham Castle belongs to the crude and robust Carolean style known as Artisan Mannerism, to be seen in the typical staircases at Thrumpton, Holme Pierrepont, and Woodborough, and in doorcases and 72 panelling at Thrumpton (1662) and Annesley (*c.* 1669). The most sophisticated late C17 house, Watnall Hall, Greasley, with fine panelling, plasterwork, and wrought-iron gates, has been demolished. On a smaller scale the surviving C17 MANOR HOUSES AND FARMHOUSES mostly date from the later C17. Early C17 examples in stone (for example Clerkson's Hall, Mansfield Woodhouse, 1631; Langford Old Hall; Costock Manor) are scarce now that several have been demolished (for example, Kirkby-in-Ashfield). Brick was adopted generally quite late (*see* Building Materials, p. 49), and even later the style is essentially

* Mr Colvin attributes to *Talman*, who was once thought to have designed Thoresby, the demolished Blyth Hall of 1684–5 (*see Dictionary of British Architects*, 1978 ed.).

Tudor or Jacobean with shaped or stepped gables and detail in
which classical elements are used in a coarse, heavy-handed, but
none the less charming way (Thrumpton Hall, 1609–18, remodelled 1662; Brewhouse Yard, No. 53 Castle Gate, and Nos. 4–
6 Wheelergate c. 1660 (demolished), Nottingham; Nos. 15–21
Millgate, Newark, 1663 (demolished); Bulwell School, 1667;
Tuxford School, c. 1669; North Wheatley Manor House, 1673;
81 Willoughby Almshouses, Cossall, 1685). Nottingham, becoming
a brick town in about 1660, was encircled by a number of contemporary manor houses; at Beeston, c. 1675; Bramcote; Chilwell,
1677 (demolished); and Stapleford, 1689 (demolished). A
favourite decorative form widespread in brick houses of c. 1700
is cogged or dentillated eaves and string courses (e.g. Highfield
Farm, Kirton; Edingley Manor Farm). At Bole, East Leake,
78 North Wheatley (1673), Rempstone, and Sutton Bonington, these
strings are taken up over the windows like vestigial pediments or
labels in a pseudo-classical manner. The favoured plan of c. 1700
is single- or double-pile with gabled end elevations and a symmetrical façade. Later in the EIGHTEENTH CENTURY the single
pile was often extended by another range with an up-to-date
façade (e.g. Caunton Grange, Gonalston Rectory, Farnsfield Hall,
Dunham House), or, alternatively, by a rear wing making a T- or
L-shaped plan. C17 H-plan houses at Caunton (Beesthorpe Hall)
and Mansfield Woodhouse (Manor House) were Georgianized
with sashes and rendering. In Notts the double-pile plan, that is a
house more or less square and two rooms deep, was covered with
the most simple form of roof: two parallel pitched roofs with a
valley between. This contrasts with the more sophisticated hipped
form with a platform or hidden valley found in the south-east,
and with the northern form, shallow enough to cover the two-
room depth. In other respects vernacular building in the county
shows affinity with the north, in the use of rear staircase projections (e.g. Manor House, Lowdham), and of timber-framed fireplace hoods. These (now rare but still found at Old House, Bleasby,
and Red Lion Cottage, Chilwell, 1678) were most easily constructed against the gable-end, which left room for a framed staircase in the centre of the house. The popularity of the arrangement accounts for gable-end chimneys becoming usual in the C18.
As the brick industry expanded in the C18, it encouraged country
builders to put up taller houses, though these were often still
double-pile. Although seen elsewhere in the Midlands (e.g.
Warwickshire), they are particularly noticeable in Notts. Early
C18 houses have up to three or four feet between the upper

windows and the eaves. Later, because brick was simpler and cheaper to use than timber, small windows were put in this space to light the attics (as in several cottages at Costock and Sutton Bonington), instead of the dormers preferred in the south-east. Except in the most 'polite' houses, any dormers are likely to be later insertions. Some farmhouses (e.g. Manor Farm, Kingston-on-Soar) are of two storeys plus garrets, others (e.g. 79 High Street, Arnold) a full three storeys. Goldhill Farm, Halam, is an ambitious example of the latter type dated 1810. One curiosity of c. 1700 should be mentioned separately: that is, the buildings designed by the local squire *Sir Thomas Parkyns* at Bunny, Bradmore, Costock, and East Leake. His solid farms and Bunny School are almost without classical references, but the extraordinary combination of features at Bunny Hall betrays some knowledge of the current native Baroque. 83

Both Nottingham and Newark have plenty of TOWN HOUSES 85, 89, 90 in the polite architecture of the CLASSICAL STYLE, beginning with the late C17 Newdigate House at Nottingham and the neglected Handley House at Newark. In Nottingham the best later houses are concentrated in two areas, around the castle (Stan- 89 ford House, Castle Gate, 1775) and around the parish church in High Pavement. Nottingham had, and Newark still has, a market place of early C18 character lined with the colonnades Jones misnamed 'piazzas'. Other towns have no C18 houses worth individual mention (except perhaps the Moot Hall (1752) and Waverley House (1754) at Mansfield), but East Retford and Tuxford have a general Georgian character because in the C18, like Newark, they were stopping-places on the Great North Road. At Southwell, the Residence and Vicars' Court (1779–85) is a neat piece of late 25 C18 planning. Cranfield House (c. 1700–20) is the best of the prebendal mansions, most of which were rebuilt or refaced during the C18. Of the same period are the rectories at Langar, Wilford, and Kirkby-in-Ashfield (1717 with a perfect s façade) and, on a slightly larger scale, the contemporary Ollerton Hall and Sutton Bonington Hall. One or two of the villages have a number of good brick houses (Collingham, Farndon), but Notts is not rich in specially pretty villages: Clifton for its verdure, and Fiskerton and 1 West Stockwith as Trent-side villages of almost Dutch character 2 may be singled out. Nottingham and Newark also have the only notable C18 PUBLIC BUILDINGS: *Gandon*'s uninspiring Nottingham Shire Hall of 1769–70, and *Carr*'s Newark Town 91 Hall of c. 1774–6.

Altogether the county possesses about fifteen CHURCHES built

between the RESTORATION AND THE EARLY NINETEENTH
CENTURY.* No one of them is architecturally important, though
77 St Nicholas Nottingham (1671–82), Morton (1756), and one or
two others have much that is lovable. Like the tower of St
Nicholas, the brick tower at Edwalton, which may well go back
to the middle of the C16, and the C17 towers at Kirklington,
Hawksworth, and Bilsthorpe still have a later Perp feel. So does
the nave at Holme Pierrepont. The chancel tracery at Barnby-in-
69 the-Willows looks distinctively post-medieval. Of classical
2 churches, the best are West Stockwith (c. 1722), Papplewick
(1795, typical small proprietary chapel of a late C18 mansion),
93 and Carr's Holy Rood (1782–3) at Ossington. Occasionally the
old nave and aisle arrangement is kept and Tuscan columns
replace the piers of the Middle Ages (East Stoke 1738, Blidworth
1739). The only church of spatially unusual form is of the very
end of the Georgian period: at Milton, West Markham, by
Smirke, 1831–2, a combined church and Newcastle Mausoleum.
The Duke's monument († 1850) in it is not worthy of the name
of the founder, although the Duchess's (now at Clumber) is quite
a touching piece by Westmacott, c. 1832. Indeed by and large
SEVENTEENTH AND EIGHTEENTH CENTURY MONUMENTS
are disappointing in Notts. At Newark in a group of three wall-
tablets († 1639, † 1659, † 1661) with busts one can see the conservative reaction to classical detail. Surprisingly, the latest monument is the most Jacobean, the earliest the most Jonesian. A
similar blend of old and new occurs, for example, at Laneham
(† 1638). Upright figures appear at Mansfield Woodhouse in 1684
and at Sturton c. 1687, semi-reclining ones surprisingly late (Blyth
86 † 1703, West Stockwith † 1722). This is the type (in an up-to-
date version influenced by Plumier's and Scheemakers's
Buckingham monument † 1721) used by William Palmer in the
87 Lexington monument (1726) at Kelham. There are few monuments by well-known sculptors and none of their best work. Most
94 accomplished are the Denison figures († 1782, † 1785) at Ossington
by Nollekens, who also did a bust at Shelford. There is a tablet
by Roubiliac at Newark († 1757); two at Holme Pierrepont (1802,
† 1811) and an early relief (1780) at Papplewick Hall by Flaxman;
a tablet at Staunton by Westmacott (1811) and a monument at
Shelford by Chantrey († 1824). Sir Thomas Parkyns's design (1715)
84 for his own monument at Bunny is as curious as his hall. Excellent

---

* The earliest Nonconformist church, the Old Meeting House (1701), is at
Mansfield, where a community (later called Unitarians) was established in
1665.

anonymous craftsmanship is found at Holme Pierrepont († 1683) 80
and Teversal († 1741), but minor c18 monuments are not at all 88
frequent, and curiously rare in the north. In the north also the
most attractive feature of Notts is absent: engraved slate tombstones. These are very usual in the south and east, so much so
that they cannot be mentioned in this book except in a few
selected places.*

As regards CHURCH FURNISHINGS of the c17 and c18, on
the other hand, Notts has a few places so complete and so unknown that attention must be emphatically drawn to them. I am
chiefly thinking of Teversal, c. 1675; but Barnby and Langar 76
(early c17); Maplebeck and Owthorpe (mid-c17); Oxton, c. 1681;
and Elston Chapel (minor late Georgian, now derelict), Papplewick, and Tythby (c18) are also worth noting. Of individual merit
are the Jacobean traceried screen at Winkburn, the reredos
(c. 1660, and just going classical) at Wollaton, the altar rails (1732) 73
at Car Colston, and the rustic achievement of 1686 at Annesley.
There is important stained glass at Southwell (Flemish and
French, c16 and c17), at Strelley (Flemish c16 and c17), and at
Babworth (by *Eginton*, 1830). Finally the series of fonts put up
immediately after the Restoration (at Southwell, East Bridg- 75
ford, Misson, Newark, Orston, Scarrington, Shelford, Sibthorpe, 74
Tuxford, Tythby, Walkeringham, and Whatton) should be
mentioned.

Notts, unlike Derbyshire, has no EIGHTEENTH CENTURY
COUNTRY HOUSES of national importance now that Thoresby
II, Worksop Manor, and Nuthall Temple have all disappeared.
Neither is there an example of the first important classical country
house style, based on Coleshill, since Averham Park (c. 1718–23)
and Winkburn Hall have been altered out of recognition.
Thoresby (*see* p. 27) represented the Baroque and, as long as
*James Paine*'s one completed wing (1761–7) of Worksop Manor
was still in existence, this was a nationally paramount example
of its style, the strictest Palladian style. If completed it would have
been the largest country house, or rather palace, since Blenheim.
All the Palladian monuments in Notts have gone. *Paine*'s Serlby
Hall (1754–73) was 'modernized' by *Lindley & Woodhead* in
1812–13; Nuthall Temple (1754–7) by *Thomas Wright*, which was
as famous for its plasterwork by *Thomas Roberts* as for belonging
to the same rare genre as Chiswick and Mereworth, has been
demolished; and two less exciting examples, Kelham Hall by *John*

* An article on them has appeared in *The Architectural Review*, vol. 107,
1950 (by M. W. Barley).

*Sanderson, c.* 1730, and Clumber House by *Stephen Wright, c.* 1760–70, were superseded by or subsumed in Victorian piles. In fact no great architecture contemporary with the great estates carved out of Sherwood Forest in the late c17 and c18 has survived the c19 and c20. Welbeck, altered but not much improved by *John James* (1741–9), *John Carr* (*c.* 1775), and *Repton* (1790–2), has a late Victorian veneer; *Carr's* Thoresby II (1767–71) was replaced by Salvin's mansion. *Carr* of York was popular in Notts. As well as the work at Grove Hall, Newark Town Hall, Thoresby, and Welbeck mentioned already, he substantially altered Blyth Hall *c.* 1770 (now demolished, though the bridge he built remains), Colwick Hall *c.* 1776, and Clifton Hall 1779–*c.* 1791, and designed *c.* 1780–90 the typically plain Langford Hall. The grandstand of *c.* 1780–90 at Nottingham racecourse was by him, and he worked in Gothic style at Budby *c.* 1789 (*see* below). Carr's pupil *Lindley* of Doncaster, who favoured Carr's 'late Adam' style, remodelled the early c18 Ossington Hall *c.* 1790 (demolished) and may have been responsible for the elegant Papplewick Hall of *c.* 1781–7. The early c19 interiors of Spital House Blyth also suggest his hand (he was working in 1812–13, with *Woodhead*, at nearby Serlby Hall). There are one or two plainer houses by lesser known local architects: Stanford Hall (1771–4) and Wilford Hall (1781) by *William Henderson* of Loughborough and Strelley Hall (1789–92) by *Thomas Gardner* of Uttoxeter. Finally a group of late c18 houses connected with the Pocklington family should be mentioned: Carlton Hall (1765), for and possibly by the banker-cum-amateur architect *Joseph Pocklington* (who designed the Bell Inn dining room at Carlton-on-Trent, 1788, and the demolished Muskham House, North Muskham, 1793) and the houses at Winthorpe built by his brother, Roger.

This brings us to the EARLY NINETEENTH CENTURY and the GREEK REVIVAL.* The most successful essay in this style is *Smirke's* Newcastle Mausoleum (*see* p. 30). *Donthorn's* villa, Upton Hall of 1830, is also neo-Greek, and *Henry Moses Wood* used the style in Nottingham for the Judges' Lodging (1833, with *Nicholson*) and very late (1857) for a lodge on the Forest Recreation Ground.

Many of the houses described had important GARDENS AND PARKS, some of which have outlived the houses. The late c17 saw formal gardens laid out on a vast scale. Thoresby had one, New-

---

* Not in this style but of 1806, Osberton Hall by *William Wilkins Jun.*, never very good and much altered *c.* 1830 by *Ambrose Poynter*, then almost rebuilt by *MacVicar Anderson* in 1877.

stead has part of one (1695), so has Serlby (1727), and Shireoaks Hall still has the remains of one laid out by the Surveyor General *Sir Thomas Hewett* on a scale that far outstripped that of the house. But the most historically important garden at Worksop Manor has gone. Designed by *Lord Petre* and laid out by *Peter Bourguinon* in 1733–44, it came mid-way between French formalism and Kent's naturalism. *Repton* was popular in Notts and by 1791 had been consulted at a number of places near to Welbeck (Babworth, Grove, Thoresby, and Wansley). At Clumber there is a fine series of classical GARDEN BUILDINGS and gates by *S. Wright* and at Rufford an unusual bath summer house (1729) by Hewett's protégé *John Hallam*. The GOTHIC REVIVAL STYLE appears early in garden buildings, in Newstead's 'silly forts' (1749), and in *Thomas Wright*'s summer house at Nuthall Temple: these survive. In the same genre is Wallingwells' C18 Castle Garden.

In country houses the Countess of Oxford was first at Welbeck Abbey, 1743–9, but the style is rare. There are a few castellated stuccoed recastings of earlier houses such as Bleasby Hall, late C18, Rosclaveston Manor, Tollerton, *c.* 1800, and Wallingwells, *c.* 1828. In emulation of what was there before are the similar façades at Holme Pierrepont, *c.* 1800 (now stripped off), Wiverton, 1814, and *Wyatville*'s Elizabethan-style interiors at Wollaton, 1801–4 and 1807. In decoration the best is the screen at Newstead Abbey of *c.* 1820. Newstead was restored and considerably 95 enlarged in 1818–19 by *John Shaw*, who included a neo-Norman tower at this early date. *Ambrose Poynter* also showed an early appreciation of the Norman style in his church at Scofton of 1833.

With that we have arrived at the CHURCH ARCHITECTURE OF THE VICTORIAN ERA. Convincing Gothic first appears in *Rickman & Hussey*'s St Stephen Sneinton (Nottingham) of 1837–9 (enlarged by *Hare*, 1912). Neo-Norman is used again clumsily by *L. N. Cottingham* at Thorney in 1849–50. Quite a number of leading church architects have had jobs in Notts, starting with *Pugin* at St Barnabas Nottingham (1841–5). *G. G. Scott* worked with *Moffatt* in 1843 at St John, Leenside, Nottingham (demolished), at Beeston in 1842–4, and on his own in restorations at Bingham 1845, Gamston 1855, Lowdham 1860, Costock 1862, and Arnold 1868–9. *Moffatt* left Scott's office in 1845 with the commission to restore St Mary Nottingham. *Oldrid Scott* and a G. G. Scott assistant, *W. S. Weatherley*, restored a number of churches, but the most prolific, and often ruthless, restorer was *Ewan Christian*, the Ecclesiastical Commissioners' Architect.

*Hodgson Fowler* was more sensitive (*see* also his new churches at Grove, 1882, St Alban Ordsall, 1901), but the best restoration, a model of SPAB 'anti-scrape', is twentieth-century, by *R. Harley 53 Smith* for Nevil Truman at Holme in 1932. *Teulon* and *Clutton* provided robust estate churches at Bestwood (1868–9) and Moorhouse (1860–1). The finest church architecture undoubtedly 100 comes late in the century. Supreme is *Bodley & Garner*'s Clumber church (1886–9), in full Ecclesiological rig. Also by *Bodley* two impressive compositions in Nottingham (St Alban Sneinton 1886–7 and the chancel of St George Kirkewhite Street 1897) and Coddington village church, which he restored and partly rebuilt in 1865–8. The decoration here (*see* below) and in Plumtree chancel (1873–4 with *Garner*) is contemporary. In 1897, *Temple Moore* designed a fine interior at Mansfield and *Christian, Caröe & Purday* a Sedding-style church at Nottingham. Well into the twentieth century (1911) comes *Paley & Austin*'s St Anne, Worksop. The churches for the Presbyterians at Nottingham (1896) and West Bridgford (1898), by the local architects, *Brewill & Baily*, are typical of the free and enterprising Nonconformist architecture of *c.* 1900.

*Comper*'s early and most inventive style appears in 1896–8 at Egmanton: his 1937 reredos at Newark is much less original. Some other CHURCH FURNISHINGS should be mentioned briefly. *Morris & Co.* did their best work at Coddington for Bodley, but there is some of their later glass (mostly *Burne-Jones* designs) at Whatton 1878, High Pavement Chapel, Nottingham 1904, Woodborough 1910, Halam 1919, and Mansfield 1913–28. There are good examples of other Victorian STAINED GLASS as well: by *Pugin* (made by *Wailes*) at St Barnabas Nottingham; by *Heaton, Butler & Bayne* (as good as Morris) at St Mary Nottingham 1867; and by *Hardman* at Newark (1862). There is a complete series (1883–95) by *Kempe* at Hucknall and a dull one (1892–6) by *Clayton & Bell* at Arnold. East Retford has an uncommonly instructive selection of glass by all these firms. The only MONUMENT worth mention is Bishop Ridding's at Southwell, designed by *Caröe* in 1907 with a bronze by *Pomeroy* who worked for Wilson at Welbeck. *Wilson*'s bronze doors at St Mary Nottingham (1904) are even finer than those at Welbeck (1909).

In VICTORIAN DOMESTIC ARCHITECTURE Notts has much to offer, even now that Clumber (remodelled by *Barry Jun.* in 1879–80) has been razed to the ground. There is Thoresby by 99 *Salvin* (1865–75), as proud a display of neo-Elizabethan grandeur as any in the country.* Then side by side in date are *Sir George Gilbert Scott*'s and *Teulon*'s neo-Gothic Kelham (1858–61) and 98 Bestwood (1862–5). Both have splendid carving, at Kelham by *Farmer & Brindley*, at Bestwood by *Earp*. *E. W. Godwin*'s romantic Beauvale House of 1871–3 shows a move towards the Domestic Revival, and for that is of national importance. Then finally among the first league is Welbeck. The underground suite of rooms (1860–79) is of interest more as a curiosity than as a work of architecture, but, towards the end of Victoria's reign in 1889–96, Welbeck was enriched by *Sedding*'s chapel and library with the details of both superb interiors by his brilliantly imaginative pupil, *Henry Wilson*. Much more conventional are the interiors and exteriors of 1900–2 by *Sir Ernest George & Yates*. In the second league, the best preserved house, both inside and out, is Flintham Hall (1853), the *chef d'œuvre* of the local *T. C. Hine* (*see* below). In neo-Elizabethan style are *Blore*'s dull Kingston Hall (1842–6), *Clutton*'s sumptuous Widmerpool Hall (1873–6), and *Devey*'s tactful additions to Hodsock Priory (1873–6). On a smaller scale, *Street*'s domestic-looking former vicarage at North Muskham, 1863.

ESTATE BUILDINGS belonging to these C18 and C19 country houses should be mentioned here. The cottages at Thrumpton (1700–45) and Sir Thomas Parkyns's buildings at Bunny, Bradmore, and Costock (*c.* 1700–41) are earliest. Next in date come William Mellish's mid-C18 rectory and cottages at Blyth, all with Gothic casements, then, in the late C18, the single village street at Strelley and Mr Acklam's hill-top farms at Wiseton. Fashionably Gothic are Earl Manvers's estate village, Budby, *c.* 1807–12, other Manvers housing at Radcliffe-on-Trent and Holme Pierrepont, and the old village of Lenton (Nottingham). Lord Belper provided houses round a green at Kingston-on-Soar (1840–5) and Earl Manvers expensive almshouses (*c.* 1890 by *W. O. Hickson*) of Perlethorpe. Most important of all is Earl Cowper of Beauvale's model hamlet of Moorgreen (1872–7). It was *Godwin*'s parsonage here that inspired J. T. Carr to commission from him designs for the first two villas for London's Bedford Park.

Other SECULAR BUILDINGS by nationally known C19 architects are few. In Nottingham the group of contemporary public buildings N of the centre (University College by *Lockwood & Mawson*, 1877–90, Guildhall by *Verity & Hunt*, 1887–8, Poor Law Offices by *A. H. Goodall*, 1887) and *Waterhouse*'s Prudential

---

* *Salvin*'s other work in this style at Rufford (1838–40) and Kelham (1844–6) has mostly gone.

perhaps should be singled out. Elsewhere there is only *George &*
101 *Peto*'s Domestic Revival Ossington Coffee Palace of 1882 at
Newark and one or two schools. Edward VI Grammar School at
East Retford by *Decimus Burton* (1855–7) and *R. H. Carpenter*'s
gaunt Worksop College (1890–5) are typical of c19 school architecture. In contrast *Hurst & Moffatt*'s school-cum-gatehouse at
Clipstone is remarkable because so eccentric. Town halls and
public buildings in the smaller towns are all disappointing.
Nottingham is predominantly a Victorian city. LOCAL ARCHI-
TECTS profited most from its c19 expansion. Both *T. C. Hine**
(1814–99) and *Watson Fothergill*‡ (1841–1928) were competent
and individual designers whose work is scarcely known outside
the Midlands. Hine's work, in Gothic for churches, usually Jacobethan or Italianate for secular buildings, can be seen throughout
the county, in churches (e.g. All Saints Nottingham 1863–4, his
best), church restorations (e.g. Holme Pierrepont, Laxton),
houses (notably Flintham Hall), stations (*c.* 1857 for the G.N.R.
at Aslockton, Bingham, Nottingham, Orston, Radcliffe-on-
Trent), commercial (e.g. Nottingham lace warehouses 1855) and
public buildings (Corn Exchange 1849–50, Castle and Shire Hall
1876–9, Nottingham), and monuments (market crosses at
Bingham and Mansfield). Fothergill tackled similar jobs with an
102 idiosyncratic combination of polychrome Gothic and half-timbering (see his own office in George Street, Nottingham, 1894–5).
The city's suburbs are interesting examples of URBAN
PLANNING. First and most impressive is the Park Estate initially
developed in 1820 but laid out on a grand scale by *Hine & Evans*
in 1856, but also worth study are Sherwood Rise 1845–50,
Mapperley Road 1852 etc., Alexandra Park *c.* 1854, and Mapperley
Park laid out *c.* 1880 by *Evans & Jolly*. In all of them there is a
good selection of houses built for affluent local manufacturers by
*Hine, Fothergill*, and other local architects, notably *Henry Sulley*,
*Arthur Marshall*, and *Brewill & Baily*.

Thus the TWENTIETH CENTURY and the end of this survey
is reached. First-rate modern architecture exists in only one place
103 so far (i.e. in 1950): at Beeston, where *Sir Owen Williams* built
factories for Boots in 1932 and 1938, with frank concrete construction. The 1930s colliery pithead baths at Blidworth,
Hucknall, Kirkby-in-Ashfield, Mansfield, West Markham, and
Warsop also deserve notice. Otherwise the c20 buildings worth

---

* In practice from 1848 to 1890; with *Robert Evans* 1857–67 and with his
son, *G. T. Hine*, 1867–90 (JPB).
‡ He changed his name from Fothergill Watson in 1892.

mentioning are still in the Arts-and-Crafts tradition: Inisdoon, Mansfield, 1904–5, one of *Barry Parker*'s best designs, and *C. C. Thompson*'s quadrangle and chapel at Kelham, 1924–8. The fittings and furnishings in both buildings (though removed from the latter) were excellent.

# POSTSCRIPT TO THE INTRODUCTION

IN 1951 the most striking twentieth-century development was the outward spread of Nottingham, which comprised two-fifths of the county's total population. Even then dormitory housing was appearing in the surrounding villages and small towns like Woodborough and Gotham. Since 1951 these places have increased in popularity, and large areas of bad housing in the city have been cleared. Nottingham's population has consequently declined from 306,055 in 1951 to 280,300 in 1976 while, during the same period, that of the county has increased from 841,211 to 977,500.* Though few places, except in the rural north-east, have no new buildings, design of both housing and amenities is uninspiring.‡

The redevelopment of parts of NOTTINGHAM has promoted very little architecture of merit. The most prominent redevelopment has been on the site of the late C19 Victoria Station: the Victoria Centre (by *Arthur Swift & Partners*, 1965–72), which incorporates high-rise flats and a shopping centre as large as the old city centre. High-rise flats have been rejected in general in favour of low-rise housing similar to the terraces it replaces. Only the *John Stedman Design Group*'s hillside housing (St Ann's Development Phase 10, 1965–78) deserves individual attention. The city has one building of which it can be proud: Nottingham Playhouse by *Peter Moro & Partners*, built in 1959–64 and still the best modern building in the county. NOTTINGHAM UNIVERSITY is disappointing. Although almost completely built since 1951, the style that prevails over most of the campus is neo-Georgian, in no example as good as Morley Horder's original university building of 1928. Among the most recent buildings are the library, a thoughtful design by *Faulkner-Brown, Hendy, Wat-* 104

---

* The county boundary remains about the same. Only Finningley has been lost to South Yorkshire but is still included in this volume.

‡ One exception is the group of houses at Lambley by the *Architects' Design Group*, 1972–3, in the neo-vernacular style beloved at the moment. It will be interesting to see how serious and long-lived this trend is.

*kinson & Stonor* (1972), and the University Hospital by the *Building Design Partnership* (1965–79), impressive because of its size. At the time of writing it is the largest group of hospital buildings in the world. Industry, with its huge financial resources, has been able to patronize internationally-known architects. On the outskirts of Nottingham two important INDUSTRIAL BUILDINGS stand side by side: Boots' cool and smoothly-detailed office build
105 ing at Beeston by the Americans *Skidmore, Owings & Merrill* in association with *Yorke Rosenberg Mardall*, 1966–8, and, in con
106 trast, *Arup Associates'* monumental John Player Horizon Factory (1968–71). Also on an imposing scale the string of POWER STATIONS along the Trent, notably at Cottam by *Yorke Rosenberg Mardall* 1964–8 and at West Burton by the *Architects' Design Group c.* 1969. There are no important new CHURCHES in Notts. *Laurence King* has completed the E end of Worksop Priory (1966–74), and *Gerard Goalen's* Good Shepherd (R.C.) at Arnold is typical of its date (1963–6). The stained glass in Goalen's church is by *Patrick Reyntiens* (1964–5), who also made windows at Hucknall (1961–2) and, to *John Piper's* design, at Misterton (1965). Finally the work of the *County Architect's Department* should be mentioned. In 1955 the CLASP* system of a light steel frame on a set module, based on that used in the Hertfordshire schools, was developed in Notts. Initially designed for school building, it is now widely used for other purposes. Among more successful results are the County Hall extension (1960–4) and Mansfield Woodhouse health centre (1972–4), where old materials have been re-used in the cladding. The latest development in school building is in the nature of a social rather than an architectural experiment. The community school (*see* the first examples at Bingham (1966–8) and Carlton (1968–72)) is used at Sutton-in-Ashfield (1971–8) as the focal point of a small industrial town.

From architecture we move briefly to planning. Nottingham and Mansfield have both been subjected to traffic schemes that have involved the destruction of a number of good buildings and the disruption, to no aesthetic advantage, of the old street patterns. In compensation, as the planners intended, both town centres are now more congenial. Nottingham was pedestrianized in 1973. Although introduced late (compared with, say, Norwich), the scheme was at the time more comprehensive and covered a larger area than that in any other town. Newark was completely

* Consortium of Local Authorities Special Programme. In 1957 the system was adopted for use in mining areas by a number of counties who, encouraged by the Ministry of Education, formed a consortium.

by-passed in the 1960s and the worst of the twentieth century hardly intrudes, except the new shopping precinct behind the Market Place (by *Gordon Benoy & Partners*, 1974–8) which, although cleverly planned to be discreetly hidden behind the famous market place, overwhelms Lombard Street at its back. Nottingham can take, and even benefits from, the monumental scale; Newark cannot. Redevelopment has meant demolition. In Nottingham the major loss has been the superb Collin's Alms- 82 houses of 1709 (demolished in 1956). Altogether ten churches (and three Nonconformist chapels) have gone, the most important to the townscape *H. I. Stevens*'s Holy Trinity of 1841. Its spire was a striking landmark N of the centre. Mansfield has lost two early Nonconformist chapels to the distributor road: the Baptist Chapel (1791) and the Friends' Meeting House (1800). In other towns losses have been fewer. In Newark good houses of 1663 in Millgate have gone, and the medieval White Hart, although not threatened with demolition, looks ready to fall down (in 1978). At Worksop the best Georgian houses in Potter Street went to make way for a civic centre too expensive to be built.

To set against the record of destruction is the restoration of a number of buildings. In Nottingham the C17 Brewhouse Yard, houses at the top of Castlegate, and the stables at Wollaton Hall have become museum departments, the timber-framed Severns restaurant has been re-erected on Castle Road, and the Theatre Royal has been preserved as part of a larger theatre by the *Renton Howard Levin Wood Partnership*. The centre in general has a well-kept air. In Newark, the Moot Hall has been completely rebuilt, and Wilson Street rehabilitated. At Papplewick one of Nottingham's two splendid pumping stations is kept in working order by a charitable trust and North Leverton Windmill is still operated commercially. The Nottingham Buildings Preservation Trust have restored several lesser-known and otherwise neglected buildings, notably Windles Square, Calverton. Three country houses have been restored (Clifton Hall, Colwick Hall, and Win- 92 thorpe Hall, all C18). Two more are well preserved (Kelham Hall 98 as the Newark District Council Offices, Welbeck Abbey as an army college). Many more have gone:* Rufford Abbey (C17, early C18, and 1830–40 by *Salvin*) except for the monastic remains and

* Destruction of the country house started early in Notts: Worksop Manor went in 1840. In total since 1900 fourteen have gone. Those demolished before 1950 were Nuthall Temple (1754–7 by *Thomas Wright*), Broxtowe Hall (mid-C17), Rampton Manor (1851–3 by *William Burn*), and Clumber (c. 1760–70 by *Stephen Wright*, remodelled in 1879 by *Charles Barry Jun.*).

outbuildings; Blyth Hall (1684–5, possibly by *Talman*); Watnall Hall, Greasley (*c.* 1690–1700); Ossington Hall (1729, altered *c.* 1790 by *Lindley* of Doncaster); Grove Hall (mostly 1762 by *Carr* of York); Bulwell Hall (1770); Thorney Hall (late C18); Sherwood Lodge, Arnold (late C18 and C19); Oxton Hall (late C18 and 1847); and Whatton Manor (1838–40). Langford Hall has been tactfully reduced in size, and two good late C17 manor houses (Chilwell 1677 and Stapleford 1689) have disappeared. No important village churches have been demolished, though one or two are redundant. The best of these, the Mausoleum at West Markham and Elston Chapel, are in the care of the Redundant Churches Fund. The wave of destruction for redevelopment seems to have ebbed slightly and often now it is neglect (for example, of the fine early C18 Winkburn Hall, and of many farm and village buildings) that threatens to lead to demolition.

## EARLY SETTLEMENT IN THE COUNTY
### BY MALCOLM TODD

THE factor which above all else has determined the overall distribution of early settlement in Nottinghamshire is the valley of the Trent, with its easily cultivable gravels and alluvium. Throughout the prehistoric and early historic periods, the most notable concentrations of human settlement are to be discovered within this relatively narrow belt of fertile ground. The earliest traces of human activity have been revealed here, though this is in considerable measure a matter of chance, since the many deep gravel-pits and other riverside workings have inevitably produced a disproportionately large number of artifacts and other finds from all periods.

The Lower (early) and Middle PALAEOLITHIC cultures are represented by finds of flint hand-axes, flakes, and waste material from several sites on the gravels, notably in the area of Attenborough and Beeston. The Upper (later) Palaeolithic is best known in the developed culture given the name Creswellian after the caves at Creswell Crags on the Derbyshire border near Welbeck. The major caves used by Palaeolithic man lie on the Derbyshire side of the Creswell gorge, but Church Hole on the Nottinghamshire flank was in use at this time, between 8750 and 7000 B.C. The succeeding MESOLITHIC and earlier NEOLITHIC cultures are very sparsely represented in the county, what we know of them being derived from small numbers of flint implements from isolated locations. The distribution of these objects suggests that the uplands of the west and centre were somewhat more favoured by the Mesolithic hunters than the valleys of the Trent and its tributaries. The earliest farming communities of the Neolithic (c. 4000 to 3000 B.C.) do betray their presence on the gravels, but as yet no settlement sites have been identified and examined. Contacts with a wider world, in the form of finely ground stone axes imported into the region from some distance, are now evident. The main sources of these, as identified by their petrological content, were the Lake District, North Wales, and Charnwood Forest in Leicestershire.

Shortly after c. 2000 B.C. the impact of the Beaker cultures was felt in this sector of the Trent basin, though the earliest phases of this influx of new settlers are as yet unrecorded in Nottinghamshire itself. Later necked Beakers, however, are known from several sites in the Trent valley and from Clumber Park in the north.

The continued importance of the Trent gravels is apparent throughout the second millennium B.C. and beyond. Air photography reveals a large number of circular barrows and other ditched monuments in the valley, many of which are likely to belong to the early and middle phases of the BRONZE AGE. But artifacts and settlement sites of this lengthy period of time, from the CI8 to the CI4 B.C., remain relatively uncommon in the county. Even the Food Vessels common in Derbyshire and Lincolnshire have only occasional counterparts in Nottinghamshire so far. This is a gap which time and further field-work will surely fill. To the middle Bronze Age belong a series of cremation burials in collared urns (e.g. Hoveringham) and, somewhat later, cremations in the bucket-shaped urns of the so-called Deverel-Rimbury culture. The latest stages of the Bronze Age are distinguished by several finds of striking metalwork. Hoards containing a variety of weapons and implements are known from Newark and Nottingham, while a fine series of Hallstatt swords and other weapons has been recovered from various points along the Trent, notably Attenborough, Clifton, Fiskerton, Holme Pierrepont, and near Newark. The Clifton site may have been a riverside settlement of some local importance in the middle and late Bronze Age, for a timber revetment for the river bank was found here as well as three canoes. Central Nottingham may also have had a Bronze Age settlement, as scattered finds of pottery intimate.

The earlier phases of the IRON AGE (i.e. the middle of the first millennium B.C.) are barely represented here, except for stray finds of pottery and two known settlements, one beneath the later Roman villa at Epperstone and the other on Red Hill, Ratcliffe-on-Soar. Without doubt, the river gravels retained their importance as areas of settlement during this time. From the C3 B.C., matters become a little clearer. Pottery vessels with scored decoration link the Trent valley with the contemporary Iron Age cultures in Lincolnshire and Leicestershire. The picture in the uplands north of the river is almost blank as yet, but it might be anticipated that further work will show that the population of these hills had much in common with settlers in Derbyshire and the south Pennines.

The later Iron Age cultures, commonly named La Tène after the Swiss type-site, are well to the fore in the Trent valley and in the Keuper Marl landscape west of the river, but scarcely at all in the uplands. A fine bronze brooch in the shape of a bird (now unfortunately lost) was found at Red Hill, Ratcliffe-on-Soar, and from the Trent at Sutton-on-Trent came a superb bronze sword scabbard. Many homestead sites of Iron Age date lie on the river gravels, their economy probably based on mixed farming. The precise details of their circumstances, however, remain to be worked out. On the Keuper Marl hills bordering Sherwood Forest to the south and east lie a group of small hill-forts which probably began their life in the Iron Age, though most of the datable finds from them are of the Roman period. The best preserved are Fox Wood (Woodborough), Old Ox (Oxton), Combs Farm (Farnsfield), and Burton Lodge (Burton Joyce). Other sites within Sherwood Forest may have been of similar character. Although these small enclosures are commonly termed 'forts', they may in reality be viewed as settlements sensibly provided with protective earthworks against the depredations of neighbours rather than against the concerted onslaughts of major forces.

By the beginning of the ROMAN period in the mid C1, the Trent basin was occupied by a people or tribe who called themselves the *Coritani* (or *Coritavi*). Much of the county probably lay within their territory, with the probable exception of the north-western hills, which, as earlier, were bound by close cultural ties to the Derbyshire uplands.

During the rapid conquest of this part of midland England in the reign of Claudius (and more specifically in the years A.D. 43–7), the area up to and including the Vale of Trent came within the orbit of Rome and was occupied by her armies. Three certain fort sites are so far known of the middle years of the C1. Two

of these, Margidunum and Thorpe (Ad Pontem), lie on the Fosse
Way, the other at Broxtowe in the northern suburbs of Nottingham. The military site at Margidunum, which was as much
supply-base as garrison-post, is the most completely examined: it
may have been founded early in the reign of Nero (c. A.D. 55) rather
than in the first campaigns of conquest. Broxtowe, too, probably
belongs to the fifties and may have been connected with the
earliest confrontation with the Brigantes of the Pennines. The
date of Thorpe is not yet clear. The site at Brough has produced
a cheek-piece from a fine decorated helmet of the later CI, possibly
betokening military use of the place. There is evidence, too, for
mid-CI occupation at Newark, though whether or not this was
military is not clear. A marching-camp at Holme, three miles N
of Newark, is fairly safe evidence for the presence of an army unit
in the period of conquest.

The Roman road-system is still imperfectly known. The Fosse
Way, one of the great routes of the province which date from the
earliest years of occupation, enters the county on its southern
border at Willoughby, runs in a straight line to Cotgrave, then
abruptly changes alignment and continues on a virtually direct
course to Lincoln, leaving Notts at Brough. Two routes led north-
westwards from the Fosse Way, the one from Thorpe crossing
the Trent and running up the valley of the Greet, the other leaving
Margidunum, crossing the river at Gunthorpe, and entering the
higher ground by way of the Dover Beck. The ultimate destination
of both roads is unknown. The first-named route probably continued east of Thorpe across the Vale of Belvoir towards Ancaster
in Lincs. In the north of the county, a major road linking Doncaster (Danum) and Lincoln (Lindum Colonia) ran from the river
Idle to the Trent at Littleborough.

The sites of some fifteen Roman villas are known in the
county and their distribution is of some interest. A considerable
number lie on the Keuper Marl lands in the centre and east, a
few on the claylands south of the Trent. With the exception of
Mansfield Woodhouse, they are absent from the poor land of
Sherwood Forest, but more significantly they are also scarce on
the rich alluvial lands of the Trent valley. Here, a dense concentration of humbler farmsteads occupied the landscape, the villas lying
generally at some distance from the river. The largest and most
sumptuous of the known villas is that at Southwell, in its final
phase evidently a well appointed courtyard house. The most completely known house and attendant farm buildings is that at Mansfield Woodhouse, oddly sited on the western edge of Sherwood.

The other, more informative villa sites are Barton-in-Fabis, Car Colston, Cromwell, Epperstone, Oldcotes, and Ruddington.

The humbler agricultural settlements, too, are naturally concentrated on the more amenable land, especially on the Trent gravels, the rich clayland of the Vale of Belvoir, and the Keuper Marl. As in earlier periods, the sandy tracts of Sherwood Forest remained very sparsely occupied. The character of the Romano-British peasant holdings is fairly clear, although few have been thoroughly excavated. Essentially, the settlement pattern is one of loose clusters of homesteads, each consisting of a few timber huts set amid stock enclosures and small fields. Apart from the introduction of a modicum of Roman equipment, pots and pans, tools, and possibly agricultural implements, the tenor and scope of life in these steadings was little altered by the Roman conquest, except in so far as their occupants had to conform to a new order and its exactions.

No large Roman urban settlement lay within the county, the centres of local administration being the *colonia* at Lincoln and the tribal capital at Leicester. Minor towns did spring up at sites on the Fosse Way earlier occupied as garrison posts by the army. These townships were Margidunum, Ad Pontem, Crococalana, and possibly Vernemetum. None of them are today eloquent of their earlier importance, there being little for the visitor to see but for slight remains of earthworks. Excavation at Margidunum and at Ad Pontem, however, has brought out something of their history. Both developed steadily as road-side villages during the C2, and Margidunum at least received defences in earthwork before A.D. 200. Slight traces of these works can still be seen on the eastern side of the Fosse Way. The site reached the peak of its development in the later C3 and its defences were then strengthened by the addition of a stone wall and a broad, deep ditch outside it. In the C4, however, the site declined as a centre of population, and was mainly used as an official staging-post on the main road. Ad Pontem is less well known, but it too was provided with earthwork defences, perhaps about A.D. 200, and these were later replaced by a stone wall on a different alignment. None of these four townships on the Fosse Way grew into medieval centres, or even villages. After their demise, their principal use to the medieval settler was as a convenient quarry for building material.

The steady accumulation of archaeological discoveries indicates that the earliest ANGLO-SAXON settlements in Nottinghamshire were established in the Trent and Soar valleys or close to their margins. The primacy of the alluvial land is thus demonstrated throughout the early history of the region. Traces of the settlements are scanty indeed, but the positions of the known cemeteries are a reasonably sure guide to the areas which attracted the c5 settlers. The largest cemetery so far recorded lay on Millgate, Newark, this one beginning early in the c5. The associated settlement may well lie, as yet undetected, beneath the medieval town, perhaps on the west side. Other cemeteries of the pagan period in or close to the Trent valley are at Bassingfield, Bingham, Holme Pierrepont, and in the Soar valley at Kingston-on-Soar and Sutton Bonington. The exceptions to this pattern are the c6 inhumation cemetery on the Fosse Way at Vernemetum, near Willoughby on the Wolds, and the c6 barrow near Oxton on the edge of Sherwood Forest. The Willoughby cemetery attests the use of land around the Roman settlement of Vernemetum in the Anglo-Saxon period, though it does not in any way demonstrate continuous occupation here. The Oxton burial appears at present as an outlier, presumably representing colonization of the wooded valleys lying north-west of the Trent.

Elements in the pottery of c5 and early c6 cemeteries reveal close links with the material from adjacent parts of Lincolnshire, especially from the limestone ridge and the Witham valley. No doubt this was due to a degree of cultural association between these two areas, but probably these similarities in basic equipment are best explained as the result of trade in these commodities along the Witham and Trent valleys. Later, in the c6, the pattern of trade seems to have altered. Now, the pottery and some of the metalwork reveal affinities with those from Northamptonshire and Leicestershire.

The scarcity of Anglo-Saxon material of this early date from Nottinghamshire north and west of the Trent is notable. Place-name evidence, in particular names suggestive of clearance, such as *leah* and *feld* names, do occur in the south of Sherwood Forest, but the absence of any archaeological support for early settlements here may mean that these clearances came in the middle or even the late Saxon period. Nottingham itself has now produced evidence for a middle Saxon occupation site beneath the later *burh*, and there is the possibility that the origins of this settlement lay still further back, in the pagan centuries. Three of the four Roman townships on the Fosse Way, Willoughby (Vernemetum), Margidunum, and Brough (Crococalana), have yielded Anglo-Saxon material, Vernemetum in its large cemetery, the other two in the form of chance finds of pottery and metalwork.

## BUILDING MATERIALS
### BY ALEC CLIFTON-TAYLOR AND MAURICE BARLEY

THE Elizabethan Sir Francis Willoughby, landowner turned coal magnate, had special reasons for using Jurassic limestone from Ancaster in Lincolnshire for his grand house, Wollaton Hall: not only was the stone of the highest quality, but whatever brought it – traditionally pack horses, but probably coal barges on the Trent as well – could also be used on the return journey to carry his coal into fuel-starved Lincolnshire. Since transport greatly increased the price of stone, distance from the quarry is usually a measure of the resources of an individual or a community, whether it be the medieval citizens of Newark, using Ancaster stone throughout the long process of rebuilding their great parish church, or Sir Jesse Boot, choosing Portland stone for the first Nottingham University building in 1922–8.

The majority of the county's churches are built of New Red sandstone, of which the best known here are the Permian sandstones of Mansfield. These occur in two distinct colours, the 'white' (which is either pale yellow or light grey) and the 'red' (a pinkish brown). The former, which is the only building stone in Nottinghamshire that is still worked, has always been the more important; it was used for such edifices as the town halls of Newark and of Mansfield itself, and is specially well seen at Southwell Minster, where the famous 'leaves', always protected from the weather, show us of what it was capable. Used externally, this fine-grained stone is more prone to decay: Newark Town Hall shows a good deal of later patching.

Triassic sandstone from the Keuper series, known locally as 'skerry', was formerly quarried at a number of places towards the centre of the county, notably Tuxford, Maplebeck and Gedling, some five miles to the east of Nottingham, where it was employed intermittently for a very long period. Like many of the New Red sandstones, the products of these quarries were not red but generally pale golden-brown. After John Cooper of Thurgarton demolished most of the remains of the medieval priory in the 1780s, the second-hand stone was used in the village for cottages and barns. An inferior sandstone from the Bunter formation was used in medieval Nottingham, for instance for the town walls, which were 7 ft thick.

Nottinghamshire has two kinds of limestone, but unfortunately lies a little too far west for the Oolite. The county's Magnesian limestone is, however, a very distinguished stone. It starts just north-west of Nottingham and broadens (also improving in quality) towards the Yorkshire border. It is a calcium magnesian carbonate which may also contain silica (sand). There used to be a flourishing quarry at Mansfield Woodhouse and another at Steetley, scarcely three miles from Worksop but a few yards inside Derbyshire. These two quarries, and no doubt others on the magnesian belt long ago abandoned, yielded a beautiful pale grey or honey-coloured stone that was a great standby in the northern part of the county. Churches which display it to good effect include Worksop Priory, Blyth Priory, East Markham and Sutton-on-Trent. Steetley stone was also used in the eighteenth century by James Paine at Worksop Manor (demolished), while Anthony Salvin employed it for all the dressings and ashlared facings at Victorian Thoresby, and so did Bodley & Garner, in conjunction with Runcorn sandstone, for the Duke of Newcastle's lavish church at Clumber. Immense quantities from Bulwell and Linby were used in Victorian Nottingham for garden walls and to line the new suburban roads cut like canyons into the sandy subsoil.

In the south-east of the county, from the Wolds to the Vale of Belvoir and northwards to Newark, considerable use was made of another Jurassic stone, the Lower or Blue Lias, which despite its name is a chilly grey, and only available as a rule in small, narrow pieces. This stone can be seen at a good many churches between Willoughby-on-the-Wolds and Hawton, in the Norman parts of Newark Castle, in the remains of the Palace of the Archbishops of York at Southwell, and in farmhouses and cottages at Collingham, Langford and South Scarle. Blue Lias limestone does not wear well, as may be observed on the inner walls of Newark Castle or the church tower at Sibthorpe. Usually, though, the dressings are of Triassic sandstone or, as at Hawton, of Ancaster limestone. Yet in the south of the county the only alternative might have been to collect rounded boulders from the Boulder Clay, as was done for part of Wysall church; so here Blue Lias was much better than nothing.

To round off the stone picture two other varieties deserve mention. Swithland, the fine Leicestershire slate, was used for roofing in Roman times and again for Georgian and Victorian houses in the southern part of the county; the demand for churchyard headstones no doubt helped to keep the quarries going. And the valley of the Trent yielded, from the Keuper, another Triassic stone, alabaster, which is a special form of gypsum (calcium sulphate). The only quarry working today (which is a mine) is at Fauld near Tutbury, in Staffordshire. But the noble columns of the Great

Hall at Kedleston in Derbyshire, of ivory-white alabaster veined with grey and dark red, came from Nottinghamshire: the quarry was on Red Hill, close to the point where the Trent is joined by the Soar. So soft a stone can of course only be used internally.

The bands of gypsum in the Keuper marls which run the length of the county were used from Tudor to mid-Victorian times to make a hard flooring material. It can be seen in Car Colston church, but was normally used only for the upstairs rooms of houses; by Victorian times it was relegated to the attics. The gypsum, which included inferior deposits and waste from the alabaster workings (and until Tudor times the red-veined variety was always rejected), was burned with clay and pounded brick and laid warm, on a layer of reeds spread across the joists. After it had set, it became very hard indeed: a smooth and shiny limestone which made an excellent floor. Such floors can almost be taken for granted in any old Nottinghamshire house, and, being very durable, a great many survive.

In the Middle Ages the usual material for domestic building in Nottinghamshire, as in most other English counties, was timber. But both in towns and villages so much rebuilding took place on the high tide of Georgian and Victorian prosperity that very few timber-framed houses survive. Newark has half a dozen (including the White Hart Inn and the Governor's House), Nottingham one example (Severn's, much restored), Southwell one (the back part only of the Saracen's Head), Retford none at all. Sometimes, as at Lowdham Hall, the timbers have been plastered over. Neither the craftsmanship nor the material was of as high a quality as in some other counties. Good oak was not plentiful here: the poor soil of the Bunter sandstone does not encourage trees to grow either tall or thickly, and the oaks of the Sherwood Forest were royal property. Moreover, timber had been used extravagantly for iron-smelting and ship construction. Thus resort to woods that were inferior to oak was frequent. A few cruck buildings from the western margins of the county are known; most have vanished. But many a modest farmhouse or cottage hides the remains of a frame under a later skin of brick, as at Clifton.

The poor quality of much of the available timber also meant that eastern Nottinghamshire shared with Lincolnshire the construction known as mud-and-stud: a slight timber frame hidden and protected outside by some six inches of mud. This technique lasted for labourers' cottages until the nineteenth century but it is doubtful whether any remain. The thatch with which all these timber-framed buildings was at one time roofed is also, in Nottinghamshire, now a rarity.

Far and away the commonest building material in the county today is brick, and since the Hall at Holme Pierrepont was stripped of its modern stucco it is evident that brick was employed there as early as about 1500. It was used about 1525 for the gatehouse at Hodsock and for a small hunting lodge at Kneesall, about 1575 for a dovecote in the village of Wollaton, and again before the end of the sixteenth century to line the rock-cut cellars at Wollaton Hall and for a manor house of the Willoughbys at Cossall. But before 1600 brick was rare, and employed only by a few of the wealthiest landowners.

From the beginning of the seventeenth century the use of brick gradually became more widespread. Thrumpton Hall, begun about 1608, and Clifton Hall, begun about 1630, relied on it entirely. After 1660 Nottingham started to become the brick-built city which it now so largely is, and a centre for brick-making; when the church of St Nicholas, destroyed in the Civil War, was rebuilt in 1671–82, this was the material to be chosen. Other notable examples from these years include the pleasant old Grammar School (now the County Library) at Tuxford, founded in 1669, the charming Willoughby Almshouses of 1685 at Cossall, and the school at Bunny, which, although it dates from 1700, is still almost entirely pre-classical.

In the Georgian period almost every house built in Nottingham was of brick, and the same is true of the whole of the alluvial valley of the Trent, with its profusion of villages. Some of this south Nottinghamshire brickwork, owing to the iron oxides in the clays, is of a startlingly bright red: for example, the church at Kinoulton, built in 1793. Plenty of Georgian brick houses of excellent quality can still be seen in Newark, as well as at Southwell and elsewhere. The bricks of the northern villages are a dull brown, similar to those of the Vale of York. By the end of the eighteenth century even the humblest weavers' cottages would be constructed of brick. But the nineteenth century witnessed a sad change for the worse. Bricks for the colliery villages were now made from the hard, local carbonaceous clays, and, although horribly durable, they are an eyesore which has done much to spoil the look of a sizeable area of western Nottinghamshire.

Except during the Victorian period, when there was a great vogue for Welsh slate, nearly all the county's brick houses have tiled roofs. In Nottingham there was already one in 1503, long before the arrival there of brick. In the eighteenth and nineteenth centuries plain tiles and pantiles were both in much demand; pantiles are normal over two-thirds of the county and make a notable contribution to the visual excellence of Newark. They first came into eastern England from Holland, along with other Dutch building practices such as curved and tumbled gables; the river Trent seems to have been the route by which they penetrated. But it was not long before pantiles were being made locally; and happily they can still be obtained. Nottinghamshire, through its Building Preservation Trust, tries by means of grants and loans to help owners to retain the traditional character of their houses. It should be much lauded for its efforts to preserve the quietly harmonious qualities of those villages which have not been overwhelmed by coal mining and urban sprawl.

The last word should be about Nottingham, a great Victorian city, full of buildings which, however aesthetically unattractive (and it is not easy to like Waterhouse's Prudential Assurance, built of those hard red bricks from the carbonaceous clays), do bear witness to the scale and quality of brick technology. Terracotta was also favoured, in the hope of resisting city grime, for a place of worship (Albert Hall), a departmental store (the Co-op in Parliament Street), a pub or two, and, inevitably, for the Midland Railway Station, built in 1904. Since this building was cleaned in 1975 its shining pink walls and dome can be seen to embody the technical skills and self-assurance of England before 1914.

# INDUSTRIAL ARCHAEOLOGY
## BY KEITH REEDMAN

THE industrial archaeology of Nottinghamshire is predominantly the remains of the early means of production of two of mankind's basic needs – food and clothing. Mineral extraction, especially coal mining, has existed since the C13, but few early remains are visible. At Strelley there are C17 bell-pit features, and relics of the industry can be seen in a museum of mining at Lound Hall near Retford. It is evident that the county is a food producer from the large number of remains of wind- and watermills. North Leverton windmill is the only one still working, and one of only two in commercial use in the country. The other is at Over mill, Cambridgeshire. One watermill at Ollerton is in working order, others, e.g. at Hoveringham, have much of their machinery left, but many are in ruins. The Dover Beck (from Hoveringham to Oxton) and the River Greet (from Rolleston to Farnsfield) are rich in sites of watermills (some converted to cotton mills). They are too numerous to list exhaustively in the gazetteer.

Malting and brewing are examples of the food industry which flourished in the county. It was in the expanding towns that the large maltings were established, having outgrown the domestic stage during the c18. Substantial remains of this period can be seen in Mansfield, Retford, and especially Newark. Malting is still carried out in Nottingham which, like Newark, remains an important brewing centre. Warwick's brewery at Newark has a particularly fine series of buildings dating from 1864 to the 1920s.

The county is well-known as the birthplace of the machine-made hosiery industry and its later offshoot machine-made lace. The stocking frame is said to have been invented by the Rev. William Lee of Calverton in 1589. Originally a domestic industry, it was well established by the mid c17 and has flourished ever since, spreading at an early date to Derbyshire and particularly to Leicestershire. The characteristically long knitters' windows lighting the frame-shops can be seen throughout the east Midlands, either on the ground floor (Calverton) or in the top storey (Stapleford). Particularly fine examples of cottages are preserved at Calverton and of workshops at Ruddington. Later in the c19 the industry was organized on a larger scale in factories (Hine & Mundella's steam-powered factory of 1851 at Nottingham) and in warehouses (Carlton Street, Nottingham). The long top-floor windows in these buildings lit the inspection shop.

It was possibly the demand for yarn for the knitting industry which persuaded Richard Arkwright to set up his first cotton-spinning mill in Goosegate, Nottingham, in 1769. This horse-powered factory has long since gone, but many early water-powered cotton mills remain (there are good examples at Linby, Mansfield, Maythorne, and Pleasley). At Robinson's mills at Papplewick, remains of which survive at Grange Farm, a rotative steam engine (by Boulton & Watt) was employed for the first time in 1786 to power a textile mill.

A development of the hosiery industry was the introduction of machine-made lace, first to Nottingham and then spreading into the hosiery districts of Derbyshire and Leicestershire. From the early c19 Nottingham became the centre for the manufacture, finishing, and merchanting of machine-made lace. Large multi-storey steam-powered factories were built in the latter half of the c19 and during the first decade of the c20. Many can still be seen in the Radford area of the city and to the west in Beeston and district. A part of the ancient centre of Nottingham round the parish church became almost exclusively occupied by those engaged in buying, finishing, and selling lace and is still known as the Lace Market. Fortunately, despite some demolition, it still exists, and has been designated a conservation area. Many fine buildings which a short time ago were decaying because of the decline of the industry have been given new uses and are being restored to their former glory. Adam's warehouse and those on Broadway, all fine designs by *T. C. Hine* (1855), bear witness to the prosperity of the lace trade.

The River Trent has been a transport artery since prehistoric times, but the remaining evidence of navigation dates from the canal age, when the Chesterfield, Grantham, and Nottingham canals were constructed between 1775 and 1796. Warehouses survive on the Nottingham Canal, on the canalized stretch of the Trent at Newark, and on the Chesterfield Canal at Worksop.

It was in Nottinghamshire in 1603–4 that the first railway or tramway in the British Isles was constructed by Sir Huntingdon Beaumont to carry coal from pits in Strelley, which Beaumont leased from Sir Percival Willoughby, for a distance of two miles to Wollaton Lane, whence it could more conveniently be carted to Nottingham or the Trent. This railway had wooden rails and horse-drawn wagons. Iron rails, invented towards the end of the C18, were used most notably on the pre-locomotive Mansfield and Pinxton railway, built by 1819. Here edge-rails were used instead of the plate rails which had been more common until then. The line, altered about 1850 and converted to locomotive operation, still has some original features, particularly a fine stone viaduct to the s of Mansfield. The first locomotive railway in the county was the Midland Counties Railway opened between Nottingham and Derby in 1839. From then on the railways continued to be built until the last major undertaking – the Great Central line from Nottingham to London, opened in 1900. The two main lines, the Midland and Great Central, had stations in Nottingham rivalling each other in grandeur: the Midland of 1904 and the Victoria of 1898–1900, both by *A. E. Lambert*. The best small station in the county is the Jacobethan one of 1850 at Worksop. *T. C. Hine* built a number of stations (at Aslockton, Bingham, Nottingham, Orston, etc.) on the Great Northern Line opened in 1852. The wrought-iron lattice-girder Bennerley Viaduct of 1887–8 (one of the last remaining) carried this line across the Erewash Valley to Derby Friargate.

Industrialization and population growth demanded public services, such as waste disposal and water supply. Nottingham was progressive with piped water supply, but the C19 population explosion demanded a large increase in volume. The Corporation sank new boreholes into the sandstones to the north of the city at Haydn Road, Basford 1857, Bestwood 1871, and Papplewick 1883) and used large steam-engine-driven pumps to raise the water into storage reservoirs. The steam engines are now out of use, but two have been preserved, one (probably the last by *James Watt & Co.*, 1884) in its engine house at Papplewick and one from Haydn Road at the Industrial Museum at Wollaton. Steam power was also used to pump sewage, and at Worksop the pumping-engine house still exists. The engine houses themselves are magnificent monuments to those responsible for public health. The one at Papplewick, with ornate cast-iron, tiles, and stained glass, is comparable with any contemporary church or town hall.

# FURTHER READING

Students of the county should first refer to Dr Robert Thoroton's 1677 *Antiquities of Nottinghamshire, edited and enlarged by John Throsby (1790–6)*, in particular for Throsby's useful descriptions and illustrations of country houses. There is a facsimile volume with a new introduction by M. W. Barley and K. S. S. Train (1972). Other literature used in the first edition was extensive. The most important books and papers were the Notts volume of the *Little Guides* (by E. L. Guilford), J. C. Cox's volume of the valuable collection *County Churches*, Arthur Mee's *Nottinghamshire*, and *Kelly's Directory* (edition of 1888). Of more specialized works the first volume of the *Victoria County History* was very valuable, as were the *Memorials of Old Nottinghamshire*, 1912, and the excellent *Transactions of the Thoroton Society*, 1898. Specially important articles in the *Memorials of Old Nottinghamshire* deal with Notts medieval church architecture in general (A. Hamilton Thompson), with Southwell (A. Hamilton Thompson), and with spires (H. Gill), in the Thoroton *Transactions* with Brasses (1913, by J. Bramley), Windows (1916, by H. Gill), Porches and Doorways (1917, by H. Gill), Military Effigies (1924, by H. Lawrence and E. I. Routh), and Easter Sepulchres (1924, by E. Woolley). An article (by C. E. Keyser) in the *Journal of the British Archaeological Association* (new series, vol. 13, 1907) sums up Norman buildings in Notts. A catalogue of Notts stained glass appeared in the *Journal of the Brit. Soc. of*

*Master Glass-Painters* (vol. 9, 1944, 1946, etc.). Dovecotes have been treated by J. Whitaker (1927), Crosses by A. Stapleton (1912, in the *Mansfield Advertiser*).

In preparing the second edition we were fortunate to have been allowed to use the unpublished results of a great deal of research. In addition the Thoroton Society Transactions (*see* above) continue to be useful. There has been little written about the buildings of the county in general. Most illuminating is Dr Norman Summers's *A Place to Live: Nottinghamshire Heritage* (1975). D. M. Smith's *Industrial Archaeology of the East Midlands* (1965) contains much about the county's industrial buildings. There is more on individual places, but not all the guidebooks and local histories can be mentioned here. On the development of Nottingham most valuable are J. D. Chambers's *A Century of Nottingham History 1851–1951* (1951) and Professor M. W. Barley's essay in *Historic Towns* (ed. M. D. Lobel, 1969). There is a good chapter in *The History of Working-Class Housing* (ed. by S. D. Chapman, 1971). M. W. Barley's *Nottingham Now* (1975), and K. S. S. Train's *Walks Around Nottingham* (1970) give a good picture of the town with much useful information. Dr Summers's *Prospect of Southwell* (1974), referred to in the gazetteer, is a thorough study of the minster, its collegiate buildings, and the town. Articles in *Country Life* were used for both editions, and Mr John Harris's article on Thoresby House in *Architectural History* (IV, 1961, pp. 11–13) was most helpful. The Royal Commission's volume on the *Civil War Siege Works* (1964) at Newark goes into more detail on this subject than we have space for in this book.

Certain older standard works have been used for all volumes in this series, such as E. W. Tristram on wall painting, Aymer Vallance on screens, Mill Stephenson on brasses, etc. For the second edition many more studies of individual periods (e.g. *Architecture in Britain 1530–1830* by Sir John Summerson) were available and the list of monographs is growing, e.g. Mark Girouard's on Robert Smythson, which together with the catalogue of drawings in the Smythson collection of the R.I.B.A. Drawings Collection (*Architectural History*, V, 1962) was particularly useful. Finally, Gunnis's dictionary of sculptors and Colvin's of architects (in the second edition, 1978) are of course indispensable.

# NOTTINGHAMSHIRE

\*

AD PONTEM *see* THORPE

## ANNESLEY

CHURCH and hall form a fine group, or formed one, before the church was allowed to decay miserably. It is not a picturesque ruin, though it could be – just an utterly neglected derelict building. Fortunately most of the remaining pieces have been salvaged and placed in the C19 church, but its best feature has been wantonly destroyed. It was the splendid five-light ogee-reticulated E window of the S aisle or Felley Chapel, founded in 1363 (cf. Woodborough *c.* 1356, Sturton, and many minor examples). The SEDILIA still remain, earlier than the window, with E.E. shafts and pointed trefoil heads, finely moulded. No cusps, no crockets: impossible after 1300.

ANNESLEY HALL is said to incorporate the walls of a medieval hall, but of medieval masonry nothing is visible. It is stone, basically C17 but much added to in the C19, and stands behind a forecourt entered through a gatehouse-cum-stable range of 1838. The centre part is C17 but of at least two builds, one mid, one late C17. The entrance (NW) façade looks regular H-plan with a few mullioned and transomed windows in the cross wing. The gabled wings (Georgianized with Venetian windows and sashes) are both said to be of 1691: the r. one may be earlier.\* On the garden side, the cross wing has four bays of mullion-and-transom cross windows lighting the Great Hall and Great Chamber, which have decoration of *c.* 1660. In the hall a two-tier wooden fireplace, and in the Great Chamber fine Restoration-type panelling with enriched pilasters, doorcases of a crude but fruity Artisan Mannerist style (cf. Thrumpton), a decorative plaster frieze, and a black marble fireplace with verses scratched on it, dated Christmas Day 1669 and signed by Patricius third Viscount Chaworth. At the NE end of the

---

\* Thoroton illustrated the house in 1676 and Throsby later copied it. In the drawing the house looks L-shaped with both wings double-pile and with a gabled staircase or porch projection in the angle. The SW part of the house as seen from the present entrance front seems to correspond with the drawing: see the projection in the angle.

cross wing on the garden front, a flat-roofed staircase projection with staggered mullion-and-transom cross windows lighting a late C17 stone staircase. Its balustrade is of surprisingly un-English design, massive and crude wrought iron with brass finials. Over the outer door a plaster panel dated 1691 with a sundial in a cartouche (cf. the achievement in the church), and, leading to the door, a stair, its parapet crowned by ball finials. At the s w end a three-storey C18 façade to the C17 wing. At each end of the building C19 additions in a Tudorbethan style, that at the NE end of 1838, the s w service wing of 1885.* Also C19 the ugly porch projection on the entrance front (early C19?) and the one-storey links between the wings. Running along the w side of the house and garden a late C17 terrace with a stone balustrade. Under the central stair, a vaulted room, and in the centre of the balustrade a fine vase. At the s lodge a solitary C17 gatepier.

The colliery opened in 1867. The colliery village is separate from the church and hall, towards the top of the hill, and it is there, in a splendid position high above the road, that a new church was built.

ALL SAINTS. 1874 by *T. G. Jackson*, partly rebuilt after a fire in 1907. NE tower with broach-spire and Dec detail. The pretty wooden porch belongs to the earlier date. – From the old church: FONT. Norman, with diagonal criss-cross and a top border of crosses. – ACHIEVEMENT, dated 1686, originally on a wooden frame inserted into the tower arch of the old church: heavily decorated plasterwork straying on to the masonry. The arms of Patricius Chaworth are supported by angels and garnished by draperies. A delightful if unsophisticated piece of work (cf. the plaster panel on the Hall). – STATUES, retrieved from Colwick church. – CHANCEL PAVEMENT and STAINED GLASS in the s chancel window; *The Builder*, 1909, says they were made by *Powell & Sons*. – s aisle window, copies made by Mrs *Sophia Musters* of the Virtues by Joshua Reynolds in the w window of New College Chapel, Oxford: removed from Colwick church *c.* 1937. – MONUMENTS. Badly preserved effigy of a lady with folded hands, C14: said to be Leonia de Raines. – Brass to William Breton † 1595. – Monument to an unknown person, alabaster, C16, a recumbent male figure in a shroud, sombre and moving. A similar monument once existed

* The s w wing will be demolished if, as planned, the Hall is converted into a hotel, the stables into four homes, and the park into a golf course. The ruin of the church may be stabilized (1978).

at Fledborough (*Gentleman's Magazine*, 1808). Unlike those to ancestors at Chesterfield and Fenny Bentley in Derbyshire, the head is shown here.

In the Park, ½ m. SE of the church, a small motte-and-bailey CASTLE.

## ARNOLD

ST MARY. As so often in the districts of modern developments in Notts, the village centre is pretty well preserved, because the new has taken place away from the old. The most important part of the church is the mid-C14 chancel with its large, tall, three-light N and S windows, the tracery ogee-reticulated (all renewed except a fragment above the organ loft), and with one of the Lincolnshire–Nottinghamshire EASTER SEPULCHRES. That at Arnold is badly preserved and deprived of all its sculpture. Originally it must have been similar to Hawton, of upright shape, tripartite, with crocketed ogee gables and tall pinnacles. The plain surfaces are partly adorned by diapering, patterns of square flowers, as we find them on the Southwell pulpitum and that at Lincoln. On the l. a tomb recess with a tomb-chest showing the same diapering. The recess has an ogee arch with double cusping. Opposite SEDILIA (the chancel floor was originally lower, which is recognizable in the sedilia as well as the tomb-chest) and a charming double (that is 'two-light') PISCINA with Dec tracery. By the same hand no doubt the head-brackets for statues l. and r. of the (new) E window. That of the woman on the r. is of very fine quality. – As to the other parts of the church, the tall N and S arcades are a little earlier than the chancel. The W tower is Perp, partly rebuilt when the church was restored by *Scott* in 1868–9. – STAINED GLASS. Window with St Agnes, 1893, by *Kempe*. – INCISED SLAB with the Virgin and Child on a bracket held by an angel: possibly 1347 for John de la Launde.

ST PAUL, Daybrook. 1892–6 by *Pearson* of Truro Cathedral, and indeed with the same tall spire on the pattern of Coutances (at the S end of the W front) added after 1896. All stone, wide and large inside, but not vaulted. The style 'Geometrical'. Ornate Dec SEDILIA, and opposite an equally ornate recess for the MONUMENT to Mrs Emily Seely, 'the gentle and good woman who inspired her husband to build and adorn this church' (by *Brock*, 1897). – STAINED GLASS. (A complete but uniformly dull scheme by *Clayton & Bell*. The E and W windows are the only ones of any ambition. RH)

THE GOOD SHEPHERD (R.C.), Thackeray Lane, Woodthorpe. By *Gerard Goalen*, 1963–6. A small church with a rather squat appearance because the entrance is banked up from the road and there are deep fascias. Needle spire with a projecting louvred bell-chamber. Inside, the double-octagon auditorium converges on the sanctuary, the diamond shell vaults are supported on slim concrete piers. The atmosphere is intimate and darkened, the simplicity relieved by a glorious display of glass by *Patrick Reyntiens*, 1964–5. His technique is *dalle-de-verre* (i.e. slabs of glass joined with concrete): the theme is the tree. (Sanctuary: the five wounds and crown of thorns superimposed on the three New Testament tree symbols – the tree of the cross, that of the mustard seed, and the vine and branches. Nave: Old Testament trees: N window tree of life and of good and evil; s window burning bush.)

(METHODIST CHURCH, Front Street. By *Bartlett & Gray*, 1966–7, commended by the Civic Trust for 'presence' in the urban scene. Circular, with tall windows and brick panels between strongly projecting brick mullions.)

ARNOLD HILL COMPREHENSIVE SCHOOL, Gedling Road. Built by *D. E. E. Gibson* (County Architect) and the Ministry of Education in 1959 as an educational experiment, i.e. the lower, middle, and sixth-form blocks clearly defined and grouped round an assembly hall. Blocks of one to three storeys, concrete and timber-clad, around courtyards.

S of St Mary in HIGH STREET, No. 79 (mid-C18, very tall, with moulded window lintels and a contemporary staircase) is the house where the painter Bonington was born. In MANSFIELD ROAD at REDHILL, an almost unspoilt terrace (Nos. 271–277) of four framework-knitters' cottages.* The usual long windows are on the ground floor here (cf. Calverton).

SHERWOOD LODGE (now Notts Constabulary H.Q.), 2 m. N of Redhill. The late C18 mansion has been replaced by a CLASP office building.‡

Nearer Nottingham at DAYBROOK, at the junction of the Mans-

---

* Opposite, No. 266 was a large early C18 brick house, built as an inn. Three storeys divided by brick bands and eight bays wide. Central gable with ball finials and a porch projection with rustic wrought-iron balcony over. The windows had C18 casements. Demolished 1978.

‡ Front with a three-bay pediment, Venetian window, and Tuscan porch. Several canted bay-windows. Doubled in size in the C19 without alteration to the C18 character. The CHURCH of St George by *Aston Webb*, 1903, has also gone.

field and Nottingham roads, a three-storey HOSIERY FAC-
TORY with decorative brickwork in the gable, built in 1885 for
I. and R. Morley, now a wire works. Alongside it a two-storey
office block with a central pediment and behind it a four-storey
building of 1901, discreetly embellished in the Byzantine style.
(Nearly opposite St Paul's church, a big 1930s model
LAUNDRY; cf. the contemporary glass and concrete factories
for Boots', Beeston, and Viyella, Nottingham. RH)
In RAMSDALE PARK, on the prominent hill-crest with fine views
to northward, an Iron Age occupation site. An C18 plan by Hay-
man Rooke shows a rectangular earthwork surrounded by two
ditches.

## ASKHAM
7070

ST NICHOLAS. Usual W tower with eight pinnacles. The unaisled church is tiled, a sign of the restoration of 1906–7 to
which the S porch also belongs. Close to the porch clearly Norman masonry in the nave wall. Chancel S wall with a double-
lancet window. Chancel E window Dec, nave windows later
C14. At the junction of nave and chancel inside on the N a pretty,
diagonally placed ogee-headed niche (cf. Elkesley). – PISCINA.
Ogee-headed niche with a fragment of an E.E. shaft-piscina in
front of it. Most of the shaft is broken off (cf. Gringley). –
ALTAR RAILS. Late C17, with heavily twisted balusters.

## ASLOCKTON
7040

ST THOMAS. 1890–2 by *Sir Reginald Blomfield*, utterly insensitive to the county or the scenery. Ancaster stone and faced
with red brick inside. No tower.
CRANMER'S MOUND. Small, well preserved motte still standing
16 ft high. To the SE, two rectangular platforms surrounded
by broad ditches may mark the sites of later houses of the
Cranmers. Archbishop Cranmer was born here. Other earthworks, medieval and probably agricultural, lie to the S and SE.
(STATION for the G.N.R. by *T. C. Hine*, 1857 (cf. Bingham,
etc.). JPB)

## ATTENBOROUGH
5030

ST MARY MAGDALENE. The tower of the same type as
across the river Trent, for example at Bunny, that is with the

buttresses connected horizontally by a band at the top, and battlements above that. Then follows a much thinner spire without broaches just as in the neighbouring churches of Wollaton (Nottingham), Stapleford, Barton-in-Fabis, Cossall, etc. The whole steeple however is larger than any of the others. It belongs to the early Perp style, it appears. An impression of largeness is also conveyed by the interior, with its exceptionally tall circular piers, four bays N and S. They date from the first half of the C13, as is proved by the foliage of the capitals on the N side, the mouldings of the arches, and the oversized billet and nailhead ornament. The most surprising thing about Attenborough is, however, that the S capitals have been redone by a workman of the C14 with fanciful heads and monsters and large leaves. The comparison between the styles of the two centuries is instructive. The tower cuts off half a bay from the arcades. The doorway into the N aisle is earlier than the arcade (round-headed, waterleaf capitals). The aisle windows mostly of the date of the steeple. At the same time nave and aisles were embattled. The chancel (much rebuilt in 1869) has a plain parapet instead and large later Perp windows, similar to Lambley. Just as there, brackets for statues were inserted l. and r. of the E window. – ALTAR TABLE. Jacobean. – FONT. Plain C13 with nothing but blank pointed arcades on the eight panels. – CHOIR STALLS. Two tall ends are preserved, with elaborate C14 blank tracery (a pentagram in a roundel for example). – The modern choir stalls contain fragments of Jacobean carvings, very worldly, with mermaids and a merman with a goatee. The initials IP point to the Powtrell family, and there is indeed a wooden memorial tablet in the church with their arms and the date 1623. – SOUTH DOOR with splendid large primitive iron scrollwork and original boards: it looks latest Romanesque. Porch rebuilt in the C18. – STAINED GLASS. Small C15 bits in the tracery of the S windows.
Many finds from the NEOLITHIC to the ROMAN period have been made in the nearby gravel-pits.

## AVERHAM

The large stuccoed Georgian-style RECTORY* (by *William Patterson*, 1838) makes a delicious group with the church. The

---

* As part of its garden wall a Perp window from Southwell, probably from the Archbishop's Palace ruined during the Civil War.

two lie at the far end of the village, with the church reaching close to the river Trent.

ST MICHAEL. In the W tower, the N and S sides of the nave, and the S side of the chancel plenty of early Norman herringbone masonry, in places laid regularly with alternating two or three straight courses. The masonry proves that the whole structure of the church is Norman, in spite of the later tower arch to the nave (decorated with heads and monsters), and of the windows, the diagonal buttresses, quatrefoil-panelled frieze (as in south Notts at Stanford-on-Soar, Langar, etc.), battlements, and eight pinnacles added to the W tower. The S porch is another addition, embattled, with gargoyles and letters and shields referring to Sir Thomas Sutton and his wife. He died in 1525. To the same period belong the well-carved corbels of the nave roof, and the other corbels now in the nave walls. The most interesting window tracery is in the chancel,* the E window of five lights, intersected but with one ogee quatrefoil at the top, typical early C14. This date also fits the S window with three round quatrefoils, not set in circles (cf. top window, corridor to the chapter house, Southwell). The Norman internal space is wide, not subdivided by aisles. Its roominess comes out specially well thanks to the simple plain benches and simple panelling all round it. The date is 1890; the work was designed by *Hodgson Fowler.* – SCREEN. Simple early Perp. – STAINED GLASS. Fragments collected in a N chancel window: amongst them C14 canopies and borders and a figure of Christ blessing, put together by the Rev. J. H. Sutton of Brant Broughton, c. 1885. – E window, the S half filled with late C15 glass from nearby Kelham Hall. – Some late C19 and early C20 glass by *Heaton, Butler & Bayne.* – One S window with early C19 glass, little copies of Italian paintings and bits in plain colours as one often sees them used domestically. – MONUMENTS. Laid in the N recess (ogee-headed with the Sutton rebus) a foliated cross slab with a Norman-French inscription. – S recess, late C14 effigy of a layman, bearded, holding his heart in his hands; quite good if not well preserved (cf. Stanford-on-Soar, West Leake). – W end, incised slab, civilian, C13. – Sir W. Sutton † 1607 and wife, recumbent alabaster effigies, columns with projecting entablatures l. and r. – Lord Lexington † 1668, wall-monument.

AVERHAM PARK FARM. On a hilltop looking over the Trent valley towards Newark, the hunting lodge of Robert Sutton

* Restored in 1857 by *C. Bailey* of Newark.

† 1723, second Lord Lexington, of nearby Kelham. Built after his retirement in 1718 from diplomatic service.* Stukeley's 1728 painting and the illustration in *Vitruvius Britannicus* vol. IV (1739) show that it was a house of the Coleshill type with two detached, flat-roofed wings standing at r. angles to and a little in advance of the main W front enclosing a *cour d'honneur*. The vanished N wing was for guests, the S a service wing connected to the house by an underground passage which was convenient without disrupting the symmetry of the design: Palladian colonnades or links had yet to become popular (Holkham, 1734). The house has lost its hipped roof with top balustrades, central lantern, panelled chimneys, and dormers, but is still characteristically two-storeyed and double-pile. Brick seven-bay façade with a pediment over the slightly broken-forward central three bays. In the pediment, which has lost its bottom moulding, one plain sash. Many blocked sash windows on the W front and untidy additions to the N side. The main door on the W led into a vestibule opening into a hall in the centre of the E front through an archway flanked by pilasters. The rooms opened straight out of the hall, not from a transverse corridor which, first at Coleshill in 1659, had introduced greater domestic comfort. In the SW corner a newel stair, and in the centre of the W front upstairs a gallery. Plain interiors apart from panels and overdoors painted by *Parmentier* in grisaille to imitate relief sculpture. The surviving S wing, now with a pitched roof, has blocked remains of five oval windows over five sashes.

STAYTHORPE POWER STATION, ½ m. S. By *Cecil Howitt*. The brick-clad 'A' station, begun in 1946, is typical of power stations of the 1930s to early 1950s with Battersea as its prototype; the 'B' station, completed *c.* 1960, with asbestos cladding.

# AWSWORTH

ST PETER. Of the brick church of 1746 built by a coalmine-owner, Richard Smedley of Risley, the chancel is preserved, looking with its gable like a Notts cottage, not at all genteel and Palladian. The E window is a curious, naïve version of Gothic too: two triangle-headed lights under a segmental arch.

---

* Professor Barley and Dr Summers (*Trans. Thor. Soc.* 1961 (65), p. 47) point out that it is exactly aligned on Newark spire and suggest that this conceit was in recognition of the part played by the first Lord Lexington in the siege of Newark.

The rest of the church was rebuilt by *Naylor & Sale* of Derby in 1902–3. A projected NW tower unbuilt. The whole a nice example of the free treatment of Gothic about 1900 (brick with stone dressings) which as a rule is found so much more frequently in Nonconformist chapels than in churches.

BENNERLEY VIADUCT. One of the two remaining wrought-iron lattice-girder bridges in the British Isles. Built in 1887–8, it crosses the Erewash valley on sixteen spans for 484 yards, carried on piers 56 ft high. The GNR line it carried from Nottingham Victoria to Derby Friargate is now abandoned.

## BABWORTH

6080

ALL SAINTS, s of Babworth Hall. Essentially Perp, with most of the usual features (e.g. the s porch of West Retford type; cf. St Mary Nottingham). Chancel, nave, N aisle and low w tower, all embattled. Square-headed windows. Late Perp (c16) priests' doors. Round-headed PISCINA in the chancel. Restored in 1859–62, with new tracery and roofs, by *J. L. Pearson*,[*] and again in 1877–8.[‡] – STAINED GLASS. Resurrection window by *Eginton*, 1830: a precious survival of late Georgian glass; E window by *Wailes*, 1855; w window by *Kempe*, 1879. – MONUMENTS of little merit to the Simpson family. The best, with an urn, to the Rev. John Simpson †1784 by *Thomas Waterworth* the elder of Doncaster.[§] – In the vestry, the base of a monument to John Bridgeman Simpson's first wife, Henrietta, †1793, inscribed *Repton-Desigt, Coade Sculpt*. The rest of it disappeared in the C19 restorations. – The rector, Richard Clyfton (1586–1605), became minister of Brewster's Separatist church at Scrooby (*see* p. 305).

BABWORTH HALL. A basically C18, two-and-a-half-storey house beautified by *Repton* in 1790 for John Bridgeman Simpson by whitening the red brick. Restored to its red brick and given plate-glass windows, top balustrade, etc., in 1850 by *William Burn*. Repton also laid out the grounds. Although the approach from the Retford road is different from that proposed, the

---

[*] According to Dr Quiney.

[‡] According to the *Notts Guardian*, 3 January 1879, this restoration was also by *Pearson*.

[§] The Rev. J. Simpson, something of a connoisseur, built the Palladian Stoke Hall (Derbyshire) and subscribed to Paine's *Plans . . . of Noblemen's and Gentlemen's Houses* (1767).

church tower still appears above the trees as it does in the Red Book sketch. To the N, the kitchen garden, walled, with stoves and flues.*

BABWORTH RECTORY (now called HAYGARTH HOUSE), S of the church. Late C18 and stuccoed, with the usual sash-windows, canted bay and semicircular bow, but in addition a C19 S wing with numerous cottagey gables echoing the C18 dormers. Gothick game-larder, now joined to the house.

RANBY HALL, 3 m, NW. C18 and early C19 plus later additions,‡ for example the Doric porch on the three-storey, seven-bay E wing. S front also seven-bay but of two storeys with a pilastered and pedimented centre. (Colonnaded staircase hall; drawing room with Corinthian columns and coffered recesses. DOE)

8050

## BALDERTON

ST GILES. Its fine steeple, of Lincolnshire–Newark type, just as needle-sharp as Newark, rises now in what has become virtually a suburb of Newark. The lower stage is evidently C13 (see the W door and the tower arch inside), but the crocketed spire with one tier of windows must be late C14 or even early C15. The chancel has E.E. lancet windows, the E triplet of 1856 by *G. G. Place*. The aisles mostly Dec; tracery of ogee reticulation.
14 The oldest part of the church, however, is its Norman doorway of high quality, at the entrance to the porch. It has an inner order of beakheads all along jambs and arch, and then two orders with decorated colonnettes and scalloped capitals; the voussoirs with zigzag. In a niche above the doorway a late
15 C12 figure of a saint in a round-headed surround, faceless and not in good condition, but once of excellent quality. N arcade on low octagonal C13 piers with double-chamfered arches, S arcade C14 with large undulating leaves on the capitals. – DOOR. C15, with a roughly carved figure of the Virgin. – FONT. Early C14, octagonal, with ballflower ornament on the shaft. – PULPIT. Plain Perp. – SCREEN. Perp, of the same design as Newark, but with a pretty little figure of the Virgin over the entrance. – BENCH ENDS. Unusual, numerous, symmetrical shape, panelled, with poppyheads. – STAINED GLASS. Many C14–16 bits in the chancel windows, for example a half-

* Bound into the Red Book unexecuted designs for a greenhouse by *William Wilkins*.
‡ Including some of *c.* 1860 by Mr Goddard.

figure, a St Michael, and a bearded head in the SE window, a feathered angel and parts of two saints in the SW window. – In a S aisle window Adoration of the Lamb by *Wailes*. – MONUMENT to Mary Sikes † 1828 by *D. W. Willson* of London.

METHODIST CHURCH, Main Street. With a little needle spire. Stone, in the free-style Gothic favoured by the Nonconformists at the turn of the century.

EARTHWORKS of the besieging Parliamentary army in the Civil War once surrounded the village, but are now largely destroyed (cf. Hawton, Farndon, Coddington, and South Muskham).

### BARNBY-IN-THE-WILLOWS 8050

ALL SAINTS. The most striking feature of the church is the chancel tracery, odd combinations of circles, segments, 69 triangles. In the E window the centre lancet has at its foot glazed semicircles. Is it C17? It seems more likely than Professor Hamilton Thompson's and others' attribution to the Middle Ages. Otherwise the church has nave and two aisles, alternating supports, circular and octagonal, plain moulded capitals; still C13. W tower ashlar, C15. N porch late C15, with pinnacles, gargoyles, and a fine wooden door. – FONT. Octagonal, with shields in panels. – Several old BENCH ENDS. – ALTAR RAILS. Early C17, with rather heavy balusters. – Of the same time the much rarer PANELLING of the altar surround. – BOX PEWS in the aisles. – MONUMENT to Mary Sharpe † 1742, with bust.

(JUBILEE SCHOOL. 1850, in classical style, with blank arched recesses.)

DOVECOTE. Circular with conical roof, only 15 ft high, but 63 ft in circumference, the smallest of the three circular dovecotes left in Notts (cf. Sibthorpe, Thoroton). Two types of nesting holes: the earlier in stone, the later of bricks and pantiles.

### BARTON-IN-FABIS 5030

ST GEORGE. An excellent high unaisled chancel of the late C14 with tall windows, SEDILIA with crocketed ogee gables, and a S doorway originally with two orders of colonnettes. The chancel arch is impressively high and narrow. C14 S arcade on octagonal piers with double-chamfered arches. In the S aisle chapel a PISCINA and AUMBRY.* A clerestory of different

* According to Mr Alvey.

rhythm was added in the C15. Of the later C14 also the ashlar-built w tower of Bunny type. Porch added in 1693. (Restored in 1877 and in 1885* by *T. C. Hine*, who built a new RECTORY (1878). JPB) – SCREEN. Restored remains of a fine rood screen. – PULPIT. Jacobean with some new panels.‡ – MONUMENTS. Several of the Sacheverell family, notably William † 1616 and wife, alabaster, obviously by the workshop which did the monuments to the same family at Ratcliffe-on-Soar. – Nice incised Swithland slate gravestones of the C18 and C19 with the engravers' signatures; at Barton, where they are inside the church, they can be studied more easily than where they are in churchyards as in so many other south Notts villages.

DOVECOTE in the farmyard of Manor Farm, visible across the fields from the road into the village. The only octagonal dovecote in Notts, of brick, originally with 1,200 plaster nesting places. Built by the Sacheverells in the late C17 or early C18.

At Glebe Farm, ¾m. s, the remains of a ROMAN VILLA were excavated in 1856 and again in 1949. Much of the main house lies beneath the modern farm buildings. Parts of one subsidiary dwelling and outbuildings have been excavated and areas of two mosaic floors revealed. The villa appears to have been occupied from the C2 to the C4.

On BRANDS HILL, remains of medieval contour ploughing. Lynchets, or small banks, mark the boundaries of small plots.

BASFORD *see* NOTTINGHAM, p. 266

BEAUVALE

In Greasley parish

BEAUVALE PRIORY. Remains of a Carthusian house, founded in 1343 by Nicholas de Cantilupe, mostly incorporated in farm buildings. One of only nine Charterhouses in England and, apart from Mount Grace, Yorks, and Hinton, Somerset, the best preserved and least encumbered. It would be very informative if excavated and laid out. Carthusian houses were quite different from those of other orders. The monks lived alone, each with his own house, arranged around a cloister, for the

---

* A. E. Street wrongly attributes the restoration to his father, *G. E. Street*, according to Paul Joyce.
‡ According to Mr Alvey.

order imposed a vow of silence and strict separation of one monk from another. Whole ranges of these houses and their gardens can be traced. The upstanding remains are part of the church, with a C15 window, a staircase doorway to the large cloister, a large part of the S wall of the small cloister, a three-storey tower house, and much of the gatehouse range incorporated in the outbuildings of the present farmhouse. The tower house, possibly the prior's lodging, has two pointed doorways and a blocked one to the ground floor, a two-light window to the first floor, and three two-light mullioned windows to the top floor. It is one of only three remains of tower houses in Notts (cf. Halloughton, Strelley). The farmhouse is built largely of materials quarried from the priory.

(MANOR FARM, S of the priory. C17. Part rubble (from an earlier house? *see* below), part brick, with modern casements. C17 staircase with splat balusters and a dog-gate. Adjoining, a two-storey red-brick gatehouse, the inner sides of the arch half-timbered. Over it a dovecote, a brewhouse/bakehouse at the side. Facing the house a ruined wall with a late medieval stone doorway with moulded jambs. NS)

BEAUVALE HOUSE. Begun in 1871 and with the date 1873 above the entrance. A small, inexpensive, but romantic retreat in a tract of Sherwood Forest for the seventh Earl Cowper, on the estate inherited from his grandmother, Lady Palmerston. He was already a considerable landowner with a family seat at Panshanger, Herts. His architect here was *E. W. Godwin*, practised designer of romantic country houses in Ireland (Dromore and Glenbegh), who in 1867–8 had built a medievalizing gatehouse and walled garden at Castle Ashby for the Earl's father-in-law, Lord Northampton.* The plan of two linked rectangles, one the main house, the other the office and stable courtyard, makes the house look larger than it is; and the composition of roof shapes building up to a high tower appearing above the trees,‡ together with the brick, tilehanging, and half-timbering, gives it its romance. It was probably the decorative half-timbering in Shaw's and in Nesfield's designs that suggested its use here, but Godwin's timbering is structural and North French rather than 'Old English' in style. The details, of no particular period, are simple, and in the interior bold and original. Over the

* There is a comprehensive but undated set of designs for Beauvale in the RIBA Drawings Collection.

‡ The chimneystack on the tower has been removed.

staircase an impressive timber barrel-vault, plain tiled or brick fireplaces, and an ingenious wooden spiral staircase in the tower. The entrance hall, with stained glass panels, was originally of two storeys and the walls were covered throughout with wallpaper designed by Godwin. Unlike Burges's medieval fantasies, this house was comfortable to live in and marks a step towards the acceptance of the Domestic Revival in secular architecture.

For the estate hamlet, Moorgreen, *see* Greasley.

## BECKINGHAM

*7090*

ALL SAINTS. The exterior appears all C15, the interior mainly C13. That is: the usual ashlared W tower with diagonal buttresses, gargoyles, paired belfry windows, battlements, and eight pinnacles, gargoyles on the S aisle too, and Perp windows everywhere. But both arcades inside have octagonal piers with moulded capitals exhibiting some dogtooth, and double-chamfered arches. The N chancel chapel very similar. Restoration 1892 by *Ewan Christian* (JPB). – SEDILIA with deeply moulded arches, and little shafts with unrestored stiff-leaf capitals. Part of the rood SCREEN, *c.* 1500, under the tower arch.

VICARAGE. 1873 by *Hine* (JPB).

## BEESTHORPE HALL *see* CAUNTON

## BEESTON*

*5030*

The anatomy of the older Beeston, although dismembered by new roads and smothered by recent suburban growth, can still be discerned. The manor house and cottages along the original main street (Middle Street and West End) belong to the rural village; the textile mills and some housing to the C19 industrial village; at the same time the railway arrived and the church was rebuilt.

ST JOHN THE BAPTIST, Chilwell Road. Rebuilt in 1842–4 by *Scott & Moffatt*, with a large SW tower and a dull Perp interior. The chancel was left standing, much lower than the new church though somewhat enlarged by *C. H. Thornton* in 1876. It has straight-headed Perp windows and pretty ogee-cusped SEDILIA, PISCINA, and AUMBRY. – FONT. Circular and fluted. – ALTAR RAILS. Late C17 with balusters.

* Professor M. W. Barley kindly amended our description of Beeston.

METHODIST CHURCH, Chilwell Road. 1902 (*W. J. Morley* of Bradford). Gothic, brick with stone details and spire.

MANOR HOUSE, No. 2 Middle Street. Brick with a continuous stone plinth. Now stripped of its C19 stucco. The main range, with Gothic glazing bars, dates from *c.* 1675 (cf. Chilwell Manor House), the short NE wing from *c.* 1700 or slightly later, possibly replacing a timber-framed wing. A Dutch gable at the S end of the main range, chimneys placed diamond-wise, and the remains of round arches over original openings. The shaped brick bands on the street side were decorative in the local Artisan Mannerist fashion (cf. East Leake, etc.). Inside, a stair and some panelling of *c.* 1700.

In WEST END several houses originally C17 and C18, including No. 6 (lobby-entrance plan with cross wing) and No. 3 (tall brick L-plan house of *c.* 1750), now smartened up. By *c.* 1830 the Nottingham end of BROADGATE had begun to be lined with houses (Nos. 40–44), and in SALTHOUSE LANE Dagfa House (now a school) and The Woodlands are two small Regency villas. The later C19 terrace housing is being replaced in 1978: REGENT STREET, old people's housing (*Elsworth Associates* in succession to *Gordon Benoy*) and SALISBURY STREET (*Architects Design Group*). A shopping centre completed in 1973 involved the demolition of one of Boots first shops.*

STATION. 1847 for the Midland Railway.

The most impressive buildings in the town are industrial. The textile industry, which migrated from Nottingham in the early C19 and again in the late C19, changed its character. Of the first period, the SILK MILL behind the properties fronting Station Road at its junction with High Road, an old (1826) but much altered building, and behind SWISS MILLS (1886), Wollaton Road, a very early lace factory of the 1820s or 1830s. Later, but more distinctive architecturally, the ANGLO- SCOTIAN MILLS of 1871. Tall, red brick, and Gothic: rigorously symmetrical, with lancet windows and castellated turrets.

The former HUMBER WORKS, Humber Road, was part of the first extensive engineering works in the east Midlands, a cycle factory built by Thomas Humber in 1885. It was abandoned in 1908 when the Humber Co. moved to Coventry. Good classi-

---

* It was of 1908, in their prestige half-timbered style, inspired by the Jacobean building they restored for use as a shop in St Albans. By *A. N. Bromley*, with statues, heraldry, and stained glass by *Morley Horder* depicting local history (cf. Shrewsbury, York, Derby).

cal façade with windows in pairs above a blank arcade and plaques showing early company trademarks.

Dwarfing Beeston by its massive industrial scale the premises of THE BOOTS COMPANY LTD, lying between the railway line and the canal s of the town. Here is some of the most important c20 work in the county: two factory buildings by *Sir Owen Williams*, civil engineer and designer of the Empire Pool, Wembley, and an office building by the internationally-esteemed American partnership *Skidmore, Owings & Merrill* (in association with *Yorke Rosenberg Mardall*).

103   Williams's buildings date from soon after Boots moved here from Station Street, Nottingham, in 1928.* The earlier factory, built in 1930–2 (for wet processes), is a milestone in modern architecture – and especially concrete architecture – in Britain. Its appearance is the direct outcome of its construction rather than recognition by Williams of the aims of the international modern movement. Reinforced concrete is used for its structural potential, whereas designers such as Behrens and Connell & Ward sought only to imitate the aesthetic appearance by using stuccoed brick. The result is powerful and startlingly modern: concrete mushroom columns carry galleries round a packing hall the full height of the building, which is wrapped in a glass curtain wall. The s front is 550 ft long, all cantilevered out over the loading dock. The projection is 30 ft. His second building of 1937–8 (for dry processes), though less acclaimed, is structurally as interesting. The long two-storeyed block, designed to be extended, is hung from vast concrete frames, again allowing a projection over the loading dock of 48 ft – Banham makes a convincing suggestion that the bold forms and mass of raw concrete in combination with glazing influenced the post-war 'New Brutalist' movement.

105   On the same site is a late example of the true International Modern Style by *Skidmore, Owings & Merrill* (1966–8), who established themselves in the late 1950s as exponents of this prestigious manner, chiefly associated with successful business.‡

* Some of their offices etc. are still there in post-war buildings by their own Architects' Department.

‡ Skidmore, Owings & Merrill in association with Yorke Rosenberg Mardall have built elsewhere in Britain for W. D. & H. O. Wills & Sons at Bristol (finished in 1973). The same exposed-frame principle has been used for both factory and office block. The glamour of this building makes an interesting contrast with the toughness of the contemporary Arup Associates' Horizon Factory for John Player at Nottingham (*see* Lenton, p. 254).

Although the output of this firm, with seven regional offices, is no longer homogeneous, the Boots building is one of the best recent examples of the style for which they became famous, i.e. rationalist architecture true to Mies van der Rohe's objectives of 'craft and purity' in all details. It is also representative of their preoccupation in the late 1960s with structure. The Chicago office particularly, which produced the Nottingham design, is responsible for buildings (e.g. John Hancock Tower, Chicago) in which the structure has become almost expressively assertive. The Boots building, closely related to that of the Armstrong Cork Co. in Lancaster, Pennsylvania, is cool and unaccented. In both, the main feature is the black painted steel frame with massive horizontal roof-plate and square steel columns that appear to support it. As in most contemporary SOM buildings, the curtain wall (here of bronze anodized glass) is set back behind it. In fact the appearance is illusory. The predominant first floor is supported on conventional concrete piers, concealed on the outside by a ramp and earth banks. The block is hollow, with both storeys expressed in the courtyard. Open-plan interior, the fittings constructed to the same 6 ft module as the whole structure, reflecting SOM's tendency towards rigid Beaux-Arts planning. The building is successful on its own terms. Whether those terms operate successfully on a bleak industrial estate is perhaps another question.

The Boots site is of interest not only to the architectural enthusiast: the development of buildings in response to the change in industrial processes is also fascinating to record. The earliest plant is the soap factory of 1928 in the SE corner of the site. The multi-storeyed factories designed in the 1930s, though still in use, are now outdated by buildings like the vast sheds (tablet factory, 1974–6) to accommodate processes all on one floor.

## BENNERLEY VIADUCT see AWSWORTH

## BESTHORPE                                         *8060*

WINDMILL at Mill Farm. The oak post (twenty-one inches square), quarter bars, and cross trees all survive intact inside a complete brick round house, now a store. The best post-mill remains in Notts.

BESTWOOD LODGE and Kelham Hall are the best examples in
   Notts of the High Victorian mansion on a lavish scale but of
   medium size. Bestwood Lodge was built for the tenth Duke
   of St Albans in 1862–5 by *S. S. Teulon*, one of the most ruthless,
   insensitive, and original of the High Victorians.* The building
   is of brick, with stone dressings, in the Gothic style, chiefly
   E.E., but not shy of Franco-Flemish dormer windows. The
   bricks are of many hues; above the windows there are, for
   example, black headers and moulded red bricks. The skyline
   defies description. There is no desire for symmetry or indeed
   balance (as Salvin for instance achieved at Thoresby). The
   clash of elements is harsh, and it is difficult for us now to
   imagine that so jarring a composition could then convey
   comfort and prosperity. And yet the Prince of Wales was
   inspired by the plans of Bestwood to employ Teulon at
   Sandringham!
      Some of the jarring notes are the result of alterations. To the
   r. a conservatory wing of after 1867, enlarged after 1896 to form
   a drill hall. The end of Teulon's wing opposite with stepped
   gable and bellcote looks like a chapel (and now is one), but it
   was built as a servants' hall and was censured by the *Ecclesiologist* for its ecclesiastical overtones. Above the wildly original
   porch with its flying buttresses, the heads of Robin Hood and
   his Merrie Men, carved (like the scenes from local history elsewhere on the building) by *Thomas Earp*. The carving inside
   is equally accomplished, although the interior in general is not
   as grand as Scott's at Kelham. Best perhaps is the entrance hall
   and the great hall with its extraordinary stepped fireplace.
   GARDENS landscaped by *Teulon* and *Thomas Church*. ALEX-
   ANDRA LODGE GATE is of 1878, a gatehouse with a half-
   timbered stage over the Gothic entrance arch.
w of the house EMMANUEL CHURCH, in E.E. style, by *Teulon*,
   1868–9. – In the apsidal chancel STAINED GLASS by *Morris
   & Co.*, 1911.
BESTWOOD PUMPING STATION, 2 m. NE, on the road to
   Mansfield. 1871–4, in an Italian Gothic style, with a tall taste-
   less chimney, standing proudly in a garden landscaped round
   its serpentine cooling pond. Iron gates and lamp standards all

---

* The Victorian house was not the first one here. There were hunting lodges
on the site from the C14. The first Duke acquired the land from his father,
Charles II.

intact. The architect is unrecorded.\* The water engineer was the famous *Thomas Hawksley*, but the machinery was removed in 1968.

BESTWOOD COLLIERY, E of the B683 N of Bulwell, is now disused, but its winding engine house is an interesting relic of the age of steam winding (not quite over) preserved complete with headstocks. Vertical engine built in 1873.

FORGE MILL, almost opposite Bestwood colliery but actually in Hucknall parish. One of the mills built by the Robinsons on the river Leen, this one well to the S of their others at Papplewick. Stone-built mill of three storeys erected in 1787. To its N an extensive silted-up mill pool. The position of the water intake to the internal wheel (or wheels) can be seen.

BILBOROUGH *see* NOTTINGHAM p. 267

## BILSTHORPE                                                    6060

ST MARGARET. W tower, nave, and chancel. The Savile transeptal chapel added (by *T. C. Hine*, who restored the church in 1873. JPB) The top of the tower was redone in 1663, still with Tudor windows, but with obelisks instead of pinnacles. – Fragment of an inscribed foliated CROSS SLAB in the porch. – Plain Norman FONT. – BENCHES. Nice plain C17, with one bolection moulding (cf. Walesby; also perhaps Hockerton). – STAINED GLASS. W window by *Kempe*, 1880.

(MANOR FARM, opposite the church, is almost all that remains of the old village. The inter-war mining village is expanding in all directions. Brick with posts and beams of the timber frame showing externally. C17, with axial stack and lobby entrance. Miscellaneous windows. NS)

## BINGHAM                                                       7030

ALL SAINTS. The steeple is of high interest, broad and strong, with pairs of corner buttresses and an additional buttress in the middle of each side. The windows are lancets and two-light lancets higher up. Corbel table with ballflower ornament and

---

\* It was probably Hawksley himself. He had been articled in Nottingham to Mr Staveley before joining with Jalland (*see* p. 237 n) in a partnership known as Staveley, Hawksley & Jalland until 1850. Hawksley was Nottingham's water engineer from 1852 until 1880, when the job was taken over by the Corporation (*see* Papplewick).

human heads (note the lady with the wimple). The battlements have on the W instead of pinnacles two (completely redone) figures of bishops. Broad, not very steep spire, broached, with three tiers of windows: the whole C13 to early C14. The nave has two aisles with arcades continued in front of the transeptal chapels. Octagonal piers, the capitals with large upright leaves, for example oak, vine, but also still one crocket capital. Even so, the date is no doubt later than the Southwell chapter house (and the quality much inferior). The windows are C14 and C15, easily recognizable as such. The best is of four lights with intersecting tracery and one quatrefoil at the top, that is c. 1300. Complete restoration by *Sir G. G. Scott*, 1845, and by *Caröe*, 1912. – Plain SEDILIA and PISCINA of c. 1300. – SCREEN. Old parts in the base, Perp, the rest by *Caröe*, who designed the REREDOS and CHOIR STALLS. – FONT. Tub on new base: the cover looks Jacobean. – STAINED GLASS. Window of 1848 with Virgin and Child, designed and painted when aged twenty-four by *Alfred Richard Mowbray*, founder of the firm of church furnishers (RH). – Chancel. Very pretty, probably of c. 1873, with small figures and groups in medallions by Mrs *Miles* († 1884) of Bingham. – S transept window designed as a memorial to his parents by her son *Frank Miles*, fashionable painter of fashionable women. E. W. Godwin designed No. 44 Tite Street, Chelsea, for him.* – Window (Jacob's Dream) by *Kempe*, 1888. – MONUMENTS. One of c. 1310, supposed to be to Sir Richard de Bingham, cross-legged, badly preserved. – Partly effaced incised slab to (?) Sir Thomas Rempstone and his wife † 1458. – LYCHGATE, with screens partly of fretwork and partly of wrought-iron, by *Frank Miles*, 1881.

The church stands E of the Market Place, and E of the church, in Crow Close, earthworks of a MEDIEVAL VILLAGE indicate that the settlement migrated westward for almost half a mile. Before this, a Romano-British rural settlement lay at the NE corner of the village.

Bingham is a small market town but, apart from the large rectangular market place and a few public buildings, it looks more like an overgrown village.‡ In the MARKET PLACE, the BUT-

---

* According to the late S. Race, who told us that church furnishings designed by the Miles family were removed before World War II. A section of WALL PAINTING by *Mrs Miles* or *Frank Miles* was restored to the church in 1976.

‡ We are grateful to Mr Adrian Henstock for providing much of the new information included in this entry.

TER CROSS, Gothic and octagonal, with a slated roof crowned by a lantern. Erected to the memory of the Earl of Chesterfield's agent, John Hassall of Shelford Manor, in 1861, probably by *Hine*. What survives of his former G. N. R. station (STATION HOUSE) of 1857 is linked to the Market Place by a contemporary axial road. Round the square, two or three late-Georgian-style houses of *c.* 1830–40 (two on the N side now District Council Offices), and on the corner the so-called MANOR HOUSE of *c.* 1700, somewhat altered but with some unusual features all in brick. Double-pile with corner pilasters and one in the centre up to first-floor level. Above it a curious bowed panel with an ornamental surround. In CHURCH STREET, the MAGISTRATES' COURTHOUSE, built as a police station and lock-up in 1852, is in an Italianate style seen elsewhere in the town (e.g. *R. C. Sutton*'s former Wesleyan school of 1859, No. 12 Kirkhill). CHURCH HOUSE, EAST STREET, is by *Scott & Moffatt* (1845–6), a typical Tudor-style C. of E. school building.

TOOTHILL COMPREHENSIVE SCHOOL, The Banks. In 1964 the County Architect (*H. T. Swain*) adopted the policy for community schools recommended by the DES. Bingham was the Architect's Department's first attempt (1966–8), in CLASP, with too great a range of cladding materials. These schools (cf. Carlton and Sutton-in-Ashfield) are not, alas, as vital to the community architecturally as they are socially and educationally.

Pagan Anglo-Saxon cremation CEMETERY on the ridge, 1 m. SE.

## BLEASBY

ST MARY. Basically C13 but almost rebuilt in the C19, i.e. restored in 1845, 1852, and more extensively (and dreadfully) in 1869 by *Ewan Christian* (JPB). N arcade of C13 type. E window of three lights with STAINED GLASS by *Whall*.

BLEASBY HALL.* The five-bay main front is early C18, as the proportions show, but 'Gothicked' with stucco, an embattled porch projection, and angle turrets in the late C18 by a Southwell speculator for a quick sale. He also pulled down rambling Jacobean parts at the rear, some of which may still exist behind the stucco. Servants' wing (W) in a similar style, dated 1836. The service wing behind has late C16 beams and door-frame.

OLD HOUSE. Records date from 1363, but the present stone

* Description kindly provided by David Durant.

structure is basically of *c.* 1500. It is a type of house rare in this part of the country and was originally divided by a surviving stud partition running up the whole height of the house into a full-height hall with a two-storey section at its s end. Also intact the roof and a timber-framed firehood at the N end of the hall. The brick gable at this end was possibly timber-framed originally. Much altered in the C17, when the upper floors were inserted, and later, when the N–S partitions and the staircase were put in. Plain C19 service wing.

# BLIDWORTH

High up in Sherwood Forest with wide views and biting winds, the old village round the church at the top, and vast amounts of colliery housing stretching down the hillside.

ST MARY OF THE PURIFICATION. Of the medieval church the W tower remains, C15, unbuttressed and much restored. Some fragments, a window, a door, and some walling have been re-erected in the churchyard, with the woods behind in the distance. The present church dates from 1739, with the usual round-headed windows and an unusual s arcade, on correct Tuscan columns (cf. East Stoke), but with chamfered arches. E end of chancel rebuilt 1839 (Colvin). – FONT. C15, with a variety of blank Perp tracery panelling. – PULPIT. Wood, neo-Dec, with crocketing, transferred from Southwell in 1900. It looks *c.* 1820 (cf. the screen at Newstead Abbey). – PANELLING in the chancel also transferred from Southwell Minster. The eight Jacobean panels may well have belonged to a pulpit. – On the reverse of the HYMN BOARD, a King David painted by *Shepperd*, 1779. – MONUMENTS. Thomas Leake † 1598, a Sherwood Forest ranger, with his hunting gear and trophies. – William Bilbie † 1777 by *Christopher Theakston* of Doncaster.

WINDMILL. Derelict brick tower mill of *c.* 1818, the shortest in the county.

(About 2 m. W of the village two completely secluded and quite inaccessible houses. RAINWORTH LODGE is C19 and C20, part colour-washed rubble, gabled and very irregular, with a little Gothick glazing. Three-bay stone barn adjoining, probably also C19. Beautiful garden with trees and lakes formed out of Rainworth Water, cf. FOUNTAIN DALE, SW of Rainworth Lodge and on the same lake system but a much superior house. Early C19, white stuccoed, with deep bracketed eaves and some

Gothick glazing. Probably the remodelling of an earlier house – see the fine range of C18 stables and outbuildings, now flats. NS)

RUFFORD PITHEAD BATHS, 2 m. N at Rainworth. 1941 by *J. W. Dudding* for the Miners' Welfare Commission.

## BLYTH

PRIORY CHURCH of St Mary and St Martin. There is nothing like Blyth in Nottinghamshire to get a feeling for early Norman grimness. The church is only a fragment of what it once was, and a sad, badly treated fragment at that. The E part was pulled down after the Dissolution, and a wall was put up W of the easternmost bay of the nave.* The owners of Blyth Hall a hundred years or so ago used the space from that wall to the huge, sheer W arch of the crossing as an aviary. So the crossing, the N and S transepts each with an apsidal E chapel, and the chancel ending in an apse and accompanied by straight-ended chancel chapels (the scheme of Bernay, the Trinité at Caen, etc., in Normandy, and for instance of Old Sarum in the C11 in England) are all gone. The nave also is deprived of its E bay, as has already been said, and moreover of its original W end by the insertion of a Perp W tower, a symbol of the civic pride which took the place of the monastic pride of the Benedictine priory. This W tower is of a usual Notts type, ashlar-faced, with pairs of corner buttresses, large bell-stage windows, battlements, and eight pinnacles.‡ What is unusual, however, is that the battlements are in a charming way connected by openwork cusped gables. There is a gabled W door too with another large window right above, and the aisle and S porch are battlemented. Another addition has to be discounted to visualize the Norman building; the proud S aisle of *c.* 1300, as wide as were the old aisle and the S transept put together, with five large three-light windows with intersecting tracery. Instead of a sixth window the customary S porch appears which has a richly moulded E.E. doorway with two orders, crocket capitals, and some nailhead. The E end of the S aisle, now walled up, was a two-bay opening with an octagonal pier into the Norman transept. The Norman work appears at its purest and most uncompromising in the S elevation of the nave. Its date cannot be determined with any cer-

* Mr Train thinks this wall was probably erected before the Dissolution: it has traces of a Doom painted on it.

‡ Bellchamber and above rebuilt in 1929–30.

tainty. Blyth was founded by Roger de Builli of Tickhill Castle
beyond the Yorkshire border in 1088. It was made subordinate
to Holy Trinity Priory at Rouen and became important because
it offered hospitality on a busy high road. Building usually
6  started at the E, so the nave may have been erected or even
designed as late as after 1100. However, the style of the work
does not make that appear probable. It is decidedly C11 in
character. So it seems that the nave was begun at once and
finished by 1100. The piers have square cores with flat projections on all four sides and a demi-shaft on each side against
this projection. The demi-shafts have unusual base mouldings:
a hollow with two rolls below. The shafts towards the nave once
led straight up to the ceiling, as they still do, for example, at
Ely. But about 1230 the ceiling was replaced by an E.E. vault
with thin, elegant ribs. These hard main vertical sections frame
arcades whose capitals are of the most rudimentary volute type
with just one upright tongue in the middle, and the arches have
only two steps. The gallery has large, gaping, completely undivided openings, as Saint-Étienne in Caen had had them some
twenty-five years before. A string course at gallery level runs
round the main dividing shafts. In the clerestory each window
7  has an order of columns inside. On the N side the aisle is completely preserved, with small windows, rude depressed transverse arches, and equally rude groined vaults. The gallery, however, has been removed and Perp windows inserted instead.*
On the S side the later aisle is so high that it takes in the arcade
as well as the gallery openings. Externally the clerestory is complete with its corbel table. What the W front was like is now
impossible to say. All that we know is that two spiral staircases
(that on the N can still be seen rising five or six feet up the Perp
W tower, of the S one only the doorway) projected holding a
main feature between, which one would like to think may have
been one of those giant niches as they occur at Lincoln and
Tewkesbury, or a simpler arrangement as at Thorney (Cambs).
Twin towers (as intended at Tewkesbury) were obviously not
planned here, because the W piers are no bigger than the other
nave piers. In any case, according to the evidence which has
come down to us, we must expect something severe and forceful, without any refinements whatsoever. – PULPITUM. The
present E wall is supposed to contain part of the pulpitum, that
is the stone chancel screen, as they survive elaborately

* The only later work, a restoration of 1861 by *J. G. Weightman* (Peter
Howell).

decorated at York, Canterbury, Southwell, Lincoln, Exeter, etc. – SCREENS. Three wooden screens remain in differing condition, the best that in the S aisle, complete with its vaulting on both sides. The pattern of the main panels not very imaginative. The others are the rood screen and the parclose screen between nave and S aisle, both also uninteresting in design. The first and the second have at the foot painted panels in the East Anglian way, very raw. – FONT. Late C17 with cherubs' heads. The cover of the usual Jacobean type. – PULPIT. First half of the C17; nothing special. – Late medieval ALMSBOX on a stone corbel, almost covered by ironwork. – PAINTING by *Fra Bartolommeo*, according to the church guidebook. – STAINED GLASS. W window 1903 by *Kempe*. – MONUMENT. Damaged effigy to a knight, a FitzWilliam, *c.* 1240, with cylindrical helmet and visor; S aisle. – A foliated cross in the tower chamber has a Norman French inscription to Francke, Marchant de (?) Bosas, *c.* 1300.* – Edward Mellish † 1703; stiffly reclining against an aedicule background with fluted Corinthian pilasters and a segmental pediment. The earliest figure in such an attitude in Notts (cf. West Stockwith). Signed by *John Hancock*. – Catherine Hornby, 1772, tablet by *J. Wood*.

Blyth, originally on the Great North Road, is now just skirted by the A1. An attractive village (really a decayed market town which grew up outside the gates of the abbey, important to medieval travellers). A broad main street bordered on the E side by a village green and with a second green round the churchyard. The HALL, built in 1684–5 by Edward Mellish † 1703, was demolished in 1972.‡ The STABLES and surviving BRIDGE of 1770 were probably built by *John Carr*, a great friend of William Mellish.

William Mellish built the former RECTORY close to the church (with a blank-arcaded façade, cupola, and Gothick casements), almshouses (demolished), and easily recognizable terraces of cottages with the same Gothic window casements; one opposite the churchyard and one, with a tall pedimented carriageway, on the E side of the green. Plainer cottages on the W side have

* According to Mr Rigold.

‡ It was seven bays wide with N and S façades both with a centre of five bays and one-bay projections at each end and then one outer bay. H. M. Colvin suggests an attribution on stylistic grounds to *Talman*. Carr added a bay-windowed drawing room with Adamish detail between two of the towers in the 1770s (payments 1773 and 1776), according to Dr R. B. Wragg. Quoins and (perhaps also *c.* 1770) square turrets in the Burlingtonian taste on the four projections.

been replaced by a row of nondescript bungalows. Also in the MAIN STREET an altered C17 house with quoins and a segmental stone doorhood, and further s a pretty octagonal early C19 cottage, stuccoed, with Gothic windows and door and a central chimney. Opposite, on the green, the former leper HOSPITAL OF ST JOHN THE EVANGELIST, refounded in 1226 but apparently rebuilt on this site in 1446 with older material. It was being used as a school in 1695. It is a rectangular building with dog-tooth ornament in its jambs and in its segmental-arched door. Hoodmoulds over the (altered) C17 windows. s of the church near the Angel Inn, a row of cottages with wooden cross windows, built as the Friends' Meeting House c. 1698.

SPITAL HOUSE, ¼ m. s. Plain but well proportioned early C19 house of two storeys and three bays. Stuccoed. Pretty interiors, possibly by *Lindley & Woodhead* of Doncaster, who worked nearby at Serlby. THE MANTLES, E of the village, is similar in appearance but not as well designed or detailed inside.*

<sub>7080</sub>                                    BOLE

ST MARTIN. Perp w tower, with the ashlaring, diagonal buttresses, and eight pinnacles which one sees so often in east Notts. Ashlar, battlements, and pinnacles also in other parts of the church. Only the chancel N wall is evidently older masonry, although most of it was rebuilt in the restoration by *Ewan Christian*, 1866. No attraction in the interior architecture: aisleless nave. – FONT. Norman, with arcades and intersecting arches. – PULPIT given by a noted local Ecclesiologist, Sir H. J. Anderson. Set in it Flemish late C16 panels with the story of Esther and Ahasuerus, very lively, if not very courtly.

MANOR FARM, E of the church. Of *c.* 1675, with fine shaped gables and diagonally-set chimneystacks. Rendered front with C19 windows, but at the back diaper-patterned brick with a moulded string course and two little triangular pediments, probably over windows originally. In the same tradition as North Wheatley.

* Information from Mr Harry Johnson.

# BOLHAM

### Part of East Retford

BOLHAM HALL, 1 m. N, in Tiln Lane. Early C18 and called Bol-
lom House in 1772. Five-bay Georgian brick house of two-and-
a-half storeys, the door surround late C18.

BOLHAM MILLS, Bolham Lane. An interesting water-powered
site at the foot of a red sandstone cliff, partly cut away to accommodate it. Of obvious antiquity, the present buildings are of
c. 1800, for paper-making. Converted in the mid-C19 to a tan-
ning mill and still used as such, although the waterworks have
been largely obliterated.

# BONINGTON see SUTTON BONINGTON

# BOTHAMSALL

ST PETER AND ST MARY. 1845; a piece of Notts imitation-Perp.
*William Wilkins*'s design of 1817 was rejected (Colvin). –
FONT. Perp, from the old church, octagonal, with various
fanciful castellated tracery patterns. – BRASS, N side of the
chancel. Two remaining parts of a brass without a matrix slab:
either the upper half or a demi-effigy of a lady of c. 1360–80
plus an inscription. If the date is correct (it may be Margaret
Buslingthorp † 1369), this would be the earliest surviving brass
of English workmanship in Notts. (An earlier one to Alan Fleming † 1363 at Newark is foreign.) If the identification is correct,
her ancestor, Sir Richard de Buslingthorpe, was commemorated
by the earliest surviving brass in Lincs.

At the E entrance to the village, houses built by the Duke of
Newcastle, who owned the village. Near-replicas of those at
Hardwick-in-Clumber.*

CASTLE HILL. A small motte-and-bailey castle, ¼ m. W, overlooking the river Meden.

LOUND HALL. *See* p. 167.

* According to Mr H. Johnson.

## BOUGHTON

6060

(St Matthew. 1867–8, by *James Fowler* of Louth.* Geometrical with spire. Excellent stained glass in the E window to W. J. Pickin † 1869, the Duke of Newcastle's agent, who built the School (now church hall) and Schoolhouse, 1861, in Pickin's Row.)

Pumping Station. 1905, red brick, with some shaped gables and a tall polygonal chimney. No machinery.

Boughton joins up with Ollerton.

## BRADMORE

5030

Only the church spire survived the fire that devastated the village in 1706. It is an interesting early specimen, unbuttressed, C13 ground floor and C14 upper floor, with two-light ogee windows and a dormerless broach-spire. A mission church of 1887 adjoins it.

Much of the village was rebuilt, to his own designs, by Sir Thomas Parkyns of Bunny. Rancliffe Farm in Farmer Street has Sir TP 1736 in black headers on the gable: double-pile and with a large barn. Also no doubt by him, although not dated or initialled, Parkyns House, Farmer Street; Tofts Farm and Debdale Farm, Loughborough Road; and Barn Close, with a barn continuous with the façade. Also in Farmer Street, Blackcliffe Farm and Rufford Lodge have the stone mullioned windows used in Parkyns's early buildings, but none of his other distinctive features in the construction.

For other buildings by Sir Thomas *see* Bunny, Costock, and East Leake.

## BRAMCOTE

5030

St Michael. Of the old church only the C14 tower, all covered in creeper, was left standing when a new church was built in 1861 by *John Johnson* of London. – The font, later C13 with a frieze of black pointed-trefoil arcades, was transferred. – Wall monument to Henry Hanley † 1650; note the inscription.

Opposite the old tower, The Grange, late Georgian, stuc-

---

* Information from Mr Keith Train and Mr Bartlam.

coed.* Five-bay façade with Venetian windows flanking and
one above a doorway of a similar shape. Shallow hipped roof
with a strangely long interval between the upper windows and
the eaves. Two-storey wing on each side, and on one side a bow-
window. Further s at the end of Town Street, the MANOR
HOUSE, in existence in 1564, though the present L-shaped
building is late C17; brick with diaperwork of vitrified
headers, steep undecorated gables, and windows with plain V-
shaped mullions. An unusual and quite conscious piece of Artisan design. Tall, of two storeys, and in the s wing, because of
the fall of the site, a semi-basement containing the kitchen
below the ground-floor dining parlour. The inner façades are
mirror-images of each other, except for the half-round steps
and entrance leading into a heated hall in the w wing. The windows centre on the angle, which means those of the w wall in
the angle are half-blocked where they abut an original internal
wall. Handsome steps up to the terrace, which has a nice early
C18 wrought-iron balustrade.

In DERBY ROAD, Nos. 139–143 are a block of three three-storey
framework-knitters' houses with the typical long windows on
the top floor. Only the centre one has all its original windows
at the front, No. 143 only the top one.

SWIMMING BATHS, Crow Hill Park. 1963–5 by *R. I. Savidge*
for the *Architects' Design Group*. A disciplined design with long
windows towards the park and plant visible from the entrance.


## BRINSLEY                                          4040

ST JAMES. 1837–8, the type of Commissioners' churches all over
the country, but looking less cheap here than usual because of
the Mansfield stone used. Oblong shape, two polygonal turrets
flanking the w front with its three lancets; lancets also along
the sides. The chancel was added in 1877.


## BROADHOLME *see* THORNEY


## BROUGH                                           8050

CHURCH. Tiny, unaisled, of 1885, with a crossing tower but
no w tower. – Iron SCREEN of the same date. – TABLET to
T. C. Smith Wooley † 1914 by *Frampton*.

---

* Probably the house advertised in the *Nottingham Journal* of 6 March 1830
as a 'newly built messuage' by *H. M. Wood* of Nottingham.

The site of the Roman roadside town of CROCOCALANA lay here. This, like Thorpe (Ad Pontem) and East Bridgford (Margidunum), may have begun as a Roman fort of the mid CI, as the cheek-piece of a fine military helmet recovered from the site strongly suggests. The later town straggled along the Fosse Way for more than half a mile. Air photographs indicate the presence of ditched defences, not yet excavated. No buildings have yet been revealed by systematic excavation.


BROXTOWE *see* NOTTINGHAM p. 268


6070                        BUDBY

Built as a model village by the first Earl Manvers of Thoresby *c.* 1807–12: just a group of simple, sizeable, two-storey, three-bay stuccoed cottages with porches.* Only the patterns of the window casements look faintly Gothic. On the other side of the main road CASTLE BUDBY (or WILLIAM), built *c.* 1789 by *Carr* of York for the clerk of works of the estate. Towered and castellated.


6040                       BULCOTE

In this hamlet, now joined to Burton Joyce on the E side, HOLY TRINITY, 1862 (aisleless and towerless), an early C18 double-pile brick MANOR HOUSE, and KINGSWOOD,‡ 1893 by *Watson Fothergill*.


BULWELL *see* NOTTINGHAM p. 267


5020                        BUNNY

Thanks to the church and its Wrestling Baronet, one of the most rewarding villages in south Notts.

ST MARY. The largest church in the neighbourhood. W tower with spire, nave and aisles of five bays, and long unaisled chancel of four windows. Mostly C14, the aisles with three-light

---

* Mr P. Middleton points out that there are similar cottages built by Earl Manvers at Holme Pierrepont, Cotgrave, and Radcliffe-on-Trent. Those at Holme Pierrepont especially resemble designs in *Gandy*'s books. Gandy did some work nearby for the Duke of Newcastle at Clumber.

‡ Information from Mr D. Kilner.

windows of intersecting tracery (probably recast in the early
C18). The chancel, reroofed by Sir Thomas in 1718, has a ten-
light straight-headed window with plain mullions of completely
domestic character. Nave with two octagonal piers (the rest
circular) and double-chamfered arches. Later porch with two
charming little Perp windows and a stone roof on transverse
ribs, not an unusual feature (see, for example, St Mary,
Nottingham). Its gable has a C17 or early C18 look. Nave and
aisles have panelled parapets, chancel and tower battlements. A
plain band connects the top of the tower buttresses below the
battlements (cf. Sutton Bonington, Barton-in-Fabis, Attenborough). The spire is crocketed, as at Newark and in Lincolnshire. – SEDILIA with ogee arches and thick finials. – PISCINA
adjacent, prettily divided into two with Dec tracery. – ROOD
SCREEN simple and partly reconstructed. – (STAINED GLASS.
E window of 1910, an early work by *Geoffrey Webb*. RH) –
MONUMENTS. Richard Parkyns † 1603, the usual kneelers facing each other, but the eight little children to their l. and r.
small and stiffly frontal (cf. Gotham). – Dame Anne Parkyns
† 1725. Wall-tablet with her figure kneeling on top; putti and
skulls at the foot. Signed by *Edward Poynton* of Nottingham
(cf. West Stockwith). – Sir Thomas Parkyns † 1741 (cf. below). 84
A standing wall-monument, two bays wide, designed by Sir
Thomas himself (sketches of 1715 and a drawing survive) and,
according to Throsby, 'wrought out of a fine piece of marble
by his chaplain in a barn'. Sir Thomas's figure looks a professional job. He stands in the l. bay, four-square and life-size,
with hands aggressively pointing forward, ready to start a
wrestling bout. In the r. bay a little figure of a man laid out on a
straw mat, and a ridiculous Father Time by his side, which
look as if they were carved by the chaplain. Elaborate inscriptions in Latin, Greek, and English above and below (for
example 'That TIME at length did throw him it is plain who lived
in hopes that he should RISE again.') – Sir Thomas Parkyns.
By *John Bacon* the younger, 1806. Kneeling mourning
woman bent over an urn. – Elizabeth Cropper † 1800 by
*J Peck* of Loughborough and a tablet by *Gaffin* of Regent
Street.

Sir Thomas Parkyns (1662–1741) was a remarkable character;
collector of stone coffins, author of a Latin grammar, trained
lawyer and enthusiastic amateur wrestler, physician and architect, 'contriving and drawing all his own plans' for the farms
on his estate. In the village he also designed and built the Hall,

the school, and, soon after 1701, the much altered old Vicarage. Home Farm of 1739 has been demolished.

83 BUNNY HALL. His Hall is as weird as his personal achievements and his monument in the church. Only the N wing of a later building but unmistakable, it is a long chequered brick wing with a tall narrow façade on the end of it crowned by a huge, elephantine semicircular pediment across the whole width (cf. Brizlincote, Derbyshire, 1714; Worcester Guildhall, 1721–3) and a massively castellated tower above it. Up to the second floor, two clumsy and pointless stone-faced stepped buttresses, apparently original although they cut into the blind windows flanking them. On each step are alcoves, the lower ones slightly pointed. At the corners of both elevations, Ionic pilasters, and on the side ones semicircular and segment-headed windows with large keystones. The decoration, especially the oversized achievement and diaper brickwork in the pediment, is still entirely in the spirit of the C17, the well-cut details illogically assembled. But the windows and tower bring to mind Vanbrugh's Claremont, Eastbury, etc., of c. 1715–20.* Bunny Hall, unlikely to have been started until after 1717, when Sir Thomas was in financial straits, was going up in 1723 (inscription on the W front) and described as unfinished in 1725. The tower must be a belvedere (cf. Thrumpton) overlooking the fine deer park. On each side between the castellations, a plain wrought-iron balcony. The only access to it was by a crude staircase (cf. Wollaton Hall) at the N (service) end of the building. The parlour occupied two-thirds of the E front, with the staircase at the S end where the main entrance presumably was and the hall ran along most of the W side next to the kitchen. It is not clear whether Sir Thomas's wing extended further S (see traces of pedimented windows on the W front of the S wing), but the present S block, adjoining the N wing at r. angles, was standing in 1791, when Throsby drew it. Irregular rear elevation and gabled stuccoed main façade turning its back on Sir Thomas's eccentricities. Enlargements, including the E entrance, begun by the second Lord Rancliffe in the early C19 were still not complete in the 1880s. The house, originally approached through massive gatepiers from the E, is now reached through

---

* According to Mr Twelvetrees, who kindly allowed us to use unpublished material from his research about the Hall and the school, there is no mention of Vanbrugh's work or the name of any architect in the Parkyns papers. He notes that the Vanbrugh building most accessible from Bunny was the 'toy castle', Somersby Manor Farm, of 1722, in Lincolnshire.

a farmyard with ranges of BARNS, one curved with part dated 1718, another inscribed *TSP 1734*, and the early C18 LAUNDRY with mullion-and-transom-cross windows.

The solid brick structures of Sir Thomas's buildings have consistent characteristics. In the earlier houses, e.g. the school, stone-mullioned windows, in the later ones wooden casements with segmental arches over them. String courses, where used, are stone and square in section except on the old vicarage, which is brick.

SCHOOL AND ALMSHOUSES. 1700, picturesquely placed between the church and the road. Brick with some black chequering. The steep-pitched roof with dormers, rusticated quoins, rusticated door surround with a competently carved achievement over it in the end elevation, and stone-mullioned windows are still entirely in the spirit of the C17. Along the string course dividing the ground floor from the first floor we read: Scientia non habet inimicum nisi ignorantem – Disce et Discede – Nemo hinc egrediatur ignarus Arithmetices. At one end the schoolroom, at the other four rooms for four widows, much more cramped quarters than the master's, which took up the whole first floor and attic.

For other buildings by Sir Thomas *see* Bradmore, East Leake, and Costock.

There are several nice C18 brick cottages and houses, but Nottingham has made itself felt in a semi-detached manner. Making the strongest contribution to the street scene, the long gabled front of the RANCLIFFE ARMS, originally at least partly timber-framed with gabled wings. Centre filled in and faced with brick in the early C18. IVY COTTAGE of *c.* 1700 has coped gables with old-fashioned kneelers and ball finials. THE GRANGE with a tented porch is later C18.

Traces of ROMANO-BRITISH RURAL SETTLEMENT have been recorded on the hill to the S of the village. This may have been a small villa.

## BURTON JOYCE                        6040

ST HELEN. Short steeple, C13 to the bell-openings, no battlements, the low broach-spire with two tiers of dormer windows a little later. N and S arcades probably of *c.* 1200, with capitals renewed out of recognition. One capital of a respond has been found with elementary knob-like leaf- or head-shapes. No

clerestory. S aisle externally* and both arcades of 1878–9 (by
*T. H. Wyatt* of London), N aisle much widened *c.* 1275: see
the spectacular early geometrical E window of four lights with
three circles at the top but no trefoils or quatrefoils in them.
A similar pattern occurs at Raunds in Northants. The other
aisle windows are mid-C14, plus one low side window. The
chancel, with later C14 windows and a wholly Perp four-light
E window, is not in line with the nave and allows for a very
large hagioscope (squint would here not be appropriate) from
the N aisle. – FONT. C13; rounded sides with projecting semicircles at the corners; no decoration at all. – STAINED GLASS.
E window, 1888, and two others, 1884 and 1888, by *Kempe*. –
MONUMENTS. Robert de Jorz, *c.* 1400(?). – Incised slabs to
Sir Brian Stapleton † 1550; to Alice Leeke, 1596; and to Alice
Lacock, 1617.

(THE HALL. A very plain late C18 three-storey, three-bay brick
house, with a Tuscan columned porch. DOE)

Much suburban-type housing for Nottingham commuters.

BURTON LODGE FARM. 1 m. NW of the village, near the crest
of a ridge, an Iron Age EARTHWORK.

BULCOTE. *See* p. 84.

# CALVERTON

Like Woodborough, Calverton was a centre of framework knitting. Here the industry was conducted in the stocking-knitters'
cottages, which have the typical broad windows behind which
the frames stood.‡ Probably more survive here than anywhere
else in the county. In WINDLES SQUARE, at the E end of Main
Street, two out of three rows of such cottages remain, built in
1834 and unusual because they have large windows front and
back on the ground floor. Now eight instead of eleven dwellings,
simply restored in 1972–4 by the Notts Buildings Preservation
Trust to designs by Nottingham University Department of
Architecture Teaching Office. More knitters' cottages in MAIN
STREET: two just past Bonner Hill, the first one apparently
very early; a well-maintained pair by Little Lane; and Nos.
221–225 dated 1857, quite late for purpose-built craftsmen's
cottages. Stocking-knitting remained a cottage industry until

---

* Part still of the 1725–9 rebuilding (see datestone), according to Mr T. L.
Butler.

‡ The stocking frame was invented in the late C16 by the Rev. William Lee,
probably a native of Calverton.

the early C20, when the Meridian factory half-way along Main Street was built, although there were some much earlier workshops using hand-frames, e.g. one of *c*. 1800–20 in Main Street, now Minta's. Further W another type of cottage: good colliery housing by *G. A. Jellicoe*, 1937, who was also responsible for the contemporary CALVERTON COLLIERY itself, a well-designed group of modern brick buildings, the detail reminiscent of Holland.

ST WILFRID. * E.E. chancel arch on Norman shafts with odd scalloped capitals with large corner volutes and in one, between the volutes, a tiny seated figure of St Wilfrid, Bishop of York, giving the blessing after a baptism. More Norman panels (mostly on the second floor of the tower), representing occupations through the year (e.g. feasting for January, reaping for August: not as consistent as the unusually complete series of Labours of the Months on the Burnham Deepdale font, Norfolk), probably formed part of the W door of the Norman tower (cf. the portal of St Margaret, Walmgate, York), from which also probably came the carved stones found under the nave floor in 1881 and erected over the door to the William Lee Annexe in 1962: note especially the cat and the cow with the human face on its nose (cf. Southwell Minster wall). The nave and tower were largely rebuilt in 1760–3, using the old stone. The chancel was rebuilt about 1835, and the whole restored in 1881. Most tower windows and the W door are surrounded by intermittent rustication *à la* Gibbs.

LODGE FARM, Oxton Lane. A fine later Georgian brick farmhouse typical of many scattered throughout the country.

## CARBURTON 6070

ST GILES. A minute Norman chapel; nave and chancel and, originally, a S arcade, now built into the S wall, with Y-tracery windows. The S aisle was removed before 1748. Exterior rendered and porch renewed *c*. 1958.‡ Three original windows in the chancel, two of them in the E wall, l. and r. of a larger late C13 window. This no doubt replaces a third plain window; so the appearance of the E wall in Norman times was as at Sookholme.

---

* This entry was kindly revised by the Rev. T. Hoyle.
‡ Information from Mr H. A. Johnson.

MANOR FARMHOUSE, E of the church. Early C18 coursed rubble, with a deep space between the eaves and the first-floor windows. Later sashes inserted into windows with chamfered surrounds and hoodmoulds.

CARBURTON GATE. *See* Clumber.

## CAR COLSTON

7040

ST MARY. The ground floor of the W tower is C13 (see the masonry and the tower arch inside). The ashlared Perp upper parts had to keep to the same slimness if complete rebuilding was to be avoided. The chancel is higher than the nave, one of the splendid mid-C14 chancels of this neighbourhood, similar to Sibthorpe and Hawton. Large windows with flowing tracery, ogee reticulations in the three-light N and S windows, five lights with a more complex pattern in the E (very similar to the S aisle at Newark). The SEDILIA and the PISCINA with its nodding ogee arch are no doubt by the master who worked at Hawton: heavily crocketed and finialled. The N aisle also has contemporary windows and a doorway with an ogee arch. Of the C14 probably the plain sturdy S door too. The N and S arcades have tall slim octagonal piers and double-chamfered arches of the C14. The clerestory windows, above the spandrels not the apexes of the arches, are later. – FONT. Plain Norman. – PULPIT. Jacobean. – ALTAR RAIL, given in 1732, with finely shaped and also twisted balusters. It has a semicircular projection in the middle, no doubt to accommodate more communicants. – BENCHES. A few of the C14. – ALMSBOX. Early C16 pillar-type. – STAINED GLASS. Chancel S 1875 by *Kempe.* – At the W end of the S aisle the COFFIN of the antiquary Dr Robert Thoroton † 1678 who lived in the village (*see* Old Hall Farm).

(CAR COLSTON HALL, at the W end of the village. Built *c.* 1838 by the Rev. Girardot. Brick and stone in a restrained Tudor-Gothic Revival style with three large gables and plain mullioned and transomed windows. NS)

The village is unusually pleasant, with good houses along a large green, especially one at the E end, BEECH CLOSE, dated 1719 on the gable end. Five-bay, brick with stone band, plinth, and quoins, hipped roof and dormers, and a shell hood.

OLD HALL FARM, between the church and Brunsell Hall. Tall, narrow, stuccoed late Georgian house (1812) with a hipped roof, on the site of Dr Thoroton's house.* Remains of its cellars are incorporated at the back, and a C17 brick wall encloses the garden.

BRUNSELL HALL, at the NE end of the village.‡ Built in 1662 by Samuel Brunsell, contemporary of Thoroton and rector of Bingham and Screveton. Remains of a sizeable H-plan C17 brick manor house. Two-thirds of it were pulled down in 1759. The brick toothing is exposed where the N wing originally joined at one end. At the other, rusticated brick quoins. Decorative brick cornice, casements, and an old C17 door in a modern porch. Inside, the principal room has contemporary panelling arcaded above a dado, an overmantel crudely but exuberantly carved with a cherub's head and swags of fruit, and a compartmented ceiling with a central rose. The hall, since divided into two, occupied the centre of the house with a staircase round three sides of it.

The outline of a ROMAN VILLA can be seen in pasture immediately E of the Large Green. It has not been excavated.

On the Large Green, traces of several HOUSE PLATFORMS, presumably of medieval date.

## CARLTON                                        6040

Despite its rather evocative name, Carlton-le-Willows, a small town indistinguishable from the suburbs of Nottingham which it adjoins on the E. The most striking building is the church.

ST PAUL, Church Street, Burton Road. A massive Romanesque basilica by a London architect, *W. A. Coombs*, built in two stages in 1885–91 and paid for by the fourth Earl of Carnarvon. Red brick striped in yellow and with lots of moulded terracotta decoration. Tall apsidal projection at the W end flanked by two porches that lead into the aisles. Round window and bellcote above. – INSCRIPTION for the choir seats by *Eric Gill*, 1903.

ST GEORGE, Netherfield. A towerless brick church of 1887 by *E. Christian*.

CAVENDISH COMPREHENSIVE SCHOOL AND CARLTON FORUM, Coningowath Road. CLASP construction and interesting because the second attempt (1968–72) by the County Architect (*H. T. Swain*) to combine a school with community sports facilities (cf. Bingham).

* According to Mr Train.
‡ Colonel T. Blagg kindly amended our description of the Hall.

On the main A612 road on the N side, a row of four adjoining
   HOSIERY FACTORIES, increasing in age to the E. The earliest
   are typical of the stage in the industry's development when
   workshops were becoming factories: still recognizably for
   framework knitters. The two intermediate buildings clearly
   show development between early and late C19. The fourth,
   early C20, could be for any textile process in the district. All
   three-storey, but each one higher than the last.
S of the A612 in Mar Hill Road, a former LAUNDRY and DYE
   WORKS (now brewery) by *Watson Fothergill*, 1899, without the
   gothicism of his earlier work (DG).
GEDLING. *See* p. 131.

5080                  CARLTON-IN-LINDRICK

ST JOHN THE EVANGELIST. The most important late Saxon
   (or more probably Saxo-Norman) monument in the county.
3  The C11 W tower is complete, except that between 1417 and
   1443 it was buttressed (diagonally), given a SW newel stair, and
   crowned with a belfry with battlements and eight pinnacles.
   The masonry, which must be of good quality to support the
   belfry (the E buttresses rest only on the nave walls), is laid in
   various ways as if to mark the four stages: carefully coursed
   rubble below, then roughly dressed rectangular blocks, then
   herringbone, and, at the top, a stage like the lowest but inter-
   spersed with herringbone. Two string courses: one square-
   sectioned, the upper one Perp. The coupled bell-openings are
   preserved too on the E and W. They have plain capless shafts
   and lintels cut away to form arches.* The W doorway, really
   the S door moved here in 1831, is late Norman, three orders
   with volute capitals, the outer voussoirs with manifold mouldings, the inner with zigzag on front and soffit, with a pointed
   roll-moulding to separate them. The door opening itself has
   zigzag accompanying it up the jambs and around the arch. On
   the inner face of the tower, the C11 tower arch is delicate and
   advanced in detail, with two moulded recessed orders supported by recessed shafts. Their bell capitals have upright lan-
   cet-like leaves, i.e. the palmette characteristic of Lincs late

---

* It has been grouped with the Lincs towers (cf. probably also the fragments
at Clayworth and Everton) but differs in two respects: there are two equal
stages with belfry openings high up instead of one tall stage with the belfry
resting on the string course; and the belfry openings are simpler and plainer
than in Lincs, with jambs constructed something like the Escomb fashion.

Saxon work, and fillets of cable mouldings. The broad low shape looks Norman and so does the angle roll of the outer mouldings, although Dr Taylor emphasizes that the construction and soffit roll are distinctively late Saxon. The doorway to the W gallery is the remains of an early opening.

Earlier than the tower, and not bonded to it, the nave W wall and probably the side walls. Also early, though probably Norman, the three deep-splayed N chancel windows, and one above the N arcade. The chancel arch jambs Transitional with finely scalloped capitals and a kind of ball decoration on the abaci. The S impost has some interlace showing Saxon survival. Transitional N arcade with round arches, circular piers, and capitals with little volute leaves, not quite leaf-crockets yet. The S arcade of 1831 imitates the original N arcade. N chancel chapel with arches from aisle to chancel which have keeled shafts and a keeled roll moulding – a complicated building history evidently between the C11 and C13. A low round-headed recess in the chancel N wall. Of later work, the E window of five lights inspires respect although it is not very inventive. Perp clerestory and C15 heraldic bosses on the renewed nave and N aisle roofs. – SCULPTURE. Stone, asymmetrical, re-used over the S chancel door recessed in a semicircular moulding, showing the sun, moon, and two stars. Outside the moulding fan-shaped sprays of foliage or birds' tails. Cross probably carved when moved. Norman. – FONT. Plain, early Norman. – ALABASTER CARVING. Trinity, Nottingham work of the C15, badly preserved. – STAINED GLASS. N chapel E window: later C15 fragments.

CARLTON HALL was demolished in 1955.*

Pleasant village with many C18 and early C19 buildings of coursed rubble, rather prettified, e.g. CARLTON MILL (now village museum), a water corn mill with a C19 cast-iron water wheel *in situ*. A large chimney in the centre for supplying supplementary steam power during drought or frost.

(S of the village, at WIGTHORPE, WIGTHORPE HALL, with an C18 N wing. Ashlar with two full-height bows and a pedimented door surround Additions of 1872. WIGTHORPE HOUSE is plain C18, stuccoed, with canted bays.)

WALLINGWELLS. *See* p. 363.

---

* The core was supposed to have been of *c.* 1650, but the house looked plain late Georgian, with a fine top-lit staircase.

7060                     CARLTON-ON-TRENT

Most of these Trent-side villages follow the old North Road running parallel to the river for several miles N of Newark. Just skirt-
ing them the more recent artery, the A1. Well cared for church,
Hall, and C18 houses all along the Great North Road.

ST MARY. 1851, an early church by *G. G. Place* of Nottingham,
   with a crocketed Dec spire on the W tower. S doorway E.E. with
   a semicircular arch, medieval. Plain aisled nave with richer Dec
   chancel. – FONT. C17, cup-shaped.
CARLTON HALL, nearly opposite the church. Large and completely of brick. According to the Architectural Publications
   Society Dictionary by *John Johnson* of Leicester, but Joseph
   Pocklington, the Newark banker for whom it was built, was an
   amateur architect himself (*see* below and North Muskham).
   To the road, five-bay, two-and-a-half storey centre, dated 1765,
   with two full-height canted bays and Venetian windows
   between. Bays linked by a Doric-columned porch. Two three-
   bay wings, possibly slightly later, each with an open pediment
   inside a larger pediment, all with modillion cornices. The garden
   front of the central block has a flat façade with a three-bay
   pediment and a stone doorcase with Doric half-columns. The
   whole composition is reminiscent of Paine. Inside, a well
   planned staircase with a wrought-iron 'crinoline' balustrade.
   Modest Georgian features in most of the rooms, except the
   drawing room, which occupies one of the wings on the garden
   front. This (nearly two storeys high) has fine plasterwork on
   walls and ceiling in provincial Adam style (cf. Muskham
   House). Marble fireplace supported by two well-carved
   Atlantes.
The BELL INN, well known to C18 travellers, is now called PARK
   FARMHOUSE. At the N end a one-storey dining room with
   Venetian windows and a Georgian plaster ceiling, designed in
   1788 by *Joseph Pocklington* of the Hall.*
It would be interesting to know for certain why the Torrington
   Diary, under 1792, pillories Mr Pocklington for having 'shewn
   more vile taste ... at and about his place ... than can be well
   imagined'; one suspects he was unjustly deriding the talents
   of this amateur architect.
On the bend of the road S of the church, two C18 houses well
   restored by the Nottinghamshire Buildings Preservation Trust:

* Information kindly given by Angus Taylor of Doncaster.

on the l. a brick house with a plain doorhood, on the r. a painted-brick three-storey house (THE GREY HOUSE) with two-storey canted bays and a pedimented window between.

THE SMITHY. Early C19 or late C18, with an archway designed as a horseshoe and worked in projecting bricks (cf. Gonalston).

WINDMILL. Tall brick seven-storey tower mill (60 ft high). No cap or sails, but a fine-looking building. Adjacent, a small brick warehouse on the bank of the Trent.

## CARRINGTON see NOTTINGHAM p. 263

## CAUNTON

7060

ST ANDREW. Prettily placed by a little stream with a footbridge over, and a good, rewarding village church, neither over-restored (1869 by *Ewan Christian*) nor neglected. To be visited in preference to a good many others, though the *Little Guide* has only five lines on it. Inside, a Norman s arcade with a little stylized foliage on the curving-in part of the capitals, as at Southwell. The N arcade is C13, and so is the W bay, on both sides isolated from the others by some wall (cf. Norwell), which indicates that the nave was extended one bay W in the C13. The chancel arch belongs to the same date, but the whole chancel, with lancet windows on all sides, is part of the C19 restoration. Semicircular recess in the s aisle wall, s door with double-cusped ogee arch, mid-C14. The low W tower mainly C15 (see the tower arch with large horizontal leaves along the embattled capitals, and the top with a quatrefoil frieze, gargoyles, and battlements, but no pinnacles). – FONT. C13. – STAINED GLASS. E window probably by *Holiday*, c. 1869.

CAUNTON MANOR. Basically an early C18 two-storey four-bay brick house, extended to an irregular nine bays after 1902 and finally completely re-Georgianized by *Houfton*. He added new windows, doorcases, modillion cornice, the pedimented central five bays on the garden front, and the huge stone porch. (Still some good C18 features inside including staircase, plasterwork, fireplace, and doorcases with cherub swags. In an upper room some painted canvas panels said to have been brought from Sweden in the early C18. DOE).

CAUNTON GRANGE. A range of rooms with a three-bay, three-storey brick façade and a pedimented Roman Doric stone door-case added c. 1785 to an older range behind (see the stonework in the s wall). A type of improvement common in Notts; cf. Gonalston Rectory, Farnsfield Hall.

WINDMILL, at Mill House, Mill Lane. Roofed and used as a store. Tarred brick, four storeys (43 ft high), with no cap or machinery but with a loading dock.

EARLSHAW FARM, ½ m. sw. An area of 100 sq. ft surrounded by a rectangular moat.

DEAN HALL FARM, ¾ m. SE. Some early C13 carved stones have been re-used in the stuccoed farmhouse. The property once belonged to the Knights Hospitaller.*

BEESTHORPE HALL, ½ m. w. A remodelled large C17 H-plan brick house, Georgianized and stuccoed in 1770–1.‡ At the back (w), the brick of the original house with traces of mullioned windows. Up to the first-floor level of the s wing, very good stonework with a string course, evidently earlier than the present brick house. In this wing a room with a C16 or C17 plaster frieze and a pretty C18 inlaid wooden fireplace. On the main front two one-storey wings attached to each of the gabled wings: the r. a dining room added in 1809, the l. a sham façade to match it behind which a ballroom was built in 1815. Some original plaster cornices and doorcases survive. To the N, joined to the house by C18 brick outbuildings, stables with a pedimented coach house with semicircular windows.

<sub>6040</sub>                   CAYTHORPE

A pleasant hamlet with a water mill opposite the Black Horse, dated 1749, not in use, and a few C18 houses, not of outstanding quality. One framework-knitter's workshop at the back of a house s of the Black Horse.

<sub>5030</sub>                   CHILWELL§

CHRISTCHURCH, High Road. Aisleless, towerless church of 1901 with Perp windows. Nothing distinctive.

The MANOR HOUSE, Clarke's Lane, built in 1677, was demolished in 1964.¶ Further w on the HIGH ROAD, two cot-

---

* According to Professor Barley.

‡ Although a rainwater head at the rear reads SB 1780.

§ We owe this revised description of Chilwell to Professor M. W. Barley.

¶ It was a double pile with plain gables. Later sashes but mullioned windows on the side.

tages and a former farmhouse survive: STONE CROFT, partly
Tudor, with a four-centred arch to its doorway; RED LION
COTTAGE, 1682, and originally timber-framed; and, opposite,
THE MEADS, a tall brick house of c. 1750 (very like No. 3 West
End, Beeston), with derelict farm buildings.

In HALLAM'S LANE, No. 35 of 1936–7 is by *Myerscough Walker*,
better known as a perspectivist. Part of an unrealized plan of
c. 1930 for a circular house. Of rendered brick. D-plan with
a roof terrace and a lantern lighting the spiral stair below.
Semicircular living room.

OLD COLLEGE HOUSE, N of the parish church, a Tudoresque
villa with shaped gables to porch and roof, is so named from
its occupation in 1860–81 by the General Baptist College;
TUDOR HOUSE of 1858 behind it, in simpler brick with
mullioned windows, housed students and staff. Beeston's textile
development stretched as far W as Neville's factory (now
MYFORD) in CHILWELL HIGH ROAD, built in two phases,
one dated 1886 in the E gable; four storeys, unaltered, with an
inspection shop. Opposite the HOP POLE INN, Gothic of
c. 1850. Next, PARK ROAD and GROVE AVENUE, of the same
age: cottages in large gardens, a modest example of the concept
of rural homesteads for industrial workers more explicit in the
later Garden Cities. Some of the original cottages survive,
among later infilling which includes No. 60 PARK ROAD by
the *Architects' Design Group*, 1968.


## CHURCH WARSOP see WARSOP


## CLARBOROUGH

7080

ST JOHN THE BAPTIST. Over-restored (in 1874 by *James
Fowler* of Louth: RH) N arcade, originally of C13 date (see the
circular piers and thin moulded capitals). The S arcade on octagonal piers is evidently later. No clerestory. W tower of the
usual type of the neighbourhood (diagonal buttresses, four
pinnacles). – FONT. Octagonal. Perp or Victorian? –
STAINED GLASS. E window by *Kempe*, 1900. – MONUMENT.
Thomas Outybridge of Bolham House † 1772, by the
*Fishers* of York. It is interesting to note that the custom of
a fashionable provincial workshop could extend as far as
this.

(At Welham, a small hamlet at the S of the village, WELHAM

GRANGE, a remarkably fine and intact house dated 1667.
T-plan, tall (three full storeys), with a symmetrical three-bay
front. Projecting string courses and decorative eaves all in brick,
tumbling (*see* North Leverton) in the gables. The outbuildings,
including a fine dovecote, mutilated by conversion into dwellings. NS)

(WELHAM HALL, 1 m. s. Large early C19 stuccoed house of
three storeys and seven bays. On the E front a semicircular bow
with a cast-iron balcony. Pretty stable block with wooden
cupola. JPB)

(Alongside Welham Hall, YEW TREE FARM, with another
lofty Notts farmhouse, three-storey and three-bay, C18.
NS)

<sub>7080</sub>                    CLAYWORTH

ST PETER. The ground floor of the tower could be pre-Conquest.
It is followed upward by different masonry with a Norman window. The top is Perp, of the kind usual in the neighbourhood,
ashlar, with eight pinnacles on the battlements. Ashlar also
appears outside the N aisle, the chancel aisle, and the Perp
clerestory. Much restoration was done in 1874–5 by *Oldrid
Scott*. The s porch, for example, with timbering and bargeboards, is entirely new, although it shelters a very plain Norman
doorway and medieval water stoup. C13 chancel arch. The
arcades of the two aisles inside are very weird and not yet fully
explained. Arches with C13 mouldings on the s, double-
chamfered on the N. Between them and the piers there are no
capitals; only a few heads which had apparently served as label
stops are inserted incongruously. The profile of the piers shows
that they are Perp. It is octagonal with two little hollows, like
reedings, in the diagonals, just as at East Markham. It has
no connection whatever with the profile of the arches. The two
N chancel chapels also have entirely different openings. It all
needs further study. – Remarkable heavy stone PARCLOSE
SCREEN between the s aisle and the s chancel chapel of St
Nicholas, founded *c.* 1388. – FONTS. One simple medieval, the
other plain with traces of painting: painted by *Scott*, according
to Kelly, though the shape looks C17. – Some C17 PEWS. –
STAINED GLASS. E window 1875, W window 1891, and two
s aisle windows 1877 and 1878, by *Kempe*. – MONUMENTS.
Humphrey Fitzwilliam † 1559. Big tomb-chest with coarse
tendril and strapwork decoration. – Brass with a half-effigy

of John Tonstall, rector, † 1630.* – Francis Otter † 1813 by *Sir Richard Westmacott.*

(CLAYWORTH HALL, s of the church. Just a plain and much altered late C18 or early C19 stuccoed house with a semicircular window lighting the original staircase. DOE)

(THE GRANGE, a farmhouse reached by a track from the Main Street. Of *c.* 1680, two storeys with attics, five bays of typical narrow sashes, and a gabled roof with brick tumbling. The best house in the village. NS)

(ROYSTON MANOR, now a country club and restaurant. The s front is said to date from 1588 (DOE), but everything visible was rebuilt in 1891. It is difficult to determine its original appearance. Sizeable, with three gabled rectangular bays on the w front and large stone mullion-and-transom windows: all the walls rendered.)

Several simple C18 houses in TOWN STREET.

CLEVELAND MILL *see* EAST MARKHAM

CLIFTON *see* NOTTINGHAM p. 268

CLIFTON (NORTH AND SOUTH)          *8070*

ST GEORGE. Entirely on its own between the two villages. A strong, broad late C15 tower, with diagonal buttresses in six set-offs, human gargoyles, battlements, and eight pinnacles. N wall lancet early C13, like the fine chancel arch with stiff-leaf. Inside, N arcade with circular and octagonal abaci, also early C13.

CLIPSTONE          *6060*

The hamlet stands ½ m. N of the large colliery village of New Clipstone.

KING JOHN'S PALACE, in a field at the junction of the roads from Warsop and New Clipstone. Three venerable walls, but nothing visible is more eloquent, which is a pity, because it was the principal royal hunting lodge in Sherwood Forest instead of Mansfield after Henry I's reign. First documented as such in 1164 and already decayed by 1525. The ruined walls, with

* According to Mr Train.

no datable features, stand up to 10 ft high, enclosing an area of 58 by 20 ft. Nearby a large hollow, probably a fishpond. Excavation in 1956 showed that the palace comprised a large group of important stone and less important timber-framed buildings, constructed at several different periods.* In the C14 they included a number of smaller chambers besides a great hall, knights' hall, queen's hall and kitchen, king's kitchen, great chamber, great chapel, long stable, great gateway, etc. There was building during at least two periods earlier than the ruin, the first in timber, the second probably of 1176–80, in stone. From the latter period, an animal-headed corbel was found. These buildings were defended by a ditch, possibly palisaded. The surviving walls belonged to an undercroft, which may represent one of the two new chambers with chapels built in 1279–90 by Edward II for himself and his queen. Repairs to and rebuilding of the buildings listed above in 1348–9, and more repairs in 1360–3 and, by *William Elmeley*, Clerk of Works, in 1367–75.

ARCHWAY LODGE, $\frac{1}{2}$ m. down a lane leading w from King John's Palace. A school (now a house) in a strange disguise. Built in imitation of the gatehouse of Worksop Priory by *Hurst & Moffatt* for the fourth Duke of Portland (1844). It has figures of Richard Cœur-de-Lion, Robin Hood, Friar Tuck, Maid Marian, Little John, and Allan-a-Dale. The schoolroom is above the arch.

At NEW CLIPSTONE the church of ALL SAINTS (1928), 1930s COLLIERY HOUSING by *Houfton & Kington* of Chesterfield, and a well-designed PITHEAD BATH of 1937.

<sub>6070</sub>
# CLUMBER

The Clumber estate formed part of Sherwood Forest until in 1707 licence was given to John Holles, created third Duke of Newcastle (of the neighbouring Welbeck Abbey), to enclose it as a park for the queen's use. In fact the land remained a sandy waste until the middle of the C18, or probably later if one is to judge from Horace Walpole's disappointment on a journey in 1772. He severely censured 'a new brick house cased with stone' which had been built *c.* 1760–70 by *Stephen Wright* for

---

* For the excavation report *see Transactions of the Thoroton Society* (64), 1960, p. 21.

the new first Duke of Newcastle (of the Pelham Clinton family).* Wright had worked for the Duke at Claremont and on Cambridge University Library when the Duke was Chancellor. In 1814 *Benjamin Dean Wyatt* made designs for alterations, followed in 1829 by a library and alterations by *Sidney Smirke*‡ and in 1857 by further designs by *Sir Charles Barry* for extensive alterations and Italianate embellishments. Only Smirke's designs were carried out, but in 1879–80 after a fire the central part of the house was rebuilt, again in an Italianate style, by the younger *Charles Barry*. It was pulled down completely *c.* 1938, the date marking the end of an era in which such vast seats were still usable and used. The C20 has few wealthy men with the inclination or means to go on with them. Fortunately the National Trust, which takes up many of the responsibilities so laid down, has preserved the park for public use.

The house was sited very near the large serpentine lake made in 1774–89.§ One tiny fragment of *Barry*'s work remains: the DUKE'S STUDY, which was set back from the main house on the E side and joined to it by low wings forming a partly enclosed garden. Its only architectural feature is a bay-window framed by plain pilasters. Behind this are the C18 and C19 STABLES and OFFICES (now National Trust Regional HQ). On the l. the C18 red brick coach house with a central pediment and cupola over the arch. In front of it the walled turning court, and behind it a quadrangle of stables etc., C18 on the N and W sides, C19 on the other two. In the NE corner nearest the church, the PARSONAGE.

Those responsible for destroying the house did not have the nerve to destroy the CHURCH as well. It was erected for the seventh Duke, an ardent Anglo-Catholic and nephew of the Ecclesiologist A. W. Beresford Hope, at a cost of £30,000 in 1886–9 by *Bodley & Garner* and remains one of their masterpieces, eclecticism at its most refined. White stone with

100

* The following notes were kindly provided by Mr Gervase Jackson-Stops:
Dills approved by *Wright* dated 1763 are for work on the best staircase, the top balustrade, and the w front of the stables and brewhouse, indicating that the house had been begun some time before this. The master mason was *Andrew Ince*. According to the Earl of Verulam, the house was 'not yet finished' in 1768.

‡ *Smirke* also submitted estimates for converting the parsonage into a *cottage orné*.

§ The foundations of the house are being excavated at the time of writing (1978) and will be left uncovered.

red Runcorn stone dressings and a spire over the crossing, also of red stone, clearly modelled on Patrington, Yorkshire. Unaisled nave with blind arcading along the walls and a wall passage above, transepts and chancel of almost the same length as the nave. The chancel is elaborately decorated with carving (ROOD SCREEN, PRIEST'S and CHOIR STALLS) by the Rev. *Ernest Geldart*, and with STAINED GLASS all by *Kempe*, Bodley's first pupil. – FONT, PULPIT, the two ALTARS, and the stone figures designed by *Bodley*. – The STATUE of the Virgin in the S aisle is by *Ninian Comper*.\* – MONUMENT, from and now back in the Newcastle Mausoleum at West Markham, to Georgiana, Duchess of Newcastle, † 1822 in childbirth. By *Westmacott*, probably not complete in 1832. Reclining marble figure, her twin children nestling close to her, turning to see a beckoning angel or allegorical figure in delicate relief as a back panel. – What makes the church unforgettable is its setting, poignantly beautiful and inappropriate: for with the house gone the church remains almost on its own, separated only by a stretch of lawn with clumps of oak and cedar from the lake, a memorial to the passing of an age.‡

Ornamenting the park several buildings by *Stephen Wright*. Opposite the church by the lake a Greek Doric TEMPLE, after Stuart's Hagley temple, and at the W end of the lake a fine three-arched stone BRIDGE and CASCADE, 1763. Also a Roman Doric SEAT ALCOVE and a GROTTO, 1765–7. There is a series of five gates by *Wright*: at the head of the magnificent Duke's Drive, four rows of lime trees three miles long, APLEYHEAD LODGE, in the form of a triumphal arch, with curved wings and lodges; towards Worksop, TRUMAN'S LODGE, a castellated archway and lodge; to the SW, CARBURTON GATE, with tiny pedimented lodges; to the SE, SOUTH NORMANTON GATE, 1785, fine gatepiers with well-carved *Coade* stone vases; and DRAYTON GATE, of particular interest because almost identical with the vanished one *Wright* designed for the Earl of Lincoln at Oatlands Park: Kentian gatepiers with niches.§

*See* p. 448

---

\* Comper and Newcastle quarrelled (which led to the end of several commissions, e.g. Egmanton) when Comper refused to alter his master's work by rebuilding the E wall at the W end and installing a large alabaster reredos.

‡ This was written in 1951. The impression is still romantic but less eerie, for the church (occasionally used for services) and park are now well frequented.

§ According to an updated memorandum in *Wright*'s hand, they were erected to a slightly adapted design by *Lord Burlington*. There was a lodge at Blyth Corner by *John Simpson* of Budby, 1787 (cf. Nottingham Hospital).

At the NE end of the lake, the late C19 estate village, HARD-WICK-IN-CLUMBER, with red brick home farm and estate workers' houses, some dated.

## CODDINGTON

8050

ALL SAINTS. The attraction of this church is not what is old, but what is relatively new, namely *Bodley*'s decoration of the chancel, commissioned from *Morris & Co.*: a lovely cambered and painted ceiling, a settle in lieu of sedilia, fine woodwork, and two exquisite windows, early *Morris* and *Burne Jones* designs (1865), that is with much transparent glass and smallish figures set in light colours.* The whole, except the screen of 1890–1, in Bodley's early French style, dates from 1864–5. The rich effect of colour and pattern that Bodley sought is muted now the stencilled wall decoration (supervised by *Kempe*) has been whitewashed. Bodley restored the old church severely and gave it steep-pitched tiled roofs. The S arcade with circular piers and simple moulded capitals and the N arcade with octagonal piers and a little nailhead in the capitals, both C13, look very new. The S door has some dogtooth. The W tower is contemporary, unbuttressed and low, but with a Perp top with eight pinnacles. – STAINED GLASS. Another window of 1865 by *Morris & Co.* in the tower, the design by *Morris* himself. – In the S aisle three windows with their more vigorous later designs, one by *Ford Madox Brown* with St Anne and St Elizabeth, and one by *Burne Jones* with David and Samuel; both 1881. – SE window 1882, a design by *Morris* and *Burne Jones*.

SE of the church OLD MANOR FARM, dated 1714, the typical Notts brick house with a steep gable and a gabled porch. Four cross casements. Behind it a rectangular gabled DOVECOTE of brick with some C17 decoration.

DICE HOUSE COUNTRY CLUB, N of the by-pass. Late C18 brick, unaltered, but sadly with nothing left of the rural character it had as New Manor Farm. The farmyard is a bleak tarmac-paved car park.

WINDMILL. A small four-storey tarred brick tower mill of c. 1859. A ruinous shell, but interesting in that the batter decreases at the second floor.

Civil War earthworks of the besieging army can be traced, with

*The panel with St Cecilia may be that exhibited on the firm's stand at the Great Exhibition of 1865.

difficulty, in the vicinity of Coddington House. A medieval moated site lay here, but was not included in the C17 works (cf. Hawton, Balderton, Farndon, and South Muskham).

COLLINGHAM

The separate parishes of North and South Collingham have been united and form one long leafy riverside village.

ALL SAINTS, North Collingham. As at South Collingham, the special point about the church is its arcades; but whereas there a contrast exists between Norman and E.E., both sides are here C13 of about the same date, though differing in design. The S side has the four major shafts enriched by fillets and the four minor ones keeled (exactly like Beverley); on the N the major ones are keeled. The S capitals have a little dogtooth, the N capitals upright leaves. The E and W responds on the N side have shaft-rings. The tower arch and chancel are E.E. too. The development can be seen to go (as so often) from E to W: the primitive waterleaf capitals of the chancel arches came first, the leaf capitals of the N arcade get more elegant towards the tower. Externally the tower is plastered. Of the late Middle Ages the best contribution is the N porch with its stone roofs and transverse ribs (cf. St Mary, Nottingham, etc.). – MISERICORDS with heraldic motifs, arranged incongruously above the chancel arch. – FONT COVER. 1684, yet still of Jacobean type. (Or is it 1638? An order for a cover was sanctioned then, and another in 1684. Perhaps the old one was found and no new one ordered?) – MONUMENTS in the porch: two badly preserved Knights in sunk relief of the same type as at Staunton.

ST JOHN THE BAPTIST, South Collingham. With a tall tower dominating the village. The Norman N arcade is adorned with zigzag and lozenge (similar to South Scarle). The one label stop is a gruesome head of a beast with a man's head in its mouth. The S arcade has piers of eight shafts, the ones in the main axes with fillets. The capitals are moulded, not high, the arches double-chamfered and with heads as label stops. Of the same date the S doorway, the tower arch (with shaft-rings to the shafts and capitals as in the crossing at Newark), and the chancel arch. The corbels supporting the old nave roof before the C15 clerestory was added can still be seen. The chancel is C14 with the usual straight-headed windows. The E window alone is Perp.

Restored in 1843 by *J. H. Hakewill* (JPB). – SCREEN by *Travers*, 1940. – STAINED GLASS. E window of the S aisle by *Ward & Hughes*.

VILLAGE CROSS of North Collingham, NE of All Saints. Only the base and the lower part of the shaft survive. The cross must originally have been of great size. The shaft was crocketed (probably C14).

A number of handsome and interesting houses not connected with farming but built by people of private means. Several in High Street and Low Street, plain Georgian with good doorcases.* Facing THE GREEN an early C19 house with end pilasters and a round-arched doorway, all in fine brickwork. YEW TREE FARM HOUSE has an C18 to early C19 façade, but a C17 wing to the rear which may have been timber-framed (see the corner-posts) and C17 outbuildings. THE NUNNERY is C16 or early C17, with a pargetted upper floor and some early leaded casements. In HIGH STREET, a one-storey cottage with a pyramidal thatched roof, a large C18 house with a one-bay pediment, and LODGE FARM HOUSE, late C18 with a nice doorcase. THICKETTS, a small 'neo-vernacular' brick and tile house by *Brian Elsworth*, 1966–7, makes a good contribution to the village scene.

## COLSTON BASSETT

ST MARY. The church has gone through many vicissitudes. It was once a stately building with two aisles and a S transept. Then the depopulation of the Wolds (*see* Upper Broughton, Wiverton, etc.) did away with the N aisle and set windows with Gibbsian intermittent rustication in the new wall. Finally, in 1892, the squire, R. Millington Knowles, decided to commemorate the death of his son and his wife by building a new church in the centre of the relatively recent estate village. The Church Commissioners ordered him to unroof the old one to convert it into a ruin. They should have gone further and attended to its decay so as to make it pleasing. The oldest visible part is the walled-up Norman N arcade with circular piers and scalloped capitals but pointed arches.‡ The S arcade was partly Transitional and partly C14. To the same century belong the chancel (see the windows) and the tower arch. But the tower itself is C15, with the typical panel frieze of this

* The late C17 BAPTIST CHAPEL in Low Street has been demolished.
‡ Which, although decayed, still could be saved (S. Rigold).

neighbourhood. The s transept must have had an uncommonly sumptuous s window. It is now all gone.* – In the churchyard, good slate HEADSTONES.

ST JOHN. 1892 by *A. W. Brewill*, a lavish design for a village church (*see* above), with crossing tower and spire and richly carved decorative detail inside. – FONT. Octagonal, with battlements and plain shields in the panels (cf. Hickling). – The MONUMENT to Alice Knowles † 1892, with a life-size Carrara angel pointing to a cross, is in the expensive cemetery style.

VILLAGE CROSS. Classical shaft of 1831 to commemorate William IV's coronation, on an old base.

THE HALL, w of St John, was built *c*. 1704 but now appears all neo-Italian Renaissance *à la* Barry, say *c*. 1860.

VICARAGE. A charming two-storeyed house with deep eaves to the hipped roof. This almost Regency grace must be due to *H. M. Wood*, 1834.

## COLWICK *see* NOTTINGHAM p. 251

4040

## COSSALL

ST CATHERINE. Small unbuttressed w steeple of the C13 with a later spire with one tier of dormers, probably late C14. The church was rebuilt in 1842 with old stone for chancel and clerestory. – FONT. C15, octagonal, with quatrefoils at foot and top and panelled battlements. – STAINED GLASS. Early C15 figure of St Catherine, s window.

81 WILLOUGHBY ALMSHOUSES. 1685, a delicious group, brick, the centre with a saddleback roof, and gabled parts on both sides, on the l. three, on the r. four slightly less in height.

Old cottages and farmhouses as well, mostly with a lobby-entrance plan.

5020

## COSTOCK

ST GILES. Now virtually C19, that is the work of *G. G. Place* in 1848 (N aisle added) and even more of *Gilbert Scott* in 1862. Old the rich C14 recess in the outer s wall in which lies a hardly

* Screen in Long Whatton church, Leics (M. W. Barley).

recognizable effigy of a priest. – BENCH ENDS. Six, poppy-headed. – MONUMENT. Large tablet to the Rev. William Wild. 1827 by *Peatts* of Nottingham.

MANOR HOUSE, at the corner of Main Street and Church Street, SW of the church. One of the most charming in the county: a stone house of the latter half of the C16 with divers gables and mullioned windows. (Late medieval plan of two cross wings linked by a central hall, now two-storeyed throughout, with minor additions and alterations. NS)

(HALL FARMHOUSE, E of the church. Somewhat later than the Manor House, i.e. early C17 (ovolo-moulded mullions, door openings). Much altered and with a brick addition of 1765. NS)

(Also in the village several tall brick cottages of two-and-a-half storeys. MWB)

HIGHFIELDS FARM, off the road to Bunny. Built in 1729 as the dower house to Bunny Hall by Sir Thomas Parkyns. Typically plain and solid (cf. his farms at Bradmore, etc.).


## COTGRAVE                                    6030

ALL SAINTS. A reminder of a C12 church the demi-columns of the chancel arch with their waterleaf capitals. The nave is wider than it was in the C12 (see the position of the chancel arch). The arcades have quatrefoil piers with fillets (cf. Fledborough, Lowdham, etc.), moulded capitals, and double-chamfered arches; late C13. The clerestory was added in the C15 as usual. Chancel windows renewed in 1877–8 by *Evans & Jolly*. The steeple has a plain C15 spire without lucarnes. It is ashlared, whereas the rest of the church is stuccoed over.

Anglo-Saxon BURIALS are recorded close to the Fosse Way, 1 m. w.


## COTHAM                                    7040

ST MICHAEL (disused). Small, with nave and chancel under one roof and W turret of 1890. Of the old tower some fragments in the churchyard. The church was probably reduced in size some time in the C18. The windows are an odd assembly now, two with flowing, the others with Perp tracery. A Norman doorway of no special interest. Inside, a crocketed C14 PISCINA, a C14 FONT, and two very damaged contemporary MONUMENTS. The only reason why the church had to be seen – the

monument to Anne Markham † 1601 – has been moved to St
Mary Magdalene, Newark. – In the churchyard slate HEAD-
STONES by *Wallis* of Newark.

# COTTAM

HOLY TRINITY. Nave and chancel under one roof with a bell-
turret of 1890. Norman masonry, Norman S doorway of two
orders. One has colonnettes. The scallops of the capitals end
at the top in a playful wavy line. The voussoirs have zigzag on
front and soffit. The other order has the same motif for jambs
and voussoirs, but capitals are inserted so oddly that it seems
justifiable to suppose interference at some later date. There
were restorations in 1869 and 1890.
(POWER STATION, close to two other huge power stations at
West Burton and High Marnham. Eight cooling towers and one
650 ft chimney. The whole power plant enveloped in a bright
amber-coloured aluminium sheeting. Architects: *Yorke
Rosenberg Mardall*, 1964–8.)

# CRESWELL

CRESWELL CRAGS. Some of the famous caves and rock-shelters
which have yielded information about Palaeolithic man lie on
the Nottinghamshire side of this gorge. The more important
caves, however, lie in Derbyshire, and the whole complex is
treated in *Buildings of England: Derbyshire*, rev. ed., 1978, p.
156.

# CROMWELL

ST GILES. Splendid but renewed five-light E window with flowing tracery. The S window of the chancel is simpler curvilinear.
W tower unbuttressed, Perp, said to be 1427, S aisle windows
with intersecting tracery, S door very plain C13. The C13 S
arcade on circular piers with moulded capitals renewed by
*Ewan Christian* in 1873–6.* Other windows Perp. – STAINED
GLASS. Minor C14–15 fragments in the chancel windows. – In
the churchyard HEADSTONE to Lucia Anne Buckley Harris

---

* According to Mr Alvey, a blocked AUMBRY on the outside of the N chancel
wall suggests a former N chancel chapel.

† 1926, with a Pietà in the Gill style by *J. Cribb* of Ditchling, 1927.

OLD RECTORY. A nice but neglected five-bay brick house with bands between storeys and a coved cornice, built *c.* 1680 as a dower house for the Earls of Clare, but in use as a rectory before 1714. Good original staircase. SE bay-window and a rear wing added in 1786–8, which may account for its description as late C18 in the *Beauties of England and Wales.* Curved wing at the NW end, 1814.*

A ROMAN VILLA is known lying within an extensive complex of fields by the Trent ½ m. from the village. It has not been excavated.

Parts of a timber and stone BRIDGE are recorded from the Trent here. A date in the Roman period is likely but not certain.

## CROPWELL BISHOP 6030

ST GILES. Perp ashlared W tower with two friezes at the top instead of the one customary in this part of Notts. The aisles are divided from the nave by four arches on low circular piers, the N arcade slightly earlier than that on the S, but both C13. There is, however, a round-headed window preserved in the N aisle wall. Most of the other windows are C14, except the clerestory, C15 as usual. Good nave ROOF on monsters' heads.‡ Chancel early C14, with a three-light E window of the ogee-reticulated type, a PISCINA, and an AUMBRY. In the N aisle a long piece of C13 wall-plate with nailhead ornament. – FONT. Octagonal, Dec, with a FONT COVER of 1662. – BENCHES with poppyheads from Colston Bassett. – SCREEN. Bits of Perp detail used in the new screen. – STAINED GLASS. Late C14 standing bearded figure in the N aisle E window. – In the churchyard, slate HEADSTONES of the Vale of Belvoir type, and by *Sparrow* of Radcliffe and *Wood* of Bingham.

THE COTTAGE, No. 24 Fern Road. Small timber-framed farmhouse with plaster infill. Modern pantile roof and dormers.

By the side of the disused Grantham canal, two BOTTLE KILNS of the shape usually found in the pottery industry. Known as Roberton kilns (after their Scottish builder), they are used for drying gypsum for the plaster works. Early C20.

---

* Information about this house was kindly given by Mr Hemingway.

‡ Repaired from time to time, see dates 1600, 1785, 1795, according to Mr Alvey.

5070          CUCKNEY

ST MARY. An unusually long nave of *c.* 1200 with a N aisle. The
arcade towards it oddly wavering in design, starting at the W
with circular piers, then two of quatrefoil plan, finally the others
octagonal. Can it really be changes in order of time, or should
one assume a local lodge trying to outdo the alternation of supports at Worksop?* The arches are all semicircular and double-
chamfered. In date the arcade seems to stand between the lower
stages of the broad, short W tower (cf. Edwinstowe) and the
S door (two orders without columns, one zigzag, the other a
thick angular rope motif) on the one hand and the upper stage
of the tower (ashlar with mid-C13 two-light windows) and the
S porch on the other. The S porch in any case seems E.E.
throughout (see its door with stiff-leaf capitals and its corbel
table). The PISCINA has dogtooth and nailhead ornament. All
windows Perp. – SCREEN now in the tower arch: only scant
remains of Perp panel tracery.

CASTLE HILL, W of the church. The motte of a castle probably
built by Thomas de Cuckney in the time of King Stephen
(1138–54). The N part of the church is built over mass burial
trenches.

PRIMARY SCHOOL. An early water-powered textile mill believed to have been built in 1723. Being used for spinning
worsted in 1786, then for cotton manufacture until 1844.
Worked by children, it was appropriately turned into a National
School by the Duke of Portland. Three-storeyed, of eight
windows' width. At the end of the pool, decorative iron railings.
Opposite, a row of three-storey stone cottages appears contemporary.‡


7070          DARLTON

ST GILES. Little of interest. W tower narrow and unbuttressed,
of the same date perhaps as the S doorway, that is Transitional
(complexly moulded round-headed arch, typical decoration of
the hoodmould, waterleaf capitals). (Much restored in 1855:

* The length and variety of detail are reminiscent of the late C12 churches
of the East Anglian fenland (BC).

‡ According to Mr R. D. Smith, they were used to accommodate the children.

nave and aisles by *Hine & Evans*, who added the pyramid cap
to the tower; chancel by *Ewan Christian*. – STAINED GLASS
in the E window by *Wailes*. JPB) – BRASSES to a Knight and
a Lady, *c.* 1510.

KINGSHAUGH HOUSE, ½m. W, S of the A57. Fragmentary
remains of a rectangular earthwork with an outer enclosure
covering seven acres. It surrounded a hunting lodge built to
serve the east, Le Clay, division of Sherwood Forest. Fortified
and held against King John's supporters during the rebellion
of 1196. The new lodge built here by King John in 1210–11
at a cost of some £550 was abandoned after the forest charter
of 1217. What appears to be a massive lump of medieval
masonry exists in the core of the present, derelict, late C17
double-pile brick farmhouse: five bays, C18 and C19 sashes,
but an original dog-leg staircase with balusters. The masonry
footings to three of the external walls are unlikely to be
medieval.


DAYBROOK *see* ARNOLD


DEAN HALL FARM *see* CAUNTON


DUNHAM-ON-TRENT                    8070

ST OSWALD. All that must be looked at is the tower, with spec-
tacularly large Perp windows on the upper stage: four lights,
one transom, and elaborate intersections in the top part (cf.,
for example, Gainsborough). It is ashlar-faced, with diagonal
buttresses, battlements, and pinnacles, as usual in this part of
the world. The rest (except for the S wall of 1805) was built
in 1861–2 by *T. C. Hine*: Dec style, not one of his most successful jobs, the striped roof especially discordant. He also
designed the VICARAGE.

(DUNHAM HOUSE must have been the parochial mansion of the
prebendary of Dunham at Southwell Minster. A late C17 range
across the back has a late medieval fireplace in brick. Front
range added or refronted in the C18. A nice Georgian façade
with a hipped roof turned to mask the rear range. NS)

EAKRING

St ANDREW. The w tower, unbuttressed, is, including the inner
    tower arch, E.E.; only its top is Perp. Unaisled nave. Much
    restoration by *St Aubyn*, 1880–1. Chancel early C14 with a re-
    markable E window, just one step beyond Southwell chapter
    house, that is with an odd, rather wilfully shaped pointed qua-
    trefoil in an otherwise correctly *c.* 1300 four-light window (cf.
    Stapleford). The N and s lancets also look *c.* 1300. – FONT.
    1674, but no distinguishing features. – PULPIT. Could be
    about the same date.
WINDMILL, at the w end of the village. Five-storey brick tower
    mill with cogged cornice. No cap, windows, or doors, but three
    bedstones, some machinery, and the curb remain.


EARLSHAW FARM *see* CAUNTON


EAST BRIDGFORD

The village is beautifully wooded above the river Trent and still
    has several Georgian cottages and houses. Its greatest archaeo-
    logical interest is not visible to the eye. It is the Roman town
    of MARGIDUNUM, 1 m. SE on the Fosse Way. (Parts of the
    site lie in the parishes of Car Colston, Bingham, and Newton.)
    It began *c.* A.D. 55 as a fort, with a large supply-base attached.
    After the army left, *c.* 70, a straggling roadside town developed,
    later receiving its own defences enclosing an area of 5
    acres. This settlement flourished in the C2–3, but by the
    end of the Roman period it was in decline. A little Anglo-
    Saxon material is known, but by 500 the place had been
    deserted.
St PETER. Excavations have shown the foundations of a cruci-
    form Saxon church. Its successor was Norman, and of this
    the chancel is standing, with a plain corbel table. Then follows
    the C14 with the usual Notts arcades of octagonal piers, the
    chancel arch, the transepts, s porch, plain ogee SEDILIA and
    PISCINA, and finally the clerestory (C15) and the w tower,
    rebuilt in 1778 by *Francis Moore* according to the inscription
    (Colvin), but on the old lines. Everything is over-restored, first
    in 1862 (chancel windows) and more completely in 1901–4 and
    1913 by *C. E. Ponting* of Wiltshire. – SCULPTURE. Small
    fragment of a Saxon shaft with interlacing. – PULPIT. Nice,

late Georgian. – FONT. From Bingham, one of the 1662–3 series (cf. Southwell). – Free-standing STOUP on a clustered shaft; E.E. – FLOOR TILES. A few of the C14 and C15 in the chancel. – STAINED GLASS. Minor C14 fragments in the chancel. – MONUMENTS. Foliated cross slab with a later inscription of 1628. – Mutilated effigy of a knight in chain mail. – John Hacker † 1620 and wife, the usual kneeling figures looking at each other across a prayer desk, kneeling children in the predella below. – Charles Beaumont † 1830, a stone on the chancel floor, still in the Georgian tradition, by *Booth* of Nottingham.

The late Georgian RECTORY close to the church is stuccoed, with a canopied veranda.

(OLD HALL, Kneeton Road. Early to mid-C18, plain five-bay brick house with sashes, hipped roof, and gabled dormers. Dentillated brick cornice running across the service wing, set back with domestic-looking casements. Good C18 wrought-iron gates.)

(MANOR HOUSE, on the road to Kneeton. Plain, stuccoed, *c.* 1830, but with some good inserted features including Adamstyle fireplaces. DOE)

BRIDGFORD HILL, next to the church and rectory. Country house of a fair size built in 1792 by the Rev. Thomas Beaumont, friend of James Paine junior. The main front has a full-height central bow.[*]

Two WINDMILLS. One, N of the village in Kneeton Road, is a tall red brick tower mill with no cap, with windows, floors intact, built in 1769 and raised from four to seven floors in 1852; two-storey mill buildings attached. The other (STOKES MILL), W of the village centre, with datestone 1828, has been unsympathetically converted into a house.

## EAST DRAYTON

ST PETER AND ST PAUL. A very complete Nottinghamshire late medieval exterior, that is, rather broad and square, embattled everywhere, with chancel lower than the nave, with S porch, and with a W tower strengthened by diagonal buttresses

---

[*] Mr T. Beaumont, who gave us this information, suggests that Thomas Beaumont designed the house himself, possibly with the help of *Paine Jun.* The plans were probably used again at Gedling House (*see* p. 131) across the Trent, but with a third storey.

and ending in eight pinnacles. The porch pinnacled too, with a stone roof on four transverse stone arches like a timber wagon roof (cf. St Mary, Nottingham, etc.). The chancel in its masonry is older (see the Transitional N door with round arch and typical ornament). The interior has C13 octagonal piers, moulded capitals, and double-chamfered arches on both sides. Differences between N and S only in detail. – SCREEN. Lively tracery similar to Ordsall. – ALTAR RAIL. With twisted balusters.

This village or Ragnall was the birthplace of Nicholas Hawksmoor.

## EAST LEAKE

5020

ST MARY. Nave N side Norman, with coarse rubble walling laid herringbone fashion, two high small windows, and a little of a former doorway. Above the later arch of the W tower also a round-headed opening into the nave. The tower is unbuttressed, that is early, and received in the C15 battlements and a plain spire. The C15 clerestory has battlements too. Lower chancel (rebuilt of old materials in 1886 by *W. S. Weatherley*) with one original, but much restored, group of three E.E. lancet windows under one arch (cf. Gedling). The E window is a sumptuous piece of decoration, five lights, all ogee reticulation, filled with pointed quatrefoils. – (Gone, STAINED GLASS by *Kempe*, also of 1886. – Three windows by *Powell* (chancel and N wall) and the W window by *Heaton, Butler & Bayne*. JPB) – FONT. E.E., very crude. – BENCHES. A number of no great importance in the nave. – VAMPING HORN or shawm (cf. South Scarle), a trumpet used in choir services, to 'vamp up' the singing. It is 7 ft 9 in. long. The only other examples in England are at Potter Hanworth and Willoughton, Lincs; Braybrooke and Harrington, Northants; Charing, Kent; Ashurst, Sussex; and Haversham, Bucks.

(GENERAL BAPTIST CHAPEL. Brick, dated 1839, but part of the 1756 chapel remains in the E wall. – Slate HEADSTONES from 1776. CS)

MANOR HOUSE. Double-pile, red-and-black chequered and diapered brick, the front range dated 1715 in the dark headers on the gable, the identical back range 1728. Three-bay front with bands and sashes in segment-headed openings.

OLD HALL FARMHOUSE, beside the church. Now a restaurant. C17, diapered brick, two storeys and four windows with decorative brick bands carried over them like vestigial segmental pediments (cf. Rempstone, Sutton Bonington, North Wheatley). (Barn, now dining room, dated 1799 on the road end, with an exposed kingpost roof. NS)

(GLEBE FARM, opposite the church. A typical lofty late C18 Notts farmhouse with a cottage adjoining. Three storeys, plain, but well proportioned and sympathetically restored. NS)

Near Glebe Farm, and in School Green, brick cottages with the remains of timber-framing.

WATER HOUSE at Rough Hill, 2 m. NE. Probably built in 1701 by Sir Thomas Parkyns of Bunny. He built a manor house in the village in 1704. It was demolished about eighty years later.


## EAST MARKHAM                                           7070

ST JOHN THE BAPTIST. Essentially of the C15, and the most splendid church in this part of the county. In more than one way out of the ordinary run. It has an unusually large nave and an unusually large chancel; and it has a clerestory duplicating the number of the bays of the arcades, a rhythm quite usual for the large parish churches of East Anglia, but rare in Notts, except in the case of as ambitious a church as Newark. Moreover, the piers of the arcades, although octagonal as in nearly every Notts village church, have sunk rectangular panels to each side and castellated capitals (cf. St Peter, Nottingham). The hoodmoulds are adorned by outstandingly good label stops, demons and portraits. (How much of them is due to *Oldrid Scott*'s careful restoration in 1883–7?) Very tall tower arch with concave profiles to piers and voussoirs and castellated capitals. All the aisle windows are of the same design, all the clerestory windows also. The chancel has a five-light late Perp E window, but its N and S windows are typical of the earliest C14 and the arch to the nave with no capitals at all to separate jambs from voussoirs could well be early C14 too. The general impression inside is roomy, stately, very light, and not very daring. Outside it is dominated by the excellent proportions of the three steps: tower to nave, nave to chancel, chancel to ground. In detail the tower is of the usual pattern (pairs of corner buttresses, corner gargoyles, eight pinnacles). What is unusual is the niche with a mutilated figure on the S side. S porch with an old timber roof. – ALTAR RAILS, PULPIT, FONT COVER. All early or mid-C17, and of the same style. – FONT. Shape probably C14, with eight flying buttresses; bowl 1686, plain, with pyramidal wooden cover. – SCREEN, moved to the S arcade. Not much old. Thin and delicate panel-type tracery. – STAINED GLASS. S aisle E window: two early C15 female saints. – Chancel E window by *Comper*, 1896, with heraldic fragments of *c.* 1380. – MONUMENTS. Tomb-chest to Sir John Markham † 1409 (Orate pro anima Johis Markham justicarii – and well may he ask; for he drew up the document deposing Richard II): shields in niches, and on the top just the inscription: the effigy has gone. – Brass to Dame Millicent Meryng † 1419, large and outstandingly good. – Stone slab to a lady, the same odd type as at North Collingham and Staunton.

S of the church, itself at the S edge of the present village, an area of disturbed meadow shows the site of the MEDIEVAL VILLAGE. (After an outbreak of plague in 1609, when more than a quarter of the population died, the village regrouped itself nearer Lincoln Road, then becoming an important local route. NS)

(MARKHAM HALL. The earliest house was of 1700, with a new range built across the front in 1777. Almost nothing pre-1777 exists now. Main façade in Flemish bond with lighter headers, of three storeys and seven bays with the centre three slightly projecting under a pediment. Doorcase with open pediment, windows above it with classical surrounds. Entrance hall with moulded plasterwork imitating panelling and a niche. Adam-style decoration and chimneypiece in the drawing room. NS)

CLEVELAND MILL, 1½ m. W. Four-storey brick tower mill of 1837 being converted sympathetically (1978) into a house. Cap and sails to be restored.

EAST RETFORD *see* RETFORD

EAST STOKE

The present village migrated from the church towards the Fosse Way in the C18, but planners have encouraged it to move back. The medieval village, now marked only by mounds on either side of a sunken road to the river, was close to the church.

ST OSWALD. Embedded in the trees of the park of Stoke Hall, the small church was largely rebuilt in 1738 (Colvin) with an arcade of Tuscan columns, round-headed windows, and a clerestory of plain mullioned windows. But the chancel has late C14 straight-headed windows with ogee tracery, and the short tower an arch towards the nave with finely moulded capitals of the C13. – CHEST. Perhaps C13. – STAINED GLASS. Some medieval fragments in the tracery lights of the SW window look C15. – MONUMENTS. Hellenic tablet to Lady Bromley † 1839 by *Nicholson & Wood* of Newark. – Tablet in coloured marbles to Geo. Wakefield † 1816 by *Henry Jackson* of Lincoln. – In the churchyard, monument to Lord Pauncefote † 1902, our first Ambassador to the United States.

STOKE HALL dates from the mid C16 or before (only re-used roof timbers and some internal walls visible) but was much enlarged by *Lewis Wyatt* in 1812.* Part two-, part three-storeyed with plain sashes. Wyatt connected the house with a formerly independent house said to be on the site of the C12 St Leonard's Hospital,‡ founded before 1135. (See a much weathered statue (St Leonard) under a canopy built into an external wall of the house; also two early medieval carved figures and some later emblems, probably in terracotta. All must be from the medieval buildings. NS) Much reduced in size in 1921–3, when the three-storey entrance block was pulled down.

In the village, a nice late C18 house next to the Pauncefote Arms.

AD PONTEM. *See* Thorpe.

## EASTWOOD

A small industrial town more famous as the birthplace of D. H. Lawrence (8a Victoria Street, restored and furnished by the District Council) than for its architecture. That is perhaps changing however. Broxtowe District Council won E.E.C. recognition for their plans to improve the town while retaining the character of Lawrence's time. Houses in Princes Street, Victoria Street, and Wellington Street have been preserved, and parts of the adjacent areas rebuilt in a sympathetic manner.

ST MARY. Only the embattled tower of the large early-Dec-style church of 1858 by *Robert Barber* of Eastwood survived the fire of 1963. New nave and chancel 1966–7 by *Royle & Whitehorn* of Nottingham.

(The old village developed down CHURCH STREET to the river

* According to APSD and Graves' *Royal Academy of Arts* (1905), a drawing was exhibited by *L. Wyatt* in 1812, but it is not included in the RA catalogue for that year.

‡ *See Trans. Thoroton Soc.*, 57 (1953), 9–12.

and Erewash Canal. Opposite the church No. 10 (IVY COTTAGE, once the manor house) is C17 under C19 cladding. Further down, three tall farmhouses of *c.* 1800 and some basically older cottages. MWB)

(EASTWOOD HALL, $\frac{1}{2}$ m. N of the centre. Early C19 stucco with Ionic-columned porch and full-height bows. The N.C.B. who own it have performed their usual trick of removing the fireplaces (cf. Clerkson's Hall, Mansfield Woodhouse) but have left a geometrical staircase with domed top-light and remains of good quality Regency plasterwork.)

## 7070        EATON

CHURCH. Rebuilt in 1860 by *G. Shaw* of Manchester at the expense of H. Bridgeman Simpson of Babworth Hall. Dec, with chancel, nave, and bell-turret. All that is old is a PISCINA and an C18 MONUMENT (in the vestry). Shaw also did the STAINED GLASS* (except the E window depicting the Transfiguration, which is by *J. R. Thompson* of Southwark, 1874. RH)

(EATON HALL (College of Education). Very Regency, long, stuccoed eight-bay façade of *c.* 1830. Pediments to the first-floor windows and a pair of large segmental bows to the ground floor with cast-iron balconies above. Hipped roof and bracketed eaves. Many modern additions.)

## 6050        EDINGLEY

ST GILES. Nave and chancel in one; chancel rebuilt 1844. W door with chevron decoration was originally to a tower. In the S wall remains of the demolished C14 S aisle (cf. Upper Broughton, Wiverton, etc.). The N wall a jumble of windows, amongst which one Norman one as narrow as an arrow-slit. All restored *c.* 1890 by *Hodgson Fowler*.

MANOR HOUSE FARM. A good example of brick building in Notts about 1700. L-plan, with high gables, bands, and cogged eaves cornice (cf. Highfield Farm, Kirton).

## 5030        EDWALTON

Part of West Bridgford. Modern housing has completely submerged the old village.

* Information from J. P. Bartlam.

HOLY ROOD. The remarkable feature of the church is the W tower: brick, English bond, diagonal buttresses. The top windows are still pointed, and of such early detail that one is tempted to suppose mid-C16 origin. The small nave with clerestory and S aisle of stone has an irregular N side of various dates. Low C14 S arcade. The chancel was built on the foundations of the medieval one, which had fallen down in the C17. By *Brewill & Baily*, 1894, harsh red brick, but with pretty neo-Perp N and S windows.

## EDWINSTOWE          6060

ST MARY. Essentially C12–13, that is a broad, strong W tower with a broad, flat staircase projection on the S side. A small pointed window on the S, round-headed inside, a tall lancet on the W, so tall that it has a transom (a very unusual detail for the C13), a Norman triplet on the top floor, and above that a spire which in its present form is certainly C19, probably re-cast from what had been done in 1680.* A plain Norman doorway on the S side of the chancel. As for the interior, the N arcade rests on circular piers with very elementary moulded capitals, the S arcade with octagonal piers is later, later also than the S windows, which are typical late C13 and thus go well with the PISCINA, the S doorway, and the S porch. The latter has exactly the same capitals as the arcade at Warsop nearby. Finally there is a Dec E window, a Perp clerestory, and Perp battlements of nave and chancel. Attached to the N aisle is the family MAUSOLEUM of the Ward family, 5/8 in plan, with typical C19 coloured glass and a free-standing canopy in the centre: c. 1831. – FONT. Dec. – PILLAR PISCINA. Fragment in the chancel, just a short part of an E.E. quatrefoil shaft. – STAINED GLASS. Fragments of C14 glass in the N aisle E window. – Foljambe Memorial window, 1873 by *Heaton, Butler & Bayne*, one of those given by C. G. Savile Foljambe in memory of his wife (cf. Wellow, Ollerton, St John Worksop).

(METHODIST CHAPEL, High Street. 1848. Rendered three-bay front with tall round-arched windows above a rusticated entrance storey. CS)

COCKGLODE, a villa built in 1778 N of the Ollerton–Edwinstowe

* According to Paul Joyce, A. E. Street includes this church in his list of *G. E. Street*'s restorations, but there is no trace of Street in the building. The most substantial renovations were done in 1897.

road, in the s outskirts of the forest, of modest size and comfortable, has been demolished.

(EDWINSTOWE HALL (NCC Children's Home), N of the church. Part early C18 (see the general proportions, the hipped roof with pedimented dormers, and some windows), but other features are mid-C18 (rainwater head dated 1757) and C19. Inside some early C18 features and a splendid two-storey drawing room of 1751, the ceiling in Rococo manner with cherubs in low relief on the central panel (DOE). Additions by the County Architect quite separate.)

In the Middle Ages, Edwinstowe was the central and most important settlement in SHERWOOD FOREST (see Introduction, p. 17). Visitors to the Forest can now resort for instruction to a VISITORS' CENTRE in the Birkland N of Edwinstowe: a series of hexagonal huts or 'pods' grouped in a compound, inspired by the dugout shelters of early forest dwellers. By *Ian Pryer, William Saunders & Partners*, 1973–6, for the County Council, who have designated the area a Country Park.

7060                           EGMANTON

ST MARY. There is no denying the fact, *Comper*'s screen, organ case, and pulpit make the church. As a piece of reconstruction the SCREEN with its rood and rood-canopy is admirable, and as pieces of medieval revival organ case and pulpit are admirable too. But as pieces of contemporary art, they are of course valueless. Their date is early in Comper's work (1896–8), during a period when he was strongly influenced by South German Gothic art. The ORGAN CASE is consequently modelled on that in Freiburg-im-Breisgau Cathedral; the PULPIT, though fortuitously with a Voyseyish look about it, on the medieval pulpit in Ghent. Also by *Comper* (who was recommended to the patron, the Duke of Newcastle, by St John Hope) are the STAINED GLASS in the E window, the ALTAR TABERNACLE, originally a hanging pyx, and the image of the Virgin in the chancel. As for the old parts, the N arcade is late C12 (circular piers, waterleaf capitals, only slightly chamfered arches), the s door probably even earlier (wholly unmoulded arch), the recess on the s side of the s transept (s aisle chantry) somewhat later. The windows in the transept are typical Notts late C14, straightheaded, and the W tower equally typical Notts C15. – ALTAR TABLE. 1685, yet still Jacobean, that is, pre-classical. –

STAINED GLASS. Fragments in the s window, s transept, for example the C14 figures of St George (well-preserved) and St Michael (over-restored). – MONUMENT. Nicholas Powtrell † 1579, justice of assize, and two wives; incised slab.

MOTTE AND BAILEY CASTLE, W of the church. One of the two best surviving examples in the county (the other is Laxton). The motte is a steep mound standing more than 20 ft high and measuring 460 ft in circumference. The bank and ditch surrounding the bailey can still be traced, except where obliterated by farm buildings.

## ELKESLEY

6070

ST GILES. The chancel windows look *c.* 1300, the nave windows humbly Dec, which would go with the N arcade. A Dec niche placed diagonally at the junction of nave N wall and chancel as at Askham. But how much belongs to the partial reconstruction of 1845? The W gallery in the tower chamber certainly, with the staircase leading to it. Perp roof bosses in the nave.

LINCOLN CORPORATION PUMPING STATION. A handsome brick building of 1908–11* which is doomed to demolition. The two large triple-expansion steam engines, working until recently, are now destined for the Welsh Industrial and Maritime Museum.

## ELSTON

7040

CHAPEL, in a field towards Stoke Field, a house near the boundary with East Stoke parish. Nave and slightly lower chancel. s wall with Norman masonry and plain zigzag decoration of jambs and arch of doorway. Windows C14. Inside it had a W gallery, box pews of deal, with hat pegs along the walls, squire's pew, pulpit with Jacobean detail, and reader's desk below: that is, a completely untouched poor village church interior of *c.* 1820.‡ Traces of C18 wall paintings.

ALL SAINTS. Perp clerestory and aisles, but all too new, i.e. restored in 1827, 1859, and 1887 (JPR), except for the tall, slim, only slightly buttressed tower of C13 date. Worth a visit because

* Possibly by *Blomfield, see Lincs, History and Archeology,* 12 (1977), 20–1.
‡ Disgracefully neglected and consequently vandalized, but the Redundant Churches Fund is now responsible for its upkeep.

of the MONUMENTS to the Darwins of the Hall. Artistically
they are not up to much (several, 1789–1816, by *Wallis* of
Newark), but the three by *Tyley* of Bristol to three Darwin
children who died at the ages of 13, 14, and 15 in 1835–8 are
of good provincial quality. One tablet to Elizabeth Hill Darwin
† 1827 by *Taylor* of York.

ELSTON HALL looks like an H-plan house, probably of *c.* 1700,
much remodelled. The main front stone, mostly of 1756, still
with gabled wings. Over the slightly projecting entrance bay,
a shaped parapet with a crude half-figure of a drummer boy.
The centre of the garden front, slightly canted out between
the wings, is brick, of 1837, with mullioned windows and
Gothic glazing to the porch. C19 gabled and other more
modern additions at each end. Birthplace of Erasmus
Darwin.

ELSTON TOWERS. The whole building is really one huge folly.
Built by Robert Middleton in 1875 in what supposedly is Tudor
Gothic, but incorporating features from every building that
caught his fancy in an excruciating design. Main rooms at first-
floor level on a podium made by the spreading ground floor:
octagonal towers at the ends, and a proliferation of metal roof
terminals. In the centre, projecting at the rear, a Baptist chapel.
Near it a tower originally with clock and bells but now with
a metal chimney.\*

ALMSHOUSES, opposite the church. Founded in 1744 by Ann
Darwin. In the village several dated early C18 brick farmhouses
and cottages and a small DOVECOTE behind cottages at the E
end of Top Street.

WINDMILL, on the road to Sibthorpe. 1844. Capless, but the
five storeys have floors, doors, and windows. In 1978 being tactfully converted into a dwelling.

7030                              ELTON

ST MICHAEL. Small, and in its present appearance primarily
the result of the restoration of 1855–7. The low tower was
rebuilt then. The exterior was plastered in imitation of ashlar.
Originally the church had a Transitional S arcade, demolished
in 1786. A still wholly Norman-looking corbel head remains,
and round arches with some nailhead built into the wall. As
so often in this neighbourhood (*see* Upper Broughton, Wiver-

---

\* Information and description kindly given by Dr Summers and Mr Train.

ton, etc.), depopulation has necessitated a reduction in size – ALTAR RAILS, C17, with balusters. – MONUMENT to Francis Launder, 1822, by *Joseph Hall* the younger of Derby.

## EPPERSTONE                          6040

HOLY CROSS. S arcade mid-C13 on quatrefoil piers with fillets (cf. Lowdham) and with capitals moulded towards the arch opening and decorated with stiff-leaf towards nave and aisle: a most unusual arrangement. N door and W steeple of the same period, the spire (type of St Peter, Nottingham) of different stone and later. Chancel rebuilt 1853–4 (RH). – MONUMENTS. Slab with foliated C13 cross. – Stone effigy, C14, hardly recognizable.

The village is uncommonly pleasing. There is a DOVECOTE opposite the Cross Keys in Main Street, rectangular and gabled with modillion string and eaves courses.

PAPER MILL. Attractive ruins of a water mill, now part of a stud farm, last operated in 1912. Probably early C19, then rebuilt after a fire in 1828. Mostly brick with stone tailrace arches. Nearby a former steam engine house: the small stream was obviously too unreliable for sustained output.

A ROMAN VILLA lies on the slopes NE of the village, about 2 m. away. The excavated building was an aisled structure, later embellished with a simple bath-suite and painted walls. It was occupied in the C2–3. Earlier, an Iron Age settlement had existed here.

## EVERTON                            6090

HOLY TRINITY. An unusual exterior with a tall, very short nave (cf. Tuxford) between the W tower and the lower chancel. The nave masonry is earlier below than above. The ashlared, embattled clerestory stage corresponds to the top parts of the tower, the embattled S porch, and the embattled, low S chancel chapel. The ground floor of the tower, however, is as old as the lower stage of the nave, and one window in the nave dates them as Norman. Inside, the tower arch to the nave is also Norman, narrow and unmoulded. To the same period belongs the chancel arch with one order and chevron ornament. Earlier still in appearance the S tympanum, Norman probably, but of

Viking descent: two horse-like dragons seemingly licking each other's muzzles in the friendliest spirit. *Kinderkunst*, one is inclined to say. In spite of all research we know very little of what made our ancestors carve such things and place them over the doors of churches. N arcade of two bays, the octagonal pier with a well crocketed capital (renewed?). The capital of the E respond is much more elementary. The corbels of the early roof survive. The chancel was extended E into a five-sided apse with half-columns between the lancets in 1841 and a Lady Chapel added. – FONT. Norman, circular, with interlaced arches on short columns; a copy in the church, the battered original in the porch. – (STAINED GLASS. W window and three lancets of the apse by *Wailes*. Poor examples by the ex-grocer and not too well preserved. RH) – MONUMENT. Incised alabaster slab to a Knight and his lady, now under the tower. Inscription obscured.

(VICARAGE. With classical decoration on a tiny scale: a 'pretty conceit' of the early C19. Stuccoed, with a hipped roof. On the road front, windows framed with little semicircular pilasters carrying shallow flat cornices. To the garden front they have segmental heads on scrolled brackets at the sides. NS)

(In HIGH STREET, opposite the recreation ground, a pair of C18 houses with a central pediment and coupled doors in a surround of reeded pilasters. DOE)

WINDMILL, at the S end of the village. Four-storey brick tower in good condition, with the framework of the cap and ball finial intact.

PUSTO HILL FARM. *See* Wiseton.

<sub>7050</sub>

# FARNDON

ST PETER. Very restored (e.g. tower repaired in 1598) and plastered, but the outside of the N wall shows early Norman herringbone masonry and a plain contemporary doorway, and inside the S arcade of three bays is on E.E. piers, circular with four detached shafts, and four major and minor shafts with fillets for the major ones: simply moulded capitals (cf. Laneham). The nave roof is of 1664. N aisle rebuilt 1897 by *Hodgson Fowler* (JPB). – In the CHURCHYARD a slate headstone by *Francis Lamb* of Bottesford. – A Viking SWORD, one of the few objects of Danish origin from the county, is recorded from the churchyard.

There are several dignified Georgian houses nearby. Worth noting individually the OLD HALL, mid-C18, with a central pediment and late C18 greenhouse; FARNDON LODGE, late C18, with a stone-columned porch and simple gazebo; and with late C18 façades and good doorcases No. 1 and No. 2 (late C17, refronted) CHURCH STREET and Nos. 8 and 9 WEST END. Also CROSS LANE FARMHOUSE, a typical lofty late C18 Notts farmhouse, and many lesser C18 brick houses, e.g. Chestnut Farm and Pilgrim Cottage.

WINDMILL. Tall red brick tower mill of five storeys. No cap, but a dentil course at the curb and a datestone 1823.

EARTHWORKS of the besieging forces in the Civil War appear once to have surrounded the village. Now, only a corner bastion is visible in a field between the roads which link the village to the Fosse Way (cf. Hawton, Balderton, Coddington, and South Muskham).

## FARNSFIELD

6050

ST MICHAEL. Perp tower, ashlar, with diagonal buttresses. The top C19, same date and same design as the rebuilding of the church: 1859–60 by *Hine & Evans*. – STAINED GLASS. (Three apse windows 1862 by *Wailes*. Very characteristic. – Nave w by *Clayton & Bell*, 1876. RH) – Leeson and Hitchbone families, 1904; an unusually good example of its date, of the Arts and Crafts rather than the Ecclesiological school, in the Crane-Sumner tradition. Designed by Mrs *E. M. Everett*, *née Leeson*.

SCHOOL by *Hine & Evans*, 1862.

(FARNSFIELD HALL comprises a late C17 farmhouse, i.e. the two-storey single range of rooms facing the road, and, built against it in the latter half of the C18, a fine new range of rooms with a central entrance, facing into a small park. Stucco probably later. The complete reorientation marks a rise in status, a common feature of Notts houses of that time – cf. Gonalston Rectory, Caunton Grange. Stuccoed and pedimented stables dated 1818. NS)

COMBS FARM, 1¼ m. SW. Small, roughly oval earthwork, surrounded by a single bank and ditch, sited on a promontory Presumably Iron Age in origin; so far, only Romano-British material is reported from the site (cf. Ramsdale Park, Arnold, Oldox, Oxton, Foxwood, Calverton). Combs Farm itself is C17 or earlier in origin.

CAMP HILL, $1\frac{1}{2}$ m. NE. Traces of two ditches in a small wood are the only visible remains of an earthwork, probably Iron Age in origin, estimated in the C18 to cover 40 acres. Romano-British material has also been recovered from the site.

A small Roman MARCHING CAMP lies $\frac{1}{2}$ m. SW of the village.

## FELLEY

4050

FELLEY PRIORY. Founded for Augustinian Canons in 1156 by Raph Brito of Annesley. Less than ten miles away and ten years later Henry II founded Newstead Priory for the same order. Little survives of Felley: four thick semicircular shafts with waterleaf and similar capitals, now gateposts of the house.

The house is extremely pretty with its long rambling front, stone below, brick for the several gables, and with stone-mullioned windows of two to four lights. It is kept so well now that it reflects more the modern nostalgia for an idealized past than the dates of its erection. The central part of three gabled bays and a large chimneystack is the most genuinely old. The stone ground floor may contain medieval fabric but has a four-centred doorway that looks C16. The gables and chimneystack (both with some figurative panels) and r. hand bay look C17 and no doubt date from the Millingtons' time. They acquired the estate in 1604. The other gables must be relatively modern. Inside, stone fireplaces including one to the main chimney-breast with a four-centred arch cut out of a foliated cross slab with Anglo-Norman inscription. C17 balusters and newel-post knobs re-used in the modern staircase. Near the house, an out-building with a four-centred arch and a mullioned window and mostly timber-framed barns.

## FENTON

### Near Sturton-le-Steeple

7080

MANOR FARM. Fragment of a C17 brick house, formerly the seat of the Thornhaughs. Now a farmhouse, it was reduced to its present size before 1700. On the W side a mullioned three-light window. Roof with stone coping and kneelers. All in moulded brick a string course of little arches on corbels and an eaves course carried on corbel brackets.

( GRANGE FARM. Stone mullioned three-light window dated 1693 WM in a C17 brick wing extended by C19 brickwork at the front.

Main range of the house C18. A much decayed coat of arms is set into the gable of a C19 outbuilding. NS)

## FINNINGLEY

Finningley lies in the reclaimed fenland which connects this northernmost corner of Notts* with Lincolnshire, and most appropriately once belonged to the great *Cornelius Vermuyden* himself, who conducted the draining operations in East Anglia about 1630–40.

HOLY TRINITY. Norman w tower right up to the bell-stage with double openings on all sides and a low unadorned tower arch inside. Norman nave walls wider than the tower. Norman s door badly preserved. Chancel *c.* 1300 and good, with window tracery just leaving the geometrical conventions, but not yet flowing. Accordingly the simple SEDILIA and PISCINA group is still C13 in character (though the capitals are omitted between the uprights and the arches). The chancel arch is steep on trefoil shafts with finely moulded capitals. The chancel has an arched roof truss with carved bosses. Old open roof with carved beams and bosses to the nave: no clerestory. – FONT. Circular, with a C17 cover. – PULPIT. 1603. – MONUMENTS. Six incised foliated cross slabs in the porch.

SCHOOL. Late C17 or early C18 barn converted to a school and given to the parish by John Harvey of Ickwell Bury, Beds., in 1855. Single-storey, four tall casements, studded door in an architrave surround.

## FISKERTON

The special character of the village is that it really lies on the river. A grass-grown footpath or promenade runs along the embankment and the houses with their gardens look over it. On the wharf, a single-storey brick WAREHOUSE and, a little further up, on a stream running into the Trent, FISKERTON MILL, a four-storey, seven-bay water corn mill, brick with a pantile roof: a classic type of larger mill building. Waterwheel disused, but the mill still worked by cheaper waterturbines.

The parish is Fiskerton-cum-Morton. For Morton, see p. 179.

The parish is Fiskerton-cum-Morton. For Morton, see p. 179.

* Now in South Yorkshire. For Finningley Park *see The Buildings of England: Yorkshire: The West Riding.*

# FLAWBOROUGH

ST PETER. An inscription says explicitly: This church rebuilt 1840. Yet it looks as if some of the windows came from a previous building. In the red brick tower a reset Norman doorway, terribly worked over, with two orders of colonnettes and two orders of zigzag arches. The little capitals are of varied design, mainly with closely ribbed leaf forms. The best thing about the church is the view over the Vale of Belvoir. – A good range of slate HEADSTONES.

# FLEDBOROUGH

ST GREGORY. A roomy nave with two aisles, both arcades identical, E.E., with unusually tall quatrefoil piers with fillets (cf. Lowdham, etc.) and double-chamfered arches. The chancel arch also E.E., though perhaps a little later. The clerestory C14, the chancel rebuilt in 1890.* Only externally will it be noticed that the W tower in its lower stage is actually the oldest part of the building. It has a blocked and pointed W door and a small lancet W window, with slight outer and deep inner splay. The tower arch also is Norman in its detail, though pointed. The upper part of the tower is C13. – The original chancel must have possessed a simplified version of an EASTER SEPULCHRE à la Hawton. Two small panels are all that remains, one with three sleeping soldiers in ogee arcades, the other, smaller still, with two censing angels and a figure of Christ rising. – STAINED GLASS. Fledborough is uncommonly rich in C14 glass. This has been connected with the foundation of the Lisures Chantry in 1343, although there is no direct evidence. The best general impression is obtained by examining the E window of the N aisle with figures under solid arcades, mostly with tower-like structures on the arches. Only St Andrew and the upper part of a knight are completely original. Fragments of shields and saints in a NE chancel window. All shields modern in the nave windows. The colouring is pale, mostly white, grey, pink, and olive-green. Much was renewed in 1852–7. – MONUMENTS. Foliated cross in the tower chamber, exceptionally rank with stiff-leaf and fruits as of maize. – Lady

---

* According to Mr Michael Brook, *J. L. Pearson*'s restoration plans of *c.* 1870 were carried out.

wearing a wimple; her garments have rippling hems on both sides; early C14. – Later C14 Knight, upper half only, alabaster.

## FLINTHAM

ST AUGUSTINE. Close to the Hall, which forms an odd foil to a church all modest 1828 except the tower. The original transepts (arches visible outside) were then pulled down and the nave entirely rebuilt by Mr *Nicholson* of Southwell. The only interesting medieval remains are the herringbone masonry of the crossing tower almost up to the belfry windows, the opening from it into the nave, and the mid-C13 tower arches with semicircular shafts with fillets and moulded capitals. Was a C12 W tower made central in the C13? Restoration 1896 by *Hodgson Fowler*. – FONT. C14, octagonal, with a C17 cover.* – ALTAR RAIL with very elementary balusters, probably *c.* 1600, and ALTAR TABLE of the same date. – MONUMENT. Effigy of *c.* 1330 of a cross-legged knight bearing a shield with the arms of Hose. – In the churchyard slate HEADSTONES including one to Henry Green † 1776 by *James Sparrow*.

FLINTHAM HALL.‡ The medieval and Jacobean house was rebuilt in 1798, enlarged by *Lewis Wyatt* in 1829, and remodelled by *T. C. Hine* in 1853 for T. B. T. Hildyard M.P. On the N front Wyatt's plain two-storey brick wings still face the stable yard; the other façades were encased by Hine in stone with heavy Italianate details and top balustrade. On the W front a porte-cochère under a square central tower. On the S front a projecting central bay with an elaborate window of curious design, and, upsetting the symmetry in a typically C19 way, a narrow canted bay on the r. Linked to this by the two-storey library wing, the *pièce-de-résistance*, a conservatory as tall as the house, no doubt inspired by the recent Crystal Palace. Conventional load-bearing walls support a barrel-vault of cast iron and glass, but the end wall and the exposed length on the W side are screens of stone tracery in imitation of cast-iron construction. More remarkable than the architecture is the authentic Victorian atmosphere of the interior. In many rooms the original decoration and furniture by *Holland & Sons*. Lighting the staircase a large tracery window filled with rich stained

* According to Mr Alvey.
‡ We are grateful to Mr Myles Hildyard for amending our account of Flintham Hall.

glass. In the library, two storeys high, the prize-winning book-case-cum-chimneypiece designed by *McQuoid* and exhibited by *Holland & Sons* at the Great Exhibition, 'the work of the greatest pretension in the collection … in full cinquecento taste'. A Venetian-palazzo-style balcony looks down on to the fountain and exotic vegetation in the conservatory. Beyond the walled garden, *Wyatt*'s aviary. Park and lake are early C19. (Two LODGES by *Hine*: w lodge Loudonesque with shaped gables, N lodge based on Hine's 'Model Cottage Design' of 1848, which won a Society of Arts competition for a labourer's cottage, an important starting point in his career. JPB)

## FOREST TOWN
### *see* MANSFIELD p. 169

## FOUNTAIN DALE
### *see* BLIDWORTH

## GAMSTON
7070

ST PETER. The *Little Guide* says 'of no interest'. Yet there is an unusually picturesque exterior, due, it is true, at least partly to *Sir George Gilbert Scott*, who restored the church in 1855. His no doubt is the tall rood stair turret (but there was no rood loft). However, what must be original is the rhythm of excessively low chancel, short, tall embattled nave (with clerestory windows influenced by East Markham), and w tower starting with pairs of corner buttresses and then going on with the more familiar diagonal buttresses. Battlements and eight pinnacles. Embattled nave, s aisle, and chancel. Inside, E.E. chancel arch and s arcade. Perp s aisle. – Good C17 CHEST carved with arcading, etc. – MONUMENTS. A prior, early C14, head on a diagonally placed pillow held by angels. – Priest with chalice, an early C14 demi-figure in a quatrefoil (cf. Tuxford) under a crocketed gable. – Important alabaster effigy with delicate chain mail, believed to be Sir Bertram Manboucher, *c.* 1420.

(COTTAGE, E of the church. C16 or C17, timber-framed with brick-nogging, rendered and colourwashed. DoE)

## GATEFORD
### *see* WORKSOP

## GEDLING 6040

ALL HALLOWS. One of the most remarkable steeples in Notts, 34 historically, visually, and archaeologically: historically in that it belongs entirely, right to the tip of the spire, to the years c. 1300–20, visually in that the spire is exceedingly thin, takes up more than half the total height of the steeple, and achieves by its broach and first tier of dormer windows at a distance an outline of the shallowest S or ogee curves. The sides of the spire actually have a slight, ingenious entasis. The effect is elegant, almost sensuous, in an Indian way, as it were. The lowest windows c. 1300, the bell-openings Dec, the battlements on a corbel table of monsters. The first tier of dormers has four real windows (Dec) and four niches for statues. The second tier high up. The steeple stands to the N of the nave front, wholly projecting, a position unique in the county. It has the advantage that it allows for a proper W front. This was begun c. 1200 (see the badly preserved and much restored doorway). The upper stage belongs to the date of the tower: a large window with ogee reticulation and two niches for statues l. and r. of it. The window has two head corbels, and its outer voussoirs are decorated with square little fleurons. Masonry of c. 1200 has also been found in the chancel and the N aisle walls. The main visible motifs of the chancel are mid-C13, the (renewed) lancet windows (the group at the E end, three separate lancets and a quatrefoil in the gable, is especially noble), the S door with shafts with fillets and stiff-leaf capitals, and the SEDILIA and PISCINA with triple shafts (with fillets) and pointed trefoil heads; a little dog-tooth decoration. Opposite a double AUMBRY with triangular heads. The nave is long and roomy, N and S arcades of five bays, identical, with tall octagonal shafts and moulded capitals of late C13 or early C14 form. The S aisle windows Early Dec, the S porch probably contemporary. It has a stone roof but no transverse ribs (cf. St Mary, Nottingham). The N windows renewed, except for the last to the E. – PULPIT. Made up from Elizabethan wildly chip-carved panels. – PAINTING. Descent from the Cross; looks Venetian early C18. – Large two-tier brass CHANDELIER in the nave. – MONUMENTS. Alabaster slab of a priest in cassock and surplice, carved partly in low relief. Assigned to c. 1200 but probably very much later and *Volkskunst*. – Foliated cross with face of a priest in a quatrefoil at the head of the cross (cf. Tuxford and Gamston).

GEDLING HOUSE (used by the County Education Resources Service). Plain stuccoed two- and three-storey house, the centre slightly curved. Very like Bridgford Hill facing it across the Trent, 3 m. or so away at East Bridgford. The same plans may have been used (*see* p. 113).

(A very similar plan is used on a smaller scale at MANOR FARMHOUSE. Three-storey centre block with one curved façade, two-storey side wings. NS)

8060                          GIRTON

(ST CECILIA. Tiny, aisleless: vestiges of E.E. and Perp. Almost rebuilt 1879 (chancel *E. Christian*, nave *H. M. Townsend*): new N wall with re-used lancets, new S windows and bellcote. JPB)

FLEET COTTAGE. A good example, now very rare, of the early north-east Notts cottage, probably C17. Ground floor limestone, upper floor timber-framed. Disposition of the main rooms original.


GOLDHILL FARM *see* HALAM


6040                       GONALSTON

ST LAWRENCE. Rebuilt in 1853 by *Hine & Evans* with a spire like Hine's at Farnsfield (JPB). The chancel walls old. In the N wall an octagonal pier has been laid bare, proving the former existence of a chancel chapel (demolished, like one aisle, in 1787: RH). The nave arcade (C14) is entirely renewed. Chancel windows with intersecting tracery, that is end of the C13, a correct restoration. – STAINED GLASS. Small fragments of *c.* 1300 in the N aisle NE window. Most of it now in Southwell chapter house. – ALTAR RAILS. 'Laudian', with balusters. – MONUMENTS. Three of the Heriz family, *c.* 1300 ('uncovered', according to Cox, in 1848 by the sculptor Westmacott: RH). The two Knights, cross-legged, are badly preserved; the Lady Mathilda has suffered unusually little. She wears a wimple, and above her head is a cusped arch on corbels, one with stiff-leaf, the other with more naturalistic foliage.

GONALSTON HALL. A remodelling in 1851–2 by *T. C. Hine*, in a style very like that of the church, of a *cottage orné* of 1837.*

* Information kindly given by Mr Train.

(OLD RECTORY. A double-pile house with entrance front, in the N range facing the village, incorporating remains of an earlier house. On the other side (S) away from the village a range of 1785. Fine symmetrical front with canted stone bay-windows to the main living rooms flanking the entrance and a small pediment in the centre of the eaves. Reorientation in this way is a common feature of many C18 improvements in Notts; cf. Farnsfield, Caunton Grange. NS)

(MANOR FARMHOUSE. Late C17; two storeys with attics, gabled ends; refenestrated with sash-windows in the C18. Central gabled porch with cogged decoration to the parapet. NS)

(A number of estate cottages and houses were built, and older ones improved in the late C19, by a philanthropic member of the Franklin family. NS)

(SMITHY, at the E end of the village. Datestone: *JP 1854*. Giant horseshoe motif round the entrance of projecting brick courses, cf. Carlton-on-Trent. NS)

CLIFF MILL. The derelict and ruinous remains of this water mill, built in the 1790s, deserve a mention as the cotton mill at which Robert Blincoe was first apprenticed. The memoirs of Robert Blincoe describing his ill-treatment at Litton Mill, Derbyshire, are well known.


GOTHAM    5030

ST LAWRENCE. A remarkable W tower of the C13, unbuttressed, with a thin corbel table, no parapet, and plain splays instead of broaches to the spire (a specially early form). The spire has two tiers of little E.E. lucarnes. The whole is of one period, earlier than, for example, at Normanton, that is, if we can trust what we see now. The steeple was actually rebuilt 'with the old materials' in the later C18, at the time when the chancel was also rebuilt (inscriptions 1789) and the aisles (like the chancel) faced with stucco. Only the clerestory with its C13 three-light windows rises above the stucco. The nave and S aisle are of *c.* 1200 (see the round piers and capitals of the arcade, one with the plainest waterleaf, one with stiff-leaf, and one with faces at the corners from which leafy tendrils sprout). Double-chamfered arches. N arcade C14 on octagonal piers. – MONUMENTS. John St Andrew † 1625 and wife, and Will. St Andrew, date illegible, also early C17. Both have the usual kneelers in profile, but in the tomb of William the two wives and children kneel on the main level and he himself above, where as a rule the achievement of the family is displayed. The John St A. monument does not have children kneeling frontal between the parents (cf. Bunny), only a baby in its cradle on the extreme l., the most appealing feature of the monument.

(MANOR HOUSE, SE of the church. Early C17, red brick, with three equal gables. Modern casements except for the stair window on the garden front, which is mullion-and-transom cross. A great deal of timber-framing, C17 or earlier, left internally, which suggests a rebuild of an earlier house, including many re-used timbers in the roof (principals, purlins, etc., and late medieval cusped wind-braces, cf. Holme Pierrepont, used in their original context). In the attic plastered enclosures, most probably grain bins. NS)

7030                              GRANBY

ALL SAINTS. One of the south Notts churches which were reduced in size in post-Reformation times (cf. Upper Brough-ton, etc.). The N arcade (C14 with octagonal piers) and N chancel arcade are now built into the stuccoed outer wall. E.E. S door-way with manifold mouldings of the arch. The terracotta E win-dow of the still roomy chancel was replaced in 1888 by one of stone.* How interesting it would have been to see this and com-pare it with the terracotta windows at Layer Marney in Essex. The W tower has Norman windows (and once had a spire). The arch into the nave is of c. 1250 with demi-columns and plain moulded capitals. The top is obviously Perp, but the whole was, we are told, repaired in 1777, the approximate date probably of the pulling down of the superfluous parts of the church. – BENCH ENDS. With poppyheads of varied design, for example mermaids. – PULPIT. 1629, not of special value (cf. for its style Syerston). – ALTAR RAILS of c. 1700. – In the churchyard, good slate HEADSTONES in the Vale of Belvoir style, e.g. Ann Hall † 1744 by *James Sparrow*, and one of 1811 by *Wood* of Bingham with an urn and pastoral scenes *à la* Samuel Palmer.

GRASSTHORPE *see* SUTTON-ON-TRENT

---

* According to Mr Alvey there are fragments of a terracotta window lying in the chancel. Two cusped heads, excellent quality terracotta, a remarkable survival in these parts.

## GREASLEY

4040

ST MARY. A proud C15 Notts tower, tall and broad, and in
a position to serve as a landmark for miles around. Ashlar, pairs
of corner buttresses, large twin two-light bell-openings, battlements, and eight pinnacles. The rest of the church 1882 and
1896, rebuilt by Earl Cowper of Beauvale. – Nice slate COM-
MANDMENT BOARDS (the slate district reaches up about as far
N as this). –(STAINED GLASS. Roundels of medieval glass
showing St Agatha and St Agnes, from Beauvale Priory. DOE)–
MONUMENT. Lancelot Rolleston † 1685, demi-figure baroque-
ly draped, with the usual pediment etc.

GREASLEY CASTLE FARM, SE of the church. Of the fortified
manor of the Cantilupe family, begun *c.*1341, some of the moat
and quite a lot of inarticulate stone walling survive. A ruined
wall and a reconstructed pointed arch are incorporated in an
outbuilding of the C18 farmhouse. The excavations of 1901
seem to point to a square plan with angle towers.

At MOORGREEN, a hamlet ½m. NW, estate cottages (Nos. 120–
122, 130–132, 134–136) built for Earl Cowper by *E. W. Godwin*
in 1872–7.* The MANSE, 1873, two storeys of brick with a
large gable on the side, is an influential *Godwin* design: the illustration of it in the *Building News* of 1874 led to the commission
for the first two prototype houses at Bedford Park, Chiswick.

BEAUVALE. *See* p. 66.

WATNALL HALL, 1 m. SE. Demolished in 1962.‡

## GRINGLEY-ON-THE-HILL

7090

A remarkable position on an E spur of the range of hills lying in
front of the Pennines. Wide views; the obvious strategical ad-
vantages were already understood when the prehistoric hill fortress was built on BEACON HILL. The village clusters round

---

* According to Mr Roger Dixon.

‡ It was a fine brick building of *c.* 1690 or 1700, the side of seven bays with
the usual two-bay projections l. and r., the usual central door with a segmental
pediment (here carried on Ionic half-columns and broken over them at the
sides), the usual modillion cornice and hipped roof (cf., for example, Ollerton
Hall). Fine contemporary interior with two panelled and pilastered rooms,
pedimented doorcases, a staircase with one turned, two twisted, balusters per
tread, and plaster ceilings with naturalistic wreaths of fruit and flowers. The
iron gates, which were moved from the flight of steps in front of the house
to the road entrance, have gone. They were by far the best in Notts.

the church, with some nice Georgian brick houses, and several farms with good barns, e.g. BEACON VIEW FARM, where an arch leads into the farmyard barns and stables. Above it a dovecote with a weathervane.

ST PETER AND ST PAUL. Norman blocked doorway on the N side of the tower, N arcade of tall circular shafts with simple moulded capitals and double-chamfered arches, pleasantly unrestored. E.E. also the remarkable PILLAR PISCINA, simply a colonnette with a capital of windswept stiff-leaf. Otherwise mostly Perp, especially the upper part of the tower, the usual pattern of east Notts. The north DOOR is classical, probably late C17.

WINDMILL. Four storeys with a skeleton cap and ball finial; c. 1830.

7070

## GROVE

ST HELEN. By *Hodgson Fowler*, 1882. Late Dec. – Good INCISED SLAB to Hugh Hercy, 1455, in civilian hat and armour, and wife with steeple headdress. Part recut.

GROVE HALL was demolished in 1951.*

6040

## GUNTHORPE

The manor belonged to Simon de Montfort. The CHURCH of 1849 is of no interest. GUNTHORPE HALL has the appearance of being a Georgian structure castellated and cemented early in the C19.

6050

## HALAM

ST MICHAEL. Norman chancel arch, very complete and satisfying: the orders with scalloped capitals, the arch with altogether four roll mouldings, three of them on the one major capital below. Contemporary probably the broad tower storeys without buttresses. Or are they C13? Truncated and very squat, with a modern pyramidal roof and ugly pinnacles. The triple-

---

* It had C16 or C17 work at the back, and *John Smythson*'s plan of 'Mr Nevelles: House at Grove' is preserved (*Archit. His.* III/3). Otherwise of 1762 by *Carr* of York: plain grey stuccoed seven-bay block, the SW front with a central canted bay, the other side with a recessed centre. *Repton* made improvements for Colonel Eyre in 1790.

chamfered tower arch seems C13 rather than C12. C13 the wall of the nave with one lancet window, the s arcade on rather broad heavy quatrefoil piers with double-chamfered arches, and the s chancel doorway with bands of chevron. Windows usual straight-headed Perp. – STAINED GLASS. In the tracery lights of a N chancel window, four good complete C14 figures: St Christopher, St Blaise, Adam naked and delving, Eve naked and spinning. The scenes lost from the main light are the Temptation of Adam and Christ blessing. – Three windows by *Morris & Co.*, 1919: nave N side, a two-light window with the Annunciation and Visitation and one lancet with St Michael; s aisle W, the Transfiguration and Ascension.

MANOR FARM. Plain stone house of 1795 with a fine medieval gargoyle built in just below eaves level at the corner. Stone barn and brick byre with dovecote over across the former farmyard.

HILL FARM. Late C17 brick (English bond) with projecting string courses and modillion eaves cornice: stone plinth. T-shaped plan with two low storeys and steep gables.

WATER MILL, N end of the village. C18, with a water-wheel, probably C19, and machinery *in situ*. Three-storey brick with lean-to wheelhouse and cottage adjoining.

(Two more DOVECOTES, one attached to a barn by Manor Farm, the other in the grounds of Halam House. Little to indicate their original use now the flight holes have been filled in. NS)

(GOLDHILL FARM, ½ m. N, on a fine site: rising ground falling away to the SE looking towards Southwell. Lofty three-storey brick house of 1810 with plain stone dressings. Monotonous but effective repetition of semicircular heads to the openings, i.e. four Venetian windows with Diocletian windows above flanking round-headed central windows and doorway. More Venetian windows in a two-storey wing. Extensive range of outbuildings ending in a large dovecote with nesting boxes of mud and stick from floor to ridge. NS)


## HALLOUGHTON

ST JAMES. Rebuilt by *Ewan Christian* (JPB) in 1879–82, except for the E wall with two lancet windows and the s doorway with simple chamfered hoodmould. – SCREEN. Low, with simple ogee tracery. – STAINED GLASS by *Barraud & Westlake*.

MANOR HOUSE. A prebendal house of the college of Southwell, incorporating a medieval tower house, rare in Notts. The only other examples are C14, in the ruins of Beauvale Priory and incorporated in Strelley Hall. The stone tower, at the N end of this rambling and fortuitously picturesque house, is entered by a raised door on the SE and lit by narrow slit windows in the SE and NE walls. The earliest fabric seems to be C13 (single lancet in the NW wall), but to the important first floor there is a two-light C14 window. The upper part of the stair to this floor remains in the thickness of the wall with arched openings in both faces, but the entrance is obscured by the addition between 1580 and 1630 of a hall with chamber over it on the SW side. In the later (c. 1790?) brick facing, some portions of the timber-framed two-and-a-half-bay hall, the carving on the timbers of a high quality unusual in Notts. SW of it more fragments of framing, including a large chimneybase, indicating what must have been the service wing, are incorporated in the 'new and neatly built farmhouse' seen by Byng in 1789. Stuccoed, with a plain seven-bay façade. Lawn in front enclosed by a ha-ha and a dovecote above stables in a two-storey brick wing. Some of the farmyard buildings have evidence of early brick-work.

# HARBY

ALL SAINTS. Cruciform church of some pretensions, built in 1875–6 by *J. T. Lee* of London. E.E. style, with a tall spire, a REREDOS by *Powell & Co.*, and STAINED GLASS in the E window by *Heaton & Butler* (JPB). The FONT is late medieval, octagonal, with shields in quatrefoil panels. – In the E wall of the tower a statue to Eleanor of Castile, who died in 1290 at the house of Richard de Weston (moated site E of the church). No trace of an Eleanor Cross here.

WINDMILL. Built c. 1877. Five storeys with a cogged cornice and cast-iron windows. No cap, but floors in good condition.

# HARWORTH

The old village with its biggish church in a field is now only an appendix to the north-westernmost colliery village of Notts – well planned on the lines of C20 city suburbs by *Philip Brundell*, 1922.

ALL SAINTS. Mostly rebuilt by *C. J. Neale* in 1869. The W tower only remains, the usual type of north and east Notts, with eight pinnacles. In the S wall a badly preserved cusped recess. The original chancel was Norman, see fragments of the old corbel table (cf. East Bridgford) and the badly worked-over chancel arch. Can the roll moulding with a kind of intermittent rustication (a pre-Serlio, pre-Gibbs motif) be in accordance with the original? The S door, Transitional, is also renewed. – FONT. C18, a big plain baluster.

## HAUGHTON 6070

Of the MANSION of the Stanhopes and, after 1537, the Holleses nothing survives. Yet it was one of the greatest in the county before the Holles family, by intermarrying with the Cavendishes, moved over to Welbeck Abbey and pulled it down in the C18. The style was Tudor (it was largely rebuilt in 1545); engravings of its exterior and a plan of 1618 by *John Smythson* for unexecuted additions (*Archit. His.* III/4) exist. Haughton Hall Farm lies on its site.

ST JAMES. This chapel or church became the domestic chapel of the Stanhopes in 1509. Before then it had been one more Notts village church of a type not at all rare. Now it is in ruins, in a secluded spot by the little river Maun, a mile E of the road. The nave walls, where they still stand, show Norman stonework everywhere, except on the N side, where a C14 arcade was blocked up when the aisle was pulled down. The Transitional chancel arch is half-filled by debris; it had moulded capitals. The Norman S doorway with its zigzag ornament lies on the ground.

½ m. S of Hall Farm and St James, the oldest DECOY (cf. the C18 Decoy House) in Notts, C17, and apparently contrived round the remains of a motte-and-bailey castle.[*]

SCHOOL, 1 m. E on the Retford Road. A modest brick building of 1692, added to in the C19.

## HAWKSWORTH 7040

ST MARY AND ALL SAINTS. Nave rebuilt in 1812–13, N aisle in 1837, and the chancel in 1851, when the rest was modernized. The brick tower, a pleasant oddity in Notts, is C17 still in the

---

[*] According to Professor Barley.

Gothic tradition. Lowest stage C13, stone. Built into the s wall
of the tower, a Norman TYMPANUM, very elaborate, exceedingly barbarous, but quite typical of provincial Anglo-Norman
sculpture of the early C12. In the tympanum proper a cross
flanked by two primitive figures. On one side an incomplete
inscription running over the lintel balanced awkwardly by a
large rosette on the other. It says that *Gauterus et uxor eius*
*Cecilina fecerunt facere ecclesiam istam* ... Along the outer edge
a border of rosettes and as a label (with label stops) a border
of stars. – CROSS SHAFT. Saxon, about 6 ft tall, with crosses
and interlace. – STAINED GLASS. E window by *Wailes*,
c. 1851.

(MANOR HOUSE. Stone, with a gabled entrance porch on the
long, low façade. Gothic glazing bars to later casements. Good
stone DOVECOTE of 1665. NS)

(MANOR FARM has a range of barns dated 1820, impressive in
size. Some queen-post roof trusses inside. Contemporary but
smaller-scale outbuildings at TOP FARM, s of the church. NS)


7050                            HAWTON

ALL SAINTS. The chancel is one of the most exciting pieces of
architecture in the country. It was built by the second Sir
Robert de Compton, who died in 1330 and was buried in it.*
It is 37 by 19 ft in size, with windows of three lights and an
E window of seven. The tracery is by no means smooth, but
rather wilful and perverse in its curves and counter-curves,
decidedly Lincolnshire style. Inside on the N side is a group
of N door, FOUNDER'S TOMB RECESS, and EASTER
SEPULCHRE under one horizontal cornice to which the pinnacles just reach up. These divide the three parts from each
other. On the brackets above the tops of the ogee arches of door
and recess stand figures. The recess is ogee-cusped, and every
cusp again sub-cusped. The effigy in the recess (cross-legged,
according to its date) is badly preserved and reminds us of what
the rest of the sculpture might be like if more and less skilful
and careful restorers had not touched it up from time to time.
The Easter Sepulchre is of a richness of appearance comparable
only with the screen at Southwell, which was no doubt made

* According to Mr Train. A memorial slab to the first Sir Robert † 1308
lies under the w tower, according to Mr George McHardy, who kindly cor-
rected the description of the Easter Sepulchre.

by the same masters. It is divided into three parts in width, with a main ogee canopy separated by pinnacles from side-pieces imitating flying buttresses. The main niche extends the width of all three. At the foot sit the sleeping soldiers in relief under nodding ogee arches, part of the Resurrection scene depicted on the back wall. The figure of Christ (in partly broken relief) is shown in the centre, rising from the tomb, with the three Maries, part of the traditional iconography, to his r. In the l. part, an ogival cusped niche in the back wall to hold the host (i.e. the body of Christ) during the Easter celebrations. Above to the l. and r. of the main canopy a relief strip of the Ascension with the Apostles gazing up at Christ. Only his feet appear (a not at all rare convention). This description can give no idea of the luxuriance of the decoration, the rank growth of crockets and finials, the patterned backgrounds with square panels (as at Southwell), rosettes, and more frequently flatly spreading thick nobbly leaves. And opposite all this, on the s side of the chancel, a display almost as glorious: the tripartite SEDILIA, again with ogee arches, surface patterning with leaves, fanciful capitals (a pelican, two boys picking grapes), and nine figures in all. They are, like those of the Sepulchre, not over-slim and of a soft rounded style with rippling draperies. Lincoln was probably the centre of the style (cf. the Easter Sepulchre there and at Heckington, Lincs). As well as the sedilia, a double PISCINA.

After the chancel a glance should be given to the late C13 N arcade of the nave, octagonal piers (but the E wall respond has a demi-column with a characteristic shaft-ring), double-chamfered arches, and a little dogtooth decoration. Other details are of the date of the chancel, especially the s arcade and the E window of the N aisle. It seems difficult not to assign a C14 date also to the w door with its blank flowing tracery. It is of course part of a much later tower, for the w tower, as ambitious of its kind as the chancel, was built in 1482 by Sir Thomas Molyneux of Hawton (and Sefton, Lancs). It has four-light windows on the bell-stage, a quatrefoil frieze, and eight, instead of the usual four, pinnacles (cf. East Markham, etc.). At about the same time the clerestory was added, and nave and aisle were battlemented. Restoration 1880–/ by *C. Hodgson Fowler* (JPB), – SCREEN. Of twelve slim bays plus entrance; Perp. – BENCHES. Plain and trustworthy. – (STAINED GLASS. Just a few old grisaille bits. RH).

CIVIL WAR REDOUBT, 300 yds NW of the church. This well-preserved earthwork, 375 by 270 ft overall, is one of the works of the besieging Parliamentarian army in 1645–6. It was established within the remains of a C15 moated site of the Molyneux family. The Hawton redoubt is one of the few visible remnants of the works which encircled Newark at a distance of 2 to 3 miles during the two great sieges (cf. Farndon, Balderton, Coddington, South Muskham).

## HAYTON

7080

ST PETER. Outside the village to the SW. The oldest parts are the late C12 S arcade and the S door. The arcade is on circular piers, one with a moulded capital, the second with upright leaves exactly as at Worksop Priory, and both with double-chamfered arches of an early design. The S door round-arched but with a zigzag of a kind of oval leaves on the hoodmould and a little dogtooth otherwise, again exactly as at Worksop. The window tracery mostly early C14 (the same date as the ashlar-faced W tower). S porch with a stone roof on transverse ribs (cf. St Mary, Nottingham). Trefoil-headed PISCINA in the chancel. – FONT. C14, octagonal, with large leaves in the panels, completely re-tooled. – STAINED GLASS. E window 1877 by *Kempe*. – MONUMENTS. Three effigies looking early C14, as far as their desperate condition allows one to judge.

## HEADON

7090

ST PETER. In an exposed position on the escarpment. Sturdy, short W tower, E.E., the top rebuilt in the 1885 restoration by *G. Somers Clarke Jun.* Also E.E. the arcades (see especially the NW respond and the very similar capitals of the octagonal piers). Double-chamfered arches. The rest of the church Perp (aisles, chancel, clerestory). – PULPIT. Nice, with a tester on two wild-man brackets, so-called Jacobean, but may of course be later.
Of HEADON HALL (the seat of the Wastneys, which Throsby says was designed by *Sir Thomas Hewett, see* Shireoaks Hall) all that survives is a fine avenue of trees in Headon Wood, ½ m. NW.
The parish is Headon-cum-Upton.

HEMPSHILL HALL *see* NUTHALL

## HICKLING

6020

St Luke. Stately ashlar-faced tower (rebuilt 1873), with the quatrefoil frieze below the crenellation which is usual in this neighbourhood. Chancel rebuilt 1845, general restoration 1886. Nave and four-bay arcade to N and S aisles, octagonal piers and moulded capitals, and two-light windows; C14. – Font. Octagonal, with plain shields in the panels (cf. Colston Bassett). – Font cover. 1665. Very simple village carpenter's work. – Fragments of a screen. The openings were depressed four-centred. – Bench ends, poppyhead, good. – Poor box. Small; of 1685, but still not at all classical. – Brass candelabra. Two in the chancel. – Stained glass. Small late medieval bits in the chancel E and N windows. – South door, with accomplished C13 iron hinges and scrolls. – Monuments. By far the most remarkable relic in the church is the Saxon coffin lid with a cross and much wild interlacing, and also two beasts' heads (dated mid C10 by T. D. Kendrick). – Outside the S aisle, an early C14 coffin lid with a foliated cross and naturalistic leaves just turning undulated. – An unusually rewarding number of engraved C18 and early C19 slate headstones in the churchyard, for example to John Smith † 1725 with inscription:

> This world's a city full of crooked streets
> Death is the market-place where all men meets.
> If life were merchandise yt men could buy
> The rich would often live and poor men die.

Hickling was apparently the home of the anonymous engraver (or engravers) who produced so many stones in the archaic style of John Smith's, with an angel in shallow relief across the top (genuine folk-art). His products are widespread in the Vale of Belvoir. Also many outstanding examples of *Charles*, *Heywood*, and *Sparrow*, and a good early stone by *Stephen Staveley* to John Hopkinson † 1728 (mwb).

### HIGH MARNHAM see MARNHAM

### HOCKERTON

7050

St Nicholas. The aisleless nave has a Norman window. Chancel arch also Norman and completely unmoulded.

Another window in the nave is C13; the chancel was redone in the C14 (see the windows and the recess with a niche, probably an EASTER SEPULCHRE). The date of the lower part of the W tower is not apparent; the upper part is C14, ashlar, with diagonal buttresses and battlements. (Restored in 1876 by *James Fowler* of Louth. RH) – BENCH END. Marked 1599, and M.O., pretty, very simply symmetrical shape, just with some widely spaced pairs of horizontal rows of carved indents. – (STAINED GLASS. E window by *Ward & Hughes*, 1876: nothing special. RH)

(HOCKERTON MANOR. A cottagey exterior but still exhibiting some diapered brickwork. Inside, a four-bay timber-frame and axial chimneystack (much re-used timber). NS)

6080

# HODSOCK PRIORY

A fictitious name. There was no priory here, but there was a large moated manor house, dating from *c.* 1250–3, that belonged to the Clifton family at the time that the GATEHOUSE was built, which is the only feature earlier than the C19. It is of brick with a diaper pattern, dates from the early C16, and is reached across a new bridge over a moat. The far side has the usual polygonal stair-turrets, the near side only two flat projections, but these rise like turrets above the general parapet level. In the piece between them the archway, with three-light windows above and a nice corbel table as the crowning motif. To the l. and r. three two-light windows above each other. In each turret a newel staircase, one with stone treads, the other with wooden ones. In the room over the archway some early Renaissance plasterwork, interesting because isolated from Court influence and yet of quite high quality. There is nothing anywhere nearby with which to compare it. Above a low diapered dado, pilaster-like strips with *all'antica* reliefs linked at window-head level by arched bands of cable moulding.

The house lies at r. angles to the gatehouse. The oldest part, facing SW, looks as if it is early C19: simple decorated cornices in the two main rooms.* The exterior was remodelled by *Devey* in 1873–6 for Mrs Mellish, who filled in the segmental window heads with brick-nogging and added corbelling as on the gatehouse. At the same time Devey replaced an earlier

---

*No sign of *Ambrose Poynter's* Gothic alterations of 1829–33 for Mrs Chambers.

(C18?) house at r. angles with the gatehouse with a larger one, Jacobean in style, with diaper brickwork and nice decorated chimneys. Not very interesting, but a conscientious response to the gatehouse (cf. his additions to Sudbury Hall, Derbyshire, 1874).

## HOLBECK                    5070

A Welbeck estate village.

ST WINIFRED.* 1913–16 by *L. Ambler* for the Duke of Portland. Towerless Norman-style stone church based on Steetley nearby in Derbyshire. – Contemporary STAINED GLASS with Faith, Hope, and Charity by *H. Hendrie of* Edinburgh. – MONUMENTS. Tablet to Major Lord William Augustus Cavendish Bentinck † 1902 by *Eric Gill*, 1929, erected 1939. – Also by *Gill*, tombstone to Lady Ottoline Morrell † 1938.

## HOLME                      8050

ST GILES. In its way one of the most remarkable churches in the county, for with the exception of the lower part of the E wall with a chevron string course and the N wall, all ashlared and with an E.E. doorway which dates it C13, and with the exception of the W steeple with a low broach-spire (one tier of small dormers close to the top), everything is Early Tudor. It is true that the chancel masonry may be even earlier than the C13, but that makes no difference to what the eye really takes in. The rebuilding of most of the church was due to a Lancashire man, John Barton, who had grown rich on the wool trade with France, died in 1491, and lies buried with his wife between the chancel which he renovated (see the N corbels carved with 53 his merchant's mark and the arms of the Staple of Calais) and the S chancel chapel which he built. It is said that there was an inscription in a window of his house at Holme which read as follows:

> I thanke God, and ever shall,
> It is the sheepe hath payed for all.

The Barton MONUMENT is in two tiers, with a rotting corpse below (cf. Wollaton) and two well-carved effigies above. The

* Information about the church kindly given by Mr H. V. Radcliffe.

E window of the church was filled with GLASS commemorating John Barton's generosity. The fragments were skilfully pieced together by Messrs. *King* of Norwich for Nevil Truman, and added to them we can see two delicious early C14 quatrefoils with the Coronation of the Virgin from Annesley, some C13 grisaille bits from Salisbury, and some C16 and C17 figure bits from Beauvais. The chancel and chancel chapel are wide and airy, with four-light and five-light Perp windows of no special ingenuity. The S aisle also belongs to Barton's time. It is separated from the nave by piers of four shafts and four hollows, just as at Newark (where the workmen perhaps came from). The nave capitals are plain, those of the chancel arcade decorated with individual leaves. A two-storeyed S porch was added, with much ornament and (probably carved *c.* 1550) a proud frieze of shields over the door, diagonal buttresses, and gargoyles. (The whole church was admirably restored in 1932 by Nevil Truman and his architect *R. Harley Smith*: a model of SPAB anti-scrape principles. RH) – The ROOFS of the nave and aisle are simple. – ROOD SCREEN and PARCLOSE SCREEN also comparatively simple. – TOWER SCREEN with Jacobean urns made out of pew panels from Attenborough. – PULPIT, incorporating Jacobean panels from Dean Hole's pulpit at Caunton. – ALTAR RAILS. C17. – CANDELABRA. Of *c.* 1690–1710. – BENCH ENDS with poppyheads, in the Lady Chapel, all intact as in *c.* 1485. At the E end of the S aisle one with much finer tracery.

A ROMAN MARCHING-CAMP lay close to the Trent, dating presumably from the earliest years of the Roman conquest.

## HOLME PIERREPONT

The church and hall form a good group a little way from the village.

ST EDMUND. Externally the impression is of a Perp ashlared tower with spire and a classical church with a certain Gothic hangover. The S aisle has three-light windows with posthumous Gothic tracery. Its W and E ends are gabled as if they had pediments; its S porch is emphasized by Tuscan columns with a bulgy cornice. The date of all this is 1666. But inside there is a complete E.E. arcade with quatrefoil piers, double-chamfered arches, and corbel heads. In 1878–81 *Hine* inserted the Dec

the chancel.* – FONT. C15, octagonal, with shields; no quatrefoils. – STAINED GLASS. E window 1913 by *Powell & Sons*
(RH). – MONUMENTS. Plenty, and some of great interest.
Recumbent stone effigy of *c.* 1300. – Upper half of a knight,
alabaster, late C14. – *Ex-situ* brass to a lady (effigy only), *c.* 1385.
– Sir Henrie Pierrepont †1499, a good, well-preserved alabaster
effigy, with calm face; shields in lozenge panels on the tomb-
chest. – Sir Henry P., 1615, husband of Frances Cavendish,
daughter of Bess of Hardwick. *John Smythson*, the son of Bess's
architect Robert Smythson, supplied the design (*Archit. His.*
III/5). Alabaster tomb-chest with seven children, upright and
stiff. The effigy recumbent on the tomb-chest; background
with inscription elaborately framed by strapwork and two
columns. – Princess Gertrude of Kingston † 1649, without
effigy. – John Oldham, the poet, † 1683, just a tablet against 80
a pier, surrounded by swags, etc., but as strikingly good as
work by Grinling Gibbons. – Duke of Kingston, *c.* 1806, by
*Michael Taylor* of York. – Hon. Evelyn P., 1802 by *Flaxman*. –
William Saltren † 1811, with a profile of a woman reading,
signed by *Flaxman*. Gothic surround no doubt later. – Lady
Sophia P. 1823 by *Pierre Bazzanti* of Florence.

HOLME PIERREPONT HALL. The red-brick S entrance range 58
(until 1975 encased in early C19 stucco) with gateway and flanking towers is the principal surviving part of a great early C16
courtyard house, built and still owned by descendants of the
Pierrepont family.‡ The N range, which contained the hall, was
rebuilt by Robert Pierrepont, first Earl of Kingston, in 1628
and demolished in the 1730s. It was rebuilt again in the 1870s
and is of no special interest. Of the C17 house Thoroton drew
a bulbous cupola at the NE angle, but all that now remains is
a projection on the E side with stone quoins (cf. Doddington,
Lincs, which may have been a 'Smythson' house; *see* the church
for a Smythson connection). Next to it a Georgian block of *c.*
1740 with a bow window on the ground floor. The rest of the
E side much altered. On the first floor a large drawing room,
with a plasterwork ceiling of *c.* 1660, brought from Wheelergate, Nottingham, awaiting restoration. At the N end a fine
staircase of about the same date resited here *c.* 1740: it has a
pierced and carved foliated scroll balustrade typical of its date,

---

* According to Mr Train.

‡ The bricks must have been made locally, though the brickmakers, who
also built the house, may have come from Norfolk, where the family had estates
round King's Lynn in the C15 and C16.

with low reliefs carved on the newels and closed strings (cf. the more luxuriant example at Thrumpton).

The SOUTH RANGE, with lodgings for retainers of the kind characteristic of late medieval houses (e.g. Haddon, Derbyshire; Thornbury, Glos), is the most interesting, not least because it is one of the earliest brick buildings known in the county.* Wide four-centred arch in the middle, and l. and r. of it four wide blank arches like fireplaces, of no known function but backing on to the fireplaces in each room inside. Flanking the gateway, three-storey towers containing garderobes ending in two-storey wings. One small ventilation window survives. Only one original window on the ground floor of the s front: stone-mullioned, with arched heads to the three lights. The brick crenellation was evidently raised to conceal the roofs *c.* 1800, when the windows were altered to sashes and stucco applied. The interior is divided by close-studded partitions with four-centred doorways into rooms varying in size but each with a fireplace and garderobe. On the l. of the entrance the lodgings remained unaltered on both floors. Two stone fireplaces with four-centred arches and moulded jambs. At the E end the inserted ceilings have been removed to reveal the stud-partition rising to the peak of the medieval roof, which has cusped braces, unusual in the east Midlands which did not possess a local tradition of high-quality carpentry (*see* Introduction, p. 48). Garden wall of 1628 with stone coping and an uncommon bond of brick. The elaborate formal garden with clipped box hedges dates from the 1870s.

In the village early C19 Manvers ESTATE HOUSING (cf. Budby and Radcliffe-on-Trent).

A NATIONAL WATERSPORTS CENTRE and country park has been carved out of a chain of gravel pits on the s bank of the Trent by Notts County Council (*H. J. Lowe*, Planning Officer, 1969–73, *Gelsthorpe & Savidge*, architects, 1971–3) and the sports council. Landscape gardening on the grandiose public scale.

Pagan Anglo-Saxon CEMETERY of the C5–6.

## HOVERINGHAM

ST MICHAEL. 1865 by *William Knight* of Nottingham. Multicoloured red brick with stripes of yellow brick and plate tracery.

---

* Date of building unknown, but Sir William P. received a licence to empark in 1518.

w bellcote. Heavy timber porch. TYMPANUM early Norman: St Michael, two dragons, and the Agnus Dei, very close in style to the tympanum at Southwell, that is close to the 'Urnes style' of the Vikings. On the lintel a strip of beasts interlace with St Peter and another nimbed ecclesiastic l. and r. (cf. at Normanton-on-Trent a prebend of Southwell). – FONT. Primitive Norman, but obviously not in its original state. – MONUMENT. Sir Robert Goushill † 1403 and his wife, Elizabeth Fitzalan, widow of Thomas Mowbray, Earl of Nottingham and Duke of Norfolk. She wears a coronet to denote her former rank. Alabaster, the effigies (mutilated at head and foot) on a tomb-chest with shields on quatrefoils.

MILL FARM MILL. A three-storey corn mill complete with wheel (undershot with wooden paddles) and machinery.

## HUCKNALL

5040

ST MARY MAGDALEN. A large church right in the (unattractive) Market Square (a rare thing in Notts). The church was very much smaller when the Victorians started on it. It consisted only of tower, nave and chancel, and N aisle. The S aisle was added in 1872–4 (by *Evans & Jolly*: JPB), the two unusually long transepts in 1887–8 by *R. C. Clarke*. What is left of the old fabric is so restored that it looks as new as the new parts. Clarke also moved the whole E end further E. Only the W tower still exhibits clearly its C12–13 work (unbuttressed, with lancet windows). The top stage, ashlar-faced with battlements and pinnacles, is C14. The N arcade was originally C13 (tall octagonal piers, moulded capitals, double-chamfered arches). The front of the S porch is an excellent piece of heavy C14 timber construction, the close-studded sides renewed. But all this is now forgotten in the C19 work, and of course for most visitors in Byron. His MEMORIAL is a simple tablet with a profile medallion above. Visually the predominant feature of the church is, however, neither the medieval building nor Lord Byron, but the twenty-five STAINED GLASS windows by *Kempe*, of his best, early period, beginning with the E window of 1883, and then mostly 1888–95, with his dark blues and brownish reds, his plenty of vegetation, and his unmistakable faces. If you want to study late Victorian stained glass at its most competent (not the genius, the innovations, the aesthetic purity of Morris, but the accepted High Church medium), Hucknall is one of the best

places to go to. – PAINTING. Christ and the woman taken
in adultery, by *Maclise*, 1869, that is at the very end of his
career.

ST JOHN EVANGELIST, Nottingham Road. 1876–7 by *Bakewell
& Bromley*.

HOLY CROSS (R.C.), Watnall Road. By *Reynolds & Scott* of
Manchester. Like the parish church, the glory of this church
is the STAINED GLASS. In the E window a large figure by
*J. E. Nuttgens*, 1960, in the last of the Arts and Crafts tradition.
In the Lady Chapel, the more vigorous contemporary work of
*Patrick Reyntiens*: nineteen panels, 1961–2.

PUBLIC LIBRARY, Market Place. 1887; Renaissance style.

Former COFFEE TAVERN AND INSTITUTE, now shops. A
modest building of 1884 by *Watson Fothergill*. The Duke of
Portland, whose cousin established the Ossington Coffee Palace
at Newark, leased the site.

Some framework-knitters' cottages on the E side of ALBERT
STREET (three-storey with long windows on the first floor at
the rear). At the end of the street on Cunnery, one with a stone
front and brick sides, three-storey, with a knitters' window on
the top floor. On the w side of the town in NOTTINGHAM
ROAD, a shortened terrace of three altered knitters' cottages,
one still with its long first-floor window.

NEWSTEAD PITHEAD BATHS, 2 m. NW. 1934 by *A. J. Saise*.
One of the many modern pithead baths erected by the Miners'
Welfare Commission.

FORGE MILL. *See* Bestwood.


HYSON GREEN
*see* NOTTINGHAM p. 255


7050                    KELHAM

Church and Hall close together, which in this case means that
the grey, moderate-sized church at first recedes into insignificance
behind Scott's baronial mansion.

ST WILFRID. Within the church the medieval work is very much
less conspicuous than the C18 Lexington Chapel added to the
s of the chancel, with round-headed windows and with coupled
niches inside on the w and E. The contrast of Ancaster and
Mansfield stone should be noted. The chapel holds the free-
87 standing MONUMENT to Robert Sutton Lord Lexington † 1723

and Lady Lexington † 1703. They are shown semi-reclining (that is, like Plumier and Scheemakers' effigy of the Duke of Buckingham † 1721), dos-à-dos, with long, far from pious inscriptions ('By his Negotiation King Philip was prevail'd upon to renounce all Claim to the Succession of ye Crown of France', etc.). Very competent marble figures by *William Palmer*, 1726. – One more monument in the church: to a daughter of the seventh Earl of Scarborough † 1864, just to show that the much patronized *Gaffin* of Regent Street could at that date work in the Gothic taste as well as the classical. – The church itself has Perp arcades of a profile simplifying that of East Markham; the arches are in accordance. Old beams in the N aisle. Chancel arch and tower arch, the whole W tower, the N and S porches, and the windows also Perp. The chancel E window by the Holme–Muskham masons. Everything embattled, which always shows late medieval activity. Restoration by *Hodgson Fowler*, 1874. – FONT. Simple large bowl, just with roll mouldings top and bottom, yet said to be after 1660. – SCREENS. Late Perp chancel screen with elaborate small panel tracery: parclose screen slightly more simple. – STAINED GLASS. Only small medieval fragments, N aisle.

KELHAM HALL (Newark District Council H.Q.). In 1857 the Palladian house of *c.* 1730 by *John Sanderson* burnt down, leaving only the rather dull Jacobean-style SERVICE WING built by *Salvin* in 1844–6, which survives on the N side of the present house. *George Gilbert Scott*, who at the time of the fire was making minor alterations to the house for John Manners-Sutton, M.P. for Newark, was given the opportunity to rebuild it.* He made his plans in 1858, the builder *William Cubitt & Co.* laid the foundations in 1859, and the work, as far as it was ever to progress, was almost finished by 1861. Manners-Sutton must have underestimated the cost of building a house that would rival the splendours of those in the Dukeries or of Harlaxton and Belvoir just outside the county to the E and S, for the planned grand staircase, the conservatory, and many details (e.g. the clock for the clock tower, and many marble columns for the interior) were never completed. Eventually (in 1898) the mortgage was foreclosed and the estate sold.

1857, the year of the fire, was also the year in which Scott published his *Remarks on Secular Domestic Architecture, Present and Future*. The house therefore is of prime importance for an

* Manners-Sutton may have heard Scott when he lectured in Newark in 1855. Scott based the first two chapters of his *Remarks* on this lecture.

understanding of Scott's ideas on the use of Gothic forms in
98  secular building. The exterior is entirely asymmetrical, that is
picturesque, tall, of unattractive red Retford brick with unattractive Ancaster stone dressings. The ornamental motifs are
C13–14, as a contemporary source (F. O. Morris) says, 'viewed
on a broad basis, and freely admitting all which can be usefully
learnt from the architecture, whether of England, France or
Italy, tho' ... as Italy is the birthplace of most modern domestic
architecture (especially) many useful hints ... might be
obtained from its productions'. The interior is equally freely
and consistently Gothic but rather C12–13, that is partly with
round arches. Like his later and famous Midland Hotel, St Pancras (1865–74), the most impressive thing about Kelham is the
irregular skyline, with its three 'grandiloquent' towers. Also like
St Pancras, the façades are otherwise weakly composed with a
plethora of different motifs on a similar scale and no strong
accent or personal hallmark. There are nine different window
designs on the E and S fronts and fourteen on the W, which well
illustrate Scott's point in his *Remarks*: 'That the number of
changes that may be rung on this one feature, the windows, are
as inexhaustible as they are charming!' Despite this variety the
N side still has the flatness and squareness of his first design
(1856) for the Foreign Office. Ornamental buttresses distinguishing the chapel and large oriel indicating the main bedroom in Pugin's 'form expressing function' tradition.

The entrance is on the N side through a covered carriage court
originally with open arcades, unimpressive externally but exotic
within, with Italian Gothic stripes of red brick and Ancaster
stone. It leads into the N staircase hall and thence into one of
the rib-vaulted corridors that form the N–S spine of the building
on both main floors. The even grander staircase was to have
been at the S end of the corridor. The main rooms, all rib-
vaulted and some with a little of their painted decoration, open
off the corridor to r. and l. On the r. the chapel, on the l. the
most complete and splendid rooms, the music room and the
drawing room. The two-storey MUSIC ROOM (now Council
Chamber) opens directly from the corridor by a cathedral-like
six-bay arcade complete with triforium. Here, as elsewhere
in the house, the capitals, carved by *Brindley* of *Farmer &
Brindley*, are naturalistic, the one thing in which the Victorians
thought they could do better than the Middle Ages, outdoing
Southwell by means of scientific progress as it were. On the
opposite wall, in Scott's strange admixture of the ecclesiastical

and the secular, a baronial fireplace. The DRAWING ROOM is the 'chapter house' to this 'cathedral', with much of its effect created by the mirrors between the windows reflecting the central column and the muted brown and gold flower-painted decoration. The fittings, doorcases, etc., are carefully detailed and well made throughout, and even the humblest bedrooms at the top of the house have massive stone door surrounds. As much attention was paid to practical matters. Firstly the whole house is fireproof, so the rib-vaulting in the main rooms is of brick or brick and stone and the rest of the house is of the iron and brick factory type construction which Scott was not abashed to reveal. Staircases are of iron and stone, floors of marble, tile, or cement. Neither was comfort neglected. Central heating (by hot air through wrought-iron grilles in the floor), gas (from Kelham's own gasworks), and water (from a tank in one of the towers) were provided, and the hollow newel of the tower staircase conceals a luggage lift.

On the N side of the house is the QUADRANGLE built in 1924–5 by the Society of the Sacred Mission who bought Kelham in 1919. Their architect was *Charles Clayton Thompson* of the Derby partnership of *Currey & Thompson* and the buildings are in their successful Arts-and-Crafts-based style (cf. St Mary, Buxton). Thompson's steep-pitched, cottagey roofs and chapel dome make an acceptable foil to Scott's uneven pile. Most interesting is the CHAPEL, built in 1927–8 and frankly imitative of the Byzantine style. Never completed, it is still weatherboarded where the N and S aisles were meant to be. Its brick and concrete interior was once very powerful in its emotional appeal, with a flying brick arch supporting rood figures by *Sargent Jagger* reflected in polished black floor tiles, and with fittings by *Thompson*. Now stripped for its secular purpose as an assembly hall, it looks dismal. Only a few pews remain.*

E of the service wing an arcaded SUMMER HOUSE which looks like *Salvin*'s, but apparently has some of Scott's spare marble columns. Near the main gate the half-timbered HOME FARM.

# KEYWORTH

6030

ST MARY MAGDALENE. The tower of the church is unique in the county. It is broad and square, with originally large ground-

---

* The rood figures have gone to the Sacred Mission's house at Milton Keynes. The later Madonna is at Southwell.

floor openings in the N and S walls (cf. Wollaton). Large Perp
W window, and on the second stage double windows separated
by an odd kind of lesene or pilaster strip with blank two-light
panelling, so long and slim that it seems like reeding or fluting.
The corner buttresses are also panelled in this way and have,
where they are set off, gables in addition. The tower ends with
a gargoyle frieze and a solid parapet, and on it rises, far recessed,
a solid octagonal upper stage with a short spire (a curious, aesthetically not very refined effect but lively and original). Comparisons with France have been suggested. Comparisons with
Hertfordshire spires are perhaps less far-fetched (Baldock,
Ashwell). The church has an early C14 chancel and later C14
N arcade. – (STAINED GLASS. An early work by *Burlison &
Grylls*, described as 'very fine' in the *British Architect* of 1874.
RH)

INSTITUTE OF GEOLOGICAL SCIENCES, on the E side of the
village. Designed in 1965–9 as the Mary Ward Teacher Training College by *Bartlett & Gray*, who are converting it (1978)
into a centre for the institute.

BARN, adjoining No. 31 MAIN STREET. Timber-framed with
a rubble plinth and herringbone brick infill. Dated 1665 and
a rare survival in south Notts; restored in 1977–8 by *F. W. B.
Charles*.


*8040*                       KILVINGTON

ST MARY. 1852. Placed entirely on its own on a hillside, with
a picturesque beauty in the Capability Brown sense. Yet it was
the medieval church this one replaced, not the Victorian architect whoever he was, that determined the site.


*4040*                        KIMBERLEY

ST WILFRID. The depopulated parish was united with Greasley
in 1448. The present church (stone, E.E style, with apsidal
chancel and bellcote) was built in 1847 for the new parish,
revived by brewing and framework knitting.

UNITED METHODIST FREE CHURCH. 1890 by *R. C. Sutton*
of Nottingham, who also designed the mortuary chapel in the
nearby cemetery, 1883.

WINDMILLS, to the N at Giltbrook. Ruins of two stone round-
houses, all that remains of three post-mills known as Lawn
Mills.

# KINGSHAUGH HOUSE see DARLTON

## KINGSTON-ON-SOAR

ST WILFRID. Mostly of 1900 by *R. Creed*,* of no intrinsic interest, but housing the most remarkable chantry chapel in the county: the BABINGTON CHANTRY of *c.* 1540. It is not in its original position, and the tomb-chest is missing. Parts of this are displayed to the W of the monument itself, which is a canopy on four columns. The columns are short and thick and covered all over with a network of hexagonal panels in which crowd Gothic tracery and little figures, much damaged. One row was a Dance of Death, the others saints and figures in contemporary dress. The capitals stick out excessively far and have babes and tuns (rebus!) as their decoration. The arches are four-centred and the vaults ribbed and provided with pendants. The top is battlemented and pinnacled. Inside against the E wall is a relief of the Last Judgement, no doubt the relief of the chantry altar and a late appearance of a religious scene connected with a tomb. Its carving is better preserved and shows how inferior the aesthetic qualities of the sculptors were. The whole, in spite of the date, has only a trace of the Renaissance: on three soffits at either end with typical Italianate arabesques and, at the E end, tragic masks and satyrs.‡ Altogether uncouth, if thoroughly meaty, provincial work.

KINGSTON HALL.§ 1842–6 by *Blore*, in his dour neo-Elizabethan style, stone, wealthy but dull. Built for Edward Strutt (created Lord Belper in 1856), a grandson of the great industrialist Jedediah Strutt of Belper in Derbyshire, and sold by Lord Belper in 1976. Now to be turned into flats. The main façades are of three storeys and five bays, the end bays emphasized by gabled projections. On the entrance front an elaborate porch with turrets and buttresses (not shown in Blore's sketch of the house). At r. angles to this front a long two-storey office and stable wing linked to the W with a large conservatory, also in Elizabethan style. It was Strutt who commissioned Loudon

---

* The nave, S aisle, and tower are the new parts. The chancel (with E.E. SEDILIA) and chancel aisle are dated by an inscription, *AB Anno Dei 1538 BF*, i.e. about contemporary with the chantry (R. Alvey).

‡ According to Mr Stanley Luff.

§ Mr Hugh Mellor kindly amended this description.

to design Derby's Arboretum, so a conservatory is not a surprising feature.*

In the VILLAGE Strutt built a symmetrical group of semi-detached gabled brick cottages, each pair of slightly different design.

MANOR FARM. Large mid-C18 farmhouse, a double-pile of two storeys and five bays, typical of the county. Open pedimented doorcase.

## KINOULTON

6030

ST LUKE. Built by the Earl of Gainsborough in 1792–3. Very red brick, round-headed windows, three on each side, and a W tower with a classical cornice below the very low pitched roof. Inside, a W gallery and a lower 3/8 chancel. The chancel is nicely, domestically panelled. – The ORGAN may well be contemporary and is Gothic.

RECTORY. 1849 by *T. C. Hine.*

OLD CHURCHYARD, on the hill W of the village, close to the Fosse Way (A46). Nothing now left except a few slate HEADSTONES, including a particularly fine one to Patrick Dee † 1703.

MOAT, 1 m. S of the village. Rectangular shaped earthwork with remains, revealed by aerial photography, of buildings to its N and S. It has been suggested that it was a grange of either Launde Abbey, Leics, or Swineshead, Lincs.

## KIRKBY-IN-ASHFIELD

4050

The village centre of Kirkby has been spoilt, but it is still a pleasant surprise in the colliery drabness of the neighbourhood. The Manor House of 1622 opposite the church was replaced in 1964 by an estate of nondescript bungalows.‡

The church (ST WILFRID) was unfortunately mostly destroyed by fire in 1907 and replaced by a building without special merit (by *L. Ambler*). The only early work is C13 masonry

---

* A large pagan ANGLO-SAXON CEMETERY of the C6 was found when the garden was laid out in 1840–4. The few surviving cremation urns are in Nottingham University Museum (M. W. Barley).

‡ The C16 and C17 Kirkby Hardwick and Kirkby Old Hall further out were also destroyed in the 1960s.

in the chancel walls and two C15 buttresses to the aisles. The broach-spire dates from 1863–7. – (STAINED GLASS in the E window, 1908, and another of 1911, by *Powell & Sons*. RH)

The RECTORY on the other hand is a perfect specimen of the early C18 (1717). Garden front of five bays, brick, with a hooded porch on scrolly brackets. The N side, although spoilt by paint and a modern lean-to, has some good original windows. Elizabethan S wing demolished in 1964.

Rural survival opposite the church: a stone PINFOLD.

CASTLE HILL CAMP. Small, rectangular, immediately S of the church, with two entrances. The remains of the C13 Stoteville Castle.

BENTINCK PITHEAD BATHS. 1934 by *A. J. Saise*. The pithead baths put up by the Miners' Welfare Commission are amongst the most gratifying modern structures in England between the two wars.

To the S, at Kirkby Woodhouse, GENERAL BAPTIST CHAPEL, 1754, sadly altered in 1866, when the brick walls were rendered and heightened, the arches of the front windows made square, and the porch added (CS).


# KIRKBY WOODHOUSE *see* KIRKBY-IN-ASHFIELD


# KIRKLINGTON                               6050

ST SWITHUN. The distinguishing feature is the C17 brick tower erected on medieval ground-courses, with a big staircase-turret. The small windows still Tudor in style. Top storey later. The body of the church consists of nave and chancel. S doorway Norman, S porch late C13. Chancel 1873–4. Built into the S vestry wall a rudely carved C12 lintel (cf. Hawksworth tympanum). – FONT. Norman, with blank intersected arches on short columns. – SOUTH DOOR. C17 panelling, rectangles within rectangles.

KIRKLINGTON HALL (Rodney School), N of the church. Called in 1797 'a large modern building', though this was the result of a thorough remodelling of an earlier one. It was then embattled and had octagonal tower-like wings. Now mostly of 1904, stuccoed, with a strong Jacobean flavour. Two-storey porte-cochère, little turret, glazed porch with balcony over on the side, and other bits of cheer. (Very little of the C18 house can be deciphered, except a fine ceiling and fireplace of *c.* 1775 in what was probably the Withdrawing Room. Nothing earlier, unless a section of exposed brickwork and timber-stud partition is accepted as genuine. NS)

HIGHFIELD FARMHOUSE, on the Southwell Road. Late C17. L-plan with projecting string courses, etc. Two-storey with attics.

(SCHOOL, on the Hockerton Road. 1840, plain stuccoed, with gabled and pedimented ends projecting either side of the entrance porch. NS)

(THE MILL and MILL FARM. A pleasant group either side of the road from Southwell where it crosses the bridge over the river Greet to enter the village. The Mill is C19, three-storeyed, with a hoist overhanging the road. Mill Farm, double-pile C18, has sash-windows: plain but well-proportioned. NS)

## KIRTON

6060

HOLY TRINITY. Much C13 work inside: N arcade (circular piers, simply moulded capitals, moulded arch with nailhead), chancel arch, N doorway, S porch doorway. Perp W tower of the usual east and south Notts type. Some windows with plate tracery, some Perp. All restored in 1865. – STAINED GLASS. Many minor fragments of the C15.

HALL FARM. The L-shaped house facing the road is C17, probably built *c.* 1630 by William Clarkson. Very plain but interesting because an early example of brick facing, bonded to thick walls of rough skerry. The windows look later, *c.* 1680–90.

HIGHFIELD FARM. A gabled C17 brick house with a banded course and cogged eaves cornice cf. Edingley Manor Farm.

## KNEESALL

7060

ST BARTHOLOMEW. A rich W tower of *c.* 1425 with the battlements developed into gabled and traceried little showpieces with animals at each corner and angel figures on each side instead of gargoyles. The chancel is probably contemporary with the chancel arch (angel corbels and an E window of five lights in the most representational Perp style). Earlier the nave, with slightly differing N and S arcades on octagonal piers and with moulded capitals and arches. Aisle windows Perp, arched heads to N aisle, straight heads to S. Perp clerestory. – Fragments of an Anglo-Saxon SHAFT, carved on one side with interlace work; nothing special. – BENCH ENDS. Eleven of the C15, of the symmetrical shape and nothing special either, though at least one finial is carved with a face.

OLD HALL FARM. At first glance it is not obvious, because of the modern roof and windows, that this is one of the earliest brick houses in Notts: first half of the C16 (English bond) (cf. Holme Pierrepont, Hodsock gatehouse). It is important in two respects: the constructional (rather than decorative) use of terracotta, and the plan. The intact sills, jambs, and heads of the original mullioned windows show that they were of terracotta. Also constructed with blocks of terracotta the newel staircase. Its use dates the house to c. 1515–40 (cf. Layer Marney, Essex) and is unique in Notts secular buildings. The early date makes it the first example of the lobby-entrance type of plan, i.e. with a lobby opening into a room on either side of a central chimneystack and staircase. Here, there is another room on the r. This plan, characteristic of modest farmhouses and cottages, was no doubt convenient for hunting boxes and occasional retreats where accommodation was required only for a much reduced household. Probably built as a hunting lodge by Sir John (later Baron) Hussey, Chief Butler of England, who held the manor in 1522–6. There was originally another storey, as at Beckley Park, Oxfordshire, a hunting lodge built by another King's man, Lord Williams of Thame, c. 1540.

## KNEETON                                        7040

ST HELEN. Virtually all 1879–90 by *Ewan Christian* (JPB), except the Perp W tower with diagonal buttresses and diagonally projecting gargoyles at the top. Aisleless and reduced in size, see the traces of an arcade on the exterior of the S wall. Inside, a completely plain, large, early medieval FONT. The best thing about the church is the view down into the Trent valley.

(OLD VICARAGE. T-plan. The stone and brick wing still has some mullioned windows, the main range is C18. Two nice C18 FARMHOUSES by the church, one with a timber-framed barn. NS)

LAMBLEY

HOLY TRINITY. One of the few almost entirely Perp village
churches in Notts, all of a piece and of felicitous proportions,
tall and upright, without being narrow, all the windows high
and spacious, three-light in the nave and chancel s, five-light
chancel E. The tracery simple, the usual panelling motif, with
just at the top in the centre of each window one motif of two
bladder-like shapes moving up towards each other. This in
itself occurs often in late C14 windows in the county, and the
tallness of the openings is typically Notts too. The only earlier
parts are the C12–13 W tower, complete from the tower arch
(with waterleaf and similar leaf-shaped capitals) to the wide
bell-openings (pointed twin windows with a round arch), and
crowned by a late C14 top. Of the earlier C14 one window in
the N wall of chancel. Originally a two-storeyed chantry (of the
Cromwells 1349; with a squint on the upper floor) must have
existed against this same wall. On the s between chancel and
nave a very prettily corbelled-out rood staircase. The whole
exterior looks strong and forceful with parapets instead of
battlements and the two diagonal buttresses of the E end
stepped up stage after stage in an almost aggressive way. Flanking the E window outside, two carved panels bearing Ralph
Cromwell's badge of a purse, representing his office of Lord
Treasurer of England. The building is due to his munificence.
He ordered the rebuilding in a codicil to his will dated 30 September 1454, but nothing was done for at least twelve years.*
– ROOD SCREEN. Dated 1377. Five slim openings on each side
of the entrance, not gathered together in the usual way into twos
or threes. – COMMUNION TABLE. 1619, with bulbous legs.
– ALTAR RAILS. 'Laudian', that is with sturdy balusters. – The
CHANCEL STALLS have some Jacobean panelling. – STAINED
GLASS in the E window: Crucifixion, may well be still in its
original position; also Virgin and Virgin with Child, both late
C14. – In the N and s chancel windows earlier C14 fragments.
– MONUMENT. Ralph Cromwell the elder, first Baron Crom-
well, † 1398 and wife. Incised slab, almost effaced.
(LAMBLEY HOUSE. Undistinguished, early C19, stuccoed.

---

* According to Dr Richard Marks, who says that in an indenture drawn
up between 30 September 1466 and 23 April 1469 by Ralph's executors, one
of the outstanding charges is £300 for building the church. Ralph was a great
builder who was also responsible for Wingfield Manor, Derbyshire, and Tat-
tershall Castle, Lincs.

Better is a late C18 outbuilding. Red brick; pedimented centre
with a large blind arch and half-pedimented wings. DOE)
Off CHURCH STREET a group of three prestigious houses in a
dip, by the *Architects' Design Group*, 1972–3, a good example
of mid-1970s neo-vernacular with red brick and pantiles.
Understated low shapes with pitched roofs, built in close relationship to the restored existing farmhouse.

## LANEHAM

*8070*

ST PETER. Essentially Norman, which is not frequent in Notts.
Norman tower, narrower than the nave, and very low tower
arch, of door size only. Norman herringbone masonry on the
S side of the nave and in the chancel. Norman chancel arch with
one order, scalloped capitals. Norman S doorway, much redone,
with an inner roll moulding and two outer orders with colonnettes. The capitals have transitional waterleaf decoration. The
arches with zigzags on fronts and soffits. The N aisle arcade is
E.E. with eight shafts, the major ones with fillets (cf. Farndon).
Square seats at the foot of the piers. A complex profile for the
arches. The S side of the chancel has one C13 lancet window.
The later Middle Ages are represented by the straight-headed
C14 N aisle and N chancel windows. Timbers of the S porch C14
too, but completely rebuilt in 1932. The W tower redone Perp
(cf. the diagonal buttresses and battlements). – FONT. Norman,
with tall arcades. – PULPIT. C17. – BENCHES. Plain and solid,
medieval or C17 to C18. – VESTRY SCREEN. Panelled C18. –
DOOR, S side, also plain, with long hinges and little scrollwork.
– CHEST. Decorated only with three rosettes. Quite possibly
C13. – STAINED GLASS. C14 fragment in a nave S window, first
from E: the Virgin enthroned. – MONUMENT to Ellis Markham
† 1638 and his father Gervase Markham. For its date, surprisingly modern and naturalistically carved. Classical aedicule
background decorated with garlands; the two men, father and
son, kneel behind each other, facing E.
The village straggles down from the main road to the Trent ferry.
(BINGE FARM. An early C18 house with modillion eaves course
and tumbling in the gables. NS)

## LANGAR

*7030*

ST ANDREW. A stately building of very complete Notts type with
transepts, low battlemented roofs, and central tower, but un-

fortunately so vigorously restored in the 1860s by the Rev. Thomas Butler that little of the original surface remains. The crossing tower is E.E., see its arches inside on attached columns with moulded capitals throughout. How good these originally were can be seen from the original capitals, between S aisle and transept (remains of red colour). Externally the bell-stage has large blank arcading. Is it a copy of something original? The tower top has the quatrefoil frieze usual in this region. Of the same date is the clerestory; the nave arcade was late C13. – SCREEN. Mostly new, but Perp fragments. – ALTAR RAIL. C17, with thick, early balusters. – PULPIT. Jacobean; of unusual shape, with back panel and book-rests on brackets on all sides. – READER'S DESK, opposite the pulpit. Also Jacobean. – ALTAR CLOTH. Italian C16 embroidery; captured by Viscount Howe. – MONUMENTS. A large number in the two transepts: N the Chaworths, S the Howes. Sir John Chaworth † 1558 with his wife. Recumbent alabaster figures, with their children stiffly on the walls of the tomb-chest (cf. the Sacheverells at Ratcliffe-on-Soar). – Sir George Chaworth † 1587. Also alabaster, recumbent on a rolled-up mat, the tomb-chest plain. – The quality of both is much inferior to that of the splendid free-standing alabaster monument of Thomas Lord Scroope † 1609 and his wife, a four-poster with a group of three columns at each corner, supporters and achievements on top. The recumbent figures and the dwarf-like bearded kneeling son at the feet of his parents are good enough to be in Westminster Abbey. – Against the S wall two Romanizing busts on tapered shafts: to Scroope Viscount Howe † 1712 and Scroope Viscount Howe † 1734. – A plain tablet commemorates Viscount Howe of the Glorious First of June.

LANGAR HALL, a plain stuccoed house mostly of c. 1828, stands within the church precinct. The kitchen wing at the back may be part of an earlier structure, pre-C17. It linked the house to the church before being curtailed by a few feet.

RECTORY, just outside the church precinct. Handsome early C18 brick double pile. Five bays with a hipped roof and dormers and a pedimented doorhood on brackets. Birthplace of Samuel Butler, the novelist, son of the Rev. Thomas Butler.

UNICORN HEAD. Plain gabled double-pile brick house, dated 1717. The windows are altered. On the adjoining low wing a chimneystack with two arcaded stages to the brewhouse.

(BOTTOM HOUSE FARMHOUSE, Cropwell Bishop Road. Plain double-pile early C18 brick house with sashes on the front.)

(Contemporary brick BARN with good earlier roof with two rows of purlins and curved wind-braces. F. W. B. Charles)

## LANGFORD

ST BARTHOLOMEW. Small and entirely on its own, some way N of the rest of the village. A N arcade and N chancel chapel were removed (cf. Upper Broughton), but in the chancel is a blocked arch with piers like the S arcade and ballflower ornament round the arch. Stuccoed, with tiled roofs. The tower C13 (see the blocked tower arch); the S arcade, with castellated abaci to the octagonal piers, the clerestory, and the chancel, with straight-headed windows, C15. Original nave roof. – MONUMENT. Knight, second half of the C14. – Tablet to Slingsby Duncombe † 1831 by *R. Marshall*.

OLD HALL, S of the church. C17; stone. Charming, despite its blocked and altered mullion-and-transom-cross windows. Three bays with gabled end elevations. Excellent central gabled porch projection, its sides corbelled out, with a heavy entrance arch.

FARMHOUSES. Three of *c.* 1700 along the main road, almost identical, local stone with brick string courses, quoins, and gables. These houses belong to a rebuilding of the village after the medieval village (now only mounds in two fields to the S) had decayed.

LANGFORD HALL, ½ m. SE. Probably begun *c.* 1780; 'newly built, at present not inhabited' in 1790. Very plain brick house by *Carr* of York for the Duncombes: three storeys, seven bays, with a three-bay pedimented centre and a simple Tuscan Doric porch. Originally much larger: a long two-storey service wing which ran parallel at the back has been demolished, and a garden now lies between the house and the original stable block. Staircase lighted by a large Venetian window. Except in the dining room, apparently Regency in decoration, the original doors and cornices still exist.[*]

## LAXTON

'Laxton is unique among the villages of England today in that here and here only has the open-field system of farming survived

---

[*] Information kindly given by Mr Patrick Radford.

unchanged in its essentials since the days long before the Norman Conquest' (C. S. and C. S. Orwin). This fact is not of an architectural nature, though of visual as well as social importance, and should not therefore, strictly speaking, have a place in this book. But the absence, by sheer accident, of enclosure either in the C16 or the even more agriculturally radical C18 is remarkable enough to be at least mentioned. Besides, the open-field system has an effect on the composition of the village street, which is lined with small farmsteads (e.g. Laxton Bar Farm 1703) with yards opening on to it instead of into surrounding fields. Laxton has other claims to consideration, too.

MOTTE-AND-BAILEY CASTLE. The largest and best-preserved in the county. The motte has a circumference of 816 ft and a total height of 71 ft. A smaller mound, 8 ft high and 147 ft in circumference, lies on its summit. Traces of a masonry wall surrounding the inner bailey may be discerned. It has not been excavated in the outer bailey.

To the s, prominent EARTHWORKS in pasture may be the remains of a later masonry residence (of the C16?).

46 ST MICHAEL. The best feature of the exterior is the nave clerestory (seen from the s), with six closely placed three-light windows, battlements elaborately decorated with blind tracery and shields, and eight pinnacles. It was built by Archbishop Rotherham who, about 1490, found himself for a short time lord of the manor.* The upper part of the rebuilt W tower goes with that (minus the Victorian pyramid roof of course). Its lower parts are E.E.; and E.E., in spite of the clerestory, is the dominant character of the interior. Tall, slender, circular piers for N and s nave arcades with simply moulded capitals, and square piers with four demi-shafts with fillets for N and s chancel arcades (cf. Mansfield, Worksop, etc.). The nave was shortened when the tower was rebuilt one bay eastward during the thorough restoration of 1859–60 by *Hine & Evans*. They also gave the chancel exterior a High Victorian veneer. It is of the early C14, see the slim Dec windows (with a transom), the miniature EASTER SEPULCHRE, an upright niche with flowing tracery, and opposite the stepped SEDILIA with crocketed and finialled gables, but a straight fleur-de-lis cresting. The seats of the sedilia are separated by stone arms. A low-side window a little farther E. The clerestory necessitated a new roof, and

* He signed his work with a panel on the N side battlements showing a bishop with stags below.

this was provided with the same lavishness as the clerestory itself. It rests on shafts decorated alternately with apostles and musician angels (sculpturally not very good). – SCREENS. Old bits in the rood screen; the N aisle screen mostly new but historically important in that it is dated 1532 and yet shows no trace of the coming of the Italian fashion. – MONUMENTS. The church is proud of its de Everingham Monuments, supposed to represent members of the family who died in 1287, 1341, 1387, and 1398, but they are in such a poor state of preservation that there is little aesthetic reward in examining them. It is, however, interesting that on the tomb of Adam († 1341) his first wife's effigy is in stone like his own, but that of his second wife in oak (the only wooden medieval effigy in the county).

LENTON see NOTTINGHAM p. 252

LINBY

5050

One of the prettiest villages on the N side of Nottingham. Stone cottages, a stream along the High Street, and two VILLAGE CROSSES, the Top Cross medieval with a base of seven steps and a shaft probably of 1869, the Bottom Cross in good condition and apparently dated 1663. The OLD RECTORY, an irregular C18 stone house made rectangular in 1856, has three stone-mullioned windows in a part-C17 rear wing.

ST MICHAEL. Unbuttressed W tower with a SW staircase, Perp bell-openings, gargoyles, battlements, and pinnacles. Norman masonry on the N side. The S door Norman of the plainest. Norman fragments also on the S side of the chancel. The arcade C13, insignificant. The most interesting features are a C14 fragment of STAINED GLASS (S aisle, E window) and the NORTH PORCH, early C16, with the stone roof supported by transverse ribs, which is not an infrequent motif in Notts (cf. St Mary, Nottingham, etc.). The N windows are typical late C18. – STAINED GLASS in the N aisle windows by *Hardman*, 1912.

LINBY HALL (HALL FARMHOUSE), Main Street. A very handsome and problematic building. Late medieval in origin, it is one wing and all that remains of the early manor. It was probably an addition to house a long gallery. The front, of ashlar, has a late C17 to early C18 appearance. Tall, with three storeys and seven bays of two-light mullioned windows. In the centre of the centre bay, a blank round panel, and at either end of the façade two slightly projecting octagonal turrets, covered with the rest by a pitched roof and containing newel staircases, one of which is still in use. The interior has been much altered and makes little sense. In the centre of the rear (E) wall a large ashlar chimneybreast supported on corbels but with no fireplace or chimneystack: not bonded into the wall, which was an internal one originally. The floor levels were changed in the C18, rooms divided up, and new windows inserted. The rest of the house may have been demolished then. On one side a plain gabled DOVECOTE which looks C17, on the other a matching BREWHOUSE. (In the farm buildings the remains of a water-driven farm-wheel used to power a number of operations: sawing, grinding, milling, etc. NS)

CASTLE MILL, at the E end of the village, halfway to Papplewick. Once, like the other Robinson mill at Papplewick, beautified in a most extraordinary way with embattled corner towers, quatrefoil openings, and pointed doorways and windows, but stripped of all this character, except the towers, when turned into flats by a 1950s 'improver' intent on making it look as much like spec. housing as possible. Unlike the other Robinson mills at Papplewick and Bestwood, this was always powered by water, not by steam.

PAPPLEWICK HALL. *See* p. 287.

PAPPLEWICK HALL. *See* p. 287.

8080

# LITTLEBOROUGH

The site of the Roman town of SEGELOCUM, of which as yet little is known. It lay where the Trent was bridged or forded by the Lincoln–Doncaster road. Defences may once have existed, but no certain trace has yet been recorded. Recent excavations have shown that the site was occupied from at least the late C1.

ST NICHOLAS. Tiny, aisleless Norman church with large areas of herringbone masonry everywhere. A few Roman tiles appear mixed up with the stonework (*see* above). Inside the church the chancel arch is Norman with one order with scalloped capitals. The arch profile and the jamb profile are strangely out of keeping.

Houses face the river, a reminder of the C18 river traffic.

## LITTLE CARLTON
*see* SOUTH MUSKHAM

## LOUND HALL

6070

### In Bothamsall parish

1937, neo-Georgian, by *Brierley, Rutherford & Syme* of York. Now a museum of mining and N.C.B. training centre.

## LOWDHAM

6040

ST MARY. Outside the village across a stream. A spacious interior with tall, wide arcades. The piers are quatrefoil with fillets up the shafts and into the capitals (cf. Cotgrave, Epperstone, Fledborough, and Basford), and carry double-chamfered arches. So this is C13 (school of Southwell). The s door belongs to the same period, the w steeple may be a little earlier. In the C15 a spire of the type of St Peter, Nottingham, was added in different stone. The s aisle has Dec windows. *Scott* restored it in 1860 and the chancel was rebuilt in 1890. – FONT. Of *c.* 1300, and the best font of its date in the county, octagonal, with richly crocketed gables starting from human faces or animals: no doubt by a minor mason from the Southwell chapter house team. – MONUMENTS. Sir John de Lowdham † 1318, cross-legged and well preserved except for the face; the inscription is Norman French (Sir Ion de Loodham git ici – De Sa Alme Deus eyt Merci). – A priest, incised slab of *c.* 1520 in the s chancel wall. – In the churchyard a number of worthwhile slate HEADSTONES, several by *Wood* of Bingham.

MANOR HOUSE. Mid-C17, timber-framed underneath the plaster, which on the N side (visible in the dairy) has a fishscale pattern. In the wing, a contemporary staircase with flat balusters. Lengthened in the C18.

At the end of MAIN STREET, on the l., a two-storey FRAME-WORK KNITTERS' WORKSHOP, now part of a stonemason's premises

WATER MILL. On a very attractive site. Three-storey brick mill, flanked by two-storey buildings.

## LOW MARNHAM *see* MARNHAM

# MANSFIELD

Mansfield is remembered by the high arches of its railway viaduct (1875) which rise right in the middle of the town and cut off the parish church from the market place. The C20's contribution to the townscape, an inner ring or distributor road (1973–6), is a less pleasing intrusion. As usual (for example at Nottingham and Derby), it makes the centre more attractive but the inner suburbs desolate, and sweeps out of its way a number of interesting buildings: here, as at Derby, early Nonconformist chapels. The town has about 57,500 inhabitants (1971): it had about 6,000 in 1801. Just at that time its industrialization set in with the introduction of the stocking-frame to Mansfield. The pre-industrial town, where some houses of up to that date may be found,* extended very little beyond the area now bounded by the ring road. It was an important royal manor in the C11 and C12.

ST PETER. Norman w tower, exceptionally complete and convincing; unbuttressed, with w door, window above, and twin bell-openings with nook-shafts. The waterleaf capitals date them as second half of the C12. The tower arch, the window above, and the former roof-line, all visible from the nave, are Norman too. So is some chancel masonry, including a little zigzag which can be seen from the present s chancel chapel. In the N aisle one lancet window; i.e. the aisle was added in the C13. But the main impression today is due to *c.* 1300. Both arcades were then built, with tall slender square piers with four attached demi-shafts with fillets (cf. Worksop, Laxton, Warsop, Teversal), moulded capitals, double-chamfered arches, and heads as label stops. The tower top is Dec, the E end Perp, *c.* 1475, the spire (with pedimented dormer windows) 1666. – ORGAN. Moved in 1971 from Clare College Cambridge, renovated by *Mander & Son*. Over-large and incongruous Baroque case. – STAINED GLASS. E window, 1905 by *Kempe*. – MONUMENTS. Incised slab to a priest, *c.* 1280, quite good. – Layman (cf. Calverton and Oxton). Late C13 or early C14. – In the s porch, two foliated cross slabs.

ST JOHN THE EVANGELIST, St John's Street. 1854–6 by *H. I. Stevens*. An expensive-looking church financed by H. Gally

* Several C17 stone houses still exist under C19 refacing, for example in Westgate.

Knight († 1846), author of *Ecclesiastical Architecture of Italy*. Built of local stone with a four-stage tower, stair-turret and spire, aisles, and a clerestory. The detail is good, with a variety of tracery patterns, especially nice the broad flowing tracery in the E windows. Set in a large grassy churchyard. – STAINED GLASS. Good W window † 1905. – E window S aisle possibly by *Holland* of Warwick, 1857. First rate.

ST MARK, Nottingham Road. By *Temple Moore*, 1897. The exterior almost conventional neo-Perp; the SE tower small and tapering, with reduced tracery. The interior is not at all what the outside would make one expect. Instead of aisles, it has square piers between side chapels or niches. These are connected by passages with round-headed arches. The W end of the nave is screened off by two arches on a central column and there is a two-bay NE chapel. The plan is that of the best late Victorian churches, one of the real contributions of their age to English church design. – The ALTAR looks like *Leslie Moore*'s work. – STAINED GLASS. Two small W windows by *Kempe*; the E windows also in his style. – Beside the church a CHURCH HALL in the same neo-Perp style.

ST ALBAN, Clipstone Road, Forest Town. 1911 by *Louis Ambler*. Towerless, rubble-built, lancet-style, the nave and aisles roofed in one. Plain plastered interior with high nave and low aisles.

OLD MEETING HOUSE. Set back in Mill Walk on the N side of Stockwell Gate just beside the ring road (Quaker Way) is the C17 Old Parsonage where meetings of the community known later as the Unitarians began in 1665. Stone, T-shaped, with a mullioned window in the rear wing. Two-storey façade with two widely spaced pairs of mullion-and-transom cross first-floor windows. Sashes and dormers later. The Meeting House lies well behind the older house. Of 1702, rubble, with four tall cross windows on the E, W, and S sides, and one-light windows above them on the S side. (It formerly had two E entrances and pulpit opposite but was re-ordered in 1870. Chancel, with two two-light mullioned windows and a round one between, added to the N side in 1882. Two original posts support the roof. PARLIAMENT CLOCK by *Thomas Haley* of Norwich. C3) STAINED GLASS. Late windows by *Morris & Co.*: N side from W, the second 1928 adapted from a *Burne Jones* and *J. H. Dearle* design, the third 1913. – S side, second from W, 1929 to a design by *Burne-Jones*, *Dearle* and *Morris*. – Mansfield was famous for its early conventicles. They could flourish here because the town was not incorporated and so not forbidden to the Puritans.*

FRIENDS' MEETING HOUSE, Rosemary Street. Built in 1972–3 (architects *Bartlett & Gray*) to replace the demolished building in Quaker Lane. A simple design in buff brick with a pitched roof raised on one side to admit a clerestory.‡

NOTTINGHAM ROAD METHODIST CHURCH, Nottingham Road. 1913. A stone church, not a chapel, in Free-style Gothic, probably by *Brewill & Baily*. At the back a square bay-window to the church rooms and nice wrought-iron eaves-brackets. Behind the church, a brick and stone CHURCH HALL in the same style with a very pretty lantern: square and tapering with a curly finial.

BRIDGE STREET METHODIST CHAPEL. In a good formal setting with a flight of steps leading to an Italianate chapel. Built in 1864. Rock-faced, rusticated, portico *in antis* with triple-light window over and curving balustrade.

TOWN HALL. *See* Perambulation, p. 171.

OLD GRAMMAR SCHOOL (St Peter's Church Parish Centre), at the back of the churchyard. Built in 1551, given its charter in 1561 (according to the inscription over the door), but rebuilt in Queen Anne's reign (schoolroom 1714, headmaster's house for boarders adjoining it 1719) in a very old-fashioned manner, and restored and extended in 1851. Plain six-bay, three-storey building. Two-light windows with unchamfered mullions. The gabled porch has a round arch with voussoirs.

NEW QUEEN ELIZABETH GRAMMAR SCHOOL, Chesterfield Road. 1875 by *Giles & Gough* of London.

(BRUNTS SCHOOL, Woodhouse Road. 1891 by *Evans & Jolly*. Stone.)

BERRY HILL SCHOOL, Black Scotch Lane. 1967–78, mostly by the County Architect, *H. T. Swain*, except part of the middle school (by *Goodwin, Warner & Associates*). The first and

* The following were demolished to make way for the distributor road: the former BAPTIST CHAPEL, Stockwell Gate, with a three-bay front, rubble with brick to the W, steeply hipped roof, built by the Methodists in 1791 and acquired by the Baptists in 1815; and the FRIENDS' MEETING HOUSE, Quaker Lane, a stone rectangle with lunette windows to N and W, S wall with a staircase porch between two rooms facing the burial ground, and the date 1800 over the entrance gate (CS).

‡ *Watson Fothergill's* CONGREGATIONAL (later UNITED REFORMED) CHURCH of 1877 in Westfield Lane is mostly disused in 1978. An entrance feature like an apse and ambulatory faces the corner. Coarse Romanesque details in Fothergill's usual striped polychrome style. Rock-faced turret and little clergy house to Wood Street.

middle schools very neat CLASP buildings with the usual irregular grouping of hall and classrooms: brown tilehung. The nursery school (1976) is a playful adaptation of an existing building into a tiled pyramid on low brick walls. On one side glass replaces tiles, forming a kind of veranda.

HEALTH CENTRE, St John's Street. Very unassuming but pleasing use of CLASP, by *H. T. Swain* (County Architect), 1966–8. Two-storey aggregate-clad blocks round a courtyard with an open stairway on one side. Nearly opposite, next to the church, are the COUNTY AREA OFFICES, similar but more ordinary; also by the County Architect.

CATTLE MARKET, Nottingham Road. 1877 by *Watson Fothergill*. Stripy red brick with a round tower.

MIDLAND STATION (now commercial premises). Stone, Italianate, 1872. Next to it the Midland Hotel, built as Broom House *c.* 1820. Large and square, with the centre bay emphasized by rusticated quoins; pedimented doorcase.

The centre of the town is the MARKET PLACE with the MOOT HALL, given in 1752 by Lady Oxford (of Welbeck Abbey), an urbane seven-bay stone house with a graceful pediment decorated in the Rococo taste, and the TOWN HALL, erected in 1836 by *W. A. Nicholson* of Lincoln in a heavy neo-classical style with a four-column Tuscan porch. The Market Place originally ran N–S with the Moot Hall on the axis: it was then enlarged and turned E–W with the new Town Hall as its *point-de-vue*. Next to the Town Hall the very competently and restrainedly designed SAVINGS BANK (now County Court offices) of 1840. In the Market Place extension by the Savings Bank some very late Georgian stuccoed houses and two hotels. In the middle a Gothic MONUMENT to Lord George Bentinck, designed by *Hine* and erected in 1849. From here the view of the Market Place is good, with hills leading up out of it and the viaduct crossing behind it. Across the bottom (N side) run Church Street and Westgate. In CHURCH STREET several C18 houses, some stone, some stuccoed, mostly with unmoulded architrave surrounds and all very plain. On the s side the SWAN HOTEL, C18, but with two gables with stone mullioned windows that look earlier: the reset datestone reads 1584. On the same side the equally big WHITE HART. Opposite the s side of the church on the corner of Midworth Street, CHURCH HOUSE, with to the side a tall round-headed staircase window of the kind common in northern counties and a plain three-storey three-bay façade. To the l. a round-arched doorway (now window) in a one-storey bay. In MIDWORTH STREET itself, an C18 or early C19 MALTINGS. Long, plain stone range to the street, gables and louvred turrets away from it. Opposite the N side of the church in BRIDGE STREET the best house in the centre of the town. It is late C17, with mullion-and-transom-cross windows on the side and back and a façade in the post-Restoration style, with hipped roof, pedimented dormers, quoins, and a segmental pediment on brackets and a big keystone to the central doorway. Earlier this century the doorway was made into a window and two new doors were made in the outer bays: sash-windows probably late C18 or early C19.

Church Street continues into Church Lane, which goes under the ring road. Off it on the r. in BRUNT STREET, No. 36 GROVE HOUSE (awaiting repair in 1978), an L-shaped composite building of several different dates. The main block is C18 (with some good panelling, fireplaces, etc.). Its façade, away from the street, moved foward in the early C19, has five bays with quoins and a (possibly re-used) pedimented doorcase with Ionic pilasters flanking a round-arched doorway: all stone and very flat. Also early C19 the short wings on this side and the r. wing with three tripartite over three Venetian windows. At the back a basically timber-framed wing (C16?) on a stone plinth, cased in C18 brick.

In the other direction from the Market Place is WESTGATE, which has been pedestrianized. On the l. a very ordinary shopping precinct, the FOUR SEASONS SHOPPING CENTRE, with a nicely scaled, undulating façade of canted bays on piers: architects, *Bernard Engle & Partners*, 1972–6. Set back and to the W of it in a small square, WAVERLEY HOUSE, a good example of a provincial town house dated 1754. Its façade is very lively but with a strange mixture of old-fashioned, pattern-book motifs. It is of two-and-a-half storeys and five bays with a pitched roof, dentil cornice, and lots of rustication (rusticated quoins and Gibbs rustication round the lower windows, forming aprons below them, and round the doorcase, which has a full Doric pediment supported on half-columns). Above the door a central window with lugged architrave and volutes, a curly pediment, and attached balustrade. The other windows have lugged architraves, and the first-floor ones also have odd-looking aprons. Original plasterwork inside (DOE). Of the plainer C18 houses on the W side of the square one also has lugged architraves. In the centre the C16 or C17 MARKET CROSS with sundial and ball finial on a tall stone shaft. At the corner of Westgate and Clumber Street, CROMWELL HOUSE, three-storey, seven-bay, with three gables, stone plinth, stuccoed above. Sash-windows to the lower storeys but mullioned windows with hoodmoulds in the gables which must date it to the C17. The plinth could be earlier. Right at the end of WESTGATE are a few more C18 stone houses. Facing down, at the corner of Westfield Lane, Nos. 1 and 1a CHESTERFIELD ROAD SOUTH, a three-storey, three-bay house with Venetian windows flanking the door and, attached, what may have been the coach house, with little quatrefoil windows under the eaves.

N of this off CHESTERFIELD ROAD, in CROW HILL DRIVE, INNISDOON, 1904–5, one of *Parker & Unwin*'s most exciting designs from the early years of the century. Its roughcast walls and tiled roof are characteristic of their houses of this period, but the L-plan is adventurous, with the space between the arms filled in by two canted bays flanking a central door, making an irregular triangular plan overall.* Familiar handling on the garden elevations: mullioned bay-windows and a continuous range of mullioned windows running across a central recess balcony on the first floor. An awkwardly shaped lobby leads into an impressive double-height living hall, its complex angles and interplay of open galleries and landings handled in a masterly fashion. The three main rooms open into each other to form one suite by means of double doors, one sliding and with its well detailed gear boldly exposed. Some detailing was almost certainly by *Cecil Hignett*, Parker's best assistant at that time, see the leaded lights in the sliding doors, the exaggerated keystone of the main inglenook fireplace, and the carving on the bressumer over the entrance. Copper-hooded fireplaces in two of the main rooms, and in general the fittings respected and intact.

Only a few pre-C20 buildings of note outside the town centre, most of them early survivals (late C18 or early C19) of the town's textile industry. Most important because probably the oldest, STANTONS MILL in BATH LANE, NE of the centre. Only the two-storey and probably earliest part, which extends over the river, has been conserved intact. On the N side the remarkably unspoilt BATH MILL.

Similar relics S of the centre. Furthest S on the road to Sutton-in-Ashfield, KING'S MILL RESERVOIR, formed by the large

* *Barry Parker* explained the practical reasons for this complicated plan (briefly the restrictions imposed by the site) in *The Craftsman*, September 1910. We owe the descriptions of Innisdoon and Inglenook (below) to Mervyn Miller.

dam of the demolished Kings Corn Mills. In the steep valley below it (just outside the town), the river is crossed by a five-arched stone VIADUCT built *c.* 1819 for the pre-locomotive Mansfield to Pinxton railway: still impressive, although supported by iron ties now. s off Sutton Road a little further N, HERMITAGE MILL in Hermitage Lane, three- and four-storey stone with a later brick extension but with its mill-dam preserved. Again a little further N still, off Sutton Road in Sheepbridge Lane, SITTLE MATLOCK MILL, small, stone-built, and still in industrial use. Sheepbridge Lane leads into High Oakham Hill, and N of it, in HIGH OAKHAM ROAD, another *Parker & Unwin* house, INGLENOOK, of 1905–6. Usual roughcast exterior with mullioned windows and tiled roof. Cruciform plan.

High Oakham Hill continues E as Atkin Lane and, E of Nottingham Road, as Berry Hill Lane. On the S side is BERRY HILL HALL (Miners' Rehabilitation Centre). Towards the road the stable-yard with an arcaded outer wall and a pretty polygonal tower with an ogee cap. The hall itself is a spacious, plain early C19 building with a pediment feature on the main front. Recent additions.

Finally, off the main road N to Mansfield Woodhouse, in Birding Street, SHERWOOD PITHEAD BATHS, 1934 by *A. J. Saise*, among the many good modern buildings put up by the Miners' Welfare Commission.

<sub>5060</sub>                    MANSFIELD WOODHOUSE

Some of the smaller places surrounding Mansfield still give quite a clear idea of their character before industrialization. Mansfield itself has lost that. But at Mansfield Woodhouse and Kirkby-in-Ashfield the C19 and C20 developments have taken place away from the old centres.

At Mansfield Woodhouse (now joined up to Mansfield), the MANOR HOUSE (Mansfield District Council Offices) stands side by side with the church. It is early C17, but much altered in late Georgian times. Of the original work the H-plan with three-storey gabled wings (double on the r.) and some mullion-and-transom-cross windows still discernible. In the alterations the centre was filled in, the wings given sash and oval windows, and the top castellated. On the side a Venetian window.

ST EDMUND. The steeple was built after a fire of 1304, the

church in 1804–10 (but much restored in 1847–50 by *Sir G. G. Scott*). The bell-openings of the tower Dec, the spire very odd, with one tier of large lucarnes right at the foot, the second tier so close to the tip and so tiny that they look from a distance like a spiky finial. Scott's design is an imitation of Notts traditions, neither original nor sensitive. – PILLAR PISCINA. Norman, in the s chancel chapel, found in 1930. – STAINED GLASS. Some arms and decoration; 1617. – MONUMENTS. Knight and Lady, *c.* 1300, in the churchyard, heads in trefoil frame, fragmentary. They must once have been of fine quality and are still more expressive than many. Should be transferred into the church. – Sir John Digby † 1684 and wife, standing figures not in an aedicule but in a frame with a curved pediment-like top, the carving atrociously provincial.

CHURCH STREET is most attractive, with some nice C18 houses, especially the one on the corner with Gibbs rustication round the door, and some sensitively designed modern buildings. The BRANCH LIBRARY is a neat tile-hung building (1960–1 by *Robert Matthew, Johnson-Marshall & Partners*), but the HEALTH CENTRE (1972–4) is better, CLASP, but cleverly integrating an existing stone wall and re-using stone and paving setts. Only the green slate-hanging seems an odd choice in this setting, although the slate was found locally at the demolished Sherwood Hall (County Architect: *H. T. Swain*). At the top of Church Street, in STATION STREET, CLERKSON'S HALL, formerly dated 1631 on a fireplace, a large and tall gabled house, with mullion-and-transom-cross windows, now belonging to the National Coal Board, who removed the dated fireplace and a fine plaster frieze. There is still panelling in the dining room and a carved and moulded beam in the parlour. Further E on the same side is WINSTANLEY'S HOUSE (No. 57 High Street), a long, low, late C16 or early C17 house with mullioned windows and a steep roof, the best of its type in the district. In the opposite direction in Debdale Lane, DEBDALE HALL, with an early Georgian core but mostly early C19 in appearance. Big canted bay on the front and a five-bay garden façade with a central three-bay pediment. To the w a good range of outbuildings of a similar date. N of the village, PARK HALL, also Georgian.

ROMAN VILLA, 1 m. NW. The first farmstead on this site consisted of a group of timber huts dating from the late C1. In the C2, a winged corridor house was built, and later still two ancillary dwellings and barns were constructed in the farmyard. The villa reached the peak of its prosperity in the late C3, but the main house was abandoned shortly after 320.

WHINNY HILL, 1 m. E, has been identified, on dubious grounds, as the site of a small Iron Age fort.

7060

# MAPLEBECK

ST RADEGUND. Much restored in 1898 by *C. Hodgson Fowler* (JPB) and architecturally of little interest. The chancel was almost rebuilt and STAINED GLASS by *Kempe* put in the E window. W tower with low, short broach-spire, probably C14. N arcade a little earlier. At the E end of the chancel just one lancet. S porch rebuilt but with the old timber roof. – Remains of a STONE ALTAR built into the N wall. – ALTAR RAILS. C17, with balusters. – SCREEN. Not complete, but what remains goes with the altar rails and also with the plain, solid BENCHES. It was a Laudian refurnishing job.

MAPPERLEY *see* NOTTINGHAM p. 263

MARGIDUNUM *see* EAST BRIDGFORD

MARKHAM CLINTON
*see* WEST MARKHAM

8060

# MARNHAM

ST WILFRID, Low Marnham. The S arcades must have been done by Lincoln masons. The piers have slim octagonal cores and four detached shafts each, an excellent, lively effect. The capitals have crocket-leaves and more elementary upright leaves. The arches are simply double-chamfered, a little disappointing after the display of the piers. The N chancel chapel is similar, and the chancel arch of the same date (that is early C13). The N arcade is C13 too, but more of the usual local kind (circular piers, E and W responds keeled, moulded capitals). Most of the windows are plainest Perp without tracery. The S door has an elaborate ogee arch and no capitals at all (not a frequent thing). – In the chancel chapel (very incongruous) an C18 crystal CHANDELIER. – STAINED GLASS. Perp figure of St James in a N window. – MONUMENTS. Two by the same able craftsman with inscription cartouches and cherubs and skulls: one to E. Nicholson † 1698, the other with an illegible inscription referring to 1694 and 1698. – William Cartwright † 1748, the father of Cartwright, the inventor of the power-loom (cf. Ossington).

(MARNHAM HALL, High Marnham, in the shadow of High Marnham Power Station, ½ m. N. Early C18, two storeys plus attics with dormers. Five-bay with a moulded brick band breaking forward over the first-floor windows. Wide rusticated brick door surround. SE room with bolection-moulded panelling. Later wing at the back with early C19 windows. DOE)

## MATTERSEY

The fame of Mattersey is its PRIORY, about 1¼ m. E of the village. The priory itself was one of the relatively few houses of the Gilbertine Order, founded by Gilbert de Sempringham in 1149. The only wholly English order, it first incorporated both nuns and canons living strictly segregated in the same monasteries. Mattersey, founded c. 1185, was a small, poor house for canons only, six in number. Of that time only the foundations of the N, S, and W walls of the unaisled church remain near the farmhouse. It was probably never rebuilt after a fire destroyed the monastery in 1279, for overlying the N wall is a tall fragment of a C15 chapel or tower with diagonal buttresses and a window jamb. The excavated fragments of the monastic buildings erected after the fire (a group round the cloister s of the church) show that the cloister arcade was C13 with pairs of dwarf columns. The W range has all but gone, but there are more substantial remains of the E and S ranges. The mid-C13 E DORTER range, a seven-bay block, has the octagonal pier bases and some responds of its vaulted two-aisled undercroft. The two N bays were divided into two chapels, perhaps to replace the destroyed church. The southernmost bays opened into the REREDORTER (see the paved drain). Best preserved is the late C13 S REFECTORY or FRATER range, also with a two-aisled vaulted undercroft: of six bays with circular piers. In the s wall, remains of four two-light windows. A block of masonry in the s walk may be the base of the stairs to frater and dorter. The KITCHEN is almost free-standing at the SW corner of the refectory. Most of the walls are late medieval, possibly dating from after the Suppression to judge from carved fragments built into them.

ALL SAINTS. The surprise of the church is two small C14 panels
in the chancel, one square with St Martin and the Beggar, the
36    other oblong with St Helena finding the True Cross. They are
unrestored work of the workshops that at the same time did
the Notts Easter Sepulchres (Hawton, etc.) and the Southwell
screen, and may have come from the priory which was dedicated to St Helen. There is little to be said about the rest of
the church. The usual Perp w tower with diagonal buttresses,
gargoyles, battlements, and four pinnacles. The N side Perp,
the s side early Dec. N chancel chapel with E.E. arcade (circular
pier with simple moulded capital and one nailhead course,
double-chamfered arches), C14 arcades to the two aisles. The
roof of 1866 on corbels with the typical highly naturalistic
foliage of that date. The same appears on the FONT. Recess
in the s aisle with ogee arch and a finial with foliage of, say,
the end of the C14.

(MATTERSEY HOUSE, on the road from Gringley to Ranskill.
Early C18, three-storey and three-bay, with small lower wings.
Simple classical door surround and little keystone blocks to the
flat brick arches over the windows. w of the church, another
tall, three-bay brick house, late C18. NS)

(MATTERSEY HILL, s of the village. Plain red brick, with the
central bay of three pedimented. DOE)

BLACO HILL FARM. See Wiseton.


MILTON see WEST MARKHAM


6090                         MISSON

ST JOHN BAPTIST. Much damaged by lightning in 1894. Nave
and aisles of three bays, octagonal piers on the s, circular on
the N, the N arches less pointed than the s. Nave, aisles, and
w tower are embattled. The tower has angle buttresses and four
pinnacles. Perp stone-vaulted porch. – FONT. 1662–3 (cf. Walkeringham). – Restored C17 PULPIT and tester with roses and
fleur-de-lys in the panels.

(COTTAGE in Slayne's Lane. The weathered lintel formerly read
1692; part demolished. Brick with stone quoins and a big keystone to the door. Three-light mullioned windows.)

(Several early C19 COTTAGES with classical door surrounds.
DOE)

## MISTERTON

ALL SAINTS. w tower and spire rebuilt in 1843–7; but evidently original fragments were used, for example the dogtooth of the tower windows, stones of the low, windowless broach-spire. The best feature of the church is the arch from the tower into the N aisle, treble-chamfered, with a dogtooth label and with heads as label stops, on stiff-leaf corbels: *c.* 1200. One pillar of the chancel arcade also of this date. N arcade and E window, with some unusual tracery, Dec. The rest Perp. – FONT. C13 base; bowl of 1660. – STAINED GLASS. Fragments of a C15 bishop in a N window. – (An important window of 1965 by *John Piper*, made by *Patrick Reyntiens*, showing the Five Wounds. RH)

(METHODIST CHURCH, on the main road. 1878. Red brick with yellow brick Corinthian pilasters with stone capitals. Fine round-headed central window of two round-headed lights divided by a marble shaft. More grey marble to the pilastered doorway. NS)

PUMP HOUSES. One on each side of the Mother Drain at Misterton Soss, built to house beam engines (now gone) which propelled scoop wheels. The building on the N side looks earlier; that on the s has a datestone reading *1828, Alfred Smith, Engineer*. To each a tall square chimney with stone-embellished 'Crown' caps.

## MOORGREEN *see* GREASLEY

## MOORHOUSE

A hamlet in Laxton parish with a CHAPEL by *Henry Clutton* built in 1860–1 at the expense of Speaker J. E. Denison (later Viscount Ossington) of Ossington Hall, 2 m. s. In the vigorous C12 French Gothic used by Clutton in his larger churches, e.g. Woburn. Local skerry with Ancaster stone dressings, heavily notched round the window openings. The division between nave and chancel marked by buttressing and a bellcote. Massive timber roof, chancel stone-vaulted on a diminutive scale.

## MORTON

ST DENIS. 1756. Charming from outside, disappointing within.

The small embattled brick tower of the type met in Thamesside villages, where wealthy Londoners lived in the c18. The body of the church also brick, with three round-headed windows on each side and a low, short, projecting apse. The interior re-pewed and devoid of appeal.

DOVECOTE (Manor House). Early brick, 17 by 17 ft.


## NETHERFIELD see CARLTON


5070                    ## NETHER LANGWITH

LANGWITH LODGE. Largish red brick neo-Georgian house of the Ernest Newton school. H-plan, of eleven bays, with the characteristic Venetian windows in the pedimented gable ends: by *Louis Ambler* for the Duke of Portland's agent, 1904.

COTTON MILL, now a barn at Langwith Mill Farm. An early water-powered example of *c.* 1780: four-storeyed and originally sixteen windows wide (quite a remarkable size as early industrial buildings in Notts go). Three rows of workers' cottages were demolished in 1964.

Upper Langwith, with the church, is in Derbyshire.


7050                    ## NEWARK

The history of Newark expresses itself to the eye clear in two structures: the castle and the church, representing the Lord of the Manor and the burgesses. The Lord of the Manor was in the Middle Ages, with short interruptions, the Bishop of Lincoln. The castle was his castle. The church was the pride of the town, a wealthy town of wool merchants dealing with sheep-breeders on the one hand, and with Flemish clothiers on the other. The brass to Alan Fleming is the most spectacular reminder of this commercial orientation of Newark. The castle is in ruins, and so now the town seems wholly centred round the church. Wool and the other staple, coal, were carried via the Trent.

The town lies within a region of dense early settlement in this fertile valley. Settlements of Bronze Age and Iron Age date are freely attested by aerial photographs and by finds from the numerous local gravel-workings. A considerable Romano-British site, with finds ranging from the c1 to the c4, grew up in the North-gate area of the town, near where the Fosse Way (from Leicester to Lincoln) crossed a prehistoric trackway (Sewstern Lane) coming

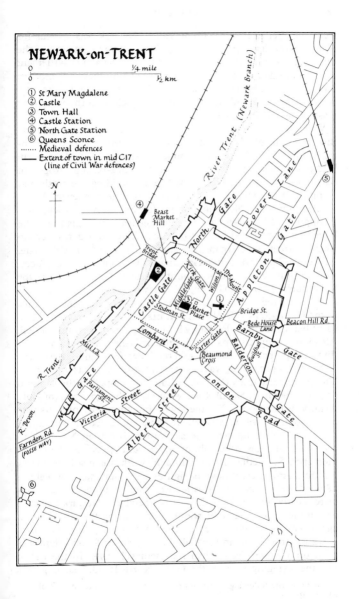

# NEWARK-on-TRENT

0            ¼ mile
0            ½ km

① St Mary Magdalene
② Castle
③ Town Hall
④ Castle Station
⑤ North Gate Station
⑥ Queens Sconce
...... Medieval defences
▬▬ Extent of town in mid C17
(line of Civil War defences)

River Trent (Newark Branch)

N

④

Beast Market Hill

Trent Bridge

② Castle Gate

North Gate

Lovers Lane

Appleton Gate

The Mount

Kirk Gate

Wilson St.

Middlegate

Stodman St.

③ Market Place

① ✠

Bridge St.

Beacon Hill Rd

Bede House Lane

Barnby Gate

Guildhall

Lombard St.

Carter Gate

Beaumond Cross

Balderton Gate

London Gate

Mill La.

R. Trent

Mill Gate

Parliament St.

Victoria Street

Albert Street

London Road

R. Devon

Farndon Rd. (FOSSE WAY)

⑥

from the Welland to the Trent Valley. Newark was a focus for
Anglo-Saxon immigrants, to judge from a large cemetery of the
C5–6 that has been excavated in Mill Gate. The actual settlement
of that period has not yet been located. The origin of the modern
Newark lies in a mid to late Saxon settlement (*Newerche*, the 'new
work' or fortification) which probably lay close to the river near
Castlegate and the castle.

William the Conqueror gave Newark and land round it to the
Bishop of Lincoln as part of the endowment for the new bishop-
ric.\* The third Norman bishop, Alexander the Magnificent
(1123–48), nephew of another great prince-bishop, Roger of
Salisbury, created the Newark we see by building the castle and
planning the town. Newark is one of the clearest examples of
towns planned by Norman bishops (cf. St Andrews, Lichfield),
distinguished by a regular and symmetrical street plan and the
large market place within the defences. The three gates were in
Bridge Street (E), Bargate (N), and at the N end of Mill Gate.
Appleton Gate and Carter Gate mark the E line of the defences,
Lombard Street the S, The Mount and Slaughterhouse Lane the
N. On the river front to the W, they may have run out to the castle
from the S; the NW rounded corner is preserved in the grounds
of the Ossington Coffee Palace. At first they consisted only of an
earth bank and ditch. Probably in the C14 a stone wall was added.
Alexander may also have strengthened the river defences by
diverting part of the Trent to join the Devon in front of the castle.

Newark's prosperity was based on its position as a route-centre.
The prehistoric track (Sewstern Lane) developed in the C13 and
C14 into the Great North Road. As early as the C13 a gild (of Holy
Trinity) is mentioned. Yet the town, though important in its part
of the country, was very small. It had about 2,000 inhabitants in
1377, and about 3,000 as late as *c.* 1600. But then Nottingham
also had no more than about 3,000 and 3,500 at these two
moments. So medieval and Tudor Newark was nearly as big as
Nottingham, whereas now the figures are about 25,000 and about
280,000. When the town was incorporated in 1549 the buildings
were mostly timber-framed. Like Nottingham, Newark began to
acquire its brick character about 1660. During the Civil War it
again was its position that gave it importance, this time as a
Royalist stronghold, and an elaborate system of fortifications was
built on a wider circuit than the medieval walls. In the C18 it
became a staging-post on the Great North Road, coaching inns

\* We owe the following information about the Norman town to Professor
M. W. Barley.

were built, the narrow medieval gates demolished, and the town
began to assume the elegant Georgian character still predominant today.

## CHURCHES

St Mary Magdalen. Among the two or three dozen grandest
parish churches of England, 222 ft long, with a spire 237 ft high.
Nothing remains of the pre-Conquest church. Four phases
appear in its architectural history, with the fourth unmistakably
dominant.

TRANSITIONAL. The CRYPT under the sanctuary, two 13
oblong, rather narrow bays with depressed rib-vaulting, the
ribs of keeled profile; two rudely decorated bosses, one with
a cable-moulding, the other with flat leaves. No transverse
arches (cf. Durham). Incorporated in the present crossing piers,
the remains of Transitional ones which, with the crypt, show
that a cruciform church was intended before 1200.

E.E. The WEST TOWER is engaged, i.e. set flush with the W 32
façade, quite a rare arrangement. The W portal is of four major
and three minor orders, that is on the most ambitious scale. In
the voussoirs of the arch several orders of dogtooth ornament.
The surrounding blank arcading, as so often in English Gothic
façades, is of a rhythm which will not make sense. Inside, the
tower, at first intended to be open to the W, N, and S, has thick
compound piers with fillets and moulded capitals. On the
second stage a large, later window and again blank arcading.
On the third stage four tall arcades, two of which have window
openings. Above, in the spandrels, a diagonal trellis pattern
which appears identically at Lincoln. The buttresses (set back
from the corners) end on this stage. Above it the C14 is reached.
The two windows on each side have ogee tracery and are
gathered together by crocketed gables. The stage ends with a
quatrefoil frieze, as so often found in Notts, and pinnacles.
Above it rises the needle-sharp SPIRE, with broaches and four
tiers of four dormer windows in alternating positions (a landmark for miles around).

E.E. also the CROSSING. Strong compound piers with one
major and two minor attached shafts towards each side. The
distance between tower and crossing shows that already in the
C13 the church was on a cathedral scale. As regards its date
within the century, it is known that Henry III (that is before
1227) gave six oaks from Sherwood Forest towards work then

going on. The early C14 by pushing up the spire to its exceptional height matched the length of the church. Dec also the SOUTH AISLE, under construction in 1312, after the completion of the spire, and probably following it immediately, remarkably wide, with pitched roof and elaborate undulating tracery. A six-light window to the w, the six s windows of four lights. The buttresses between them have niches with ogee arches, gargoyles, and steep canopies. The later s porch (cf. below) cuts into the third bay from the w. The rest of the building is Perp, which means that as far as the interior is concerned the general impression is wholly Perp. Approximate dates are known: nave and N aisle probably before 1460 (payments to woodworkers for roofs), in any case before 1487, when the church was described as lately rebuilt; chancel largely rebuilt c. 1487–1500.*

52     NAVE. Although entirely of the C15, its proportions are determined by the s aisle of more than a hundred years before. It was the generation of c. 1310 that decided on a new church of much wider, airier character. The nave piers are so slim and the outer windows so large that nave and aisle appear all as one room. That is typical of the late as against the high middle ages, in which a clear separation between the three parallel eastward streams of the nave and aisles is always kept. The profile of the piers (four shafts and four hollows between them) also allows the eye to slide round them. A glance at the solidity of the C13 piers of tower and crossing shows up the difference at once. But while the room feels broad, it does not feel low. The aisle windows have two-centred arches, that is emphasis on their vertical growth; the piers are tall and lead the eye up just as vigorously as across the aisles. However, once the apexes of the arches are reached the close row of clerestory windows (twice as many as there are arcade openings) adds an energetic horizontal accent, and externally the roofs have a low pitch and decorated battlements. The design of the nave suggests that it was begun well before 1460, when the roofs were being made, for it resembles in general proportions and in various details the nave of Holy Trinity, Hull, begun in the last decade of the C14.‡ In common with Holy Trinity it has small foliage capitals

---

* Rebuilding bequest 1483; rebuilding deed (lost) 1487; glass for E window ready 1490; bequest for reredos and stalls 1493; Thomas Meyring buried on the N side of the high altar 1500; reredos finished 1508; glazing continued until 1539.

‡ The resemblance was pointed out by Mr Chrisopher Wilson.

to each shaft of the piers with small faces in between, and the separation of clerestory windows by chamfered projections. The wooden roofs are also similar. The tracery is not particularly close, but the embattled transoms appeared first in the late C14 chapter house at Howden in the East Riding and became very popular in the first half of the C15 in east Yorkshire (Selby Abbey N window) and in Lincolnshire (Croyland Abbey).

NAVE FURNISHINGS. FONT. Shaft C15 with figures; bowl 74 dated 1660, of Restoration type with cherubs' heads, etc., the product of a local campaign to make good Puritan damage (cf. Southwell). – (STAINED GLASS, from the E. S aisle: SE by *Wailes*, to T. S. Godfrey † 1859. Medallions in rich geometrical settings. – Second window to Elizabeth Gilstrap † 1869 by *Alfred Gerente* of Paris. Medallions with intricate figures on vivid blue backgrounds in a C13 French style characteristic of Gerente, one of the most medievalizing of the many C19 glasspainters. – Third window by *Wailes*, to Geo. Hodgkinson † 1865. Two tiers of canopied panels with Old Testament scenes. – Fifth and sixth windows by *Kempe*, given in 1901. – The W windows of nave and aisles (N † 1888, S † 1894) look like *Burlison & Grylls*'s work. RH) – PAINTING, N aisle. Raising of Lazarus by a local artist, *William Hilton*; large. – MONUMENT, near to the font, to Anne Markham † 1601, re- 68 moved from Cotham. Of the very best workmanship; a walltablet with the lady in relief kneeling and her children in front of and behind her, the whole with drapery above and two slim Corinthian columns and a pediment, not at all provincial in quality, very knowledgeable of classical detail, and very elegant in the shaping of the figures.

S PORCH two-storeyed with a depressed window arch and the Virgin in a niche above. Four- and five-light Perp windows. Library (given by Bishop White, 1698) on the upper floor.

CHANCEL AND CHANCEL AISLES (completed by 1498). The external E view is impressive but not particularly happy. 51 The aisles are so wide and their six-light windows so broad that they make the chancel itself, with its enormous seven-light window filling almost the whole height of the wall, appear narrow and squeezed in. A figure of the Magdalen in the niche above the apex of the E window reaching up higher than the battlements. Inside, the three E windows are all flanked by niches with canopies. N and S sides with two-centred five-light windows and buttresses between each with two thin tall pinnacles. The piers as in the nave, only shorter, because the floor is raised.

Window shapes and tracery and clerestory windows also as in the nave, except that the clerestory windows are a little higher. The roof-line of the nave and chancel runs through without any break, a very impressive line externally, when seen from a distance.

CHANCEL AND CHANCEL AISLE FURNISHINGS. The high altar is not placed against the E wall. Behind it is enough space (without any strictly structural division) for an ambulatory and an E chapel, the LADY CHAPEL, which has a MONUMENT to Robert Brown, High Sheriff, † 1532, black Purbeck marble with quatrefoil decoration, no effigy. – NE CHAPEL. Woodwork by *Caröe* (cf. Southwell, Bishop's Palace, etc.). – MONUMENTS. J. Johnson † 1659. Bust in an oval niche; triangular pediment. – W. E. Tallents † 1837, by *Bedford*. Nice profile surrounded by a wreath, half hidden by drapery. – STAINED GLASS. N chancel chapel E by *Hardman*, disappointing and muddy compared with the firm's earlier chancel E window (RH). – SE CHAPEL. Woodwork by *Comper*, 1930. – STAINED GLASS. In the chancel chapel E window fragments of medieval glass from several windows rearranged by *Joan Howson*, 1957. Two main groups, one of *c.* 1300 (centre panels: Creation, Expulsion, Adam delving and Eve spinning, Adoration of the Magi, Christ in the Temple, Agony in the Garden, Three Marys at the Sepulchre, Noli me Tangere, and other fragments); the other early C15 (side panels, Virgin Mary scenes: Suitors in the Temple, Annunciation, Visitation, Funeral; Christ scenes: Massacre of the Innocents, Crucifixion, Deposition, and Ascension, with figures of Anger, Gluttony, and Lust from a Seven Deadly Sins series plus other heads in the tracery). – (Chancel E window. 1862. An important *Hardman* design given as a memorial of the Prince Consort. Strong, deeply glowing, somewhat strident colour. – S chapel SE to J. M. Walker † 1929. Very light, luminous design that looks like a *Percy Bacon Bros.* production. RH) – SCULPTURE. Fragment of a reclining Virgin on a couch. – MONUMENT. Hercules Clay † 1644. Tablet with garland. – In both chancel aisles BENCH ENDS with poppyheads. – HIGH ALTAR with seats under ogee arches against the back of its base, that is towards the E (cf., for example, Lincoln, Southwell). – REREDOS by *Comper*, 1937, a shameless imitation of the late C14, all glistering with gold. It is only when one gets near it that one recognizes in the figures the feeble drawing of a late follower of pre-Raphaelite traditions instead of an expected handwriting similar to that of the

Wilton Diptych. The back part is signed by *James Powell & Sons*, 1912.* – ROOD SCREEN. 1508 by *Thomas Drawswerd* of York, the only surviving work by one of the most famous firms of its time. Coping to W and E continued for two bays to the E on the N as well as the S side. In the coping, small traceried roundels of gilded lead. Narrow panels with slim ogee arches and close Perp panelling in the spandrels.‡ – CHOIR STALLS. Of *c.* 1500, with twenty-six misericords representing, for example, angels, an owl, a 'green man', an eagle, a man on a lion attacking a monster with a lance, a dragon, and also foliage. – CHANTRY CHAPELS. Thomas Meyring † 1500, between choir and N choir aisle. Built out of the selling-out of all his clipped wool and his whole flock of sheep: four-centred arch towards the altar, towards the aisle two bays above the base completely filled by five-light transomed openings; battlemented top; a workmanlike, somewhat pedestrian job. – Robert Markham, *c.* 1508. Similar to the Meyring Chapel towards the altar, but the four-centred arch panelled, not moulded, and four stone seats, the SEDILIA, partly hiding it. Towards the aisle six-light instead of five-light openings, that is a slimmer appearance and a lighter cresting on top. – PAINTINGS. Two stone panels of a very naively painted C16 Dance of Death in the openings of the Markham Chapel, one showing death, the other a richly attired gallant. No evidence of more scenes in this series, which according to Mr Rouse is one of only two surviving in England (cf. Hexham). – MONUMENTS. Chancel W piers. R. Ramsey † 1639 and T. Atkinson † 1661, both, like the Johnson monument of 1659 (cf. above), busts in oval niches. Curiously enough the monument of 1661 is the most conservative of the three, still quite early C17 in its details. The Ramsey monument on the other hand already has a broken segmental pediment and scrolls *à la* Inigo Jones.

TRANSEPTS. The latest and boldest part of the building. They were begun after 1500. The N and S windows are as large as they could possibly be made: seven lights, with depressed four-centred arches emphasizing their breadth rather than their height. The impression inside is of a glasshouse. Nothing like it was tried again (except perhaps by Robert Smythson) until the time of the Crystal Palace.

FURNISHINGS. SCULPTURE (S transept). War Memorial, 1939–45, by *Robert Kiddey*. Incised slab of the Gill type. –

MONUMENTS. Brass to Alan Fleming † 1363, a merchant of
Newark, made in Flanders. One of the largest brasses in England (9 ft 4 in. by 5 ft 7 in.), the main figure flanked by broad
piers each with several tiers of double niches with figures; in
niches above his head also a row of small figures, in composition
and details similar to Elsing, Norfolk, 1347, and St Margaret,
Kings Lynn, 1364. – D. Crayle † 1727. Excellent bust under
a broken triangular pediment. – Anne Taylor † 1757 by *Roubiliac*. Rococo shape, with profile medallion; nothing special in
the *œuvre* of the great sculptor. – Albina Fisher † 1806; but
the monument is late Victorian, by *Forsyth*, with two sentimental angels in flowing robes framing the inscription.

CHRISTCHURCH. *See* Perambulation, p. 196.

ST LEONARD, North Gate. By *Evans & Jolly* of Nottingham,
who won the competition of 1871 judged by *Sir G. G. Scott*.
A simple town church, stone, with mechanical detail. Now
demolished. – STAINED GLASS. E window 1895 by Mr *Tute*,
in Kempe's style. – Two windows by *Christopher Webb*:
S aisle E, 1931, and N aisle, 1941.

HOLY TRINITY (R.C.), Boundary Road. By *Horsley & Currall*,
begun in 1975, unfinished at the time of writing (1979). Polygonal church of pinkish brick with a conical roof topped by a
lantern and spirelet. Basically an octagon with top-lit chancel
and chapels projecting on four sides, and with long windows
on the others. Interior spoilt by sub-Perp woodwork.

BEDE HOUSE CHAPEL, Bede House Lane. The Bede House,
founded in 1556, has been demolished, but the small stone
chapel remains, and in 1978 awaits a new use.

WESLEYAN CHAPEL, Barnby Gate. Of the prosperous Victorian
type with large stone Doric porches. Built in 1844 by *J. Simpson*
of Leeds. Nice interior with oval gallery and coffered ceiling.
– Late *Morris & Co.* STAINED GLASS, N side (behind pulpit):
1922.

BAPTIST CHAPEL, Albert Street. 1876 by *Drury & Mortimer*
of Lincoln. Undistinguished red brick.


PUBLIC BUILDINGS

CASTLE.\* Large and roughly oblong in plan, on a cliff above the
river and commanding the crossing from northern England.
After slighting at the end of the Civil War, all that remains is

\* We owe this account of the castle to Professor M. W. Barley.

the gatehouse (there was no keep) and, running W from it and
then S to the SW turret, the curtain wall. Splendid high river
front (265 ft long, 170 ft high) with a watergate in it, beaten
only by Warwick, Durham, and perhaps Chepstow. Raised
from c. 1133 by a great builder, Alexander, Bishop of Lincoln,
† 1148, who at the same time was planning the town.* How
much he completed is uncertain. The gatehouse is certainly his,
and also a vanished free-standing chapel. (The stones for its
doorway, of three orders, are stacked in the undercroft.) By
1139 it could be called 'a magnificent castle of very ornate construction'. The GATEHOUSE, as at Richmond and Ludlow, was
the strong point, its front face remarkable for fine jointed ashlar,
the rear largely rubble (limestone) with ashlar dressings. It has
a plain entrance passage, not vaulted, and two upper floors
reached by a newel stair in a turret at the rear of the E side. The
larger of the two rooms at first-floor level was the bishop's private CHAPEL, open to the roof, unheated, and lighted to the
S by a wheel window, still with nook-shafts, scalloped capitals,
and a roll moulding. The smaller outer room, perhaps for a chaplain, had a fireplace. The westernmost of three large single-
light windows overlooking the entrance (blocked in the C16)
shows the quality of Alexander's work: square-headed inside,
with nook-shaft, scalloped capital, and nook roll, and an arch
of two orders outside, its hoodmould with pellet ornament
identical to that on the chapel doorway. The upper levels com-
municated with rooms to the W, both within the wall thickness,
by a timber gallery corbelled out from the outer face. Also C12
the SW TURRET with altered openings. In the basement a
dungeon, and at both upper levels chambers, for sleeping
because each has a garderobe.

A later bishop, perhaps Henry de Burghersh (1320–40),
rebuilt the curtain wall, including the NW and central TURRETS
but stopping short of the SW turret: a grand operation in polychrome masonry with oolite and sandstone (the dominant
material), but undocumented and with no datable stylistic features. Only three large, equally spaced openings with a hint of
reticulated tracery shown in Buck's drawing of c. 1724 suggest
an early C14 date. They must have lighted two HALLS, at first-
floor level from the bailey, separated by the middle turret and
each open to the roof (for the duplication of halls see Southwell,
p. 329). That to the N was the more private, with space beyond

* Alexander was also responsible for Banbury Castle, the castle and town
at Sleaford, and the W portals of Lincoln Cathedral.

it for two rooms for the bishop's use, one above the other. The kitchens cannot be located. At the lowest level of the NW turret a dungeon, with another between it and the undercroft. The UNDERCROFT, of four by two vaulted bays, was also part of this rebuilding. Reached by the watergate, it provided storage beneath the hall. The last alterations made by a bishop were those of Thomas Rotherham (1471–80), before his translation to York. He inserted an upper floor into part or all of the northerly hall and provided new windows, including a two-storey oriel, to light it.

Under Henry VIII, who took over castle and town in 1547, the castle was allowed to deteriorate. In 1581 the Earl of Rutland leased it. He may have reduced a tower on the town side (for building material) and certainly modernized what was left for residence, with a new doorway and window to the SW turret, a window in the middle turret, two windows at top level over the hall, and with new windows and a fireplace in the gatehouse. His gatehouse windows, of two to four lights with round heads and sunk spandrels, must be more or less contemporary with the transomed river-front windows, although by different masons. *Salvin* confused the evidence by his restoration in 1845–8.* His work, in light-coloured, comparatively un-weathered oolite, includes the anomalous upper-level window nearest the NW turret and the strengthening of the buttresses flanking the gatehouse N entrance. In 1889 Newark corporation acquired the castle and *H. E. Milner* laid out the grounds: the castle was repaired by an unknown architect in Yorkshire sandstone which now looks sadly unsuitable. In 1979, a new programme of restoration by the DOE and the local authorities has started.

BEAUMOND CROSS, London Road Gardens, moved from the S end of Carter Gate. Weathered C15 shaft, repaired and ornamented in 1778, restored again in 1801. A very slender, slightly tapering, fluted shaft, with a niche for a statue at the foot and a lantern top below a knob-like finial. No cross.

91 TOWN HALL, Market Place. Palladian, built *c.* 1774–6 of Mansfield stone by *Carr* of York, and a fine example of its type and period. Seven bays. Ground floor with large smooth rustication and arched windows. The centre is a three-bay loggia with original iron grilles. Above it, another, with tall, slim Doric

---

* Newark, Carisbrooke, and Caernarvon were the first medieval castles to be restored by the government in the C19, excluding those occupied by the Crown.

columns rising through both upper storeys, and a pediment with a figure of Justice. Ingenious T-plan incorporating a columned butchers' market or shambles stretching out at r. angles behind the shallow main block. The unusual engaged columns of the 'aisles' first appeared at Mereworth church, Kent (1744–6), probably inspired by Sangallo's entrance to the Palazzo Farnese. Above the market a fine assembly hall with two pairs of giant Corinthian columns screening off apses or niches in the Robert Adam manner. Pilasters in pairs between the windows. Compartmented ceiling (rather poor in quality, probably because of successive restoration) by *Kilminster* of Derby: Carr's version of Adam's ceiling in the old library at Harewood. Doorcases also with Adam-style decoration. At one end windows over the mantelshelves, at the other a bust of George III by *Peter Turnerelli*, 1809, and one of the fourth Duke of Newcastle, 1823. Facing the Market Place behind the loggia a small Council Chamber with good doorcases. Behind the butchers' hall, a MARKET HALL of 1884 by *Charles Bell*, opening on to Middle Gate.

Former CORN EXCHANGE, Castle Gate (now bingo hall). A focal point at the end of Stodman Street, on the riverside. 1847–8 by *Duesbury*, with Italian Baroque features. Massive proportions compared with the adjacent c18 houses. Single-storey, stone, with three large double doors in three shell-headed alcoves. Flanking the central tower figures with corn by *John Bell*, 1843. At the back brick, with a tall tower. Inside, a ridge and furrow part-glazed roof.

GILSTRAP LIBRARY, Castle Gate. A pretty little stone building in an Arts and Crafts Jacobean style with much naturalistic carving. 1882–3 by *Henman & Beddoes* of Birmingham.

LILLEY AND STONE SCHOOL, London Road. Built in 1898 as the School of Science and Art by *Mallows & Grocock* of Bedford. A good example of the work of a talented architect, *C. Mallows*, little known today, but an excellent draughtsman whose work can be seen in various architectural periodicals of the day. Queen Anne style with some fancy Art Nouveau style ironwork over the porch.

MOUNT SCHOOL. *See* Perambulation, p. 195.

COUNTY JUNIOR SCHOOL, Lovers Lane. A well designed board school of 1889 by *Hine & Son*. Queen-Anne-style details, a pilastered feature on each main façade, and a lantern.

GENERAL HOSPITAL, London Road. 1879–81 by *William Bliss*

*Sanders.* * Rather grandiose, with 'Wrenaissance' detail in fiery red brick.

HAWTONVILLE HOSPITAL (former Union Infirmary), Boundary Road. By *A. Marshall*, opened in 1905. In the style of Marshall's suburban houses, with Dutch gables and bay-windows.

CASTLE RAILWAY STATION. 1846. Early Italianate; well preserved.

TRENT BRIDGE. Brick with stone dressings. Built in 1775 by *Stephen Wright* (Colvin). Footways and railings dated 1848.

LONGSTONE BRIDGE, below the castle, parallel with Mill Gate. Built in 1819 by the Newark Navigation Co. Seven arches in stone.

VIADUCT (or Flood Road). By *Smeaton*, 1770. Carries sections of the Great North Road across the flood plain of the Trent, NW of the town (widened on the W side).

PERAMBULATION

The perambulation begins in the MARKET PLACE which, in spite of insensitive C19 additions, is still a joy to examine. The shape is an irregular rectangle with an island of C17, C18, and C19 buildings in the NW corner. On the W side is the strictly Palladian TOWN HALL (*see* Public Buildings). But only a little N of this proud monument of a metropolitan taste, the half-timbering of an earlier age peeps in (all restored in 1960): the QUEEN'S HEAD, C16, with continuous jetties to its two upper storeys, close-studded walls, and an interesting hybrid roof with diminished principles (which can be seen for the price of a drink); and the cottage in QUEEN'S HEAD YARD. The theme is taken up by the WHITE HART INN in the SE corner of the Market Place, one of the paramount examples of late C15 timber-framed architecture in England, but at the time of writing in a sadly dilapidated state crying out for restoration. Of four bays, the fourth, apparently in its original state, hidden behind the return angle of the square. Highly decorated main front. The upper storeys, mostly intact, have twenty-four closely-placed uprights with tiny terracotta figures of saints, one with a book, the other with a palm, repeated time and time again. They may be later additions. Under the eaves a row of windows, unusual for the date, recalling those of the Priors'

---

* Sanders is best remembered for his scholarly *Examples of Carved Oak Woodwork in the Houses and Furniture of the C16 and C17*, to which Ruskin wrote an introduction.

House at Much Wenlock. Ground floor entirely modern (bays three and four replaced by cast-iron and steel columns, 1850–1900), but still with its gate-passage. At the back, the first and second floors were entered by galleries, now glazed, although the turned balusters suggest that they were once open. Inside, a superb purlin roof of *c.* 1500, originally open to the upper rooms. The front range is not the oldest part of the building:* inside the s range are the remains of a crown-post roof of *c.* 1350 (the timber-framed walls rebuilt in brick) which may have belonged to the great hall of an earlier inn. A floor was inserted later, possibly when the front range was built. Some framing and part of a similar roof also in the E wing. The rest of the s side of the Market Place is completely dominated by two big inns: the former SARACEN'S HEAD, 1721, and the CLINTON ARMS. Their size and prominent position are characteristic of towns on the Great North Road. The Clinton Arms had ninety horses about the year 1800. Both buildings stand on colonnades or loggias, or, as C17 England called them, piazzas (cf. Market Place, Nottingham), with Tuscan columns and no arches, and both date from the early C18, the Clinton Arms with fashionable alternating Gibbs rustication on columns and window surrounds and Palladian pediments to the main windows. Behind on the s side a shopping development by *Gordon Benoy & Partners*, 1977–8. The architects and planners had the right idea (cf. Salisbury, 1973; Chesterfield, 1977). The buildings on the Market Place screen the inevitable blank back walls and multi-storey car park, but the development breaks out behind with harsh-coloured brick and details out of scale with C18 and early C19 Lombard Street. Altogether too many neo-vernacular gimmicks.

The 'piazza' motif appears again on one of the island buildings of *c.* 1710 and on the N side, where otherwise there is much less of interest. Here stands the MOOT HALL, a replica (1967) of the original of 1708, with the arms of John Holles, Duke of Newcastle, whose manorial moot hall it was. It has seven bays, the Saracen's Head eight and no dormer windows; otherwise they are almost identical, brick with quoins and dormer windows in the roof. In the NW corner, behind the island of encroachment, the grey brick pedimented former Subscription Library, *c.* 1830 by *William Fowler*. Also on the N side the early C18 No. 25 has a fine staircase with alternating plain, fluted, and turned balusters on a cut string (DOE). On the E side one

* According to F. W. B. Charles.

opulent early C18 house (Nos. 27–28) with a stately doorcase. Segmental hood with a bull's-eye window in the tympanum, on elaborate double consoles, one pair at r. angles, the other flush to the wall. Quoins, keystone, coved cornice, and a nice pedimented dormer. Inside, a staircase similar to that in No. 25.* From here another good early C18 house looks down into the Market Place from the top of BRIDGE STREET. Important to the composition of the Market Place, it is large (of seven bays) but plain, with a panelled parapet. Modern shopfront.

Nos. 27–28 leads on to the others in CHURCH WALK and APPLETON GATE which form a close behind the church. Most of them are plain and distinguished only by their doorcases, e.g. the VICARAGE (No. 10), more important-looking, with a nice wooden doorcase and some original features inside including an early C18 staircase, and Nos. 9 and 9A, late C17, with a modillion cornice. Further up, the grammar school, founded in 1529 and built in 1532. Now called TUDOR HALL, it is used as part of Newark District Council Museum. Only the s end is visible from the street. Of stone, with a stepped brick chimneystack, the remains of the original street gateway set back into the façade, and an original doorway at the back. Inside, a timber-framed room partly overhanging the one large hall. In 1817, when the headmaster was attempting to establish a fee-paying boarding school concentrating on the classics, the plain brick headmaster's house was built in front of the old school on Appleton Gate by *John Sadler Sheppard*. The doorcase with an open pediment on brackets rising from pilasters is a common feature of Newark houses – in this instance, of stone. N of and at r. angles to the headmaster's house, the English school (now museum) of 1835, marking the introduction of modern subjects into the curriculum. Red brick with tall windows and a master's alcove on the N side. Behind, the art room, 1902. Next, in extensive gardens enclosed by old stone walls, the FRIARY, on the site of a vanished house of Observant (1507), then Austin (1534) Friars. It is a rambling stone building, C17 in its earliest parts to judge from the small stone mullioned windows on the N side above the C19 porch and at the back, for example to the C17 staircase. On the ground floor a fine panelled room with pilasters and other enrichments. This core was remodelled c. 1720 with wooden mullion-and-transom-cross windows at the back (E) and on the N, the latter lighting

* The building had a printing press (now in Newark Museum) on which the first of Byron's poems ('Hours of Idleness', 1806) was produced.

an upstairs room with bolection-moulded panelling. On the w, traces of quoins where a short front wing was added later. N and E wings and probably the entrance hall and porch date from 1868–77. To the s an outbuilding called the OLD CHAPEL with an undercroft and C17 mullioned windows.*

Off the w side of Appleton Gate N of the church, in THE MOUNT, the early C19 MOUNT SCHOOL (C of E): the boys' school of 1826 by *W. M. Fowler*, chiefly a one-storey school-room with a stuccoed and pilastered façade, and the brick girls' school of 1838 with a staircase tower of 1877 at the back. WILSON STREET to the w was built in 1766 by Dr Bernard Wilson, vicar of St Mary Magdalene and an extremely wealthy pluralist of questionable character. The narrow street had a tunnel-like quality, with identical terraces of sixteen tall houses facing each other, brick, with the least possible of accents. Now only the w terrace, with one house breaking forward slightly at each end, and the corresponding pavilions of the E terrace remain, so that the original effect is lost.‡ In the church-yard on the E side an ugly view of the back of the red-brick Tudor-style SONG SCHOOL built in 1866. At the end of KIRK GATE, which leads off Wilson Street opposite the w end of the church, the former NOTTINGHAM & NOTTS BANK, 1887, in *Watson Fothergill*'s usual idiosyncratic manner, nearly con-temporary with the Ossington Coffee Palace (*see* p. 199), but a very different thing to the Palace's Domestic Revival style: Italian Gothic, with large biforated windows to the fine bank-ing hall (with polychrome brick walls, a coved wooden ceiling, and ornate ironwork) and a fancy tower, reduced in height in 1957. The manager's house, with its oriel window, forms part of the composition. All now the Newark Technical College school of violin-making, a very suitable new use. Also in Kirk Gate early to mid C18 houses, several of the smaller ones timber-framed inside. On the N side two box-framed C16 and C17 houses now thrown into one, the earlier (No. 39, w) with moulded timbering and some internal wall-painting, the later (No. 37, E) with a crown-post roof with no purlins (cf. Severn's Restaurant, Nottingham).§ Further down on the same side,

* Parallel with Appleton Gate to the w in Lovers Lane (Tithe Barn Court) stood the aisled rectorial TITHE BARN. Part of it was moved to Hillside, Bea-con Hill Road, but has since collapsed (1978).

‡ The houses are being refurbished, some without their chimneys, all with-out their shutters.

§ The later house is said to have been the residence of Lady Leake, with whom Henrietta Maria stayed when she was at Newark during the Civil War.

the OLD KING'S ARMS, an early C18 inn with cast-iron royal arms and a blank arcade on the ground floor, and PUREFOY HOUSE, an early C19 two-bay stuccoed front with pilasters supporting a pediment over all. On the opposite side, at the corner of MIDDLE GATE, a C15 timber-framed building. Jettied upper storey, with some curved braces; modern ground floor. In Middle Gate itself not much except a mid-C18 house of ample proportions with a pediment over the centre three bays and a Roman Doric half-columned doorcase, and the entrance to the Market Hall behind the Town Hall (*see* Public Buildings).

Middle Gate ends at STODMAN STREET. Nos. 37 and 37a is the best Georgian house, early C18, with panelling and a staircase of the period. Also two good timber-framed houses. The WOOLPACK INN at the w end apparently dates from 1489 (DOE). Although stuccoed now, it is clearly the r. half of a Wealden-type building, i.e. with a jettied wing alongside a recessed section. More impressive is GOVERNOR'S HOUSE at the Market Place end, C16, with a coved and oversailing upper storey. It was associated with the Governors of Newark during the sieges of 1643–6. Here, St Mark's Lane leads s past the shopping development (*see* p. 193) to LOMBARD STREET, on the periphery of the old town. Mostly late C18 or early C19 houses (Nos. 31–33 is early C18, three storeys, five bays, good moulded doorcase). On the N side the former CHRISTCHURCH of 1836–7 by *J. D. Paine*, E.E. style, with three gables in stock brick and groups of three lancets at each end. Galleries on cast-iron columns and a tall lancet arch to the straight-ended chancel. Behind to its NW REGENT HOUSE, the former Congregational church, built as an independent chapel in 1822 by *W. Wallen*, plain red brick with pilasters between the three round-headed windows. Two porches with pilasters and pediments; arcaded at the side. The interior is well worth preserving, with a gallery running all round on cast-iron columns, and a tall elliptical arch articulating the end wall. Remains of a burial ground. Both churches are now warehouses. Adjacent on the N side nearer Beaumond Cross a very large pedimented early C19 house (Nos. 40–46) with lower wings. On the corner of ALBERT STREET and BEAUMOND CROSS, at the E end of Lombard Street, the CASTLE BREWERY OFFICES, built in 1882 by *William Bradford* for Caparn & Hankey, a French Renaissance-style composition in stone made splendid by a lot of vermiculation, marble, and red composition. In the pediment a sensitive relief of Newark Castle and, dominating the whole, a large central clock tower. Offices and brewhouse of 1889 at the back, on the site of the early C19 Union Workhouse, originally U-shaped, with two long wings stretching back from a block where the offices now stand. The l. wing survives. From the E side of Beaumond Cross LONDON ROAD leads out of the town. It has some early C19 stuccoed classical villas (Nos. 39–55) and a nice brick terrace (Nos. 57–62) with cast-iron balconies. Off London Road down a path near the Girls' School, the CLUB HOUSE of an early bowling club: a pretty brick building of 1809 with stone castellations, Gothic glazing, and a delicate cast-iron veranda inscribed with an appropriate admonition: LET NO MAN BE BIASSED.* N of Beaumond Cross CARTER GATE is the only street in the old centre completely spoilt by mediocre commercial development. Above modern shops on the W wide, the restored upper storeys of a timber-framed house with a fine moulded bressumer over the yard gate between the shops.

At the point where Carter Gate leads into Appleton Gate, running SE, BALDERTON GATE, the medieval road to London. As in London Road, the houses are mostly late C18 or C19 (see Nos. 117–119 and 121 on the NE side with cast-iron balconies). Set back on the SW side the COUNTY OFFICES occupy Dr Wilson's mid-C18 mansion (*see* Wilson Street). Three storeys, five bays, plain except for the parapet with blind panels and rusticated quoins and spoilt by facsimile wings and porch. Opposite, GUILDHALL STREET links Balderton Gate with BARNBY GATE to its N. In Guildhall Street, on the site of the hall of the medieval Holy Trinity Guild, a former METHODIST CHAPEL, plain red brick of two storeys with a round-arched door and windows, some with Gothick tracery. In Barnby Gate, a large detached early C18 house, much altered, but with its original staircase. At the W end a pretty yard to the RUTLAND ARMS.

The second part of the perambulation takes in the long riverside road (part of the Fosse Way) which changes its name from FARNDON ROAD at the S end, to MILL GATE, then to

* Further E, Bowbridge Road leads S from London Road. At its junction with Boundary Road the HAWTONVILLE ESTATE, 1919–20, one of a series of council estates designed and planned by *Barry Parker* after his partnership with Raymond Unwin ended in 1914. Pleasant if somewhat bland, the houses showing Parker's concern for sensitive placing of windows and profiling of hipped roofs. The house types developed for this project were used in Parker's municipal work throughout the 1920s (Mervyn Miller).

CASTLE GATE under the castle, and to NORTH GATE past the town bridge. We begin S of FARNDON ROAD in Devon Park at the QUEEN'S SCONCE. The Civil War fortifications round Newark, a Royalist stronghold, remain the most impressive in England. There are several small redoubts, batteries, and sconces in the fields round the town, but this is the most impressive survivor: a small fort with a large pointed bastion at each corner. In Farndon Road itself a solid, plain three-bay brick house with a wooden doorcase, its capitals decorated with Prince of Wales feathers.* A date plaque at the back reads G M S 1806. It was the master's house of George and Mary Scales Hawton Bleachworks and Linen Manufactory, which with its workers' cottages once lay between Farndon Road and the River Devon.‡ At the bottom of MILL GATE on the site of the former SOUTHFIELD HOUSE, sheltered housing for old people by *Gordon Benoy & Partners* for Newark Housing Association, 1969–70, a group of brick-built flats round a courtyard of two and three storeys, rather blocky with square bay-windows projecting on all floors. On the site the S boundary of the Anglo-Saxon cemetery was determined (*see* p. 182). Round the corner in VICTORIA STREET there are some mid-C19 houses that follow the Georgian pattern. Off the E side of Mill Gate in PARLIAMENT STREET, the OLD HALL (R.C. presbytery), a double-pile C17 brick house of three storeys with two stone-capped gables, stone string course and plinth. Inside, the original staircase of two parallel flights, the newel posts ending in lovely big knobs (cf. The Friary, Appleton Gate). Mill Gate itself has a villagey atmosphere, with many modest Georgian houses and cottages. The larger houses have a concentration of decoration on the doorcases. Worth picking out (from the S end, E side): No. 107 of chequered brick, early C19; Nos. 69–71, late C18 or early C19, two houses divided by a wide coach arch with a blind recess over, containing a semicircular window; No. 65 built as a Methodist Chapel in 1776 before the one in Guildhall Street; No. 23, detached and with a good pedimented doorcase.§ On the W side: Nos. 78–82, the centre house slightly broken forward, and, more important, the TRENT

---

* Further W, Farndon WINDMILL, no cap. Dated 1823.

‡ The manufacture of blue linen smocks was a staple Newark industry in the C18 and C19.

§ A particularly good house, Nos. 15–21, was demolished in 1965. Said to have been built in 1663, it had two-storey canted bay-windows (cf. Stamford) and shaped gables. (Adjacent cottages to the N also had shaped gables. MWB)

NAVIGATION CANAL WAREHOUSE and adjacent mill, 1870, tidied up by *Guy St John Taylor Associates* (1975–9) for the District Council. In the warehouses round a courtyard, craft workshops, and a folk museum. To one side in MILL LANE a row of late C18 or early C19 cottages. C19 warehousing lines the canalized stretch of the river which runs alongside the Trent behind Mill Gate. Between the canal and the river by the millrace, the foundations and wheelpits of a large C19 water mill burnt down in 1965. CASTLE GATE, at the junction of Lombard Street, is more stately than Mill Gate. Near the S end two C16 timber-framed cottages (Nos. 40–44), but the houses are mostly plain C18, with slightly elaborate doorcases and some central pediments (e.g. Nos. 21–31), a fine setting for the castle. The much altered No. 11 was once a charming early C18 house, a focal point with the church spire behind it for those crossing Trent Bridge. Still with its hipped roof and pedimented central bay outlined by stone quoins, it has been restored to its former glory. On the S side of BEAST MARKET HILL leading up to Castle Gate from the bridge a pretty little two-storey early C19 TOLL HOUSE (Women's Institute County House). Opposite, a building on a totally different scale, the OSSINGTON COFFEE PALACE of 1882, Newark's outstanding Victorian building, given by Viscountess Ossington, widow of Speaker Denison and sister of the 'burrowing' fifth Earl of Portland (*see* Welbeck Abbey), and designed by one of the most expensive London firms of architects, *Ernest George & Peto*. In a prominent position, just at the end of the bridge and opposite the castle, it was intended to demonstrate loudly against strong drink and uphold the banner of coffee. Although it offered the amenities of a good-class hotel, as so often was the case with such ventures, it was not a success, and is now offices. Ernest George made an excellent job of it, as he did with his earlier temperance hotels, the Cocoa Tree, Pinner (1877–8), and the Beehive, Streatham (1878). It is a happy, very ingenious composition with manifold gables and chimneys, the first floor all of those oriel windows which Norman Shaw had just made popular. The handwriting is heavier than Shaw's, though equally deft. Towards the river a terraced tea garden bounded by a curving wall in stripes of stone and brick, which preserves the line and level of the medieval town wall. Behind, a bowling alley and tile-hung stables.

Then on into NORTH GATE, a mixture of substantial houses, C17 to early C19, and some early industrial premises. At the

s end, w side, Nos. 1 and 3 (TRANSPORT HOUSE), late C18
red brick. Inside, a good C17 staircase and two early C18
panelled rooms. Next No. 5, C17, with mostly C18 features including a good panelled room. Stone-built (the town walls came
by here, see the plaque on the opposite corner). Set back,
HANDLEY HOUSE (No. 7), a handsome-looking late C17 house
which must at one time have been rather grand. Two storeys,
hipped roof with dormers and modillion cornice, rusticated
doorcase and quoins. At the back an C18 wing. Half the plan,
of the usual sort, is well-preserved. In the two r. hand rooms
original panelling, cupboards, etc., in the hall plasterwork
with allegorical scenes. Once terraced gardens sloping down
to the river. Opposite, the late C18 NORTH GATE HOUSE,
large and very plain, of five bays and three and a half storeys,
with a panelled attic. Further on the best Georgian house, No.
38, late C18, with a moulded pediment and cornice and two-
storey wings. No. 40 is of four bays, slightly earlier but with
a similar doorcase. On the other side is one of the earliest surviving BREWERIES (now a store but almost untouched). Courtyard with a late C18 or early C19 house on one side, three-storey
maltings and a kiln of the same date on the other three. The
perambulation ends with another and more important monument to the Newark brewing industry which began in 1776
when Samuel Sketchley came from Burton-on-Trent to establish his brewery near the Town Wharf. This business passed
through the Handley family to Richard Warwick, who in 1882–
90 built a splendid new brewery on the w side of North Gate.
His office, parallel to the street, was built in 1890 by *William
Bliss Sanders* (*see* General Hospital) to whose *Examples of
Carved Oak Woodwork* three of the Warwick family subscribed.
The style is the current Queen Anne, in brick, with an oriel
over the entrance and long windows with shell-like tracery in
the heads lighting the office which occupies almost all the first
floor. Here all the original fittings are fine, from the woodwork,
curving counter, and grand staircase to the radiators with castellated tops in tiled recesses. Behind, the brewhouse of 1882,
also by *Sanders*. Further back on the site the bottling stores
of 1920, the earlier 'semi-Greek style' maltings of 1864, and
nearer the river Trent House, the earliest part of the brewery,
which became the master brewer's house, very mutilated. On
the other side of the river (best seen from Trent Bridge), concrete maltings built *c.* 1890.

## NEWSTEAD ABBEY*                    5050

Not an abbey. It was founded between 1163 and 1173 by Henry II as a priory of Augustinian Canons. The first church seems to have had no aisles: the N aisle was probably added in the late C13. During that century extensive rebuilding took place in the claustral area. What survives of that date are the blocked W and E processional doors from cloister to church (*see* below), the C13 chapter house, the entrance to the slype next to it, the dorter undercroft (E), the shafts of the blocked dorter stairs (SE), and the undercroft of the great hall (W).

This period of building activity included the provision of a new façade for the church, an exceptionally perfect example 26 of a late C13 church front. Nothing of the bittiness which mars so many E.E. façades, even Salisbury, even Lincoln. A few large, logically composed motifs, broadly laid out, easily and lightly carried through. Narrow buttresses divide the front into three parts. Ground floor with tall steep blank arcading, cusped where the arches are broader. The capitals are partly still stiff-leaf, partly naturalistic (vine with grapes), partly figurated. Central portal of many orders and extremely finely moulded in the voussoirs. No recourse to ornamentation. A mullion divides the portal into two, slim and quatrefoil in section, as at the chapter house entrance of Southwell. Just as at Southwell, a quatrefoil appears in the tympanum. But it is not yet composed solely of tracery. It is still, exactly as at the S portal to the Angel Choir at Lincoln, a blank quatrefoil (pointed at the top) with a seated figure of Christ. The first floor had a vast six-light window, as big as any of the Perpendicular style, with geometrical and, it seems, intersecting tracery. Dogtooth decoration in the outer voussoir. L. and r. specially high blank four-light windows with sexfoil and cinquefoil circles in the tracery, exactly like the Salisbury chapter house of *c.* 1270, and decidedly earlier in style than the Southwell chapter house. The only feature which is not exactly in symmetry now is the side portals. That into the N aisle still exists, much simpler than the central one, but that which probably existed on the S side has gone. It would, however, never have led into a S aisle, for the whole of the S side of the façade is a sham. Behind it there simply was the N end of the W range, and behind that, occupy-

* We thank Dr Rosalys Coope and Miss Pamela Wood for thoroughly revising this description.

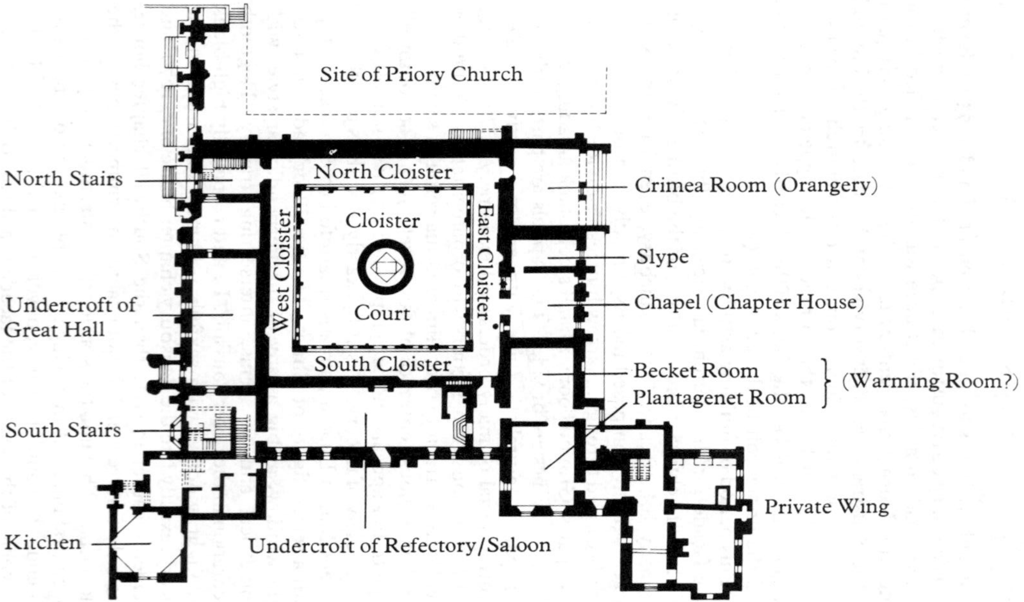

Site of Priory Church

Crimea Room (Orangery)

Slype

Chapel (Chapter House)

Becket Room

Plantagenet Room

(Warming Room?)

Private Wing

East Cloister

North Cloister

Cloister
Court

South Cloister

West Cloister

Undercroft of Refectory/Saloon

North Stairs

Undercroft of
Great Hall

South Stairs

Kitchen

Ground Floor

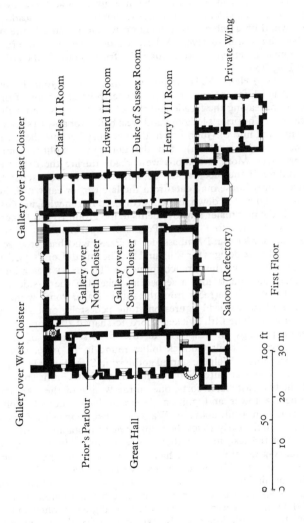

Gallery over West Cloister

Gallery over East Cloister

Charles II Room

Edward III Room

Duke of Sussex Room

Henry VII Room

Private Wing

Prior's Parlour

Great Hall

Gallery over
North Cloister

Gallery over
South Cloister

Saloon (Refectory)

First Floor

| 0 | 10 | 20 | 50 | 100 ft |
| 5 | | | 30 m | |

ing the place of an aisle, the N walk of the cloisters. This remarkable early instance of preference given to aesthetic over
functional considerations is worth remembering. The façade is
crowned by a gable with a niche in which a seated figure of
the Virgin still survives. A Perp window has been inserted
below it, and the openwork quatrefoil frieze on top of the aisles
is Perp too.

In 1539 Henry VIII granted the priory to Sir John Byron
of Colwick for the sum of £810. He destroyed the body of the
church, leaving the façade and the adjacent ranges round the
cloister. The prior's lodgings and great hall (probably C15) were
converted into Sir John's own, the refectory became the great
chamber (later saloon), and the dorter was split up into
chambers. More alterations were made during the C17; the
building of the block at the SE corner resembling a separate
two-storey house may date from the late C17 or early C18. So
Newstead passed down to the fourth Lord Byron who, in 1695,
made the first major improvements to the grounds. His father-
in-law was the first Earl of Portland, superintendent of the
Royal Gardens and Ambassador to Paris, who had procured
the Le Nôtre designs for William III. The fourth Lord's garden
certainly shows this French influence. To the SE was a long
canal, later made into a serpentine lake. On the E side the
garden rises in terraces from the square Eagle Pond, with, to
the E of it, two lead figures on stone pedestals, probably by
*John Nost*. The fifth 'wicked' Lord re-shaped the upper lake
and, perhaps in response to the first stirrings of neo-
medievalism, built Gothick follies round it. In 1749, that is
before Horace Walpole started gothicizing Strawberry Hill and
only a few years after Sanderson Miller's first Gothicisms, he
built two castellated forts, one on the W side of the lake, the
other, a tower and gun-emplacement later dubbed 'Folly
Castle', on a hill above it. Walpole called them 'silly forts!'.
Later, in the early 1770s, he transformed the stables on the NE
side of the lake into another 'castle' or fort. He also kept a
twenty-gun ship afloat (he had been in the Navy when young)
and entertained his acquaintances with mock battles. However,
late in his life, he wantonly neglected the house and stripped
his estate of deer and trees so ruining his heir's inheritance.
When the poet Byron, the sixth Lord and great-nephew of the
'wicked Lord', inherited Newstead in 1798 the house was
in a ruinous state. The rooms which he restored for his own
use in the NW corner and those which he fitted up for guests

in the SE part of the building were more of an oasis in this scene of decay than we can now imagine. In 1808 Byron buried his dog Boatswain; his neat classical monument stands sacrilegiously near the high altar of the old church, though some way to the SE of it.

That the mansion at Newstead appears to us as complete as it does is due to the poet's schoolfellow, Colonel Wildman, who purchased the Abbey in 1817 and set to work at once. His architect was *John Shaw*, the architect of St Dunstan-in-the-West and many country houses. He made complete plans for restorations and additions (dated 1818 and 1819 and preserved in the Abbey and in a private collection) and largely finished them by 1829. The pivot of his composition is a feature that was created by him, the SUSSEX TOWER, a Norman-revival piece. The building 'of rich and rare mix'd Gothic' as we walk through it today is as much his as the priors' or the Byrons'. Shaw's was an unusually broad-minded revivalism. Colonel Wildman's successor, Mr Webb, who owned it from 1860 to 1899, made only minor contributions, for example the bay-window which extends through two storeys on the S façade of the private wing.

So to examine the EXTERIOR of the house. Shaw's Sussex Tower stands at the S end of the WEST FRONT, balancing the intricate and paper-thin church façade on the opposite side. Between them lies the prior's lodgings with, at the N end, the canted bay lighting prior's chamber and parlour, and next the three long oriel windows of the hall, carried on a low arcade of pre-C18 date, extended S by Shaw c.1820. Here, only the northernmost window which lighted the dais end existed before the Byrons. A second one was added in place of the exterior chimneybreast some time before 1730, and Shaw added the third in place of the original entrance. A flight of steps led up to a C17 porch at hall level according to representations by Buck (1726) and Tillemans (c. 1730). Buck shows the hall with its one original bay, central chimneybreast, and first-floor entrance. By the time Tillemans painted the same view c. 1730 the chimneybreast had been replaced by the second window.

Shaw transferred the entrance to the ground floor, giving it a vaulted Gothic porch. Between it and the tower a semicircular bay-window behind which is the main staircase. He moved the old C17 entrance porch to the E side. The N front is almost plain except for two oriel windows, an outside staircase, and a semicircular gable added to the N end of the prior's lodgings, all C19. The EAST FRONT, overlooking the formal garden, has at the N end the C19/early C20 addition of a large bay-window and, at the S end, the private wing with C17 entrance porch already mentioned. Towards the N end of the E range, between three buttresses, three lancets with simple C19 tracery lighting the chapter house. The SOUTH FRONT is the one which Shaw altered most radically. Its original undistinguished appearance is recorded in an early C18 watercolour in the Abbey. At the W end is Shaw's kitchen, polygonal and almost free-standing, imitating the abbot's kitchen at Glastonbury. Finally back to the W front. The lower storey of the wing that encloses the S side of the forecourt, very stark with small lancets, is Shaw's; the upper was added by Mr Webb after 1860.

The INTERIOR is entered by the W porch which leads into the much restored C13 UNDERCROFT beneath the great hall (eight rib-vaulted bays carried on three octagonal columns without imposts). Here three Byron MONUMENTS from Colwick church have been put up: to Sir John † 1567, an alabaster tomb-chest with little kneeling figures against the chest walls and an incised slab on top; to Sir John † 1604, a large standing wall-monument with two recumbent effigies between baluster columns with obelisks and achievement on top (cf. Averham); and to the two Sir Johns who died in 1624 and 1625 and their wives, one of the usual small wall-monuments with figures kneeling opposite each other, one generation above, the other below. From the entrance hall one enters the N walk of the CLOISTER. Over the cloister walks are galleries, but whether these predate alterations by the first Sir John is a vexed question.* The lower windows are early C15, the upper ones of c. 1540, yet the wall is apparently all of one build. In the centre of the cloister garth is a hexagonal conduit, with shell niches on each side of the lowest stage, a frieze of quatrefoil, and then a battlemented parapet. The upper stage has a parapet decorated with lozenges, and each stage is topped by six grotesque figures. The inscription on it reads W B 1720, but Walpole in 1760 called it an 'ancient cistern' and the ornamentation of the top suggests an early C16 date. The C18 date may refer to a restoration or possibly the removal of the conduit to the W front (where it is shown in Tillemans' painting). In the depth of the N wall of the cloister (i.e. the S wall of the church) are the shafts of the E and W doorways to the nave, already mentioned. At the E end of the N walk, on the site of the transept, the ORANGERY with a possibly re-used ceiling in an apparently C19 imitation

* New evidence shows the galleries are post-Dissolution.

of late C17 style plasterwork. Next along the E walk one passes the Gothic doorway formerly to the slype or passage into the churchyard (this now blocked and a C19 doorway inserted), then the doorway to the CHAPTER HOUSE (a rectangle with six ribbed vaults on two slender composite shafts: circular core and four detached shafts with shaft-rings and stiff-leaf capitals). Converted by the early Byrons into a chapel, the gallery was added by Colonel Wildman and the whole chapel was decorated in polychrome in Butterfield's manner for Mr Webb in the 1860s: rich tiling within the arcade above the sedilia, stencilled patterns on walls and ceiling, stained glass *à la* Hardman, and traceried pews. At the end of the E walk is the archway into the original 'dark entry' to the cloister walk. Opening off the l. of it, rooms traditionally known as the priory WARMING ROOM. Originally one large vaulted hall with two central columns and stone vaults, it formed in part the undercroft to the dorter above. Now it is divided into two, the BECKET ROOM and the PLANTAGENET ROOM. In the S walk, to the W of the 'dark entry', are the shafts of the blocked dorter stairs and the stone staircase that replaced it. Beyond, the stone ledge of the lavatory.

From the C19 N staircase (off the W walk) one reaches the galleries above the cloisters. From here a spiral stair goes up to the PRIOR'S CHAMBER (Byron's bedroom), lighted by the N bay of the W range. Below it is the prior's parlour. The gallery over the N cloister, converted into the library in the early C19, has an C18 marble fireplace, probably by *Thomas Carter*. Off the E gallery the main bedrooms of the house made out of the dorter in the C16 and restored by Shaw. These are raised above the level of the gallery because of the height of the vaulted rooms below and are reached by short flights of steps. The CHARLES II ROOM has a Kentian ceiling of before 1720, painted with grisaille grotesques (cf. Belisarius Room, Raynham Hall, 1730). In the next two rooms (the EDWARD III and DUKE OF SUSSEX ROOMS), two of the three early C16 overmantels believed to have been brought from Colwick Hall when the Byrons sold it in the C18: oak carved in panels with hideously comic figures gaudily painted (and repainted). That in the Edward III Room has projecting busts in the manner of terracotta busts by Giuliano da Maiano at Hampton Court. At the end of the E gallery a staircase leads up to the SALOON in the S range (the refectory of the priory) with its ceiling dated 1631 and 1633. The wooden braces have tracery in the spandrels and very Jacobean-style pendants from the beams. Only eight of the plaster panels at the E end of the room are original: strapwork surrounding crude *all'antica* busts. They are for some unknown reason more elaborate and different in subject matter from the other panels (replicas made after a fire in 1965), which have large coarse plaster vases containing foliage, flanked by grotesques, birds, and animals. The fire exposed painted wall-decoration, probably late C12, in a brick pattern with a scrolly border, seen to the r. of the fine mid-C18 fireplace attributed to *Thomas Carter*. From the W gallery one enters the GREAT HALL. To the N of it the PRIOR'S PARLOUR, with the third of the crude and gaudy C16 overmantels, this one dated 1556. The great hall was thoroughly refitted for Col. Wildman: the screen, particularly, is a surprisingly competent piece of Gothick woodcarving.* The C19 staircase beyond the screen, with its curved bay-window, leads down again to the entrance. Working drawings for this staircase are in the Abbey collections dated 1830 and inscribed TW (Thomas Wildman).

The SE wing, which was opened to the public post-1979, was certainly in the C19, and probably before, used as the residential quarters of the owners. It contains another mid-C16 overmantel and some early panelling re-used, a wealth of interesting carved overmantels and wall panels made for Colonel Wildman, and also interesting plasterwork.

In the grounds, Wildman made the middle (garden) lake below the S front out of the existing stream. The suitably light and fanciful STABLES with a spire by the upper lake were built in 1862–3 by *M. E. Hadfield* for the Webbs. Pretty LODGES at the main (E) and the W entrances by *C. A. Buckler*, 1860s.

The delights of the grounds range from C17 basins and yew tunnels, C18 Gothick waterfalls and follies to Webb's C19 Japanese rockeries and fernery. The last have been restored to as perfect a condition as any gardener could desire. The house is the epitome of the picturesque and romantically medieval so

---

* Before the chimneystack was removed (*see* p. 205) there was probably a chimneypiece by *Nicholas Stone*, who supplied one between 1635 and 1638 through his brother-in-law Hendrik II De Keyser, who is said to have come to England *c.* 1634, and was involved in the building operations at Newstead in 1638 according to Stone's accounts. He was still there in 1639, when he married a local girl and was described as 'of Newstead, gent.'. But no work can be connected with him. He moved to Nottingham *c.* 1640 before returning to Holland in 1647. (This information was kindly given by Mr H. J. Louw.)

admired in the late C18 and early C19. It makes a poignant contrast with the raw ugliness of Annesley Colliery through which you pass if you approach from the w.

The rest of the story is quickly told. Newstead passed through the Webbs' heirs until it was bought by Sir Julien Cahn, a Nottingham businessman; he presented it to the City of Nottingham in 1931. The Roe Byron Collection of manuscripts, books, and pictures was bequeathed in 1937 and is exhibited in the house together with the Frazer Collection of personal relics of the poet and the Gatty Collection of Byron and Webb family furniture.

In the grounds N of the house, ABBEYWOOD HOUSE by *Bartlett & Gray*, built in 1954–6 and typical of that date, with solid–void interest on the main upper storey.


## NORMANTON-ON-SOAR                    5020

ST JAMES. The chief attraction of the church is its crossing tower with spire, a rarity in Nottinghamshire (but cf. Whatton). Its date is C13, as appears clearly from the strong piers inside with their fillets and moulded capitals, and the decoration in the abaci. The arches are double-chamfered. Broach-spire with one tier of two-light lucarnes. The church is aisleless (though Throsby says that it had one aisle) and also of the C13 (see the s door originally with two orders of colonnettes, and the lancet windows of the chancel). E window of four lancet lights with three quatrefoils above. Nave clerestory Perp. N transept 1889–90 by *W. S. Weatherley*. – FONT. Octagonal, C14, with tracery panels. – BENCH ENDS. A few old, plain ones. – ROYAL ARMS above the chancel arch, plaster, 1683. – STAINED GLASS. One window with St Paul, 1889 by *Kempe*. – MONUMENTS. To Frances Willoughby (later Columbell) † 1606 and to W. Willoughby and wife, 1636, both the usual type with kneeling figures. The latter has a curious steep ogee arch at its top.

MANOR HOUSE. A modern rebuild, but a medieval stone DOVECOTE, with C17 shaped gables in brick, stands in the garden.

ON MAIN STREET a good timber-framed COTTAGE with a jettied front, and two early C18 FARMHOUSES, No. 51 spoilt by modern windows, and No. 76 (the Post Office) with decorative brick strings and eaves cornice.

## NORMANTON-ON-TRENT

ST MATTHEW. The tower is surrounded by tall old beech and elm trees. N arcade C13, with low alternating supports. The W arch is cut into by the later tower. There follow an octagonal, a circular, an octagonal pier, and a semicircular E respond. Plainly moulded capitals and double-chamfered arches. S arcade later, all on octagonal piers. The clerestory as usual is Perp. – STAINED GLASS. Hope and Faith (chancel, N side) by *Mayer* of Munich, 1855. – MONUMENT. Robert Curtys † 1680. A slate inscription plate, surrounded by a broad stone frame with tendrils, etc., still entirely in the Jacobean tradition.

The village is well away from the river.

THE HALL, at the N end of South Street, next to the church. Dated 1820 over a chimneypiece (DOE). Plain, stuccoed, with Doric pilasters to a pedimented stone door surround. Contemporary lodge with blank arcaded wall to South Street.

THE GRANGE, at the S end of South Street. 1747 on a rainwater head (DOE), and possibly of this date the parapet with a band of diapering in blue and white brick and the sashes. The basic structure with tall narrow window openings looks earlier, c. 1700. An exceedingly attractive but very plain five-bay house.

SCHOOL. Opposite the E end of the church: just a plain brick cottage (now altered) of two storeys with door and one window l. and r. 1776.

(N of the church, a tall narrow five-bay brick house with gabled ends. Tall, narrow mullion-and-transom-cross windows replace the originals: late C17. NS)


## NORTH CLIFTON *see* CLIFTON


## NORTH COLLINGHAM *see* COLLINGHAM

## NORTH LEVERTON

ST MARTIN. Although the W tower is Perp, ashlar-faced, with diagonal buttresses and battlements, as usual in this part of the county, the interest of the church is the contributions of c. 1300-40, that is the intersected, repetitive tracery of the S aisle (arcade of octagonal piers with quite finely moulded capitals inside) and the fantastically curved tracery of the chancel.

Only the aisle E window must be posthumous. S doorway of c. 1200 with crocket capitals, but a round arch with dogtooth.

DOVECOTE, in High Street. C18, rectangular, with corbelled cornice and three gabled dormers.

As in many north Notts villages, good C17–18 brickwork (cf. North Wheatley). Gables of the Dutch, Lincs, and east Yorks kind where the bricks are laid in sloping courses at r. angles to the edge of the gables in a series of triangles, i.e. tumbling, and at the rear of a cottage on Mill Road a stepped and curved gable.

HABBLESTHORPE MANOR. Small, early C17, whitewashed brick house. Two mullioned windows in the gable end, one an excellent four-light affair, the others modern but still with hoodmoulds. Jacobean overmantel and some panelling in the parlour.

(CORNER FARM, at the crossroads in the centre of the village. Early C19, simple two-storey, three-bay house with a fine dovecote standing high above outbuildings on one side and a large barn, all in an impressive single range. NS)

WINDMILL, ½ m. W. The only working windmill in the county, built by subscription in 1812–15 and still owned by a syndicate of farmers. Brick three-storey tower tapering from the base but parallel towards the top (cf. the only other example, at Farndon): it was heightened in 1884. Tarred black, traditional for waterproofing. Ogee cap, four patent sails, and a fantail.

## NORTH MUSKHAM     7050

ST WILFRID. The building lies quite close to the river Trent, as most of the churches in this part of the county are. According to Thoroton, in the C16 the river changed its course just N of North Muskham and cut off Holme, which until then had been on the same bank as Muskham. North Muskham church is all embattled, and was apparently specially cared for in the late Middle Ages (cf. Holme). Only the lower part of the tower and the N arcade are older, the latter archaeologically of interest in that the waterleaf capitals date it late C12, but that it possesses octagonal piers, probably the earliest in Notts. The arches are double-chamfered. Tower arch of the same type as the N arcade. The S arcade, on the other hand, possesses piers of an odd Perp shape similar to St Mary, Nottingham: lozenges with the nar-

row sides towards nave and aisle and attached shafts to mark
the arch opening. Capitals only for these; the main profiles run
up uninterrupted into the arches. Clerestory with three-light
windows and contemporary timber roof. Grand chancel with
four-light windows N and S and a five-light E window, all with
tracery of the most matter-of-fact kind and no cusping at all:
exactly the same elementary pattern as at Holme. Now Holme
was embellished by the Bartons, and the Bartons' coat of arms
also appears on a buttress on the N aisle at North Muskham,
where the N windows are of the same type. The E window, on
the other hand, with the curves of the pointed arches replaced
by straight lines, is as at Sutton-on-Trent, Norwell, Colwick
(Nottingham), and Sutton-in-Ashfield. The S porch with
castellated capitals, gargoyles, and battlements belongs to the
same date. – FONT. 1662. – PULPIT. Probably late C17, perhaps contemporary with the ALTAR RAILS, with strong but
already quite elegant balusters. – SCREEN. Exceptionally fully
cusped. – STAINED GLASS. Very little of late medieval date;
two N aisle windows and the S aisle E window with the Barton
rebus. – MONUMENT to John Smithe † 1583, a very squat
pyramid on the ground, standing up only about 18 in. with its
pedestal. Long inscription quoting from his will.

EDGEFIELD HOUSE, the former Vicarage, in Vicarage Lane.
Designed by *G. E. Street* in 1863 for the Rev. Winstanley Hall.*
An excellent red brick house in Street's typical small-scale
domestic style. Varied roof levels with gables and half-hipping,
tiled. Big plain chimneystacks, straight-headed doors: the only
Gothic motif a discharging arch over an upper window on the
garden front. On this front also, a projecting bay has timber-
framing with brick-nogging. Very pretty half-hipped coach
house beside the entrance drive, also by *Street*. A charming,
though strong, composition.

(OLD HALL, opposite the church. The structure is at least as
old as 1676 (dated staircase). Remodelled garden front, porch
added, etc., *c.* 1820. Brick, with some earlier stonework incorporated. NS)

(OLD VICARAGE, on the old Great North Road. Colourwashed
brickwork with a symmetrical front, mid-to-late C18. C19 addition at the S end, with a cruciform pattern recessed in the roof
parapet and Gothick glazing bars. NS)

MUSKHAM HOUSE. Built to his own designs by *Joseph Pock-*

---

* We owe this description to Mr Paul Joyce.

*lington* in 1793.* Throsby described it as 'one of the most spacious and commodious houses ... in the county'. It was demolished as early as *c.* 1840.

MUSKHAM GRANGE was built *c.* 1819 and demolished in 1963.‡

## NORTH WHEATLEY    7080

ST PETER AND ST PAUL. Chancel of 1825, but not pretty. W tower ashlared, with top windows of the early C14; N and S walls of the wide, aisleless nave also ashlared. The late Perp windows have depressed ogee heads. Restored in 1896 by *C. Hodgson Fowler* (JPB) and again in 1927. – PULPIT. 1604. – BENCH ENDS from West Burton, with panelling which looks *c.* 1300. – A curious and impressive, very primitive-looking LADDER or staircase in the tower.

MANOR HOUSE, Low Street. Dated 1673 with the Cartwright 78 arms in a panel above the door; a wonderful specimen of decorative brickwork. In spite of an untiring display of modillions, not yet correctly classical. The windows have brick mullions and transoms, the porch absurd Ionic pilasters not carrying anything, and obelisks in flat brick relief. Between the ground floor and the upper floor a broad frieze of lunettes (all modillioned). On the l. and r. corners the series begins and ends with half-lunettes. The top of the house seems to have been altered or left unfinished: one would expect to see the end walls and porch carried up into gables. If the roof is later, so must the decorative eaves course be.

(A number of villages in the north of the county have buildings of fine late C17 and early C18 brickwork, the gables often with tumbling (*see* North Leverton). North Wheatley has more of these than anywhere. Another feature of this village are the numerous DOVECOTES: nearly every sizeable farm has one, either as a separate building or above farm buildings. NS)

## NORWELL    7060

ST LAWRENCE. Quite a large church, with a broad, that is early, W tower, transeptal chapels, and one of the tall, short naves with

* According to Angus Taylor.

§ The main front was pedimented, with two one-storey pavilions, the Great North Road front with two full-height bows under separate pyramidal roofs at either end. Nice interiors in a provincial version of the Adam style.

elaborate clerestory that are frequent in the neighbourhood.
The w tower* has lancet windows up to and including the bell-
stage (two separate lancets on each side there) and a tower arch
towards the nave which is also typical C13 (demi-shafts with
fillets running up into the moulded capitals, as at Southwell).
To the same phase belongs the chancel with lancets and a good
chancel arch. Earlier still by a few decades the s door with a
round arch and waterleaf capitals, and the s arcade of three bays
with slender circular piers, 'water-holding' bases, and capitals
similar to the waterleaf type. The arches are double-chamfered.
About 1300 the five-light E window was inserted, large, with
geometrical tracery. The C14 added the N arcade of four bays
(octagonal piers, complex moulded capitals), the fourth bay of
the s arcade, the outer walls of the aisles, the N transept, and
the s porch. Then the C15 came and gave the tower its diagonal
buttresses and a top stage with three-light windows, battlements, corner gargoyles, and pinnacles. Nave and aisles are also
embattled. But the best feature of the church is its late Perp
clerestory, five windows close together and with all the Gothic
curves replaced by straight lines, although cusps still abound
(cf. North Muskham). Considerable restoration in 1874–5 by
*Ewan Christian*, including the stone PULPIT. – Three E.E.
RECESSES with short shafts and segmental tops, two in the s
aisle, one in the N transept. – PISCINA and AUMBRY above
it in the s chapel with early C14 carving in the spandrels. –
STAINED GLASS. Windows 1903 and 1908 by *Kempe*. – MONU-
MENTS. Well preserved (or recut?) foliated cross slab. – Lady
35    with a wimple in a s aisle recess; early C14 and quite exceptionally well preserved, very slim, with the conventional arrangement of the drapery of its date. – Cross-legged knight, s aisle
recess, supposed to be Sir John di Lisure † 1330; not good.
The back of the recess has trefoil moulding. – C14 head on a
pillow placed diagonally (in the porch). – Simple wall-tablet
to Elizabeth Ayloff † 1629.

(MOATED SITES of the church and on the N side of the village
street behind the houses probably represent the parochial
manors of Norwell Overhall and Norwell Tertia Pars, prebendal estates of the collegiate church of Southwell. A third
moated manor (at the prebend of Norwell Pallishall), s of
the village on the road to North Muskham, still has remains
of a late medieval timber-framed and stone house, with a C17

---

*Partly rebuilt? The s buttress is dated 1713 (R. Alvey).

timber-framed addition: at the time of writing, in urgent need of restoration. NS)

(In the village a number of C17 and early C18 cottages and farmhouses still exhibit traces of timber-framing, the infill panels mostly replaced by brick in the C18. NS)

WINDMILL, W of the church. 1852. 30 ft high, with three of its four storeys. Roofed over and used as a store.

Unusual circular brick PINFOLD, late C18 or early C19.


NORWOOD PARK *see* SOUTHWELL

## NOTTINGHAM

The city of Nottingham comprises the old town; the areas immediately N, S, and W of it, developed during the C19 (the N and
W as desirable residential areas, the E and S with working-class
housing); the villages and suburbs further out that have long been
absorbed into the city (Sneinton, Basford, Bulwell, Radford, and
Lenton since 1877); and even further out the villages with their
C20 housing estates that have only recently been taken within the
city boundary. It is most convenient to divide the description of
the city into these categories, subdividing them topographically
as follows:

*Centre:*
1. The old town
2. N of the centre
3. W of the centre
4. S of the centre

*Outer Nottingham:*
1. E: Sneinton – Colwick
2. W: Lenton – Radford – Hyson Green – The University
3. NE: St Ann's – Carrington, Mapperley, Sherwood
4. NW: Basford – Bulwell

*Villages:*
Bilborough
Clifton
Wilford
Wollaton

### INTRODUCTION

Although now primarily regarded as an industrial city, Nottingham is, in contrast to Birmingham or Liverpool, a medieval town
in origin.* Occasional finds of prehistoric and Roman material
have been made within the area of the city, but it is not until the
Saxon period that Nottingham certainly became a major settlement site. Recent excavations suggest that an area of early to mid
Saxon settlement lay on the eastern side of the hill, in due course
occupied by the late Saxon *burh*, in the area of Belward Street and

---

*We owe the following information about medieval Nottingham to Pro-
fessor M. W. Barley.

Bellar Gate. This early settlement may have been surrounded by a ditched earthwork. The defences of the late Saxon *burh* enclosed the hill on the N, W, and E sides.* In the S sector, a fairly steep cliff rendered them unnecessary.‡ These defences, which date from the C9 or C10, consisted of a ditch with presumably a bank along the inner side. After 918 Nottingham became one of the five chief Danish boroughs in England (together with Stamford, Lincoln, Derby, and Leicester). On the virtually impregnable Castle Rock, a Norman fortress was built by William Peverel, whom the Conqueror had left 'to bridle the English' (Camden). That task was completed by planting another, French, borough alongside the English and under the shadow of the castle. The planned layout of the French borough included a triangular market place, one of the largest in England, and two new parish churches, St Peter and St Nicholas. Rebuilding of the castle in stone began under Henry II; a C13 chronicler could say that 'fortified both by art and nature' it 'had no peer in the Kingdom of England'. The double borough was also fortified, first by bank and ditch, then from *c.* 1267 by a wall.§ The first charter dates from 1157. There are no visible remains of the main religious houses. The Franciscans, founded *c.* 1230, began their first stone building in Broadmarsh in 1256, and the Carmelites were established before 1272 between St James Street and Friar Lane. The two most important hospitals (Holy Sepulchre, Augustinian, *c.* 1170, and St John Baptist, *c.* 1200) were extra-mural.

The Trent fostered trade and Nottingham prospered in industry and commerce, chiefly wool-dyeing and cloth-making. Weavers are mentioned in a Pipe Roll as early as 1155 and dyers at the same time. A Merchant Gild was sanctioned by King John. Later in the Middle Ages power was concentrated in the hands of a few leading families, all wool dealers, the Samons, Thurlands, and Plumptres. The mother church, St Mary, is evidence of that

* They ran between parallel streets: Warser Gate–Woolpack Lane and Goosegate on the N; on the W between Bridlesmith Gate and Fletcher Gate (here a drop in the level of about 10 ft between the two may indicate the height of the rampart); and on the E, probably between Carter Gate and Sneinton Street–Water Lane.

‡ Because the Bunter Sandstone on which Nottingham stands is easy and safe to cut, the whole central area is honeycombed with caves of every age, many still in use. The cave-dwellings were known to a C10 writer (Asser), and in the C18 Stukeley engraved some which are still there, behind a petrol station on Castle Boulevard. Part of a system below the Broadmarsh Centre is open to the public.

§ Considerable lengths have been excavated and reburied. The line is marked on the flanks of an underpass in front of the Theatre Royal.

prosperity. Also important from *c.* 1367 to 1530 was the trade, much for export, in alabaster panels and figures made from material brought from the quarries at Chellaston near Derby via the Trent.

After the Civil War, during which the town had been first a Royalist, then a Parliamentarian stronghold, two fashionable quarters grew up, one round St Mary's church, the other round the rebuilt castle, and the mainly timber-framed buildings were replaced by brick. Celia Fiennes in 1694 called Nottingham 'the neatest town I have ever seen', and Defoe, thirty years later, 'one of the most pleasant towns in England'. It must have been extremely pretty with its steep streets, its castle and church standing in elevated positions, and its many large mansions with their own pleasure gardens, but transformation into an industrial city began in the C18: textiles (the domestic framework-knitting industry), pottery (salt-glazed stoneware), and brick-making at Mapperley. Coal-mining, developing in adjacent parishes to the N W, provided the incentive to improve Trent navigation (1766–77) and to build the Nottingham (1793) and Beeston (1796) canals. By the late C18 there was no room for the expansion of the framework knitting and bobbin lace trade, so industrial communities grew up first at Arnold and Bulwell and then, in the 1820s, elsewhere along the River Leen at New Radford, at Carrington, and, to the E, at New Sneinton. By the late 1830s the common land round the old city had still not been enclosed and the slums were a severe problem. The population had increased from *c.* 11,000 in 1750 to 60,000 in 1850, yet the area had increased by only a third. The Enclosure Act when it came in 1845 was enlightened. Nearly 100 acres in the Sandfield and Clayfield district N of the town were left as open areas, which included, for example, the Arboretum, Elm Avenue, Corporation Oaks, and Robin Hood Chase, and, just to the N, Forest Recreation Ground. Some areas, for example the Meadows and St Ann's, which had their own factories, were laid out with working-class housing of a good standard. Others were developed as desirable residential districts: the Park, Mapperley Park, Alexandra Park, and Sherwood Rise. The 1870s saw a spate of public works (Trent Bridge (1871), the first Board School (1874), the first industrial dwellings (1876–7), University College (1877–81), and so on) and, in 1877, the extension of the borough to include Sneinton, Basford, Bulwell, Radford, and Lenton. This extended borough was welded together in 1881–4 by the construction of the boulevards.

After the exodus of large numbers of people to the new suburbs, the lace trade took over the streets round St Mary's church for its warehouses: the area became known as the Lace Market. This trade has now declined, and the largest employers are the industries started in the late C19 by local men: Boots (at Beeston), Players, and Raleigh. Nottingham became a city in 1897, but its population increased most significantly when more of the surrounding villages were incorporated (Bilborough in 1932, Clifton in 1952, Colwick and Wollaton in 1933). The old town has become just the commercial and leisure centre for sprawling suburbs, most of it in the stranglehold of the inner ring road. Just as in 1897 the G.C.R. cutting broke through the middle of the town,* Maid Marian Way disrupts the old town plan. The centre, with restricted streets partly pedestrianized, is peaceful, well preserved, and attractively fossilized, with a reasonable standard of modern building, but the ugliness of the road is too great a price to pay.

## THE OLD TOWN

### CHURCHES

ST MARY, High Pavement. Next to Newark, the largest parish 48 church in the county. Probably a Saxon minster rebuilt in Norman times. One fragment of the C12 survives in two arches built into the plain mid-Victorian brick wall of Birkin's warehouse in Broadway (*see* Perambulation, p. 231). They have no capitals between jambs and voussoirs. With the exception of the W front and the clerestory tracery, both by *W. B. Moffatt* (1845–53)‡ in imitation of what had been there originally,§ the S chancel chapel by *Temple Moore* (1912–13), and the chapter house by *Bodley* (1890), the church is almost entirely C15, the century of greatest prosperity. Cruciform plan. Nave of six bays and aisles, aisleless chancel (originally), and transepts. The tower over the crossing, not at the W end. The earliest parts of the present building are the SOUTH PORCH and a RECESS in the 47 S wall of the S transept, which, being bonded into the wall, proves that the wall is contemporary. Both are early C15, with ogee arches and some Perp panelling. The porch has a stone roof with four rolls as transverse arches, the inner doorway is

* The Midland Railway from Derby arrived in 1839, its competitor on the London route, the G.N.R., in 1852.

‡ This was one of the jobs Moffatt took out of Scott's office when the partnership was severed in 1846 (P. Joyce).

§ Moffatt's W end replaced a classical one of 1762 by '*Hirons*' (Hiorne) of Warwick.

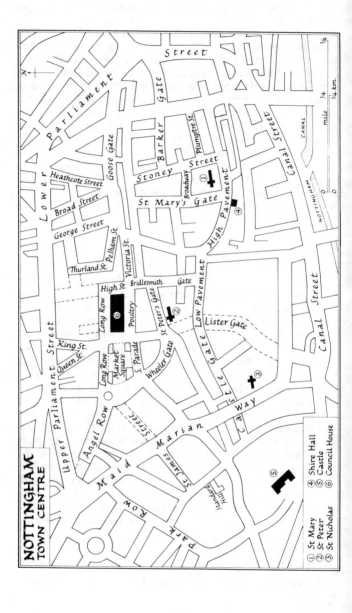

NOTTINGHAM
TOWN CENTRE

① St Mary
② St Peter
③ St Nicholas

④ Shire Hall
⑤ Castle
⑥ Council House

enriched by niches placed diagonally in the typical C14 way. The voussoirs of the arch are decorated by large square fleurons. The recess carries its panelling into the soffit of the arch.

The rest of the building can be treated as one. All windows 50 are wholly Perp. In the chancel they are of four lights, tall, with two transoms and two-centred arches, with the exception of the E window which goes to nine lights and three transoms. The N and s windows of the transepts are huge (twelve lights, 49 three transoms, depressed four-centred tops) and create the impression of the glasshouse which we also get at Newark. Even in the aisles there are no windows of less than three lights (s aisle; earlier than the N aisle with four lights).* The nave piers are slim, of graceful, essentially lozenge shape, with the thin sides pointing towards nave and aisle and only a few meagre capitals, that is mostly running through from shaft to arch without a break. The clerestory stands immediately on the apex of the arcade and the windows are doubled in number. The peculiar character of the church is determined by a system of rectangular panelling of the walls, the panels being framed by plain rolls. The windows of the aisles, for example (also double in number as against the arcades), appear set into this framework. The same is very noticeable on the E walls of the transepts. The uprights and horizontals of this scaffolding give the church a solid, four-square appearance, very different, for example, from Newark, and also from Melton Mowbray in Leicestershire, with which, on the other hand, on the other hand, the fenestration of the clerestory and the emphasis on, and detail of, the crossing tower are evidently connected. At St Mary's the tower rests on broad composite piers (underpinned in 1843–8)‡ and has a fanvault (cf. Rotherham) inside. The vault is a replica by *Stretton* in wood and plaster of the original which collapsed in 1558. Outside, the tower is of three stages, the first with a blank arcade, the second with one large window (like the chancel, N and s) on each side, the third with four arcades of which the two middle ones are pierced, the others blank. The tower is crowned by battlements and eight pinnacles. The body of the church is also castellated, the chancel plainly, the nave and aisles with panelled battlements. The panelling extends to the but

* The s aisle was refaced by *William Stretton*, architect and churchwarden, in 1818–20. Were the windows altered at all then?

‡ By *Scott & Moffatt*, after being declared unsafe by *L. N. Cottingham* in 1842.

tresses too. The richest decoration is lavished on the show-fronts of the transepts: ogee gables and pinnacles. – The VESTRY also belongs to the original building (see its Perp window). Its plaster ceiling is early C18. – The CHAPTER HOUSE adjoining was built in 1890 by *Bodley* in anticipation that the church would be the cathedral of the diocese of Southwell, created in 1884.

FURNISHINGS. ALTAR TABLE, N transept. Jacobean. – FONT. Octagonal, C15, with Perp panelling under ogee arches. – REREDOS and CHANCEL SCREEN. 1885 by *Bodley & Garner*. – CHANCEL ROOF. 1872 by *Sir G. G. Scott*, decorated by *Lawrence Bond*, 1965. – BISHOP'S THRONE. By *Bodley*, 1890. – CHOIR STALLS. 1872 by *Scott*. – ROYAL ARMS. Lion and Unicorn, free-standing isolated figures, *c.* 1710. – ORGAN, E wall of transept. The first in this country by *Marcussen* of Denmark, installed in 1973. – STAINED GLASS. Unimportant C15 fragments in several windows of the s chapel. – C19 series of unusual extent and completeness. Only some examples can here be mentioned: *Burlison & Grylls* (s transept: first, 1903, and second, 1882, E windows from the s; s aisle: tenth from E, 1882); *Clayton & Bell* (chancel: first s, 1888, and third, 1891, and fourth, 1880, N from the E; N transept: N window and second and fourth E windows, all 1876; s aisle: eleventh, 1888, and twelfth, 1900, windows from the E; w end, first, 1887, and second, 1884, s windows; s transept: third, 1878, and fourth, 1873, E windows); *Hardman* (chancel E, 1865 to the Prince Consort, s second from E, 1878; w centre to Thomas Adams the lace manufacturer, 1876); *Heaton, Butler & Bayne* (s transept s, 1867, a major mid-Victorian design, as exciting as the very different early ones by Morris & Co. and in a wide and glowing colour range: RH); *Kempe* (s aisle, fourth to eighth from E, 1895–1905); *Ward & Hughes* (chancel s, third and fourth from E, both of 1868). – PAINTING. Seated Madonna, whole figure, school of *Fra Bartolommeo*, given to the church in 1839. – SCULPTURE. Small alabaster panel of usual Nottingham C15 style (s chancel chapel), possibly part of a reredos, found under the sanctuary floor. It shows St Thomas's resignation of his see. – In the s chapel a small terracotta maquette for the Prodigal Son by *G. Tinworth* of Lambeth, exhibited at the Royal Academy in 1875. – SOUTH DOOR. Bronze, very sumptuous; 1904 by *Henry Wilson*. Scenes of Christ with Our Lady in panels surmounted by a Pietà in a vesicle. Tautly-drawn low relief figures with great expression (cf. Welbeck Abbey). –

CURIOSUM, N aisle. Vestry clock, late C18 or early C19. –
MONUMENTS. Battered alabaster effigy in the N aisle, later
C14. – John Samon † 1413, three times mayor of Nottingham,
alabaster; in the S transept recess mentioned above. – Opposite,
in the N transept, a similar, later recess with niches and mutilated angel figures in the gable, perhaps erected for the tomb of
Thomas Thurland † 1473. In it now an alabaster tomb-chest
made probably for John de Tannesly † 1414 and his wife.
Quatrefoil panels with shields and small figures of the Annunciation. On this Purbeck slab not belonging to it and probably
from the tomb of William Amyas † *c.* 1348–69, originally in the
S transept. At the back a small early C15 figure of a bishop in
alabaster under an arch possibly from the tomb-chest of Robert
English † 1475. – Robert Plumptre † 1693. Marble tablet with
broken pediment composed of acanthus scrolls (N transept). –
Many minor early C19 tablets in the N aisle. – In the churchyard, by the NW doorway into the church, a nice collection of
typical Notts slates and a terracotta (pipe-clay) HEADSTONE
to two sisters, the stone made and fired by their father, *W.
Sefton,* a well-known pipe-maker.

ST PETER. St Mary is an exceptional church in the county; St
Peter is the current type and might easily stand in any prosperous Notts village: W steeple with pairs of angle buttresses
and a thin tall spire (often repaired) rising above the battlements. Unusually elaborate W door with pinnacles and niches.
Embattled nave, aisles, and chancel. Inside, the nave is not high
for its length and width. The S arcade has C13 piers with four
filleted shafts and four deep hollows (cf. Rolleston, South
Scarle, and Upton; the source is Lincoln, for example St Mary
Magdalene). The capitals are partly moulded and partly stiff-
leaf, the arches double-chamfered. N arcade of 1360, repaired
in 1495, with castellated thin capitals (cf. East Markham) and
taller arches on E.E. piers. The roofs of the nave and S aisle
are Perp by *Nicholas Strelley,* 1501–9 (on demi-figures of
angels). N clerestory renewed in 1699, the exterior of the S aisle
and the whole chancel too by *Evans & Jolly* in 1875. Chancel
repaired again by *Dykes-Bower* in 1951. – WEST DOOR with
fine ironwork by *Richard Bentley* of Derbyshire, 1977. –
FONT. Octagonal C17 bowl, with a stylized rosette in each bulg-
ing panel, on a C14 base. – ORGAN CASE by *Schnetzler,* 1770,
brought here in 1812. Pretty acanthus scrollwork. – ALTAR-
PIECE in the S aisle, former Rostrum of the Archdeacon's
Court, at the W end of the S aisle; 1672. – STAINED GLASS.

E window 1878 by *Ward & Hughes*; S windows (Almond *c.* 1858
and Howard *c.* 1866) by *Heaton, Butler & Bayne*; S aisle, E end,
1881 by *Burlison & Grylls*; tower W window by *Powell, c.* 1906,
an interesting example of a genuine development from Morris's
teachings; N aisle windows by *Bucknall* to *Comper*'s designs
with figures and grisaille medallions of local views set in clear
glass. From E to W 1964, 1969, and 1963. – Baptistery window
by *Margaret Trahearne*, 1976. – PAINTINGS. Last Supper, an
altarpiece of 1720 by *Edward Dovey*, who worked near by in
Bridlesmith Gate. – Agony in the Garden by *Thomas Barber*,
1816. – MONUMENTS. Margaret Saunders † 1633 and Jane
Ellis † 1639, wives of Sir John Locke. – Lady Gardner † 1811
by *John Bacon Jun.*

ST NICHOLAS. The old church was razed by Colonel Hutchinson in the Civil War. The new church is of 1671–82,* with C18
aisles (S 1756, N 1783) reflecting its increase in social status.
It lies on the ascent to the hill on which the castle stands and
served the fashionable C18 quarter. Now only a few trees partly
screen it from Maid Marian Way, and heavy traffic thunders
past its once-peaceful churchyard. The W tower has still
decidedly Perp bell-openings besides quoins and straight
mullioned-and-transomed windows. At the E end also a
window of five lights with transom. The aisles, with round-
headed windows and battlements, are separated from the nave
by Tuscan columns. The roof is sadly messed up. The chancel,
with an C18 plaster ceiling, opens from the nave by a segmental
arch. – PULPIT. Nicely inlaid; 1783. – COMMUNION RAIL.
Late C17, with balusters, every second twisted. The panelling
of the chancel of the same date.

HIGH PAVEMENT CHAPEL (Unitarian). 1876 by *Stuart Colman*
of Bristol. Gothic, with a prominent spire. Of no special architectural merit, but with a (ritual) E window with STAINED
GLASS by *Morris & Co.*, 1904. Twenty-one figures in three
tiers: top tier (Truth, Light, etc.) and middle tier (Justice,
Courage, etc.) by *Burne-Jones*, bottom tier (Theology, Labour,
Philosophy) by *Burne-Jones* and *J. H. Dearle*. – N aisle window
also by *Morris & Co.*, 1907: David and Jonathan by *Burne-
Jones*. – Other less important glass: N transept window 1890,
designed by *H. Enfield* and made in Düsseldorf; N aisle 1925

---

* The first rector was instituted in January 1683, but the first baptism had
already taken place in December 1682. The date on the chancel window reads
1699.

1 *Villagescape:* Clifton (Nottingham)

2 *Villagescape:* West Stockwith

3 Carlton-in-Lindrick, St John Evangelist, tower, eleventh century and 1417–43

4 Stapleford, churchyard, cross, probably *c.* 1050

5 Shelford, St Peter, relief of the Virgin and Child, Anglo-Saxon

6 Blyth Priory Church,
  nave, eleventh century

7 Blyth Priory Church,
  aisle, eleventh century

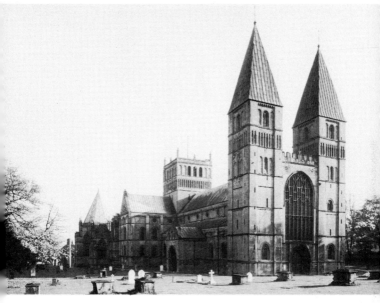

8 Southwell Minster, early
  twelfth century

9 Southwell Minster,
  north transept, early
  twelfth century

10 Southwell Minster, nave, early twelfth century

11 Southwell Minster, tympanum in the north transept, early twelfth century

12 Hawksworth, St Mary and All Saints, tympanum, early twelfth century

13 Newark, St Mary Magdalen, crypt, early twelfth century

14 Balderton, St Giles, doorway, twelfth century

15 Balderton, St Giles, Saint, late twelfth century

16 Lenton (Nottingham), Holy Trinity, font from Lenton Priory, mid twelfth century

7 Newark Castle, gatehouse c. 1133–9, curtain wall early fourteenth century

8 South Scarle, St Helen, arcade, late twelfth century

9 Worksop Priory Church, nave, late twelfth century

20 Worksop Priory Church, late twelfth century

21 Worksop Priory Church, Lady Chapel, mid thirteenth century

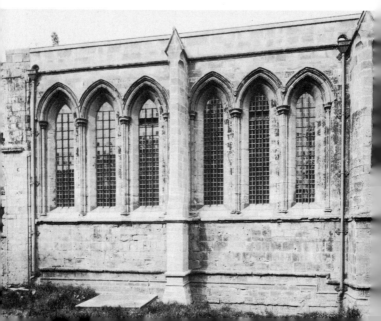

22 Southwell Minster,
   Lady Chapel, capitals,
   mid thirteenth century

23 Southwell Minster,
   Lady Chapel, begun
   1234

24 Sutton-in-Ashfield, St Mary Magdalene, capital, mid thirteenth century

25 Southwell Minster, east end 1234–c. 1300, chapter house c. 1290 (Vicars' Close 1779–81

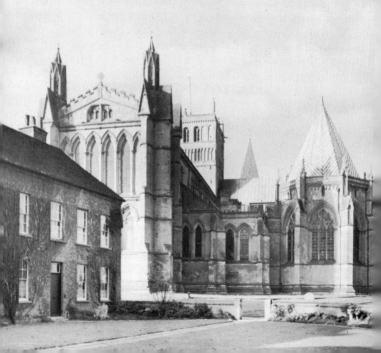

6 Newstead Abbey, façade of former priory church,
late thirteenth century

27 Southwell Minster, chapter house, *c.* 1290, doorway

28 Southwell Minster, chapter house, *c.* 1290, capital

29 Southwell Minster, chapter house, *c.* 1290

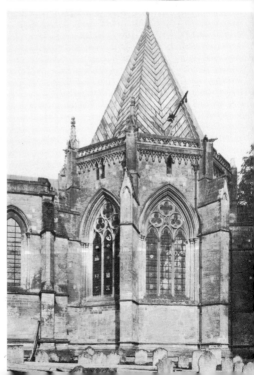

30 Whatton, St John,
corbel with King
David, *c.* 1300

31 Skegby, St Andrew,
monument to an
official of Sherwood
Forest, *c.* 1300

32 Newark, St Mary Magdalen, tower, thirteenth and fourteenth centuries

33 Attenborough, St Mary Magdalene, capital, fourteenth century

34 Gedling, All Hallows, tower, early fourteenth century

35 Norwell, St Lawrence,
monument to a lady,
early fourteenth
century

36 Mattersey, All Saints,
relief panel with St
Helena, fourteenth
century

37 Southwell Minster, pulpitum, *c.* 1320–40, detail
38 Southwell Minster, pulpitum, *c.* 1320–40, rib-vault with flying ribs
39 Hawton, All Saints, Easter Sepulchre, shortly after 1330, detail

40 Hawton, All Saints,
east window, shortly
after 1330

41 Car Colston, St Mary,
east window, c. 1330–40

42 Bibthorpe, dovecote, thirteenth or fourteenth century

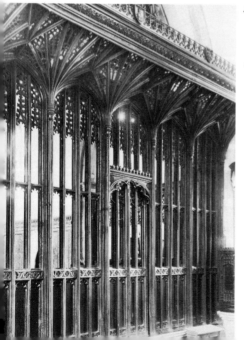

43 Strelley, All Saints,
monument to Sir Sampson
de Strelley † c. 1390
and his wife † 1405

44 Strelley, All Saints,
screen, late fourteenth
century

45 East Markham, St John the Baptist, brass to Dame Millicent Merying † 1419

46 Laxton, St Michael, chancel early fourteenth century, nave clerestory late fifteenth century

47 Nottingham, St Mary, south porch, early fifteenth century

48 Nottingham, St Mary, fifteenth century

49 Nottingham, St Mary, north transept, fifteenth century

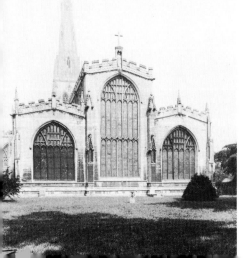

50 Nottingham, St Mary, fifteenth century

51 Newark, St Mary Magdalen, east end, c. 1487–1500

52 Newark, St Mary Magdalen, nave c. 1460, chancel c. 1487–1500

53 Holme, St Giles, late
fifteenth century, east end,
with monument to John
Barton † 1491

54 Holme, St Giles, porch,
late fifteenth century

55 Newark, White Hart Inn, Market Place, front range late fifteenth century

56 Strelley, All Saints, monument to John de Strelley † 1501
57 Strelley, All Saints, monument to John de Strelley † 1501, detail
58 Holme Pierrepont Hall, gatehouse range, early sixteenth century

59 Wollaton (Nottingham), St Leonard, monument to Henry Willoughby
† 1528 and his wives

60 Annesley, All Saints, monument to an unknown man, sixteenth
century

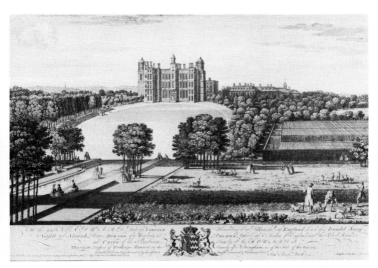

61 Worksop Manor, by Robert Smythson, completed 1585–6, altered 1701 (view by Buck) *(Copyright Country Life)*

62 Worksop, Manor Lodge, late sixteenth century

63 Wollaton Hall (Nottingham), by Robert Smythson, 1580–8

4 Wollaton Hall (Nottingham), by Robert Smythson, 1580–8, roofscape
*(Copyright Country Life)*

65 Clifton (Nottingham), St Mary, monument to Sir Gervase Clifton † 1587 and his wives

66 Southwell Minster, monument to Archbishop Sandys † 1588

67 Sibthorpe, St Peter, monument to Edward Burnell, 1590

68 Newark, St Mary Magdalen,
   monument to Anne Markham
   † 1601 (formerly at Cotham)

69 Barnby-in-the-Willows,
   All Saints, chancel window,
   probably seventeenth century

70 Newstead Abbey,
saloon, plaster ceiling,
1631 and 1633

71 Clifton (Nottingham),
St Mary, monument to
the first three wives of
Sir Gervase Clifton,
1631, detail

72 Thrumpton Hall, staircase, *c.* 1660 *(Copyright Country Life)*

73 Wollaton (Nottingham), St Leonard, reredos, *c.* 1660

74 Newark, St Mary Magdalen, font, base fifteenth century, bowl 1660

75 Southwell Minster, font, 1661

76 Teversal, St Catherine, thirteenth and fourteenth centuries,
with furnishings of *c.* 1675

77 Nottingham, St Nicholas, 1671–82, south aisle 1756

80 Holme Pierrepont, St
Edmund, monument to
John Oldham † 1683

81 Cossall, Willoughby
Almshouses, 1685

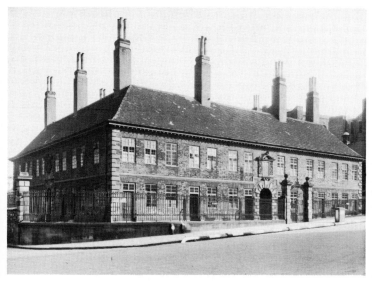

82 Nottingham, Collin's Almshouses, 1709 (demolished)

83 Bunny Hall, by Sir Thomas Parkyns, *c.* 1720, north front

84 Bunny, St Mary, monument to Sir Thomas Parkyns † 1741,
   designed by himself, 1715

85 Newark, Appleton Gate, house of the early eighteenth century

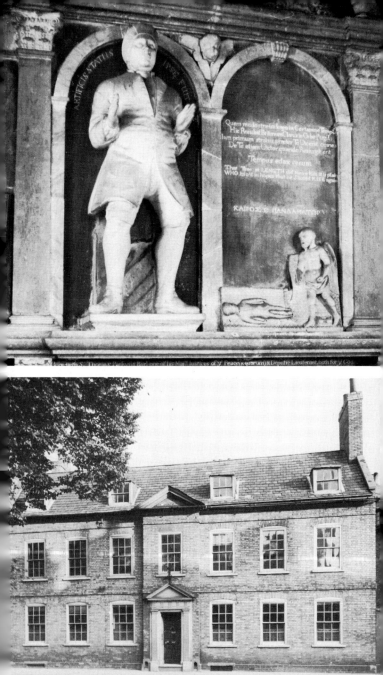

86 West Stockwith, St Mary, monument to William Huntington † 1691, by Edward Poynton

87 Kelham, St Wilfrid, monument to Lord Lexington and his wife, by William Palmer, 1726

88 Teversal, St Catherine, monument to Sir John Molyneux † 1741 and his wife

89 Nottingham, Stanford House, Castle Gate, 1775

90 Nottingham, No. 18 Low Pavement, early eighteenth century

91 Newark, Town Hall, by John Carr, *c.* 1774–6

92 Nottingham, Colwick Hall, by John Carr, *c.* 1776, south front

93 Ossington, Holy Rood,
   by John Carr, 1782–3

94 Ossington, Holy Rood,
   monument to Robert
   Denison † 1785, by
   Joseph Nollekens

95 Newstead Abbey, west wing, fifteenth to seventeenth centuries, remodelled by John Shaw, 1818–29 *(Copyright Country Life)*

96 Nottingham, Judges' Lodging, High Pavement, judges' dining room, by Wood & Nicholson, 1833

97 Beeston, Anglo-Scotian Mills, 1871

98 Kelham Hall, by Sir George Gilbert Scott, begun 1859

99 Thoresby, by Anthony Salvin, 1865–75

100 Clumber church, by Bodley & Garner, 1886–9 (stable and offices
eighteenth and nineteenth centuries)

101 Newark, Ossington Coffee Palace, by George & Peto, 1882

102 Nottingham, Queen's Chambers, Long Row, by Watson Fothergill, 1897

103 Beeston, Boots Factory, by Sir Owen Williams, 1930–2

104 Nottingham Playhouse, by Peter Moro & Partners, 1959–64

105 Beeston, Boots Offices, by Skidmore, Owings & Merrill in association with Yorke Rosenberg Mardall, 1966–8

106 Nottingham, John Player Horizon Factory, by Arup Associates, 1968–71

by *Kempe & Co.*; Sunday School centenary memorial by *Holiday*, 1906.

PARLIAMENT STREET METHODIST CHURCH. 1874 by *R. C. Sutton*. Stands well at the corner of George Street. Pinkish brick, tower with a pyramidal cap.

WESLEY CHAPEL (former), Broad Street. *See* Perambulation.

ROMAN CATHOLIC CHAPEL (former), George Street. *See* Perambulation.

BAPTIST CHAPEL (former), George Street. *See* Perambulation.*

PUBLIC BUILDINGS

SHIRE HALL, High Pavement. 1770–2 by *Gandon* (of the Dublin Customs House), built by *Joseph Pickford* of Derby. Small and not specially distinguished, though in the good taste of the age. The simplified front with attached Ionic portico and an ample expanse of bare wall shows the influence of French neo-classicism evident in many features of his public buildings. The façade is now only just recognizable as Gandon's. The alterations, including the Italianate extensions and the centre of the building inside are by *T. C. Hine*, 1876–9.

COUNCIL HOUSE, Market Place. 1927–9 by *T. Cecil Howitt*. Not much can be said in defence of this kind of neo-Baroque display at a date when the Stockholm Town Hall was complete and a style congenial to the C20 established. Wren has to answer for much, once the connection between Greenwich and this dome (via the Old Bailey?) is noted. The Ionic columniation is no more inspiring or truthful than the interiors. The only positive interest lies in the plan of the building. Its centre is a shopping arcade of great height with a glass roof, and shops run all along the ground floor on the N and S sides.

CASTLE. The plan of the medieval castle is known, but very little of it remains above ground except the foundation of the tower built in 1212–13 W of the present castle and the C14 GATEWAY into the outer bailey, and this in so restored a state that it can

---

* Other chapels: HOCKLEY CHAPEL (formerly Methodist), Goose Gate, 1782, a plain house completely altered in 1959 for 'Ideal Homes'; CITY TEMPLE, Halifax Place (demolished), by *J. Simpson*, 1847, built for the Methodists, a two-storeyed brick and stone block of five by six bays, with one-storey Ionic portico, very secular-looking; CONGREGATIONAL CHAPEL, Castle Gate, 1863 by *R. C. Sutton*, Italianate, disused but still standing (1978).

hardly be counted.* Whether the dramatic capture of Roger Mortimer and the guilty Queen in 1330 really took place through the underground passage known as Mortimer's Hole is doubtful. It seems that this was a goods entrance from the river Leen, and that the original passage into the inner bailey was long ago blocked. Nottingham continued to be the principal fortress in the Midlands during the reigns of Henry VII and Henry VIII, but by 1525 all the buildings and defences were 'in great ruyne & dekay'. The outer defences were repaired in 1536, before an expedition to crush the Pilgrimage of Grace, and twice during Elizabeth I's reign. More repairs and some demolition (probably including the hall) took place in the C17 before Charles I raised his standard at Nottingham on 22 August 1642. There was much fighting in and around the town. The castle was held for the Roundheads by Colonel Hutchinson, and after the end of the war the Council of State ordered it to be slighted.

In 1663 William Cavendish, first Duke of Newcastle, bought the site (and its park to the W) and began in 1674 to build a palace on it which was completed in 1679 at a cost of £14,000. It looks at first, that is in its general shape with the top balustrade, as if it stood in north Italy or Prague. It is a rectangle (nine bays long) with short projecting wings (of three by three bays) at the back. The end bays of the wings themselves project slightly on the inner face. There is no doubt that the long E front facing the town is the showpiece. The other sides are relatively plain, with rusticated quoins and intermittent rustication to the window surrounds only on the outer faces of the wings. On the main façade a congestion of features, everything done to increase life and movement in the way the Continental Baroque tried to do it everywhere. The bays are broad, the outermost defined by pilasters (coupled at the ends), the others separated by engaged columns of the composite order, carrying impost blocks. The heavy modillion cornice breaks forward over these. The columns and pilasters seem to sink into the stone mass of channelled rustication, large on the basement, scaled down above. Basement doorway and keystones to the windows also rusticated. The piano nobile is heavily stressed, its long mullion and transom cross windows with alternating broken triangular and segmental pediments originally carrying

* Excavations since 1976 have begun to expose the remains of the wall of the middle bailey and cleared one of its towers. Further excavation is planned (MWB).

busts, and balustraded sills. In the centre, flanking the window, two columns support only a sill on which stands a mutilated equestrian statue of the Duke, set against a recessed panel. According to Deering in 1757, the statue is by *Sir William Wilson*. Nothing can now be judged of its quality. The details have all been renewed (see below) but some can be trusted, i.e. the first-floor windows and the almost square upper ones surrounded by fleshy strapwork, typical of the native mid-C17 style characterized as Artisan Mannerism. Other details are still Jacobean in character, e.g. the balustraded sills and lights to the upper windows, and the parapet recalls the medievalizing details of the earliest work at Bolsover. For, despite the Continental influences (and some of the details are reminiscent of ornament by Alessi in Rubens's *Palazzi di Genova*), the English accent can nowhere be mistaken. The comparison that comes to mind at once is with the later Cavendish buildings at Bolsover, especially with the state rooms, which have fewer of the eccentricities of John Smythson's long gallery and more of the fleshy strapwork and mouldings typical of Artisan Mannerism. An excess of rustication is found through all these later buildings. Neither the exact date (some time after 1630) nor the designer of the Bolsover state rooms and riding school are known, but according to Deering, the Duke's builder at Nottingham was the Lincoln mason *Samuel Marsh*.* But how much part did the Duke himself take in designing his buildings, which are consistent enough in style to suggest the direction of one mind? When the Duke died in 1676, the castle was incomplete, and in his will he left instructions that it 'may be finished according to the model by me laid down and designed'.‡ It would not have been at all unusual in those days before the establishment of a clearly defined architectural profession, for the Duke to have chosen the form of the building from a pattern book such as Rubens's *Palazzi di Genova* or from buildings he had seen for himself, for example Michelangelo's Capitoline palaces in Rome. The low, rectangular silhouette and Baroque references were novel in England, anticipating Office of Works designs for Hampton Court and possibly Thoresby and Talman's for Chatsworth. The details are not reliable, though, for the castle was fired during the Reform Bill riots of 1831,

---

* Vertue says that *Marsh* also worked for the Duke at Bolsover.

‡ A model in this case can of course mean the general form or design or, more specifically, an architectural model. An actual model does exist in the castle, and this may be the original, altered to show the damage of 1831.

reducing it to a shell, and virtually rebuilt only in 1876–8 for the purpose of making it into a museum.* It became the first municipal museum of art in England. At that time the roof was altered, the three storeys reduced to two, the curving Baroque staircase to the first-floor entrance on the w side removed,‡ and a semicircular colonnade added on the w side to shelter the new ground-floor entrance. The architect was *T. C. Hine*, and many of the details now are distinctively his, e.g. the tracery in the blind windows of the top floor of the back and sides (cf. Flintham Hall and the Lace Market warehouses).

CORN EXCHANGE (now County Sales), Thurland Street. 1849–50 by *T. C. Hine*. Latest classical, with heavy quoins and heavy segmental window pediments, but at the top not a classical cornice: instead, playful brickwork of Jacobean derivation (typical of the date). New for the date is the use of polychromy, i.e. specially designed encaustic tiles decorated with wheatsheaves used around windows and along the string course.

PLUMPTRE HOSPITAL, Plumptre Square. 1823 by *Edward Staveley*, Surveyor to the Corporation from 1796 and one of a Leicestershire family of monumental masons and surveyors. Cemented front with Perp windows but a central pediment.

82 COLLIN'S ALMSHOUSES, Friar Lane. Tragically demolished in 1956.§

PERAMBULATION

The area of the old town originally within the medieval walls is bounded by Upper and Lower Parliament Streets, the castle, and Park Row. Since the arterial road, Maid Marian Way, was constructed to complete a ring road round the city centre (1958–66), the w side of the area has been cut off from the rest. Two of the

---

* The now destroyed interiors had previously been altered by *Vanbrugh*, in 1719.

‡ The e one was removed in the 1860s.

§ It was a lovely group of 1709, one of the best almshouses of its date in England: a two-storeyed block of eleven by fifteen bays with hipped roof, quoins, and casement windows; cartouches to stress the entrances into the completely plain quadrangle, with just a limetree walk across to the Hounds Gate entrance. Here was a second group of two detached houses of four bays each, facing Hounds Gate and, on the w side of the court, the chapel and a block of 'offices'. Also demolished, in 1954, the new buildings for Collin's Almshouses in Carrington Street of 1831. Two long ranges behind each other, cemented according to its date with rusticated entrance.

The WALTER FOUNTAIN, Greyfriars Gate and Carrington Street, 1866, Gothic of four tiers, by *R. C. Sutton*, was demolished in 1950.

best streets, St James's Street and Castle Gate, are bisected by it. Maid Marian Way, devoid of interesting buildings, has rightly been called 'one of the ugliest roads in Europe'. The perambulation begins in the new road-defined centre and ends on the w side of Maid Marian Way near the castle.

## (1) Market Place and Streets NE and E of it

We begin near the Market Place in ANGEL ROW, in the fashionable C18 quarter (w of the Wheeler Gate/Lister Gate/Angel Row line) now bisected by Maid Marian Way. BROMLEY HOUSE on the s side was built for Sir George Smith, the banker, by a Mr *Taylor* (Sir Robert Taylor?) in 1752. Very civilized and not at all provincial, as indeed all the best Nottingham houses are, with an elegant and very restrained doorway (now sandwiched between shopfronts) and Palladian triangular pediments to the first floor. The interiors have charming Rococo plasterwork and chimneypieces. The rectangular top-lit staircase hall is particularly rewarding. In the C18 the MARKET SQUARE, although so large, had a nice homely appearance, with an Exchange (1724–6) and plain houses mostly resting on arcades, in emulation (cf. Newark) of Inigo Jones's Covent Garden piazza which introduced the fashion. Most of the C18 has gone, but some C19 successors maintain the theme. On the e side near Bromley House is the pedimented and stuccoed BELL INN of c. 1830 (partly medieval within), with nice Egyptian lettering, and a late C17 or early C18 house, now without its arcade but still with a modillion cornice and some wooden casement windows.* Opposite, a pretty colonnade with iron columns in front of Yates's Wine Lodge, 1876, and inside it a cast-iron gallery all round. On the s side of this public space, in SOUTH PARADE, the best building is the NATIONAL WESTMINSTER (formerly Samuel Smith & Co.) BANK, a stone palazzo in the manner of Gibson by *G. R. Isborn*, 1878. Further e in POULTRY the FLYING HORSE HOTEL, a very restored timber-framed building with the centre of the upper storey oversailing on three Tuscan columns. Facsimile plasterwork and modern w bay. The e extension, late C18, of two bays, also projects over the pavement on columns. At the end of Poultry in BRIDLESMITH GATE a Victorian pub, the DOG AND BEAR HOTEL (1876), fancifully ignorant, with Bacchanalian masks and ornate capitals to the rusticated ground floor,

* Excavations for an extension to Lloyds Bank revealed the remains of the Carmelite friary.

and the upper floors rock-faced, with the Italianate two-light windows going all queer with wavy hoodmoulds. (Opposite the pub, Nos. 1–9, a shop and office building of *c.* 1895 by *G. S. Doughty*, finished with a row of shaped gables. Just past the pub near the top of ST PETER'S GATE, two more Victorian buildings face each other across the cobbled Bank Place: the Italianate COUNTY COURT of *c.* 1875 by *J. C. Sorby*, and the former WATERWORKS OFFICES (now Barclays Bank) by *Arthur Hawksley*, 1874, in a well-detailed Venetian Gothic. JPB) Bridlesmith Gate continues to LOW PAVEMENT. To the W, near the corner of Lister Gate, No. 9, formerly the ASSEMBLY ROOMS (now Post Office), built in the C18, altered by *John Carr* in 1790, and repaired and enlarged in 1807; only the handsome façade with giant attached Corinthian columns (of 1836 by *Thomas Winter*) is now old. Next to it the plainly classical SAVINGS BANK of 1836. Opposite, on the S side, No. 10 (1876) is a wild version of the Butterfield type of Gothicism by one of the less squeamish designers (*Alfred Smith* of Nottingham).* Further E No. 16, a good Edwardian brick and stone building of 1910 with some free Baroque detail. Entrance passage revamped. There are several buildings of a similar age and quality in the city centre, e.g. in Bridlesmith Gate and Long Row. On the S side the most imposing building is WILLOUGHBY HOUSE (Nos. 20–22), built *c.* 1738 by Rothwell Willoughby, younger brother of the second Lord Middleton, set back behind a small courtyard with fine wrought-iron railings and gate. Red brick. Main doorcase with broken segmental pediment and moulded keystone on Roman Ionic columns; frost work on the garden doorway. Ionic columns appear in the next-door house, No. 18, also early C18, with Venetian windows on each of the three floors. In the lowest the centre light breaks through a pediment. Rear wing dated 1760, probably a separate house. On the other side of Willoughby House, VAULT HALL, *c.* 1733, a good pair of houses in one eight-bay building, named after the extensive rock cellars (Vaults of the Woolstaplers) beneath. No. 24 has a doorcase with columns like those of No. 18 and Willoughby House, No. 26, a Roman Doric doorcase. Very good ironwork to the forecourt.

HIGH PAVEMENT begins to the E across the main road. Past the chapel, No. 14 has an elaborate wooden doorcase with a blind ornamental fanlight. Opposite, the COUNTY HOUSE, built as

* According to Mr Train.

*See* p. 448

90

a private house *c.* 1728–30 and altered in 1833 by *Moses Wood & James Nicholson* to form the Judges' Lodging. From the early C18 they retained the main staircase. The façade of the County House still has its original proportions, but with the thin detail (moulded window surrounds, delicate segmental iron balcony, etc.) added by Wood & Nicholson. In contrast the E extension of 1833 is robust: squat neo-Greek Doric columns of cast-iron 96 supporting an upper floor with three two-storey windows. It looks like an Athenaeum or Literary Institute and in fact housed the judges' dining room. Inside, Greek Revival decoration. Nos. 26–52 are C18 and early C19 houses, nothing special. Behind No. 42 is COMMERCE SQUARE, a small square comprising almost entirely C18 and early C19 red brick office buildings of good size and proportion. From here a steep pathway leads down to Narrow Marsh from the cliff on which the buildings of High Pavement and the adjoining streets stand. Back in High Pavement, No. 54 is of four storeys, with an unusual arrangement of windows on the upper floors, two Venetian windows with a round-headed window sandwiched between, and on the top floor the same arrangement but with Diocletian instead of Venetian windows. At the E end the street divides. SHORT HILL continues on the same level. No. 2 with Venetian windows may have been an C18 merchant hosier's house and warehouses. At the rear an attic with a long inspection window. HOLLOW STONE, parallel to Short Hill, descends the cliff with, on the N side, a tall terrace of C19 lace warehouses standing imposingly on ground which falls steeply away.

The heart of the LACE MARKET lies to the N of High Pavement. In ST MARY'S GATE, near the corner of Broadway, No. 27 is quite a rarity in the Victorian industrial area, just surviving but dilapidated. Its late C18 stucco façade was once rather elegant: shallow Corinthian pilasters, Adamish frieze, and round windows in the attic. Inside, a wrought-iron staircase, lantern-lit, and plaster panelling. Following the S-shaped curve of BROADWAY tall red brick warehouses of 1855 by *T. C. Hine*, that on the r. for Richard Birkin on the site of Colen Campbell's Plumptre House of 1730. Inside the gateway two arches of the previous St Mary's church (*see* p. 219) and the coat of arms of the Plumptre family. That on the l. is ingeniously adapted to the bend in the street, its façade almost symmetrical, with two curved corners. STONEY STREET and the streets adjoining are lined with similar warehouses. Off the E side of Stoney

Street near the top of Broadway in PLUMPTRE PLACE and PLUMPTRE STREET, two Edwardian warehouses with good Art Nouveau wrought-iron work, the gates of the Mills Building (1906) in Plumptre Place particularly magnificent. But the most monumental design is another of 1855 by *Hine* for Adams Page & Co. at the top of Stoney Street on the l. To the entrance at first-floor level a grand flight of steps. Over it a bowed window (as later used by Norman Shaw) lit a large open-plan sale room. Attached to the central block two long curving wings. In the basement of the r. wing a library, classroom, tearoom, and, nearest the street, the works chapel (see the tracery windows and door). Even the rear, with its large doorway to admit dray-loads of lace, has elegance. In style like the Broadway warehouses, this façade has continuous attic windows lighting the mending and inspection rooms. Much expensive ironwork and stone reliefs carved with subjects appropriate to the industry. Additions to Warser Gate made in 1865. At the corner of Barker Gate a *Fothergill* warehouse, 1897, with his usual mixture of polychrome brick and Domestic Revival detail in the upper floors.* Oriels on the corner distinguish the sales offices. In BARKER GATE, the NATIONAL SCHOOL, very plain, with pediment and pilasters all in brick. Built in 1834.

Continuing N up Stoney Street and up the pedestrian way opposite the end of it, we arrive at HEATHCOTE STREET, which forks r. on the N side of Goose Gate. Here is the PEOPLE'S HALL (an C18 house named thus in 1857), with heavily rusticated corner pilasters and doorcase. Next to it, set back in a forecourt with good railing and gate, No. 11, a plain late C18 stuccoed house. Inside, a fireplace with a Rococo plasterwork overmantel. Back to Goose Gate and up BROAD STREET, where the GENERAL DISPENSARY of 1841–3 by *Nicholson & Goddard* of London has a plainly classical rendered front (full-height pilasters above a rusticated basement). Further N the Wesleyan Chapel (now Co-operative Educational Centre) of 1839 by *S. S. Rawlinson* has been demolished. It had a grand order of attached columns. Next door was the former Sunday School. Back again to Goose Gate and along Carlton Street to GEORGE STREET. Here are two more former chapels, the BAPTIST CHAPEL (now Co-op Arts Theatre), 1815 by *Edward Staveley*, with Tuscan-columned porch blinded and generally

---

* There is another *Fothergill* warehouse (Milbie House 1882–3) in PILCHER GATE, off the w side of St Mary's Gate. Very different, with a mostly glazed façade and stripped classical articulation.

defaced, and the R. C. CHAPEL (now a wholesale stationers) of *c.* 1825–8. The stone façade, with paper-thin Gothick and classical details, is by *Edward Willson* of Lincoln, who collaborated with Britton and Pugin.* On the opposite side *Watson Fothergill's* own office (1894–5), overtly advertising his personal taste and skills.‡ Polychrome stripes, lower floors Gothic with much carving, including representations of his mentors: a medieval architect in a niche, busts of Pugin and Street, and the inscribed names of Scott, Burges, and Shaw. Below the first-floor windows, four reliefs, each one showing a building (classical, medieval, and Renaissance) under construction. In strange contrast with this, timber-framed gables and bargeboards in the attic storey. In THURLAND STREET (off George Street via Lincoln Street) one of *Fothergill's* earlier buildings (now the NATIONAL WESTMINSTER BANK), done in 1878–82 when he was still known by his real name of Fothergill Watson. Very monumental, with a large central feature and tower symmetrically over it. Lively sculptured friezes on the gables and the tower. Fine circular banking hall with massive polished granite columns supporting the domed upper part. The bank's E.E. style is more sophisticated and restrained than that of JOURNAL CHAMBERS at the bottom of Thurland Street in PELHAM STREET. This is of 1860, with multi-coloured bricks a little *à la* Butterfield and prettily decorated dormers. The neo-High Renaissance started by Barry appears in the insurance and banking buildings in VICTORIA STREET (parallel to Pelham Street), especially the ROYAL INSURANCE CO. (now Art Gallery) by *Evans & Jolly*, 1872, very refined for these architects, with a separate order and pediment for each doorway and each first-floor window.

Long Row, on the N side of the Market Square, is reached via High Street at the w end of Victoria Street. In HIGH STREET, MAPLES STORE, a chemist shop of 1904, splendid with terracotta and Art Nouveau windows, carefully restored by the *Architects Design Group* (1974), and in LONG ROW an altered but fine late C18 house or pair of houses bridging Greyhound Street. Red brick, four storeys projecting over the street on columns. What remains is the central decorative feature with an arched niche with a swan-neck pediment to the first floor, and above it a blind panel with a wavy floating cornice over

* There was also a C. of E. chapel-of-ease (St Paul) in this street by *William Wilkins*, 1821–3, now demolished.
‡ For this exuberant Nottingham architect *see* Introduction (p. 36).

an exuberant frieze. On the corner of Long Row and King
Street a *Watson Fothergill* building (QUEEN'S CHAMBERS,
1897), following Norman Shaw in its whimsical detail. Large
projecting half-timbered gables; a brick tower towards King
Street. The Domestic Revival style occurs again in KING
STREET in *Fothergill*'s similar Jessops Drapery Store (now
Waring & Gillow) of 1895–7, with gables, towers, and oriels
to the staff quarters of the shop, concealing iron and concrete
construction. Between King Street and Queen Street and facing
down prominently into the Market Square is *Waterhouse*'s
PRUDENTIAL ASSURANCE, of the same type as the head-
quarters building in London. Filling the rest of this island
between streets, with the main façade to Upper Parliament
Street, is the former ELITE CINEMA (now Bingo and Social
Club), 1921 by *Adamson & Kinns*, faced with white faience.
The blank return to Queen Street is most remarkable; Art
Nouveau frieze, and figures in oddly shaped niches at roof
level. Most of the other side of QUEEN STREET is occupied
by the former GPO, 1895 by *Tanner* of the Office of Works.
Huge, blackened stone with Jacobean details. In UPPER
PARLIAMENT STREET, *Fothergill*'s very early EXPRESS
CHAMBERS, 1876, with the first hint of his idiosyncratic style
in the corner feature.

### (2) *Streets SW of the Market Place*

Back to the Market Place. On the s side is WHEELER GATE.
In this street the only noteworthy building is ELDON
CHAMBERS (No. 18), with some shaped glazing bars in a Dio-
cletian window.* Wheeler Gate carries on s into LISTER-
GATE. At the bottom of this pedestrianized street is the
BROADMARSH CENTRE, 1965–75 by *Turner, Lansdown, Holt
& Paterson*, one of the first covered shopping precincts in the
city, replacing a popular shopping area. Unprepossessing,
especially when compared with the more ambitious Victoria
Centre (*see* p. 241). CASTLE GATE, one of the best streets in
Nottingham, begins at the top of Lister Gate. Under the
modern office block at No. 8 C13 rock-cut cellars with crudely
cut pillars, wells, and a garderobe. Further on a number of fine
C18 houses. No. 19 (STANFORD HOUSE), built by William
Stanford in 1775, is of red brick with stone and stucco dressings.

* No. 18 was much remodelled in 1867, probably by *Robert Evans*, who had
his office here in 1871. Nos. 4–6 were demolished in 1960. They comprised
a tall house with three shaped gables. Its magnificent if coarse plaster ceiling
of *c.* 1660 is to be re-erected at Holme Pierrepont Hall.

Three storeys and five bays with a straight parapet. The shape
of the window lintels is a survival from Bromley House (*see* p.
229), but the features of the slightly broken-forward centre bay
are up-to-date and Adamish. Above the tripartite pedimented
doorway, a tripartite window with a large elaborate fanlight
over it. The rear elevation with a central bow is also reminiscent
of Adam.* Next to Stanford House, No. 17 has shaped stucco
lintels and a Venetian-window-type doorway. Nos. 29-31 look
only slightly less grand than No. 19, but the impression they
give is the result of alterations: it really is a pair of houses of
1794 heightened by two storeys and with a central doorcase inserted between the two original ones, making an unusual and
definitely attractive feature. On the N side of the street early
c18 houses (Nos. 32 and 34), No. 32 with a good doorcase and
Venetian windows, No. 34 with a hood on wrought-iron brackets
and wrought-iron passage gates.

The W end of Castle Gate is divided from the rest by Maid Marian
Way. Before crossing note the SALUTATION INN, stranded
here in St Nicholas Street. Over-carefully restored and
extended, but still perhaps an approach to the appearance of
Nottingham in the c16. Plastered; wooden window frames with
arched lights. A medieval roof visible in an upstairs bar, two
levels of rock-cut cellars below (MWB). In CASTLE GATE on
the W side of Maid Marian Way, the stately NEWDIGATE
HOUSE (No. 64). Typical of its date (*c.* 1675–80), it has three
storeys and five bays, angle quoins, and a hipped roof with
modillion cornice and pedimented dormers. Probably once
brick, though now rendered, it displays features typical of Artisan Mannerism, but in a refined fashion: that is, the alternating
pediments (cf. Tyttenhanger, Herts, *c.* 1655–60) to the two
lower floors, the moulded and lugged architrave surrounds to
the upper windows and the door, the volutes on the door surround, and the broken pediment, originally containing a bust,
over the doorway. The wrought-iron screen and gates, some
of the best ironwork in the city, are almost certainly by *Francis
Foulgham.*‡ The garden, laid out in the French style with

* Stanford House stands on the corner of STANFORD STREET, which has
a complete series of c19 lace warehouses along the W side.

‡ According to Mr Edward Saunders, Foulgham, who worked in Nottingham from about 1710 until his death in 1749, did the ironwork at Arbury,
Warwicks, in 1719 for Sir Richard Newdigate, an uncle of Thomas Newdigate
† 1722 who built this house. The garden screen at Arbury is almost identical
to the screen here. In the Castle Museum is a dismantled gate from Colwick
Hall, also very similar to the Arbury screen and also probably by *Foulgham.*

miniature *broderies* by *London & Wise* and illustrated in their *The Retired Gardener* of 1706, disappeared early. Opposite, a row of c18 houses all used by the City Leisure Services. The terrace of plain brick houses with elegant doorcases (Costume Museum) has a datestone 1788 with the initials of Cornelius and Mary Launder (see No. 64 St James Street). The fittings in one of the front parlours are intact. The interior of Nos. 49–51 was gutted by the City Architect's Department *c.* 1970 and replaced by a wooden substructure of open galleries, etc. No. 53 has late c17 gables and brick keystones similar to those in Brewhouse Yard. Under the castle walls runs Castle Road. At the s end of Castle Rock the TRIP TO JERUSALEM INN, mostly c17 but reputedly founded during the Crusades and with rock-cut cellars. Behind it in BREWHOUSE YARD a group of late c17 houses in one H-shaped block (carefully restored in 1977 as a museum of social history).* Well detailed with plain gables, brick bands, projecting keystones, and redder brick dressings to the upper windows. Further N on the opposite side a timber-framed building (SEVERNS) of *c.* 1450 from Middle Pavement re-erected here in 1968 by *F. W. B. Charles.* It is the front or solar wing of a substantial house. Three bays and tall, with curved braces and wooden tracery windows (reconstructed on the pattern of No. 24 Westgate, Exeter) on the upper storey. Crown-post roof without purlins inside – unusual at this date in the east Midlands and more common in southeast England. Further N a harmonious and picturesque terrace of brick cottages (MORTIMER HOUSE) by *Fothergill,* 1883.

Opposite the entrance to the castle in King Charles Street, Standard Hill, ST MARY AND ST PETER'S VICARAGE, one tall brick double house of ten bays, built between 1808 and 1810. Further up Standard Hill and in St James Terrace and St James Street more nice c18 houses in an area made fashionable by the Dukes' residence. Byron lived in No. 76 ST JAMES STREET, w of Maid Marian Way. Several houses have good internal features, including No. 72 (elaborate façade with ground-floor windows set in a rusticated arcade with stucco ornament in the tympana, neo-classical fireplaces) and No. 64 (centre bay pedimented below the parapet and central arched recess with Diocletian window above a window and doorway framed together). At the back the datestone reads c1767L. Built

---

* Another terrace, almost identical but with renewed top floor, stands to the w. According to Mrs Postles they were probably all built shortly before 1680.

and occupied by Cornelius Launder (High Sheriff 1775) from
1768 until his death in 1806.* Inside, doorcases, overmantels
with some lovely Rococo details, and an original staircase.‡ Finally, at the bottom of the street and overshadowing it, one of
the ill-conceived and poorly designed multi-storey buildings
that line Maid Marian Way and break up the pattern and scale
of the whole castle area.

## N OF THE CENTRE

### CHURCHES

ALL SAINTS, Raleigh Street. 1863–4 by *Hine & Evans*. Large,
well composed C14-style church with W tower, broach-spire,
and a polygonal apse to the chancel. Rock-faced with bands of
sandstone. – TRIPTYCH by a local artist, *Hammersley Ball*. –
FONT COVER by *Harry Gill*. – STAINED GLASS in the Lady
Chapel by Miss *Townsend* and Miss *Howson* of London. –
Matching school with round tower, vicarage, and church institute make a fine group.

ST ANDREW, Mansfield Road. 1869–71 by *William Knight*.
Rather ugly C13-style church with some Romanesque detail in
the crossing tower; blunt broach-spire. Cruciform, with very
low aisles and a tall clerestory, and chancel chapels. W extension
by *S. R. Stevenson*, 1884. – (STAINED GLASS. W window by
*Heaton, Butler & Bayne*, 1871. RH)§

MANSFIELD ROAD CHRISTIAN SCIENCE (formerly Presbyterian) CHURCH. 1896 by *Brewill & Baily*. Stone in an Art-
Nouveau-influenced Gothic with some characteristic ironwork,
e.g. rainwater heads and pipes.

---

* According to Mr Train.

‡ In St James Street E of Maid Marian Way, Nos. 7–11 is a battered late
C18 group, seven bays wide, Nos. 9–11 with good doorcases.

§ HOLY TRINITY, Trinity Square. 1841 by *H. I. Stevens*. Like his other
churches, dark grey stone with lancet windows; a serious job. The W tower
with an octagonal upper stage was a fine accent on the skyline of Nottingham.
Demolished for a car park in 1958.

ST MARK, Huntingdon Street. 1855 by *Jalland*; still the Commissioners'
type, with angle turrets à la King's College, Cambridge. Stone and not at all
cheaply done; all windows Perp. (Chancel of the 1870s by *Isaacll* JPB)
Demolished in 1958.

ST MATTHEW, Talbot Street. 1853 by *H. Roberts*. Lancet style, with a
tall broad spire at the NE and a W front with two very low turrets. Demolished
1956.

CONGREGATIONAL CHURCH, Addison Street (now a warehouse). 1883
by *Henry Sulley* of Nottingham.

SYNAGOGUE, Shakespeare Street. Built as the Wesleyan Reform
Chapel by *Simpson*, 1854. Classical façade with a giant order
of fluted Corinthian pilasters supporting a pediment.

CHURCH CEMETERY, Mansfield Road. With a wealth of Picturesque features: a circular catacomb *à la* Highgate, caves, and
lush conifers. (Landscaped by *Edwin Patchitt* of Nottingham,
1856. JPB) The chapel by *E. W. Godwin*, 1878–9, has gone.
It was cruciform, with a spire.

GENERAL CEMETERY. *See* W of centre, p. 243.


### PUBLIC BUILDINGS

Although Shire Hall is in the centre of the old town, the accumulation of public buildings on one spot is outside its old boundaries,
just N of it in Shakespeare Street, Burton Street, and South Sherwood Street. They were not designed together as a Civic Centre,
and although at one time it was proposed to incorporate and
extend them, the Art College now fills the intended site instead.
The location of these buildings here betrays their relative youth
(they date from the 1880s on), and none is especially good.

GUILDHALL, Burton Street. 1887–8 by *Verity & Hunt*. Stone,
French Renaissance style.

POOR LAW OFFICES (former; now City Registrar's Office),
South Sherwood Street. By *A. H. Goodall*, 1887, in a red-brick
Scott-type Gothic.

TRENT POLYTECHNIC now occupies the large High Gothic
building on the corner of South Sherwood Street. Well sited
with lawns in front and well detailed, it originally incorporated
the public library, University College (moved to University
Park in 1928), technical and trade schools, and the Natural History Museum (now in Wollaton Hall). Begun in 1877 by *Lockwood & Mawson*, it first opened in 1881, closed two years later
because of structural defects, and re-opened in 1890. The
NEWTON BUILDING, next to it but facing Burton Street,
looks like a 1930s period piece but, surprisingly, was built in
1956–8 by *Cecil Howitt*. Portland stone with a central tower
which has glazed sides. Behind it and best seen from Shakespeare Street are the new buildings for the polytechnic, including the COLLEGE OF ART, by *David Jenkin* (City Architect),
1965–78, a group including hostels which centre on the lecture
hall, canteens, and other amenities. Informally designed to be
capable of expansion and consequently messy-looking. Most of

the buildings, in red brick, are at least partly below road level, with large semi-basement communal areas lighted by mono-pitch glass roofs. The former College of Art in Waverley Street (now WAVERLEY ANNEXE), built in 1863–5 by *Frederick Bakewell* of Nottingham for the encouragement of design in lace, etc., is ornately Italianate with named busts of architects and artists round the upper storey.

POLICE HEADQUARTERS, Shakespeare Street. 1940 by *R. M. Finch* (City Engineer); deadly dull.

NOTTINGHAM UNIVERSITY (Department of Adult Education), Shakespeare Street. Unorthodox mid-C19 Palladian façade with two giant Corinthian columns *in antis*.

HIGH SCHOOL, Arboretum Street. Fancifully castellated main front with mullioned windows by *T. Simpson* assisted by *Hine & Evans*, 1866–7. Either side of the central tower were the classical (w, now classrooms) and English (E, now library) schools. To the N a classroom wing with an upper storey (drawing and writing schools) of 1880. The basement was excavated in the 1870s and 1880s for science teaching. An interesting record of the development of the C19 school curriculum. Much later building.

GIRLS' HIGH SCHOOL, Arboretum Street, has occupied Clarence Lodge, built for the lace manufacturer James Hartshorn by *Emile Vandenberg* of Lille in 1875, since the 1880s. The noteworthy feature is the iron railings, in one of Hartshorn's lace designs.

THEATRE ROYAL, Upper Parliament Street. Built in 1865 in the tradition of Nash's Haymarket by *C. J. Phipps*, the most successful London theatre architect. Its grand Corinthian portico is all that remains intact. The interior was remodelled opulently in 1897 by *Frank Matcham*, who demolished the old backstage accommodation to make way for the Empire Theatre (demolished 1969) alongside. The theatre, benefiting no doubt from the 1970s renaissance in provincial theatres (e.g. at Sheffield, Leeds, Birmingham, Leicester, etc.), has again been remodelled and extended: 1976–8.* The architects (*Renton Howard Levin Wood Partnership*) have used the formula that was so effective at their Crucible Theatre, Sheffield, of 1970, i.e. foyers, bars, dressing rooms and so on grouped round the

---

* Nottingham Corporation, which subsidized the remodelling, has a good record of patronage in this field. They also built the civic theatre, the Nottingham Playhouse (*see* p. 243).

auditorium (here the C19 one) and expressed on the outside as an irregular polygon. Although, like the Crucible, on an island site, the result is less successful. The portico stands out self-consciously and the additions too tactfully sweep away from it in a series of curves. Stark white mosaic cladding against the cream-painted portico. It is not fair, however, to criticize the handling of scale without noting that this is only part of the original, temporarily abandoned design. The C19 theatre would have been balanced by a huge, fan-shaped concert hall and large fly tower behind it. The interior has some neat details, but the decoration, a modern counterpart to Matcham's lushness, is redolent of a luxury hotel. The auditorium has been slightly altered: boxes and the proscenium arch, a bit of incorrect classicism, are new.

ARBORETUM. Laid out by *Samuel Curtis* concurrently with Waverley Street, Forest Road, and Sherwood Rise (*see* p. 264), the surrounding wealthy suburbs, and opened in 1852. Lodges and castellated brick refreshment rooms by *Moses Wood*. Pagoda by *M. O. Tarbotton*, 1863.

FOREST RECREATION GROUND. On the site of the Nottingham racecourse, for which *John Carr* designed a grandstand in 1777. It was built by *Samuel Stretton* but does not survive. A LODGE, 1857 by *Moses Wood*, is there on the Mansfield Road side: cruciform, stucco, and of the Greek Revival type (cf. Judges' Lodging, High Pavement). Fluted Doric portico on one side and unfluted porticoes on the others, the whole only the size of a cottage.*

PERAMBULATION

(The s edge of the Forest Recreation Ground is lined with villas of the same prosperous C19 type as those in Mapperley Road on the other side of Mansfield Road (*see* Outer Nottingham: North-East). In FOREST ROAD EAST they are mainly Italianate (e.g. Nos. 61 and 67), with a notable exception, UPNAH HOUSE by *Henry Sulley*, 1877. In FOREST ROAD WEST a variety of styles (e.g. No. 91, with a tower; No. 93, MCIVOR HOUSE, Gothic, by *S. R. Stevenson*, 1874; and No. 111, 'Queen Anne', with a good wrought-iron gate). To the s in RALEIGH STREET, near *T. C. Hine*'s All Saints, No. 73 (SIMLA VILLA),

* The MECHANICS' INSTITUTE, Trinity Square, 1869 by *Thomas Simpson* of Nottingham and surprisingly late classical for its date, was demolished in 1964.

the house he built in 1870 for his son, G. T. Hine. It has a tripartite French Gothic doorway. JPB)

In this N area the most important C20 development has been the VICTORIA CENTRE on the site of the old Victoria Station (demolished in 1967).* The centre, by *Arthur Swift & Partners*, 1965–72, incorporates shopping malls, covered market, bus station and car park fitted underneath in the former railway cutting, and flats. It covers a huge area between Mansfield Road and Upper Parliament Street, as long as the old town centre from N to S. The scale of the design is similarly huge, brutally so in the parts that abut the street. Above the chunky grey-textured exterior of the two-storey shopping centre rise five slab blocks of flats, linked to give an irregular skyline that dominates the city. The whole exterior has an admirable monumentality rare in most modern city-centre building. The malls inside are simple and spacious, darkened to focus attention on the two storeys of lighted shops. On the Mansfield Road side all that remains of Victoria Station are the red brick clock tower and the Victoria Hotel by *R. W. Edis* dated 1901. Further up Mansfield Road some light relief: THE YORKER (formerly Rose of England), 1898 by *Watson Fothergill*. To the W, in TALBOT STREET, the former LAMBERT BLEACHING FACTORY, an imposing five-storey brick building with, at an angle on the corner, a tall clock tower strongly reminiscent of the tower at Wollaton Hall. The datestone reads 1863.

## W OF THE CENTRE

ST BARNABAS (R.C. Cathedral), Derby Road. 1841–4 by *A. W. Pugin*, financed largely by the Earl of Shrewsbury. 190 ft long (like a large parish church),‡ cruciform in the E.E. style, and less cheaply executed than most of his major churches. It is good ashlar, with a proud steeple (150 ft high) above the crossing and with a fine rhythm of breaks in height between the various parts, though individually the façades are rather papery. The interior is less successful, modelled on the Notts custom (octagonal piers, double-chamfered arches, twice as many

*VICTORIA STATION was of 1898–1900 by *A. E. Lambert* for the G. C. R. Like the Midland Station (*see* p. 247), it was a screen in front of a porte-cochère, but in rather the mixed Loire-Château and Baroque style of, say, the Imperial Institute. The tower, which remains, was placed asymmetrically.

‡ Not made a cathedral until 1851.

clerestory windows as arcade openings). The transept lancet windows are impressive and the varied roof-trusses nice *See* p. 448 scholarly exercises. The E end, almost as large as the nave, is square, with an ambulatory and E chapels. Unfortunately not all the chapels were decorated as Pugin intended, and the parts of the church that were have vanished in successive rearrangements and redecorations,* the first in the late C19 when the chancel screen, rood, and high altar were removed. *F. A. Walters*'s 1927 restoration of some Pugin features was undone again in 1961–2. All that remains is the original CRUCIFIX, now hanging from the chancel arch, and some of the twenty-six STAINED GLASS windows designed by *Pugin* and made by *Wailes*. Of these the aisle windows survive. Those in the transepts are by *Nuttgens* and of the early 1940s. The modern decoration is harsh and crude. The altar has been moved under the crossing to suit present liturgical needs, and the whole effect could hardly be farther from the richness of decoration and atmosphere that Pugin intended. Only the decoration of the Holy Sacrament Chapel, with red, gold, and green stencilled wall patterns, looks typically Pugin and splendid: it was painted and restored by *Alphege Pippet* in 1933. – CATHEDRAL HALL. 1976–7, a brick octagon, by *Eberlin & Partners*.

Behind the cathedral in College Road the PRESBYTERY, 1844, and the CONVENT OF OUR LADY OF MERCY, also by *Pugin*, 1845–50. Austere red brick with Dec chapel windows and fittings by *Hardman*. S and W sides later.

ALBERT HALL METHODIST MISSION, North Circus Street. Designed by *A. E. Lambert* and built in 1907–9 in the typical style of the Edwardian theatre or music hall, and in fact concerts and other events were put on there in the practice of temperance halls. Plenty of buff terracotta as they liked it at that time. The motifs come from Mountford, etc.: intermittent rustication, boldly curved pediment, asymmetrical tower.

SOCIETY OF FRIENDS' MEETING HOUSE, Clarendon Street, nestling into a corner of the General Cemetery. 1960–2 by *Bartlett & Gray*. A simple design in keeping with the Friends' form of worship: a rectangular brick block with a glass foyer and a parabolic shell dome over the meeting hall.‡

* Details of these were supplied by Mr Roderick O'Donnell.

‡ The SCOTCH BAPTIST CHAPEL, East Circus Street, has been replaced by the Playhouse. It was by *Booker*, 1858–9, but looked older. Externally with two giant Tuscan columns *in antis*, internally Ionic pilasters along all four walls. The W end had a semicircular bay which projected into the loggia behind the giant columns.

GENERAL CEMETERY, Alfreton Road. Started in 1837–40. The chapel by *S. S. Rawlinson*, stucco, neo-Greek, with an attached Ionic portico, was demolished in 1958. Rawlinson's entrance feature, Canning Terrace (the name dates it), has the debased classical details familiar from Loudon's *Encyclopaedia*. Two wings of six almshouses, each wing pedimented, flanking an entrance gate.

NOTTINGHAM PLAYHOUSE, Wellington Circus. 1959–64 by *Peter Moro & Partners*, the only modern building of national importance in the city centre. One of the first civic theatres to be built after the post-war slump in live theatre's popularity, and still one of the best. It was the earliest design to resolve the controversy between the proponents of the traditional proscenium-arch stage and those of the new thrust (or peninsular) type. The thrust stage, used experimentally by Sir Tyrone Guthrie at the Edinburgh Festival in 1947, was not incorporated in a purpose-built theatre until Powell & Moya used it in their Chichester Festival Theatre opened in 1962. The Playhouse, like Chichester, has aesthetic value as well as historical importance. The exterior demonstrates a clear separation of parts. The concrete drum of the auditorium is the dominant element in the design, the lower part enclosed in the glass cube of the foyer. Behind and appearing above the drum a square aluminium-clad fly tower, along the side a black brick rectangular mass of dressing rooms, etc., and, projecting from the front and enclosing a segment of the circus, a wing of bars and restaurants. On the main façade the upper foyer is cantilevered out over the entrance. Its cladding, alternate panels of opaque and clear glass, acts as a positive feature during the day but negatively at night, when it becomes transparent and reveals the integrity of the drum. The foyer levels are constructed around the drum in an ingenious way. From the outside, steps lead down to the lowest stalls foyer, then up to a mezzanine-level balcony entrance, and up again to an upper foyer running the whole length of the façade. An aluminium relief on the drum (by *Geoffrey Clarke*) penetrates all levels. The predominance of the cylindrical form is as obvious inside the auditorium as outside. Nothing (except the forestage when in use) breaks into the space. The balcony sweeps round in a continuous curve, the boxes at stalls level are recessed, the walls are covered in slatted black screens. Lighting concealed behind them breaks through in horizontal bands which encircle the auditorium, and stage lighting is suspended in a central drum echoing the 104 total shape. The geometrical clarity of the forms is reminiscent of the very first 'New Brutalist' tendencies in post-1945 architecture, for example in the Smithsons' Hunstanton School of 1949, but the shuttered concrete finish of the drum is used for aesthetic reasons rather than for truth to materials.

GENERAL HOSPITAL, Postern Street. The large block of 1781–2, built by *John Simpson* of Budby on land given jointly by the third Duke of Newcastle and Nottingham Corporation, still stands. It was an eleven-bay pedimented block with angle pavilions, much extended at one end between 1787 and 1824 and heightened by a third storey in 1854–5 by *Hine*, who added a chapel and, in 1877, a new wing. The main façade remained more or less intact until 1897–1900, when *Waterhouse* disrupted it with his Jubilee Wing: completely circular, of five storeys, with central ducts and flues, and still 'a joy to work in' in 1951. By *Hine* the Postern Street entrance and the former Children's Hospital in Postern Street, 1869, enlarged by *Evans & Jolly* in 1877.* (STAINED GLASS in the chapel by *Shrigley & Hunt*. RH) Large block completed in 1971 by *Cartwright, Woollat & Partners*.

THE PARK ESTATE. The hospital now occupies several wealthy villas to its N, i.e. to the NW of the fashionable C18 suburb round the castle. The castle had a park from the C12, and it survived into the C19, when the Duke decided to develop it as a residential area. In 1825 Mr *Hakewill*‡ was in correspondence with the Duke and visited the Park. In 1827 the first houses on the Ropewalk and in Park Row (now Park Terrace, probably Nos. 11 and 12) were built, closely followed by Nos. 1–10. Most of the rest of the stuccoed villas in Newcastle and Park Terraces, Nos. 15, 17, and 19 Park Valley, and the remaining houses on the Ropewalk went up in the next ten years. Many of them are of odd proportions because of their position on

---

* According to Mr D. Golberg, the Tower House at the Park Row entrance bears all the characteristics of alterations by *Watson Fothergill*.

‡ According to Miss L. Russenberger, who has given us details of the early years of the Park, probably *Henry Hakewill* of Warwick, who in 1817 drew up a plan of the Willes Estate, Quarry Fields, near Leamington Spa. An unsigned, unused plan, showing a dull layout round a square, may be his. (The earliest house designs seem to have been by *Peter Frederick Robinson* (1796–1856), a pupil of Henry Holland. He was surveyor to the fourth Duke, published a design for a villa in the Park in his *New Series of Designs*, 1838, part 11, and was replaced by *Hine* at the fifth Duke's accession. JPB)

the cliff. Squat on the road side, they are as high as seven storeys towards their gardens. After the first spate of building, development was interrupted until 1851, probably because of a loan contingent on the sale of the Park taken by the financially insecure fourth Duke.

Then in 1850–1 the Lammas Fields district, centring on Wellington Circus NE of the Ropewalk, was laid out as a sort of prelude to the development of the rest of the Park. Most of the houses are plain late Georgian in style, despite the late date. By *Hine*, surveyor to the Newcastle estates, Nos. 1–11 REGENT STREET, a tall Jacobean terrace with shaped gables, and No. 25, his own house, Ecclesiological, with a corner turret and vaulted drawing room. The Park itself was laid out only after 1856, an unfortunate date for the packing of houses into a landscape. Even so, as a piece of planned villa siting so close to the city centre, the Nottingham Park is something that historians of 'urbanism' should take more notice of. It was laid out by *Hine & Evans*. Presumably they were somewhat influenced by Nash and his plan for Regent's Park, for they adopted a scheme with a pattern of roads intersected by others radiating from two central circuses. However the Nottingham Park does not have Nash's generous distances, although the roads are on a terraced principle (which involved immense earth-moving operations) giving a very high and, at the time, almost unique standard of privacy to each house. Neither do the houses have Nash's white 'compo' fronts. The whiteness and the pilasters and columns have given way to brick and Gothic or Tudor detail. The main entrances are through lodge gates on Derby Road and immediately w of the castle in Castle Boulevard.

Much of the building activity took place in 1856, when Newcastle Terrace was lowered and many of the houses along the outer crescents were built. Approximately 200 houses are by *Hine*, some individually designed and some, e.g. in Pelham Crescent, identical rows of villas. Most notable are those below the castle in CASTLE GROVE (The Lodge and Nos. 1–7, 1856; Elizabethan, white brick, with shaped gables and some foliated detail), in DUKE WILLIAM MOUNT (Nos. 1–3, opulent red brick Elizabethan), several with very odd features in LENTON ROAD (Nos. 17, 21, 31–32), and others with open Italianate towers, such as the now stuccoed Peveril Tower in CAVENDISH CRESCENT NORTH which has an elaborate interior. Hine seems to have taken great pleasure in building on difficult sites, as at Nos. 1–3 NEWCASTLE DRIVE, which have seven or eight floors and the front door opening from the Drive on the fourth floor.*

Later houses, of the boom years 1880–95 when wealthy industrialists moved in, include several by *Arthur Marshall* of Nottingham, usually in a cheerful combination of hot red brick and yellow stone with fancy gables and much early Renaissance ornament: e.g. Brightlands, CLUMBER ROAD EAST, 1885 for the photographer Samuel Bourne. (Marshall himself was a keen photographer.) (There are also houses in *Watson Fothergill*'s idiosyncratic style along NEWCASTLE DRIVE: e.g. Nos. 21, 23, 27, and 39 (1886). Nos. 5 and 7 LENTON ROAD are his earliest surviving buildings (1873), very restrained; Nos. 1–5 SOUTH ROAD form one of his largest, most irregular houses. DG) Also distinctive, No. 14 CAVENDISH ROAD EAST: steeply pitched gables with very deep eaves and much openwork timbering. Above the entrance an interesting asymmetrical arrangement of windows and moulded brick panels. The estate also has its picturesque aspects. There is a tunnel carriage drive to Derby Road made in 1856 but later abandoned to pedestrians, and, linking the Ropewalk with Tunnel Road, a tunnel with roaring lions carved out of its cave-like walls. It was made *c.* 1856 by the alderman who lived in the house above in the Ropewalk. Only a few houses were built after 1900, e.g. CLARE VALLEY, and in the 1930s small terrace houses in HOPE and HAMILTON TERRACES. Since 1945 there has been some ugly infill, built without respect for the original planning or standard of architecture, in the gardens of the houses deemed too large for present-day use.

N of the roundabout at the bottom of Park Row is CITY GATE, one of the city's more sophisticated office developments (1973–6 by *Ian Fraser, John Roberts & Partners*), slightly oppressive in its bulk and dark colour and with ugly screening to the ground-level car park. W of this in Derby Road, Alfreton Road, and Ilkeston Road survive a few stuccoed and classical villas

---

* The following are also by *Hine* according to Mr Bartlam: Haddon House and Nos. 1–2, 10–12 Cavendish Crescent North; Nos. 13, 17–19, 23, and Holyrood House, Cavendish House, Overdale House, Elmhurst in Cavendish Crescent South; No. 31 Cavendish Road East; Clumber House and Nos. 5–7, Clumber Road South; Linden House and Holly Lodge, Clumber Road West; The Chestnuts, Kenilworth Road; Queen Anne style houses in Lenton Avenue; Lincoln Circus; Nos. 3–9, 25, 29–33 Newcastle Terrace; Nos. 5–7 North Road; No. 1 Park Ravine; No. 1 and Ashley House (1877) Park Drive; Nos. 3–5, 25, and Valley Grange, Park Valley.

and terraces. To the N of it, in CLARENDON STREET, more of the same and the sumptuous Victorian TERRACE ROYAL by *Wilson & Dutton-Walker* of Nottingham, 1863. Eight houses, Dec Gothic with elaborate carving, by *Smith* of Nottingham, much praised in *The Builder* (JPB). S of the Park on CASTLE BOULEVARD a towered warehouse by *Fothergill*, 1894, and VIYELLA HOUSE of 1933, like Boots' Beeston factory, a building that was genuinely modern at the time, all glass except the entrance feature, four storeys and four square.

## S OF THE CENTRE

ST GEORGE, Kirkwhite Street West. By *R. C. Sutton*, 1887–91; chancel by *Bodley*, 1897, tall and plain, with a very tall separate altar niche possessing only one window high up, an impressive composition.

ST SAVIOUR, Arkwright Street. 1863–4 by *R. C. Sutton*. Simple; w end with lancets, and an entrance through the SW tower.

ST FAITH, Collygate Road. 1913–15, aisle 1939, by *Sutton & Gregory* of Nottingham.

OUR LADY AND ST PATRICK (R.C.), London Road. 1880 by *Evans & Jolly*. Demolished.*

BRIDGEWAY HALL METHODIST MISSION, Arkwright Street. Built in 1963–7 by *Terry Bestwick*, to serve a C19 working-class suburb; now in the midst of its 1970s successor (*see* below). Its 'aggressive evangelism' suits both. Red brick, with a curved altar end to the street corner. The interior can be glimpsed through full-height slit windows.

MIDLAND STATION. 1904 by *A. E. Lambert*. One-storeyed in the Edwardian manner, with an arcaded *porte-cochère*. Terracotta with plenty of intermittent rustication of columns and window surrounds and a domed turret. Large Art-Nouveau-style wrought-iron gates.

GREAT NORTHERN STATION (now Goods Depot). 1857 by *Hine*. Venetian windows and a central shaped gable.‡

---

* ST JOHN THE BAPTIST, Canal Street, by *G. G. Scott & Moffatt*, 1843–4, badly war-damaged, has been demolished. It was never of special artistic interest. The style was E.E.

‡ Across the canal from London Road, the C19 CORPORATION DEPOT (East Croft), with clock tower, stabling, etc., is virtually derelict (MWB).

TRENT BRIDGE. 1871 by *M. O. Tarbotton* (Corporation
Engineer), with ornamental cast-iron work by *Handyside* of
Derby.

Along the canal near the station some INDUSTRIAL BUILDINGS
of interest. W of Carrington Street, the premises of Fellows,
Morton & Clayton Ltd, canal carriers. Facing Canal Street a
two-storey office block (No. 54) dated 1895. The four-storey
warehouse W of the offices backs on to the canal wharf, complete
with two canal-type cranes. An arm of the canal enters the
building via a large arch. The window pattern (semicircular on
the top floor but otherwise segmental) is typical of its date in
local industrial buildings. In the yard W of the Midland Station
a huge late C19 former grain warehouse and provender mill of
eight storeys formerly with a canal connection to the Nottingham canal. E of the station much has been demolished (e.g. the
historically important Hine & Mundella early steam-powered
hosiery factory of 1851 by *T. C. Hine\**), but at the corner of
Queens Road and London Road is an interesting group of what
were once probably lace factories. The best is in London Road
dated 1873 in the scrolly pediment. Off London Road, further
S, MEADOW LANE BRIDGE, one of the original stone canal
bridges.

Much of the housing in THE MEADOWS area SW of the London
Road has also been flattened (1972–7), and council estates by
the City Architect *David Jenkin* are taking its place. The red
and yellow brick terraces with pitched roofs and small walled
backyards are not unlike their Victorian predecessors. Only the
planning is more informal. To the W a desolate industrial area,
but to the S the VICTORIA EMBANKMENT, landscaped on
a generous scale thanks to Jesse Boot, who inaugurated the
scheme in 1920. The WAR MEMORIAL here is a belatedly
classical triumphal-arch affair by *T. Wallis Gordon*, 1927, with
magnificent wrought-iron gates. Also worth noting, a good
STATUE of Queen Victoria by *Albert Toft*, 1905, moved from
the Market Square in 1953, and the SUSPENSION BRIDGE of
1906.

---

\* Burnt down in 1859. T. C. Hine probably also designed the replacement
according to Michael Brook.

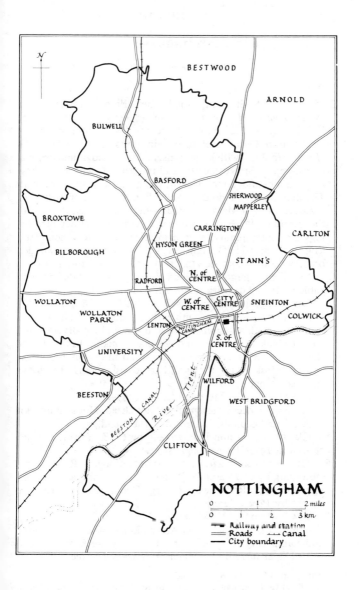

N

BESTWOOD

ARNOLD

BULWELL

BASFORD

SHERWOOD
MAPPERLEY

BROXTOWE

CARRINGTON

CARLTON

BILBOROUGH

HYSON GREEN

ST ANN'S

RADFORD

N. of
CENTRE

WOLLATON

WOLLATON
PARK

W. of
CENTRE

CITY
CENTRE

SNEINTON

COLWICK

LENTON

NOTTINGHAM
CANAL

S. of
CENTRE

UNIVERSITY

BEESTON CANAL

River Trent

WILFORD

WEST BRIDGFORD

BEESTON

CLIFTON

NOTTINGHAM

0          1          2 miles
0     1     2     3 km
━━━ Railway and station
═══ Roads      ┈┈ Canal
━━━ City boundary

OUTER NOTTINGHAM: EAST

SNEINTON—COLWICK

*Sneinton*

St Stephen, St Stephen's Road. The dark grey crossing tower by *Rickman & Hussey*, 1837–9, of respectable size with large E.E. openings. According to Hine, the first example of the revival of pure Gothic architecture in Notts. The rest by *C. G. Hare*, 1912, Dec, with large transepts, tall arcades, and original pier shapes. – BENCH ENDS and misericords with a monkey, a fox on a hound, a ram, jack-in-the-green, a head, a lion with a lamb in its jaws, a donkey, and a lion. Late C15 or early C16; removed from St Mary's *c.* 1848. – PAINTING. Assumption of the Virgin by *W. Hilton*, probably *c.* 1837–8. – Other furnishings all contemporary, so the interior looks very complete: REREDOS carved in Oberammergau, elaborate painted wooden ORGAN CASE, FONT COVER, NAVE ROOF, and PANELLING. – Opposite the large countrified churchyard, the tall brick and gabled VICARAGE with Tudorish windows, 1843.

St Alban, Bond Street (not used by C of E). 1886–7 by *Bodley*. Brick and stone dressings with early C14 detail, tall but without clerestory, with a wagon roof high up. W and E walls stark and almost blank except for windows placed high. On the W wall the outlines of the tenements that used to cluster round the church. Masking the SW side, later parish rooms. To the SE the Lady Chapel, 1898.

(St Matthias, St Matthias Road. 1867–9 by *T. C. Hine*.\* Rock-faced, lancet style, small but not cheap. Unusual interior with foliated capitals. Extended at the E end.)

(St Cyprian, Carlton Hill. 1934–5 by *C. E. Howitt*. A brick church in 1930s Romanesque style.)

(St Christopher and St Philip, Colwick Road. 1910; rebuilding by *C. Howitt & Partners* after bomb damage completed in 1952. Red brick with large Dec interior. – STAINED GLASS by *Pope & Parr*.)‡

William Booth Memorial Centre, Notintone Place, Windmill Lane. A Salvation Army old people's home, hostel, and community centre built in 1969–71 by the Army's Architect's Department under Major *D. Blackwell* (project architect

---

\* Information from Mr Bartlam and Mr Alvey.

‡ St Philip, Pennyfoot Street, 1879 by *R. C. Sutton*, was demolished in 1963.

*D. Greenwood*). Two- to four-storey red brick buildings of rectangular outline and with long wooden-framed windows, grouped round a terrace of three late Georgian brick houses where Booth was born in 1829 (now a museum). A pleasing combination.

Sneinton (Snotington) was a subsidiary Anglo-Saxon settlement to Nottingham (Snotingham). In the early C19 it became a fashionable suburb. Near the church some Georgian houses from the days of its prosperity. Up BELVOIR HILL a decayed terrace of *c.* 1820 with urns on the parapet commanded a view of the countryside to the E. Demolished. At the top, a fully restored five-storey brick tower WINDMILL, sole survivor of a number which once ringed the city, built *c.* 1807 by George Green, whose MILL HOUSE of 1817–18 stands to the E.

### Colwick

Church and Hall once made a famous picture near the river Trent. Now the church is unroofed and the Hall, which has been recently restored by Home Breweries, serves the racecourse and nature reserve in its park.

CHURCH (formerly ST JOHN THE BAPTIST).* Perp nave with the typical tall Notts windows and W tower, and chancel of 1684 embattled and with round-headed windows. The tower has buttresses of pilaster slimness. The Byron monuments have been transferred to Newstead Abbey and those of the Musters to All Saints, Annesley, but in the churchyard slate HEADSTONES by *James Sparrow* of Radcliffe and *John Harvey* of Nottingham.

COLWICK HALL. A medium-size Georgian mansion, brick with stone dressings. Apparently early C18,‡ it was extensively and impressively remodelled for John Musters *c.* 1776 by *Carr* of York. His builder was the local man, *Samuel Stretton.*§ The original house was a roughly square block of two equal storeys. On the entrance (N) front, a deep recess five bays wide, with the three corner bays forming wings two bays deep (cf. Melbourne Hall, Derbyshire, E front, remodelled 1706 by Smith of Warwick). The windows have simple stone surrounds and

* The present small modern church of St John the Baptist is just outside Nottingham in Colwick village, which is now just a collection of modern houses.

‡ There is a fine early C18 wrought-iron gate in the Castle Museum from Colwick (*see* footnote on p. 235).

§ The date is supported by a painting by Stubbs which shows the S front in its present form.

the angles quoins. The only later additions on this façade (Carr's or even later) are the balustraded parapet, the short one-storey wings at each side, and the covered colonnade running from the front door to a screen of Corinthian columns across the recess. The original graceful central cupola has gone. The s front, overlooking a serpentine lake, is more important and more completely transformed. To the main block of nine bays was added an attached Ionic portico with pretty Rococo leaf decoration round an *œil-de-bœuf* window in the tympanum. Ionic pilasters mark the angles of the block. The ground-floor windows have cornices, the upper ones are plain. Flanking the main block, in an arrangement reminiscent of Kenwood as altered by Adam, two five-bay wings of one tall storey, with Doric pilasters between round-headed windows.

The interior is unspoilt and very fine, in Carr's version of the Adam style. In most of the rooms at least fireplaces and cornices survive, and the main rooms are splendid. Along most of the s front is the library, with fine plasterwork and carved panelling (more of the same in the central entrance hall). At each end a columned screen, and at the E end a Chinese-style bookcase. The ballroom in the w wing leads off it. Apses at each end screened by Corinthian columns, fine plasterwork, but a plain coved ceiling. The main staircase, off the w side of the entrance hall, has branching flights with three fluted balusters to each tread. An odd feature of the irregular and probably early c18 plan is the second staircase against the s front. Rather grand, cantilevered round three sides of a square stairwell, and with a simple wrought-iron balustrade.

OUTER NOTTINGHAM: WEST

LENTON – RADFORD – HYSON GREEN

*Lenton*

LENTON PRIORY,* Gregory Street, Old Lenton. Of the old Cluniac priory founded by William Peverel in 1102–8 we know from excavations‡ and from slight remains above ground. It

---

* The house called LENTON PRIORY, built by *William Stretton* for himself, has been entirely submerged in the modern NAZARETH HOUSE in Priory Street.

‡ Partial excavation in 1936, 1943–51, 1954, and 1962–4 showed that the c12 church had a choir of three bays with apse, ambulatory, and chapels, transepts with chapels, and a ten-bay nave. The first three piers w of the cross-

was the most powerful monastic house in Notts and, for example, held all three Nottingham parish livings. In a patch of grass at the corner of Old Church Street and Priory Street lies the lower part of an easterly pier of the ambulatory. Buildings in Priory Street occupy the site of the nave, and up to 7 ft of the N and W walls are incorporated in the S boundary of the churchyard together with 9 ft of the W buttress. The so-called PRIORY CHURCH is largely a building of 1883, small and towerless, with a little bell-spike and Dec windows, but it has a C12 chancel with a PISCINA, one old lancet, and Norman carving on the altar step. It was part of the monastic buildings, possibly the chapel of the Hospital of St Anthony founded before 1108. Foundations of an attached building (the hospital hall?) were found 3 ft inside the present nave. Stone churchyard wall and nice gates of 1811.

HOLY TRINITY, Church Street, New Lenton. In 1842 a new church was built by *H. I. Stevens*. Large, with a large W tower, all of dark grey stone, and all with lancet windows, solidly and well done. The interior has tall quatrefoil piers. But the church is not visited for its architecture. It holds the mid-C12 FONT from the old priory, without doubt one of the most interesting in the country and one of only five rectangular narrative fonts. It is almost square, of stone, 34 by 28 by 30 in. high. The N side has only a foliated cross, the others all figure scenes. On the E, eleven arcades in two tiers, each filled by a row of cherubim with a row of seraphim beneath, except the centre of the lower tier, which shows the Baptism of Christ in a central arch of double width. On the S: the Crucifixion (with the soul of the penitent thief emerging from his mouth and soaring upwards, that of the impenitent thief being consumed by a large dragon). On the W: three scenes divided by a foliated cross, 16 at the top the Resurrection and a combined scene of the Entombment and Resurrection, and below two panels showing

---

ing were of a curious compound type, the main face consisting of a large three-quarter column attached to a rectangular core with smaller shafts on the other sides. This appears to be a unique form, although comparable in principle to the complicated compound piers found in eastern England (Ely, Castle Acre). The fourth pier was of a different design and may have belonged to a different building phase. Between the N transept chapel and the choir a recess was found, possibly for a staircase (cf. Norwich Cathedral). Remains of a stone screen were found between the second piers W of the crossing. Excavations in 1976 confirmed the existence of an E chapel.

the three Marys at the Sepulchre. The carving (with traces of original colour) is typically Cluniac in its richness but the style has no parallel in England. Clapham says it has Spanish origins. The bowl is quatrefoil, evidently intended for complete immersion as it measures 30 by 26 by 18 inches. – STAINED GLASS. Unusual and attractive floral glass in the E window to Francis Wright, the church's founder, † 1873.

Lenton village originally consisted only of GREGORY STREET. It must have been quite picturesque, with a Gothick character given to it by the Gregorys in the early C19. From Derby Road, Nos. 2a, 4, and 12 are stuccoed cottages with hipped roofs and Gothick glazing. On the opposite side, the so-called OLD MANOR HOUSE (the real Manor House has been demolished), a row of brick cottages made into one house, with gabled dormers and very pretty Gothick glazing. At the corner of SHERWIN ROAD, another house with a bow towards the garden, and further on the plainer late Georgian WHITE HART INN, the former Lenton Coffee House. At the back a mid-C17 brick wing with a Dutch gable, recently stuccoed. Opposite, a gabled brick C17 cottage.* To the N, rising suddenly out of the red brick suburbs of New Lenton, in WILLOUGHBY STREET, stark white concrete high-rise housing of 1967 by the City Architect, *David Jenkin*.

To the W, at the end of WOLLATON HALL DRIVE, Wollaton Park Gates and Lodge (*see* p. 280).

106 JOHN PLAYER HORIZON FACTORY, Lenton Industrial Estate. A huge, dramatic-looking factory with a bold outline, clearly articulated structure, and precise detailing that give impact from a distance and close to. Features like the outside staircases and chimneys add excitement. Inside, the space is organized for production on one floor without structural interruptions, so the service core runs horizontally through the building. Architects: *Arup Associates*, 1968–71.

For Lenton Abbey and other outlying houses, *see* p. 259.

*Radford*

ST PETER, Hartley Road, Old Radford. 1812 by *H. M. Wood*. Still the Georgian embattled rectangle with an embattled W tower. Only the windows are of a two-light minimum Gothic

---

* Right at the other end of Sherwin Road, just in CASTLE BOULEVARD, the tall, square chimney of a textile factory, LENTON WORKS, with the extraordinarily early date 1825 just above the plinth, very handsome and easily seen from Abbey Bridge, was demolished in 1978.

character (the same as at Papplewick twenty-five years earlier). The gallery has gone. Chancel 1871.*

Throsby described Radford village as a 'little paradise', landscaped by the owner, Mr Eliot. It was swept away by the lace industry, and now much of the area is covered by the premises of JOHN PLAYER & SONS‡ and the RALEIGH CYCLE WORKS. John Player transferred his business from the Broadmarsh to one of the three factories he built on RADFORD BOULEVARD in 1883–4. The Castle Tobacco Factory (Factory 1 on the E side) was opened in 1884 and gradually extended until 1935. No. 2 Factory of 1932 on the opposite side, by the Imperial Tobacco Company's own architects, is the most stylish and expensive of the group, with the No. 3 Factory of 1938–9 behind it. (Raleigh's office building farther up the boulevard is in just the same vein: by *C. E. & T. C. Howitt*, 1931.) Head Office, opposite No. 2 Factory, was completed in 1967 by *McMorran & Whitby* (cf. Nottingham University), an unexpected design for the area: white and weatherboarded, almost colonial in style. Further out on Ilkeston Road, the fortress-like concrete Bonded Warehouses, 1938. For the John Player Horizon Factory, *see* Lenton, p. 254.

From this point on Radford Boulevard, Hartley Road leads E. At its E end, in an area redeveloped with modern housing, one of the large tenement lace factories (CLYDE WORKS) still stands. Five storeys of orangey-red brick. Opposite the junction of Hartley Road with ALFRETON ROAD, in a terrace of early C19 houses, No. 238 is one of the few surviving framework-knitting shops left in the county, with its typical long upper windows intact both front and back.

*Hyson Green*

ST PAUL, Radford Road. 1844 by *Stevens*; stone, aisleless, still with the sense of plain surfaces of the Georgians. Only single starved lancets. The tower attached to the nave at the SW, behind the front with a W porch. Chancel 1889–91.

---

* CHRISTCHURCH, Ilkeston Road, New Radford, was demolished in 1950. It was of 1847 by *Stevens* of Derby, with his characteristic restraint in decoration. One wide low-pitched roof covered nave and aisles. The aisled E end was lower, ending in a polygonal apse. Bellcote; no tower.

ST MICHAEL AND ALL ANGELS, on the corner of Hartley Road and Alfreton Road, of 1888–9 by *W. G. Habershon*, was demolished in 1975 and the site acquired by the G.P.O. It was a chapel-of-ease to St Peter, serving Player's factory workers. Stone church of no particular merit.

‡ Demolished post-1979.

St Stephen, Bobbers Mill Road. 1897 by *Christian, Caröe & Purday*. It seems to be by *Caröe* and it is very typical of his style, with a very fanciful broad crossing turret, very low aisles with broad windows, a w front with a naughty buttress right up the centre of the central window (a Sedding motif), and detail of the characteristic Arts and Crafts Gothic of *c.* 1900. There are surely some good fittings.

The Victorian HOUSING round St Stephen has been completely demolished and new housing and factories are planned for completion in 1979.

*University of Nottingham*

University College was founded in 1877, contemporary with the other civic universities at Birmingham, Leeds, and Sheffield, and was built in 1881 alongside the Public Library and Natural History Museum in Nottingham's new civic area N of the old centre (*see* p. 238). Its removal to the park at Lenton and the first building there was due to the benefaction of Jesse Boot, who at the same time brought his factory from Nottingham to the site s of University Park (*see* Beeston). His reward was to be created Lord Trent after George V had opened the University building in 1928.

In 1920 Boot acquired a large estate at Highfields, w of Lenton village, intending to build on it an industrial estate and model town for his workers in the manner of the enlightened C19 industrialists like Salt, Cadbury, and Lever. The factory was begun on former farmland between the railway line, University Park, and the canals and river. Boot was to live in Lenton House (*see* p. 259), with the model town in the surrounding parkland, but Mrs Boot refused to move from Nottingham's Park Estate. In 1921 he revealed a scheme for driving a new boulevard through the estate and making a public pleasure park, with ornamental lake, on either side of it, and with a new university college in 60 acres of the park. *W. H. Radford*, the famous Nottingham engineer, built the boulevard and excavated the lake in the fields below the college, and *Morley Horder*, designer for Boots' Tudor-style shops and architect of private houses in the Cotswold style, designed the new 'palace of education'. The TRENT BUILDING was begun in 1922. It is of the classical re-revival, a style considered to confer academic respectability on new universities, and is handsomely carried out in good grey Portland stone. Very subdued ornament in the wings; the centre is stressed by a four-column por-

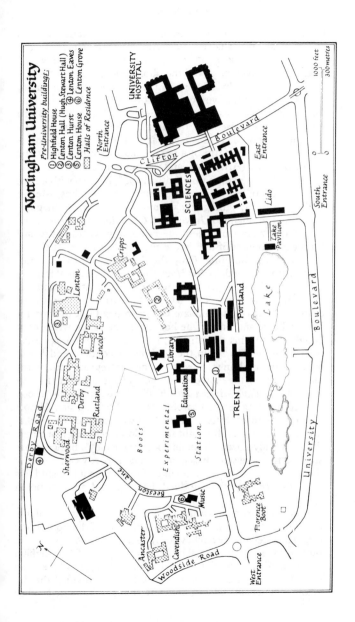

# Nottingham University

Pre-University buildings:—
1. Highfield House
2. Lenton Hall (Hugh Stewart Hall)
3. Lenton Hurst
4. Lenton Eaves
5. Lenton House
6. Lenton Grove

▨ Halls of Residence

UNIVERSITY HOSPITAL

North Entrance

Clifton Boulevard

SCIENCES

East Entrance

South Entrance

Lido

Cripps

Lenton

Lincoln

Library

Portland

Lake Pavilion

Lake

Derby Road

Sherwood

Rutland

Derby

Boots'

Experimental

Education

Station

TRENT

Beeston Lane

Music

Ancaster

Cavendish

Florence Boot

University Boulevard

West Entrance

Woodside Road

N

1000 feet
300 metres

tico with pediment and a tall tower with Lutyensesque aedicules
and a curiously-Italianate roof. Also of this first phase the
Lutyensesque LAKESIDE PAVILION (1926, originally red
brick) and LIDO that served the public park; and FLORENCE
BOOT HALL (also by *Horder*) to the W, large and utilitarian,
with Georgian-type windows and of no special merit. Unfortunately it was this dreary neo-Georgian that set the pattern
for most of the subsequent buildings. It is perhaps most convenient, and not too confusing as far as chronology goes, to examine these in the form of a perambulation beginning at the
Trent Building (Arts, Law, and Administration).

   The college became a university in 1948, by then with a park
of 175 acres. In 1955–6 (i.e. at the time when Gollins, Melvin
& Ward were designing frankly modern buildings, imaginatively sited, at Sheffield University), *Cecil Howitt* continued the
classical theme in a much less interesting way, with scant regard
for the possibilities of the site, in the PORTLAND BUILDING,
E of the Trent Building. Only the decoration of the interior,
now largely changed, by Sir *Hugh Casson* and a team of interior
designers acknowledged the modern movement. Behind the
Trent Building to the NW, HIGHFIELD HOUSE (Vice-Chan-
cellor's residence), a plain late Georgian box built in 1797 for
Joseph Lowe and one of the houses on the estate when Boot
bought it. N of this the EDUCATION BLOCK by *Farquharson,
McMorran & Whitby*, in the weak neo-Georgian used for so
many of the buildings. Next to it the centrepiece and, at the
moment (1978), the showpiece of the University: the LIBRARY
(1972) by *Faulkner-Brown, Hendy, Watkinson & Stonor*, a cool,
studied building set on a carefully shaped sloping site. Almost
a square, with chamfered corners. Two heavy concrete-clad
upper storeys with full-height slit windows overhang two others
that are totally glazed, the main floor, reached by a bridge, more
stressed than the semi-basement, which is partly concealed by
the fall of the site. Inside, the main floor has an air of studious
calm induced by the subdued lighting and uninterrupted
spaces.

   N of the library and round the N and W perimeter of the
campus are the HALLS OF RESIDENCE. NE of the library, the
original castellated seven bays of HUGH STEWART HALL were
built in 1804 as Lenton Hall by *William Stretton* of Nottingham
for John Wright. N of it, six halls built in 1954–60 by a team
of architects under *Sir Percy Thomas*, who provided the development scheme when university status was granted. They

were built on the collegiate plan in 'Wrenaissance' style, with
formal gardens and quadrangles totally at odds with the landscaping of this part of the park (by *G. A. Jellicoe*, 1954, revised
by *McMorran*, 1959).\* What a chance was missed to exploit
the informal possibilities of modern architecture. A walk up
Lenton Hall Drive from Hugh Stewart Hall, along the drive
parallel with Derby Road, and down Beeston Lane takes us past
both the halls of residence and the pre-University buildings
that have survived. In Lenton Hall Drive, the first of the six
and the most rigidly formal, CRIPPS HALL by *D. H. McMorran*,
with segmental window heads, the same *leitmotif* as on the
Education Block. N of the drive LENTON HALL, also by
*McMorran*, and opposite LINCOLN HALL (by *Frank Woolley*)
and DERBY HALL (by *Brian O'Rorke*). After a bend in the
drive, SHERWOOD AND RUTLAND HALLS show the freest
interpretation of the chosen style, with dark brick, white
timbering, and silly versions of the obligatory lanterns. Rutland
Hall (*Fletcher, Watson & Partners*, 1965) has a weatherboarded
octagonal gatehouse with a shiny black conical roof. N of the
halls along DERBY ROAD are several of the original houses of
the Lenton area. Furthest E, LENTON HURST, a large red-
brick house by *Arthur Marshall*, *c.* 1900 (now part of Lenton
Hall), its garden laid out by *Gertrude Jekyll*; then a pair of
C19 cottages, one stone and castellated, the other a *cottage orné*;
then LENTON EAVES (*c.* 1877, and, just outside the campus,
the stuccoed LENTON ABBEY of *c.* 1800, probably built on the
site of an abbey grange.
    There are more houses along BEESTON LANE, the original
country lane that begins just w of Rutland Hall. First on the
l. LENTON HOUSE, within its own grounds, which Boot intended to be his home and which still belongs to Boots Company (Experimental Station). By the entrance a pretty stuccoed
lodge with Gothick glazing bars and a group of farm buildings.
The house itself is Regency, black and white, with full-height
bow and bay windows, the two-storey w block of 1800, the
three-storey extension of 1816.‡ Opposite, more University
buildings: NIGHTINGALE HALL by *Cecil Howitt*, 1955–6
again neo-Georgian, but this time on a star plan. s of it a short
drive leads to WILLOUGHBY, CAVENDISH, and ANCASTER
HALLS. Cavendish and Ancaster (by *Williamson, Faulkner
Brown & Partners*, 1965–6) mirror each other, still neo-Geor-

gian in character, with rectangular windows and a hipped roof behind a heavy cornice, but, like Rutland and Sherwood Halls, more domestic in scale and with some more frankly modern features. In Beeston Lane again, LENTON GROVE (Department of Music), late Georgian and stuccoed.

West and East Drive lead from here, past the Trent Building, to the agglomeration of SCIENCE BUILDINGS, known to students as Science City. Nottingham University is traditionally biased towards science and technology, and its science buildings, concentrated on the E of the campus, far outnumber the other faculty buildings. Behind the brown brick NATURAL SCIENCE BUILDINGS of no great distinction* (completed in 1954–5) on South Drive are three parallel three-storey blocks (Schools of Mining, Thermodynamics, Engineering, and Medical Science and Pharmacy), linked at one end to a long spine block (Applied Sciences) at right angles to them. Simple and effective modular building by *Andrew Renton & Associates*, who took over from *Basil Spence & Partners* from 1961 to 1966. To Spence's designs (1956) only the courtyard block and chemistry buildings (*see* below). Grey brick end walls and glass curtain walls with black mullions to the three short blocks, grey brick cladding to the main part of the spine. The overall effect is spoilt on the E side by unappealing and noisy ground-level service areas and by the temporary buildings that interrupt the layout.‡ On the N side of the spine a similar courtyard block linked to the spine by a staircase hall, almost transparent in dark tinted glass, with a skeleton of staircases and open walkways. The spine and courtyard block form one side of a grassy open court with buildings arranged round it in a formal way, completely different from the landscaping of the rest of the campus. In fact there is a dichotomy between the modern science buildings and the retardataire buildings on the rest of the campus which marks a change of planners, from McMorran to Spence. On the other sides of the court a number of buildings of differing quality by the same architects. To the NE a tall slim TOWER BLOCK (Electrical Engineering and Architecture) with a grid pattern of strongly pronounced horizontals and verticals uniformly clad in dark grey aggregate, its monumentality enhanced by its setting in a slightly sunken well of smooth grey tiles. NW

* A more exciting design for this crucial site by *David du R. Aberdeen* was abandoned when the architect withdrew.

‡ The layout was in fact planned to accommodate these temporary buildings, which were to be demolished in 1970 but are still there in 1978.

of the tower block, nondescript Chemistry, Mathematics and Physics Blocks, and raised above the courtyard in the middle of the w end, the SCIENCE LIBRARY (completed 1964, extended 1969–70), similar to the tower block but only three storeys high. Glazed between projecting beams carried on above the roof-line like battlements.*

Just outside the campus, on the other side of Clifton Boulevard, which runs along the E side, the QUEENS MEDICAL CENTRE, a teaching hospital and medical school. First stage 1971–7 by the *Building Design Partnership*. When completed in 1979 it was the largest group of hospital buildings in the world. The hospital itself is vast, the design of it stark and repetitive: bands of golden brick and dark tinted windows with a halo of white asbestos cladding on the top floor. There are three hollow blocks and another one of six storeys, attached to the corners of a central block (diagnostic centre). Towards Abbey Street, STAFF HOUSING, offices and a social centre, grouped together in a much more villagey atmosphere. Small-scale buildings in brick and white weatherboarding round small courtyards, the planned neo-vernacular character in strong contrast with the starkness of the hospital. *See* p. 448

ST ANN'S – CARRINGTON – MAPPERLEY – SHERWOOD

## St Ann's

ST CATHERINE, St Ann's Well Road. 1896 by *R. C. Clarke*. Plain stone church, towerless, but with a bell-turret. E.E. interior with clustered columns.‡ Plain C13 FONT from South

---

* Between East Drive and Cutthrough Lane the deserted medieval village of Keighton was excavated and tile kilns of Lenton Priory found. The site was occupied by the mid C12 until the third quarter of the C15. The tiles were made to patterns supplied by Malvern craftsmen, and many patterns are identical to those made there, even down to the date on the canopy tile of a group of five. 1457–8

‡ ST ANN, St Ann's Well Road. 1864 by *R. C. Clarke*; Dec. N transept 1879, N aisle 1882, chancel enlarged 1896. Demolished 1971.

ST BARTHOLOMEW, Blue Bell Hill Road. Designed in 1894 by *Pearson*, but not built until 1900–3 by *F. L. Pearson*, according to Mr Quiney. Not one of his important churches. Demolished in 1971.

EMMANUEL CHURCH, Woodborough Road. By *Watson Fothergill*, 1883–92 and 1898. Demolished 1972. The interior was of a very ambitious and busy design, with lots of patterned brick and a curious tripartite chancel arch.

Wheatley. – STAINED GLASS. W window by *Kempe*, 1899.

ST AUGUSTINE OF ENGLAND (R.C.), Woodborough Road.
1921–3 by *Sidney Brocklesby*. Truncated W end that looks incomplete. Interior in 'the Romanesque idiom of Périgueux'.
Two large bays with saucer domes and a five-bay arcade dividing chancel from ambulatory. Low arcades with a small window
over each arch and piers ranging from square at the W end to
quatrefoil near the altar. – Fine C12-style STAINED GLASS: by
whom? That in the Lady Chapel is by *John Hardman Studios*,
1922.

BAPTIST CHAPEL (now Pakistani League of Friends), Woodborough Road. One of the few old buildings surviving the massive redevelopment of the area. A huge chapel of 1893–4 with
the usual interesting *Watson Fothergill* details and an eccentric
tower. Apse to Albert Street North and arcading all along the
side at the street-level entrance to the basement. Inside, the
nave divided from the aisles by cast-iron columns, too slender
for the brick arches they support, and with the gallery bolted
to them in an obvious way.

Most of the C19 working-class housing that covered this area has
been swept away since 1967 and replaced largely by very ordinary council housing. Phase 10, on the W side of Woodborough
Road, by the *John Stedman Design Group* (1965–78) is the only
part of the redevelopment that makes effective use of the sloping
site and is comparable with Stedman's closely-textured 'hill village' of Kingswood at Corby (1965–72). The scheme begins
with most originality at the top of the hill, across the cliff
below Cranmer Street, where groups of small dwellings are
stepped down under a continuous monopitched roof, each
group divided from the next by a narrow flight of steps. Unfortunately the tightness of this design is broken irresolutely on
Woodborough Road by a fringe of much more ordinary houses.
Similar conventional though well laid-out houses, together with
a children's home, a handicapped persons' home, and a pub by
the City Architect, cover the rest, i.e. nine-tenths, of the site.
The self-effacing quality of this scheme forms an instructive
contrast with the monumental flats over the Victoria Centre.
Cutting through the council housing, two grand tree-lined
avenues, ELM AVENUE and ROBIN HOOD CHASE, tracts of
forest specially designated for recreation in the 1845 Enclosure
Act.

In the SE of the area, towards Sneinton, still a few C19 buildings.
In BATH STREET, Nottingham Corporation's first indus-

trial dwellings, VICTORIA DWELLINGS of 1876–7 by *Bake-well & Bromley*, with a striking end elevation of a giant lancet framing open balconies and flanked by two towers. Also in Bath Street the first Board School, 1874 by *Evans & Jolly*. From the front of Victoria Dwellings can be seen the distinctive continuous row of windows lighting the top-floor inspection shop of BANCROFT'S LACE FACTORY, 1869, in Robin Hood Street (MWB).

*Carrington – Mapperley – Sherwood*

ST JOHN EVANGELIST, Mansfield Road, Carrington. 1843 by *Surplice* of Nottingham, stone, in the usual lancet style of that date, with a little bellcote. Chancel added in 1866–77 by *Jackson & Heazell*, re-using the E window. N aisle in an unrelated style, 1922 by *A. E. Heazell & Son*. – (STAINED GLASS. E window 1948 by the local firm of *Pope & Parr*. RH)

ST JUDE, Woodborough Road, Mapperley. Large, low, and rambling red brick church built over a long period. Nave part of a cruciform plan by *Evans & Jolly*, 1877, later abandoned. Chancel 1892 and organ chamber 1897 by *W. A. Heazell*. Aisles 1916, chapel 1922, vestries 1925, and final bay of nave 1929 by *A. E. Heazell & Son*. Towerless, but with a little conical cap to the bellcote. Every other bay of the aisles gabled. Plain but spacious interior. Next to it an incongruous neo-Georgian church hall, 1970 by *Eberlin & Partners*, not even in the right colour brick.

ST MARTIN, Trevose Gardens, Sherwood. 1937 by *E. H. Heazell*. Straightforward 1930s Byzantine style in brick. Arched narthex, and chancel with a bold apse. The nave has a high barrel-vault.

CITY HOSPITAL, Edward's Lane. The earliest parts were built in 1889–91 as the City Isolation Hospital and Sanatorium, to which the Bagthorpe Workhouse was added in 1903 by *Arthur Marshall*. The only later addition worth mentioning is the MEDICAL EDUCATION CENTRE, 1970–1 by *George Grey & Partners* Simple interlocking brick and white-painted timber-clad blocks.

COPPICE HOSPITAL, Ransom Road, Mapperley. The former County Lunatic Asylum; by *T. C. Hine*, 1857–9. Plain four-storey elevation enlivened with bands of patterned brickwork. Some large mullioned windows in the centre and Elizabethan gables on the other sides. Two large wings by *G. T. Hine*, T.C.'s son.

MAPPERLEY HOSPITAL, Porchester Road, Mapperley. 1887.
Vast and gloomy; the prizewinning design which launched
G. T. Hine as consulting architect to H.M. Commissioners in
Lunacy (JPB).

This area, once forest, became the 'rus in urbe' of the Nottingham
lace manufacturers after the enclosure act was passed in 1845.*
The first estate of large villas was SHERWOOD RISE, developed by the Duke of Newcastle N of the racecourse at Carrington. The earliest houses, of c. 1845–50, in the first four
avenues W of SHERWOOD RISE, are stuccoed and classical, the
later ones High Victorian. On the E side of Sherwood Rise,
released for building in 1882, ELMSLEIGH, HAMILTON
ROAD, built in 1883 for Joseph White, a director of Thomas
Adams, by *Henry Sulley*, an aggressive design with steep gables
and huge ugly bargeboards, and an interior with Byzantine
columns and a conservatory with a smoking gallery. Later still
are Nos. 1–3 Sherwood Rise (1894) and the cheerful NORRIS
LADIES' HOMES (1892), just in Berridge Road, by *Watson
Fothergill*, and FOREST LODGE, Sherwood Rise, probably by
*Arthur Marshall*.‡ The E side of the estate has suffered
badly from later development, which began in 1895 with the
Great Central Railway cutting. The estate was wound up in
1962.

Next to be developed, c. 1854, on a speculative basis by the
brothers B. H. & J. G. Hine (proprietors of the family hosiery
business) was the secluded and still private ALEXANDRA
PARK, E of Woodborough Road, the layout and first houses
designed by the Hines' elder brother *T. C. Hine*. Among Hine's
houses, the neo-Elizabethan SPRINGFIELD§ and SUNNY-
HOLME (now Trent House) and, in Woodborough Road,
FERNLEIGH for the patron of All Saints' church, William
Windley, later altered, with tile-hanging and pargetting, and
extended by *Arthur Marshall* c. 1895–1906 for J. D. Player.
RISEHOLME is by *A. W. Brewill*: not outstanding. The main
CRESCENT, a winding drive lined with laurels and trees like
the approach to a country house, Hine intended to be much
longer, stretching E to the Coppice Hospital, but this plan was
revised c. 1900 and the estate completed to the N with the cul-

---

* Most of the following information about the development of this area was
kindly given to us by Mr J. P. Bartlam.

‡ Off Berridge Road to the E in FOXHALL ROAD a terrace by *Fothergill*,
1901: modest, but with quirky gables.

§ Lavishly altered c. 1900.

de-sacs (e.g. Dagmar Grove) leading off Woodborough Road.
MAPPERLEY ROAD, continuing SW from Woodborough Road,
was yet another manufacturers' Belgravia, with houses built
from 1852 onwards ranging from stuccoed classical (CLAY-
FIELD HOUSE, CRANMER HOUSE, and Nos. 20 and 22 with
details from Loudon) to the fine BEECHWOOD with a corner
turret. The most magnificent house (MALVERN HOUSE, No.
39) was built in 1874, probably by *Henry Sulley* of Nottingham,
for the manufacturer T. B. Cutts. There is subtle polychromy
in the stonework, very Dec detail, and lots of sculpture inside
and out. To the r. of the house two half-timbered gatehouses
facing a walled court, and in front of the carriage sweep Gothic
gatepiers and wrought-iron gates. Behind were terraced gardens
commanding a panoramic view of the valley. Also in Mapperley
Road the Elizabethan-style former CONVENT OF THE
SISTERS OF ST JOSEPH by *Hine*, c. 1870.*

MAPPERLEY PARK, at the N end of Mapperley Road, was developed in the grounds of MAPPERLEY HALL, built c. 1792
by the Wright family of bankers. The Hall in Lucknow Avenue
is latest C18 stuccoed, with a top floor and Italianate details
added to the garden front c. 1845. Extended by *Robert Evans*
in 1889–90. To the r. of the façade a tripartite screen with Doric
columns flanking the central arch may have been the entrance
feature originally. The first land (in Magdala Road) was released
for building c. 1880,‡ and in 1903 the Wrights sold the Hall and
130 acres to a group of business men who were responsible for
many of the roads and houses in an Edwardian free-classical
style. Among the earlier houses, worthy of note are OAKFIELD,
CYPRUS ROAD (rock-faced, High Victorian, and no doubt by
*Henry Sulley*, 1882); No. 2 LUCKNOW DRIVE by *Hine*, 1882,
with good details, strapwork, and shaped gables; No. 1 MAG-
DALA ROAD by *Brewill & Baily*; and CLAREMONT, ELM
BANK, with elaborate Italianate gardens. On the W side of
MANSFIELD ROAD a few oddments: by *Watson Fothergill*,
CLAWSON LODGE (No. 403), 1885 for Mr Doubleday, a lace
manufacturer, and Nos. 409–411, 1881–2. N of Mapperley
Park, round PRIVATE ROAD, an earlier private estate origin-
ally called Mapperley Place, developed on the Duke of New-

* For Forest Road, the continuation of Mapperley Road W of Mansfield
Road, *see* N of centre (p. 240).
‡ There is a design in the Nottingham County Record Office of the earliest
(S) part of the estate by *Evans & Jolly* dated 1882, so one must presume that
it was they who laid out this part (JPB).

castle's land. The houses (e.g. MAPPERLEY HOUSE, MAP-PERLEY PLACE, and a cottage of 1825 in Mansfield Road) are mostly stuccoed classical. Other opulent houses in the Domestic Revival style of all dates from the 1880s to the 1930s.

### OUTER NOTTINGHAM: NORTH-WEST

### BASFORD – BULWELL

*Basford*

ST LEODEGARIUS. The N and S arcades have very slim quatrefoil shafts and fillets (cf. Rolleston, Lowdham, Cotgrave, Fledborough) of *c.* 1250, the arches double-chamfered.* Stiff-leaf capitals with figures on the SE pier. The chancel perhaps a little earlier, with single lancets grouped (cf. Southwell choir) and a priest's door with waterleaf capitals. Chancel repaired in 1900. S aisle windows C14, straight-headed, of a usual pattern. The N aisle and N arcade were rebuilt in 1858–9 by *Arthur Wilson* and the whole church was restored, except the tower, which fell in 1859 and was rebuilt in 1859–61 by *Thomas Allom* in a congested E.E. style. Built into the E jamb of the E.E. S door, a PORPHYRY SLAB, possibly a pax. – STAINED GLASS. S aisle, W of the door, a window by *Kempe & Co.* – In the churchyard some good slate HEADSTONES, the best perhaps to William Adkinson † 1777 by *Radcliffe*.

(ST AIDAN, Arnold Road, Basford. 1905 by Messrs *Evans*. Simple Gothic with Dec windows. KT)

ST AUGUSTINE OF CANTERBURY, High Church Street, New Basford. 1859 by *G. G. Place*, 'designed so that hereafter it can be enlarged if necessary': and so it was. In 1877 Place's nave became the S aisle when a new nave was built. N aisle 1884, chancel 1895, E window 1910.‡ – (STAINED GLASS by *Alexander Gasgcoyne*, 1911, in the E window. RH)

(CHRISTCHURCH, Nuthall Road, Cinderhill. 1856. The Duke of Newcastle gave the site, so his architect *T. C. Hine* designed the church. Rock-faced, plate tracery, octagonal bell-turret.

---

* Mr Train suggests that the arches, which are of local stone and slightly overhang the capitals, are contemporary with the chancel, and that the shafts, of magnesian limestone and probably carved off-site, are a later modification to the piers.

‡ Information from Mr Bartlam and Mr Alvey. Demolished.

Arcades with *Minton* tiles in the place of hoodmoulds. – PULPIT. Heavily carved by *Thomas Earp.* JPB)

ST MARGARET, Aspley Lane, Aspley. 1934–6 by *E. H. Heazell.* Brick, typical reduced Gothic of the period.

A few old houses near the church in OLD BASFORD. Opposite the church the MANOR HOUSE, a rare and good example of a house of *c.* 1700: seven bays, two and a half storeys, brick, with a decorative iron gate of the same date. In BAILEY STREET, CHURCHFIELD has an early C18 staircase. Further away in SOUTHWARK STREET Nos. 1–11, brick cottages of *c.* 1700.

*Bulwell*

ST MARY AND ALL SOULS. 1849–50 by *H. I. Stevens* of Derby. Stone, Dec, with w tower and aisled nave. N chapel 1946.

ST JOHN THE DIVINE, Quarry Road. 1884–5 by *William Knight.* – (Some *Powell* STAINED GLASS of 1892. RH)

BULWELL HALL was demolished in 1958.*

OLD GRAMMAR SCHOOL, Strelley Street. 1669, and very characteristic of Notts brick building at that date: a small house with a gabled porch on the long side, not in its centre, and two gables on the short sides. These gables are all curved and stepped, shaped gables as they are usually called. There is brick rustication besides. Nothing classical at all yet. Original lead guttering. Stone outbuildings behind.

OUTER NOTTINGHAM – VILLAGES

BILBOROUGH

ST MARTIN, St Martin's Road. Essentially a late C14 church (see the windows in nave and chancel, and also the handsome S porch with a crocketed ogee niche over the entrance), restored in 1887–9 by *J. E. Newbury.* w tower a later medieval replacement of one of the same date, two stages embattled, *c.* 1450. Church extended in 1972. On the N side of the chancel, wall MONUMENT to Sir Edmund Helwys of Broxtowe† 1590.

The only village houses that remain are the VICARAGE of 1842,

---

* It was a handsome stuccoed house of 1770, of five bays, two and a half storeys, with a one-storey porch, a central Venetian window, and wings at r. angles but connected by curving colonnades. (The additions of 1879, heavy balustrade, and clock tower, may have been by *Hine.* JPB)

late Georgian style, stucco, with full-height bow, and ST MAR-
TINS COTTAGES, a row of brick cottages along one side of the
churchyard. This village core is surrounded by post-First-and-
Second-World-War housing and industrial estates. The best of
the housing is THE WILLOWS Old People's Estate, Ambergate
Road, SE of the village centre, with bungalows and a hostel
round a green. Brick with tiled roofs and plenty of advance and
recession in the layout. The boiler house, given a steep conical
roof and seating under the eaves, has been cleverly used as the
focal point of this inward-looking and, seemingly, rather isolated group. Designed by *David Jenkin* (City Architect), 1967–
9. The best industrial building is FARRAND'S in Wigman
Road, unusual when it was built in 1957 (by *J. M. Austin-Smith
& Partners*) because the warehouse was given as much emphasis
and attention as the linked office block. It stands out as bold
and precise in dreary surroundings.

N of Bilborough, BROXTOWE is also an area of C20 housing
estates. BROXTOWE HALL was demolished in 1937 to make
way for one of them.*

Under the housing estates, the site of a mid-C1 ROMAN FORT.
Two or three phases of occupation seem to be represented here
in the period A.D. 50–75.

## CLIFTON

1 A delightful riverside village with the grassy terraces of the Hall
ending at quite some height above the river and the celebrated
Clifton Grove following the river down towards Wilford for a
mile. The village is still separate from the vast housing estates
to the N, S, and E. It has a spacious green with a brick DOVE-
COTE on it (the largest in Notts, with 2,300 nesting places, 38
by 18 ft, probably early C18) and, facing it, the GEORGE
WELLS ALMSHOUSES (founded 1709, with a wide central
gable and two odd two-storeyed little gazebos or plaisaunces
isolated on the r. and l. of the large forecourt-garden. At the
further corners, smaller necessary houses. Adjacent two smaller
windowless gazebos, now derelict). Next to it an early C19
house, the OLD RECTORY. From here, VILLAGE ROAD
passes some thatched, timber-framed cottages, refaced in brick.

---

* It was mid-C17 with a richly decorated, still Jacobean-style gateway and
an entrance porch crowned by an achievement. Its newer gables replaced an
original upper storey. It was the home of Thomas Helwys, leader of the early
Baptists, whose father is buried in Bilborough church.

No. 56, refaced in 1707 by Thomas and John Lambert (see gable TIL 1707), has a C14 hall (with end frames of aisled construction incorporated in the end walls, and a base-cruck middle frame) and cross wing of *c*. 1600. The timber framing of Nos. 27 and 29 is C16, but with too-obvious modern infilling. Thus the Hall is reached, with the church close to it.

St Mary. A large, cruciform building with an impressively tall crossing tower (cf. Langar and also St Mary, Nottingham). The oldest part is the N arcade of three bays, Transitional, with the central capitals emphasized by waterleaf, and two still entirely Norman-looking corbel heads above. The arcade with one order of nailhead and a keeled roll-moulding between two hollows is worth remembering. The s arcade is later, with octagonal piers and large nobbly horizontal leaves covering the capitals. Late C14 clerestory. The chancel was enlarged when a chantry college was founded by Sir Robert Clifton in 1476. It has a good flat timber ROOF, with bosses, and plain SEDILIA. The s door of the chancel is dated 1632, yet still entirely Perp in character. – (SCREENS by *Hodgson Fowler* of Durham, who restored the church in 1873–4. JPB) – Previous restoration by *Cottingham*, 1846, a further restoration in 1884 by *Bodley*, and another in 1965–75 by *G. G. Pace*, continued in 1975–9 by *Ronald Sims*, in which the church was reordered with the sanctuary under the tower and the chancel arch glazed to form a separate chapel. – Over the E side of the chancel arch a very rare DEVICE, the coat of arms of Christ surmounted by a spitting Jew, carved in low relief and painted; mid C15. – *Marcussen* ORGAN, 1973, which benefits from the acoustics designed by *David Jones*. – STAINED GLASS with St Oswald and St Alban, 1898 by *Kempe*. – MONUMENTS. A proud display of an unbroken family tradition. – Incised foliated cross. – Alabaster Knight (Sir Gervase C.?), late C14. – Dame Alice Nevill, alabaster, on a tomb-chest, late C14, with hair net and expressionless features, angels holding her pillow, a lamb at her feet. – Sir Robert Clifton † 1478, Sir Gervase Clifton † 1491, both brasses, same workshop as Strelley. – Incised slab to Eleanor Milford, *c*. 1520. – George Clifton † 1587 and wife, brass. – Sir Gervase † 1587 and his two wives, three recumbent effigies on a tomb-chest, alabaster, stiff children against chest front, the features of all the figures also expressionless. By *Garrat Hollemans* of Burton on Trent. – A later Sir Gervase's first three wives (he had seven), 1631, no effigies, but at the foot a hideous glimpse into a charnel chamber with bones and skulls. Also angels with reversed torches and

hourglasses. L. and r. free-standing obelisks with coat of arms. –
Sir Gervase himself † 1666, bust in oval niche between columns,
same hand as at Teversal.

CLIFTON HALL (Department of Education, Trent Polytechnic). One of the largest Georgian mansions remaining in
Notts. Remodelled several times, its main façades are unusually self-effacing and utilitarian, not perhaps surprising,
since the house received its present form under *John Carr* of
York in 1778–97. It incorporates part of an earlier building,
probably part of that surveyed by John Thorpe or of its early
C17 successor. In Hollar's view the W side of this appears to
have had a N half with a straight parapet and tall tower
(reminiscent of Robert Smythson's designs; cf. Hardwick) and
a S half with five gables of the usual late C16 or early C17 type.
It is most of the S side that has been incorporated in subsequent remodellings and betrays its presence by its brickwork
in English bond, by a fragment of sill, probably of an attic
window, on the E façade, by quoins up to supposed gable level
at the NE angle, and by the hoodmould over the first-floor
windows on the W side. Yet it is impossible to relate Hollar's
drawing exactly to what remains. Carr gave at least the E front
a regular appearance (two wings five bays wide and projecting
by only one bay, and a recessed centre of five bays with a one-
storey colonnade of Tuscan columns linking the wings in front)
and added a full-height stone-faced bow to the S side. The
central section is only a screen wall with some false windows
masking the octagonal hall inserted between the wings about
1750:* see the relieving arch at first-floor level.

In the S wing, the rooms have C17, early C18, and Carr's
fittings and decoration. The interior of the N wing is mostly C19.
On the first floor, running from back to front of the cross wing
S of the octagonal hall, the C17 GREAT CHAMBER (now library)
with original decoration reordered to accommodate new windows etc.: panelling articulated by pilasters and a frieze of crisp
strapwork framing representations of the gentlemanly arts (the
martial arts, music, literature, etc.). The ceiling, though not perhaps the central portrait medallion of Gervase Clifton † 1666,
is C19.‡ The fireplace is a magnificent two-storey job of black

---

* According to Mr Colvin.

‡ Possibly lowered. There is a significantly large gap between the ceiling
and the original plaster floor of the room above, which is of the same dimensions but lower, and no doubt cut down in the C18. The C18 spiral staircase
in the angle of the octagon is possibly C17 in origin.

and white marble, attributed by Dr Girouard to *John Smythson*, who did drawings, dated 1632, for a banqueting house and stables here (*Archit. His.* III 1–3), part of building activities connected with the visit of Charles I in 1632 or 1633. Adjoining, in the NE angle of the S wing, the exquisite little PAGES' ROOM with a set of lively paintings after engravings of 1608 by Jacob van Gheyn, illustrating the handling of the pike, musket, etc., set into the panelling. This is painted to simulate white marble, picked out in black with pilasters identical to those in the Great Chamber. The floor is black and white marble. The plaster frieze with the Seven Deadly Sins has fleshy strapwork of a slightly later type than that in the other room. To the r. of the fireplace a doorcase with half-columns embossed with vine trails and with painted heraldry on the lintel. The black and white scheme is typical of its date (cf. the Marble Closet at Bolsover), but the present arrangement of panelling and doorcase (probably C16) cannot be original because both have been cut to fit this room. They seem to have been moved from elsewhere. Several rooms have cornices, doorcases, and fireplaces of the early C18, when the gables were probably built up to form a third storey. In the room at the SE angle of the S wing a good plaster ceiling of *c.* 1675, inappropriately painted, and a bolection-moulded fireplace.* In a sitting room (now dean's study) on the W front, an overmantel with Rococo plasterwork surrounding a portrait attributed to *Romney*. On the ground floor below the Great Chamber, the MORNING ROOM (now Board Room) has a Rococo marble chimneypiece crowned by a portrait medallion supported by cherubs, and in the NW room are imposing doorcases and an overmantel with broken pediments. The most splendid room is the OCTAGONAL HALL, which goes through the height of the building and effectively divides it in half. Restricted light comes in through Diocletian windows below the dome (not expressed outside), and between them are emblems of the martial arts in delicate plasterwork garlands by *Dugdale*, 1779. The plasterwork lower down looks earlier, more robust, with vases of naturalistic flowers in high relief. Between the doors and a fireplace on four of the walls, statues in niches. The hall leads to the very modest staircase behind it, with an early C19 wrought-iron balustrade. The most elaborate of the rooms refurbished by Carr is the BOW ROOM on the ground floor. Here

---

* The accounts show minor payments in 1672, 1674, and 1688, according to Mr H. J. Louw, but there is no mention of this plasterwork.

the decoration is in a very thin Adam style, the embossed ornament on the doors and chimneypiece in applied pewter (indistinguishable from plaster or wood) by the *Westwoods* of Birmingham, 1779. In the next room unfinished and very naïve overdoor paintings of hunting scenes.

The GARDEN has as its most remarkable feature (at the time of writing in great disrepair) a double-curved stairway of C18 origin with stone balustrade, vases and statuary. The classical summer house has gone,* and so has the C19 hothouse attached to the house.

E of the green, a vast amount of C20 housing, and ST FRANCIS, 1952 by *Vernon Royle*.

CLIFTON BRIDGE. One long, elegant, cantilevered span. 1958 by *R. M. Finch* (City Engineer) in association with *R. Travers Morgan & Partners*.

In 1938–41 a fine series of Bronze Age metal implements was recovered from the river during construction. Three dug-out canoes (Castle Museum), and traces of a pile revetment for the river bank suggested a settlement nearby.

## WILFORD

Wilford must have once been as pretty a riverside village as Clifton. Until 1988 the Nottingham Power Station across the river crushed the church, and though the church, the RECTORY (of *c.* 1700, double-pile brick), its outbuildings, and the whitewashed FERRY INN (possibly C17) make a pleasing group, modern housing interferes everywhere. The MAIN ROAD has far more recent houses than old cottages (No. 36, dated 1828, Tudor style, probably built as a school, No. 136, C18 with simple doorhood, No. 138 with a good shell doorhood). At the S end a cottage dated 1724, and round the corner WILFORD HALL, 1781, a red brick box with some modest Adamish trim on the entrance, designed by *William Henderson* of Loughborough and built by *Samuel Stretton*. Nice stables with arcaded ground floor, central archway, and pediment.

ST WILFRID. Dark grey stone, with a NW tower, very much

---

* It was demolished in 1969. According to the *Travel Journal of Philip Yorke*, he saw the 'Summer House designed by Lord Burlington' in 1744. Sir Robert Clifton was a guest at Londesborough in 1735. From what remains in the house it does not seem likely that Burlington had anything to do with the early C18 remodelling.

restored. C14 nave with arcade on octagonal piers. Clerestory and chancel followed in the C15, battlemented outside without a break. The chancel of excellent proportions. (The aisles were rebuilt in 1890–1 by *Naylor & Sale* of Derby. JPB) – PISCINA in the S aisle with two fragments of a little Norman arch used as its pointed head. – STAINED GLASS. The Kirke White memorial window by *O'Connor* in glaring colours (Three Magi). – In the churchyard a magnificent slate HEADSTONE by *F. Radcliffe*, a Nottingham woodcarver.

ST PATRICK'S R.C. PRIMARY SCHOOL, Coronation Avenue. 1968–9 by *Bartlett & Gray*. An interesting organic grouping of octagonal classrooms and assembly areas.

WILFORD BRIDGE. A toll bridge by *E. W. Hughes* with ironwork cast by *Andrew Handyside* of Derby, 1870.


## WOLLATON

ST LEONARD. The steeple of the familiar type of this neighbourhood, that is with battlements and a much slimmer spire without broaches. The special feature at Wollaton is that on the ground floor there are open arches (now alas glazed) to the N and S, presumably for processional reasons, or because the village street was so narrow. The tracery of the bell-openings dates the steeple as late C14. Of the same date the body of the church, although the masonry of the chancel must be much older, as there is a S doorway of *c.* 1200. SEDILIA again C14. The N aisle was renewed *c.* 1500 (see the arcade with the very curious profiles of the piers – the capitals do not seem to belong – and the N windows). The S chapel (to accommodate the Willoughby monuments) and S aisle 1885–7 by *James Fowler* of Louth, who restored the church. – REREDOS. Very rare in the county and 73 beyond the county: a classical composition with fluted Corinthian columns dividing the side parts from the centre and a broken segmental pediment emphasizing the centre, but all three parts filled by large cartouches still entirely of strapwork – *c.* 1660, one is inclined to say. With that date the ALTAR RAILS in the S aisle would also go.* – MONUMENTS. An exceptional number in a county not rich in monuments. Richard Willoughby † 1471 and wife, two brasses of good

* The WOLLATON ANTIPHONAL, first half of the C15, written for a member of the Chaworth family of Wiverton, but in the possession of the rector of Wollaton as early as 1460, has been deposited in Nottingham University Department of Manuscripts.

quality, probably by the same workshop as those of Sir Robert Strelley at Strelley, and Sir Robert and Sir Gervase Clifton at Clifton. The brasses are on a raised stone slab beneath which lies a cadaver (cf. Holme). The lavish canopy also like Strelley, but in this case the tomb of John Strelley † 1501, that is, over the horizontal top of the recess three demi-figures of angels, then an elaborate cresting, and above that a panelled canopy with three niches for statuettes. – Henry Willoughby † 1528 and his wives, between chancel and s chancel chapel and visible from both sides. The tomb-chest has openwork arches between which statuettes of mourners of unusually fine quality and behind which a cadaver. On the chest the effigy of Henry Willoughby, and to his l. and r. his four wives, portrayed half his size to fit them in neatly. The canopy surprisingly simple. All faces unfortunately severely damaged. – Robert Smythson † 1614, 'architector and surveyor' of Wollaton Hall, as he calls himself, a strictly architectural framework of a square inscription tablet. – Henry Lord Middleton † 1800, by *John Bacon*, an urn on a large pedestal and two vases l. and r. with pretty flower garlands, all in relief; no figures. – Henry, sixth Baron Middleton, † 1835, by *Sir R. Westmacott*, with two genii bending towards each other with a fine romantic sentiment. – In the churchyard a good slate HEADSTONE to Richard Attenborough (Attonbrow) † 1728.

(ST MARY, Wollaton Park.* Quite a substantial church of 1937–9 by *Cecil Howitt*. – All STAINED GLASS by the London firm of *A. J. Dix*, 1937. – FONT. Elaborate, with low-relief carving, modelled on the form of Lenton Abbey font. RH)

COTTAGE (No. 737 Wollaton Road), opposite the church. Stone patched with brick. Part medieval, with one original door and window; possibly the C15 chantry house.

Round the attractive village square C18 brick cottages, with a pump of the same date in the middle. SCHOOL by *James Fowler* of Louth, 1866.

DOVECOTE, Dovecote Drive. 1585. Large, rectangular, of brick, built by Sir Francis Willoughby (date and initials FW in dark headers on the s wall under the ivy) and connected with the Old Hall. This, first mentioned in 1283, occupied an area N and SE of the church. The Old Rectory, the Admiral Rodney, and the cottages in Rectory Lane cover parts of the site. Repaired and altered by Sir Francis between 1550 and 1585,

---

* Wollaton Park is an area of suburban housing on land purchased from Lord Middleton in 1924 by the corporation.

it was used as guest accommodation after the new Hall was finished in 1588 (cf. Hardwick Old Hall, Derbyshire).

WOLLATON HALL is the most important Elizabethan house in 63 Notts and one of the most important in England. It was built between 1580 and 1588 by *Robert Smythson* for Sir Francis Willoughby, a great coal magnate, who paid for the building (over £8,000) out of the profits from coal extraction on his own vast estates. Although an industrialist, Sir Francis was by no means *nouveau riche*, for his aristocratic connections included the Dudleys, the Seymours, and Lady Jane Grey, his first cousin. A wish to stress this impressive lineage may have inspired some of the medievalizing aspects of his house. It is extremely showy, erected of expensive Ancaster stone in a prominent position, far above the old hall of the Willoughbys down by the church. There seems to be a strange kinship between Wollaton Hall and some of the imitation-Tudor *châteaux* built by prosperous Victorians. Wollaton of course was one of their favourite models. Robert Smythson, a mason of high standing, was the designer of that other most spectacular Midlands house, Hardwick Hall. He first appears at Longleat in 1568, then at Wardour, where he did minor work for Sir Francis's cousin and brother-in-law, Sir Matthew Arundell, about 1576. He moved from there to the Midlands, where his name is connected with a number of stylistically related houses, e.g. Worksop Manor, Barlborough Hall, Hardwick Hall, etc., and settled at Wollaton.* His memorial in the church reads 'Architector and surveyor unto yee most worthy house of Wollaton with divers others of great account'. That he was Sir Francis's master mason is confirmed in the building accounts (1582–8), but at his death three decades later he was honoured with the title 'architector', an early indication of the rise of the mason's status under the influence of Renaissance ideas.

Wollaton is distinguished from earlier Elizabethan houses by its spectacular all-round symmetry and raised central hall with turreted prospect room above. The ground plan, basically a rectangle with four almost free-standing towers attached at each corner, does not seem to have been Smythson's own idea, but to have been adapted from two plans in du Cerceau's *Premier Livre* of 1559, one of the most popular source books of the period and known to have been in Willoughby's library. A close variant of these combined plans, in an unknown hand on paper dated

* Worksop Manor, not Wollaton, may have been *Smythson*'s first house; see p. 390.

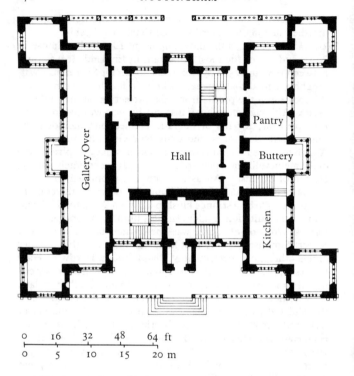

Gallery Over

Pantry

Buttery

Hall

Kitchen

| 0 | 16 | 32 | 48 | 64 ft |
| 0 | 5 | 10 | 15 | 20 m |

*c.* 1577–94, has been found.* On the reverse is a pedigree of the Northamptonshire Willoughbys in Sir Francis's own hand. Smythson adopted this plan (*Archit. His.* 1/25(1)),‡ using the service basement and central hall. He compromised between a

* By Mr David Durant (*Trans. Thor. Soc.*, 76, 1972, p. 13). He proposes that the very French plan may be by the Longleat mason, *Allen Maynard*, but there is no firm reason to suppose that it was made by a professional architect-mason. Dr Girouard thinks that the form of central clerestory-lit hall and corner towers was originally suggested by Mount Edgcumbe, Cornwall, begun in 1546 by a distant relative of Sir Matthew Arundell.

‡ The plan varies only slightly from what was built. The major difference is the lack of the courtyards intended to surround the house. The entrance staircase was built as a straight instead of a three-sided flight, and of the three main staircases round open wells one survives. The others were not built or were rebuilt as dog-leg flights (see Thorpe's survey. The arrangement he shows was altered in the C17 and C19). See ground-floor plan above.

central position for the hall and the medieval position with the entrance at one end. The hall is still parallel to the front but set back with an L-shaped passage connecting the central porch to the screens passage at one end. At Hardwick he took this desire for symmetry a stage further, with the hall placed both centrally and axially and entered on the short side, with the screen forming a lobby inside the door. Usually in Elizabethan houses (unlike in medieval ones) the entrance was central, opening into the screens passage at one end of the hall, which extended asymmetrically parallel to the main frontage. The change from this arrangement was determined partly by the desire for symmetry in the plan, and partly because of a social change which meant that the hall declined in importance as the main room in the house until it became in the later C17 only the prelude to the reception rooms. The central position of the hall is not its only unusual feature. It is three storeys tall, so tall in fact that it projects above the roof of the centre block and gets all its light via clerestory windows. Above the hall rises a huge 'prospect room', used it seems solely for the view it afforded, since it is reached only by one narrow newel staircase and has no decoration or fireplace. Like the rooftop banqueting houses at Longleat or the upper stages of the towers at Hardwick, it tells of the C16 love of panoramic views (*vide* the paintings of Coninxloo).

*Smythson* transformed the revolutionary but anonymously devised elevations of Longleat into a very individual statement probably more expressive of Sir Francis's character and aspirations than his own (cf. Hardwick where, although the symmetrical plan and towered silhouette are characteristically 'Smythson', the appearance of the building is as hard and uncompromising as its builder, Bess of Hardwick). Wollaton's outward-looking façades, storeys of almost equal height articulated by pilasters of the correct classical orders (here divided by niches), large square mullioned-and-transomed windows (larger to the main rooms on the first floor), and straight parapet are derived from Longleat. But Longleat's smooth classicism has been replaced by a more dramatic, more medieval, towered silhouette. The excrescences on the tops of the towers add to the complication of the silhouette: curved gables and groups 64 of chimneys brought together in a form reminiscent of medieval market crosses or conduit heads. The tracery windows of hall and prospect room, the form of the latter recalling the C15 Prior Overton's tower at Repton or the tower at Mackworth, both nearby in Derbyshire, the silhouette and chimneys are (like the Keep at Bolsover) clear evidence of a conscious medieval revival: a revival paralleled in court ceremonial and literature. As at Bolsover, where Robert Smythson's son John adapted the medieval-type fireplaces from illustrations by Serlio, the tracery windows here are derived from a contemporary pattern-book: Vredeman de Vries's *Variae Architecturae Formae*. The classical column chimneys and busts of Plato, Aristotle, Diana, Virgil, Hercules and many others come from Longleat, but the rest of the ornament is gaudy and Netherlandish, with any amount of strapwork in the Dutch gables, angular bands round the pilasters (cf. Wardour), cartouches, etc., all ultimately though not exactly taken from de Vries. On the central bays of the E and W fronts, extraordinary parapets which almost raise these entrance bays to the status of frontispieces. They are topped with an odd mixture of classical forms: little pedimented tabernacles supporting classical vases and statues and, in the centre, the Willoughby arms. The exterior details were being carved in 1582–3 by *Christopher Lovell* and *John* and *Christopher Rodes* (a father and son, who had been at Longleat, the son going later to Hardwick). *Thomas Accres*, who did so much decorative sculpture at Hardwick, worked as a mason at Wollaton in 1584–5. In 1588 *William Styles*, who first appeared in 1584 and 1585, took over as master mason, and Robert Smythson's son *John*, paid as a labourer in 1585, was mentioned as a mason. The terrace on the W front was created by *Wyatville* in 1823 by building an extension to the service basement. He may have refaced some of this front at the same time, but fortunately he did not carry out Lord Middleton's plan to create a new entrance façade in line with the corner towers.

The INTERIOR, now used as the City of Nottingham Natural History Museum, is disappointing, except for the HALL with its odd, somewhat uncomfortable proportions, 60 by 30 by 50 ft high. At one end the stone SCREEN, classical, with metopes and strapwork panels from de Vries.\* The design, with figures in the spandrels, like that, for example, in Middle Temple Hall, comes originally from French choir screens. The roof is a fake hammerbeam one like that at Longleat, made after Serlio's method of mortising together short lengths of timber. It was carved by *Lewis*, possibly the son of John Lewis, head

---

\* In the RIBA drawings by *Robert Smythson* include a design for the hall screen (1/25(7)) and details from de Vries for the hall screen (1/25 (2 or 4)) and tower cartouches (1/25(2)).

carpenter at Longleat.* It was certainly open originally, and was altered to an unknown extent by *Wyatville*, who added the shields and tracery panels in 1832. He also gave the screen its balustrade and renewed the panelling. Serlio's Book III provided the pattern for the Doric fireplace which, with the screen and roof, is the only original fitting in the whole house. The interior was refurbished after a fire in 1642 and again by *Wyatville* between 1801–4 and 1807. He opened up the central way through the hall, basing the design of his doors on that of the prospect room windows, and made the EN-TRANCE HALL in the centre of the front. There are Elizabethan details in the plaster and woodwork here, but the staircase has a Regency-style wrought-iron balustrade. Ceiling with a 'Toilet of Venus' by *Thornhill*. Above the GRAND STAIRCASE, a ceiling of *c.* 1699 by *Laguerre*, originally showing an 'Assembly of the Gods' but altered by *Thornhill* to include 'Prometheus stealing the Fire'. Walls painted by Thornhill with other Prometheus scenes and restored by *Rigaud*.

Smythson's arrangement of formal courtyards was apparently never carried out, and the surroundings are now landscaped. STABLES and OFFICES were built away from the house in 1794. Plain red brick block with stone s front. This has arched openings on the ground floor with an engaged Ionic portico above, crowned by a pediment with a richly carved tympanum. Since 1969–70 they have housed an INDUSTRIAL MUSEUM. Note the BEAM ENGINE HOUSE by *Terry Bestwick*, 1972–6. Just a glass showcase for a piece of machinery (from Haydn Road Pumping Station, Basford), decorative in itself, attached to the AGRICULTURAL MUSEUM, by the same architect. Beneath the terrace to the E of the house, the large CAMELLIA HOUSE, an early example of iron and glass construction. It is an irregular octagon with longer walls front and back. Only the back wall, built into rising ground, of brick: the rest of ironwork with faintly Elizabethan details.‡ Rows of iron columns with foliage capitals divide the interior into a passage round the periphery and two cross-passages, barrel-vaulted with iron plates. Over the resulting four flowerbed sections, shallow glazed pyramids. Heating (installed by *Harrison* of

---

* The head carpenter was *Crispin*, possibly *Richard Crispin*, who had been second carpenter at Longleat with Smythson. The roof now hangs from iron tie-rods, spanning the prospect room at waist level.

‡ The design may be by *Wyatville*, although his other conservatories, e.g. at Belton, Lincs, had structural members of brick.

Derby, possibly also the ironfounder) came through decorative bronze floor grilles. An avenue with four rows of limes connects the house with the main GATES (by *William Stretton*, 1790). WYATVILLE'S LODGE of 1823–5 is in Elizabethan turreted form reminiscent of the prospect room. By him also the BEESTON LODGE on Derby Road, one of a pair of tower-like lodges.

5040

# NUTHALL

The reason why visitors used to visit Nuthall was to see NUTHALL TEMPLE, one of the four or five English descendants of Palladio's Villa Rotonda: or, in this case, a descendant of a descendant of the villa, Scamozzi's Rocca Pisana. It was built for Sir Charles Sedley in 1754–7 by *Thomas Wright*, astronomer, architect, and landscape gardener, whose grottoes, Gothick arbours, and mock castles embellished the parks of several aristocratic patrons, and was demolished in 1929: a disgrace. Its site is now covered by the northbound carriageway of the M1. The glorious stuccowork inside (by *Thomas Roberts* of Oxford, who worked in many Oxford colleges and houses in that area) and the garden front with projecting bow and rusticated window surrounds reflected the Rococo style that Wright, although basically a Palladian, favoured. The dining room was redecorated and the garden front altered *c.* 1780. What survives of Wright's garden design is only a battlemented Gothic SUMMER HOUSE, 1759, in the grounds of The Yews, a GATEPIER, E of the Three Ponds public house, and the LAKE in the park.

ST PATRICK. Low, squat C13 tower, the upper part rebuilt in the C18. The chancel N arcade, s windows, and s doorway all point to *c.* 1400. The s door, similar to that in the N chancel aisle at Southwell, has two crowned heads as label stops and little square fleurons on the inner chamfer of the arch. Restored in 1884 by *James Fowler* of Louth. – SCREEN. C15, probably early. – STAINED GLASS. Late C15. Crucifixion in the E window. Some heraldic glass in a s window. – MONUMENTS. Unusual large C13 slab with an ornamented rectangle instead of a cross and some arcading each side of the shaft. To a priest? – Sir Robert Cokefield † after 1392, alabaster, by the same hand as the Samson de Strelley at Strelley. – Incised slab to Edward Boun † 1558 and wife.

Next to the church, the fine stone OLD RECTORY of 1761 with

an open pediment containing a round-headed window over the centre of the three-bay front and Venetian windows flanking the door. Stone façade, all the window jambs plain and unmoulded in the North Derbyshire–Yorkshire tradition, the rest brick.

(HEMPSHILL HALL, Nottingham Road, E of the M1. Roughcast façade to a much altered and extended double-pile house, with other walls of brick and stone. A C17 timber frame exists throughout, possibly adapted from an earlier building on the site to judge from the structure. The only old features visible externally are two large stone buttresses against the s wall. Only a garden left of a once considerable park. No. 129 Nottingham Road is the former lodge. NS)

## OLDCOTES                                              5080

The parish is Styrrup-with-Oldcotes.

ST HELEN (R.C.), Main Street. By *S. J. Nicholl*, 1869–71.* An inadequately explored and thus imperfectly known ROMAN VILLA to the w. Two more mosaics existed.

WATER MILL. Stone, now a house, with one of its two wheels still *in situ*, with all its machinery driving three pairs of stones. Probably late C19, an enclosed low-breast iron wheel by John Thornton of Worksop.

## OLLERTON                                              6060

ST GILES. Built soon after 1780.‡ A plain preaching-house, without any internal subdivisions, low and wide, with a narrower and lower chancel, and a w tower. Chancel arch and tower arch are round-headed, but light comes in through groups of entirely unmoulded pointed windows, and the w tower is modelled on the C13 Notts type, unbuttressed, with battlements and a kind of minimum pinnacles. – STAINED GLASS. E window painted in 1873 by *C. G. S. Foljambe* in memory of his first wife † 1871.§ – SE nave window by *Heaton, Butler & Bayne* given by G. S. Foljambe in 1875.

* According to Mr R. O'Donnell.
† According to Mr H. M. Colvin and Mr R. M. Robbins.
§ All these memorial windows were thought to have been painted by Foljambe himself in several different styles. In fact he commissioned most of them from various firms, e.g. Kempe (Wellow) and Heaton, Butler & Bayne (Edwinstowe; Tideswell, Derbyshire) (RH).

OLLERTON HALL, to the SE, on the A616. A fine house of late
C17 character, nine bays wide with outer bays projecting,
hipped roof, modillion frieze, the three central bays emphasized
by giant pilasters and the door by a heavy segmental pediment.
In poor condition.

In the old village centre, the HOP POLE HOTEL, a large, handsome, three-storey C18 house with a pediment, lower wings,
and attached stable block. Opposite, FOREST HOUSE, a
smaller late C17 farmhouse with hipped roof and quoins, and a
WATER MILL in complete working order with an iron breast
wheel.

NEW OLLERTON COMPREHENSIVE SCHOOL, New Ollerton.
To cater to a village much expanded by the mining community.
1969-70 by *H. T. Swain* (County Architect). CLASP, neat and
formal, but without appeal to children's taste.

<sub>6060</sub>

## OMPTON

A small hamlet with a red-brick CHAPEL of 1860 and, ½ m. W,
a WATER PUMPING STATION by *David Jenkin*, Nottingham
City Architect, 1965-8. As self-conscious in design as its
Victorian predecessors at Bestwood and Papplewick, but a
landscape feature rather than a monumental pile. Tiled pyramid
on a low glazed plinth raised on grass banking.

<sub>7070</sub>

## ORDSALL

ALL SAINTS. The usual W tower of the neighbourhood (ashlared, diagonal buttresses, battlements, eight pinnacles). The
rest very new-looking (the result of two restorations), but the
interior reveals C13 work: N arcade and a little later S arcade,
both with octagonal piers and (differently) moulded arches. In
1876 *T. C. Hine & Son* widened the S aisle, partially rebuilt
the tower, and replaced the E window. Further restoration by
*Hodgson Fowler* in 1880 (JPB). – SCREEN. With a little more
fun in the design of the tracery (trefoils, daggers) than just the
panel pattern usual in the Newark School (cf. East Drayton
nearby). – STAINED GLASS. E window 1905 and N chancel 1906
by *Kempe*. – MONUMENT. Kneeling gentleman between unfluted columns; top achievement between obelisks; supposed
to be Samuel Bevercotes † 1603.

ST ALBAN, London Road. 1901-3 by *Hodgson Fowler*. Ashlar,

Perp, with a large w window. Nave and aisles, but instead of a tower a little spire on the tall n transept.

(ORDSALL HOUSE (old rectory). Two-storey stucco house of excellent proportions, built *c.* 1815.)


## ORSTON

ST MARY. Stone tower of 1766 with quoins and round-headed windows and a roomy nave with aisles and clerestory. The N aisle has its arcade on circular piers with plainly moulded capitals and arches of a more complex C13 profile. The S arcade with one circular and one octagonal pier and capitals similar to those on the N. The chancel is E.E. too, with lancet windows throughout. The tracery of the aisle windows is of very odd Dec varieties (perhaps the fancy of the restorer in 1889–90?) and Perp at the E and W ends. In the S aisle a PISCINA with a cinquefoil head. Nave and N aisle with old roofs. – FONT 'given by Mrs Constantia Kerchevall 1662', octagonal, with angels' heads and flowers in round-headed panels (cf. Southwell). – Late C18 COMMANDMENTS BOARD and ROYAL ARMS of George III, 1786. – MONUMENTS. One to a priest; under a nodding ogee arch with two little angels, badly preserved. – Broken effigy of a lady, C14. – A DRUM from the battle of Waterloo is kept in the church. – In the churchyard, slate HEADSTONES by *Francis & George Lamb* of Bottesford (MWB).

(Good stone, gabled VICARAGE by *Charles Bailey* of Newark. JPB)

STATION, S of the village. By *T. C. Hine* for the GNR, *c.* 1855.

THE GABLES. Brick, mostly modern but with one late C17 shaped gable at the rear which has a simple curved profile rather than the more usual stepped and curved type.


## OSBERTON HALL*

No visible signs of the C18 house, although parts of it were to have been retained in an unexecuted scheme by *William Porden* in 1792. In 1806 *William Wilkins Jun.* carried out a similar plan: main block of seven bays, the central three with a Greek Doric portico, and an extension wing on the S side. It proved too

---

* Mr H. A. Johnson kindly provided this new description.

small when completed, even with another storey added to the s wing by *Ambrose Poynter*, and was virtually rebuilt in 1877 by *MacVicar Anderson*, who gave it a big *porte-cochère*, large canted bay-windows, a new roof, etc. Wilkins's work is still visible in the main block. Brick with stone quoins, the central three bays pedimented and a Diocletian window in the pediment above a Venetian one. To the E, stone stables round a courtyard by *William Lindley* of Doncaster.

The CHURCH in the grounds was built in 1833 for George Savile Foljambe, whose son gave many memorial windows to his wife (*see* Wellow, Edwinstowe, etc.). It is a remarkable building in that it shows a very early appreciation of the Norman style, treated not fancifully or romantically, but rather drily: w tower (with pinnacles!), nave and aisles with circular piers. The architect was *Ambrose Poynter*.

The parish is Scofton-with-Osberton.

7060

## OSSINGTON

The church stands away from the village but was close to the HALL, which was demolished in 1963.*

93 HOLY ROOD. 1782–3 by *Carr* of York, purely classical, buff stone. w tower with a top stage. This consists of a circular lantern crowned by a little dome. The lower part has a rectangular screen of coupled Tuscan columns. The body of the church is a rectangle with round-headed windows recessed in arches and a pedimented Tuscan columned porch. Chancel divided by three simple arches on Tuscan columns.‡ – ALTAR PAINTING by a Tuscan late Mannerist. – MONUMENTS. Tomb-chest with tracery and shields and on it brasses to R. Peckham † 1551 and

---

* It was a large plain brick house of 1729, altered by *Lindley* of Doncaster *c.* 1790. Garden front of nine bays, two storeys with pedimented dormers in the hipped roof. One-storey late Georgian wings at both ends. On the much remodelled entrance side (N), the forecourt was enclosed by a w wing of *c.* 1700, joined to the house by a blind-arcaded link, and by a later blind-arcaded block replacing the matching wing. Inside, a fine staircase with two turned and one open spiral baluster to each tread, some c18 fireplaces, and mostly c19 plasterwork. The dining room in one wing was the finest room: octagonal ends, a fine chimneypiece and doors. Three urns from the garden were removed to Flintham Hall. Mr H. Johnson has found drawings at Nottingham University for a garden temple by *Carr*, dated 1782 and 1786. Lindley was Carr's assistant from *c.* 1754 to 1774.

‡ According to Dr Wragg a domed octagonal mausoleum attached to the E end was demolished in 1838. By *Carr* but slightly later.

wife. – William Cartwright † 1602 and wife, an ambitious standing wall-tomb in three stages. In the 'predella' the twelve children kneel frontally; above, the two main figures kneel, facing
each other; above them inscriptions and pediment. The three
columns flanking the figures and between them have boldly projecting bits of entablature. – George Cartwright † 1743, an unusual composition with two very thin, tall obelisks. The Cart-
wrights are the family of Edmund, the inventor of the power
loom. The estate then went in 1768 to William Denison, a wool
merchant from Leeds. Against the w wall two accomplished
statues by *Nollekens*, William Denison † 1782 and Robert Deni- 94
son † 1785. Both are wholly worldly, with no religious connota-
tions whatever in their attitudes, features, or any paraphernalia.
William holds a sheet with six verses of Pope's *Universal Prayer*,
and on the base of the statue is a relief with a ship, wool-bales,
and sheep. – In the churchyard a baluster SUNDIAL, 1812 by
one *Arthur Buckle* (DOE).


OWTHORPE                                    6030

ST MARGARET. Isolated in a field behind a farm. Partly rebuilt
with a short w tower, probably *c.* 1630–50.* Hipped roof and
plain parapet, slightly curved (almost like a shaped gable) where
it goes up to meet the tower. Simple intersecting tracery in
pointed windows. The N wall looks old, see the C14 buttresses,
and of the old building some of the materials were used (cf.
the beautiful bracket above the w entrance with two angels
holding a shield). The old church was larger than the new (*see*
the notes *à propos* Upper Broughton, Wiverton, etc.). The new
one has no aisles and no separate chancel. – Jacobean PULPIT
in a composition with READER'S DESK below. – The severe,
arched timber SCREEN to mark the entrance to the chancel bay
goes well with a C17 date. So do the ALTAR RAILS. – FONT.
C15, octagonal, castellated, with tracery and a tree motif. – Two
Hutchinson MONUMENTS, one of them to the Colonel John
Hutchinson † 1664 of the 'Memoirs', who built a house here
*c.* 1650, and spent his retirement 'laying out gardens and planting avenues'.


* According to Mr Alvey, at the E end is a stone inscribed C1629W: RHIG.

# OXTON

ST PETER. Plain, low, unmoulded Norman chancel arch. In the chancel a blocked Norman doorway, window, and PILLAR PISCINA, a rare survival. One C13 window, the rest Dec. The N and S arcades C14, formerly four, now three and a half bays. The Perp W tower takes up the space of the half-bay. S aisle widened, probably, in the late C17 or early C18 (see the windows with segmental heads and plain mullions). – COMMUNION TABLE. C17. – BOX PEWS. Plain in the nave, rich but rustic in the chancel, those flanking the chancel arch with ugly terms and balusters. Matching PRIE-DIEU dated 1681.* – ROYAL ARMS of George II, altered to George III's, and Sherbrooke HATCHMENTS. – MONUMENT to a layman, said to be Robert de Nottingham, C14, unimportant (cf. Calverton and Mansfield). – In the churchyard a large slate HEADSTONE by *Stretton* of Nottingham.‡

(WESLEYAN CHAPEL. 1839. Brick, three bays with side gables. Porch of 1889. CS)

OXTON HALL, the seat of the Sherbrookes, was demolished in 1957.§ The stuccoed stables with a central lantern survive. (So does the tomb of Robert Sherbrooke † 1710, surrounded by cast-iron railings, close to the lane. It is a table tomb probably erected by a descendant to mark the grave, although there are no other signs of the Quaker burial ground that once existed in the woodyard. NS)

(MANOR HOUSE, SW of the church. Probably C18, with extensive outbuildings approached through an arched carriageway in the front range. Gothick glazing bars to the windows, repeated *ad nauseam* in the later additions. NS)

S of the churchyard, CHURCH FARM, a good example of late C17 or early C18 brickwork, gabled. Windows renewed in the C19 or C20.

OLDOX CAMP (i.e. Old Works), 1 m. N of the village. Sub-rectangular earthwork of about 3 acres extent surrounded by one rampart and ditch in its present state, but with a double rampart and ditch at the SE angle. The position is interesting, not adopt-

---

* Connected with William Savile † 1681, buried in the nave? (R. Alvey).
‡ According to Professor Barley.
§ It was late C18, seven bays, two and a half storeys. Centre three bays almost entirely glazed, divided by Doric half-columns on the ground floor, Ionic pilasters above, and with a Diocletian window on the top floor below the pediment. Altered on the other sides after 1847 with 'large, bold bay windows'.

ing one of the nearby crests, but nestling in a sheltered combe and thus overlooked from three sides. There has been no excavation here and no datable objects have yet been recorded. Like other similar earthworks in this part of the county, however, Oldox probably originated in the Iron Age, perhaps continuing into the Romano-British period.

Another earthwork earlier recorded at LONELY GRANGE, ½ m. w of Oldox, has now vanished without trace.

Also, 1 m. N was an Anglo-Saxon barrow containing shield, sword, gaming pieces, and knife. The site, the only certain Anglo-Saxon barrow in the county, is now lost.


## PAPPLEWICK

5050

PAPPLEWICK HALL. Probably begun in 1781 or 1782, under construction in 1784, and completed, according to Throsby, in 1787. The owner, the Hon. Frederick Montagu, was a friend of the poets Thomas Gray and William Mason. Mason was his mentor in matters of taste. Although Montagu may well have gone to a first-rate London man at his suggestion, a slight clumsiness in proportion and handling suggests that the architect was a provincial one.* The faults are negligible, for the building, though modest in size and restrained in decoration, in general is excellent. It is an almost square block. Garden façade (w) of five bays with a rusticated ground floor and giant Ionic pilasters above supporting a pediment. The entrance front has a different rhythm: three wide bays with a rusticated porch projecting in the centre and, above it, a pedimented window with a balustraded sill (quite an old-fashioned feature), flanked by coupled pilasters. Asymmetrical ENTRANCE HALL in the centre of the E front, one wall curved and carrying a cantilevered staircase with a light wrought-iron balustrade. It is in fitting both staircase and doors into the space that the architect shows some ineptness. The LIBRARY is a simplified version of Adam's at Harewood House, with recessed arched compartments for bookcases and a fireplace in an arched recess on the curved end wall. The decoration throughout is Adamish, with some fine doorcases in the principal rooms, those to the staircase hall curved. In the MORNING ROOM, an early *Flaxman* relief (1780)

---

* *Carr* of York designed Mason's rectory at Aston, Yorks, *c.* 1770, but the house is definitely not in his style. The Adam-influenced design and finely detailed interiors are more characteristic of Carr's one-time assistant *Lindley* of Doncaster (cf. Serlby Hall, especially its curved staircase hall).

commissioned by Montagu. In the grounds an URN to the memory of Mason (the one to Gray is now at Eton College) and a diminutive GARDENER'S COTTAGE. Pieces of a little Tuscan temple, built before 1756, in the stable yard. At the Hall gates, TOP FARM HOUSE (the Home Farm?). Stucco, with a Diocletian window in the wide gable. Later glazing and bargeboards.

ST JAMES. Built by the same Frederick Montagu in 1795, also in the grounds of the Hall, away from the village: the model of a modest proprietary chapel. At first the exterior looks the usual Notts village church: W tower with two-light Dec bell-stage openings, battlements, S porch. But the battlements of the nave curve up towards the corners, a thing unheard of in the Middle Ages, and on the S porch they form a kind of central pediment. The entrance to the porch has a crocketed ogee arch, very Gothick. The windows are of two pointed lights under one pointed arch, with the spandrel simply left open, the most elementary form of tracery, as typical of 1290 as it is of 1790. Inside, a gallery runs all along the N wall and then turns to the W. The SQUIRE'S PEW at the E end of the gallery has a fireplace. The nave has been repewed. – PULPIT. Oak, with ogee panels. – FONTS. Small bowl on wooden column. – The medieval font has been preserved too, ten times the size of the other, of tub-shape with very elementary incised decoration. – STAINED GLASS. Four C15 panels, a kneeling knight, a kneeling family, St Peter, St Stephen. – Hope and Faith in the E window by *F. Eginton*, after Reynolds's window at New College Chapel, Oxford; purely pictorial and lush in the colours, without any regard for the demands of glass painting. – SCULPTURE. Two small Norman figures over the S door. – MONUMENTS. Four incised slabs, two to Sherwood Forest officials, one with sling, bow, and arrow, the other with a knife, and two in the porch with bellows.

Papplewick is an attractive stone-built village with one or two rows of C18 cottages and one pretty house, THE LODGE, with full-height square bays and some Gothick glazing.

PAPPLEWICK PUMPING STATION, 1¼ m. E, in Longdale Lane, Ravenshead. One of three pumping stations built to serve C19 Nottingham.* One other survives at Bestwood. This one, built by *Ogle Tarbotton* (corporation engineer) in 1881–5, still has its

---

* The earliest, in Hadyn Road, Basford, Nottingham, was demolished *c.* 1970; one of its beam-engines is in the Industrial Museum in Wollaton Park (MWB).

twin beam-engines of 1884, probably the last built by *James Watt & Co.*, and gear incorporated in the roof beams for handling the machinery.* But the decoration is more breathtaking than the engines, with an amazing luxuriance of naturalistic detail in the cast-iron galleries and fittings: water plants and water birds‡ on the capitals of the columns, the same flora and fauna entwined with classical motifs on the lacquered cast-brass infill to the column sides, all in watery greens and cream. All the fittings and the pine furniture were specially made and this temple of hygiene even boasts stained glass and, like Bestwood, is set in a garden by an ornamental cooling pond with its own workshop, smithy, and workers' houses.

(GRANGE FARM, s of the village. The outbuildings here seem to have been the offices and warehouses of Grange Mill, where the first Boulton & Watt rotative steam engine to provide power for the cotton industry was installed in 1786. Brick with stone dressings and the same lancet and quatrefoil windows (all blocked) as Castle Mill to the N. NMR)

GRANGE COTTAGES. Two rows of late C18 millworkers' cottages at r. angles to each other. Fairly well preserved.

CASTLE MILLS. *See* Linby.

DOVECOTE, at Forest Farm, 1½ m. s. C19, probably one of the last great dovecotes to be built.

## PERLETHORPE 6070

ST JOHN. 1876 by *Salvin*. Not so close to Thoresby as Clumber church was to Clumber House, but the same story of the great Victorian nobleman who feels it his duty to build a goodly church for his tenants after having built a magnificent mansion for himself. Perlethorpe is more realistic than Clumber, large, but on a manageable scale, in a reasonable position, and of a reasonable parish church plan. W spire, nave with aisles, lower chancel. A conventional Dec of Notts idiom, well provided inside with carved capitals, carved head label stops, and so on.

ESTATE HOUSING of *c.* 1890 by *W. O. Hickson* of Nottingham, e.g. the rich half-timbered almshouses near the church.§ In the

* The Pumping Station, cared for by a charitable trust, is open and the engines in steam at certain times of the year.
‡ Cranes: Mr Crane was chairman of the committee.
§ According to J. P. Bartlam.

Gothick style of the early C19 estate houses at Budby, THORESBY HOME FARM.

## PLEASLEY

*4060*

Dominating the valley 1¼ m. NE of the village are stone-built TEX-TILE MILLS, mid-C19 successors to those founded *c.* 1780 by William Hollins of Viyella fame. Also mid-C19 company housing and amenities.

## PLUMTREE

*6030*

ST MARY. The tower is remarkable for its large-scale Norman blank arcading on the whole height of the ground floor. The masonry looks typically Norman too, though it was rebuilt in 1906,* fortunately by a sensitive architect, *P. H. Currey* of Derby. On the W side is a doorway which originally had one order of colonnettes with scalloped capitals. The arch between tower and nave is of slightly horseshoe shape on the simplest responds. C13–14 nave and aisles, the aisles with circular piers on the S, octagonal on the (rebuilt) N side. Arcades double-chamfered on both sides, slightly lower and broader on the S. The chancel (with SEDILIA and PISCINA) has an arch resting on C13 corbels. Perp clerestory. The church was restored in 1873–4 by *Bodley & Garner*, who rebuilt and extended the N aisle with stone from the medieval Trent Bridge in Nottingham. – In the nave two iron CANDELABRA (*c.* 1860), and, of the date of the restoration, the pretty SCREEN by *Bodley & Garner*, the STAINED GLASS in the E window by *Burlison & Grylls*, and the stencilled decoration on the roof by *Leach & Co.* of Cambridge. – N aisle E window 1865 by *Powell & Sons*. – In the churchyard good SLATE HEADSTONES signed by *Sparrow*, *Heywood*, and *Charles*.‡

(OLD RECTORY. Late C18 or early C19. Two-storey garden front with four Ionic pilasters supporting the central pediment. Good internal fittings and an open-well, cut-string staircase with a wrought-iron balustrade. NS)

(SCHOOL. 1840. Classical, stuccoed, with a hipped roof. NS)

A prominent BANK AND DITCH runs along the NW boundary of the village and may originally have enclosed it. This is

---

* When traces of Saxon foundations were found.
‡ According to Professor Barley.

presumably a medieval earthwork (cf. Saxondale), perhaps marking off the home-closes from the arable and pasture beyond.

## RADCLIFFE-ON-TRENT

ST MARY. By *Goddard & Paget* of Leicester, 1879–80, not at all a village church, townish and prosperous, with a thoroughly rock-faced exterior. E.E. detail and a tall tower (with a saddle-back roof, of all things). – BRASS to Anne Ballard † 1626, rectangular plate. – Good slate HEADSTONES by *James Sparrow*, the most individual of the Notts slateworkers, who lived and worked here through most of the C18.

THE LODGE. A long, low, late Georgian house in wooded grounds. Stuccoed, with a cast-iron balustraded veranda above a central bow on the ground floor.

(MANVERS ARMS. An identical design (stuccoed with a full-height porch projection) to a farm at Budby, which, like Radcliffe and Holme Pierrepont, is a Manvers estate village. NS)

STATION, in the village. Another by *Hine* for the GNR (*see* Nottingham, Orston, etc.). The RAILWAY BRIDGE over the Trent still has its original ribs, cast in 1851 by *Clayton, Shuttleworth & Co.* of Lincoln.*

## RADFORD *see* NOTTINGHAM p. 254

## RAGNALL

ST LEONARD. Much restored, with new chancel and s aisle, in 1864–7 by *Ewan Christian*. Some windows still straight-headed late Dec in the Notts way. w tower low and un-buttressed. – STAINED GLASS. E window 1864–7 by *Wailes*. – MONUMENT to William Mellish † 1692. Wall-tablet with stiff swags of fruit and cherubs' heads by *William Stanton*, 1690.

(RAGNALL HALL, at the s end of the village. The present farm-house is early C19. Between it and a malting range, the steep gable and one mullion-and-transom-cross window (with a small lunette above) of the early C17 hall, facing the road. The main

---

* According to Mr C. W. Sex.

parts of the old hall survive as barns: two brick ranges, with
stone mullion-and-transom-cross windows, at r. angles to
each other. In the short cross wing, two doors with four-centred
heads. NS)

The Hawksmoors were yeomen farmers in the Tuxford area, and
Nicholas Hawksmoor was born either in this village or at East
Drayton.


RAINWORTH see BLIDWORTH


7070                          RAMPTON

The church makes a good group with the gateway formerly to
the Manor House. But the gateway is a C19 imitation of the
real GATEWAY, hidden between the churchyard and the yard
of the early C18 HILL'S FARM, which must have been the
access of the people from the house, the de Ramptons and
later the Eyres, to the church. It is an uncommonly lavish piece
of Early Tudor brickwork, rising in three stepped stages and
adorned with corbelled-out panels of terracotta with coats of
arms. One of these is that of the Babingtons, and it seems more
than likely that the designer of the Babington Chantry at
Kingston-on-Soar also designed this gateway. What may he
have done at the Manor House? It was replaced in 1851–3
by *Burn* with a neo-Elizabethan building, now demolished.

ALL SAINTS. w tower slim, E.E. in masonry and proportions.
At the bell-stage two-light windows of *c.* 1300. The ground-
floor window is Perp: so are s porch and chancel E window.
But the s doorway is E.E. again, although the sculptured heads
to l. and r., once apparently of good quality, must be C15. The
s windows look redone C17 or C18. Of the nave arcades the N
is of *c.* 1300, the s C15, both with octagonal piers and double-
chamfered arches (a proof of how persistent that convention
was in Notts). – FONT. Norman, with curiously cusped
(retooled?) arches on short shafts. – COMMUNION TABLE.
Elizabethan, in the N aisle. – The Eyre MONUMENTS are all
minor.

RAMPTON MENTAL HOSPITAL, 3 m. w, at Woodbeck. From
the road it looks like a garden suburb, thanks to *F. W. Troup*.
Many buildings date from after *c.* 1920 when the Office of
Works took over, for example the institutional-looking neo-
Georgian administration block (by *J. H. Markham*, *c.* 1927).

Numerous traces of prehistoric and Roman SETTLEMENT occur on the river terrace and below. One settlement of timber huts, dating from the mid CI, has been excavated.

## RANBY HALL *see* BABWORTH

## RANSKILL

6080

ST BARNABAS. 1878 by *Ewan Christian*, of stone, with nave, chancel, and bellcote.

THE OLD HALL. A three-storey late C18 brick house with high brick walls and a very tall brick dovecote towards the road.

## RATCLIFFE-ON-SOAR

4020

HOLY TRINITY. The church is visited on account of the Sacheverell monuments and the W tower. The latter is C13 (note the absence of buttresses, the lower windows, the quoins, the corbel table, and the shafts with shaft-rings in the tower arch inside). Plain broach-spire of the early C14, with lucarnes in two tiers. The corner pinnacles are themselves minute broached spires. C14 arcades with octagonal piers. The arches are, strangely enough, round-headed on the N side. Old (C15) roofs in nave and chancel. The chancel windows are E.E., that in the E of four lights with geometrical tracery of *c.* 1300, quite spectacular, the aisle windows of three lights with ogee reticulation, that is early C14. – SEDILIA. Plain E.E., same date as the low recess opposite. – FONT. C14, with cover of 1660. – COMMUNION TABLE and COMMUNION RAILS. C17. – MONUMENTS. All alabaster. Greenhill lists eleven incised slabs of between *c.* 1480 and 1524, all badly worn or broken. The following monuments are to members of the Sacheverell family: Ralph S. † 1539, and wife. Tomb-chest in a niche. On the chest walls tracery and shields in panels. The niche with a depressed arch and Gothic ornamentation. Recumbent effigies. Nothing of the Renaissance yet. – Sir Henry S † 1558, and wife. Tomb-chest with recumbent effigies. On the chest walls the seventeen children all holding shields. Stiff figures, and only at the corners the crudest Early Renaissance vase or baluster decoration. – Henry S. † 1580, and wife. Still recumbent on a tomb-chest, still stiff figures of children against the chest front. The ornament is strapwork now, but an understanding of what the Renaissance meant has not yet been achieved. – Henry S. † 1625, and wife. He lies on a tomb-chest, his three wives kneel behind each other above the chest in an aedicule with columns. – Obviously one alabaster workshop provided all this work (and that at Barton-in-Fabis, and others outside the county), a provincial, but very competent workshop, only distantly echoing what was happening between 1540 and 1625 in London.

(MANOR FARM. According to Throsby built in 1719 on the site of the manor house by Sir Nathaniel Curzon, but dated 1715 on the building. Double pile and exactly square on plan with the entrance in the gabled elevation. Sashes to the ground floor, three wooden cross casements above, simple staircase.)

RED HILL, 1 m. N. The site of a Romano-British hill-top temple, overlying an Iron Age site. The temple was of Romano-Celtic type, with a square *cella* surrounded by an ambulatory. Romano-British occupation was widespread on the hill.

## REMPSTONE

5020

ALL SAINTS. Tower dated 1771, church consecrated in 1773. A complete village church of that date is rare in Notts, and with so much of the original furnishings rarer still. The W tower has classical windows but battlements and pinnacles. The body of the church is an aisleless rectangle with quoins and three windows on each side with surrounds of intermittent rustication, *a la* Gibbs. Pedimented E end with a low 3/8 apse beneath. The pulpit with reader's desk attached rises on the l. above the parson's pew; the squire's pew is opposite. – Nice slate TOMBSTONES in the churchyard.

(REMPSTONE HALL, W of the church. 1796 (rainwater head). Long, painted brick façade with two-bay projecting wings at each end, an Ionic colonnade between them and pilasters above. Pilastered and pedimented windows in the outer wings and a balustrade over all. DOE)

The village migrated ½ m. SE. Near Sheepwash Brook earthworks show where it originally stood.

(TOP FARM. C17 brick with brick string courses continuous with arched pediments over the windows, all in projecting courses: a pseudo-classical touch of the country builder (cf. East Leake, Sutton Bonington, North Wheatley). NS)

There are some other good houses in the village (a timber-framed

COTTAGE in Main Street with an upper cruck in the gable, and
SILVER BIRCHES, a tall late C18 Notts farmhouse), but one
or two have been spoilt (the once-fine C18 HREMIS FARM,
and ELMS FARM, another tall C18 farmhouse).*

# RETFORD

The market town of East Retford and the village of West Retford
stand on opposite banks of the river Idle. Although now entirely
one, their individual characters can still be discerned.

## EAST RETFORD

ST SWITHUN. Big, but also unrewarding, except for its value in
the townscape. It stands very proudly in a large churchyard
close to the Market Place. It is almost completely the work of
restorers of 1658, 1854–5, and 1905. The crossing tower collapsed in 1651, causing the chancel and 'the greatest part' to be
'very ruinous ... shaken and much injured'. It must have been
E.E. (Cox says founded in 1258 by Roger, Archbishop of York)
according to the remains of the strong piers. The C17 (1658)
rebuilt them and could not refrain from just one slight innovation in the capitals: a smooth double curve, with even a little
volute on the E ones, utterly alien to the High Middle Ages.
The oldest virtually untouched part is the N transept. On its
E side two arches and an octagonal pier complete with (recut)
vine-leaf decoration on the capital. It was revealed when *G. F.
Bodley* rebuilt the chantry chapel in 1873. He also refurbished
the chancel. Of 1852 the S porch, and of 1854–5 the rebuilt N
aisle (with capitals imitating the C13 ones) and N porch, the N
chancel aisle, clerestory, and battlements, and the E window of
re-used C13 stonework. Architect: *G. G. Place*. All this was
renovated in 1905. – The Victorian STAINED GLAS is uncommonly instructive: sanctuary E by *Clayton & Bell*, 1874
(but centre light by *O'Connor*, 1855), N and S by *Wailes*, 1858;
S transept S by *Kempe* as a Boer war memorial, 1903, SE by
*Wailes*, 1847, NE by *Hardman*, 1866; S aisle, first from W by
*O'Connor*, second by *Wailes*, third by *Clayton & Bell*, fourth
by *O'Connor*; N transept N by *Kempe & Co.* as a Great War
memorial, E windows by *Kempe & Co.*, c. 1920; N aisle first
from W by *O'Connor*, second and third by *Clayton & Bell*; W

* Information from Dr Summers.

front centre by *Clayton & Bell*, N by *O'Connor*, baptistery by *Kempe*, 1877. One window by a local, *George Shaw* of Saddleworth, 1858. – Some medieval fragments in the S transept W window of the C14 and early C15, collected in 1862 from St Martin, Canterbury, Tickhill, Yorks, a monastery in Normandy, and other places. – The MONUMENTS are insignificant. In the N transept an incised slab to Henry Smyth† 1496. – Sir Wharton Amcotts † 1807 by *William Kinnard*, architect.

ST ALBAN, London Road. *See* Ordsall, p. 282.

ST SAVIOUR, Lidget Lane. 1827–9 by *E. J. Willson* of Lincoln. His first major project. Commissioners'-type, yellow brick, with two turrets flanking the nave on the W side and narrow Perp windows. Restored and refitted in 1877–9. Contemporary VICARAGE with classical door surround next to the church in Welham Road.

WESLEYAN CHURCH, Grove Street. 1879–80 by *Bellamy & Hardy* and, like the town hall, coarse and domineering. Inside, an oval gallery and ceiling like one in the town hall. Fronting Union Street, the old WESLEYAN SCHOOL, 1823. The earlier chapel of 1789 in Spa Road is now a warehouse.

KING EDWARD VI GRAMMAR SCHOOL, London Road. Founded in 1552. The present neo-Tudor red-brick building with a central Gothic lantern and spire is of 1855–7 by *Decimus Burton*. Four classrooms on two floors to the l. of the entrance, the former hall to the r., and the headmaster's house next to it on the SE corner. Behind, a former boarding-house wing extended in 1874. In the wing on the l., extending to the road, science rooms and gymnasium of 1896, and a new hall of 1937, partly incorporating earlier cloisters, all in a larger version of the original style. CLASP buildings behind.

SLOSWICKE'S HOSPITAL (MEASE DE DIEU), Churchgate. Founded in 1657, rebuilt in 1806, and altered in 1819. Brick with Gothic windows but a Georgian central pediment; set back from the street. In 1819 a pair of houses was built, one NW and one SW of the main building. To the r. of the façade an extension dated 1835.

The town received its charter in 1246, but owed its Georgian prosperity to its position on the Great North Road, diverted through it in 1766, and on the Chesterfield Canal opened in 1777. Some of its Georgian character remains, although most of the C18 and early C19 houses are modest and altered. The centre is the MARKET PLACE, of promising L-shape and spacious, but with not much to take advantage of it. The TOWN HALL, of 1866–

8 by *Bellamy & Hardy* of Lincoln in François I style, is without any of the Victorian qualities which we appreciate today: a bad mansard roof and a bad lantern. Next to it the OLD BANK (now municipal offices) by *Chorley & Connon*, 1887, fiery red brick in the Waterhouse style. Several altered Georgian houses, a few with some pretensions, e.g. on the W side next to the bank Nos. 18–18a, early C18, of seven bays with a carriageway and pediment to the centre bay, but otherwise very plain and altered. Set back at the other end of the same side, in THE SQUARE, a town house of *c.* 1811 (see the datestone on the attached garden wall and gateway). Plain pedimented doorcase on the façade, but a better one with Ionic columns on the W side. On the N side, a mid-C18 house (TRUSTEE SAVINGS BANK) with a pedimented central bay and rusticated pilasters, and the YORKSHIRE BANK, of chequered brick on the upper floors, modern below. GROVE STREET, leading off the E side of the Market Place, has one or two houses with nice features: Nos. 5–7 with a cast-iron balcony between bow-windows, No. 25 (THE POPLARS), a plain detached late C18 house, and, further down on the other side, AMCOTT HOUSE, mid-C18, altered, but with a central open pediment and Venetian openings to central window and door. CHURCH GATE has more character than the surrounding streets, especially round the church itself, but no houses deserve special mention. Off Church Gate behind the glass merchants in LITTLE LANE a surprising little Gothic cottage of 1834. Expensive moulded brick decoration (canopies, a frieze, and so on) and Gothick windows with original glazing, all with an ecclesiastical flavour. On the other side of the church in CHAPELGATE, the OLD SUN INN, a low, basically timber-framed building, now stuccoed, probably C16. Further out in LONDON ROAD (really in Ordsall parish) some larger detached late C18 and early C19 villas and terraces, e.g. on the W side ORDSALL HOUSE, its lodge engulfed by the Northern Rubber Works in Thrumpton Lane, the ELMS HOTEL (with good internal features: DOE), and a late C18 brick house with a good doorcase. Opposite, HOLLY MOUNT, a stuccoed terrace (Nos. 87–95), and STORCROFT HOUSE.

CASTLE HILL, 1½ m. E. Small earthwork, possibly of Iron Age or Romano-British origin, but several phases are evident, and the site may thus have been re-used in the medieval period or in the Civil War of the 1640s.

BOLHAM. *See* p. 81.

WEST RETFORD

ST MICHAEL. A church of considerable interest: the account in the *Little Guide* is quite inadequate. As for the exterior, the W tower with spire is ashlared, with diagonal buttresses and a crocketed needle-shaped spire (*à la* Lincolnshire) with one tier of lucarnes. The most remarkable feature is the broach which is placed below the battlements so that the corner pinnacles find space on it and are then connected by means of little flying buttresses with another set of slim pinnacles accompanying the diagonals of the spire a certain part of the way up (cf. Scrooby). The N aisle externally Dec, the S aisle Perp (Piercy in his *History of Retford*, 1828, says C16) with an uncommonly large porch with a stone roof on three transverse ribs (cf. St Mary, Nottingham). The S arcade is worth closer study, all Perp, all slim, of no great bodily presence, but with slight differences from pier to pier. There is a prevalence of the concave everywhere; also the shape of most of the piers is a lozenge with the thin side towards the nave. Again in some piers a few mouldings are not caught by capitals but run straight into the arches. The N aisle was added in the 1863 restoration. Its arcade has quatrefoil piers and typically mid-Victorian naturalistic foliage. S aisle heavily restored in 1863 and chancel almost entirely rebuilt. It was extended again in 1890. – CHANCEL SCREEN. 1899 by *Hodgson Fowler*.

WEST RETFORD HALL, S of the church. Now divided up and known as Nos. 1–10 Rectory Road. Brick, nine bays with corner pilasters, of 1669. Original staircase and some C18 panelled rooms. Late C18 bows on the E and S sides. C18 stables with Gothic windows.

WEST RETFORD HOUSE (Restaurant), Great North Road. Large brick mansion built in 1762 for Alexander Emerson, of three storeys with two-storey C19 wings. Interior refitted in the C19. To the road the wall of the stable block, with a blank arcade.

HOLY TRINITY HOSPITAL, Hospital Road, opposite the Hall. 1832–3 by *Blore*, whose interest in this area must have been the result of his marriage to the daughter of the vicar of Mattersey. The usual long, low shape with projecting wings and screen wall (of before 1828). Neo-Tudor brick with stone dressings. To any observer of some experience it will be clear that the central feature must be later. 1833 would have made it sym-

metrical. It is indeed 1872, though the chapel on the ground
floor is the remodelled common room of 1833.

## ROCKLEY see WEST DRAYTON

## ROLLESTON                                              7050

HOLY TRINITY. The interest of the church is its two arcades,
with a variety of C13 pier shapes, those on the s (rebuilt in 1895–
6) a simplified form of Southwell chancel: quatrefoil with deep
hollows separating and partly undercutting the four shafts (cf.
St Peter, Nottingham). Capitals moulded with a little dogtooth
or with crocket leaves or freer stiff-leaf. E respond with more
realistic foliage. So the whole must be pretty late in the century.
The N arcade has two plain quatrefoil piers and one octagonal
with concave sides and shafts placed into four of the concavities
(a Lincoln idea). Moulded, deeply overhanging capitals. All
arches double-chamfered. Lancet windows occur in the s and N
aisles and on the N side of the chancel. Yet the masonry of the
building is at least partly older, for early Norman herringbone
pattern has been found at the E end of the N aisle, and the s
door is Norman too. The billet motif on the hoodmoulding is
familiar from Southwell. Tower base also Norman (see the narrow windows re-cut in the C14). The top of the tower is of the
proudest Trent valley type, with two large two-light transomed
Perp bell-stage openings on each side, battlements, and eight
pinnacles (rebuilt in 1889–90). The middle pinnacles are corbelled out, the corbels starting out of the ogee arches which
tie the two windows together (an original and successful motif).
The clerestory of course also Perp. Restored in the 1890s by
*C. Hodgson Fowler*, born at Rolleston, where his father and
grandfather were vicars (JPB). – FONT COVER. C17. – PULPIT.
The simplest later C17 type. – SCREEN. With very little play
in the tracery. – ALTAR RAILS. With early or mid-C17
balusters. – CROSS SHAFT (N aisle). Fragmentary, Saxon, with
crossed lines and interlace, signed *Radulfus me fe (cit)*. –
STAINED GLASS. E window, Saints 1878, Ressurrection 1885,
by *Kempe*.

WATER CORN MILL. Brick and pantile, one- and two-storey,
with sliding casements. Disused water wheel, gearing and
stones, still in position. The adjoining buildings are now a farm.

RUDDINGTON

ST PETER. The chapel of St Mary became the parish church when St Peter, Flawford, was demolished in 1773.\* Rebuilt in 1887–8 by *Bell & Roper* of Manchester in Dec style. Quite large NW tower and spire, battlemented all round. Simple arcades of unchamfered piers without capitals. – Medieval FONT possibly from Flawford.

SOUTH MANOR (Old People's Home). An early C18 four-bay, three-storey house much enlarged, with elaborate landscaping, by *T. C. Hine* for Sir Thomas Parkyns in 1852. CLASP additions fortunately stand detached.

(THE HERMITAGE. Irregular gabled front, mostly C19, but incorporating at the W end remains of the oldest building in the village with part of a medieval hall, partly timber-framed, with wattle and daub.‡ W wing remodelled in 1708. NS)

RUDDINGTON HOUSE. An attractive and unsophisticated stuccoed house of *c.* 1770. (*Morris* wallpaper in the drawing room. DOE)

(RUDDINGTON HALL, E of the A60, N of the village. Now a convalescent home. Built in 1860 by Thomas Cross, a Nottingham banker, in a heavy classical manner. NS)

(EASTHORPE HOUSE, E of the A60. In a Regency style familiar from the south-west of England. Five bays, with the entrance in a full-height centre bow. Bracketed eaves. DOE)

Ruddington is a large and complete nucleated village which has not grown into a town. (In the centre, CHURCHSIDE, a small mid-C17 brick and timber-framed cottage by the church; a group of four small but charming mid-C19 ALMSHOUSES in Vicarage Lane; and ST PETER'S SCHOOL, opposite the church, Gothic, a well-controlled design for Sir Thomas Parkyns, 1852. NS) Next to the school, a row of three houses, which

---

\* The remains, 1 m. E of the present village, have been excavated. The earliest fabric, nothing of which remains above ground level, was that of a Saxon church, consisting of nave (9 by 5.40 m.) and chancel (3.90 by 4.20 m); later in the Saxon period a W tower and a small sanctuary (3.30 m. square) were added. Chancel and sanctuary were replaced by a large early medieval chancel, the tower by one with a spire, probably of the broach type. S aisle added in 1280, the N aisle probably C14. The floor of the church was laid only 12 to 15 cm. above the tessellated pavement of a Roman villa. A well-known group of alabaster figures (Our Lady, St Peter, and an unknown bishop), ascribed to *Peter Maceon* of Nottingham, were discovered on the site in 1773, and are now in Nottingham Castle Museum.

‡ A medieval well and an excavation yielded datable C13 and C14 material.

look plain but have a surprising rear elevation. At their E end the late C17 MANOR FARMHOUSE.

Once an important centre of framework knitting, Ruddington, unlike Calverton, had its frames in workshops, not cottages. The best examples, in Chapel Street, are preserved as a Framework Knitters' Shops Museum. Two two-storey workshops, purpose-built in 1829, rebuilt c. 1860 face each other across a yard closed at the end by workers' cottages. Two more mid-C19 workshops between the Green and Parkyns Street; one, with its continuous top-floor window, is well seen from the Green. Another small workshop, behind No. 11 High Street, can be seen from Easthorpe Street. At the corner of Clifton Road and Wilford Road a hosiery factory, still on a small scale, but showing the change from hand- to steam-power in knitting. An even earlier factory in Kirk Lane is possibly the first stage in the transition. Different from the workshops e.g. on the green, it has cast-iron windows, large on the first floor, very small on the ground floor.

## RUFFORD ABBEY 6060

Rufford Abbey, the seat of the Saviles from the C17, was a large rambling house built at several different periods and called by Byng in 1789 'gloomy and ill-managed' and 'very melancholy'.*

* The building history was never fully explored, which is a great pity, because the fabric suggested a fascinating story. Most of the house was apparently early to mid C17, though the core may have been earlier: it belonged to the Shrewsburys until the early C17. On plan it looks like a very large H-plan house with many alterations and additions. The centre (which survives) has a much-renewed two-storey porch projection with barley-sugar columns and some strapwork and, to its l., eight bays with large windows of two mullions and two transoms taking up two storeys above a basement and lighting what appears from the plan to have been the Great Hall. Straight parapet except for two gables at the N end like those over the other bays of this C17 part. R. of the porch were three bays of two storeys plus basement and attic with two gables and mullioned and mullion-and-transom-cross windows tied to string courses, i.e. in this area probably early-to-mid-C17. At each end of the whole length of the C17 façade gabled bays formed a widespread H-plan, the l. one tied into an independently roofed late C17 or early C18 block. Three storeys, eight by nine bays, with a hipped roof, alternating pediments to the dormers, and sashes in slightly lugged surrounds: very plain but handsome. At either end of the E front of this block projected two bays (H-plan again), the S one remodelled by Salvin in 1838–40 as his staircase projection. The rest of the E front of the C17 block was even more confusing than the W side of it. Most of it was remodelled some time in the C18, with sashes at a slightly higher level than the original windows (e.g. the altered window surrounds) and with a basement entrance. On the parapet a strange Artisan-Mannerist-

In 1959 the early C18 N end of it was completely demolished, leaving the shell of the basically C17 range and, under it, the medieval remains of the Cistercian abbey founded by Gilbert de Gant in 1146. They comprise the lower part of the W range of the cloisters with undercroft (groin-vaulted on three octagonal piers) including cellarium, lay-brothers' frater, and axial night stair, and follow an arrangement very close to that at Fountains Abbey, with the night stair carried on a block in the cellar pierced by a barrel-vault and, it seems likely, a pantry and buttery in the S bays of the cellar used jointly by the lay-brothers' and the monks' fraters. The lay-brothers' frater is one of the best preserved in England, with spoon and linen cupboards in the N wall, the split cell of the vault against the S wall indicating the position of a reredos or crucifix over the high table, and traces of the day-stair treads on the W wall. *Ex-situ* some shaped floor tiles, like those from mosaic tile pavements used in some Cistercian houses. Excavations revealed that, as expected, the abbey church, with a rectangular E end and transepts each with two E chapels, lay to the N of the cloister, that is to the NE of the house. Its plan however differed from the typical Bernardine type in having an enlarged W end, its walls not aligned with those of the E end. The E end seems to have been widened in the later Middle Ages, taking in one of the S transept chapels. The S nave arcade had compound piers, the N cylindrical. The cloisters followed the usual Cistercian arrangement: in the E range the sacristy-library, rectangular chapter house, parlour, and undercroft; in the S the warming house, frater, and kitchen.

The upper floors of the house over this, now roofless, are to be made into a large hall.

In the park (now a Notts County Council country park), a GARDENER'S COTTAGE with deep eaves and strapwork, no doubt by *Salvin*. S of the house, a group of late Victorian stables, coach house, brewhouse, and water tower by *John Birch*, all red brick Jacobethan. The orangery (1889) was made round *John Hallam*'s* unusual BATH SUMMER HOUSE of 1729. The

---

style achievement. At the S end three bays with two gables and mullion-and-transom-cross windows. The levels here as well had been changed; this is still obvious on the remaining S façade where the cross-windows are all higher up in the E half of the façade. Large central gable crowned by a *Salvin* cupola and at the W end two original C17 gabled dormers.

* 'A poor mean country joyner', in Vanbrugh's jaundiced view, Hallam had worked at Chatsworth and became Secretary to the Board of Works under the patronage of Sir Thomas Hewett (see Shireoaks Hall).

bath house itself is remarkably intact, though roofless and in
need of restoration. The shallow end of the long sunken bath or
canal penetrated a three-bay Tuscan loggia between two three-
storey towers with *œil-de-bœuf* windows. Doors in the towers
originally led on to a walk above the loggia. The back half of
the building is a three-sided canted bay enclosed by a fountain
pool (with C19 fountain). On each face a large original sash.
The Cistercians created a large LAKE by damming Rainworth
Water. On its present site it is early C18, reconstructed by the
County Council in 1972–4.

RUFFORD PITHEAD BATHS. *See* Blidworth.

## SAUNDBY

ST MARTIN. The magnificent yew trees that surrounded it are
now depleted. Chancel restored and nearly rebuilt by *Pearson*,
1885–6. The Perp w tower of the usual east Notts type (ashlared, diagonal buttresses, battlements, eight pinnacles), dated
1504, survived him. The N side is all new, by *W. S. Weatherley
& Jones*, 1891–2; the s side goes with the tower. Inside, the
N arcade with circular piers and low moulded capitals was
originally E.E. – FONT. Norman, with a small kind of lozenge
frieze at the top. – ALTAR TABLE. Elizabethan. – STAINED
GLASS. Small C14 and C15 fragments in the tower window. –
Nave windows, 1886 and 1890, and two chancel windows, 1885,
by *Kempe*; the E window by *Clayton & Bell*, 1865. Comparisons
are instructive. – MONUMENT. Mutilated effigy of a Knight,
second half of the C14. – John Helwys † 1599, alabaster. The
effigy has gone. The background, with two flanking balusters
and a steep pediment, is pleasing. – In the churchyard, early
C18 slate HEADSTONES in the style of the anonymous craftsman of Bingham.

GAINSBOROUGH BRIDGE, right in the N corner of the parish,
crossing the Trent and county boundary into Gainsborough.
1791, ashlar, with niches in the piers and a balustraded parapet.
Three segmental arches.

## SAXONDALE

A well-preserved bank once bounded the hamlet and a length survives on the s side, possibly a remnant of a medieval boundary
earthwork like that at Plumtree.

## SCAFTWORTH

ROMAN FORTLET, ½ m. NW. Late Roman material only has so far been recorded from this small, triple-ditched enclosure by the river Idle.

## SCARRINGTON

ST JOHN OF BEVERLEY. W steeple with a typical Notts spire, not too steep and not too tall. Three tiers of lucarnes in it. The date of the structure is indicated by the ballflower ornament of the W door and the two-light window above it. The lucarnes have ogee tops; that is, first half of the C14. The body of the church was rebuilt in 1867–9 by *J. H. Hakewill* (JPB). – FONT. 1662, of the Southwell type, but much simpler.

(SCARRINGTON HOUSE, ½ m. N, towards Hawksworth. Another typical Notts lofty three-storey gabled house. Three bays with a portico on Doric columns. Fine outbuildings including a pigeon loft over the coach house. NS)

## SCREVETON

ST WILFRED. A small church in a pretty churchyard. C15 W tower, said to have been altered in Elizabethan times. Interior mainly early C13; nave and aisles divided by circular piers with double-chamfered arches. At the E end of the S aisle a PISCINA with leaf carving around the drain. – FONT. C12, with short columns and interlaced arches to decorate the bowl. – MIS-ERICORDS. Only one old one (C15, on the N side of the chancel) with a man seated before a fire. The one with St Wilfrid (S side) is modern. – ROYAL ARMS of Charles II, 1684. – CHEST. Good, large, iron-bound, C15. – ROYAL ARMS. 1684. – MONU-MENTS. Saxon fragment with interlacing, probably from a tomb. – C12 slab with incised cross head. – Worn but good incised slab of *c.* 1410 to a man in armour and two wives. – Richard Whalley † 1583, with three wives and twenty-five children (under the tower, but originally in the chancel): recumbent alabaster effigy, the wives and children in three panels against the back wall. – In the churchyard, a slate HEAD-STONE with masonic emblems (1819) by *Wood* of Bingham.\*

---

\* According to Professor Barley.

PRIEST'S HOUSE, at the E end of the churchyard. A good
example of a small C16–17 timber-framed house with three
rooms and an outshut. It appears to have 1607 carved on the
wall-plate. Modern brick infill and tiles. There is no evidence
that it was a priest's house.

## SCROOBY

ST WILFRID. The steeple has one unusual feature: the transition
from the square to the octagonal spire. It is handled on the pattern of West Retford. Embattled tower, nave, and S aisle.
The church is Perp throughout. The S porch carries its stone
roof on two transverse ribs (cf. St Mary, Nottingham, etc.).
Inside a contemporary arcade on octagonal piers. Restored in
1864 by *C. J. Neale* (JPB). – BENCH ENDS prettily panelled.
(METHODIST CHAPEL. A typical small three-bay chapel of
*c.* 1830. CS).

There is no provable connection with William Brewster, the Pilgrim Father, in the church or the so-called manor house. Yet
the sentimental attraction remains the same. The Puritan group
did not of course reach Massachusetts direct from Scrooby.
They tried to flee to Holland in 1608, were arrested, tried again,
reached Amsterdam, settled at Leyden, and finally sailed in
1620. Their last port of call was Plymouth.

## SELSTON

ST HELEN. Except for the C14 tower with diagonal buttresses
and a C15 top, the exterior of the church looks entirely new
(restoration and enlargement 1899). Yet on entering it, one is
in a building exceptionally all of a piece. It must all be C13, even
the N arcade, which seems at first well back in the C12 with
its almost unmoulded arches (one step and only the slightest
chamfer), and its low circular piers with entirely Norman-looking capitals. One has at the eight corners eight small heads,
another eight faces of monsters, yet another elementary leaves.
But the E and W responds have demi-shafts keeled in such a
way as is impossible, as far as we know, before the C13. The
S arcade also still has round-headed arches, but now double-
chamfered, and the circular piers, capitals, and responds are
more clearly E.E. The chancel arch and both the chancel aisles
belong to this phase. The window above the chancel arch is
very picturesque and quite recent (1904–6). – MONUMENTS.

Two incised slabs: one with a unique kind of wheel-cross, a shaft carrying a circle with in it originally, it seems, eight stars; the other one of the earliest incised slabs with a figure: to a priest, c. 1150. – Sir William Willoughby † 1630 and wife. Two recumbent alabaster effigies on a large, plain (ill-preserved) tomb-chest, the background with black columns and a round-headed, vaulted niche. The decoration as far as can be recognized still strapwork. Sir William's funeral helmet opposite the tomb against the chancel wall.

TOAD HOLE. Four pretty half-timbered thatched cottages.

The two most interesting domestic buildings in this parish were Selston Hall (a manor house of c. 1600, demolished) and Wansley Hall (the remains of an important house of the Wandesly family, apparently mostly C15), now derelict.

## SERLBY HALL

According to Throsby, the first Viscount Galway, who bought the estate in 1727, 'laid the foundation of a mansion house where the new one is now built'.* This 'however ... was removed' and a new house by *James Paine* 'built piecemeal' by the second Viscount, who inherited in 1751. Throsby's statement is endorsed by the building accounts, which show that the E wing, containing kitchen, library, and business room, was built first in 1754–5. It was followed in 1759–65 by the body of the house, apart from the largest room, which, first intended as a saloon, was fitted up in 1777, as the 'Great Dining Room'. The private W wing, also built in 1771, was not fitted internally until 1773 by the third Viscount.‡

The house we now see standing amongst trees high up on a ridge above the river Ryton is a remodelling of the C18 house

---

* Dr Leach, who provided the new information contained in this entry, puts forward the possibility that Paine also designed the first house, although this seems unlikely in view of the new start. He could have been in contact with the family from c. 1745, when the Hon. Richard Arundell, a relative of Lord Galway, helped him secure his first appointment in the Office of Works. In any case Paine's Nostell Priory was near the former Galway seat, Hodroyd Hall.

‡ The main craftsmen were: (E wing) *Francis Day*, joiner; *Thomas Ledger*, plasterer; (body of the house) *John Watson*, mason and carver; *Peter Robinson* and *Gervase Ledger*, plasterers; (W wing) *William Battersby*, mason; *Thomas Ledger*, plasterer; *Anthony Hall*, bricklayer, and *John Billington*, carpenter, worked on the body of the house and the W wing.

by *Lindley & Woodhead* of Doncaster in 1812. (Lindley had added an attic storey to Paine's Doncaster Mansion House in 1801.) Paine's design was an example of the type first used at Holkham and subsequently much favoured by the mid-century Palladians; that is, a villa, like Chiswick designed for occasional use, expanded to country-house size by accommodation provided in pavilions linked to the house by wings, different from Palladio's villas, where the 'outhouses' were only farm buildings. The main block was brick with stone dressings, of two-and-a-half storeys and five bays. Over the central three bays of each main façade, vast double interlocking pediments of slightly different form, a motif used by Paine to break up the façade and avoid the static effect of one too-massive pediment (cf. his Cusworth Park, c. 1740, and Doncaster Mansion House, 1745–8). A half-sunk rusticated service basement linked the main block, the two-storey wings, and the pedimented pavilions. Above, the features were Kentian in variety, with doors and windows in arched recesses and, typical of Paine, ball machicolation on the wings, bow windows, and broken and floating cornices. Of the original house only the central block remains: the wings were demolished in 1812. In order to concentrate all the accommodation previously provided in the wings into the central block, *Lindley & Woodhead* extended it at both ends by two bays and raised the attic to a full storey, leaving only a shallow pediment in the middle of each façade. The result is a somewhat barrack-like appearance, with none of the 'movement' Paine strove so hard to achieve. They kept and repeated on both façades the original ground-floor treatment of windows with balustraded sills, and the N front still has Paine's large arched and recessed central window. But the S front they altered completely, by adding four pilasters between the central five bays which rest on arched rustication and support the central pediment, as well as a porch of paired Tuscan columns with a typically Regency ironwork balcony over. The whole house was stuccoed (removed in 1911). For 1812 the alterations look rather old-fashioned, but by then Lindley was an old man still faithful to the Adam-influenced style of the late c18.

A circular STAIRCASE HALL originally occupied the centre of the central square block, replacing the Palladian central saloon which at Chiswick and Mereworth recalled the Villa Rotonda. In 1812 the vestibule was thrown into it and a new cantilever staircase with wrought-iron balustrade built. Paine's plan can still be traced by the wide elliptical arch that marks the position of the vestibule wall, the arch above the staircase which led from his stairs to the bedrooms, and by the screen of columns on the landing in place of his dressing-room wall. Paine's GREAT DINING ROOM in the centre of the N front has its original ceiling (paintings attributed to *Zucchi*), doorcase with fluted half-columns, and an inlaid fireplace.* Its wall decoration is of 1906. Also by *Paine* a number of marble fireplaces and the SMALL DRAWING ROOM, l. of the original entrance, with a ceiling of simple panelled plasterwork. The w-facing DRAWING ROOM of 1812 (with Adamish decoration – some re-used?) has a screen of Corinthian columns and a fireplace with fine Bacchic carvings from a house in Hanover Square. On one side of the 1911 entrance hall, the chapel, remodelled then with panelling from Hodroyd Hall, some of which is also in the Oak Room.

N of the house, below the hillside laid out in formal terraces by the first Lord Galway, the remains of an C18 GROTTO, lying on the axis of the house at the end of a long canal which with time has become a natural lake. Due of N of this on the brow of the hill and now in trees, the ruins of a GOTHICK EYE-CATCHER. Further picturesque improvements of *c.* 1812 were by *Stother* of Yorkshire and *John Webb* of Staffordshire. The C18 STABLE QUADRANGLE is of the usual sort with pediments on each side, the entrance one surmounted by a cupola, and below the house to the NE lies the part of the earlier house, incorporated into a clubroom in 1911.

## SHELFORD

*6040*

ST PETER. So ruthlessly restored by the callous Mr *Christian* in 1876–8 that little remains for enjoyment, except the situation by the river meadows of the Trent. The chancel is entirely new. The C14 windows of flowing tracery all renewed too. According to Cox, the E window is of 1897. C15 tower, its arch to the nave tall and with no capitals between jambs and voussoirs. – FONT. One of the set of 1662 fonts (cf. Southwell, etc.). –
5    SCULPTURE. An extremely interesting Anglo-Saxon relief of

---

* It was finished by *Christopher Theakston*, carver, *John Green*, joiner, and *Peter Robinson*, plasterer.

the Virgin, with the Child seated in profile. On the reverse, an angel holding a book. The edges have knotwork. Remains of a cross shaft? – FUNERAL ARMOUR with the Stanhope arms. – STAINED GLASS. E window 1897 and four others 1898–1902 by *Kempe*. – MONUMENTS. Lady Anne Stanhope † 1587, alabaster, with her eight children kneeling all in one direction against the N side of the tomb-chest, and three more swathed on the W. This arrangement of the children is not usual in Notts (but cf. Archbishop Sandys at Southwell † 1588). The face of Lady Anne is all rubbed off. – In the Stanhope Chapel, an undated bust of Mrs Welbore-Ellis by *Nollekens*. – Lady Georgina West † 1824 by *Chantrey*, a kneeling woman hiding her face in her hands.

SHELFORD MANOR. C17–18, ashlar-faced, with some mullioned and transomed windows, much altered. Incorporating masonry of Shelford Priory, an Augustinian priory founded *c.* 1160–80.

WINDMILL, 1 m. E at Newton. All that remains of this post-mill is the brick round-house, in good repair, which contains the cross trees, and part of the machinery, in the Science Museum at South Kensington.


## SHELTON                7040

ST MARY. Small, with a bellcote after the W tower was removed in 1837. On the S side a Norman doorway, not very rewarding, with two orders of roughly carved colonnettes. S arcade of circular piers with simply moulded capitals and single-chamfered arches. They are early C13, as are the fine trefoil PISCINA in the aisle and the three single, rather short lancet windows with heads as label stops. Above these a plain contemporary corbel table. – Saxon CROSS SHAFT in two pieces with interlace work.

(SHELTON HALL, W of the church. Late C18. Five bays, three storeys, stuccoed, with an open loggia of Roman Doric columns on one side. A good open-well staircase with iron balusters and some cornices remain. NS)


## SHERWOOD
see NOTTINGHAM p. 263


## SHERWOOD FOREST
see EDWINSTOWE

## SHERWOOD LODGE see ARNOLD

## SHIREOAKS

ST LUKE. 1861–2 by *T. C. Hine*. An expensive rock-faced Dec church provided for the mining community by the Duke of Newcastle, who opened a colliery in 1845. The church lost any charm when its spire was demolished in 1973 because of mining subsidence.

Opposite the church a long terrace of MINERS' COTTAGES built by the Duke in 1864. Of good design, though now altered.

PRIMARY SCHOOL (C of E). The chapel of ease of 1810, superseded by Hine's church and converted to a school in 1883. Ashlar. E end pedimented, with Gothick glazing in the E window. Other windows of three oddly elongated round-headed lights, almost lancets. Once a Gothick domed bell-turret over the W end.

SHIREOAKS HALL. Important because of its resemblance to houses by *Robert Smythson* and because of the impressive scale of its water gardens. The house has suffered so many vicissitudes that the Hewetts, who built it *c.* 1600, would hardly recognize it. It was altered *c.* 1700, partly demolished and gutted after the last Hewett's death in 1811, then patched up for the Duke of Norfolk's agent, who bought it *c.* 1812.

There was much building in the neighbourhood during the late C16 by members of the Shrewsbury circle (*see* Introduction, p. 26) to which the Hewetts, too, belonged. Sir William Hewett, brother of the Thomas who acquired the Manor in 1546, was a close friend of the Earl, whose Worksop Manor stood only two miles away. This connection, together with the structural evidence of the Hall, strongly recommends an attribution to Robert Smythson.* Originally entered from the SE, the main elevation is now the SW SIDE: very plain late Georgian, three storeys and five days, with an off-centre door, straight parapet, and plain sashes. But several inconsistencies give a clue to its real age. To the first-floor windows C16 double-chamfered reveals and heads, the staircase window showing their original height. Below it a blocked two-light mullioned,

---

* There is no documentary evidence for date or designer. Shireoaks most resembles Bolsover Keep, not begun until 1612–13 for Sir Charles Cavendish, Bess of Hardwick's son. Unfortunately the originator of this design is unrecorded as well. The plan is characteristic of Robert Smythson, † 1614, but the interior and certain external details were finished by his son John.

formerly basement, window. Top-floor windows blocked and
mock-painted early this century. Of the NE SIDE, only the
basement survived the alterations of *c.* 1812, on to which the
Victorians built one storey with a pitched roof. Discernible on
the blank wall above it, some C16 floor levels and ashlar door
surrounds. The NW SIDE has four of its six bays. Here the basement is a full storey because of the sloping site, with the remains
of one of two three-storey wings, built *c.* 1700, at its base. *
The SE FAÇADE, only two-thirds intact, gives the most clues to the
Hall's C16 appearance. Of six equal bays, the centre two projecting by one bay, it strongly resembled in form and detail the
façade of Bolsover Keep. The present fenestration relates to
the changed floor levels, but several C16 windows survive
blocked. They increased in height from two-light in the basement, to four-light on the ground floor, to six-light on the first
floor (cf. Bolsover, Hardwick, and Wollaton, where the tallest
windows light the state rooms). A sash-window breaks through
the string course indicating the C16 first-floor level, and inside,
part of an arch and its correctly classical stone impost shows
that the entrance was raised above the basement and reached
by a flight of steps (of the same dimensions and shape as those
at Bolsover Keep). On the parapet, lozenge-decorated stones
from the stair balustrade (cf. those in the same position at
Bolsover). No doubt there was another storey (the present
parapet is badly made up of re-used coping stones like those on
Bolsover forecourt walls), but only an *ex-situ* triangular coping
stone (cf. Bolsover) suggests battlements.

The original plan, reconstructed from the almost intact basement,‡ was also similar to the Bolsover Keep design, but cross-
shaped, because the principal stair (some treads of which
remain) was housed in a wing corresponding to the porch pro-

---

* Part of alterations probably made by *Sir Thomas Hewett* (b. 1656), Surveyor of Woods North of the Trent to William III, then from 1719 Surveyor
General to George I. Although he inherited in 1660, as an adult he did not
live permanently at Shireoaks until after 1689. He probably remodelled the
SW front, added the NW wings, the pavilions and outbuildings, refitted the
interior, and began to lay out his magnificent water garden soon after. The
provincial style of the remodelling seems inconsistent with what we know of
his architectural taste as connoisseur and member of the new 'Junta for architecture' (see Colvin's *Dictionary*, 1978 ed.) and suggests that his taste changed
and he adopted his new ideas quite late in life. More representative of the
strict classicism the 'Junta' promoted was the Banqueting House (see below).

‡ By Leopold Godlewski, who has kindly provided from his research all the
information about the Hewetts, their Hall and garden, included in this description.

jection instead of in a tower to one side as at Bolsover.* However, the overall dimensions without projections were very close: 63 by 53 ft at Shireoaks, 68 by 56¾ ft at Bolsover. There were other similarities: i.e. the arrangement and details of the kitchens, larder, etc., with a stone newel stair in the s corner and a separate buttery stair; the narrow central spine containing closets and flues; the layout of the rooms and some of their dimensions; and certain details (e.g. the porch impost, stair construction, and doorways). Here, as at Bolsover, the Great Hall on the first floor occupies the whole area on one (s w) side of the spine, with two lower rooms on the n e side and above them the Great Chamber linked by steps across the spine to rooms over the Great Hall. In both buildings identical room heights and an almost identical difference in first-floor levels. But the interior here, unlike John Smythson's at Bolsover, seems to have been very plain. In the Great Chamber evidence of an applied marble fireplace, and in the Withdrawing Room, plaster lined-out to imitate ashlar above three-quarter panelling.

The present makeshift construction of the INTERIOR dates from *c.* 1812, with new floor levels and some salvaged fittings of *c.* 1700 re-used. The low cellar is the lower half of the Elizabethan basement; the ground and first floors occupy its upper part plus the ground floor, with the attics at original first-floor level. On the ground floor, a typical c19 arrangement of rooms with some of the re-used fittings, e.g. a bolection-moulded fireplace, fielded doors and shutters, panelling, and Artisan-Mannerist style volutes from a doorcase used as a kind of pediment over the French doors of the dining room. On the first floor, some Elizabethan panelling, suggesting that some c16 rooms were intact until *c.* 1812.

Of the COURTS and GARDENS that surrounded most Elizabethan houses of any pretension, the rear (now entrance) court and n e terrace leading to walled gardens survive. The pavilions flanking the courtyard gate and facing into the courtyard are late c17 or early c18 (see the plain mullions and big dropped keystones), as are the outbuildings outside the gate and the coach house, workshops, and stores (now cottages) further away between the ponds. Sir Thomas's magnificent WATER GARDEN was desolate and neglected when Holland saw it about

---

* It seems impossible to tell whether Bolsover or Shireoaks came first. Henry Hewett, † 1599, son of Thomas, has perhaps the best claim to be the builder of Shireoaks. For a plan of Bolsover Castle *see Buildings of England: Derbyshire*, rev. ed., 1978.

1825 with 'the glittering cascade ... gone to ruin: the lake ... stagnant', a contrast indeed to the intended geometrical precision. The *patte d'oie* layout had an axial long canal and beech avenues radiating from the s w front. Water descended from a great stone-lined basin, half hidden in a wood, for $\frac{1}{2}$ m. towards the s w front in a series of thirty-four cascades with twelve oval and circular ponds ending in a long canal. Flanking the cascades an avenue of alternating yews and limes, changing where the canal began to rows of clipped yews. Two triangular bosquets between the yews and the canal penetrated the lawns before the house. On the far (NE) side of the house, a rectangular fountain pond, and on the former road (SE) side a huge hexagon of trees completed the composition. Sadly, all that remains is the basin, cascades, and canal, the site of the fountain pond with one wooden fountain pipe and nozzle, one or two trees marking the avenues, and a fragment of the once-large Scratta Wood.*
On the N w side the symmetry was lost with large stone-edged pools, possibly made from the ponds of the C16 house. Of the mysterious BANQUETING HOUSE, 1 m. away in Scratta Wood, only a mound remains to mark where it stood near to the *rond-point* of intersecting avenues. Vertue in 1725–6 called it 'a Greek tempietto', but we know only that it was rectangular, with flights of steps to entrances at each end and, inside, a different classical order in each of the three rooms, marble walls and floors, ceilings painted by *Trench*, and a bust of Sir Thomas by *Rysbrack*.

In a farmyard E of the hall, a timber-framed BARN, originally of twelve bays, now nine, and the remains of a large aisled one.

## SIBTHORPE

ST PETER. C13 W tower. Mean C18 nave, with the simplest intersecting tracery in round-headed windows. A N arcade which existed was taken down and only its Dec aisle windows with ogee reticulations re-used. Traces of the arcade and PISCINA still visible. The splendid chancel is now all the more exciting. It was built in connection with the foundation of a college of priests in 1335. Its large windows with flowing tracery of Lincolnshire character have three lights on the N and S, five on the E. Inside against the N wall one of the Lincolnshire–Nott-

* In Scratta Wood, an Iron Age and Romano-British SETTLEMENT SITE surrounded by a bank and ditch.

inghamshire EASTER SEPULCHRES, not one of the best: a low recess below, then a small ogee niche with the sleeping soldiers in small panels to the l. and r., and a tall steep crocketed canopy above with the figure of Christ and two censing angels (a severely abridged edition of Hawton and sculpturally not supreme). – FONT. One of the 1662 series (cf. Southwell). –

67  MONUMENTS. To Edward Burnell † 1589, 'made anno domini 1590', alabaster and very good: putti against the front of the tomb-chest holding a shield, the back panel with a shield, a rich wreath, and the upright panel at the head of the effigy also with a shield (cf. the Markham monument once at Cotham and perhaps the date plate 1573 at Staunton Hall). Only the effigy itself is poor at Sibthorpe.

42 DOVECOTE, in a field E of the church. A splendid utilitarian C13 or C14 building, nearly 31 ft in diameter and 60 ft high, with conical roof, most impressive in its isolation and simplicity. The largest of three circular dovecotes in Notts (cf. Thoroton), it contains 1,260 nesting-places in twenty-eight tiers. It belonged to the buildings of the collegiate church. A moat, 620 ft long, has been traced.

# SKEGBY

ST ANDREW. The W tower in its main masonry probably C13, the rest restored out of existence. The s aisle seems to have had an arcade with octagonal piers, and single-chamfered arches. One pier with an odd decoration of balls in the capitals. – STAINED GLASS. E window 1893 by *Kempe*. – MONUMENTS.

31  Two, to a man and a woman, *c.* 1300, probably not of the Spigurnell family as tradition upholds.* He carries the horn of an official of Sherwood Forest and is supported on the l. and r. by two angels. – Tablet to John Lindley † 1797 by *William Stretton* of Nottingham.

SKEGBY HALL (School). Early C18, five by five bays, two-and-a-half storeys, quoins, no visible roof. Rusticated lintels and keystone; segmental pedimented door to the s. (Good original dog-leg staircase. DOE) Wing by *E. W. Roberts*, 1950, and separate tile-hung CLASP buildings for the school.

Just before the village on the road from Mansfield, DALES-TORTH HOUSE, set in a walled, well-treed garden. Three

---

* According to Mr Patmore. Apparently the only member of the family to hold forest office did so for a few weeks as an interim measure in 1236.

storeys and five bays, brick. A very plain but handsome late
C18 house.

(E of the Hall the ruins of the old MANOR HOUSE of the Lindleys.
Only a few walls with blocked windows remain. Also E of the
Hall, on the opposite side of the Mansfield Road in Old Road,
KRUCK COTTAGE, partly-timber-framed C16; and the
exposed cruck of a barn against the dovecote and barns which
with the house form a courtyard. In Back Lane, MANOR
FARM, C17 stone with small mullioned windows NS)

BRANCH LIBRARY, Mansfield Road. By *M. S. Hessey* (Sutton-
in-Ashfield U.D.C. Architect), 1965–7. Small but unusual.
Nearly circular, with long mullioned windows all round, the
flat roof slightly tipped towards the entrance.


## SNEINTON *see* NOTTINGHAM p. 250


## SOOKHOLME                                    5060

SS PETER AND PAUL. An aisleless Norman chapel consisting
of nave and chancel. The chancel arch is simple enough to be
as early as about 1100. The three E windows are also preserved,
two below and one above and between the others (cf. Carburton). An interesting SEDILE against the S wall, just a stone seat
with low arms (cf. Laxton). Some Dec windows, two old roof
beams.


## SOUTH CLIFTON *see* CLIFTON


## SOUTH COLLINGHAM *see* COLLINGHAM


## SOUTH LEVERTON                               7080

ALL SAINTS. A Norman W tower, a rarity in Notts, unbuttressed
and slim, and Norman from the blocked W door, into which
a C13 lancet cuts, to the bell-stage with large twin openings tied
together by one larger arch. Only the top is Perp. Norman also
the S doorway. It is late C12 according to the moulding of the
arch. Two orders, the inner with decorated zigzag on front and
soffit. The nave is spacious, with C13 arcades to communicate
with the aisles but no chancel arch. The piers are unusual in
shape, square but placed diagonally and with shafts attached
to the angles, just as at St Mary-le-Wigford in Lincoln. The

capitals have strong upright stiff-leaf. The arch is complex in its mouldings, with three rolls for the inner soffit, all with fillets. The tower arch is contemporary (see its capitals). A puzzling problem is the blocked arch at the w end of the s aisle.* The s aisle has repetitive early C14 tracery (and a good cusped PISCINA in the E wall), the w window of the N aisle a flowing design. The N windows are late C14. Chancel restored by *Ewan Christian* in 1868. The rest of the church restored in 1897–8 by *C. Schofield*.

In the village, much good brickwork, including the DOVECOTE with stepped gables, standing high above former farm buildings in Retford Road at the N end of the village, and the DIAMOND HOUSE (the Old School), 1691, with a string course with a segmental pediment over the front entrance.

MANOR HOUSE. The only old feature a shaped gable facing the road.

7050                    SOUTH MUSKHAM

ST WILFRID. W tower below C13 (with only a narrow doorway into the nave), above Perp with two two-light windows, a local type. The two arcades inside C14, also the customary type. Chancel late C13, lancet windows N and s with nook-shafts and originally presumably three lancets at the E end. Now instead of that a large five-light Perp window, by the masons of Holme and North Muskham churches. – FONT. Octagonal, either Norman much pulled about or, more likely, a C17 imitation of Norman. – BENCH ENDS. Some of poppyhead type, a few with hideous monsters, in the chancel. – SOUTH DOOR. Medieval, without specially decorative ironwork. – MONUMENT in coloured marble to Elizabeth Beevor † 1819 by *Wallis & Marshall* of Newark. – STAINED GLASS. C15 fragments in a s aisle window.

1 m. w at Little Carlton, THE GABLES FARM, a yeoman's house of c. 1600, and with a C14 core. Timber frame, concealed by brick on the ground floor. Original plan of hall and two cross wings. Open frames in the joists of the wings show where ladders went before the staircase was inserted c. 1700 and the hall

* Professor Barley suggests that this led into an extension s of the tower (as on the N side) and was blocked later, probably in the C19. The roof-line visible outside probably represents the height of the C13 aisle. When widened in the C14, it was given a separate roof span.

divided into two storeys. The hall fireplace backs on to the through passage characteristic of the North.

## SOUTH SCARLE

8060

ST HELEN. Battlemented nave, aisles, S porch, and W tower (with eight pinnacles). All this is late medieval, but inside the church is a splendid Norman N arcade, two bays only, very similar to South Collingham, but if anything richer still: circular piers with elementary leaf capitals, and one of a playful variety of the scalloped kind, and arches with coffered diapers in two orders on the front as well as the soffit. S arcade, last separate bay of N arcade, chancel, and chancel arch all E.E. The arcade has its pier with four shafts with deep hollows between and fillets (cf. St Peter, Nottingham). The capital is moulded, the base rests on a large square seat, and the arches are double-chamfered. The tower arch has dogtooth, the chancel all lancet windows and a very pretty DOUBLE PISCINA with free-standing central shaft. The clerestory and the roof of the nave are Perp. – The shaft of the FONT with eight shafts seems E.E. too; but not much of it is left. – SCREEN. Perp. – Eleven medieval PEWS. – COMMANDMENT TABLES with paintings of Moses and Aaron. – VAMPING HORN (cf. East Leake) found when the N aisle was converted into a parish room. Possibly C18. Nine are now known: outside the county at Potter Hanworth and Willoughton, Lincs; Braybrooke and Harrington, Northants; Haversham, Bucks; Ashurst, Sussex; Charing, Kent. – INCISED SLAB to William Meryng, 1510, very good quality.

CHURCH FARMHOUSE, S of the church.* Part stone, part brick, with one C17 shaped gable.

OLD VICARAGE, N of the church. With C17 timber-framing under the plaster.

HALL FARMHOUSE, away from the buildings of Hall Farm on the W edge of the village. A late C17 L-plan stone house with the E wall repaired in brick.

Roofless remains of a rectangular medieval stone DOVECOTE in the grounds of the Hall. Still lined with nest-holes.

DOVECOTE in the outbuildings at Beecher's Farm. Stone, square, two-storey, with a pyramidal roof.

---

* The following descriptions were kindly provided by Dr Summers.

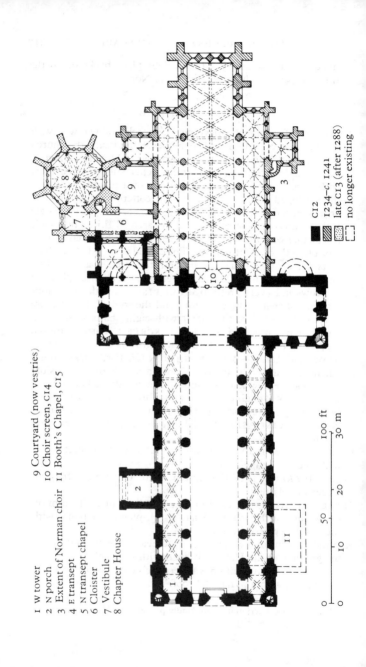

1 W tower
2 N porch
3 Extent of Norman choir
4 E transept
5 N transept chapel
6 Cloister
7 Vestibule
8 Chapter House
9 Courtyard (now vestries)
10 Choir screen, C14
11 Booth's Chapel, C15

■ C12
▨ 1234–c. 1241
▤ late C13 (after 1288)
▢ no longer existing

0    10    20    50    100 ft
0         10    20    30 m

## SOUTHWELL                                    7050

Although the minster has always had a *cathedra*, it was raised
to be head of a see only in 1884. In appearance the town is like,
say, Sherborne or Selby, a country town with the overpowering
presence of a large medieval church.

### THE MINSTER

Plenty of legends about the foundation and earliest history of the
minster exist. The first date which can be accepted as probable
is 956 for the grant of the Manor of Southwell with much land
around by Eadwig, King of the English, to Oskytel, Archbishop
of York, although the original charter has been lost.* By the
early C11 St Eadburh, daughter of the Anglian King and Abbess
of Repton, had been buried here. Then, between 1050 and
1060, we hear, Archbishop Kinsius gave bells to the *monas-
terium*. In spite of this designation the establishment at Southwell was apparently never monastic: it seems always to have
been collegiate, that is, a church to which a college of secular
canons, priests not monks, was attached. In 1108–14 it became
the mother church of the county and was obviously one of the
major churches in the province of York; just like the chapters
of Ripon and Beverley, its chapter was after 1171, except for
occasional visitation, entirely independent of York. It owned
or controlled about one-quarter of Notts and had certainly all
the regional influence of a cathedral (without incidentally possessing either a Dean or a Provost). The buildings, as we see
them, belong chiefly to three periods: (*a*) from 1108 onwards,
(*b*) from 1234 onwards, and (*c*) about 1288. These periods refer
respectively to (*a*) façade, nave, crossing, crossing tower, and
transepts, (*b*) E arm, and (*c*) chapter house.

NORMAN. Building began about 1108 under Archbishop 8
Thomas of York. Usually work started from the E, and of the
E end of Norman Southwell we know only from excavations.
It had a straight-ended chancel, not an apse, an arrangement
then almost unique in England, chancel aisles with apses, and
little apses attached to the transepts, that is (save for the chancel
ending) the same composition as many a major Romanesque
church in England and France (in Notts, for example, Blyth).
Whether a change of plan occurred between the chancel and
the surviving parts farther W, we cannot say, but it is a fact that

*According to a report of 1853 some late Saxon carved stones were re-used
in rebuilding the central piers. The dating cannot now be verified.

the decoration of all that exists now is of one kind, with the exception of the historiated capitals of the E CROSSING PIERS. Each of the capitals, with strong volutes and more old-fashioned than the scallop capitals in the rest of the minster, is carved with one scene. With one exception the iconography is quite simple but without continuity from one scene to the next. The scenes are the Last Supper, an unidentified scene including an Annunciation, a procession relating to the Entry of Jerusalem on the next capital, the Agnus Dei, and the Washing of Feet. They are among the most important examples of such capitals in England, comparable with those at Hereford (perhaps the first c. 1115), Westminster Abbey, and Reading. The technique of these, based on manuscript-drawing technique, is extremely linear, a criss-cross of folds in the draperies without any comprehension or system, and faces with large, staring eyes, consistent with a date of c. 1120. Most impressive of all are perhaps the N and S crossing arches, on enormously tall semicircular piers. The capitals consist of such tiny scallops and so many of them that they are only a fringe, not independent members of the structure (mass-effects rather than effects of articulation). The two stages of the central tower which appear inside have cable and wave decoration on the lower stage (the earliest in England, according to Sir Alfred Clapham), and zigzag on the upper stage. The composition of the TRANSEPTS is very strong and simple too: blank arcading the whole height of the ground floor, carrying a narrow gallery on the N side of the N transept and the S side of the S transept. Clerestory with wall-passage (cf. nave). The windows with one order and a roll-moulding in the arch or with big cable-mouldings or billet-friezes on the labels as their only ornaments. The W and E walls have the plainest entries into the aisles and chancel aisles, but on the E there was, farther away from the crossing, a larger opening into a chapel, both in the N and S transepts. In the N transept this was redone about 1260, and in the S transept it is blocked and was besides, before it was blocked, altered, for it now has zigzag decoration for the large arch and in addition a smaller doorway again with zigzag. Zigzag does not seem to occur at Southwell before about 1140 or 1150 (cf. the top storey of the crossing tower mentioned above), and so one must presume some later adjustment.* Above the larger openings on

9

---

* When the two acutely pointed and uneven arches with which the E chapel arch of the S transept had been filled were removed in the C19, the incomplete detail was invented.

the ground floor is a triple arch with a wall-passage behind which led from the S and N galleries to the galleries above the chancel aisles – a handsome motif, though a little out of keeping with the rest of the composition at Southwell.

The NAVE (144 ft long)* has seven bays plus the bay farthest w between the two w towers which is separated from the others by some solid wall carried up to the ceiling as pilasters towards the nave, necessary to help in abutting the towers. The slightly narrower w bay is different only in details from the others. Their system is as follows. The arcade has short circular piers, very short if compared with those at the crossing (S and N; for E and W are composite), and again insignificantly small many-scalloped capitals, some with a very minimum of decoration in the scallops. The arches have a billet frieze outside and then straight steps with a thin angle roll and a double soffit roll. The aisles are rib-vaulted, the technique of the vaulting still awkward, but the rib profile no longer of the most elementary: two ridges between two rolls (roll-ridge-ridge-roll). The aisle windows are quite large (but only the one farthest N W is original). To continue now with the elevation of the nave, the gallery above the ground-floor arcade appears to have the same undivided seven (or eight) openings on each side. But they were not originally meant to be like that. Corbels on the sides and an odd stump of a shaft downwards from the apex of the arch show that the intention was to subdivide the opening by twin arches on a colonnette (as, for example, at Peterborough and in many other places) and then leave the tympanum above these arches open and divide it only by another colonnette standing on the first and connecting it with the apex of the main arch. It seems an odd, uncalled-for idea, but it would not have been unique; for at Romsey in Hampshire it can actually still be seen executed about 1150, probably under immediate influence from Southwell (cf. the straight end to the chancel and at the beginning of the nave the very tall circular piers with small, many-scalloped capitals). The clerestory has much plain wall. The round-headed window openings have one order of short scalloped shafts. The wagon roof was only put in in 1880, but finishes the composition quite successfully.

It is a composition which combines in a remarkable way the robust with the lively. Although the piers of the nave are short and thick, the impression is not overpowering. The gallery is so proportioned as to let its arches appear to skip elastically to

* The other dimensions are width 63 ft, height 50 ft, tower 105 ft.

the E instead of weighing down on the ground-floor arcade. With the twin openings as projected the effect would of course have been even more agile. The same can be seen in the aisles, where the ribs create a busy shuttling forward and backward, very different from the inert masses of the groined vaults at Blyth. Altogether a comparison of Blyth and Southwell will elucidate the difference between the C11 and the more vivacious early C12.

Strangely, the clerestory windows are circular outside. Otherwise the side elevations are very plain, the aisle windows with a zigzag surround and then an order of colonnettes, the roof on a wavy corbel table. The N side has in addition a large, sumptuously zigzag-decorated NORTH PORCH, tunnel-vaulted (something very rare in England). Its lower storey is decorated by blank arcades inside with intersected arches and its upper storey by little windows facing N and again plenty of zigzag. The circular chimneys with conical tops are restored but based on original work. The transept gables have large horizontal zigzag bands with bands of dots between, slightly different on the N from the S. The central crossing tower has two orders, arcades with intersected and above with plain arches. To visualize its original appearance it should be imagined with a pyramidal roof.

The FAÇADE is unique in having pyramidal roofs to its towers. They were rebuilt in 1880 by *Ewan Christian*, the Ecclesiastical Commissioners' architect, on the pattern which they had until a fire of 1711.* To reconstruct in one's mind the original appearance of Norman churches it is essential to forget about the flat tops of the towers which we now see nearly everywhere, or indeed the needle-sharp spires of the type of, say, Norwich. Southwell comes much nearer to the ideal of the C12, and, indeed, the towers are the only ones besides Worksop surviving in full. In other ways the façade can now hardly be used to re-evoke Norman ideals, for the large central window belongs of course to the C15. The towers, slightly different from each other in detail, climb up with flat buttresses, without set-offs, but with six string courses crossing them, the lowest two continued from the aisle elevation. On the sixth stage, blank arcading carried all round, even over the buttresses. All the capitals

* The date of their construction is unknown. They are shown in Hollar's engraving in Dugdale's *Monasticon*, after a drawing, not correct in all details, by Hall. They were rebuilt after the 1711 fire and again, with flat roofs, in 1802 by *Richard Ingleman* (surveyor to the fabric 1801–8).

are of cushion type, and decoration here and in the central portal is again chiefly zigzag. There are five orders of columns to the portal, the capitals scalloped with little bits of ornament in the scallops. Inside it is of two orders, the outer one with pleated capitals and more zigzag, the inner one a continuous roll curiously broken at the haunches. Aisle-end windows C19, copied from the other aisle windows. They were three-light Dec before.

EARLY ENGLISH. In 1234 Walter de Grey, Archbishop of York (who rebuilt the transepts there), decided to pull down the Norman E end and replace it by a larger new one in an up-to-date style. The E ARM was lengthened by four bays, the new 23, 25 E CHAPEL, and a pair of E TRANSEPTS finished c. 1241.* The ensuing pattern is identical, for example, with Beverley and also Salisbury, that is, quite a usual pattern of the E.E. style, if quite impossible in any other country but Britain. Neither the double transepts nor the straight-headed chancel and E chapel found favour anywhere on the Continent. The elevation of the South-well E arm is something almost unique for its date in England. It is two-storeyed, not three-storeyed, that is it has no middle storey in the sense in which Lincoln and Salisbury and West-minster Abbey have them. Instead, the whole height of the nave wall is pulled together into two stages, the ground-floor arcade 22 with piers consisting of four major and four minor filleted shafts and deep hollows between (cf. Lincoln, St Hugh's Choir), moulded capitals, and finely profiled multiform arches, and the upper floor with a tall order of twin lancets for each bay, so tall that in it there are small insignificant openings from the exist-ing gallery behind, and above them, clerestory windows and a wall-passage in front of them. The idea may have come from Ripon, where c. 1175 an aisleless nave was for the eye divided in two instead of three storeys in a comparable way. Pershore in Worcestershire (1223–39) is more similar to Southwell, but probably independent. The E end at Southwell, which is aisle-less, is also two-storeyed, with two tiers of lancet windows. The shafts are mostly filleted, the capitals mostly moulded. Stiff-leaf capitals, however, also occur, especially close to the E end, and in the S aisle more than the N aisle. Otherwise there is dog-tooth and nailhead decoration and no other ornamental motif. The nave as well as the aisles are rib-vaulted, with slim,

---

* A slight break in level will be noticed in the sill of the upper storey where the replacement of the old meets the entirely new. There is a similar break in level further E which is unexplained.

resilient ribs springing from shafts which rest on corbels, that is are not carried down into the ground-floor piers. The vaults have ridge-ribs everywhere, an innovation of Lincoln of *c.* 1210, very un-French, but accepted almost at once everywhere in England. At the crossings of the ribs fine foliage bosses. With the exception of this motif the style of Southwell points clearly to Yorkshire. The designer's predilection for lancets and a rapid succession of upward-shooting lines is North English and different from the happy breadth of Lincoln. It is this emphasis on fine perpendicular lines which one remembers in thinking of the Southwell E arm. All shafts are duplicated or triplicated. All main mouldings are cut up into thin stringy lines. Even the consistent use of fillets on shafts acts that way: the eye perceives three lines instead of one. The appreciation of the solid drum-shape of a pier or shaft, which the Norman masons of the nave had so obviously possessed, has gone completely. Instead of it the love of the C13 belongs to the line, the line tensely stretched and carrying currents of energy. However, the general shape of the space is not as excessively tall as in contemporary French work; it is rather broad and shows, specially at the E end, a very clear horizontal division. So there is no excess either way.

The E arm stands as a monument to this style, the classic English Early Gothic style. To it also belongs the N transept chapel of two bays, opening towards the transept in two exceedingly steep arches. The detail inside, such as shafts (keeled), capitals, and vaults with ridge-ribs and foliated bosses, also dates this chapel as *c.* 1250 or 1260. Originally a pulpitum or stone screen between chancel and crossing of the same style may have existed (see the concealed stairs on the N wall by the SE pier of the crossing).

By *c.* 1260, we can assume, the building was once again complete. Nothing then happened to it until about 1288, when Archbishop John de la Romaine gave the decree to build a new
29    CHAPTER HOUSE. On the N side it was to be connected with the E arm by a corridor looking with a few cloistral openings on to a little courtyard W of the E transept. The courtyard is now alas taken up by vestries. A double doorway opened out of the chancel aisle into the corridor. The corridor leads to a vestibule, and the entrance to the chapter house itself is at right angles to this. The chapter house is polygonal, as English chapter houses are, but it differs from most others in that it is built without a central pier. That gives it a delicious feeling of airiness and breadth, although its size is not great. The glory

of the chapter house, the vestibule, the corridor, and the doorway from the E arm, however, is their decoration, exquisite and
by no means excessive. It consists almost entirely of foliage 28
carved with supreme skill to emulate nature. This realism was
the new ambition of the late C13, inspired by French mid-C13
innovations which English masons must have known. The
plants represented are chiefly maple, oak, hawthorn, ranun-
culus and potentilla, vine, ivy, and hop. It will never be possible
to determine how far they were copied from sketches in notebooks made during French apprenticeship or journeys, and
how far from nature. Both methods were no doubt used. That
the result is classic Gothic and not Victorian, that it has a soul
and does not only please the senses, is due to the fact that the
carvers were never satisfied with mere imitation but succeeded
in keeping stone as stone, in preserving intact the smoothness
and firmness of surfaces; in short, they achieved a synthesis
of nature and style. The climax of the whole is the chapter house 27
portal. Here alone Purbeck marble is used of which the Lincoln
architects were so fond. The contrast between the slimness of
the chancel with its majority of purely moulded capitals and
minority of stylized stiff-leaf and the ease with which the whole
chapter house and each capital spread themselves out is remarkable, a contrast which characterizes 1275–1300 as against 1200–
50 (see the Angel Choir in comparison with St Hugh's Choir
and nave at Lincoln). The development of the windows and
their tracery deserves attention too. Instead of the exclusive use
of lancets, there are now three lights grouped together with,
above, two circles containing trefoils, the topmost one a quatrefoil. That is in principle what the chapter houses at Westminster and Salisbury also do, and most richly the Angel Choir
at Lincoln. But in a few details Southwell goes beyond the
smiling classicity of these buildings of 1250–75. The designer
places a pointed trefoil above the middle light of the three into
its top, thereby breaking the perfect harmony. Similarly in the
vestibule (upper N window) there are trefoils not surrounded
by circles. Evidently the faith in perfection was wavering, and
indeed only ten or fifteen years after the completion of the
chapter house the clarity of the Early English style had finally
given way to the intricacies of the DECORATED.

Of this also Southwell possesses an outstanding example, the
PULPITUM or stone rood screen which was erected c. 1320– 37
40 to replace the one of c. 1240 or 1250* and restored in 1820 by

* Stone for it was being carried in 1337.

the *Bernasconi* brothers, who renewed the heads etc. The pulpitum is of the 'veranda type', that is with a w and an e façade connected by vaults. These little vaults possess flying ribs (like the Easter Sepulchre at Lincoln), rare in English architecture. The n and s walls have blank tracery with plenty of ogee, that is double-curved forms, the chief innovation of *c.* 1300 in tracery design. The w façade has two blank bays and three large openings with openwork ogee cusping. The e side is even richer, a two-storeyed composition with niches on the ground floor (one of them adorned with a diaper pattern of large undulating leaves, again very similar to Lincoln) and gables with blank flowing tracery on the upper floor. In the centre are much restored figures. Apart from these there are masses of small heads used in the same way as the c13 had already profusely used them. The crocketing of the gables of the pulpitum is prodigious, perhaps even more luxuriant than in the Lincoln pulpitum but very similar to the Percy tomb at Beverley on the one hand, the Lady Chapel at Ely on the other. It was evidently an East Anglian School which was called to do decorative work from Yorkshire to Cambridgeshire. Its genius is unquestioned, even if one cannot fail to realize how licentious 1320 was as compared with the nobler and more disciplined c13.

The SEDILIA must be by the same masons. The seats (unusual because there are five of them) are separated by freestanding buttress-shaped shafts connected with the wall by little embattled bridges. The stories told in many figures in the spandrels were so freely restored by the *Bernasconis* in 1820 that little remains of their original character.* Besides pulpitum and sedilia the early c14 contributed only the three windows of the n transept chapel. Their restless shapes need only be compared with the windows of the aisles added more than a hundred years later to understand the difference between the age of Edward II and the matter-of-fact, prosperous, this-worldly c15.

The PERPENDICULAR style, however, did more than that to the church. By knocking out nearly the whole of the centre of the Norman front and replacing it by one gigantic seven-light window with a broad, but still two-centred pointed arch, floods of light were admitted into the dark interior, but its original character was ruthlessly disturbed. The window is of a curious design. It has two transoms, the lower running through as usual, but the upper at alternating heights in the seven lights. A castellated pattern is thus formed, and the tracery details con-

*Ewan Christian* removed the Bernasconis' excellent plaster choir stalls.

tinue this up-and-down rhythm. It is entertaining, if somewhat hard. In addition, the C15 built a large chapel along the S aisle which was pulled down in 1784, and a pretty doorway in the S chancel aisle with good heads of a king and queen as label stops.

FURNISHINGS. Tessellated pavement, found on the W side of the S transept.* – TYMPANUM in the N transept. Too wide 11 for its present position, it seems to have been a triangular-headed lintel tympanum. Carved with St Michael and the dragon and, to the l., David rescuing his flock from the lion, the latter scene rare in sculpture but not in manuscripts and metalwork. Early C12 in style, with traces of the Anglo-Saxon Urnes style, e.g. in the entwined tail of the dragon. Underside unusually carved with bands of rich ornament. Not like the crossing capitals and possibly slightly earlier (from the previous church?), but very close indeed to the tympanum at Hoveringham (see p. 149). – FONT. 1661; octagonal; one of many put 75 up in Notts immediately after the Restoration (the same type at East Bridgford, Walkeringham, Newark, Orston, Scarrington, Shelford, Sibthorpe, Tythby, Whatton). Their plain panels with bands forming diagonal crosses with roses, fleurs-de-lys, and often cherubs' heads are easily recognized. The cover belongs to the font. – EAGLE LECTERN. Brass, c. 1510, found in the lake at Newstead c. 1780 and given to Southwell in 1805. One of a series made in the late C15 and early C16, probably in East Anglia, which includes those at Oxburgh, Norfolk, St Gregory Norwich, Holy Trinity Coventry, Lowestoft, Dundee, Newcastle Cathedral, St Michael Southampton, and Urbino Cathedral. – CANDLESTICKS, also brass; c. 1500. – BENCH ENDS. The usual poppyhead type; S transept. – MISERICORDS. Six of the C14 on the E side of the choir screen, part of the original stalls and all with human figures. – WEST DOOR. A superb example of an original C12 door with extensive large and simple scrolls developing out of the iron hinges. – NORTH DOOR to the porch, C14, with a pattern of ogee reticulation all over. – ORGAN CASE. One by W. D. Caröe. – SCULPTURE. Large wooden Virgin and Child by Alan Coleman, 1952, by the SE crossing pier. Brought from the chapel at Kelham Hall in 1974. – STAINED GLASS. The medieval glass gathered together in a S chancel aisle window is just a jumble, visually enjoyable for reasons quite independent of the original

* Saxon, according to Dr Ralegh Radford, and possibly part of the paving of a transept of the pre-Norman church.

composition of the pieces. – E window. The four lower lights contain important C16 French glass given in 1818 by Henry Gally Knight, who bought it in Paris with a provenance from the Temple church, demolished in 1795.* The scenes, with large figures in Mannerist attitudes, are, from l. to r., the Baptism of Christ, the Resurrection of Lazarus, the Entry into Jerusalem, and the Mocking of Christ. (Restored and adapted for their present position by *Miller* of London. RH) Upper lights 1876 by *Clayton & Bell*. – (E arm. Heraldic glass in the three N lancets possibly by *Miller*. RH) – Chapter house. Many small fragments without much interest arranged symmetrically in the large windows. Mostly Flemish C16–17, but in windows one and two fragments of English C13–15 glass and in window three C13 and C14 fragments including a large incomplete panel of the Betrayal of Christ and an Adoration of the Magi of *c.* 1300 from Gonalston. – VICTORIAN GLASS. In the nave aisles much brightly coloured glass by *O'Connor*, providing an excellent review of the firm's work (RH). Healing the Sick, Raising the Dead and Preaching to the Poor were shown at the 1851 Exhibition. – By *Kempe*, N and S aisle E windows, 1875 and 1880, good early work; S side sanctuary, 1898; westernmost N transept, 1907; N chapel, three windows. – MONUMENTS. Slab with a foliated cross in a round-arched recess in the N aisle. – Two incomplete incised slabs of *c.* 1300. – Headless alabaster figure of an Archbishop (*c.* 1450) in the S aisle of the E arm. – Archbishop Sandys † 1588. Alabaster, very lifelike, with the four small angels at his head and feet, on a richly moulded tomb-chest against the wall of which small figures of the members of his family kneel. The composition is nothing unusual, but the execution is better than most of the Elizabethan alabaster-work in Notts. There is (no wonder, one should probably say) nothing provincial about it. Repaired in 1852 by *Joseph Hall* the younger of Derby. – Bishop Ridding † 1904. Large bronze figure with a finely characterized head, by *Pomeroy*, 1907, kneeling at an alabaster prie-dieu on a tomb-chest; an altogether striking composition devised by *Caröe*. – Bishop Hoskyns † 1925. Bronze bust by *W. Reynolds Stephens*.

A large ROMAN VILLA lies beneath the minster and its cemetery. This may have been a courtyard house and is the largest villa yet known in the county. Part of one wing, containing a suite of baths, was excavated in 1959. A reconstruction of the

---

* See *Country Life*, CXIII, 1953, p. 896. The windows went to Lenoir's famous 'Musée des Monuments Français' which was broken up in 1814.

painted plaster from one of the rooms in the baths hangs on the S choir aisle in the minster. After the Roman building had fallen into ruins, at least one Saxon hut was erected on its site.

SURROUNDINGS OF THE MINSTER. The buildings that surround the minster reflect its medieval origins and collegiate status (cf. Lichfield). To the S, the remains of the medieval Archbishop of York's Palace, round the minster yard the prebendal houses of the non-resident canons who held livings from the minster, and to the NE the houses of the Vicars Choral who did the church offices of those non-resident canons.

BISHOP'S PALACE, on the S side of the minster. The Bishop lives in a large country-house-looking mansion, a remodelling by *Caröe* in 1907–9 of an C18 predecessor.* But this very informal gabled and roughcast building occupies and incorporates the W half of the remains of the Archbishop of York's remarkably large and monumental palace, rebuilt in the last half of the C14‡ and given its final shape (possibly largely rebuilt) by John Kemp (1426–52). It was almost finished in 1436. The N, S, and E outer walls of the courtyard-plan palace, destroyed in the Civil War, survive as the walled garden of Caröe's house. The original W range comprised the GREAT HALL in the centre with two-storeyed sections to the N and S of it.§ Incorporated into the porch of the modern house, the jambs of the doorway into the screens passage and, inside, the three-arched openings into the buttery and pantry and into the N–S passage between them. On the S side, now opening into the garden, the outside doorway to a detached kitchen which has vanished. Over this service end, the only medieval CHAMBER that survives intact. One jamb of the hall's tall W window nearest to the chamber can be seen. To the N of where the hall stood, on the first floor, is the Archbishop's PRIVATE CHAMBER (now wrongly called the Great Hall). The exterior walls of the S and E ranges survive up to the eaves. The S range contained two-storey LODGINGS for the Archbishop's staff: as well as window openings and fire-

---

* Recent unfortunate alterations, e.g. the removal of a S chimneystack to the E gable end (P. Howell).

‡ The earliest parts were attributed to Archbishop Thoresby (1353–73) but, although his extensive building work at York is well documented, there is no reference to any building by him at Southwell. Other candidates are Alexander Neville (1373–87) who sanctioned the building of a new college for the Vicars Choral in 1379 or Archbishop Arundel (1388–96) who 'while he was at Yorks he bestowed much building on divers of his houses'. *See* Dr Summers's *Prospect of Southwell.*

§ We owe this description of the medieval palace to Professor M. W. Barley.

places, there survive a double garderobe and, at the SE corner, a GARDEROBE TOWER entered by a flight of eight steps with a unique group of four closets round a central shaft. Above it a chamber with a newel stair corbelled out from the inner corner and leading to the roof. Along the E side were grand rooms at first-floor level, and at the NE corner the ARCHBISHOP'S CHAPEL: see the five-light window in the gable, an image bracket, and the remains of a gable cross and bell-turret. At the S end, probably belonging to his PRIVATE HALL, carved

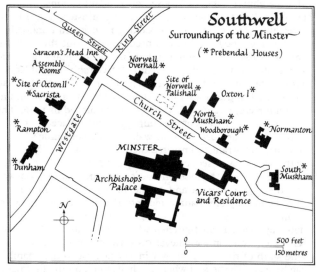

Southwell
Surroundings of the Minster
( * Prebendal Houses )

Queen Street
King Street
Saracen's Head Inn
Assembly Rooms
*Site of Oxton II
*Sacrista
Norwell Overhall *
Site of Norwell Palishall *
Oxton I *
North Muskham *
Woodborough *
Normanton *
* Rampton
Westgate
Church Street
* Dunham
MINSTER
Archbishop's Palace
Vicars' Court and Residence
South Muskham *
N
0        500 feet
0        150 metres

corbels on the S wall, a four-light window in the gable (balancing that in the chapel), and a well-carved doorway to the chamber in the garderobe tower. Between the chapel and private hall, a single garderobe, a fireplace with elaborate jambs, and the reveals of one seven-light or paired two-light windows indicate what may have been a STATE CHAMBER. The naming of these rooms is hypothetical: a great ecclesiastic would have required several suites of such rooms. The N wall, now very low, has only two fireplaces; there must have been more lodgings here. The fabric supports the assumption of two building periods. The plinth of the external walls and lower parts of the chimneystacks together with porch jambs and the archways to the service block look later C14, the remains of the windows and doorways in the s and e wall c15. Apparently between the two in date, the windows in the Archbishop's Chamber.

The PREBENDAL HOUSES are set back from the road on the N and W sides of the churchyard, not on a precinctual plan but in an informal arrangement resulting from the layout of the sites farmed by the prebendaries. Even the houses of little visual importance are of architectural interest for, although mostly brick and Georgian in external appearance, many contain evidence of their medieval origins.* At the e end of CHURCH STREET, SOUTH MUSKHAM PREBEND is gabled and H-plan and basically medieval, but with stucco and sashes of before 1814 and an early c18 staircase. In the w gable some timber-framing and part of a crown-post roof (cf. Severns, Nottingham). The next two houses have handsome classical façades: NORMANTON PREBEND a three-storeyed façade of c. 1765 with a central Doric columned porch, and WOODBOROUGH PREBEND a new front added to an older house by *Richard Ingleman* between 1819 and 1838. Five bays and three storeys with a pedimented doorcase and outer ground-floor windows in recessed blank arches. OXTON I (now CRANFIELD HOUSE) is the best design of all, remarkably fashionable for c. 1700–20, especially when compared with the old-fashioned late c17 Residence (*see* below). Probably built by Canon George Mompesson, wealthy son of William.‡ Brick with stone dressings, two-storeyed, with a hipped roof with dormers, one segmental pediment over the door, and another above the first-floor central window which breaks into the cornice. Next, NORTH MUSKHAM PREBEND has a façade of c. 1809 with a central pedimented bay, overlaying a house of c. 1769 which in turn may have been added to a c17 house. W of it, WILLOUGHBY HOUSE and PALISHALL HOUSE of 1794–6 on the site of Norwell Palishall, and, on the corner of King Street, NORWELL OVERHALL, divided into the NATWEST BANK and MINSTER LODGE. Behind the plain ten-bay façade of 1784 and the modern addition for the bank, there is some very old fabric, the only house with stone construction. The other houses seem to have been timber framed. The E and N walls are rubble, over 2 ft thick, up to first-floor level, with rubble foundations on the E side to within 5 ft of the front wall. At

---

* As Dr Summers has discovered; *see Prospect of Southwell.*

‡ At the same time, 1701, another member of the family was building the more ambitious Mompesson House in the close at Salisbury.

ground level on the E a C14 two-light window, and in the brick W wall a timber post.

Past the Saracen's Head and the Assembly Rooms in WESTGATE until 1970 stood OXTON II or the RED PREBEND,* and next to that SACRISTA PREBEND (Minster School Headmaster's House) with a stuccoed Tudor-Gothic exterior to a range of rooms built across the front between 1774 and 1798. On the S side a range probably of c. 1818 and in the angle older fabric. RAMPTON PREBEND next to it is early C17, brick and gabled, with an early C19 stuccoed façade, and last is DUNHAM HOUSE (now offices): a plain seven-bay front of c. 1780 concealing a C16 or C17 range one room deep. Regency range with semicircular ends and plasterwork of 1805. Entrance porch also 1805. Unfortunate extension by the District Council c. 1970.

25 VICARS' COURT AND THE RESIDENCE is a delightful group of well-proportioned but entirely unembellished five-bay brick houses with hipped roofs, two l., two r., with the Residence at the far end in the middle: the very *beau idéal* of what the designers of Welwyn Garden City were trying to achieve. The building history is more complicated than the harmony of the group suggests. The Residence was built in 1689–95 on the site of the Vicars' Hall for the prebendaries who had no residences after the Civil War, the construction supervised by the famous William Mompesson of Eyam, and the work surveyed in 1690 by *William Johnson* of Nottingham. In 1772 a rear wing was added by *William Handley* of Newark to the totally irregular C17 building, and in 1779–81 the present four houses of the Vicars Choral were built.‡ Then, in 1783, *Carr* of York was paid £15 for surveying the Residence and for designing additions to it. The Carr-influenced design finally accepted in 1785 was by *William Lumby*, Surveyor and Clerk of Works at Lincoln Cathedral.§ Lumby squared up the façade to the court (the windows S of the entrance light only a tapering passage) and

---

* This had a façade of c. 1808 masking what must have been the earliest brick building in Southwell. It was already referred to in 1553 as 'Le Reed Prebende' and was of English bond with timber-framing in the gable, and first-floor beams similar to those of c. 1510 in the cloister walk at Jesus College Cambridge. This brick part was possibly built against a timber-framed hall replaced in the C17.

‡ *Francis Ingleman* was consulted about the design, but the handwriting on the drawing looks like *William Lumby*'s (*see* Dr Summers's *Prospect of Southwell, op. cit.*).

§ *Lumby* had previously taken over a commission from *Carr*. Carr made designs for Lincoln Gaol in 1774, but it was built in 1785 to Lumby's design.

altered the interior. But these were not the last alterations, for in 1806–9 *Richard Ingleman* raised the roof, made a carriage entrance on the W, rebuilt the NE wing and added another 'for the uniformity of the E front'. In 1956 both wings were demolished, leaving their façades as screen walls linking the E façade to the vicars' houses; architects, *Broadhead & Royle*.


### THE TOWN

HOLY TRINITY. 1844–6 by *Hadfield*, in an unimaginative Notts C13 style.

(BAPTIST CHAPEL, Nottingham Road. Long stuccoed rectangle of three storeys with the centre bay projecting at front and back. Built in 1808 as the parish workhouse and converted *c.* 1839, with the chapel occupying the full height of the S wing and rounded centrepiece. Manse at the N end. CS)

(METHODIST CHAPEL, Prebend Passage. 1839, brick, with front pediment and entrance loggia. CS)

Of the other buildings in the town, the SARACEN'S HEAD and the ASSEMBLY ROOMS in WESTGATE have already been mentioned in passing. The former is a coaching inn with an unpretentious long cottagey front with a C16 close-studded timber-framed first floor, originally jettied but underbuilt in brick and stuccoed in the late C17 (date plaque 1693). Original carriage-arch into a yard flanked by framed buildings. Much of the internal structure destroyed by alterations. The Assembly Rooms, by its side and now part of the hotel, were built in 1805 by *Richard Ingleman*, architect to the minster chapter, with a small, plain, but formal façade. To the N of the Saracen's Head evidence of C17 timber-framing (Nos. 1 and 3 Market Place). C17 brick in Queen Street (a moulded label over a gable window, *c.* 1630) and in King Street (No. 58 and the Wheatsheaf opposite with plain gables and string courses. Almost every substantial house in the town was built between 1790 and *c.* 1820 (e.g. in Westgate, Clyde House, Norwell House, and Kelham House, and in Queen Street, Hardwick House).

Further N BURGAGE GREEN is reached, and here is the severe rusticated gateway to the former HOUSE OF CORRECTION, designed by *Richard Ingleman* in 1807, extended in 1817 and again in 1868 by *R. C. Sutton* of Nottingham. Here also some late Georgian houses: BURGAGE MANOR (where Byron's mother lived *c.* 1810), Regency and stuccoed, THE BURGAGE, and ELMFIELD HOUSE. In Burgage Lane, BURGAGE COURT, very ugly, with Venetian and Diocletian windows flanking a central bay on the main façade, and HILL HOUSE. The general impression of the town is not inspiring but pleasant in a friendly way. John Byng would still be right who wrote in 1789: 'A well-built clean town such a one as a quiet distressed family ought to retire to.'

### OUTSIDE THE TOWN CENTRE

NORWOOD PARK, to the NW. Five-bay brick house in Carr of York's manner (cf. The Residence). Two and a half storeys high, with a pediment for the three central bays. In this case the central window is of the Venetian pattern. The supposed date is 1763–4. *See* p. 448

GREET HOUSE (former Thurgarton Union Workhouse), just in Upton parish. 1824, brick, three storeys, with seven-bay wings flanking a full-height canted bay faced with a blind-arched recess.

MAYTHORNE MILLS. An industrial hamlet built by the river Greet N of the town for water power, probably first for cotton spinning but certainly later for silk, for which it is well known. Two mills stand end to end, one (N) three-storey, the other four-storey. There are two blocks of cottages opposite the mills; another range of buildings contains a manager's house and agricultural buildings which appear to be of slightly later date.

On the river Greet below Maythorne Mills, a large water-powered CORN MILL dated 1867 but with many additions. It has been used, augmented with steam and more recently electricity, for milling other products.

## SOUTH WHEATLEY

7080

ST HELEN. A ruin since 1883. What remains is the Norman chancel arch, low, of two orders, very decayed, and the W tower, ashlared and unbuttressed, with thickets of elder at its foot. The village almost joins up with North Wheatley.

## STANFORD-ON-SOAR

5020

ST JOHN THE BAPTIST. C13 S arcade of round piers with moulded capitals and double-chamfered arches, C14 N arcade of octagonal piers with finely moulded capitals and double-chamfered arches. Two-light Dec windows in the N aisle, three-light Perp in the S aisle and the clerestory. The church is much restored, by *W. S. Weatherley* in 1893–4, and the chancel virtually new. A few minor C13 fragments built into the vestry. The W tower has diagonal buttresses and battlements with a panel frieze below. – MONUMENTS. Brass to a priest; *c.* 1400. – Incised slab to an Illyngworth and wife, 1408, unique because the only alabaster slab with indents for brass inlays. – Recumbent effigy of a civilian holding his heart in his hand (cf. West Leake, Averham); late C14. – Thomas Lewes † 1694. Cartouche with heads of putti and two skulls. – Caroline Dashwood † 1840 by *Thomas & Edward Gaffin*. – In the churchyard, good slate HEADSTONES, including the first work (to Henry Fawks † 1730) by *William Charles*, with a motif much used later, the winged hourglass.

THE MANOR HOUSE, across the lawn. Late Georgian, stuccoed, and of villa size. (Facing the churchyard two blocks of cottages and a pumphouse, dated 1836 and 1839, built to match an adjacent early C18 house with oval panels in the gabled wings. DOE)

STANFORD HALL (Co-operative College), 2 m. NE in a fine landscaped park. Brick mansion of Charles Vere Dashwood, 1771–4 by *Henderson* of Loughborough. Originally very plain (cf. Wilford Hall), but much altered and extended *c.* 1892 by *W. H. Fletcher*, altered again for Sir Julien Cahn by Messrs. *Allom* in the late 1930s and extended for the college. The original entrance side has forward-curving wings, only the lower part of them C18. Centre of seven bays divided by modern giant Ionic pilasters and with a pediment containing a coat of arms. C19 or C20 outer wings of three storeys. The garden side, also with later outer wings, is much less formal, with a 3/8 bay-window as its centre motif. Allom's interiors are in various styles. His theatre (1937–8) in one wing is one of the best private theatres of the period. Three good C18 fireplaces.

## STANTON-ON-THE-WOLDS     6030

ALL SAINTS. The old village has all but gone owing to the depopulation on the Wolds which is noticeable in other places as well (*see* Upper Broughton, Wiverton, and many others), but new housing has sprung up nearby. The exterior of the tiny church is lushly overgrown, but the Norman masonry of the

S side can still be seen. There is no division between nave and chancel, and instead of a W tower only a turret. – FONT. Norman, arcaded, but very badly preserved. – STAINED GLASS in the E window by *Powell & Sons* with angels by *Henry Holiday*, 1868.

4030

## STAPLEFORD

ST HELEN. The typical steeple of west Notts: battlemented tower and much thinner spire without broaches. The lower part of the tower C13 (see, for example, the W door in a very fragmentary state), the bell-stage early C14. Nave, aisles, and chancel must also have grown to what they are now in the course of the C13. The S and N arcades both have octagonal piers and double-chamfered arches, but differ in the capitals. Spectacular chancel E window of *c.* 1290 or 1300, five lights with intersecting tracery except at the very top, where wilfully (it is the perversity of East Anglian flowing tracery which is heralded) just one pointed quatrefoil is inserted (cf., for example, Averham). Restoration of 1878 by *T. G. Jackson*,* who also designed the memorial chapel of 1923. – FONT COVER. Copper with a wooden knob; second half of the C17. – RELIEF. Wood-carving, Last Supper, C18 (Flemish?). – MONUMENTS. Good incised slab to Robert Tevery, in armour, and wife, 1571. – Gervase Tevery † 1639 and wife, alabaster, two recumbent effigies in front of an aedicule background. With four figures of children kneeling frontally below the slab on which their parents lie. The original composition not known; much changed about.‡ – George John Borlase Warren † 1801 in action after landing at Aboukir, by *Bacon Jun.* Low urn against the usual obelisk. – CROSS in the
4 churchyard. By far the most important pre-Conquest monument in Notts. A large shaft with base and top, renewed in 1820. The original shaft still 10 ft high, with rounded corners and strongly tapering. The decoration mostly interlacings, but on one face is a doll-like figure at the top. The date may be as late as *c.* 1050. – CHURCHYARD GATE. Nice early Victorian ironwork transferred from Wellington College in 1922.

(WESLEY PLACE CHAPEL. Rendered three-bay front with pediment, dated 1782–1842. CS)

* According to Mr Roger Dixon.

‡ According to Mr H. J. Louw it seems close in style to work by *Hendrik de Keyser*, who worked 10 m. away at Newstead in 1636–9 and was living in Nottingham in 1643.

The MANOR HOUSE was demolished in 1977.*

As at Beeston, the most interesting buildings are industrial. An important group of FRAMEWORK KNITTERS' COTTAGES in Nottingham Road, mainly on the S side at the bottom of a steep rise. Nos. 106–112 is a terrace of four three-storey cottages all with the original and typical long top windows back and front. No. 106 has toothing for a potential W extension. Nos. 118–120 have had their long top windows and central tunnel entrance altered, but No. 122 is intact. Opposite, Nos. 119–121 only have the original knitters' windows at the back. No. 124 is more complicated: two-storey with modern bay-windows at the front but knitters' windows on the ground floor at the back. To the E an arched entry with frame-shop over, and in the garden a decaying two-storey frame-shop with long top-floor windows.

On the S side of Derby Road at Broad Oak Drive, a two-storey office building, the last remains of a large late C19 LACE FACTORY; demolished. The factory was as decorative as the offices, in polychrome brick with stone dressings and glazed tiles at eaves level.

## STAUNTON-IN-THE-VALE                    8040

The church forms an exquisite group with Staunton Hall, although both buildings are, strictly speaking, altered and restored almost out of recognition.

ST MARY. Much rebuilt in 1854 by E. J. Wilson of Lincoln (JPB), on the same lines as before, with the Perp tower at the E end of the N aisle. Corbel table with gargoyles. The N arcade with octagonal piers C14. N doorway with ivy leaves in the capitals. – FONT. Norman, with intersecting arches on little columns. – SCREEN. 1519, interesting in comparison with other similar and undated Notts screens. – MONUMENTS. Plenty to various Stauntons. – Coffin lid with stylized cross. – Cross-legged knight, c. 1300, with very painstakingly carved (or re-carved?) chain-mail. – Lower half of another. – Lady with wimple. – Knight in sunk relief; a hand runs across his body decorated with a heraldic shield so that the middle part of the body is hidden and only the upper part and feet appear; c. 1330 (cf. North Collingham, also Gilling, Yorks). – Job Staunton

* Double pile, brick and stone dressings, 1689. Symmetrical fenestration was the only thing in which the late date came out. Otherwise still the plain undecorated gables of the Jacobean time and still mullions.

Charlton, Esq., and his wife. Standing figure of Faith by *West-macott*, 1811.

STAUNTON HALL.* The main alterations were made in 1794, when bay-windows were added, the interior arrangements changed, and the upper floor heightened so that all gables except that of the porch projection disappeared. Six mullioned windows of three to five lights, all with arched heads (i.e. early), survive at random on the stone cement and brick patched front. An inscription records building in 1554, another on the porch 1573, the latter a finely carved panel. The back with a canted bay and projecting wings is all late Georgian.

DOVECOTE, at Staunton Grange. Brick, unusually tall, with 1,100 nesting places; C17.

A ROMANO-BRITISH RURAL SETTLEMENT, occupied mainly in the C4, lay ½ m. w of the village on a site now obliterated by gypsum extraction.


STAYTHORPE *see* AVERHAM


6040                    STOKE BARDOLPH

Only a plain brick CHAPEL of 1844.
The medieval house of the Bardolphs stood here.‡


7070                       STOKEHAM

ST PETER. Just nave and chancel; restored in 1928. A s aisle was pulled down in the C17 or C18 according to the s nave windows (cf. Upper Broughton, etc.). As to nave and chancel, the masonry and two lancet windows prove a C13 date. – CHEST. Long, rough, and absolutely undecorated. Can it also be C13?


5040                       STRELLEY

ALL SAINTS. Without any doubt the most important church on the w outskirts of Nottingham. Its importance lies in its chancel, endowed in 1356 by Samson de Strelley who died

---

* Said to be the Willingham of Scott's 'Heart of Midlothian'. A print of it in the Abbotsford edition (vol. 2, p. 124) is clearly recognizable.

‡ Excavations (1957) revealed a rectangular C12 great hall extended *c.* 1200 by a two-storey wing at the E end. Occupation ceased with the attainder of the Bardolph barons soon after 1400.

about 1390 and lies buried with his wife (who died in 1405) in the centre of his chancel. The chancel is large and wide, of a type not rare in C14 Notts. The E window is new, the N and S windows large, of four lights, straight-headed, without any display of tracery. N and S transepts still with late flowing tracery, but of a kind often to be found in the second half of the century. Aisle windows and nave arcades of the same period too. The S porch also, with a steep stone roof without transverse ribs, has nothing that would contradict the C14. Only the W tower in its lower part, including the arch into the nave, is considerably earlier (C13). It may have received its battlements and eight pinnacles at the time when nave, aisles, and chancel were completed and embattled. The clerestory is the only addition to the church later than c. 1400. It was restored c. 1850 by G. G. *Place* and again in 1895 by C. *Hodgson Fowler*. – PULPIT. Jacobean back panel and sounding board. – FONT. Exceptional in shape: eight-sided, almost undecorated bowl on nine supports with ogee arches to connect them. – ROYAL ARMS. C16; well preserved. – STAINED GLASS. Scattered fragments in N windows: one a St Ugbertus, C14. – In the S chapel E window some good Flemish panels, C16 and C17. – (N chapel E to someone † 1856; looks like *Warrington*. – E window 1914, surely by *Burlison & Grylls*. RH)

We can now return to the chancel, the furnishings of which afford the most complete example in Notts of the riches of art which a generous and pious family would bestow on the church of its manor. Sir Sampson de Strelley built the church. So his MONUMENT is the centre: an alabaster tomb-chest with angels 43 standing quietly and holding shields (cf. Willoughby-on-the-Wolds) and with the two recumbent effigies, he in the armour of c. 1400, she wearing a fantastic, Phoenician-looking headdress. Their faces are of English immobility, but their hands are united. His feet lie against a lion, hers against two pet puppies. Under his head an infidel head. On the floor surrounding this tomb are incised alabaster slabs to John de Strelley † 1421, and another now unrecognizable, and a double brass of good quality to Sir Robert Strelley † 1487 and his wife. Same workshop as at Clifton and Wollaton. Moreover, in an unusually splendid recess (very similar to that of Richard Willoughby at Wollaton) lies John de Strelley † 1501, with his head, like 56, 57 Sir Sampson's, on that of an infidel. The recess has a horizontal top with three demi-figures of angels and elaborate cresting. Above this a canopy, panelled and with well preserved little figures of the two St Johns and Abraham with souls in his bosom. John Strelley's helmet is hung up against the facing wall.

All this display of family pride and anxiety for well-being after death is separated from the congregation by the best preserved ROOD SCREEN in Notts. It is very tall, in five broad divisions each subdivided into four extremely slender panels, their mullions running up to the top of the main arches. Each panel has an ogee arch thickly crocketed and otherwise chiefly trefoil and quatrefoil motifs (none of the Perp panelling yet which is so predominant, for example, at Newark). The openwork coving is especially enchanting. The cresting is restored, the rood new.

STRELLEY HALL, next to the church. Medieval walls (stone with buttresses) of some buildings connected with the old hall incorporated in the roadside wing of the C18 brick stables of the new hall. By *Thomas Gardner* of Uttoxeter, 1789–92 (Colvin), a large, absolutely plain brick house of seven by five bays and two-and-a-half storeys, now all cemented. Entrance and garden fronts pedimented. Stone porch ornamented with angle pilasters, half-columns, and niches. In the SW corner a vaulted room, much earlier in date.* Beautifully landscaped park with sunken road and orchard wall hidden by an earth bank. Round the Broad Oak pub in the single village street, some late C18 brick ESTATE COTTAGES built by the Edge family of the Hall.‡

BELL PITS. In the grounds of the school, earthworks mark the site of C17 coal-working.

# STURTON-LE-STEEPLE

ST PETER AND ST PAUL. No steeple in fact, but the tall tower with twelve pinnacles can be seen for miles. As one comes nearer it appears finely set back across a field. The bell-stage windows of three lights are almost as tall as at Dunham. Lower stages mid-C14. The rest of the church is by *Hodgson Fowler*, built after a fire in 1901–2.§ Only the N chancel wall survives (see the Norman window and doorway). Small fragments with beak-

---

* According to Dr Summers and Professor Barley the remains of a medieval tower have been incorporated here.

‡ According to Professor Barley.

§ He faithfully reconstructed the appearance of the church before the restoration of 1870 by *Ewan Christian*, who removed the clerestory etc.

head and chevron from a Norman doorway or chancel arch are built into a vestry wall. The present five-light E window with ogee reticulation (cf. Annesley) appears on old photographs as originally on the S side of the chancel. The N arcade was *c.* 1200 (see the tall circular piers and crocket-like leaves of the capitals). The W respond is original. The rebuilt S arcade C14. – The pre-1901 STAINED GLASS has been reproduced: W window, original to Richard Battye † 1873 by *Clayton & Bell*, reproduction by *Heaton, Butler & Bayne*; SE window, one of the Foljambe Memorial windows (cf. Ollerton, Wellow, etc.) by *Heaton, Butler & Bayne*, the original 1875; chancel window, reproduced from the original cartoon probably of *c.* 1870 by Messrs *Drake*. – NW window 1901–2 by Messrs *Newberry*; E window 1925 by *Kempe & Co.* – MONUMENTS. Lady Oliva de Montbegon † *c.* 1236. Mutilated female effigy with Lombardic inscription, against the N wall of the tower. – Dame Frances Earle † *c.* 1687, a life-size standing figure like a Roman matron against an altar background with columns and a segmental pediment.

TOLLHOUSE. Thought to be the only turnpike tollhouse left in the county. Pentagonal, two-storey.

FENTON. *See* p. 126.

## SUTTON BONINGTON

ST ANNE. The church of Sutton, back from the road, on the hillside, small, with a W bellcote, much restored. It is, however, still recognizable that the N arcade with circular and octagonal piers and moulded capitals and the aisle belonging to it are C13. The chancel cannot be much later, judging by one of its windows. The nave must be early C14. – FONT. Octagonal, with quatrefoil panels. – STAINED GLASS. Three windows 1897 and 1901 by *Kempe*. – MONUMENT to a man in armour, alabaster, in a recess in the chancel, *c.* 1475.

ST MICHAEL. The church of Bonington, larger, and with a W tower facing the road. Its spire is 135 ft high, ashlar-built, C15, with angle buttresses at the corners and battlements. Band below the battlements as at Bunny. The arcade to the S aisle is C13 with circular piers and moulded capitals, that to the N aisle C14 with octagonal piers and leaf capitals. The E respond, however, with upright stiff-leaf must have been left over from an earlier arcade. The arches also are identical with those on the S side: double-chamfered. Seats run round the piers. The

aisle windows are C14 with ogee reticulation, the clerestory is
C15, chancel 1878. – SCREEN and PULPIT date from the restoration of 1895 by *W. S. Weatherley*, assistant in the 1870s
to G. G. Scott Junior. – FONT. C14, with quatrefoil panels and
three projections for book, salt, and candle. – STAINED GLASS
by *Kempe*: E window 1897; a N window 1901.

Sutton and Bonington are one village with a long main street. It
was one of the best villages in the county until spoilt by post-
war suburban growth and the loss of a considerable number of
timber-framed cottages, several of cruck construction.

(THE HALL, Main Street. The most important house in the village, and very attractive. Earliest part late C17 or early C18, two-
storey with attics, roof with dormers covered in Swithland
slates. Symmetrical brick façade with stone quoins, stone window surrounds refitted with sashes, and segmental pediment
over the doorway. Considerable late C18 alterations and additions. An excellent open-well staircase with turned balusters,
late C17–early C18, in the inner hall; nice panelled doors and
linings; late C18 wood and marble fireplace surrounds etc. THE
STABLES (No. 88 Main Street, now flats) are later C18 than
the main house, of ambitious two-storeyed design, with
grooms' quarters over the carriage arch and blank arcading to
both floors. NS)

Also in MAIN STREET (from the N end) on the E side: No. 118,
early C18, plain brick with projecting strings; opposite, No. 143,
late C17 brick with ornamental string courses carried over the
windows as labels (cf. East Leake, Rempstone, North Wheatley) and the adjoining Primitive Methodist Chapel of 1832, now
part of the house. No. 145 (WHITE HOUSE) is a plain late
C18 house with two bows to the garden and a pilastered doorcase. Well proportioned and well preserved, including its fine
semicircular staircase. On the corner of BUCKS LANE, a late
medieval timber-framed house, gabled and jettied to the Main
Street: now possibly the oldest house in the village. In PARK
LANE, S of Main Street, Nos. 6–8 (HOBGOBLINS), unusual
for being stone-built in this area. Probably late C17, double pile,
with wooden cross-windows. (Large chimneybreast on the rear
elevation, and inside a two-tier stone chimneypiece ornamented
with Ionic pilasters. In the garden old walling and a medieval
doorway: it is said that there was a monastic grange on the site.
DOE) SOAR LANE runs N from the top of Main Street. No.
I is timber-framed with brick-nogging on a rubble plinth.

Jettied over the street and dated 1661 on the bressumer. The long first-floor windows of sliding casements are probably a later insertion to light a framework-knitting shop.

Pagan ANGLO-SAXON CEMETERY of the C5 to C6.

## SUTTON-CUM-LOUND

6080

ST BARTHOLOMEW. The chancel windows repay a visit to Sutton. Five-light in the E, three-light in the S, and with the most unbridled curvilinear tracery, sinuous leaf shapes, one might say, in long-drawn-out lines, very much in the Lincolnshire and South Yorkshire style. The SEDILIA and PISCINA group inside is somewhat disappointing after this. Otherwise a Norman chancel arch, wholly rebuilt, with two shafts on each side. For the rest Perp: the usual arcade, the usual W tower with pairs of angle buttresses, battlements, and eight pinnacles. Nave, aisle, and chancel also display battlements and pinnacles. The embattled low S porch has a stone roof supported on transverse arches (cf. St Mary, Nottingham). – SCREEN. Of c. 1500. – BENCH ENDS. Of the asymmetrical type, with tracery panels and poppyheads. – SOUTH DOOR also late medieval; no ironwork display. – STAINED GLASS. E window by *O'Connor*, 1856.

## SUTTON-IN-ASHFIELD

4050

ST MARY MAGDALENE. One stone with some Norman zigzag in the W wall. The PILLAR PISCINA also C12. N arcade with circular piers and very elementary waterleaf capitals, but an E respond with a graceful triple shaft and a delightful mid-C13 capital with stiff-leaf and human heads. The N door and the uninteresting S arcade C13 too. Of the C14 a three-light window with ogee reticulation re-erected against the S chancel wall. Then in 1391 a sum of money was left for the 'making and completion' of the steeple. The buttresses are diagonally placed, the spire rises behind the battlements without broach (the usual type of the district). Two-light bell-openings, the arch-curves replaced by straight lines (cf. North Muskham), a late feature which makes a very slow completion of the job probable. Of the C15 the clerestory and the aisle windows. Chancel rebuilt 1854, aisles 1867, enlarged E window 1907.

UNITED REFORMED CHURCH, High Pavement. 1905–6 by

*George Baines & Son.*\* In the fanciful free-style Gothic popular at the time. Red brick with stone dressings.

ST MICHAEL AND ALL ANGELS, Outram Street. The nave and the NW tower added to chancel (1886–7, *James Fowler* of Louth) by *Louis Ambler* 1905–9. All C13 and very conventional, without a spire. Stone.

ST JOHN'S METHODIST CHURCH, Brook Street. 1966 by *Terry Bestwick*, who has produced some other successful designs for the Methodists (cf. Nottingham and Ilkeston, Derbys). This one is intriguing. Block walls support a complicated system of tie-beam trusses, but the roof is glazed, so the church comes into its own at night when lit inside.

The old part of the town to the NW round the church is quite villagey. The church is up a leafy lane with the Victorian school building distinctly Tudor-Gothic, on one side. Opposite the lane is CHURCH LANE which leads to CHURCH STREET. Here (next to the Pantiles), a small gabled late C17 or early C18 house, the windows altered, but still with the low shape and hoodmoulds. One mullioned window visible in an earlier wing at the back. The best house is above the road at the corner of DEVONSHIRE SQUARE. Low two-storey house with three-light mullioned windows under continuous hoodmoulds, i.e. early C17. E of this the IDLEWELL CENTRE, an inward-looking shopping precinct and civic offices which makes no contribution to the townscape: architects *Archer, Boxer Partners*, 1969–73. In fact the town seems to lack a real centre, which the SUTTON CENTRE, between the Idlewell Centre and High Pavement, tries to remedy. It is one of the early attempts to weld together community facilities and a comprehensive school, and is apparently quite successful. The school, day and sports centres, and theatre are imaginatively laid out on a sloping site. Towards High Pavement some ugly features: on the roof fibre-glass pyramids lighting the sports hall, boxy windows on the first floor. CLASP clad in red aggregate, by *H. T. Swain* (County Architect) in three stages, 1971–3, 1972–7, 1976–8.

WINDMILL. The shell of a four-storey stone tower mill of *c.* 1820–30. Beside the pool near Lucknow Drive, Eastfield Side, the remains of Samuel Unwin's large COTTON MILL of 1770. The remains are slight, but the Gothic style can be discerned.

\* According to Christopher Wakeling.

## SUTTON-ON-TRENT 7060

Between the river and the A1: the church and the old part of the village nearest the river, the newer developments following the old North Road. A few pleasant houses including a timber-framed cottage and the pretty early C19 NAGS HEAD with veranda.

ALL SAINTS. This is the unusual case of a restoration by a good SPAB 'anti-scrape' man (*William Weir*, 1932) which succeeded in leaving the impression of the old and time-worn. The S porch, for example, was left as curiously unfinished as it was found, with no gable at all above the depressed arch of the entrance. The W tower was rebuilt in 1902–3 (traces of Saxon foundations were found underneath it), but except for the buttresses and the top stage, it still looks C13 (see the two-light bell-stage openings, still without tracery, and see also the tower arch). As one would assume, this actually represents a stage of development (single-chamfer) about fifty years earlier than the upper part of the tower. The chancel arch and the nave arcades, S as well as N, correspond to the later stage (circular piers, moulded capitals, double-chamfered arches, E and W responds keeled). The most splendid part of the church, however, is the MERING CHAPEL of c. 1525, externally with elaborately panelled battlements, pinnacles growing out of the buttresses, and late Perp four-light windows, and internally with a two-bay arcade whose pier is panelled and has a castellated capital. The arches are finely moulded, the outer walls also partially panelled and provided with several castellated brackets for statues. The tomb-chest has a Purbeck marble top but no effigies. The SCREEN towards the aisle is exceptionally elaborate and in its tracery and leaf friezes so close to that at Laxton, dated 1532, that the assumed date of the architecture is confirmed. The whole represents the stage just before the last flourish of late Gothic in the Babington Chantry at Kingston-on-Soar and then the coming of the Renaissance. The clerestory incidentally, of six closely set three-light windows, must be about contemporary, and also the five-light chancel E window with its straight-sided arch. The same really ungothic shape in the N window arches of the chancel (cf. North Muskham). – STAINED GLASS. Small old fragments in the chancel. – (Two E chancel windows 1875, surely by *Wailes*. – N aisle E, 1927 by *Geoffrey Webb*. RH) – BENCH ENDS. A few old ones with tracery and poppyheads in the chancel. Good for Notts.

WINDMILL, S end of the village. Brick tower mill of *c.* 1814. No cap, but floors remain, with a loading dock, one pair of stones, and bridge tree *in situ.*

MANOR HOUSE at Grassthorpe, ¾ m. N. Brick, of 1697, with C18 outbuildings. Sashes on the plain five-bay front replace mullion-and-transom cross windows.

7040                              SYERSTON

ALL SAINTS. Virtually new, though the late C14 straight-headed windows with ogee tracery in the aisleless nave represent the old ones. C13 W tower, slim, unbuttressed, and unstepped. Porch rebuilt in 1724. – PULPIT. 1636, with tester. – CREDENCE TABLE. 1629. – FONT. Octagonal, with some tracery.

SYERSTON HALL. Built by the Fillinghams, agents of the Duke of Rutland. Simple five-bay, two-storey brick block with a stone-columned porch; 1793–6. Across the back a one-bay-deep extension of 1812 with a pilastered doorcase.* The DOVE-COTE with blank arcades outside, COACH HOUSE, and GARDEN HOUSE betray a professional hand, that of Mr *Griffiths.* Extensive farm buildings of 1809 and after. (Jacobean panelling in the stable block. DOE)

4060                              TEVERSAL

76 ST CATHERINE. One of the most rewarding village churches in the county, chiefly because of the exceptional completeness of its C17 furnishings. The structure of the church goes back to the C12. Norman S doorway, not in its original order: the outer order quite jumbled up, and the inner with allegorical representations in medallions (lamb, dove, serpent, cross, three fishes, standing saint) also of doubtful logicality. The church was provided with aisles in the C13. The S arcade comes first: circular piers and double-chamfered arches, but one pier quatrefoil (or rather square with strong demi-shafts on all four sides; cf. Mansfield), the shafts with fillets carried up into the

---

* Several plans are dated 1793, including a sketch plan signed WG, possibly *William Gauntley* of Bakewell who was closely associated with the Fillinghams and who made a proposal for the 1812 extension. The house as built conforms more closely to a 'plan of the house by Mr *Kirk*', the carpenter.

moulded capitals. The N arcade also has circular piers, with dogtooth and nailhead ornament, crudely carved heads as label stops, and double-chamfered arches. One lancet window in the chancel. Many of the windows renewed late in the C17, when the interior was redone. (Incidentally, could the odd imitation-Gothic tracery in the chancel S window also be of that date?) Box-pewed, altar rails with balusters, a short altar table with bulbous legs, a combined pulpit and reading desk, plenty of large pews for special people, the squire's pew with large, tall, unglazed window openings towards the nave, and at the corners twisted columns, and a specially pewed-off space for the font, W of the squire's pew. In addition there is a C17 timber roof (with indications of Gothic detail) and a W gallery. The most likely date is *c.* 1675. Indeed the most ambitious of the MONU-MENTS in the church are those to Sir John Molyneux † 1691 and his wife, excellent workmanship in the cartouches and the two busts in niches; broken pediment, curved upwards. – Sir Francis Molyneux † 1674. Bust in oval medallion, quite absurdly bad, especially in the draperies. Same hand as at Clifton (Nottingham) † 1666. – Sir John Molyneux † 1741 and his wife. Also busts, but free-standing against a conventional background. – Sir Francis Molyneux, Gentleman Usher of the Black Rod. 1812 by *Josephus Kendrick*; profile in oval medallion formed by the Garter. – Two incised alabaster slabs with early Renaissance detail: Roger Greenhalgh † 1563 and his wife † 1538. – SOUTH DOOR. May well be C13; just upright battens and very little of curving of the iron hinges. – In the churchyard, two of the earliest slate HEADSTONES in the county, one dated 1631 (MWB).

THE MANOR (formerly TEVERSAL HALL). Now looks neo-Jacobean, due to a remodelling in 1896 by *MacVicar Anderson*, but basically an older house previously remodelled in 1767.

(RECTORY. Late C17, altered in the C19 and C20. Five-bay façade with sashes. In the stone outbuildings one small mullioned window. NS)

A rural backwater, reached only by country lanes and isolated from C19 urban development in the W of the county. Its stone buildings have more affinity with the Derbyshire stone tradition than with Notts brick building.

# THORESBY

Thoresby was enclosed out of Sherwood Forest in 1683 by William Pierrepont, fourth Earl of Kingston. Of his house,* destroyed by fire in 1745, nothing remains. It was remodelled in 1685–7 from one built in Charles I's reign by a team of the most excellent craftsmen, several of whom were first employed at Court and are later found at Chatsworth: *Benjamin Jackson*, master mason; *Edward Goudge*, plasterer; *John Nost* and *C. G. Cibber*, carvers; *Verrio & Laguerre*, painters; and *Rene Cousin*, gilder. According to *Vitruvius Britannicus* (vols. I and III), the front was executed by the same hand that afterwards built Chatsworth.‡ This has been taken to mean *William Talman*, son of a Wiltshire gentleman and officer in the Customs, who rose quickly, almost from nowhere, to become Comptroller of the King's Works with Wren at Hampton Court in 1689. And yet the drawing of the front is among Wren's at All Souls' College, Oxford, and is not in Talman's hand, which brings into question whether it was Talman Campbell was referring to. More probably he meant *Benjamin Jackson*, mason at Thoresby and Chatsworth. The design, conceived at the same time as Wren's similar designs for Winchester Palace, bears a resemblance to later designs by the Office of Works (Hampton Court, Greenwich) and by its members, Wren, Hawksmoor, and Vanbrugh (e.g. Castle Howard, Easton Neston). Talman is not mentioned in the accounts; only a payment of five guineas to 'Sir Christopher Wren's man', possibly Hawksmoor, in June 1686. It seems that the Office of Works, rather than Talman, formulated this novel and influential country house type. C17 Thoresby was of brick with stone dressings (cf. Hampton Court), on a courtyard plan, with a main front of thirteen bays and two storeys plus an attic crowned by a massive balustraded parapet.§ The rectangular silhouette used for a house was preceded only by the Duke of Newcastle's Nottingham Castle of 1674 (and possibly by the undated state rooms at Bolsover), which, like Thoresby, recognizes Italian palaces as the source

* In which Lady Mary Wortley Montagu was brought up.

‡ It also gives the date as 1671, which does not agree with the accounts dated 1685–7 or with the succession of William Pierrepont to the earldom and the enclosure of the park.

§ Hawksmoor, writing in 1731, said that the house burned down as soon as it was finished and an attic storey, which existed by 1690, was added at the refitting. Was *Talman* involved at this or a later stage? Vanbrugh includes the fifth Earl among those who regretted employing Talman.

of the design. Thoresby, although more refined than Nottingham Castle, had to some degree a coarseness of detail characteristic of the Artisan Mannerist style, with closely spaced windows, a congestion of pediments on the first floor, and busts in broken pediments. Of *Cibber*'s garden and architectural sculpture a sphinx survives.

The second house, by *Carr*, 1767–71, of red brick with a stone basement and a central feature of four Ionic columns, was modest in size (like one in St James's Square, said John Byng in 1789). The grounds gave Horace Walpole in 1772 'no temptation to stop'.*

In 1865–75 a new stone mansion was erected, far more ambitious than any other of the Victorian age in the county, and a lasting monument to the self-confidence of at least one section of the C19 nobility. The third Earl Manvers, who commissioned the building from *Anthony Salvin*, champion of early and mid-Victorian neo-Tudor design in England (ever since his Harlaxton, Lincolnshire), must have strongly felt what of representational dignity he owed to his station. The church at Perlethorpe on the Thoresby estate bears witness to that almost as strongly as the house. The main fronts are on the S and E, 182 and 180 ft long respectively. The entrance is on the E under a central tower of Burghley style; the windows l. and r. are symmetrical too, but to achieve the irregularity so desirable to Victorian designers, the corner motifs differ conspicuously. The S side is conceived on the same principle: dominant central motif, symmetrical fenestration, but very unequal corner effects. On the l. behind the corner appears the main tower over the staircase adding yet another bold accent. The detail is disappointing, especially in comparison with the ingenuity of the detail at Harlaxton. Most of it is probably by Salvin's son *Osbert*. The plan follows the formula used at Harlaxton and at Keele. The fall of the ground from W to E (together with an artificially-made terrace on the S side) is employed to create a plan in which the first floor is at ground level on the S and W fronts. A large internal courtyard goes down to the ground floor, lighting the large number of service rooms which are conveniently out of the way under the main rooms on the first floor, but without a basement outlook. In the parts with no outlook on the E, S, and W were the storerooms and cellars. The arrangement of rooms (although altered somewhat on the ground floor

---

* *Capability Brown* made proposals for improvements c. 1759, which were amended by *Repton* in 1791, but he only altered the C17 cascade.

to accommodate visitors) still reflects the organization of vast Victorian households.*

The dramatic feature of the plan is the ascent from the low entrance hall on the E front into the three-storey great hall on the first floor. This has a bay-window 24 ft high, a hammerbeam roof, and an elaborate fireplace (by *Daymond* of London), but most satisfying is the organization of space, with the staircase and bedrooms connected to the hall by low arcades leading to galleries that overlook the hall. The main staircase rises in a series of double flights under the central tower. S of the hall is the main suite of rooms: drawing room, library (with an incredibly elaborate fireplace showing Robin Hood and Little John and Major Oak, carved in oak by a Mansfield carver), breakfast room and dining room, all rising through two storeys with the best bedrooms above them. In one of the bedrooms, an C18 fireplace by *John de Val* from the second Thoresby. W of the staircase is the family wing (still used as such) with what was Lord and Lady Manvers's suite on the level of the hall and the nursery and schoolroom suites above. Altogether there are twenty-nine rooms on the *piano nobile*, and it would be tedious to count the rooms on the other floors. The style of the interior is mainly Jacobean with some C18-style reception rooms, e.g. the Blue Drawing Room, where the ceiling plasterwork is Rococo-ish to complement the C18 wall panels and chandeliers brought from the Château de Coigny.

On the S front a pair of arched GAZEBOS with strapwork cornices (cf. Kelham Hall). Of the Georgian buildings the KENNELS, with rusticated pilasters on a two-storey gatehouse feature, survive at the far end of the E axis, and the BRIDGE over the lake. (The late C18 or early C19 BUCK GATES, re-erected on a new site in 1959, have good C18 lead statues of bucks. Also early C19, MONUMENT to Spencer Perceval † 1812 with a fine sarcophagus on a pedestal; a VASE by *Coade & Sealey*, 1802; the NELSON PYRAMID, covered with slates and with a plain domed room inside; and a fluted DORIC COLUMN to a horse, 1834. DOE) The STABLES are contemporary with the house.

BUDBY. *See* p. 84.
PERLETHORPE. *See* p. 289.

---

* Indeed the house was completely inhabited and used as it was when the era of Disraeli conceived it until the 1950s, a rare occurrence. It is still in private hands, and not now open to the public.

# THORNEY

St Helen. 1845–50 by *Cottingham*, who is better known for his
writings than his buildings. Sumptuous hamfisted Norman
exterior with w façade and bellcote. Unaisled interior with big
roof, the sort of thing which in the later C19 was designed for
the *Sängerkrieg* in *Die Meistersinger*. Of the old church two C15
arcades have been re-erected in the churchyard.

Thorney Hall was demolished *c.* 1964.*

Thorney Hall Cottages, just across the Lincs border.
Brick, dated 1649, but still with steep gable and low triangular pediment incorporated in the cornice band between
storeys – that is, of Elizabethan type. Originally the manor
house.

2 m. e at Broadholme was a house of Premonstratensian
canonesses founded in 1135–54. A brick farmhouse on the site
incorporates some carved medieval stones in the walls.


# THOROTON

St Helen. The w tower shows by the unique feature of its mid-
C14 ogee-headed w niche that the workshop of Southwell screen
and Hawton chancel was responsible for it. The niche itself is
provided with a tripartite pedestal for statuary. To its l. and
r. are small panels with figures of angels. Angels also to l. and
r. of the ogee arch. The whole is crowned by the typical steep
crocketed gable as at Southwell and Hawton, and the figures
have the same rippling hems of the draperies down both sides.
The bell-stage has two-light windows with ogee reticulation.
There follows a pierced quatrefoil frieze and gargoyles, and
then the spire with three tiers of dormers. Of an earlier church
a minute double-splayed C13 window built into the e wall of
the present vestry and a small piece of a displaced Norman
arch bear witness. The n arcade of circular piers and double-
chamfered arches with moulded capitals was once E.E. too, but
is terribly restored (in 1868–9 by *J. H. Hakewill*, who rebuilt
the chancel. Of this date STAINED GLASS in four windows by
*Lavers & Barraud.* JPB)

Dovecote, in a farmyard. Circular, medieval, stone, the same

* It was a seven-bay brick block of two-and-a-half storeys with segment-
headed windows and pedimented doorcase on the front. On the side four
Venetian windows, and at the back sashes with rusticated voussoirs, a Venetian
window over the door, and a round window in the central pediment.

type as Sibthorpe. Only the ground floor and half the first floor survive; with a thatched roof.

THORPE

The Roman town of AD PONTEM* lay on the Fosse Way ½ m. w. Like Margidunum (*see* East Bridgford), the first Roman occupation of the site was in the form of a fort, with a large annexe on its northern side. This work is not precisely dated but probably belongs to the period A.D. 50–75. Thereafter, following a familiar pattern, a road-side township grew up, eventually to receive defences, first in earthwork, later in stone. There is as yet no evidence that the site was occupied after the Roman period, but little excavation has been carried out inside the defences.

ST LAWRENCE. Tower C13 with diagonal buttresses, with a roof added when the tower was restored and the church rebuilt in 1873–7. – FONT. Made up of two fragments, with an unusually pretty C17 cover in the form of open ribs curving to the top knob. – MONUMENT. To the wife of Sir William de Thorpe (chancel s side). Much damaged; later C14.

THORPE-IN-THE-GLEBE *see* WILLOUGHBY-ON-THE-WOLDS

THRUMPTON

ALL SAINTS. Unbuttressed w tower with the typical masonry windows and quoins of the C13 to early C14. (Restored by *Street*, who rebuilt the chancel at the expense of Lady Byron in 1871. His fittings include the alabaster REREDOS, PULPIT, ORGAN CASE, FONT, and STAINED GLASS: E window by *Hardman*. P. Joyce) – MONUMENT to Gervase Pigot † 1669. Large inscription plate. At the top two angels hold up drapery. A stylized tree and swags at the foot. – In the churchyard a decaying medieval FONT, carved with an arcade and three crosses.‡

THRUMPTON HALL. Built between 1609 and 1616–17 by Ger-

* A bridge across the Trent here carried the Roman road from Ancaster towards Southwell.
‡ Information from R. Alvey.

vase Pigot from Weston-on-Trent across the river in Derbyshire and brought up to date by his son shortly after the Restoration. A rainwater head on the N front is dated 1662. Brick with
stone dressings. A symmetrical plan of the H-type, once thought
to incorporate the mansion of the Powtrell family that stood on
the site.* Loggia on the entrance (s) side between the wings
(two columns supporting three arches) brought forward before
1791 and glazed c. 1830. On this side the mullioned-and-transomed windows are of three lights in the wings and of the cross-
type above the loggia.‡ The N side was altered in the C18 with
Gothic glazing to the windows and to the loggia, which was
probably added at that time. It was Gervase Pigot II († 1669)
who gave the gables their fashionable Flemish outline by adding
the wavy cresting that Hollar shows in his engraving. To
accommodate a new staircase he also rebuilt the W wall with
a straight parapet between two chimneystacks masking the
gable and a little belvedere tower, but this was altered in the
C18 by the removal of the belvedere and the addition of a balustraded parapet. The staggered mullion-and-transom-cross
windows light the new staircase, of generous proportions, 72
square, with an open well and balustrade fully carved with
acanthus scrolls (cf. the contemporary examples at Thorpe
Hall, Eltham Lodge, and Forde Abbey).§ The Artisan Mannerist style doorcases with lugged architraves and side scrolls
in the staircase hall are also familiar from Thorpe Hall. The
saloon doorcase and its fireplace (with marble medallions of
c. 1785) are the most classically refined. More robust woodwork
in the Oak Room, and in the N W corner of it an early C17 spiral
stair to the cellars and the upper floor, broken off when the W
wall was constructed. The hall of the Jacobean house may have
occupied the whole of the cross wing, now divided into hall
and library. On the N side of the hall two pillars supporting
the upper floor suggest that the cross wing was widened at some
time (perhaps to accommodate two rooms on the upper floor),

---

* Mr Oswald (*Country Life*, 21 May, 1959, p. 1138) disagrees with the con-
clusion that the close-studded partitions and linings to the walls inside antedate
the Jacobean structure. During the transition between timber and brick building many houses, even in the early C18, had stud and plaster internal walls
(MWB).

‡ The latter light the post-Restoration saloon, and it is difficult to believe
that this was ever lighted by the two storeys of two-light windows that Hollar
shows in his engraving of 1676.

§ And in Notts at Woodborough Hall and Holme Pierrepont (p. 147) (similar
but simpler).

presumably by Gervase II, as the panelling is of that date. At the E end of the hall the original early C17 dog-leg staircase with a solid, and perhaps original, balustrade. Adjoining, outbuildings with Flemish gables, built in 1830–1 but faithful to the style of Gervase I's surviving dairy. Turreted gatehouse of c. 1830. The whole picturesque group lies by a lake, formerly a backwater of a peaceful stretch of the Trent.

In the village street almost all the gabled brick houses were built c. 1700–45 by John Emerton of the Hall, whose initials are carved on the datestones. Most houses are slightly altered, some with the Gothic glazing familiar from the Hall. Among the best in the county of early C18 estate building (cf. Bunny and Bradmore).*

On Redhill, the N portals of the London to Derby RAILWAY TUNNEL, almost baronial castellated structures. The original portal of 1839 had one tower only containing rooms. It was copied, to make a symmetrical composition, in 1901, when the line was doubled.

# THURGARTON

PRIORY CHURCH OF ST PETER. Thurgarton was founded as an Augustinian priory in 1119–39. What remains now is a terribly mangled fragment of a building of about 1230, and as nothing E of the third bay of the nave survives, it is quite possible that excavations, which could easily be carried out in the gardens of the house, known as Thurgarton Priory, would reveal the original plan of the E parts of the C12. The church must at one time have been quite large. The two-tower W front, deprived entirely of its S tower, had about the same width as Southwell, and the size of the bays is, if anything, larger than at Southwell. The elevation of the surviving bays is again not wholly preserved. The N arcade is renewed (by Hine, 1852–3), the S arcade original. Its first bay, that is tower bay, has strong composite piers with fillets on the shafts and continued into the capitals; and these capitals are overhanging, just as at Southwell. The other two piers are very thick, one octagonal with four thin attached shafts (like St Benedict, Lincoln), the other quatrefoil with thin diagonal shafts with shaft-rings in the four hollows. All arches are simply double-chamfered. On them there was a twin-opened gallery (see the S side of the N

* According to Professor Barley.

tower, inside) and presumably a clerestory. Now the vaulting-shafts which stand on the capitals simply carry a Victorian timber roof. The chancel is Victorian too (by *Hine*), and the centre of the w front was altered at the same time. The group of five lancets cannot have been there. As broken-off fragments on the l. higher up show, there was an arcading beginning there. So presumably a small blind arcade stood where the lancets stand now, and above it the main windows and gable rose higher. The w portals are genuine and of impeccable E.E. taste, the middle one with nine colonnettes on each side, the N one with five. The N porch and N doorway again of the same type. The NW tower, on the other hand, is oddly bitty in design (a frequent E.E. shortcoming). The outer buttress is wider than the inner, and the blank arcading and fenestration of the two and of the centre betray no system whatever. Maybe the s tower would have balanced these discrepancies to a certain extent, but the whole would never have made a really unified composition. But then, has the E.E. façade of Lincoln that quality? In spite of the comparison with Lincoln which, owing to the date of Thurgarton, one is always inclined to make, there is not really much connection. The main piers especially, which are so massive as to appear Norman in character if not in detail, and the amount of plain wall above them are derived neither from Lincoln nor from Southwell. – BRACKET AND CANOPY, E wall of the chancel. An elaborate, beautiful, and unrestored piece of decoration of about 1330. – Three CHOIR STALLS with misericords, probably C15, salvaged and put up in the chancel; from the E, a man with outstretched hands, a bearded man's face, and foliage. A fourth, in another hand, with two wrestlers (window shelf behind stalls).

THURGARTON PRIORY was bought after the Dissolution by William Cooper. The present house, built in 1777 by John Gilbert, stands in almost the same relationship to the church as the house at Newstead, i.e. over the undercroft of the w range of the medieval cloister. But here, for all its enthusiasm for ruins, the C18 did not allow such sentiments to interfere with domestic comforts. The usual C18 classical scale of the façade is unrelated to that of the church. Brick, seven bays, two and a half storeys, with a projecting pedimented three-bay centre. The windows, Venetian on the first floor, semicircular above, and the pilastered and pedimented porch mark the centre by their shapes. Later, one-and-a-half-storey wings on the N and s, the latter built over the foundations of the s tower of the church. The *ex-situ* stone in the cellar, with the initials W C and date 1589, is meaningless in the history of the present house, which was built from scratch.

CASTLE HILL, in Thurgarton Park. Small, square earthwork set on a spur. A Romano-British phase was succeeded by an early medieval cemetery. Later occupation included metalworking activity. A medieval rectangular building may have been a mortuary chapel of Thurgarton Priory.

STATION, SE of the village. A specially nice example of the early neo-Tudor stations on the Nottingham–Lincoln line: 1849.

THURGARTON DUMBLE. Late C17 or early C18 sheepwash of unusual and complicated construction.

A ROMAN VILLA lay in Wood Meadow, 1 m. SW of the village. It was of the winged corridor type.

6030                 TOLLERTON

Safely away from the main Nottingham–Melton Mowbray road stands the group of Rosclaveston Manor and Tollerton church with its early C18 rectory.

ST PETER. Rebuilt *c.* 1812. The stuccoed outer walls and W tower witness that date. The tower has odd, stiffly Gothic windows, archaeologically highly incorrect. On the first floor over the W entrance porch the SQUIRE'S PEW, with fireplace, opens towards the nave. The nave arcades are still recognizably C13 (though rebuilt in 1908), as is the blocked E window of the N aisle. The most interesting feature is the MAUSOLEUM to Pendock Barry's wife Susannah † 1811. It is separated from the S aisle by a good neo-Greek iron gate. The interior has a glass ceiling on three semicircular arches. In two niches, N and S, obelisks with inscriptions. All the details poor. – PISCINA. In the chancel: one of the rare Norman shaft-piscinae, the shaft diapered, the capital-like top with scrolls.

ROSCLAVESTON MANOR* (St Hugh's College). Built *c.* 1675, much altered under George II, when it was known as Tollerton Hall, and again by Pendock Neale Barry *c.* 1800. Throsby illustrates it in 1791 in its Palladian pre-Pendock Barry form, i.e. three-and-a-half-storey central block of three bays with Vene-

---

* The name is a corruption of Troclauestune (Domesday Book), probably applied by Barry in a spirit of antiquarian snobbery (NS).

tian and Diocletian windows and three-bay, one-and-a-half-storey link wings to slightly taller one-bay pavilions.* It is shown after alteration in a watercolour by Thomas Hearne † 1817. In the remodelling of the garden front, the pavilions were removed, and the links were raised to the height of the main block, which was given a canted bay-window. Bays articulated by thin square turrets, the angles by octagonal buttresses. The entrance front is entirely new and not exactly aligned. Symmetrical and heavily castellated, of nine bays with a central *porte-cochère*, its Gothic arches now glazed, a central tower, and a higher stair-turret on one side. Gothic tracery in the lower windows. The symmetry of the stuccoed façade, too prim to be truly picturesque, is made picturesque by a wing projecting on the r. at an angle and continued in a (derelict) cloister, which leads to the church. The group is, however, now divided in two by a brick wall across. Nasty extension on the garden front and some of the turrets on the central and staircase towers removed. Inside, the best room, the library, is classical.

## TRESWELL 7070

ST JOHN THE BAPTIST. General appearance Perp, that is w tower ashlar-faced with diagonal buttresses and battlements. Battlements on nave and s porch too. The arcade between nave and N aisle is also Perp (see the battlemented corbels at the E and W ends of the arcade). Octagonal piers, double-chamfered arches. Battlemented corbels also in tower arch and chancel arch. The s door is, however, C13, and the chancel (the only piece of worthwhile architecture in the church) early C14, with intersected and elaborately cusped window tracery (five lights in the E window). – FONT. Octagonal, with quatrefoil panels with shields.

## TROWELL 4030

ST HELEN. Chancel C13 (see the lancets of the N wall and the simple SEDILIA with pointed trefoil niches of curved plan). Porch with stone roof on four transverse ribs, in detail unusually early (cf. St Mary, Nottingham). Arcade C14; clerestory,

---

* Throsby's illustration is probably not accurate. He based it on a 'field picture' by the engraver, Wigley.

w tower, and most windows Perp. Restoration of 1890 by *Hodg-son Fowler*. – FONT. Octagonal, C15, with quatrefoils and battlements. – STAINED GLASS. E window 1892 by *Kempe*.

Good FARMHOUSE with C18 windows, modillion cornice, and pedimented dormers, opposite the church.

(TROWELL HALL, ½ m. E, on the other side of the M1. Mid-Victorian Elizabethan-style house in brick and stone. Looks very like *Hine*'s work, cf. especially Flintham Hall. JPB)

# TUXFORD

ST NICHOLAS. All embattled except the chancel. A nice, uncommon effect is the rood-stair turret rising above the nave roof. S porch with two large square niches l. and r. of the entrance. The generally unified external appearance is deceptive. The steeple is an early example of its type. It has the diagonal buttresses of so many Notts late C15 towers, but W door and windows prove it to belong to the early C14. The broad spire with its one tier of dormers is of *c.* 1357. Nave rather short and tall, with four largish clerestory windows. The chancel, dated 1495 (the gift of Thomas Gunthorpe), has the same five-light E window as East Markham. The side windows are generously spaced too. Inside, the N arcade with circular piers, double-chamfered arches, and moulded capitals is clearly C13, the S arcade with octagonal piers may be *c.* 1300; the chancel arch and the N chancel chapel stand between. – FONT. 1662, with conical cover dated 1673. – At the E end of the S aisle STONE CARVING of St Lawrence on the grid, badly preserved and apparently bad anyway. Above it STAINED GLASS *c.* 1500: figure of St Lawrence. To the r. SEATED FIGURE on a head-corbel, probably a Virgin; only the lower part preserved, seems good C14. – SCREEN. Perp, of unusual tracery detail. – MONUMENTS. Built into the N wall of the N porch demi-figure of a priest in a quatrefoil (cf. Gamston, also Gedling). – Cross-legged Knight, bad condition, C14. – Alabaster Lady, C14, also badly preserved. – Sir John White † 1625 and wife, recumbent effigies, not too good, he on a tier a little higher than hers and behind her. Framed by Corinthian columns and with a deep semicircular arch.

An attractive centre with an urban feel, said to have been completely rebuilt after a fire in 1702 and certainly Georgian in character, no doubt because of the position at the crossing of the Great North and Lincoln Roads.

Opposite the church the C18 OLD VICARAGE behind big trees. Nice doorcase.

GRAMMAR SCHOOL (County Council Offices, Library, etc.), Lincoln Street. Founded 1669 by Charles Read and built soon afterwards (cf. Read's stone grammar school at Corby, Lincs, founded in 1673). The type of five-bay, two-storey brick house with hipped roof and dormer windows which appeared all over England in the last quarter of the C17. Brick quoins and an odd bit of 'Artisan Mannerism' about the doorway: rusticated brick pilasters with knob finials to l. and r. and a floating segmental arch over the inscription under the eaves. Inside, the school-room on one side, the master's house on the other, and between them an enormous chimney and formerly a bell-turret. At the back a projection with original staircase with thin, diminishing, turned balusters.

TUXFORD HALL, Lincoln Street. Plain façade but eccentric at the back, with two huge one-bay bows flanking the entrance with stepped castellations and Gothic glazing.

NEWCASTLE ARMS, Market Place. Broad, simple, Georgian seven-bay front, plastered, with porch and two canted bays flanking it.

LOCKUP, Newcastle Street. 1823. Brick, with two blank panels each side of the door corresponding to the cells inside.

Two brick WINDMILLS without caps or sails. Longbottom's Mill at Mill Mount (N on the B1164), possibly the only restorable mill in the county, has more machinery than any mill except North Leverton. Weston Mill, 1 m. s at Stone Road End, is mid-C19 (cf. Harby).

WESTWOOD FARM, 1½ m. w. A large series of earthworks. Undated, but probably Romano-British or medieval.

## TYTHBY 6030

HOLY TRINITY. With a small W tower, brick above, stone below. The N arcade is rebuilt, the s arcade of two bays, C14, which goes well with the tracery of the chancel windows. Those of the s aisle are C18. But the main point about the church is its Georgian FURNISHINGS: pulpit with reader's desk, high deal box pews, squire's pew, high chancel rail, W gallery. – The

FONT is octagonal, with the date 1662 on the panels (cf. Southwell).* – One poppyhead BENCH END.

# UNDERWOOD

4050

(ST MICHAEL AND ALL ANGELS. 1889–90 by *J. A. Chatwin* of Birmingham for Earl Cowper of Beauvale. Ambitious Dec. Massive SE tower with an open belfry. Oak-shingled spire added in 1891.)

# UPPER BROUGHTON

6020

ST LUKE. A small church built of a strangely coloured brown sandstone (ironstone) so badly weathered that the white outer surface is now a delight to the painter and a despair to the antiquarian. The buttresses of the lowly tower are virtually worn off. Quatrefoil frieze below the battlements as usual in this part of the county. More fragments of such a frieze built into the porch of 1733. In the porch a fragmentary Norman tympanum with vertical stripes, vertical rows of diapers, and a very crude figure in the r. corner. The church originally had two aisles. The S aisle was pulled down when the porch was built. The wolds were going through a poor time then: medieval prosperity was gone, and new agricultural methods were only just beginning to appear (*see*, for example, Wiverton). Of the S arcade only one bay survives, built into the wall. The double-chamfered arch is round, the capital moulded, but still with dogtooth (Transitional, *c.* 1200 or a little later). The N arcade is later still, but also C13, octagonal piers and a little nailhead decoration in the capitals. (N aisle and chancel rebuilt in 1854 by *S. S. Teulon*. – PULPIT, PRAYER DESK, and LECTERN after the designs of the late Mr *Wyatt*, architect – which one? JPB) – FONT. Octagonal, with C14 tracery. – Many early C18 slate HEADSTONES with raised inscriptions by the same anonymous craftsman as at Hickling.

(GENERAL BAPTIST CHAPEL, S of the church. 1795, brick with unsympathetic cement rendering. Galleries destroyed and interior turned round. CS)

Several timber-framed cottages, some perhaps as late as the early C18, many modernized. (WILLOW COTTAGE on CROSS GREEN is C17, with very large square panels and diagonal braces at eaves level. DOE)

* It could be a re-carved medieval font, according to Professor Barley.

# UPTON
## Near Southwell

ST PETER. The W tower made conspicuous by not eight, as bigger churches in this part of Notts often have, but nine pinnacles, that is eight and one bigger and taller one in the middle. The bell-stage openings large, Perp, three-light, with one transom. The tower was also intended to be used as a dovecote. The windows of the church much renewed, but the Perp S window of four lights (cf. Holme and the Muskhams) certainly original. As for the interior, the N arcade and tower arch are good C13. Piers with four shafts between deep hollows (cf. St Peter, Nottingham). The W piers have these shafts round, the E ones keeled. Moulded capitals, double-chamfered arches. N transeptal chapel with two segment-headed recesses in the N wall and a squint towards the chancel. Low-side window in the S wall of the chancel. Chancel windows C14. Restoration 1893 by *Hodgson Fowler*. – CHEST. With star-shaped iron decoration. May well be early C13.

UPTON HALL (Royal Horological Institute HQ). A stuccoed neo-Greek villa of *c.* 1830 by *W. J. Donthorn*. On the garden front an impressive portico of fluted Ionic columns in the recessed central bays. On the main front the domed centre projects. Interior probably remodelled in 1895, when additions were made for a Mr Warwick.* (At the rear, a C17 mullioned window indicates remains of an earlier house. DOE)

KELHAM HOUSE, Mickleborough Hill, ½ m. NE of the village. Good neo-Queen Anne, 1903 by *H. Baily* (of *Brewill & Baily*).

CROSS KEYS INN. Built *c.* 1700–25, perhaps as an inn, unaltered in its shell and outbuildings (including the DOVECOTE). The long village street gives an impression of a later C18 rebuilding.

WINDMILL. 1814. Only the brick two-storey roundhouse remains of this former post-mill.

GREET HOUSE (former Thurgarton Union Workhouse). *See* Southwell.

# VERNEMETUM
## *see* WILLOUGHBY-ON-THE-WOLDS

---

* This information was kindly supplied by Mr R. McD. O'Donnell.

# WALESBY

ST EDMUND. The N aspect is exceptional, just the Perp nave windows and the differently spaced clerestory windows above. No evidence appears of a former N aisle,* but the whole N wall was probably rebuilt with old materials early in the C16 by the Stanhopes of Haughton, whose arms are on the Perp tower. The chancel windows are clearly *c.* 1300 (intersecting tracery). The chancel arch inside as at East Markham, without any capitals between jambs and voussoirs (most probably early C14 too). The nave has a C13 S arcade with circular piers, simply moulded capitals, and double-chamfered arches. Tower and tower arch Perp. – PULPIT. C17, pre-classical. – BENCHES, S aisle. Plain, with just one bolection-moulding, C17, just like Bilsthorpe (cf. also Hockerton, 1599). – MONUMENT. Lady with wimple; from the ruined chapel at Haughton.

# WALKERINGHAM

ST MARY MAGDALEN. The exterior all late medieval, with the W tower of east Notts type (ashlar-faced, diagonal buttresses, eight pinnacles) and battlements everywhere. The interior has the two aisle arcades identical or nearly identical, with octagonal piers, C13 capitals, and odd square 'broached' bases. C13 also the arcade to the N chancel chapel. The clerestory is Perp, and so are the nave and chancel roofs with carved bosses and the tower arch on embattled corbels. – FONT. 1663, octagonal, undecorated. – PULPIT. Late C17. – SCREEN, now in the N chancel aisle. Late Perp. – (STAINED GLASS. E window by *Wailes, c.* 1857. RH) – MONUMENT to Francis Williamson † 1639 and his wife by *Edward Marshall,* 1659. Two life-size kneeling figures facing each other, as was the Elizabethan and Jacobean tradition. Below three kneeling children, also in the round; classical aedicule background. The quality of the figures not specially good.

(THE MANOR HOUSE, beside the church on the main road. Brick, English bond, with excellent stone mullion-and-transom windows: single pile. NS)

---

* Professor Barley notes an *ex-situ* respond in the S aisle, identical to those of the S arcade but for a narrower pier.

## WALLINGWELLS
### w of Carlton-in-Lindrick

No visible remains of the small Benedictine priory of nuns founded here by Ralph de Chevrolcourt about 1140–4, but a puzzling house set in a large park. Sir Richard Pipe, a Lord Mayor of London, bought the property in 1578. His, or a slightly later, house is shown on a plan of 1682. H-plan with a little internal courtyard. Its gabled roof-line can still be seen, inadequately masked by the present façades. Those on the W and S look early to mid C18, probably added by John White who succeeded in 1732. On the former entrance front (W) plain three-storey, three-bay faces to the two original projecting wings with stone quoins, plinth, and straight parapets. The four central bays on the E side crowned by a sham pediment. Both façades of brick, probably stuccoed in 1828, when a new entrance façade was made on the E: Tudor-Gothic, of seven bays, four gables, and buttresses carried up into little turrets between gables, a turreted porch, and plain sashes with labels over them. A little turret was added for symmetry to the SW corner of the S side. Inside, nothing of the earlier house except the roof structure: it was remodelled in 1828 (plain fittings survive) and subdivided into four houses in 1925. The pre-1682 coachyard on the S side has gone, but on the N the stone-built office wing remains, made into cottages. N of this, mid-C18 stables in fine ashlar with wings enclosing a forecourt. In the C17 the large park was laid out formally. Near the house, a canal enclosing three sides of a court on the E side, ending to the S in a great basin at the head of the kitchen garden. Two avenues intersected on axis with it. To the N, a wood crossed by avenues radiating from a *rond-point*. All this disappeared in the C18, but some picturesque features remain. Hidden by trees NW of the house the CASTLE GARDEN, a walled garden at the head of a large quarry. Flanking the entrance to it, two stone pavilions, one Gothick, the other Tudor. Until they dried up earlier this century, springs fed a series of pools down to the house and beyond to its S. By the largest of these, a serpentine lake on the site of the great basin, a large GROTTO of rough hewn rocks, circular inside, with a domical vault and five niches. Originally lined with mineral crystals and hung with stalactites. Towards Carlton, a stuccoed lodge like the E front of the house.

# WARSOP

ST PETER AND ST PAUL. The church with its broad massive w tower and its long, embattled nave and chancel lies against the hillside, higher up than the new colliery housing of Warsop. The tower is evidently early Norman (except, of course, for its buttresses and top) – see the renewed w door and window above, and even more the tower arch towards the nave, quite an important example of the style. It has the rudimentary moulding of the arch, and the crudest, biggest zigzag. Norman also the plain N and S chancel doors. Then follow the E.E. contributions: S door (with a little nailhead) and S porch, one renewed S window, and the S arcade of quatrefoil piers (or, to be more exact, square piers with four broad demi-shafts; cf. Mansfield) with circular seats at their bases and moulded capitals exactly as in the porch at Edwinstowe nearby. The arches are double-chamfered. N arcade and N windows C14. The E window, and of course the clerestory and the present roof, are later, Perp; and the pretty, low, castellated vestry was added after 1500. – SEDILIA and PISCINA under one straight hoodmould; C14. – STAINED GLASS. A few old fragments in the vestry. – (E window by *Shrigley & Hunt*, 1906. RH) – In the churchyard one good slate HEADSTONE † 1754 signed *W. Charles*.

Church Warsop, the settlement of old stone houses and farms round the church, is quite separate from the town of Warsop below it, where there is nothing of interest. Warsop is about on the N border of the stone district of Notts.

OLD HALL and BARN. Part of a group of farm buildings immediately NW of the church that have been made into a Parish Centre (1971–3). The buttressed N wall of the C17 barn, facing the road, has been mostly rebuilt. The S front of the Old Hall, on the opposite side of the former stockyard, has features dating from the C14 to the C16, so reshuffled in the C19 that the archaeology of the house is quite illegible. In the centre section, an early C14 trefoil-headed light in the angle of the cross wing and early masonry in the chimneystack. The cross wing is a jumble: Victorian lights on the ground floor, re-used C16 ones above, and an oddly placed medieval one in the gable. The W bay, probably a C16 addition, has original arched lights in the upper part, C19 ones below. Inside, two pointed stone doorways at the head of the staircase, one with some nailhead decoration.

WINDMILL, at Bradmer Hill. Stone tower mill of three storeys (28 ft high) with a brick top. No cap.

On the road between the town and the church an C18 WATER CORN MILL, still in use but powered by electricity. A water turbine is *in situ*. Stone steps to the first floor, stone mullioned windows, and a datestone which reads 1767.

PITHEAD BATHS at WELBECK COLLIERY VILLAGE (3 m. N of Warsop) and WARSOP MAIN (2 m. W of Warsop), both among the remarkably well designed buildings put up by the Miners' Welfare Commission in many parts of the country. The former 1938, the latter 1933, both by *A. J. Saise.*

## WATNALL HALL *see* GREASLEY

## WELBECK ABBEY

5070

Of the large private estates created out of Sherwood Forest after the enclosure of Thoresby Park in 1683, the central in position and importance is the Welbeck Abbey estate of nearly 3,000 acres, with the mansion (now partly an army college and partly still in private hands) near its centre. The present neither imposing or attractive appearance of the house is the result of a complicated and still not fully explored building history, with evidence of the C16 to C19 overlaid by a veneer applied by *Sir Ernest George* (then of *George & Yates*) in 1900–2 after a disastrous fire. Approached from the W, it comprises two stone-built wings arranged in an L-shape, the E wing basically C17 and C18 but much altered in the C19 and C20, the S wing mainly C18 remodelling of a C16 wing.

The mansion was originally a Premonstratensian house, founded in 1153–4 and by 1512 recognized as the head house of the order in England. Very little of it survives: seven bays of the undercroft dating from *c.* 1250, the southernmost three bays with original vaulting, the rest with C18 vaults; and an older doorway of *c.* 1180, of one order with a round head, cut to take a later door and with a C17 jamb oddly placed next to it. These remains are in what is now the basement at the S end of the E wing in an area completely rebuilt in the C18 as kitchens and then altered again in the C19.

At the Dissolution the estate came into private hands and after several changes into those of Sir Charles Cavendish, son of Bess of Hardwick, who leased it from his brother-in-law Gilbert Talbot in 1597 and bought it ten years later. The architect *Robert Smythson*, favoured by both Sir Charles's parents, provided a plan for rebuilding on a vast scale (*Archit. His.* 1/23). Although the elevation had a number of 'Smythson' features (towers, bay-windows, cupolas, and balustrading, cf. Hardwick and Worksop Manor) the plan was untypical. Unlike Hardwick, Worksop, Wollaton, or even Sir Charles's own Bolsover Keep, which in Midlands tradition are all tall and compact, this house was to be a low and spreading courtyard house incorporating the medieval cloisters, more on the lines of Theobalds and Burghley. Only a tiny part of the plan, a short wing projecting to the W of the main building, was executed. This still exists as the basis of the S wing, remodelled by Lady Oxford in 1741–52 and so known as the OXFORD WING. Features of the wing drawn by Grimm before 1740 can be recognized even in the wing's present form: the three storeys, the lantern and cupola over a newel stair, the two projecting bays carried up into towers on the S side. Lady Oxford left Smythson's plan at the W end of the wing almost intact, just adding two rooms on the N side at this end to iron out the C16 asymmetry.

Sir Charles's son, Sir William (created Duke of Newcastle in 1665), devotee of the 'Haute École' and author of the famous treatise on the subject, 'La Nouvelle Méthode', published in 1657, built himself a riding school and stables, counterparts of those at Bolsover. His architect was Robert Smythson's son *John*, whom he had employed at Bolsover since about 1613 to complete the Keep and to build the adjoining terrace range and long gallery. The stables of 1625 were demolished in the C18,[*] but the RIDING SCHOOL, dated 1622 on Smythson's drawing (*Archit. His.* 111/15 (3)), still stands to the NW of the house. Remodelled in the C18 and C19, this embattled and utilitarian-

---

[*] An engraving in the Duke's treatise and a *Smythson* drawing (*Archit. His.* 111/155) show them to have had some classical detail as well as an odd pair of little round towers with ogee caps. Attached to the stables, according to the engraving, was a range of grooms' quarters, granaries, etc., with a central gatehouse surmounted by four Dutch gables of the rather early type used by Robert Smythson at Wollaton forty-five years before. The evidence of engraving must be taken with a pinch of salt. Diepenbecke, who illustrated the Duke's treatise with pictures of the Duke's horses against views of his properties, apparently never came to England, so his views of Welbeck must have been composed from topographical drawings of unknown accuracy or from designs. Indeed, details of his view of the house conflict with those in Grimm's early C18 drawings, and those in his view of the stables differ slightly from those in Smythson's drawing. There is no evidence of any work by the Duke's architect at Nottingham Castle, *Samuel Marsh*, who was summoned to Welbeck to 'make a draughte, for the making good of a stare to my Riding House Chamber'.

looking block now has only its basic Jacobean shape and some details (e.g. the W doorway with an open pediment rising to support another pediment and thereby framing a niche above the door: cf. Bolsover long gallery for similar eccentricities). Grimm shows it to have had a hammerbeam roof inside (cf. Bolsover), but not like the C18 or C19 version that now exists above the C19 ceiling. Of *John Smythson*'s work on the E range very little survives Lady Oxford's and subsequent remodellings. Both Diepenbecke and Grimm show it to have been a long, rambling building with parts of various dates. Grimm's view from the W shows a building of two storeys, plus a basement and dormers, with a taller central section capped by Dutch gables more advanced than those on the stables apparently of the type introduced about 1620. Between this range and the C16 wing he shows a traditional hall with a steep-pitched roof. Nothing in this view can be confidently ascribed to *John Smythson* except the porch into the hall, which looks remarkably like the 'Porch at Welbeck' in two of his drawings (*Archit. His.* 111/15 1 & 2).* But inside work of his remains at the N end of the E wing, rooms with decoration closely comparable to that he did for Sir William in Bolsover Keep. In the basement is vaulting very similar to that in the basement at Bolsover, and above it, on the ground floor, an elaborately decorated little room (BURSAR'S STUDY).‡ This has a sexpartite stone rib-vault decorated with Cavendish and Ogle crests and a large pendant boss, a stone tablet carved with the Cavendish stag on the wall above the later fireplace, and panelling which is on the same pattern as the incomplete panelling in the Star Chamber at Bolsover, and which may have been removed from there. The room above has a massive stone chimneypiece similar in general type to the Serlian Doric type used by Robert Smythson at Wollaton but with a moulded surround like those in the Keep at Bolsover. In the room next to it panelling with stencilled decoration (cf. Bolsover) and a plaster frieze. On the N side of the NW corner, opening now into the C19 quadrant wing, a rusticated Doric arch, dated 1749, probably based on a C17 original like the entrance arch shown by Diepenbecke.

* This porch may be the one that survives at Whitwell Manor House, just over the border in Derbyshire, but still on the edge of the estate and used as a school run by the ladies of Welbeck in the C19. Its parapet, with strange corbelled projections, is reminiscent of the parapets on the long gallery at Bolsover.

‡ The present names of the rooms accord with their use by the army college.

The house so far described had the basic L-plan it still has today. In 1703 *Vanbrugh* and *Talman* were discussing with the Earl of Clare (created third Duke) the possibility of rebuilding the house on a scale to vie with Castle Howard, but it was left to his daughter, who married the Earl of Oxford, to do any building work. In 1741 she called in *John James* to make an initial survey, and from then until his death in 1746 James received occasional payments of one hundred to three hundred pounds. The foreman was *Thomas Dixon*, succeeded in 1743 by *James Ellins*, with *Anthony* and *Thomas Ince* as master masons. As already described, she only remodelled the existing building, beginning in 1742 with the W end of the s wing.* The insignificant central door on the s front is dated 1743 and the rebuilt C16 lantern has her initials, portrait, and the date 1749.‡ Work on the E wing began in 1743 with the ENTRANCE HALL, which still has part of its *Thomas Carter* fireplace finished in the following year. In 1749 the old great hall to the right of the entrance hall was demolished and the two-storey GOTHIC HALL built in its place. This room must have been very pretty until it was fatally bowdlerized by *George & Yates* in 1900–2. Now only the plaster fan-vault and the upper part of the fireplace (1748–51) by *Christopher Richardson* (which Walpole found 'extremely like mine in the library') are still intact; the rest was kept Gothic but without any delicacy. The other rooms in this wing along the E front were remodelled for the third Duke of Portland by *Carr* in 1775–7, but little remains of his suite (drawing room and anteroom, dining room and library) after *George & Yates* went to work on it, except a few simple cornices and fireplaces. The MASTERS' COMMON ROOM (formerly drawing room) is the most Edwardian, with lots of panelling and a heavily classical ceiling. By 1752 Lady Oxford's work was being completed, the riding school turned into stables, and a range of offices built facing it by the mason *William Birch*.

Even after the alterations the exterior of the house was by no means handsome; John Byng in 1789 called it outright 'mean, ugly and ill-built'. The only embellishment (by *Carr*) of the plain façades was on the W side, a battlemented parapet

---

* The additional tower here does not appear on a plan of about 1800 in the NMR so presumably is neither Smythson's nor Lady Oxford's work.

‡ I was not permitted to see the interior of this wing but I am told by Mr Myles Hildyard that the C18-style decoration is of 1900–2 by *George & Yates*. Red Drawing Room: ceiling painted with flowers, masks, musical instruments, etc., to complement a set of Boucher-Neilson Gobelins tapestries, 1783. Former Swan Drawing Room: a magnificent chinoiserie chimneypiece.

and a central entrance porch into the hall with a simple segmental arch and battlements.

Lady Oxford did not neglect the GROUNDS, either, and the garden designer *Francis Richardson* was employed first to lay out the kitchen garden in 1744 and then to plant the ground E of the house where the present Shrubbery Lake was made. Richardson's two elaborate plans, which seem to have been carried out, show the C17 formal gardens and water gardens swept away and a lake on the site of the present Great Lake.* *Repton* was responsible for further 'improvements' in 1790–2, as his existing notebooks of 1789 prove. Earth was moved to the W front of the building, the Mall, turning the ground floor into a basement. He also deepened and extended the lakes, which now extend for more than three miles.

The predominant human and visual interest of Welbeck is Victorian, as it is at Thoresby and Clumber. It is connected with the mysterious fifth Duke of Portland, a handsome but 'lonely, self-isolated man', as the step-sister of the sixth Duke, Lady Ottoline Morrell, described him. Most of the strange features of his character are known to us from her, though local legends may gradually have added a great deal. He lived in four or five rooms only, separated from the outer world by a door with two letter-boxes, one for messages and mail in, one out. The rest of the house was mostly empty except for conveniences placed into the corners of the rooms. The Gothic Hall was stacked full of furniture. The Duke travelled to London in his carriage, which at Worksop was placed on a railway truck, the sun blinds carefully drawn. In the park such acquaintances as the Vicar had orders not to see him when he passed them. On the other hand he was on friendly and natural terms with the hundreds of workmen employed on his vast and crazy enterprises. Each workman received a donkey and an umbrella when he started work so as to make travelling through the park more comfortable.

The fifth Duke's buildings extend below ground to the W of the house. Among the miles of tunnels one stretches 1¼ m. to the old Worksop road. It is wide enough for two carriages to pass, and dips down where it meets the lake. It conveyed the Duke to Worksop safe and unseen whenever a journey could not be avoided. Other tunnels ran to the stables and new riding

---

* In 1765 *Mylne* designed an elegant bridge. It was completed in 1767, but when Walpole saw it in 1768 it had just collapsed. (Information from Mr Christopher Gotch.)

school. These excavations, by traction engines, steam plough, and teams of Irish navvies, were begun in 1860, six years after the Duke inherited. They were lit by huge glass bullseyes above the ground. The new RIDING SCHOOL, 385 by 112 ft and 52 ft high, has cast-iron columns and a glass and iron vault. Also above ground are the remains of ranges of HOTHOUSES 800 ft in length. The Duke liked to grow his own fruit, and so also devised fruit forcing walls with glass roofs, 700 ft long. Of other buildings above ground the various LODGES in neo-Tudor style may be mentioned, more than one can count. In 1875, four years before the death of the Duke, there were thirty-five, and six under construction.

His first work, about 1860, in the house was the demolition of Carr's one-storey chapel of 1763 at the lake end of the S wing and the erection of three-storey additions in its place. The rest of the building was fitted with gas-lighting and modern plumbing, including the extraordinary water-closets, and railway lines to carry food from the kitchens to the Gothic Hall and dining room were laid! Now for the UNDERGROUND ROOMS projecting W from the house and connected to it by underground passages. The first was the suite of LIBRARY ROOMS (now classrooms). These are 236 ft long and lie S of the Smythson riding school. In 1875 a chapel was begun to the W of the library rooms. This room, 154 by 64 ft with sober classical decoration, was soon converted into a BALLROOM and the library suite into supper rooms opening off one side of the glass-roofed Glass Corridor or Long Conservatory by which they were reached from the ballroom. On the other side of the ballroom, the Rose Corridor, a similar conservatory, runs W to what was meant to be a huge Bachelors' Hall (*see* below).

A tour through these vast halls is a little disappointing. The results of the Duke's burrowing are much less cavernous than one might expect (or hope). The rooms are not too low down for skylights and are not, therefore, gloomy during the day. At night they were illuminated by literally thousands of gas jets (1,100 alone in the three original library rooms). Their heating was by hot air.

What then made the Duke go underground? Some said that he was concerned about unemployment and wanted to give as many men work as possible, others suggested that he did not want to spoil the original appearance of the house, an unlikely reason considering the singularly unattractive frontages of Welbeck Abbey. May it not rather be suggested that the Duke in his excessive, morbid shyness wanted to indulge his *mania aedi-ficandi* without appearing showy? In the C18 he might have erected a Castle Howard or a Wentworth Woodhouse. Now he chose to hide his buildings, as he chose to hide himself.

When he died in 1879, excavations had just begun for an enormous Bachelors' Hall. Then building stopped at once. The new Duke on his arrival found 'the front drive a grass-grown morass covered with builders' rubbish'. The foundation walls of the sunk hall were converted into an Italianate SUNKEN GARDEN, with a wooden pavilion and pergolas, and the house was made habitable again by the young Duke's stepmother, Lady Bolsover. Then peace reigned again for a while. Building was resumed in 1891, when a library and chapel were fitted into Smythson's riding school.* The designs (1889) were by *Sedding*, an architect no doubt chosen by Lady Bolsover, but he died before work started, and all the details are by his favourite and most brilliant pupil, *Henry Wilson*. The two rooms were complete in 1896. The CHAPEL gave Wilson a splendid opportunity to develop the richness of his Byzantiniz-ing style. It has a tunnel-vault on bulgy Ionic columns of pink marble. There is also much dark marble and some sumptuous and imaginative bronze work. The ALTAR CROSS, rather stiff in Wilson's early style, was exhibited together with the lectern, the font, and possibly the light fittings at the Arts and Crafts exhibition of 1893. The FONT was a collaborative effort, the brass bowl and enamel panel by *Henry Longdon & Co.* of Shef-field, the inlay round the bowl by *F. Davidson*, the inlaid sym-bols by *P. Wilson*, and the sculpture by *F. W. Pomeroy*. The bronze LECTERN was by *Wilson* himself; the BRONZE GATES (1909) were designed by *Wilson* and executed by *Pomeroy*. Compared with the expressive and free style of the doors at St Mary, Nottingham (1904), the figure design on these is classical and frieze-like. Also by *Wilson*, CHANCEL STALLS, beaten BRASS DOOR with formalized plant motifs, and LIGHT FITTINGS (much altered since). The ALTARPIECE is by *Hont-horst* (Adoration of the Shepherds). The LIBRARY is less formal and equally successful, with an inglenook and a lux-uriantly carved alabaster fireplace (by *Pomeroy*) as charming as anything which that moment of Art Nouveau or the English revolt from period imitation produced. The chapel and library are linked to the house by a contemporary wing (the VIRGINS'

* Information about the library and chapel comes from notes written for the Victorian Society by Mrs Shirley Bury.

WING) with quarters for maidservants. In the main corridor nice plasterwork with stylized plant forms and figures. It is perhaps a pity that the sixth Duke chose a much more conventional architect, *Sir Ernest George*, to repair the fire damage of 1900–2 and to embellish the façades. To the w front of the E wing he added a central pediment and a heavily rusticated *porte-cochère*: to the E front of the same wing a similar central feature with pediment and rustication, with to the r. a projecting bay with a Venetian window and to the l. a columned portico. Flanking the towers on the s façade he put two-bay pedimented wings with rusticated quoins.

The building history of Welbeck ends in a mood characteristic of the C20. The late Duke (when Marquess of Titchfield) built for himself in 1930–2 a house in the grounds known as WELBECK WOODHOUSE. It is no larger than a wealthy suburban villa in an industrial town (architects *Brierley & Rutherford*). The main pictures are kept there. Of Welbeck Abbey itself only the inaccessible state rooms of the Oxford wing belong to the family. The rest, with the underground rooms and the grounds, is beautifully maintained as an Army College and seems likely to remain so.*

## WELHAM see CLARBOROUGH

6060

## WELLOW

A pretty village, the green with a maypole, several good cottages and houses, some brick, some timber-framed (ROCK HOUSE, Wellow Road), and a PRIMITIVE METHODIST CHAPEL of 1847, still entirely in the Georgian tradition. Notts villages are on the whole poor in Nonconformist chapels of that type. The picture of the green is somewhat spoilt by modern houses near the church.

ST SWITHIN. Much restored and given a new chancel by *Ewan Christian*, 1878–9. The tower s w, not w. It is C12 on the ground floor (see tower arch), then C13 (see bell-stage), and Perp in the usual way at the top. In the N wall one C13 window; the s aisle (restored 1968–9) windows with intersecting tracery, that is *c.* 1300. The arcade looks rather later. – In the chancel FIGURES

---

* In 1952 Welbeck's fate, like that of so many other large houses, hung in the balance. In this case an institutional use for part of the building was its salvation. Few private individuals could have afforded to maintain it so well.

over the reredos from Pearson's demolished St Bartholomew, Nottingham. – FONT. Norman, on an odd plan, rectangular, with a semicircular projection in the middle of one side. – STAINED GLASS. E window 1878 by *Kempe*, one of the many windows given by C. G. S. Foljambe in memory of his wife (cf. Edwinstowe, Ollerton, St John Worksop, Tideswell, Derbys). – MONUMENT to Elizabeth Peel † 1851, with a carefully and sentimentally carved rose, by *Edwin Smith* of Sheffield. – In the churchyard at the E end of the church, an ALTAR TOMB of 1651 removed from inside the church.

WELLOW HALL, NW of the green. Plaque inscribed 1700 and a staircase of that date. Remodelled in the C18. Plain brick façade towards the road with a stuccoed canted bay at one end. C19 wing behind.

On the E and S sides of the village the remains of a defensive dry ditch that once surrounded the whole of the village. Probably made to protect the inhabitants during a dispute with Rufford Abbey. To the S the deserted medieval village of GRIMSTON, probably abandoned in favour of Wellow.

JORDAN CASTLE, ½ m. NE. Circular earthworks, surrounded by a bank and ditch: most probably Nottinghamshire's only known example of a Norman ring-work. It has not been excavated.

## WEST BRIDGFORD

5030

ST GILES. Mostly of 1896–1911 by *Naylor & Sale*. It incorporates part of the medieval church, namely its dark grey W tower and its S aisle and nave separated by an arcade with octagonal piers, restored in 1872 by *T. C. Hine*. The nave has become the inner S aisle of the new church. The plain two-seat SEDILIA prove the chancel to be C14. – In the new E chapel of the N aisle a severely damaged EFFIGY of a cross-legged knight, the so-called Stone Man, supposed to be Sir Robert de Luttrell, *c.* 1298. – SCREEN. Late C14, good, with four tall, slim openings l. and r. of the entrance. They are all ogee-shaped and cusped. Only the centre has Perp features. – (STAINED GLASS. Several windows by *Powell* of Whitefriars, 1946–60, and one of 1971 by *Alfred Fisher*, the firm's last designer at the Whitefriars Studio at Wealdstone. RH) – A specially enjoyable selection of engraved SLATE HEADSTONES in the churchyard.

UNITED REFORMED (formerly PRESBYTERIAN) CHURCH,

Musters Road. 1898 by *Brewill & Baily* (cf. the former Presbyterian church, Mansfield Road, Nottingham). Low tower with ornate cap. Inside, low arcades of segmental arches carried on cylindrical piers.

COUNTY HALL, Melton Road. Begun in 1937 and then and now as dead as mutton. By *E. Vincent Harris*. Work stopped from 1940 to 1945 and the building was incomplete when first used in 1946. It was finished in 1965 except for a suite of committee rooms not fitted up until 1975. The extension of 1960–4 – in CLASP, by the County Architect (*W. D. Lacey*) – is preferable to the ponderous neo-Georgian original, its lighter vein quite appropriate to the riverside.

WEST BRIDGFORD HALL (Rushcliffe District Council Offices), Bridgford Road. A plain five-bay brick box of 1768–74, with intermittent rustication of the door surround. Later additions.

TRENT BRIDGE. Two arches of the medieval bridge stranded on a traffic roundabout by County Hall.

EDWALTON. *See* p. 118.


WEST BURTON

Substantial earthen mounds and sunken roads mark where the village stood on the w bank of the Trent, until the early C19. The church was demolished in 1885, leaving the graveyard.

Overshadowing it completely, the huge WEST BURTON POWER STATION, the eight towers and two chimneys grouped effectively, the surroundings well planted. Designed by the *Architects Design Group*, landscaped by *Derek Lovejoy & Associates*, it won a Civic Trust award in 1969.


WEST DRAYTON

ST PAUL. Nave and chancel in one; Norman masonry apparent. The s doorway, with a scalloped label moulding and zigzag on front and soffit above the one order, is in a very decayed state. C15 windows.

(MARKHAM MOOR HOUSE, ½ m. SE. An early C19 brick box with a hipped roof and a good group of outbuildings round a courtyard. NS)

ROCKLEY HOUSE, ¼ m. E, at Rockley. 1826, red brick, of two

storeys and three bays, with a hipped roof. Highly decorative arcaded porch with clustered columns, garlands, fluted keyblocks, trellis spandrels, etc., and a half-conical lead roof carrying a low-relief urn. Paved yard with pedimented coach house. Cottage of 1826 in the grounds.*

## WEST LEAKE

5020

A quiet backwater, compared with the growing suburban East Leake, with some nice C18 and C19 cottages and houses.

ST HELEN. Towerless. Norman, the nave with one small window and the scanty remains of a doorway. Late C14 S arcade on low octagonal piers. Clerestory. The whole church was much restored and the N transept etc. built in 1878 (by *Henry Hall* for Lord Belper: JPB). – STAINED GLASS. A few old fragments in a N chancel window.‡ – MONUMENTS. Lady of the late C13, effigy in shallow relief under a crocketed and pinnacled gable, trefoiled inside. When in a better state of preservation it must have been a very good example of the sculptor's art. – C14 civilian, under a heavy nodding ogee arch. He holds his heart in his hands (cf. Stanford-on-Soar, Averham); two little angels to the l. and r. of his head, carrying up his tiny soul. – Thomas Mansfield, erected 1743, with portrait bust at the top. – Tablet to the Rev. T. Hastings † 1804 by *J. Peck* of Loughborough.

## WEST MARKHAM

7070

The parish is known as Markham Clinton.

ALL SAINTS. Small, with Transitional S doorway and S chancel doorway. W gable and porch half-timbered. Above the W gable a pretty weatherboarded turret. Subjected to a 'folkcrafty' restoration (according to Betjeman) in 1930–45. – FONT. Norman, of unusual interest, with very barbaric figures under arcades (cf. examples at Hereford; in Gloucestershire at Newnham, Rendcombe, and Stanley St Leonard; at Stoneleigh, Warwicks, and Pershore, Worcs; and lead fonts at Ashover, Derbys, and Dorchester, Oxon). – Old ROOF BOSSES. – Some BENCHES old and very appealing in their pale natural oak

---

* The contemporary farm, cottages, and chapel that formed a group with Rockley House have been altered out of recognition.

‡ According to Mr Alvey.

colour. – MONUMENT to a Priest, with angels holding his pillow, very defaced.

PITHEAD BATHS, Markham Colliery. 1935 by *A. J. Saise.*

At MILTON, ½ m. NW, along one of the fourth Duke of Newcastle's avenues of Lombardy poplars (a tree despised by all picturesque gardeners) stands the MAUSOLEUM which he got *Sir Robert Smirke*, the architect of the British Museum, the old General Post Office, and several of the more expensive Commissioners' churches in London, to build in 1831–2 for the tomb of the Duchess who had died in 1822. The building looks entirely as if it stood at Hackney or Wandsworth; an incongruous sight, all on its own in a field and now disused. It is a clever combination of church and mausoleum, meant to replace All Saints. The nave of four windows is entered from the W, and one would expect it to lead on to a dome; for externally an octagonal lantern of two stages, the lower one with free-standing Greek Doric columns at the corners, appears E of the nave above a crossing with apparently transepts and an E chancel attached to it. In fact the circular crossing is divided off. The church ends with an Ionic reredos W of it. The mausoleum part has its entrance at the E end, and here appears a solemn Greek Doric four-column prostyle portico, whereas the W, S, and N ends have only pilasters. From the portico the rotunda is reached, and to the N and S the tomb chambers. The monument to the Duchess, by *Westmacott,* has returned from Clumber (*see* p. 102). That to the Duke † 1851 has two sentimental young medieval pages and an ogee arch, the whole of wood and a perfect example of the taste of the 1851 Exhibition at its chastest.

RECTORY, next to the church. Also designed by *Smirke* in 1831-2. Totally different from the neo-Greek mausoleum, in a 'supposedly Swiss version of the Jacobean style'.

# WESTON-ON-TRENT

One of a chain of pretty Trent valley villages. At the SE end of the village, three tenements built with cruck trusses probably in the C16, now brick-walled.

ALL SAINTS. W steeple with battlemented parapet and plain needle-shaped spire. The tower C13 below, C14 higher up; spire C14. Nave with battlements and pinnacles; chancel embattled too. The arcades on both sides of the nave late C13 or a little later, with octagonal piers, double-chamfered arches, and simply moulded capitals (those of the s a little more elaborate). – STAINED GLASS. Tiny medieval fragments in the chancel.

## WEST RETFORD see RETFORD

## WEST STOCKWITH 3090

Notts at its most Lincolnshire, that is a riverside village all of 2 brick, almost as if it were in Holland.* The church fits perfectly into this picture.

ST MARY. Built in 1722 by the executors of William Huntington, a ship carpenter, as he is called on his MONUMENT. 86 He reclines on his elbow and holds a paper with a ship in his hand. The artist was *E. Poynton*. The church (restored in 1963) is a brick rectangle with three round-headed windows on each side and a pretty bell-turret. The altar place is emphasized by two Ionic pilasters.

## WHATTON 7030

ST JOHN OF BEVERLEY. Architecturally almost wholly ruined by several restorations and alterations. The chancel and s aisle were rebuilt in 1846, the rest gone over in 1866–7 and again severely ('by an amateur': JPB) in 1870. The most interesting feature of the plan was the central tower with spire (cf. Normanton), rebuilt in 1870. The best preserved is the Dec N aisle with a good reticulated window. A little Norman work from the s transept arch was built into the N one. – FONT. 1662; for the type (octagonal with simple decoration in the panels) *see* Southwell, p. 327. – SCULPTURE, E end N aisle. Above all, two exquisite CORBELS, one with King David, the other with a musician 30 angel, Lincoln style, and worthy of the cathedral workshop, *c.* 1300. Two canopies belong to them. The corbels show painfully of what the restorations have deprived us. – Head of a LANTERN CROSS: was it the original village cross or rather a churchyard cross? – STAINED GLASS. E end of s aisle, 1878 by *Morris & Co.* to completely new designs by *Burne-Jones*. In three lights St Peter, St John, Christ with the face of a Pre-

* It was an inland port with a barge basin and warehouses at the junction of the rivers Idle and Trent and the Chesterfield Canal, opened in 1775.

Raphaelite maiden, three stories underneath (Blind Bartimaeus, Raising of Lazarus, St Peter healing the Cripple at the Beautiful Gate) and three angels at the top. – The other windows are by leading C19 glass-painters too (for example, Innocent window by *Heaton, Butler & Bayne* and, later (1900), the chancel window by *Kempe & Co*. A comparison with the work of the Morris firm betrays their weakness*). – MONUMENTS. N aisle: Priest, supposed to be a canon of Welbeck who was vicar of Whatton in 1304–10; cross-legged knight (Hugh de Newmarch?) on a tomb-chest with shields, first half of the C14. – S aisle: Sir Richard de Whatton, late C14, alabaster, also with shields on the tomb-chest; Thomas Cranmer † 1501, good incised slab to the father of Archbishop Cranmer.

WHATTON MANOR, ½ m. S of the A52, was demolished *c*. 1966. The stable courtyard is all that remains.‡

WINDMILL, Conery Lane. Erected *c*. 1820. Five storeys with no cap but with all its floors and original iron windows.

<sub>6020</sub>

# WIDMERPOOL

ST PETER AND ST PAUL. Completely hidden from the village and close to the Hall N of it. Thoroughly restored, almost rebuilt, at great expense (£10,000) in 1888–95.§ The chancel windows were given marble nook-shafts. But the tower with corner buttresses and diagonally projecting corner pinnacles is C14. – MONUMENT to Mrs Robertson † 1891, Italian marble, recumbent effigy on a couch with many pillows.

WIDMERPOOL HALL (A.A. Patrol Service Training HQ). Sumptuous stone neo-Elizabethan by *Henry Clutton* for Major Robertson, 1872–3. At the junction of the main three-gabled block and a lower wing, a very tall Italianate tower.

(NEW INN MANOR. Near the junction of the A606 and the Fosse Way (A46). C18, three-bay stone and stuccoed farmhouse with an arched doorway. NS)

WIGTHORPE *see* CARLTON-IN-LINDRICK

---

* This cannot be taken as a general rule; *see*, for example, the excellent glass by *Heaton, Butler & Bayne* at St Mary, Nottingham (p. 222).

‡ The house was neo-Elizabethan, symmetrical, of 1838–40, a comparatively early date for the use of this style (cf. for example Harlaxton, nearby in Lincs. Could the architect have been *Salvin*?).

§ By *T. N. Huskinson* (nave) and *J. A. Reeve* (chancel etc.), following an 1835–6 restoration (see e.g. tower details).

WILFORD *see* NOTTINGHAM p. 272

## WILLOUGHBY-ON-THE-WOLDS          6020

ST MARY AND ALL SAINTS. The pride of the church is the Willoughby MONUMENTS in the N transept and N chapel. Too often medieval effigies in village churches are admitted only for their venerable age. Here is really high artistic quality, even if not well enough preserved to appreciate its details. The oldest are in stone, two ladies wearing wimples (their garments arranged in the two most usual conventions of drapery of *c.* 1300 and after), and one couple, both exceedingly slim, he a knight, cross-legged, she fashionably dressed. The details are terribly worn off, but the original elegance can still be seen. Moreover, one more knight, supposed to be Sir Richard † 1326. The rest is alabaster: Richard, a judge, † 1362, with a beautifully carved face and careful detail of costume, and Sir Hugh † 1445 and his wife, together on a tomb-chest, with mitred angels holding rectangular shields. At the W end a Trinity, at the E end a seated figure of the Virgin, both as good as any contemporary alabaster altar panels. The effigies also are well carved, much better than those done by the Elizabethan carvers of Nottinghamshire.

Architecturally also the church deserves inspection. Nave and aisles separated by circular piers. Just one capital has primitive upright leaves: others are octagonal, as if alternating supports had been considered. The date is *c.* 1200 or a little later. Next in date comes the N chapel, whose blind arcading at the W side without any capitals is an early C13 West English convention (but cf. arches from St Mary, Nottingham, in Birkin's warehouse, *see* Nottingham, p. 231). Its pier and arches towards the N aisle also belong to the C13 rather than the C14. The chancel is C13 too (windows partly later), and so is the spire with two tiers of lucarnes (very similar to Normanton-on-Soar). Clerestory and nave roof C15. – FONT. Octagonal, with simple trefoil panels. – TILES. A few medieval between N aisle and N chapel.

The MANOR HOUSE, which stood close to the church, was demolished except for a small S wing in 1978.*

---

* It was a good mid-C17 L-plan house. From the front only the gable of the lesser arm was seen. At the back the long range of the L with the recession filled in by three C18 cottages. A row of three gables with finials disappeared in the re-roofing of *c.* 1900.

THORPE-IN-THE-GLEBE, 1½ m. W. One of the best deserted medieval village sites in the Midlands, but its earthworks (a long sunken road with rectangular enclosures either side) under grass. The remains of the church, still occasionally used in 1743, lie in the farmyard of Churchside Farm. (The farmhouse itself is late C17 with some interesting timber-framed cross-walls exposed on the upper floors. NS)

The Roman roadside settlement of VERNEMETUM lay on the Fosse Way, ½ m. W of the village. Excavation has shown a series of timber buildings on the road frontage. No defences are recorded. In the C6, an ANGLO-SAXON CEMETERY occupied part of the site.

7050                          WINKBURN

Hall and church close together in lovely but overgrown parkland.

ST JOHN OF JERUSALEM.* A Norman W tower rebuilt according to an inscription on the N side in 1632 (or is it 1612 or 1692?). The tower arch has zigzag decoration in jambs and voussoirs, not *in situ* and probably re-used from the original W door. The twin openings at the bell-stage are provided with the rope moulding for the arches which we are familiar with from nearby Southwell. The church itself is a simple box, with a completely 'unrestored' interior, consisting only of nave and chancel separated by the wooden screen. S door decorated with beakheads. One lancet window in the nave. – SCREEN. Probably Jacobean; just three large round-headed openings and very little posthumously Gothic tracery. – PULPIT. Perhaps of the same date, anyway elaborately Jacobean, with tester. – ALTAR RAILS. Of c. 1700, with twisted balusters. – BOX PEWS. Contemporary. One opposite the W door has twisted balusters. – MONUMENTS. William Burnell, 1570. Incised slab on a chest in the chancel. – William Burnell † 1609 (date now defaced). The usual kneeling figure between columns, life-size. – D'Arcy Burnell † 1774, a fine thing, with the figures of Death (young and holding a reversed torch) and Fame (holding the profile portrait of Mr Burnell) l. and r. of the curved pedestal of an urn. Lines from Pope at the end of the inscription. Who may the sculptor be?

WINKBURN HALL. A fine building left empty to decay at the

* There was a camera of the Knights Hospitaller here, c. 1199–1382.

time of writing. It is an interesting house of about 1700 or somewhat earlier. Brick, two-storeyed, with an attic above a wooden
modillion cornice. On both the main seven-bay fronts slightly
advancing wings with stone quoins. Towards the garden a
central door with a large broken segmental pediment and a
finely carved keystone; to the E a plainer pedimented doorcase,
and to the N a Victorian porch with stone Tuscan columns. The
attic is a later addition, shown on a design of 1805 (a date on
the leads reads 1772). The wooden cornice suggests that the
house was originally of the two-storey Coleshill or Belton type
with a hipped roof with balustraded parapet and cupola, and
indeed it is depicted so in a mid-C18 drawing.* Inside, most
of the ground-floor rooms have mid-C18 chimneypieces and
pretty little *sopraporte* with Rococo landscape motifs, exquisitely carved in the SE room, not so good in the staircase hall,
which however has a fine Rococo ceiling. The staircase is a C19
wrought-iron version of the Carolean type with rich scrollwork
balustrade that the house may have originally possessed. In the
centre of the S front the saloon, with original cornices, doorcases, and overmantel; in the NE wing, the library, with later
C18 decoration but with an original marble fireplace with tropi-
cal scene and wigwam.

WINTHORPE                    *8050*

Bisected by the A1 (Newark by-pass), but with the old nucleus
of the village on the N side.

ALL SAINTS. 1886–8 by *S. G. Parry*; brick, with a SE spire. –
In the churchyard an ALTAR TOMB with well-carved urn to
Sarah Thompson † 1809, signed by *Richard Chamberlain* of
Newark.

WINTHORPE HALL. A Palladian villa on a hill, probably started
in 1761 for Dr Robert Taylor of Newark, physician to George
II. From his connections, one might assume his architect to
have been a prominent one, but no name is recorded. Taylor
was comparatively poor, if not bankrupt, at his death in 1762,
so the house may have been unfinished when sold to Roger
Pocklington, the Newark banker. (His brother Joseph built the

* (This also shows E and W wings (stables and kitchens) connected by quadrant colonnades. Only the stable block was built, and a C19 wing connected
it with the W side of the house. The original design may have been abandoned
because it involved the destruction of the church. NS)

almost contemporary Carlton Hall and the later Muskham House at North Muskham.) Of Mansfield stone, five bays, one and a half storeys above a rusticated basement. On the entrance front (N) a double flight of stone steps up to a Venetian window with a Diocletian window above in the slightly projecting, pedimented central bay. S and E fronts each with a deep canted bay. Entered from the N, the hall, with an Ionic screen, opens axially into a semi-octagonal saloon in the centre of the S front. In the centre of the W side the staircase (of the type with three balusters to a tread). Along nearly the whole of the E front, a room extending L-wise into the canted bay. Dull panelled ceilings throughout, richest in the saloon, where the chimneypiece has a scallop shell disgorging fruit from within a broken pediment. Parkland ruined, and semi-detacheds creeping up to the house.*

(Roger Pocklington's building activities were not confined to the Hall. Also his projects: Grove House, said to have been built for his son, Low Wood, and possibly the Dial House, all shown with the Hall in a print of c. 1800. GROVE HOUSE is a villa of c. 1800. A perron leads up to a pedimented entrance into the piano nobile rather as at Winthorpe, though totally without its elegance. Three-light sashes to the main floor, with semicircular windows above. No grandeur about the plan either: just a narrow hall with a plain dog-leg stair. LOW WOOD, down a lane just below the Grove, is dated 1787. Two storeys with hipped roof and modilion cornice, the centre two projecting bays of the four originally pedimented. DIAL HOUSE, at the corner of Gainsborough Road and Holme Lane, was originally single-storey but with central pedimented bays as at Low Wood. Later raised to two storeys, and the pediment, with its sundial, replaced at the new roof-line. NS)

(In the village, WINTHORPE HOUSE: late C18 garden façade with a classical eaves cornice and a graceful door surround; the rest C19 and C20. Next to it, the early C18 LORD NELSON pub. Also early C18 the OLD RECTORY. In Chapel Lane, the former BREWERS CHARITY ALMSHOUSES, 1616, a group of cottages commendably restored by a housing association. NS)

## WISETON

A completely unspoilt village of C18 and C19 cottages. The plain, five-bay, two-and-a-half-storey brick WISETON HALL, dated

* Restoration is under way (1978).

1771, was demolished in 1960, but the late C18 stables survive across the road from the Hall gates. In the Hall during the late C18 lived Mr Acklam, who did much for his estate. His hand is visible in the WHITE SWAN HOTEL, at Drakeholes, an inn placed in a conspicuous position at the junction of the road and the Chesterfield Canal NW of where the Hall stood and made more conspicuous by a composition in three steps. One-storey outer wings, two-storey wings with half-pediments building up to a two-and-a-half-storey centre with a façade of three sides of an octagon, articulated by a blind arch on each side with a round attic window above. The entrance door heavily rusticated. Opposite a pair of LODGES (formerly to the Hall?) with pedimented porticoes. Mr Acklam also built farmhouses 'on all the surrounding eminences'. PUSTO HILL FARM is one of them, also a neat little composition, with a pediment and two wings to the l. and r. all under one sweeping roof with the gable walls broken so the central block appears to be pedimented. Rusticated quoins. (BLACO HILL FARM, s of the village, is no doubt another. Two tower-like projections and pedimented ends to a long range of house and outbuildings. NS)

## WIVERTON HALL

7030

1814, symmetrical, castellated and stuccoed. Of five bays and two storeys with turrets flanking the central feature of *porte-cochère* and large Gothic window, and marking each end of the façade. Other windows with arched heads to the lights. On the l. a one-bay, one-storey wing. This side imitates in a thin early C19 way the later C15 (MWB) gatehouse of the Chaworth mansion* which the new house was built on to. Stone, with round angle-turrets, mullioned windows with straight-headed lights, and string courses. The l. bay has gone and the gateway, with a stone groin-vaulted ceiling, has been blocked to form a dining room. The gate arch is also visible from the inner hall of the later block. Here, a Regency well-staircase, several good inserted fireplaces, and an entrance hall with plaster vault and Gothic doors. The rest of the C17 mansion was pulled down in 1645 during the Civil War. The moat remains to the N, and to the E a Civil War earthwork. A V-shaped mound represents a half-moon battery, formerly matched by one to the W.

* It is shown in *John Smythson*'s sketch plan (survey?) of the house. He also proposed alterations in 1615 (*Archit. His.* III/18 1–2).

The church and village of Wiverton have completely disappeared except for low banks defining the medieval lane between the Hall and the straightened course of the river. Thoroton comments 150 years later in 1676, 'the necessary consequence of inclosure of good land in these parts' (cf. Upper Broughton, etc.).

## WOLLATON *see* NOTTINGHAM p. 273

## WOODBECK *see* RAMPTON

6040

## WOODBOROUGH

ST SWITHUN. The best piece is the chancel, built in the mid C14. It is wide and high and receives its light from a large five-light E window with the wildest of flowing tracery, and three-light N and S windows with ogee-reticulated tracery. In the E gable an additional triangular window with curved sides and flowing tracery which leads into the roof. Inside to the l. and r. of the E window brackets for statues. The PISCINA is a little ogee niche into which a short filleted shaft reaches up (a combination of the shaft and niche types). The SEDILIA must be new. Big W tower, C13 below (see tower arch), Perp above. The arcades of the nave also Perp of the usual Notts type. The oldest feature of the church is the N door: Norman, of three orders, with colonnettes with scalloped capitals and cable and zigzag mouldings of the voussoirs. – FONT. Also Norman, of the usual tub-shape, but decorated with crosses at top and bottom and three rows of zigzags between. – COMMUNION TABLE. Given by John Wood, Recorder of Newark, that is after 1660 (but probably of Jacobean date). – CHOIR STALLS carved by *Mansfield Parkyns*, mid-C19 owner of the Hall. – STAINED GLASS. Early C14 tracery panels in the chancel S side windows (Agony in the Garden, Sleeping Disciples (?), Noli me tangere, Doubting Thomas) and in one N side window (St Catherine and St Margaret). – In the E window, mostly by *Kempe*, 1897, a cherub. – Window of 1910 by *Morris & Co.*, N side of chancel, with saints and prophets, to a *Burne-Jones* design; Virgin and Child by *J. H. Dearle*.

(WOODBOROUGH HALL, at the W end of the village. Built *c.* 1660–70 for Philip Lacock to replace an earlier house of the Strelley family made square and Tudor *c.* 1850 for Mansfield

Parkyns.* The oldest and best feature is the fine well STAIR-
CASE with a scrolled foliage balustrade and carved pots of
flowers on each newel (cf. Thrumpton). On the landing the
main door is enriched; the others have carved and pierced
wooden fanlights. In the DRAWING ROOM an elaborate
pilastered two-tier fireplace (its segmental pediment and coat
of arms have been removed). Simpler, probably restored, two-
tier fireplaces in the staircase hall, dining room, and study
downstairs. In the dining room a sideboard by *Mansfield Parkyns* (cf. the choir stalls in the church).)

(HALL FARMHOUSE. With a plaque under the ivy that reads
'Philip Lacock Esquire 1710'. Brick, three-storey, with two
gables and a central gabled porch. DOE)

Another framework-knitting village, but with fewer remains than
nearby Calverton. At the junction of High Street and Shelt Hill
a group of two-storey cottages with ground-floor knitters' windows. Further W, a first-floor workshop at the rear of No. 117
High Street. Opposite, a row formerly with many long ground-
floor windows, now completely modernized.

FOX WOOD, I m. NW. A small oval hill-fort, one of a group on
the southern fringes of Sherwood Forest. Bivallate, the
defences well preserved on the N and W sides. The site presumably dates from the Iron Age, but there has as yet been no
orderly excavation here. Roman finds, including a stone building, have been made in the interior, so that occupation of this
hill-top may have been prolonged.


WOODTHORPE *see* ARNOLD


WORKSOP                                              5070

RADFORD PRIORY, now known as WORKSOP PRIORY or the 20
CHURCH OF SS. CUTHBERT AND MARY. The placing of the
priory is not happy as it appears now. The market cross by the
gatehouse (near to but not exactly in its original position) shows
that the medieval town lay just outside its precinct. The centre
has migrated W. The town has made a well-meaning effort to
create a civic composition with a Memorial Avenue flanked by
hospital and museum and library, and leading to the façade of
the priory. But that is not the way in which such a building

* According to Mr Myles Hildyard, probably by *T. C. Hine.*

should be seen. It reduces it to being merely the dominant accent in a typically C20 group.

The priory was founded *c.* 1120 by William de Lovetot as an Augustinian house. The nave as we see it now belongs to a second, not the first building. The first was, as excavations have shown, much smaller and had three parallel apses. The second had the more ambitious plan of Cluny, the greatest monastery of France, before it was rebuilt at the end of the C11, that is an apse, flanked by straight-ended chancel chapels, and additional E apses to the transepts. It is the same plan as has been discussed at Blyth. At Worksop this E end in its turn was replaced by a yet larger and grander one in the C13. However, of all that nothing remains except the Lady Chapel, which is a long chapel attached to the S transept. The church in its heyday was 360 ft long; the surviving nave is 135 ft in length. The Lady Chapel lay roofless, ruined, and detached from the C16 until the C20, divided from the nave by a wall built in 1564–7 and replaced in *Rundbogenstil* by *R. Nicholson* of Lincoln in 1845–9. *Sir Harold Brakspear* restored the chapel in 1922 and, in 1929, joined it to the nave by a S transept, reconstructed on the strength of, on the whole, reliable evidence. In 1935 he added a N transept, and in 1970–4 *Laurence King* provided a new E end. The scale and simplicity of the squat tower (with thin flèche), gable-ended choir, and two-storeyed sacristy and vestries are right: the details reveal what a limited vocabulary modern architecture has where conventional materials are required.

19    The Norman building to which the NAVE belongs was probably, as was usual, started at the E. The evidence of style proves that the earliest upright parts were the crossing and the transepts. The transepts had large blank arcading on the ground floor. Capitals scalloped. The arches from the aisles into the transepts are decorated with zigzag. The first bay of the nave belongs to the same design. It also has Norman decoration. But then the plan was changed, and the rest of the interior is latest Norman, or rather Transitional. The nave is long and not excessively high, very busy with decoration, but a decoration no longer as fanciful and noisy as that of Norman masons had been. It is in fact curiously unimaginative (on the whole just a repeat of the nailhead motif). It would be tedious to enumerate all the places where it occurs. The elevation of the nave consists, from E to W, of nine bays on alternating supports, circular and octagonal (cf. Peterborough transepts), and then, after a short

stretch of wall, one more bay opening into the ground-floor chambers of the two towers. The capitals have sparse stylized upright leaves, very elementary, the arches a fairly complex moulding. The hoodmoulds are all nailhead. The aisles are vaulted, the N aisle before the S (see the profiles of the ribs). Above the aisles a gallery opening towards the nave in a most curious fashion, not as just one large arch as at Blyth and Southwell, nor subdivided into two as, say, at Peterborough, but in a tripartite rhythm with a big unbroken central arch, not quite as wide as the arch below, and then a small arch on each side. The whole makes an ABAB, etc., rhythm, and, to add yet more variety, the large arches cut into the clerestory zone, and the clerestory windows (with one order of shafts) are placed above the small, not the large gallery arches, that is above the columns of the ground floor, not the apexes of the arcade (an odd, somewhat wilful composition), a 'Baroque' late phase of Norman, one is tempted to say, just before the new classicity of the early Gothic became the ideal.

The FAÇADE rises in the greyness of its ashlarwork, rigid and flat to the height of the towers. Only their tops are Perp. The buttresses are as shallow as Normandy made them in the C11, and have no set-offs on their way up. Apart from the unique feature of both a central portal and one into the N aisle, there is nothing to interrupt the bareness of this wall but one large central window, the only such survivor. The window has nailhead decoration and the modest central portal is decidedly Transitional: slender shafts with waterleaf capitals and waterholding bases; more nailhead. Only on the voussoirs are more truly Norman geometrical patterns. On the inner face of the W wall, the responds and jambs break the coursing as if they were inserted later. The keeled mouldings are not a logical response to the W pier demi-column either. In the upper stages, more Transitional features: two round-headed windows of two pointed lights in the top stage and several single lancets below. The outer aisle walls also have these flat buttresses, and wavy corbel tables. Their windows incidentally are imitations by *Nicholson*. until he replaced them, the N ones were Dec anyway. Further doorways, also late C12 in style, are on the N and S sides.

The LADY CHAPEL is of exquisite C13 design, closely con- 21 nected with contemporary Southwell and Yorkshire: tall, slim, nobly erect forms, and an almost complete absence of ornamentation (for instance moulded capitals throughout). There are three parallel lancet windows to the E and twice three to the s. Inside, SEDILIA and PISCINA have two orders of colon-nettes. The shafts here and everywhere have fillets, also outside between the lancets. These fillets, which occur in many east Notts churches of the C13, are a characteristic early Gothic conception. The stoutness of the circular pier seemed too brutal; a fillet (or simply a keeling) added shadows and emphasized line instead of mass. And such a composition as this Lady Chapel is eminently a matter of vigorous, sharp lines, as against the broader effects of the earlier nave. Vaulting was intended, but apparently given up before the walls were quite up.

The contents are sadly disappointing. Nothing at all special except the splendid late C12 SOUTH DOOR (in an early C13 porch), with elaborate scrollwork, always four small scrolls branching off from and curling into one large one (the pattern also appearing at Southwell and in other places). – REREDOS, moved from the high altar to the N transept. Rich Dec work by *Sir G. G. Scott*. – Jacobean COMMUNION TABLE, S transept. – (All the Victorian STAINED GLASS reset, alas, in 1968 and the panels made to float in clear-glazed settings: a pernicious practice intended to admit more light. – Crude E window by *John Hayward*, 1968. – W window, 1868, perhaps by *O'Connor*. RH) – MONUMENTS to Sir Thomas Neville, High Treasurer of England, † 1406, his wife, and her brother Lord Furnival † 1366; badly damaged but not to be despised.

Hardly any of the MONASTIC BUILDINGS survive. The CLOISTERS were on the N side, i.e. a reversal of the normal layout. Only the three-bay rib-vaulted parlour survives intact as the VESTRY. W of it a well-constructed chimney may indicate the prior's lodgings; on the N are the door and some windows of the cellarium; and, to the E, the foundations of the kitchens lie under the Abbey School.

GATEHOUSE, to the S. Broad and stately, early C14 in its structure, mid-C14 in the addition of the precious porch (which gave access to a chapel in the SE angle) with curvilinear tracery, miniature diagonal buttresses, and a relief panel of the Adoration of the Magi. Inside, a rich lierne-vault, canopied niche, and enriched doorway to the chapel. Three statues left in the three niches of the S side, only Gabriel from an Annunciation group on the N. The gateway itself still E.E. in its jambs and arches. The arch-braced ceiling beams with carved stone corbels are original. The main window above the entrance, Perp of seven lights, is to a hall with a fine untouched fireplace.

ST JOHN, Gateford Road. With a tall spire. 1867–8 by *R. C. Clarke*

*& Son*; berated by contemporary opinion. – STAINED GLASS (E window) given by C. G. S. Foljambe in memory of his wife Louisa Blanche † 1871.

ST ANNE, Newcastle Avenue. 1911 by *Paley & Austin*; neo-Perp, large, with a big NW tower. The interior as one might expect, large and dull; the best feature is the tall arches into the N transept. No fittings of interest.

ST MARY (R.C.), Park Street. 1838–9 by *M. E. Hadfield* for the Duke of Norfolk, the interior still of the 1820 type, that is, rather thin and timid (unaisled, of five bays with a hammerbeam roof), but the front unusually solid and serious with its Perp window and bellcote.

ST JOSEPH THE WORKER (R.C.), Blyth Road. By *Horsley & Currall*, 1969–70. Brick, octagonal, with a central spirelet, much simpler than their church at Newark.

UNITED REFORMED CHURCH, Queen Street. By *Bartlett & Gray*, 1965–7. Badly placed at the back of the site, offering no street façade.

WORKSOP COLLEGE, S of the town. Opened in 1895 as St Cuthbert's College. The earliest buildings, including the hall, on the W side are by *R. H. Carpenter*, 1890–5, hard and sharp scholastic neo-Tudor in red brick, a sort of superior Board School style. Headmaster's house (1926) and N side of the quadrangle up to the clock tower 1897. The rest of the quadrangle 1929–34. 1920s work by *B. D. Thompson*. On the S side, the CHAPEL by *Aston Webb*, 1907–11. – STAINED GLASS in the E window by *Kempe & Co*, 1913.

ABBEY GIRLS' SCHOOL, Priorswell Road. 1841, a good example of Victorian E.E. with lancet windows. Originally one large room in the corner of the priory churchyard, extended by a classroom towards the road in 1878.

A walk through the streets is unrewarding. The town spreads out in a spider fashion and has a neglected air. The MARKET PLACE is not a centre. The dull Italianate-cum-Jacobean TOWN HALL (built as the Corn Exchange by *Charles Gilbert* in 1851) presents only its side to it. The only remaining and much restored timber-framed house, the OLD SHIP INN, has genuine framing on the ground floor with a little carving on the timbers; much rebuilt above. POTTER STREET, leading out of the Market Place to the E, has some Georgian houses. The best stretch, Nos. 40–44, and several others have been demolished.* Also gone is the most notable No. 5. Nos. 33–

*The site is to be redeveloped with offices.

35 is a seven-bay stone house built in the early C18 and enlarged in the late C18 or early C19. On the façade most of the features are early C18: alternating pediments to the three dormers, quoins, flat string courses between the two storeys. Three centre bays set closer together, and a Roman Doric porch with doorways altered to serve two houses. These made a grander composition at the back, with two quadrant wings (r. one demolished). A few more altered Georgian properties in West-gate, Newgate Street, Park Street, and in BRIDGE STREET, perhaps the best of these streets: on a hill and nothing much of interest but nothing really out of scale. On the l. the late neo-classical TRUSTEE SAVINGS BANK, 1843, one of the few stone buildings in the town. Almost opposite, the YORKSHIRE BANK (1859), a later example of the same neo-classical mode in brick and stone. Further s in PARK STREET a nice late Georgian terrace with segmental pedimented doorhoods on brackets.

Worth mentioning also are the few industrial monuments. In NORFOLK STREET, a terrace of millworkers' cottages curiously of stone with brick dressings and laid out with two two-storey terraces each ending in three-storey pavilions on either side of the street.* Spanning the Chesterfield Canal near the town centre a well-known CANAL DEPOSITORY with adjacent offices. Early C19, of yellowish brick which stands out in this red-brick town. The arch has fine stone voussoirs and under it huge wooden beams and a trap-door for loading. The RAILWAY STATION, 1850 by *James Drabble* of Carlton, of good solid Steetley stone in the Derbyshire–Yorkshire Jacobean, has been exceptionally well treated by British Rail. Further out towards Kilton, the empty but as yet intact BRACEBRIDGE SEWAGE PUMPING STATION of 1881 with its fine tall square chimney on an ashlar pedestal. A good example with simple Lombard Romanesque details all in brick, and inside a gallery on cast-iron columns and a spiral stair.‡

WORKSOP MANOR. The fourth Earl of Shrewsbury's 'fair lodge at Wyrksoppe Park, not yet finished' was mentioned by Leland in his *Itinerary* (1534–43). It was swallowed up in the sixth Earl's magnificent late C16 mansion which we know only from illustrations: by Hall, who seems to show some of the earlier fabric (in Thoroton's *History ... of Nottinghamshire*, 1676), and

---

* Both mills set up in the town failed and were converted to other uses. Information about Norfolk Street from Mr P. Middleton.

‡ Threatened in 1978, but it could be adapted for recreational use in association with the nearby canal.

by Buck and Couse in the early C18. To judge from these illus- 61
trations and from drawings for the screen (*Archit. His.* 1/26),
it was designed by the Shrewsbury protégé *Robert Smythson*. In style and in plan it comes between Longleat, where
Smythson worked in 1572, and his Hardwick Hall, begun for
the Countess of Shrewsbury in 1590.* Among all the tall
Smythson-type houses (*see* p. 26), Worksop was prodigiously
tall, with a narrow central tower in the centre of each façade
capped by a domed lantern and, on the ends of the long façades,
projecting square bays. Like Hardwick, the façades were without ornament, and the design was dependent for its effect on
the symmetrical towered silhouette and huge mullioned windows. The long gallery, famous throughout England, ran along
the top floor and, like the domed lanterns, the Longleat rooftop
banqueting houses, the Wollaton prospect room, etc., afforded
the magnificent views so admired.

The manor devolved upon Shrewsbury's granddaughter and
by marriage upon the Dukes of Norfolk. The first to build there
was probably the eighth Duke, who succeeded in 1701. He
modernized the house, putting in sashes and squaring off the
towers to achieve the fashionable rectangular silhouette, and
created *cours d'honneur* at the back and front. The best feature
was the main staircase painted in 1709 by *Jacques Parmentier*
(cf. Averham), who spent twenty years working in Yorkshire.
The early C18 formal garden was relaid on a vast and expensive
scale between 1733 and 1744 by *Lord Petre*, who had already
designed his own garden at Thorndon Hall, Essex. The design
(drawn out by *Peter Bourguinon*) is novel and important because
it marks a move towards English naturalism, still geometrical,
'but the compass had succeeded the set square', and with lots
of surprise elements. Of this nothing can be seen. The eighth
Duke's STABLE AND OFFICE COURT still survives: typical
of its date, with an archway crowned by a cupola, plain sashes
and pedimented dormers on all sides, and segmental pediments
to some doors.

The house was consumed by fire in 1761 and was replaced
by part of a splendid Palladian composition by *James Paine*,

* When it was begun is unknown. Only four documents definitely relate
to the building of Worksop Manor, and all refer to its completion in 1585–
6. Mary Queen of Scots stayed there in 1583, which suggests that the house
was substantially complete. David Durant (*see Bess of Hardwick*, 1977, p. 106–
7) believes it was begun *c.* 1575, prompted by Elizabeth I's Midlands progress
in that year. Two documents referring to building work at an unspecified
house, dated 1577 and 1580, are inconclusive evidence.

who had been redecorating the apartments in the old house since *c.* 1756. It was the largest country house commission since Blenheim and, like Blenheim, would have been a palace rather than a country house. Paine's quadrangular designs seem to have been informed by the major unrealized C17 and C18 palace designs: Jones's for Whitehall, Chambers's for Richmond, Kent's for Hyde Park. Four ranges were to be linked by an Egyptian Hall on the model of Burlington's York Assembly Rooms. After only one wing was finished, the death of the heir in 1767 stopped the Duchess's enthusiasm for the new house.*
She had been the prime mover behind the scheme, conceiving and sketching the basic ideas which Paine improved and refined. Then, in 1839, the estate was sold to the Duke of Newcastle who, having come into Clumber nearby, was not at all interested in keeping up Worksop. So the wing of twenty-three bays was pulled down. All that remains is the rusticated basement of the N side with one room behind it; the pieced-together sculpture of the pediment, drawn by the Duchess and carved by *William Collins* in 1765; and Paine's splendid screen, with its Doric columns and triumphal-arch feature, designed to conceal the stable court and originally matched by another on the E side.

CASTLE FARM, ½ m. SE of the house (in Gothic style), was designed in 1758 by the Duchess, obviously no mean amateur architect.

62      MANOR LODGE, Haggonfields Lane, off the A60 opposite the walls of Worksop Manor park, was originally a lodge to the C16 Worksop Manor, though for what purpose is not clear; possibly a hunting or guest lodge. Big for a lodge, with a large number of small rooms of equal size, and plainly, though admirably, built. The ingenious plan suggests that *Robert Smythson,* who built the Manor, was also responsible for the lodge. Like Shireoaks Hall, which can be seen 1½ m. away to the NW, the plan is a cross but of a different shape: the cross wing short and wide, the side wings long and narrow. Exceptionally tall, with a basement (made into the ground floor in the C18) and four storeys of small rooms in each wing above it. John Holland in his *History of Worksop* (1826) says that there were originally two more storeys. There must have been at least one more, for the main staircase breaks off suddenly in the attic under a later

* Dr Leach, who has kindly provided all the information about Paine included in this account, thinks that no more building may have been intended, at least at that time. The wing was a house in itself, and Paine's agreement for six years covered precisely the time of the executed work, 1761–7.

gabled roof. The original roof-line was no doubt flat, possibly with a battlemented parapet. (A coping stone is built into the garden wall.) Filling the cross wing above the basement two vast double-height rooms (the Great Hall and Great Chamber), one above the other, corresponding to, respectively, the first and second floors and third and fourth floors in the wings. The lost top floors may have contained a gallery. The main (now first) floor of the cross wing was entered by a flight of steps leading to a central round-headed door (cf., for example, Smythson's Barlborough Hall and Bolsover Keep, Derbys, and Shireoaks Hall). The doorway, replaced in the c18 by a window, opened into a lobby which filled the front projection. From here the Great Hall was entered in the middle of its short side, a novel arrangement paralleled only by that at Hardwick Old and New Halls.* As at Hardwick, the two halves of the house were completely separated by the Hall and Chamber, with no direct communication between the second and fourth floors on either side.‡ The Hall and Great Chamber are lit by huge mullioned-and-transomed windows of the Hardwick type, now partly blocked, the rooms in the wings by low three-light mullioned ones. At the back, another curious feature of the plan: two projections corbelled out from second-floor level containing closets, each lit by a single-light window, and flues. In the w wing the main staircase with a stone newel, as at Shireoaks, but on a grander scale and with wooden treads. There has been more alteration than first appears from the remarkably intact exterior. Floor levels have been changed, the back of the Great Hall made two-storey and subdivided, and the entrance lobby made one with it. But the Great Chamber, though stripped of its decoration, is still its full size. All the smaller rooms totally plain, with simple chamfered stone doorcases and fireplaces.

On the A57 w of Worksop at GATEFORD, three interesting houses.§ GATEFORD HALL is a long, low house with a coursed rubble façade, altered in the c17, but with remains of the medieval manor house: the stone walling, internal timber-framing, and part of the moat. GATEFORD HOUSE, E of it,

* There is no date for the lodge, but presumably it is roughly contemporary with Worksop Manor, or at least built before the Earl's death in 1590. Alterations to Hardwick Old Hall were begun in 1584, but the axial hall may have been part of the plans of John Hardwick's previous manor house.

‡ There is no trace of any connection between the wings, not even via a gallery over a hall screen at second-floor level, or of an original main staircase in the E wing.

§ Mr J. V. Machin kindly provided the details about these houses.

is a double-pile brick house of two-and-a-half storeys. Flemish bond with light headers giving a speckled effect. Gabled rear range of *c.* 1700 to which a front range with hipped roof, plain sashes, and pedimented doorcase was added *c.* 1720–40. GATE-FORD HILL, high up behind Gateford Hall, built in 1824 by *George Crockney* for Henry Machin, has quite a handsome façade with a large porch of coupled Greek Doric columns. Office additions of 1959–63.

# WYSALL

HOLY TRINITY. The N side should be inspected first: rough Norman masonry with a tiny Norman window and a doorway. C13 W tower with spire and one lancet window. The chancel is C14, the S arcade (octagonal piers and capitals with large horizontal nobbly leaves) C15, as are the chancel roof, the clerestory, the PULPIT with tracery panels, and the SCREEN (of the same type as Newark), which has four MISERICORDS (one with a face, the rest with leaves) at its back. But to some visitors an odder piece of woodwork will be even more attractive: the LADDER into the bell-chamber of the tower, which may well be as old as the tower itself. – FONT. E.E. – STOUP in the chancel, with an early C14 head. – CANDELABRA (chancel). Small and pretty, brass, 1773. – MONUMENTS. Hugh Armstrong † 1572 and wife, alabaster, with figures holding shields along the tomb-chest walls (cf. Ratcliffe † 1558). The faces of the two effigies far from lively. – (Heraldic wooden tablet to George Widmerpool † 1689. KT)

(MANOR HOUSE, next to the Post Office and with a fine brick barn towards the road. C16 or C17 front wall roughcast over timber-framing. Central gabled entrance and one gabled wing both with jettied upper floors. Balancing wing probably demolished when the brick cottages were built. NS)

(MANOR FARMHOUSE, N of the church. A substantial house with C17 diaper-patterned brickwork on a stone plinth with areas of older stone walling in the rear wall and stair-turret, possibly from an earlier house here. Mouldings of late medieval type to a main ground-floor beam. Many later additions. NS)

(COTTAGE (The Nook) dated 1718, brick, with an angled hood-mould to the gable window, showing the persistence of medieval traditions. MWB)

# GLOSSARY

Particular types of an architectural element are often defined under the name of the element iself; e.g. for 'dog-leg stair' see STAIR. Literal meanings, where specially relevant, are indicated by the abbreviation *lit.*

For further reference (especially for style terms) the following are a selection of books that can be consulted: *A Dictionary of Architecture* (N. Pevsner, J. Fleming, H. Honour, 1975); *The Illustrated Glossary of Architecture* (J. Harris and J. Lever, 1966); *Encyclopedia of Modern Architecture* (edited by Wolfgang Pehnt, 1963); *The Classical Language of Architecture* (J. Summerson, 1964); *The Dictionary of Ornament* (M. Stafford and D. Ware, 1974); *Illustrated Handbook of Vernacular Architecture* (R. W. Brunskill, 1976); *English Brickwork* (A. Clifton Taylor and R. W. Brunskill, 1977); *A Pattern of English Building* (A. Clifton Taylor, 1972).

ABACUS (*lit.* tablet): flat slab forming the top of a capital; *see* Orders (fig. 17).

ABUTMENT: the meeting of an arch or vault with its solid lateral support, or the support itself.

ACANTHUS: formalized leaf ornament with thick veins and frilled edge, e.g. on a Corinthian capital.

ACHIEVEMENT OF ARMS: in heraldry, a complete display of armorial bearings.

ACROTERION (*lit.* peak): plinth for a statue or ornament placed at the apex or ends of a pediment; also, loosely and more usually, both the plinths and what stands on them.

ADDORSED: description of two figures placed symmetrically back to back

AEDICULE (*lit.* little building): architectural surround, consisting usually of two columns or pilasters supporting a pediment, framing a niche or opening. *See also* Tabernacle.

AFFRONTED: description of two figures placed symmetrically face to face.

AGGER (*lit.* rampart): Latin term for the built-up foundations of Roman roads; also sometimes applied to the ramparts of hill-forts or other earthworks.

AGGREGATE: small stones added to a binding material, e.g. in concrete. In modern architecture used alone to describe concrete with an aggregate of stone chippings, e.g. granite, quartz, etc.

AISLE (*lit.* wing): passage alongside the nave, choir, or transept of a church, or the main body of some other building, separated from it by columns, piers, or posts.

AMBULATORY (*lit.* walkway): aisle at the E end of a chancel, sometimes surrounding an apse and therefore semicircular or polygonal in plan

AMORINI: *see* Putto.

ANGLE ROLL: roll moulding in the angle between two planes, e.g. between the orders of an arch.

ANNULET (*lit.* ring): shaft-ring (*see* Shaft).

ANSE DE PANIER (*lit.* basket handle): basket arch (*see* Arch).

ANTAE: flat pilasters with capitals different from the order they accompany, placed at the ends of the short projecting walls of a portico or of a colonnade which is then called *In Antis*.

ANTEFIXAE: ornaments projecting at regular intervals above a classical cornice, originally to conceal the ends of roof tiles.

ANTEPENDIUM: *see* Frontal.

ANTHEMION (*lit.* honeysuckle): classical ornament like a honeysuckle flower (*see* fig. 1).

Fig. 1. Anthemion and Palmette Frieze

APRON: raised panel below a window-sill, sometimes shaped and decorated.

A.P.S.D.: Architectural Publications Society Dictionary.

APSE: semicircular (i.e. apsidal) extension of an apartment: *see also* Exedra. A term first used of the magistrate's end of a Roman basilica, and thence especially of the vaulted semicircular or polygonal end of a chancel or a chapel.

ARABESQUE: type of painted or carved surface decoration consisting of flowing lines and intertwined foliage scrolls etc., generally based on geometrical patterns. Cf. Grotesque.

ARCADE: (1) series of arches supported by piers or columns. *Blind Arcade:* the same applied to the surface of a wall. *Wall Arcade:* in medieval churches, a blind arcade forming a dado below

windows. (2) a covered shopping street.

ARCH: for the various forms *see* fig. 2. The term *Basket Arch* refers to a basket handle and is sometimes applied to a three-centred or depressed arch as well as to the type with a flat middle. A *Transverse Arch* runs across the main axis of an interior space. The term is used especially for the arches between the compartments of tunnel- or groin-vaulting. *Diaphragm Arch:* transverse arch with solid spandrels spanning an otherwise wooden-roofed interior. *Chancel Arch:* w opening from the chancel into the nave. *Relieving* (or *Discharging*) *Arch:* incorporated in a wall, to carry some of its weight, some way above an opening. *Strainer Arch:* inserted across an opening to resist any inward pressure of the side members. *Triumphal Arch:* Imperial Roman monument whose elevation supplied a motif for many later classical compositions.

ARCHITRAVE: (1) formalized lintel, the lowest member of the classical entablature (*see* Orders, fig. 17); (2) moulded frame of a door or window (often borrowing the profile of an architrave in the strict sense). Also *Lugged Architrave*, where the top is prolonged into lugs (*lit.* ears) at the sides; *Shouldered*, where the frame rises vertically at the top angles and returns horizontally at the sides forming shoulders (*see* fig. 3).

ARCHIVOLT: architrave moulding when it follows the line of an arch.

ARCUATED: dependent structurally on the use of arches or the arch principle; cf. Trabeated.

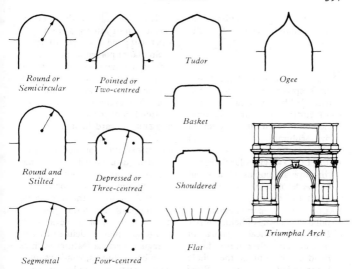

*Round or Semicircular*   *Pointed or Two-centred*   *Tudor*   *Ogee*

*Round and Stilted*   *Depressed or Three-centred*   *Basket*   *Shouldered*

*Segmental*   *Four-centred*   *Flat*   *Triumphal Arch*

Fig. 2. Arch

ARRIS (*lit.* stop): sharp edge at the meeting of two surfaces.

ASHLAR: masonry of large blocks wrought to even faces and square edges.

ASTRAGAL (*lit.* knuckle): moulding of semicircular section often with bead-and-reel enrichment.

ASTYLAR: term used to describe an elevation that has no columns or similar vertical features.

ATLANTES (*lit.* Atlas figures, from the god Atlas carrying the globe): male counterparts of caryatids (q.v.), often in a more demonstrative attitude of support.

ATRIUM: inner court of a Roman house; also open court in front of a church.

ATTACHED: *see* Engaged Column.

ATTIC: (1) small top storey, especially within a sloping roof; (2) in classical architecture, a storey above the main entablature of the façade, as in a triumphal arch (*see* fig. 2).

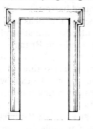

**Lugged**

**Shouldered**

Fig. 3. Architrave

AUMBRY: recess or cupboard to hold sacred vessels for the Mass.

BAILEY: area around the motte or keep (qq.v.) of a castle, defended by a wall and ditch.

BALDACCHINO: free-standing canopy over an altar supported by columns. Also called *Ciborium* (q.v.).

BALLFLOWER: globular flower of three petals enclosing a small ball. A decoration used in the first quarter of the C14.

BALUSTER (*lit.* pomegranate): a pillar or pedestal of bellied form. *Balusters:* vertical supports of this or any other form, for a handrail or coping, the whole being called a *Balustrade. Blind Balustrade:* the same with a wall behind.

BARBICAN: outwork defending the entrance to a castle.

BARGEBOARDS: corruption of vergeboards. Boards, often carved or fretted, fixed beneath the eaves of a gable to cover and protect the rafters.

BARROW: burial mound; *see* Bell, Bowl, Disc, Long, and Pond Barrow.

BARTIZAN (*lit.* battlement): corbelled turret, square or round, frequently at a corner, hence *Corner Bartizan.*

BASE: moulded foot of a column or other order. For its use in classical architecture *see* Orders (fig. 17).

BASEMENT: lowest, subordinate storey of a building, and hence the lowest part of an elevation, below the main floor.

BASILICA (*lit.* royal building): a Roman public hall; hence an aisled building with a clerestory, most often a church.

BASTION: one of a series of semi-circular or polygonal projections from the main wall of a fortress or city, placed at intervals in such a manner as to enable the garrison to cover the intervening stretches of the wall.

BATTER: inward inclination of a wall.

BATTLEMENT: fortified parapet, indented or crenellated so that archers could shoot through the indentations (crenels or embrasures) between the projecting solid portions (merlons).

BAYS: divisions of an elevation or interior space as defined by any regular vertical features such as arches, columns, windows, etc.

BAY-WINDOW: window of one or more storeys projecting from the face of a building at ground level, and either rectangular or polygonal on plan. A *Canted Bay-window* has a straight front and angled sides. A *Bow Window* is curved. An *Oriel Window* projects on corbels or brackets and does not start from the ground.

BEAKER FOLK: late Neolithic settlers from western Europe named after a distinctive type of pottery vessel found in their funerary monuments (often round barrows) and their settlements. The Beaker period saw a wider dissemination of metal implements in Britain.

BEAKHEAD: Norman ornamental motif consisting of a row of bird or beast heads with beaks, usually biting into a roll moulding.

BELFRY: (1) bell-turret set on a roof or gable (*see also* Bellcote); (2) room or stage in a tower where bells are hung; (3) bell-tower in a general sense.

BELGAE : Iron Age tribes living in north-eastern Gaul, from which settlers came into Britain between 100 and 55 B.C. and later. These immigrants may not have been numerous, but their impact on material culture in southern Britain was marked.

BELL BARROW : early Bronze Age round barrow in which the mound is separated from its encircling ditch by a flat platform or berm (q.v.).

BELL CAPITAL : see fig. 7.

BELLCOTE : belfry as (1) above, sometimes with the character of a small house for the bell(s).

BERM : level area separating ditch from bank on a hill-fort or barrow.

BILLET (*lit.* log or block) FRIEZE : Norman ornament consisting of

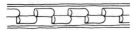

Fig. 4. Billet Frieze

small half-cylindrical or rectangular blocks placed at regular intervals (*see* fig. 4).

BIVALLATE : (of a hill-fort) defended by two concentric banks and ditches.

BLIND : *see* Arcade, Balustrade, Portico.

BLOCK CAPITAL : *see* fig. 7.

BLOCKED : term applied to columns etc. that are interrupted by regular projecting blocks, e.g. the sides of a Gibbs surround (*see* fig. 11).

BLOCKING COURSE : plain course of stones, or equivalent, on top of a cornice and crowning the wall.

BOLECTION MOULDING : convex moulding covering the joint between two different planes and overlapping the higher as well as the lower one, used especially in the late C17 and early C18.

BOND : in brickwork, the pattern of long sides (stretchers) and short ends (headers) produced on

*English*

*Flemish*

Fig. 5. Bond

the face of a wall by laying bricks in a particular way. For the two most common bonds *see* fig. 5.

BOSS : knob or projection usually placed at the intersection of ribs in a vault.

BOW WINDOW : *see* Bay-window.

BOWL BARROW : round barrow surrounded by a quarry ditch. Introduced in late Neolithic times, the form continued until the Saxon period.

BOX FRAME : (1) timber-framed construction in which vertical and horizontal wall members support the roof. (2) in modern architecture, a box-like form of concrete construction where the loads are taken on cross walls, suitable only for buildings consisting of repetitive small cells. Also called *Cross-wall Construction*.

BOX PEW : pew enclosed by a high wooden back and ends, the latter having doors.

BRACE: subsidiary timber set diagonally to strengthen a timber frame. It can be curved or straight. *See also* Roofs (3) and figs. 22–6.

BRACKET: small supporting piece of stone, etc., to carry a projecting horizontal member.

BRATTISHING: ornamental cresting on a wall, usually formed of leaves or Tudor flowers or miniature battlements.

BRESSUMER (*lit.* breast-beam): big horizontal beam, usually set forward from the lower part of a building, supporting the wall above.

BROACH: *see* Spire.

BRONZE AGE: in Britain, the period from *c.* 2000 to 600 B.C.

BUCRANIUM: ox skull used decoratively in classical friezes.

BULLSEYE WINDOW: small circular or oval window, e.g. in the tympanum of a pediment. Also called *Œil de Bœuf*.

BUTTRESS: vertical member projecting from a wall to stabilize it or to resist the lateral thrust of an arch, roof, or vault. For different types used at the corners of a building, especially a tower, *see* fig. 6. A *Flying Buttress* transmits the thrust to a heavy abutment by means of an arch or half-arch.

CABLE MOULDING: originally a Norman moulding, imitating the twisted strands of a rope. Also called *Rope Moulding*.

CAIRN: a mound of stones usually covering a burial.

CALEFACTORY: room in a monastery where a fire burned for the comfort of the monks. Also called *Warming Room*.

CAMBER: slight rise or upward curve in place of a horizontal line or plane.

CAMES: *see* Quarries.

CAMPANILE: free-standing bell-tower.

CANOPY: projection or hood usually over an altar, pulpit, niche, statue, etc.

CANTED: tilted, generally on a vertical axis to produce an obtuse angle on plan, e.g. of a canted bay-window.

CANTILEVER: horizontal projection (e.g. step, canopy) supported by a downward force behind the fulcrum. It is without external bracing and thus appears to be self-supporting.

CAPITAL: head or crowning feature of a column or pilaster; for classical types *see* Orders (fig. 17); for medieval types *see* fig. 7.

CARREL: (1) niche in a cloister where a monk could sit to work or read; (2) similar feature in open-plan offices and libraries.

CARTOUCHE: tablet with ornate frame, usually of elliptical shape and bearing a coat of arms or inscription.

*Angle Buttresses*

*Diagonal Buttresses*

*Setback Buttresses*

*Clasping Buttresses*

Fig. 6. Buttresses

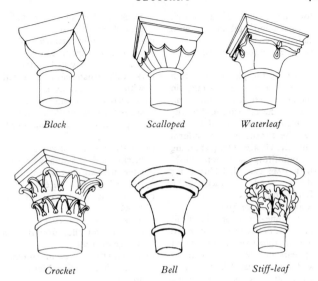

Block   Scalloped   Waterleaf

Crocket   Bell   Stiff-leaf

Fig. 7. Capitals

CARYATIDS (*lit.* daughters of the village of Caryae): female figures supporting an entablature, counterparts of Atlantes (q.v.).

CASEMATE: in military architecture, a vaulted chamber, with embrasures for defence, built into the thickness of the wall of a castle or fortress or projecting from it.

CASEMENT: (1) window hinged at the side; (2) in Gothic architecture, a concave moulding framing a window.

CASTELLATED: battlemented.

CAVETTO: concave moulding of quarter-round section.

CELURE OR CEILURE: panelled and adorned part of a wagon roof above the rood or the altar.

CENOTAPH (*lit.* empty tomb): funerary monument which is not a burying place.

CENTERING: wooden support for the building of an arch or vault, removed after completion.

CHAMBERED TOMB: Neolithic burial mound with a stone-built chamber and entrance passage covered by an earthen barrow or stone cairn.

CHAMFER (*lit.* corner-break): surface formed by cutting off a square edge, usually at an angle of forty-five degrees.

CHANCEL (*lit.* enclosure): that part of the E end of a church in which the main altar is placed. Except in cathedral and monastic churches, usually applied to the whole continuation of the nave E of the crossing.

CHANTRY CHAPEL: chapel, often attached to or inside a church, endowed for the celebration of masses for the soul of the founder or others.

CHEVET (*lit.* head): French term

for the E end of a church (chancel and ambulatory with radiating chapels).

CHEVRON: zigzag Norman ornament.

CHOIR: (1) the part of a church where services are sung; in monastic churches this can occupy the crossing and/or the easternmost bays of the nave; (2) the E arm of a cruciform church (a usage of long standing though liturgically anomalous).

CIBORIUM: canopied shrine for the reserved sacrament or a Baldacchino (q.v.).

CINQUEFOIL: see Foil.

CIST: stone-lined or slab-built grave. If below ground, covered with a protective barrow. It first appears in late Neolithic times and was also used in the Early Christian period in West Britain.

CLADDING: external covering or skin applied to a structure, especially framed buildings (q.v.), for aesthetic or protective purposes.

CLAPPER BRIDGE: bridge made of large slabs of stone, some making rough piers, with longer ones laid on top to make the roadway.

CLASP: see Industrialized Building.

CLASSIC: term for the moment of highest achievement of a style.

CLASSICAL: term for Greek and Roman architecture and any subsequent styles inspired by it.

CLERESTORY: upper storey of the nave walls of a church, pierced by windows. Also applied to high-level windows in domestic architecture.

CLUSTER BLOCK: multi-storey building in which individual blocks of flats cluster round a central service core.

COADE STONE: artificial (cast) stone made from c. 1769 by Coade and Sealy in London.

COB: walling material of clay mixed with straw and gravel.

COFFERING: arrangement of sunken panels (coffers), square or polygonal, decorating a ceiling, vault, or arch.

COGGING: a decorative course of bricks laid diagonally as an alternative to dentilation (q.v.). Also called *Dogtooth Brickwork*.

COLLAR: see Roofs (3) and figs. 23–6.

COLLEGIATE CHURCH: church endowed for the support of a college of priests.

COLONNADE: range of columns supporting an entablature or arches.

COLONNETTE: in medieval architecture, a small column or shaft.

COLOSSAL ORDER: see Order.

COLUMN: in classical architecture, an upright structural member of round section with a shaft, a capital, and usually a base. *See* Orders (fig. 17).

COLUMN FIGURE: in medieval architecture, carved figure attached to a column or shaft flanking a doorway.

COMPOSITE: see Orders.

COMPOUND PIER: a pier consisting of a bundle of shafts (q.v.), or of a solid core surrounded by attached or detached shafts.

CONSOLE: ornamental bracket of compound curved outline (*see* fig. 8).

COPING (*lit.* capping): course of stones, or equivalent, on top of a wall.

CORBEL: block of stone projecting from a wall, supporting some

Fig. 8. Consoles

feature on its horizontal top surface. *Corbel Course:* continuous projecting course of stones or bricks fulfilling the same function. *Corbel Table:* series of corbels to carry a parapet or a wall-plate; for the latter *see* Roofs (3) and figs. 22–5. *Corbelling:* brick or masonry courses built out beyond one another like a series of corbels to support a chimneystack, window, etc.

CORINTHIAN: *see* Orders (fig. 17).

CORNICE: (1) moulded ledge, projecting along the top of a building or feature, especially as the highest member of the classical entablature (*see* Orders, fig. 17); (2) decorative moulding in the angle between wall and ceiling.

CORPS-DE-LOGIS: French term for the main building(s) as distinct from the wings or pavilions.

COTTAGE ORNÉ: an artfully rustic building usually of asymmetrical plan. A product of the late C18 and early C19 picturesque.

COUNTERSCARP BANK: small bank on the downhill or outer side of a hill-fort ditch.

COUR D'HONNEUR: entrance court before a house in the French manner, usually with wings enclosing the sides and a screen wall or low range of buildings across the front.

COURSE: continuous layer of stones etc. in a wall.

COVE: a concave moulding on a large scale, e.g. in a *Coved Ceiling*, which has a pronounced cove joining the walls to a flat central area.

CRADLE ROOF: *see* Wagon Roof.

CREDENCE: in a church or chapel, a side table, or often a recess, for the sacramental elements before consecration.

CRENELLATION: *see* Battlement.

CREST, CRESTING: ornamental finish along the top of a screen, etc.

CRINKLE-CRANKLE WALL: wall undulating in a series of serpentine curves.

CROCKETS (*lit.* hooks), CROCKETING: in Gothic architecture, leafy knobs on the edges of any sloping feature. *Crocket Capital: see* Capital (fig. 7).

CROMLECH: word of Celtic origin still occasionally used of single free-standing stones ascribed to the Neolithic or Bronze Age.

CROSSING: in a church, central space at the junction of the nave, chancel, and transepts. *Crossing Tower:* tower above a crossing.

CROSS-WINDOWS: windows with one mullion and one transom (qq.v.)

CROWSTEPS: squared stones set like steps e.g. on a gable or gateway; *see* Gable (fig. 10).

CRUCKS (*lit.* crooked): pairs of inclined timbers, usually curved, which are set at bay-length intervals in a building and support the timbers of the roof (q.v.). The individual cruck is known as a blade. *Base:* blades which rise from ground level to a tie- or collar-beam upon which the roof truss is carried; in timber buildings they support the walls. *Full:* blades rising from ground level to the apex of a building; they serve as the main members roof truss and in timber buildings they support the walls. *Jointed:* blades formed from more than one timber; the lower member normally rises from ground level and acts as a wall-post; it is usually elbowed at wall-plate level and jointed just above. *Middle:* blades rising from half-way up the walls to a tie- or collar-beam upon which the roof truss is supported. *Raised:* blades rising from half-way up the walls to the apex. *Upper:* blades supported on a tie-beam and rising to the apex.

CRYPT: underground or half-underground room usually below the E end of a church. *Ring Crypt:* early medieval semicircular or polygonal corridor crypt surrounding the apse of a church, often associated with chambers for relics.

CUPOLA (*lit.* dome): especially a small dome on a circular or polygonal base crowning a larger dome, roof, or turret.

CURTAIN WALL: (1) connecting wall between the towers of a castle; (2) in modern building, a non-load-bearing external wall composed of repeating modular elements applied to a steel-framed structure.

CURVILINEAR: *see* Tracery.

CUSP: projecting point formed by the foils within the divisions of Gothic tracery, also used as a decorative edging to the soffits of the Gothic arches of tomb recesses, sedilia, etc.

CYCLOPEAN MASONRY: built with large irregular polygonal

stones, but smooth and finely jointed.

CYMA RECTA and CYMA REVERSA: *see* Ogee.

Dado: the finishing of the lower part of an interior wall (sometimes used to support an applied order). *Dado Rail:* the moulding along the top of the dado.

DAGGER: *see* Tracery.

DAIS: raised platform at one end of a room.

DEC (DECORATED): historical division of English Gothic architecture covering the period from *c.* 1290 to *c.* 1350. The name is derived from the type of window tracery used during the period (*see also* Tracery).

DEMI-COLUMNS: engaged columns (q.v.) only half of whose circumference projects from the wall. Also called *Half-Columns*.

DENTIL: small square block used in series in classical cornices, rarely in Doric. In brickwork *dentilation* is produced by the projection of alternating headers or blocks along cornices or string courses.

DIAPER (*lit.* figured cloth): repetitive surface decoration of lozenges or squares either flat or in relief. Achieved in brickwork with bricks of two colours.

DIOCLETIAN WINDOW: semicircular window with two mullions, so-called because of its use in the Baths of Diocletian in Rome. Also called a *Thermae Window*.

DISC BARROW: Bronze Age round barrow with an inconspicuous central mound surrounded by a bank and ditch.

DISTYLE: having two columns.

DOGTOOTH: typical E.E. decoration of a moulding, consisting of

Fig. 9. Dogtooth

a series of squares, their centres raised like pyramids and their edges indented (*see* fig. 9). *See also* Cogging.

DOME: vault of even curvature erected on a circular base. The section can be segmental (e.g. saucer dome), semicircular, pointed, or bulbous (onion dome).

DONJON: *see* Keep.

DORIC: *see* Orders (fig. 17).

DORMER WINDOW: window standing up vertically from the slope of a roof and lighting a room within it. *Dormer Head:* gable above this window, often formed as a pediment.

DORTER: dormitory; sleeping quarters of a monastery.

DOUBLE PILE: *see* Pile.

DRAGON BEAM: *see* Jetty.

DRESSINGS: smoothly worked stones, used e.g. for quoins or string courses, projecting from the wall and sometimes of different material, colour, or texture.

DRIPSTONE: moulded stone projecting from a wall to protect the lower parts from water; *see also* Hoodmould.

DRUM: (1) circular or polygonal wall supporting a dome or cupola; (2) one of the stones forming the shaft of a column.

DRYSTONE: stone construction without mortar.

DUTCH GABLE: *see* Gable (fig. 10).

EASTER SEPULCHRE: recess, usually in the wall of a chancel, with a tomb-chest to receive an effigy of Christ for Easter celebrations.

EAVES: overhanging edge of a roof; hence *Eaves Cornice* in this position.

ECHINUS (*lit.* sea-urchin): ovolo moulding (q.v.) below the abacus of a Greek Doric capital; *see* Orders (fig. 17).

E.E. (EARLY ENGLISH): historical division of English Gothic architecture covering the period *c.* 1190–1250.

ELEVATION: (1) any side of a building; (2) in a drawing, the same or any part of it, accurately represented in two dimensions.

EMBATTLED: furnished with battlements.

EMBRASURE (*lit.* splay): small splayed opening in the wall or battlement of a fortified building.

ENCAUSTIC TILES: glazed and decorated earthenware tiles used for paving.

EN DELIT (*lit.* in error): term used in Gothic architecture to describe stone shafts whose grain runs vertically instead of horizontally, against normal building practice.

ENGAGED COLUMN: one that is partly merged into a wall or pier. Also called *Attached Column.*

ENGINEERING BRICKS: dense bricks of uniform size, high crushing strength, and low porosity. Originally used mostly for railway viaducts etc.

ENTABLATURE: in classical architecture, collective name for the three horizontal members (architrave, frieze, and cornice) above a column; *see* Orders (fig. 17).

ENTASIS: very slight convex deviation from a straight line; used on classical columns and sometimes on spires to prevent an optical illusion of concavity.

ENTRESOL: mezzanine storey within or above the ground storey.

EPITAPH (*lit.* on a tomb): inscription in that position.

ESCUTCHEON: shield for armorial bearings.

EXEDRA: apsidal end of an apartment; *see* Apse.

EXTRADOS: outer curved face of an arch or vault.

EXTRUDED CORNER: right-angled (or circular) projection from the inner angle of a building with advancing wings, usually in C16 or C17 plans.

EYECATCHER: decorative building (often a sham ruin) usually on an eminence to terminate a park or garden layout.

FASCIA: plain horizontal band, e.g. in an architrave (q.v.) or on a shopfront.

FENESTRATION: the arrangement of windows in a building.

FERETORY: (1) place behind the high altar where the chief shrine of a church is kept; (2) wooden or metal container for relics.

FESTOON: ornament, usually in high or low relief, in the form of a garland of flowers and/or fruit, hung up at both ends; *see also* Swag.

FIBREGLASS (or glass-reinforced polyester (GRP)): synthetic resin reinforced with glass fibre, formed in moulds, often simulating the outward appearance of traditional materials. GRC (glass-reinforced concrete) is also formed in moulds and used for components (cladding etc.) in industrialized building.

FIELDED: *see* Raised and Fielded.

FILLET: in medieval architecture, a narrow flat band running down a shaft or along a roll moulding. In classical architecture it separates larger curved mouldings in cornices or bases.

FINIAL: decorative topmost feature, e.g. above a gable, spire, or cupola.

FLAMBOYANT: properly the latest phase of French Gothic architecture where the window tracery takes on undulating lines, based on the use of flowing curves.

FLÈCHE (*lit.* arrow): slender spire on the centre of a roof. Also called *Spirelet*.

FLEUR-DE-LYS: in heraldry, a formalized lily, as in the royal arms of France.

FLEURON: decorative carved flower or leaf.

FLOWING: *see* Tracery (Curvilinear).

FLUSHWORK: flint used decoratively in conjunction with dressed stone so as to form patterns: tracery, initials, etc.

FLUTING: series of concave grooves, their common edges sharp (arris) or blunt (fillet).

FOIL (*lit.* leaf): lobe formed by the cusping of a circular or other shape in tracery. *Trefoil* (three), *quatrefoil* (four), *cinquefoil* (five), and *multifoil* express the number of lobes in a shape. *See also* Tracery.

FOLIATED: decorated, especially carved, with leaves.

FORMWORK: commonly called shuttering; the temporary frame of braced timber or metal into which wet concrete is poured. The texture of the framework material depends on the imprint required.

FRAMED BUILDING: where the structure is carried by the framework – e.g. of steel, reinforced concrete, timber – instead of by load-bearing walls.

FRATER: *see* Refectory.

FREESTONE: stone that is cut, or can be cut, in all directions, usually fine-grained sandstone or limestone.

FRESCO: *al fresco:* painting executed on wet plaster. *Fresco secco:* painting executed on dry plaster, more common in Britain.

FRIEZE: horizontal band of ornament, especially the middle member of the classical entablature; *see* Orders (fig. 17). *Pulvinated Frieze* (*lit.* cushioned): frieze of bold convex profile.

FRONTAL: covering for the front of an altar. Also called *Antependium*.

FRONTISPIECE: in C16 and C17 buildings the central feature of doorway and windows above it linked in one composition.

GABLE: (1) area of wall, often triangular, at the end of a double-pitch roof; *Dutch Gable*, characteristic of *c.* 1580–1680: *Shaped Gable*, characteristic of *c.* 1620–80 (*see* fig. 10). *Gablet:* small gable. *See also* Roofs.

GADROONING: ribbed ornament, e.g. on the lid or base of an urn, flowing into a lobed edge.

GALILEE: chapel or vestibule usually at the W end of a church enclosing the porch.

GALLERY: balcony or passage, but with certain special meanings, e.g. (1) upper storey above the aisle of a church, looking through arches to the nave; also called tribune and often erroneously triforium; (2) balcony or mezzanine, often with seats, overlooking the main interior space of a building; (3) external walkway, often projecting from a wall.

GALLERY GRAVE: chambered tomb (q.v.) in which there is a little or no differentiation between the entrance passage and the actual burial chamber(s).

GALLETING: decorative use of small stones in a mortar course.

GARDEROBE (*lit.* wardrobe): medieval privy.

GARGOYLE: water spout projecting from the parapet of a wall or tower, often carved into human or animal shape.

GAUGED BRICKWORK: soft brick sawn roughly, then rubbed to a smooth, precise (gauged) surface with a stone or another brick. Mostly used for door or window openings. Also called *Rubbed Brickwork*.

GAZEBO (jocular Latin, 'I shall gaze'): lookout tower or raised

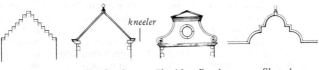

| Crowstep | Kneelered | Flemish or Dutch | Shaped |

Fig. 10. Gables

summer house usually in a park or garden.

GEOMETRIC: historical division of English Gothic architecture covering the period *c.* 1250–90. *See also* Tracery. For another meaning, *see* Stair.

GIANT ORDER: *see* Order.

GIBBS SURROUND: C18 treatment of a door or window surround,

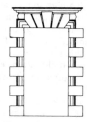

Fig. 11. Gibbs Surround

seen particularly in the work of James Gibbs (1682–1754) (*see* fig. 11).

GOTHIC: the period of medieval architecture characterized by the use of the pointed arch. For its subdivisions *see* E.E., Geometric, Dec, Perp, Flamboyant.

GRANGE (monastic): farm owned and run by members of a religious order.

GRC and GRP: *see* Fibreglass.

GROIN: sharp edge at the meeting of two cells of a cross-vault; *see* Vault (fig. 32).

GROTESQUE (*lit.* grotto-esque): classical wall decoration in paint or stucco adopted from Roman examples, particularly by Raphael. Its foliage scrolls, unlike arabesque, incorporate ornaments and human figures.

GROTTO: artificial cavern usually decorated with rock- or shell-work, especially popular in the late C17 and C18.

GUILLOCHE: running classical ornament of interlaced bands forming a plait (*see* fig. 12).

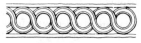

Fig. 12. Guilloche

GUNLOOP: opening for a firearm.

GUTTAE: *see* Orders (fig. 17).

HAGIOSCOPE: *see* Squint.

HALF-TIMBERING: archaic term for Timber-framing (q.v.). Sometimes used for non-structural decorative timberwork, e.g. in gables etc. of the late C19.

HALL CHURCH: medieval or Gothic Revival church whose nave and aisles are of equal height or approximately so.

HAMMERBEAM: *see* Roofs (fig. 26).

HEADER: *see* Bond.

HENGE: ritual earthwork with a surrounding bank and ditch, the bank being on the outer side.

HERM (*lit.* the god Hermes): male head or bust on a pedestal.

HERRINGBONE WORK: masonry or brickwork in zigzag courses.

HEXASTYLE: *see* Portico.

HILL-FORT: later Bronze Age and Iron Age earthwork enclosed by a ditch and bank system; in the later part of the period the defences multiplied in size and complexity. Varying from about an acre to over fifty acres in area, they are usually built with careful regard to natural elevations or promontories and range in character from powerful strongholds to protected farmsteads.

HIPPED ROOF: *see* Roofs (1) (fig. 21).

HOODMOULD: projecting moulding above an arch or lintel to throw off water. When the moulding is horizontal it is often called a *Label. See also* Label Stop.

HUSK GARLAND: festoon of nutshells diminishing towards the ends.

HYPOCAUST (*lit.* under-burning): Roman underfloor heating system. The floor is supported on pillars and the space thus formed is connected to a flue.

ICONOGRAPHY: description of the subject matter of works of the visual arts.

IMPOST (*lit.* imposition): horizontal moulding at the springing of an arch.

IMPOST BLOCK: block with splayed sides between abacus and capital.

IN ANTIS: *see* Antae.

INDENT: (1) shape chiselled out of a stone to match and receive a brass; (2) in restoration, a section of new stone inserted as a patch into older work.

INDUSTRIALIZED BUILDING (system building): the use of a system of manufactured units assembled on site. One of the most popular is the CLASP (Consortium Local Authorities Special Programme) system of light steel framing suitable for schools etc.

INGLENOOK (*lit.* fire-corner): recess for a hearth with provision for seating.

INTARSIA: *see* Marquetry.

INTERCOLUMNIATION: interval between columns.

INTRADOS: *see* Soffit.

IONIC: *see* Orders (fig. 17).

IRON AGE: in Britain, the period from *c.* 600 B.C. to the coming of the Romans. The term is also used for those un-Romanized native communities which survived until the Saxon incursions especially beyond the Roman frontiers.

JAMB (*lit.* leg): one of the straight sides of an opening.

JETTY: in a timber-framed building, the projection of an upper storey beyond the storey below made by the beams and joists of the lower storey oversailing the external wall. On their outer ends is placed the sill of the walling for the storey above. Buildings can be jettied on several sides, in which case a *Dragon Beam* is set diagonally at the corner to carry the joists to either side.

JOGGLE: mason's term for joining two stones to prevent them slipping or sliding by means of a notch in one and a corresponding projection in the other.

KEEL MOULDING: moulding whose outline is in section like that of the keel of a ship (fig. 13).

Fig. 13. Keel Moulding

KEEP: principal tower of a castle. Also called *Donjon*.

KEY PATTERN: *see* fig. 14.

KEYSTONE: middle and topmost stone in an arch or vault.

Fig. 14. Key Pattern

KINGPOST: *see* Roofs (3) and fig. 22.

KNEELER: horizontal projection at the base of a gable. *See* Gable (fig. 10).

LABEL: *see* Hoodmould. *Label Stop:* ornamental boss at the end of a hoodmould.

LACED WINDOWS: windows pulled visually together by strips of brickwork, usually of a different colour, which continue vertically the lines of the vertical parts of the window surround. Typical of *c.* 1720.

LACING COURSE: one or more bricks serving as horizontal reinforcement to flint, cobble, etc., walls.

LADY CHAPEL: chapel dedicated to the Virgin Mary (Our Lady).

LANCET WINDOW: slender pointed-arched window.

LANTERN: small circular or polygonal turret with windows all round crowning a roof or a dome.

LANTERN CROSS: churchyard cross with lantern-shaped top usually with sculptured representations on the sides of the top.

LAVATORIUM: in a monastery, a washing place adjacent to the refectory.

LEAN-TO: *see* Roofs (1).

LESENE (*lit.* a mean thing): pilaster without base or capital. Also called *Pilaster Strip.*

LIERNE: *see* Vault (fig. 33).

LIGHT: compartment of a window.

LINENFOLD: Tudor panelling where each panel is ornamented with a conventional representation of a piece of linen laid in vertical folds.

LINTEL: horizontal beam or stone bridging an opening.

LOGGIA: gallery open along one side of a building, usually arcaded or colonnaded. It may be a separate structure, usually in a garden.

LONG BARROW: unchambered Neolithic communal burial mound, often wedge-shaped in plan, with the burial and occasional other structures massed at the broader end, from which the mound itself tapers in height; quarry ditches flank the mound.

LONG-AND-SHORT WORK: quoins consisting of stones placed with the long sides alternately upright and horizontal, especially in Saxon building.

LOUVRE: (1) opening, often with lantern over, in the roof of a building to let the smoke from a central hearth escape; (2) one of a series of overlapping boards or panes of glass placed in a window to allow ventilation but keep the rain out.

LOWER PALAEOLITHIC: *see* Palaeolithic.

LOZENGE: diamond shape.

LUCARNE (*lit.* dormer): small window in a roof or spire.

LUGGED: *see* Architrave.

LUNETTE (*lit.* half or crescent moon): (1) semicircular window; (2) semicircular or crescent-shaped surface.

LYCHGATE (*lit.* corpse-gate): roofed wooden gateway at the entrance to a churchyard for the reception of a coffin.

LYNCHET: long terraced strip of soil accumulating on the downward side of prehistoric and medieval fields due to soil creep from continuous ploughing along the contours.

MACHICOLATIONS (*lit.* mashing devices): in medieval military architecture, a series of openings under a projecting parapet between the corbels that support it, through which missiles can be dropped.

MAJOLICA: ornamented glazed earthenware.

MANSARD: *see* Roofs (1) (fig. 21).

MARQUETRY: inlay in various woods. Also called *Intarsia*.

MATHEMATICAL TILES: facing tiles with one face moulded to look like a header or stretcher, most often hung on laths applied to timber-framed walls to make them appear brick-built.

MAUSOLEUM: monumental tomb, so named after that of Mausolus, king of Caria, at Halicarnassus.

MEGALITHIC (*lit.* of large stones): archaeological term referring to the use of such stones, singly or together.

MEGALITHIC TOMB: massive stone-built Neolithic burial chamber covered by an earth or stone mound.

MERLON: *see* Battlement.

MESOLITHIC: 'Middle Stone' Age; the post-glacial period of hunting and fishing communities dating in Britain from *c.* 8000 B.C. to the arrival of the Neolithic (q.v.) communities, with whom they must have considerably overlapped in many areas.

METOPES: spaces between the triglyphs in a Doric frieze; *see* Orders (fig. 17).

MEZZANINE: (1) low storey between two higher ones; (2) low upper storey within the height of a high one, not extending over its whole area. *See also* Entresol.

MISERERE: *see* Misericord.

MISERICORD (*lit.* mercy): shelf placed on the underside of a hinged choir stall seat which, when turned up, supported the occupant during long periods of standing. Also called *Miserere*.

MODILLIONS: small consoles (q.v.) at regular intervals along the underside of the cornice of the Corinthian or Composite orders.

MODULE: in industrialized building (q.v.), a predetermined standard size for co-ordinating the dimensions of components of a building with the spaces into which they have to fit.

MOTTE: steep mound forming the main feature of C11 and C12 castles.

MOTTE-AND-BAILEY: post-Roman and Norman defence system consisting of an earthen mound (motte) topped with a wooden tower within a bailey, with enclosure ditch and palisade, and with the rare addition of an internal bank.

MOUCHETTE: *see* Tracery (fig. 31).

MOULDING: ornament of continuous section; *see* e.g. Cavetto, Ogee, Ovolo, Roll.

MULLION: vertical member between the lights in a window opening.

MULTI-STOREY: modern term denoting five or more storeys. *See* Cluster, Slab, and Point Blocks.

MULTIVALLATE: (of a hill-fort) defended by three or more concentric banks and ditches.

MUNTIN: vertical part in the framing of a door, screen, panelling, etc., butting into or stopped by the horizontal rails.

NAILHEAD MOULDING: E.E. ornamental motif consisting of small pyramids regularly repeated (*see* fig. 15).

Fig. 15. Nailhead Moulding

NARTHEX: enclosed vestibule or covered porch at the main entrance to a church.

NAVE: the middle vessel of the limb of a church W of the crossing or chancel and flanked by the aisles.

NECESSARIUM: *see* Reredorter.

NEOLITHIC: term applied to the New Stone Age, dating in Britain from the appearance of the first settled farming communities from the continent *c.* 4000–3500 B.C. until the beginning of the Bronze Age. *See also* Mesolithic.

NEWEL: central post in a circular or winding staircase; also the principal post where a flight of stairs meets a landing. *See* Stair (fig. 28).

NICHE (*lit.* shell): vertical recess in a wall, sometimes for a statue.

NIGHT STAIR: stair by which monks entered the transept of their church from their dormi-tory to celebrate night services.

NOGGING: *see* Timber-framing.

NOOK-SHAFT: shaft set in the angle of a pier or respond or wall, or the angle of the jamb of a window or doorway.

NORMAN: *see* Romanesque.

NOSING: projection of the tread of a step. A *Bottle Nosing* is half-round in section.

NUTMEG MOULDING: consisting of a chain of tiny triangles placed obliquely.

OBELISK: lofty pillar of square section tapering at the top and ending pyramidally.

ŒIL DE BŒUF: *see* Bullseye Window.

OGEE: double curve, bending first one way and then the other. Applied to mouldings, also called *Cyma Recta*. A reverse ogee moulding with a double curve also called *Cyma Reversa* (*see* fig. 16). *Ogee* or *Ogival Arch*: *see* Arch.

ORATORY: (1) small private chapel in a church or a house; (2) church of the Oratorian Order.

ORDER: (1) upright structural member formally related to others, e.g. in classical architecture a column, pilaster, or anta; (2) especially in medieval architecture, one of a series of recessed arches and jambs forming a splayed opening. *Giant* or *Colossal Order*: classical order

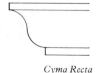

*Cyma Recta*

*Cyma Reversa*

Fig. 16. Ogee Mouldings

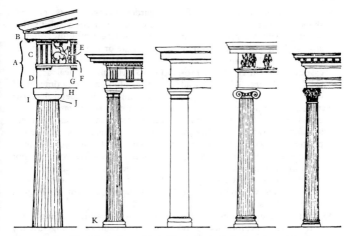

Fig. 17. Orders (Greek Doric, Roman Doric, Tuscan Doric, Ionic, Corinthian) A Entablature; B Cornice; C Frieze; D Architrave; E Metope; F Triglyph; G Guttae; H Abacus; I Capital; J Echinus; K Base

whose height is that of two or more storeys of a building.

ORDERS: in classical architecture, the differently formalized versions of the basic post-and-lintel (column and entablature) structure, each having its own rules for design and proportion. For examples of the main types *see* fig. 17. In the *Composite*, the capital combines Ionic volutes with Corinthian foliage. *Superimposed Orders:* term for the use of Orders on successive levels, usually in the upward sequence of Doric, Ionic, Corinthian.

ORIEL: *see* Bay-window.

OVERDOOR: *see* Sopraporta.

OVERHANG. *see* Jetty

OVERSAILING COURSES: *see* Corbel (Corbelling).

OVERTHROW: decorative fixed arch between two gatepiers or above a wrought-iron gate.

OVOLO MOULDING: wide convex moulding.

PALAEOLITHIC: 'Old Stone' Age; the first period of human culture, commencing in the Ice Age and immediately prior to the Mesolithic; the Lower Palaeolithic is the older phase, the Upper Palaeolithic the later.

PALIMPSEST(*lit.* erased work): re-use of a surface. (1) of a brass: where a metal plate has been reused by turning over and engraving on the back; (2) of a wall painting: where one overlaps and partly obscures an earlier one.

PALLADIAN: architecture following the examples and principles of Andrea Palladio (1508–80).

PALMETTE: classical ornament like a symmetrical palm shoot; for illustration *see* fig. 1.

PANELLING: wooden lining to interior walls, made up of vertical members (muntins q.v.) and horizontals (rails) framing panels (*see* linenfold; raised and fielded). Also called *Wainscot*.

PANTILE: roof tile of curved S-shaped section.

PARAPET: wall for protection at any sudden drop, e.g. on a bridge or at the wall-head of a castle; in the latter case it protects the *Parapet Walk* or wall walk.

PARCLOSE: *see* Screen.

PARGETTING (*lit.* plastering): in timber-framed buildings, plasterwork with patterns and ornaments either moulded in relief or incised on it.

PARLOUR: in a monastery, room where monks were permitted to talk to visitors.

PARTERRE: level space in a garden laid out with low, formal beds of plants.

PATERA (*lit.* plate): round or oval ornament in shallow relief, especially in classical architecture.

PAVILION: (1) ornamental building for occasional use in a garden, park, sports ground, etc.; (2) projecting subdivision of some larger building, often at an angle or terminating wings.

PEBBLEDASHING: *see* Rendering.

PEDESTAL: in classical architecture, a tall base sometimes used to support an order; also, the base for a statue, vase, etc.

PEDIMENT: in classical architecture, a formalized gable derived from that of a temple, also used over doors, windows, etc. For variations of type *see* fig. 18.

PEEL (*lit.* palisade): stone tower, e.g. near the Scottish–English border.

PENDANT: feature hanging down from a vault or ceiling, usually ending in a boss.

PENDENTIVE: spandrel formed as part of a hemisphere between arches meeting at an angle, supporting a drum or dome (*see* fig. 19).

PENTHOUSE: subsidiary structure

*Broken*

*Open*

*Segmental*

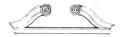

*Scrolled*

Fig. 18. Pediments

Fig. 19. Pendentive

with a lean-to roof; in modern architecture, a separately roofed structure on top of a multi-storey block.

PERISTYLE: in classical architecture, a range of columns all round a building, e.g. a temple, or an interior space, e.g. a courtyard.

PERP (PERPENDICULAR): historical division of English Gothic architecture covering the period from c. 1335–50 to c. 1530. The name is derived from the upright tracery panels used during the period (see Tracery).

PERRON: see Stair.

PIANO NOBILE: principal floor, usually with a ground floor or basement underneath and a lesser storey overhead.

PIAZZA: open space surrounded by buildings; in the C17 and C18 used erroneously to mean an arcaded ground floor, especially adjoining or around an open space.

PIER: strong, solid support, usually round or square in section. See also Compound Pier.

PIETRA DURA: ornamental or scenic inlay by means of thin slabs of stone.

PILASTER: representation of a classical column in flat relief against a wall. Pilastrade: series of pilasters, equivalent to a colonnade. Pilaster Strip: see Lesene.

PILE: row of rooms. The important use of the term is in Double Pile, describing a house that is two rows thick.

PILLAR: free-standing upright member of any section, not conforming to one of the Orders.

PILLAR PISCINA: free-standing piscina on a pillar.

PILOTIS: French term used in modern architecture for pillars or stilts that carry a building to first-floor level leaving the ground floor open.

PINNACLE: tapering finial, e.g. on a buttress or the corner of a tower, sometimes decorated with crockets.

PISCINA: basin for washing the communion or mass vessels, provided with a drain; generally set in or against the wall to the S of an altar.

PLAISANCE: summer house, pleasure house near a mansion.

PLINTH: projecting base beneath a wall or column, generally chamfered or moulded at the top.

PODIUM: continuous raised platform supporting a building. In modern architecture often a large block of two or three storeys beneath a multi-storey block covering a smaller area.

POINT BLOCK: high block of housing in which the flats fan out from a central core of lifts, staircases, etc.

POINTING: exposed mortar jointing of masonry or brickwork. The finished form is of various types, e.g. Flush Pointing, Recessed Pointing.

POND BARROW: rare Bronze Age barrow type consisting of a

circular depression, usually paved, and containing a number of cremation burials.

POPPYHEAD: carved ornament of leaves and flowers as a finial for the end of a bench or stall.

PORCH: covered projecting entrance to a building.

PORTAL FRAME: in modern architecture a basic form of construction in which a series of precast concrete beams, placed in pairs to form 'portals', support the walls and roof. The upper part of each beam is angled up to where they meet at the roof ridge.

PORTCULLIS: gate constructed to rise and fall in vertical grooves at the entry to a castle.

PORTICO: a porch, open on one side at least, and enclosed by a row of columns which also support the roof and frequently a pediment. When the front of it is on the same level as the front of the building it is described as a *Portico in Antis* (Antae q.v.). Porticoes are described by the number of frontal columns, e.g. Tetrastyle (four), Hexastyle (six). *Blind Portico:* the front features of a portico attached to a wall so that it is no longer a proper porch.

POSTERN: small gateway at the back of a building.

PRECAST CONCRETE: concrete components cast before being placed in position.

PREDELLA: (1) step or platform on which an altar stands; hence (2) in an altarpiece, the horizontal strip below the main representation, often used for a number of subsidiary representations in a row.

PREFABRICATION: manufacture of buildings or components

off-site for assembly on-site. *See also* Industrialized Building.

PRESBYTERY: (1) part of a church lying E of the choir where the main altar is placed; (2) a priest's residence.

PRESTRESSED CONCRETE: *see* Reinforced Concrete.

PRINCIPAL: *see* Roofs (3) and figs. 22, 25.

PRIORY: monastic house whose head is a prior or prioress, not an abbot or abbess.

PROSTYLE: with a free-standing row of columns in front.

PULPITUM: stone screen in a major church provided to shut off the choir from the nave and also as a backing for the return choir stalls.

PULVINATED: *see* Frieze.

PURLIN: *see* Roofs (3) and figs. 22–5.

PUTHOLES or PUTLOCK HOLES: holes in the wall to receive putlocks, the short horizontal timbers which scaffolding boards rest on. They are often not filled in after construction is complete.

PUTTO: small naked boy (plural: putti. Also called *Amorini*.)

QUADRANGLE: rectangular inner courtyard in a large building.

QUARRIES (*lit.* squares): (1) square (or diamond-shaped) panes of glass supported by lead strips which are called *Cames*; (2) square floor-slabs or tiles.

QUATREFOIL: *see* Foil.

QUEENPOSTS: *see* Roofs (3) and fig. 24.

QUIRK: sharp groove to one side of a convex moulding, e.g. beside a roll moulding, which is then said to be quirked.

QUOINS: dressed stones at the

angles of a building. They may be alternately long and short, especially when rusticated.

RADIATING CHAPELS: chapels projecting radially from an ambulatory or an apse; *see* Chevet.

RAFTER: *see* Roofs (3) and figs. 22–6.

RAGGLE: groove cut in masonry, especially to receive the edge of glass or roof-covering.

RAIL: *see* Muntin.

RAISED AND FIELDED: of a wooden panel with a raised square or rectangular central area (field) surrounded by a narrow moulding.

RAKE: slope or pitch.

RAMPART: wall of stone or earth surrounding a hill-fort, castle, fortress, or fortified city. *Rampart Walk:* path along the inner face of a rampart.

REBATE: rectangular section cut out of a masonry edge to receive a shutter, door, window, etc.

REBUS: a heraldic pun, e.g. a fiery cock as a badge for Cockburn.

REEDING: series of convex mouldings; the reverse of fluting.

REFECTORY: dining hall of a monastery or similar establishment. Also called *Frater.*

REINFORCED CONCRETE: concrete reinforced with steel rods to take the tensile stress. A later development is *Prestressed Concrete,* reinforced by wire cables which can be stretched to induce compression in the tension area of the concrete before it is loaded.

RENDERING: the process of covering outside walls with a uniform surface or skin for protection from the weather. *Stucco,* originally a fine lime plaster worked to a smooth surface, is the finest rendered external finish, characteristic of many late C18 and C19 classical buildings. It is usually painted. *Cement Rendering* is a cheaper and more recent substitute for stucco, usually with a grainy texture and often left unpainted. In more simple buildings the wall surface may be roughly *Lime-plastered* (and then whitewashed), or covered with plaster mixed with a coarse aggregate such as gravel. This latter is known as *Roughcast.* A variant, fashionable in the early C20, is *Pebbledashing:* here the stones of the aggregate are kept separate and are thrown at the wet plastered wall to create a decorative effect.

REPOUSSÉ: decoration of metalwork by relief designs, formed by beating the metal from the back.

REREDORTER (*lit.* behind the dormitory): medieval euphemism for latrines in a monastery. Also called *Necessarium.*

REREDOS: painted and/or sculptured screen behind and above an altar.

RESPOND: half-pier bonded into a wall and carrying one end of an arch.

RETABLE: altarpiece, a picture or piece of carving standing behind and attached to an altar.

RETROCHOIR: in a major church, the space between the high altar and an E chapel, like a square ambulatory.

REVEAL: the inward plane of a jamb, between the edge of an external wall and the frame of a door or window that is set in it.

RIB-VAULT: *see* Vault.

RINCEAU (*lit.* little branch) or

Fig. 20. Rinceau

antique foliage: classical ornament, usually on a frieze, of leafy scrolls branching alternately to left and right (*see* fig. 20).

RISER: vertical face of a step.

ROCK-FACED: term used to describe masonry which is cleft to produce a natural rugged appearance.

ROCOCO (*lit.* rocky): latest phase of the Baroque style, current in most Continental countries between *c.* 1720 and *c.* 1760, and showing itself in Britain mainly in playful, scrolled decoration, especially plasterwork.

ROLL MOULDING: moulding of curved section used in medieval architecture.

ROMANESQUE: that style in architecture (in England often called Norman) which was current in the C11 and C12 and preceded the Gothic style. (Some scholars extend the use of the term Romanesque back to the C10 or C9.) *See also* Saxo-Norman.

ROMANO-BRITISH: general term applied to the period and cultural features of Britain affected by the Roman occupation of the C1–5 A.D.

ROOD: cross or crucifix, usually over the entry into the chancel. The *Rood Screen* beneath it may have a *Rood Loft* along the top, reached by a *Rood Stair.*

ROOFS: (*1*) *Shape:* for the external shapes and terms used to describe them *see* fig. 21. *Helm:* roof with four inclined faces joined at the top, with a gable at the foot of each. *Hipped* (fig. 21): roof with sloped instead of vertical ends. *Lean-to:* roof with one slope only, built against a vertical wall: term also applied to the part of the building such a roof covers. *Mansard* (fig. 21): roof with a double slope, the lower one larger and steeper than the upper. *Saddleback:* the name given to a normal pitched roof when used over a tower. *See also* Wagon Roof.

(*2*) *Construction:* Roofs are generally called after the principal structural component, e.g. *crown-post, hammerbeam, king-post,* etc. See below under *Elements* and figs. 22–6.

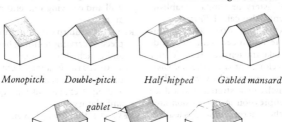

Monopitch     Double-pitch     Half-hipped     Gabled mansard

gablet

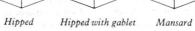

Hipped     Hipped with gablet     Mansard

Fig. 21. Roofs: external forms

A *single-framed* roof is constructed with no main trusses. The rafters may be fixed to a wall-plate or ridge, or longitudinal timbers may be absent altogether. A *common rafter* roof is one in which pairs of rafters are not connected by a collar-beam. A *coupled rafter* roof is one in which the rafters are connected by collar-beams.

A *double-framed* roof is constructed with longitudinal members such as purlins. Generally there are principals or principal rafters supporting the longitudinal members and dividing the length of the roof into bays.

(*3*) *Elements: Ashlar piece.* A short vertical timber connecting an inner wall-plate or timber pad to a rafter above.

*Braces.* Subsidiary timbers set diagonally to strengthen the frame. *Arched braces:* a pair of curved braces forming an arch, usually connecting the wall or post below with the tie- or collar-beam above. *Passing braces:* straight braces of considerable length, passing across other members of the truss. *Scissor braces:* a pair of braces which cross diagonally between pairs of rafters or principals. *Wind-braces:* short, usually curved braces connecting side purlins with principals. They are sometimes decorated with cusping.

*Collar-beam.* A horizontal transverse timber connecting a pair of rafters or principals at a height between the apex and the wall-plate.

*Crown-post.* A vertical timber standing centrally on a tie-beam and supporting a collar purlin. Longitudinal braces usually rise from the crown-post to the collar purlin. When the truss is open lateral braces generally rise to the collar-beam, and when the truss is closed they go down to the tie-beam.

*Hammerbeams.* Horizontal brackets projecting at wall-plate level on opposite sides of the wall like a tie-beam with the centre cut away. The inner ends carry vertical timbers called hammerposts and braces to a collar-beam.

*Hammerpost.* A vertical timber set on the inner end of a hammer-beam to support a purlin; it is braced to a collar-beam above.

*Kingpost.* A vertical timber standing centrally on a tie- or collar-beam and rising to the apex of the roof where it supports a ridge.

*Principals.* The pair of inclined lateral timbers of a truss which carry common rafters. Usually they support side purlins and their position corresponds to the main bay division of the space below.

*Purlin.* A horizontal longitudinal timber. *Collar purlin:* a single central timber which carries collar-beams and is itself supported by crown-posts. *Side purlins:* pairs of timbers occurring some way up the slope of the roof. They carry the common rafters and are supported in a number of ways: *butt purlins* are tenoned into either side of the principals; *clasped purlins* rest on queenposts or are carried in the angles between the principals and the collar; *laid-on purlins* lie on the backs of the principals;

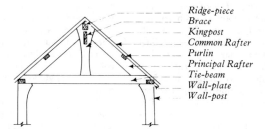

Ridge-piece
Brace
Kingpost
Common Rafter
Purlin
Principal Rafter
Tie-beam
Wall-plate
Wall-post

Fig. 22. Kingpost Roof

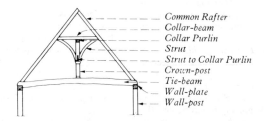

Common Rafter
Collar-beam
Collar Purlin
Strut
Strut to Collar Purlin
Crown-post
Tie-beam
Wall-plate
Wall-post

Fig. 23. Crown-post Roof

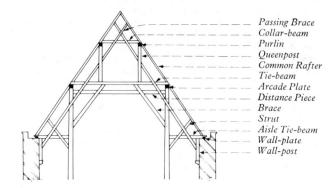

Passing Brace
Collar-beam
Purlin
Queenpost
Common Rafter
Tie-beam
Arcade Plate
Distance Piece
Brace
Strut
Aisle Tie-beam
Wall-plate
Wall-post

Fig. 24. Queenpost Roof

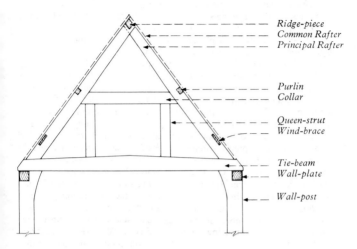

Ridge-piece
Common Rafter
Principal Rafter

Purlin
Collar

Queen-strut
Wind-brace

Tie-beam
Wall-plate

Wall-post

Fig. 25. Queen-strut Roof

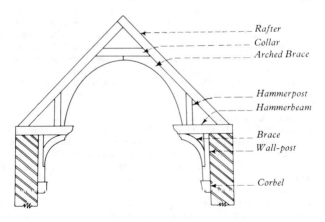

Rafter
Collar
Arched Brace

Hammerpost
Hammerbeam

Brace
Wall-post

Corbel

Fig. 26. Hammerbeam Roof

*trenched purlins* are trenched into the backs of the principals.

*Queenposts.* A pair of vertical, or near-vertical, timbers placed symmetrically on a tie-beam and supporting side purlins.

*Rafters.* Inclined lateral timbers sloping from wall-top to apex and supporting the roof covering. *Common rafters:* rafters of equal scantling found along the length of a roof or sometimes interrupted by main trusses containing principal rafters. *Principal rafters:* rafters which act as principals but also serve as common rafters.

*Ridge, ridge-piece.* A horizontal, longitudinal timber at the apex of a roof supporting the ends of the rafters.

*Sprocket.* A short timber placed on the back and at the foot of a rafter to form projecting eaves.

*Strut.* A vertical or oblique timber which runs between two members of a roof truss but does not directly support longitudinal timbers.

*Tie-beam.* The main horizontal, transverse timber which carries the feet of the principals at wall-plate level.

*Truss.* A rigid framework of timbers which is placed laterally across the building to carry the longitudinal roof timbers which support the common rafters.

*Wall-plate.* A timber laid longitudinally on the top of a wall to receive the ends of the rafters. In a timber-framed building the posts and studs of the wall below are tenoned into it.

ROPE MOULDING: *see* Cable Moulding.

ROSE WINDOW: circular window with patterned tracery about the centre.

ROTUNDA: building circular in plan.

ROUGHCAST: *see* Rendering.

RUBBLE: masonry whose stones are wholly or partly in a rough state. *Coursed Rubble:* of coursed stones with rough faces. *Random Rubble:* of uncoursed stones in a random pattern. *Snecked Rubble* has courses frequently broken by smaller stones (snecks).

RUSTICATION: treatment of joints and/or faces of masonry to give an effect of strength. In the most usual kind the joints are recessed by V-section chamfering or square-section channelling. *Banded Rustication* has only the horizontal joints emphasized in this way. The faces may be flat, but there are many other forms, e.g. *Diamond-faced*, like a shallow pyramid, *Vermiculated*, with a stylized texture like worms or worm-holes, and *Glacial* (frostwork) like icicles or stalactites. *Rusticated Columns* may have their joints and drums treated in any of these ways.

S ACRISTY: room in a church for sacred vessels and vestments.

SADDLEBACK: *see* Roofs (1).

SALTIRE CROSS: with diagonal limbs.

SANCTUARY: (1) area around the main altar of a church (*see* Presbytery); (2) sacred site consisting of wood or stone uprights enclosed by a circular bank and ditch. Beginning in the Neolithic, they were elaborated in the succeeding Bronze Age. The best known examples are Stonehenge and Avebury.

SARCOPHAGUS (*lit.* flesh-consuming): coffin of stone or other durable material.

SAUCER DOME: *see* Dome.

SAXO-NORMAN: transitional Romanesque style combining Anglo-Saxon and Norman features, current *c.* 1060–1100.

SCAGLIOLA: composition imitating marble.

SCALLOPED CAPITAL: *see* fig. 7.

SCARP: artificial cutting away of the ground to form a steep slope.

SCREEN: in a church, structure usually at the entry to the chancel; *see* Rood (Screen) *and* Pulpitum. A *Parclose Screen* separates a chapel from the rest of the church.

SCREENS or SCREENS PASSAGE: screened-off entrance passage between the hall and the service rooms in a medieval house.

SECTION: two-dimensional representation of a building, moulding, etc., revealed by cutting across it.

SEDILIA: seats for the priests (usually three) on the S side of the chancel of a church; a plural word that has become a singular, collective one.

SET-OFF: *see* Weathering.

SGRAFFITO: scratched pattern, often in plaster.

SHAFT: upright member of round section, especially the main part of a classical column. *Shaft-ring:* ring like a belt round a circular pier or a circular shaft attached to a pier, characteristic of the C12 and C13.

SHARAWAGGI: a term, first used *c.* 1685 in Sir William Temple's *Essay on Gardening*, which describes an irregular or asymmetrical composition.

SHEILA-NA-GIG: female fertility figure, usually with legs wide open.

SHOULDERED: *see* Arch (fig. 2), Architrave (fig. 3).

SHUTTERED CONCRETE: *see* Formwork.

SILL: (1) horizontal member at the bottom of a window or door-frame; (2) the horizontal member at the base of a timber-framed wall into which the posts and studs (q.v.) are tenoned.

SLAB BLOCK: rectangular multi-storey block of housing or offices.

SLATE-HANGING: covering of overlapping slates on a wall, which is then said to be *slate-hung*. *Tile-hanging* is similar.

SLYPE: covered way or passage, especially in a cathedral or monastic church, leading E from the cloisters between transept and chapter house.

SNECKED: *see* Rubble.

SOFFIT (*lit.* ceiling): underside of an arch (also called *Intrados*), lintel, etc. *Soffit Roll:* roll moulding on a soffit.

SOLAR (*lit.* sun-room): upper living room or withdrawing room of a medieval house, accessible from the high table end of the hall.

SOPRAPORTA (*lit.* over door): painting or relief above the door of a room, usual in the C17 and C18.

SOUNDING-BOARD: horizontal board or canopy over a pulpit; also called *Tester*.

SOUTERRAIN: underground stone-lined passage and chamber.

S.P.A.B.: Society for the Protection of Ancient Buildings.

SPANDRELS: roughly triangular

spaces between an arch and its
containing rectangle, or between
adjacent arches. In modern
architecture the non-structural
panels under the windows in a
framed building.

SPERE: a fixed structure which
serves as a screen at the lower end
of an open medieval hall between
the hall proper and the screens
passage. It has a wide central
opening, often with a movable
screen, between posts and short
screen walls. The top member is
often the tie-beam of the roof
truss above; screen and truss are
then called a *Spere-truss*.

SPIRE: tall pyramidal or conical
feature built on a tower or turret.
*Broach Spire:* starting from a
square base, then carried into an
octagonal section by means of
triangular faces. The *Splayed-
foot Spire* is a variation of the
broach form, found principally
in the south-eastern counties, in
which the four cardinal faces are
splayed out near their base, to
cover the corners, while oblique
(or intermediate) faces taper
away to a point. *Needle Spire:*
thin spire rising from the centre
of a tower roof, well inside the
parapet.

SPIRELET: *see* Flèche.

SPLAY: chamfer, usually of a
reveal.

SPRING or SPRINGING: level at
which an arch or vault rises from
its supports. *Springers:* the first
stones of an arch or vaulting-rib
above the spring.

SQUINCH: arch or series of arches
thrown across an angle between
two walls to support a super-
structure of polygonal or round
plan over a rectangular space,
e.g. a dome (*see* fig. 27).

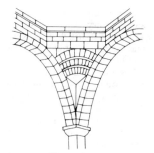

Fig. 27. Squinch

SQUINT: hole cut in a wall or
through a pier to allow a view of
the main altar of a church from
places whence it could not otherwise be seen. Also called *Hagioscope*.

STAIR: *see* fig. 28. A *Dog-leg stair*
has parallel zigzag flights without
an open well. *Newel stair:*
ascending round a central supporting newel (q.v.), called a
*Spiral Stair* when in a circular
shaft. *Well Stair:* term applied
to any stair contained in an open
well, but generally to one that
climbs up three sides of a well
with corner landings, e.g. the
*timber-framed newel stair,* common from the C17 on. *Flying
Stair:* cantilevered from the
wall of a stairwell, without
newels. *Geometric Stair:* flying
stair whose inner edge describes
a curve. *Perron (lit.* of stone):
external stair leading to a doorway, usually of double-curved
plan.

STALL: seat for clergy, choir, etc.,
distinctively treated in its own
right or as one of a row.

STANCHION: upright structural
member, of iron or steel or reinforced concrete.

STEEPLE: tower together with a

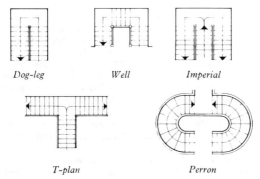

*Dog-leg*　　　　*Well*　　　　*Imperial*

*T-plan*　　　　　　　*Perron*

Fig. 28. Stairs

spire or other tall feature on top of it.

STIFF-LEAF: type of E.E. foliage decoration. *Stiff-leaf Capital: see* fig. 7.

STOUP: vessel for the reception of holy water, usually placed near a door.

STRAINER: *see* Arch.

STRAPWORK: C16 and C17 decoration used also in the C19 Jacobean revival, resembling interlaced bands of cut leather.

STRETCHER: *see* Bond.

STRING COURSE: intermediate stone course or moulding projecting from the surface of a wall.

STRINGS: two sloping members which carry the ends of the treads and risers of a staircase. Closed strings enclose the treads and risers; in the later open string staircase the steps project above the strings.

STUCCO (*lit.* plaster): *see* Rendering.

STUDS: subsidiary vertical timbers of a timber-framed wall or partition.

STYLOBATE: solid platform on which a colonnade stands.

SWAG (*lit.* bundle): like a festoon (q.v.), but also a cloth bundle in relief, hung up at both ends.

SYSTEM BUILDING: *see* Industrialized Building.

TABERNACLE (*lit.* tent): (1) canopied structure, especially on a small scale, to contain the reserved sacrament or a relic; (2) architectural frame, e.g. of a statue on a wall or free-standing, with flanking orders. In classical architecture also called an *Aedicule*.

TABLET FLOWER: medieval ornament of a four-leaved flower with a raised or sunk centre.

TAS-DE-CHARGE: stone(s) forming the springers of more than one vaulting-rib.

TERMINAL FIGURE: pedestal or pilaster which tapers towards the bottom, usually with the upper part of a human figure growing out of it. Also called *Term*.

TERRACOTTA: moulded and fired clay ornament or cladding, usually unglazed.

TESSELLATED        PAVEMENT:

mosaic flooring, particularly Roman, consisting of small *Tesserae*, i.e. cubes of glass, stone, or brick.

TESTER (*lit.* head): bracketed canopy over a tomb and especially over a pulpit, where it is also called a *Sounding-board*.

TETRASTYLE: *see* Portico.

THERMAE WINDOW (*lit.* of a Roman bath): *see* Diocletian Window.

THREE-DECKER PULPIT: pulpit with clerk's stall below and reading desk below the clerk's stall.

TIE-BEAM: *see* Roofs (3) and figs. 22–5.

TIERCERON: *see* Vault (fig. 33).

TILE-HANGING: *see* Slate-hanging.

TIMBER-FRAMING: method of construction where walls are built of interlocking vertical and horizontal timbers. The spaces are filled with non-structural walling of wattle and daub, lath and plaster, brickwork (known as nogging), etc. Sometimes the timber is covered over by plaster, boarding laid horizontally (weatherboarding q.v.), or tiles.

TOMB-CHEST: chest-shaped stone coffin, the most usual medieval form of funerary monument.

TORUS: large convex moulding usually used on a column base.

TOUCH: soft black marble quarried near Tournai.

TOURELLE: turret corbelled out from the wall.

TOWER HOUSE: compact medieval fortified house with the main hall raised above the ground and at least one more storey above it. The type survives in odd examples into the C16 and C17.

TRABEATED: depends structurally on the use of the post and lintel; cf. Arcuated.

TRACERY: intersecting ribwork in the upper part of a window, or used decoratively in blank arches, on vaults, etc. *Plate tracery: see* fig. 29(*a*). Early form of tracery where decoratively shaped openings are cut through the solid stone infilling in a window head. *Bar tracery:* a form introduced into England *c.* 1250. Intersecting ribwork made up of slender shafts, continuing the lines of the mullions of windows up to a decorative mesh in the head of the window. *Geometrical tracery: see* fig. 29(*b*). Tracery characteristic of *c.* 1250–1310 consisting chiefly of circles or foiled circles. *Y-tracery: see* fig. 29(*c*). Tracery consisting of a mullion which branches into two forming a Y shape; typical of *c.* 1300. *Intersecting tracery: see* fig. 29(*d*). Tracery in which each mullion

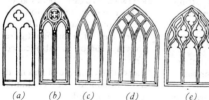

(*a*)     (*b*)     (*c*)     (*d*)     (*e*)     (*f*)     (*g*)

Fig. 29. Tracery

of a window branches out into two curved bars in such a way that every one of them is drawn with the same radius from a different centre. The result is that every light of the window is a lancet and every two, three, four, etc., lights together form a pointed arch. This treatment also is typical of *c.* 1300. *Reticulated tracery: see* fig. 29(*e*). Tracery typical of the early C14 consisting entirely of circles drawn at top and bottom into ogee shapes so that a net-like appearance results. *Panel tracery: see* fig. 29(*f*) and (*g*). Perp tracery, which is formed of upright straight-sided panels above lights of a window. *Dagger:* Dec tracery motif; *see* fig. 30. *Mouchette:* curved version of the dagger form, especially popular in the early C14; *see* fig. 31.

Fig. 30. Dagger

Fig. 31. Mouchette

TRANSEPTS (*lit.* cross-enclosures): transverse portions of a cross-shaped church.

TRANSITIONAL: transitional phase between two styles, used most often for the phase between Romanesque and Early English (*c.* 1175–*c.* 1200).

TRANSOM: horizontal member between the lights in a window opening.

TREAD: horizontal part of the step

of a staircase. The *Tread End* may be carved.

TREFOIL: *see* Foil.

TRIBUNE: *see* Gallery (1).

TRIFORIUM (*lit.* three openings): middle storey of a church treated as an arcaded wall passage or blind arcade, its height corresponding to that of the aisle roof.

TRIGLYPHS (*lit.* three-grooved tablets): stylized beam-ends in the Doric frieze, with metopes between; *see* Orders (fig. 17).

TRIUMPHAL ARCH: *see* Arch.

TROPHY: sculptured group of arms or armour as a memorial of victory.

TRUMEAU: central stone mullion supporting the tympanum of a wide doorway. *Trumeau Figure:* carved figure attached to a trumeau (cf. Column Figure).

TUDOR FLOWER: late Gothic ornament of a flower with square flat petals or foliage.

TUMBLING or TUMBLING-IN: term used to describe courses of brickwork laid at right angles to the slope of a gable and forming triangles by tapering into horizontal courses.

TUMULUS (*lit.* mound): barrow.

TURRET: small tower, usually attached to a building.

TUSCAN: *see* Orders (fig. 17).

TYMPANUM (*lit.* drum): as of a drum-skin, the surface between a lintel and the arch above it or within a pediment.

UNDERCROFT: vaulted room, sometimes underground, below the main upper room.

UNIVALLATE: (of a hill-fort) defended by a single bank and ditch.

*Cross- or Groin-Vault*     *Tunnel- or Barrel-Vault*     *Pointed Barrel-Vault*

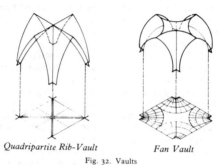

*Quadripartite Rib-Vault*          *Fan Vault*

Fig. 32. Vaults

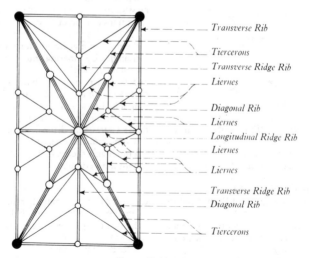

*Transverse Rib*

*Tiercerons*

*Transverse Ridge Rib*

*Liernes*

*Diagonal Rib*

*Liernes*

*Longitudinal Ridge Rib*

*Liernes*

*Liernes*

*Transverse Ridge Rib*

*Diagonal Rib*

*Tiercerons*

Fig. 33. Vaulting ribs

UPPER PALAEOLITHIC: *see* Palaeolithic.

**V**AULT: ceiling of stone formed like arches (sometimes imitated in timber or plaster); *see* fig. 32. *Tunnel-* or *Barrel-Vault:* the simplest kind of vault, in effect a continuous semicircular arch. *Groin-Vaults* (usually called *Cross-Vaults* in classical architecture) have four curving triangular surfaces produced by the intersection of two tunnel-vaults at right angles. The curved lines at the intersections are called groins. In *Quadripartite Rib-Vaults* the four sections are divided by their arches or ribs springing from the corners of the bay. *Sexpartite Rib-Vaults,* most often used over paired bays, have an extra pair of ribs which spring from between the bays and meet the other four ribs at the crown of the vault. The main types of rib are shown in fig. 33: *transverse ribs, wall ribs, diagonal ribs,* and *ridge ribs. Tiercerons* are extra, decorative ribs springing from the corners of a bay. *Liernes* are decorative ribs in the crown of a vault which are not linked to any of the springing points. In a *Stellar Vault* the liernes are arranged in a star formation as in fig. 33. *Fan-Vaults* are peculiar to English Perpendicular architecture in consisting not of ribs and infilling but of halved concave cones with decorative blind tracery carved on their surfaces.

VAULTING-SHAFT: shaft leading up to the springer of a vault.

VENETIAN WINDOW: a form derived from an invention by

Fig. 34. Venetian Window

Serlio, also called a Serlian or Palladian window. The same motif is used for other openings (*see* fig. 34).

VERANDA(H): shelter or gallery against a building, its roof supported by thin vertical members.

VERMICULATION: *see* Rustication.

VERNACULAR ARCHITECTURE: design by one without any training in design, guided by a series of conventions built up in a locality (Brunskill).

VESICA: oval with pointed head and foot, usually of a window or tracery.

VESTIBULE: anteroom or entrance hall.

VILLA: originally (1) a Romano-British farm or country house. The term is one of convenience and covers a wide spectrum of sites, ranging from humble farmsteads to sumptuous mansions associated with large estates. Various architectural traditions, including both classical and vernacular, are evident in villas, but all display some pretension towards fundamental Roman standards. (2) the C16 Venetian type with office wings, derived from Roman models and made grander by Palladio's varied application of a central portico. It became an important type in C18 Britain, often with the special meaning of (3) a country house which is not a principal residence. Gwilt (1842) defined the villa as 'a country house for the residence of opulent persons'. But devaluation had already begun, and the term also implied, as now, (4) a more or less pretentious suburban house.

VITRIFIED: hardened or fused into a glass-like state.

VITRUVIAN OPENING: door or window which diminishes towards the top, as advocated by Vitruvius, book IV, chapter VI.

VITRUVIAN SCROLL: running ornament of curly waves, on a classical frieze (*see* fig. 35).

Fig. 35. Vitruvian Scroll

VOLUTES: spiral scrolls on the front and back of a Greek Ionic capital, also on the sides of a Roman one. *Angle Volute:* pair of volutes turned outwards to meet at the corner of a capital. Volutes were also used individually as decoration in C17 and C18 architecture.

VOUSSOIRS: wedge-shaped stones forming an arch.

WAGON ROOF: roof in which closely set rafters with arched braces give the appearance of the inside of a canvas tilt over a wagon. Wagon roofs can be panelled or plastered (ceiled) or left uncovered. Also called *Cradle Roof.*

WAINSCOT: *see* Panelling.

WALL-PLATE: *see* Roofs (3) and figs. 22–5.

WARMING ROOM: *see* Calefactory.

WATERHOLDING BASE: type of early Gothic base in which the upper and lower mouldings are separated by a hollow so deep as to be capable of retaining water.

WATERLEAF CAPITAL: *see* fig. 7.

WEALDEN HOUSE: medieval timber-framed house of distinctive form. It has a central open hall flanked by bays of two storeys. The end bays are jettied to the front, but a single roof covers the whole building, thus producing an exceptionally wide overhang to the eaves in front of the hall.

WEATHERBOARDING: overlapping horizontal boards, covering a timber-framed wall, most common after the mid C18.

WEATHERING: inclined, projecting surface to keep water away from wall and joints below. Also called *Set-off.*

WEEPERS: small figures placed in niches along the sides of some medieval tombs. Also called *Mourners.*

WHEEL WINDOW: circular window with tracery of radiating shafts like the spokes of a wheel. *See also* Rose Window.

# INDEX OF PLATES

# INDEX OF ARTISTS

# INDEX OF PLACES

# ADDENDA

## MAY 1979

p. 102 [Clumber]. The gatepiers now at this entrance are of *c.* 1700, all of stone, equally fine, with well carved vases. The tradition that they came from the garden of Shireoaks Hall seems plausible. They probably replaced the late C18 gatepiers some time after 1949 when the Duke of Newcastle sold Shireoaks.

p. 230 [Nottingham, former Waterworks Offices.] *The Architect* (1874) gives Arthur Hawksley as the architect. This may be a mistake for the engineer *Thomas Hawksley* (*see* Bestwood). Arthur Hawksley of Nottingham was a painter active in the 1880s.

p. 242 [Nottingham, St Barnabas.] Dr Gomme notes that the E end is richer architecturally, with quatrefoil piers instead of octagonal ones in the chancel, Geometrical detail (including two wall arcades) in the E chapels, unusual stilted openings into the E ambulatory from the transepts, and a large rose window in the choir.

p. 261 [Nottingham, University Medical School and Teaching Hospital.] CHAPEL. Ten stained glass windows and forty-five canvases by *Brian Clarke*, refreshingly non-figurative.

p. 334 [Southwell, Norwood Park.] According to Professor Barley, the entry on p. 334 describes only the centre block. Originally it had two pavilions (stables and kitchens) linked to the house by passages, later raised to two storeys. Stable pavilion replaced *c.* 1800 by a new block to the N. The house was built for one of the Suttons (cf. Averham Park). Porticoed temple on a high point to the S (with a view of Southwell, Newark, and Lincoln), an icehouse to the E.